The Theory of Taxation
for Developing Countries

A WORLD BANK RESEARCH PUBLICATION

With contributions by

Ehtisham Ahmad	Choong Yong Ahn	Jane Armitage
Anthony Atkinson	Christopher Bliss	Avishay Braverman
Angus Deaton	Peter Diamond	Gary Fields
Mark Gersovitz	Francisco Gil Díaz	Jeffrey Hammer
Christopher Heady	Gordon Hughes	Michael Katz
Pradeep Mitra	Richard Musgrave	Richard Sabot
Raaj Kumar Sah	Joseph Stiglitz	Vito Tanzi
	Sweder van Wijnbergen	

The
Theory of Taxation
for
Developing Countries

Edited by
David Newbery
Nicholas Stern

PUBLISHED FOR THE WORLD BANK

Oxford University Press

Oxford University Press

NEW YORK OXFORD LONDON GLASGOW
TORONTO MELBOURNE WELLINGTON HONG KONG
TOKYO KUALA LUMPUR SINGAPORE JAKARTA
DELHI BOMBAY CALCUTTA MADRAS KARACHI
NAIROBI DAR ES SALAAM CAPE TOWN

Manufactured in the United States of America
First printing hardcover
and paperback editions
July 1987
Second paperback printing July 1988

Library of Congress Cataloging-in-Publication Data

The Theory of taxation for developing countries.

Includes bibliographies and index.
1. Taxation—Developing countries.   I. Newbery,
David M. G.   II. Stern, N. H. (Nicholas Herbert)
HJ2351.7.T47   1987   336.2'009172'4   87-11106
ISBN 0-19-520498-0
ISBN 0-19-520541-3 (pbk.)

Contents

v

Preface

ALL GOVERNMENTS NEED RESOURCES, but the problems of raising revenue are particularly severe in developing countries. These problems have been somewhat neglected in the past because work in public economics, both theoretical and applied, has concentrated on developed countries and taxation has not been a central concern in development economics. The past twenty-five years, however, have seen much progress in both fields, with a greater emphasis on construction of simple but clearly articulated models of the economies of developing countries that take into account the goals of, and constraints on, governments. It is now possible to investigate systematically such basic questions of public finance as which goods should be taxed, how tax systems should be reformed, and where additional resources should be sought. In this volume many of the economists whose work has been central to recent developments examine these issues, review progress in specific areas, and discuss directions for further work.

Parts 1 and 2 describe basic theories, facts, and experience; parts 3 through 6 deal with applications to particular countries and problems. Among the subjects covered are general tax theory, along with data requirements and the use of economic models in applications of the theory; the advantages and disadvantages of various taxes; the special characteristics of individual countries' tax systems and revenue sources; tax reform in general and practical experience in India, the Republic of Korea, and Mexico; the problems of taxing agriculture; and the pricing of publicly provided goods and services.

The book as a whole focuses, as the title implies, on taxation in developing countries, with a view to determining what can be achieved by applying the methods of public economics. No attempt has been made to impose a single, uniform view, but most of the authors share a concern with identifying the government's objectives and how they can best be achieved with the available resources, institutional arrangements, data, and tax instruments.

This book has several purposes. Because it uses modern methods and contains both new research and an assessment of the state of the art, it will be useful for economists and graduate students interested in development and taxation, and in particular for economists in governments, international organizations, and consultancies who wish to keep abreast of theoretical and empirical developments in contemporary research and adapt them for practical use. The book may also help to persuade academic economists and research students that taxation is a stimulating and important area for research, and it provides useful analytical tools for solving a broad range of problems. Finally, the collection, with its case studies in economic theory and econometrics, should be valuable as a textbook for courses in both public economics and development economics.

Many of the chapters in this book are necessarily technical because they contain the formal expressions and theoretical arguments that are quantified in the empirical analysis. In almost all cases, however, the discussions are not mathematically difficult. The main requirements of the reader are familiarity with partial differentiation and with the standard results of microeconomic theory as set forth in any standard textbook in which the properties of direct and indirect utility functions are derived. Although we have attempted to use consistent notation throughout the book, practical limitations and the wide range of subjects covered have made complete uniformity impossible. The discussion of "Notation and Terminology," below, provides a brief description of symbols and conventions, and we have also explained the notation as it appears in each chapter.

The immediate origins of this book were in a workshop held in the Development Research Department of the World Bank in June 1982, at which some of the leading exponents of public finance were invited to offer their views on ways of analyzing proposed tax reforms in developing countries. There were two reasons for interest in this topic: the Division of Public Economics, recently established within the Development Research Department, was then in the process of formulating its research program, and there was a sense within the development community that the rapid advances in the theory of public finance that had been made in the 1970s could fruitfully be applied to developing countries. Following the workshop the Research Committee of the World Bank decided to support the production of this book. A number of authors were commissioned to write chapters on specific topics, and the two editors undertook to provide an appropriate framework. The first draft of the manuscript was discussed at a conference held at the World Bank in June 1984 and was revised over the next twelve months. The editors are grateful for the authors' cooperation and patience during this process.

One of the goals of the project was to survey existing research and put it in a more accessible form. In addition, the book extends and adapts theory so that it can contribute more directly to the problems that face policymakers in developing countries. Much of the work of this kind reported here draws on research that was already under way at the time of the original workshop, some of it funded under other World Bank research projects. The study on India (chapter 11) was supported by the British Economic and Social Research Council and the Overseas Development Administration. This empirical work, and the project as a whole, raised many interesting additional questions, which form a considerable research agenda. The ideas presented here, however, in themselves provide both useful insights and a framework for constructive applied work.

We are grateful to the authors for their contributions, their involvement in revising their own chapters, and their detailed comments on other parts of the work. We also owe thanks to many individuals and institutions, most of all to the Development Research Department of the World Bank.

During the course of the work Newbery was at the World Bank, at Churchill College, Cambridge University, and at the Woodrow Wilson School of Public and International Affairs, Princeton University. He is currently a reader in economics at Cambridge University. Stern was at the University of Warwick, spent part of the summer of 1983 as a visiting scholar in the Fiscal Affairs Department of the International Monetary Fund, and visited the World Bank on other occasions. Since January 1986 he has been at the London School of Economics. Our associates at these and other institutions have been unfailingly helpful. In particular, we thank Bela Balassa, Esra Bennathan, Nancy Birdsall, Roger Bowden, John Duloy, Gregory Ingram, Nizar Jethar, Anne Krueger, Deepak Lal, Ricardo Martin, Graham Pyatt, Marcello Selowsky, Zmarak Shalizi, Lyn Squire, Mateen Thobani, and Arvind Virmani, all of the World Bank, and Ved Gandhi, Peter Heller, and Alan Tait of the International Monetary Fund for their comments on various chapters and for other help. Robin Boadway of Queen's University, David Bradford of Princeton University, Lawrence Lau of Stanford University, and Jesus Seade of Warwick University provided helpful advice. In addition to contributing to the volume and providing valuable comments on a number of chapters, Pradeep Mitra took responsibility for the World Bank administration of the project after Newbery returned to Cambridge in September 1983. We are greatly indebted to him. We are also particularly grateful to Geoffrey Frewer, who read the text in detail, standardized the notation, and prepared the preliminary index. Special thanks are due to James Mirrlees for guidance and encouragement throughout. We also thank Marcia Brubeck for her great care, skill, patience, and judgment in carrying through a most difficult copyediting task on a lengthy and technical volume by disparate contributors with individual preferences and idiosyncrasies. Finally, we are grateful for the kindness and support of the secretaries who have been involved in this work: Susan Buonocore, Vivian Couchoud, and Mary Ann Heraud at the World Bank, Connie Dent at Princeton University, and Jenny Johnson and Liz Thompson at Warwick University.

Notation and Terminology

WE HAVE ATTEMPTED to impose a consistent system of notation throughout the book, occasionally overriding the preferences of individual authors to do so. The main peculiarity is that q is invariably a price (not a quantity) and is the price facing consumers, as distinguished from p, the producer price. In addition, x is individual consumption or net demand and never expenditure, y is individual production, m is money income, and t is almost always a tax rate (but briefly appears as time in chapter 5). The Greek character τ is often an ad valorem tax rate. Capital letters are used for aggregate quantities (but P is the world price); R is government revenue. The shadow price of government revenue or the marginal social cost of raising revenue is always λ or λ_i. Other conventions are that ϵ, ϵ_i, and ϵ_{ij} are usually demand price elasticities (but ϵ is also the elasticity of the social marginal utility of income or the coefficient of inequality aversion) and that η, η_i, and η_{ij} are price elasticities of supply. Subscripts usually refer to goods but sometimes indicate derivatives, whereas superscripts refer to households or sectors. Vectors are usually not distinguished from scalars except that, for special emphasis, the former, where they are denoted by letters of the Latin alphabet, appear in boldface type. Other systematic usage may be detected, but the limited number of distinctive characters available precludes complete consistency. Variables are defined in each chapter.

A tonne is a metric ton.

Abbreviations

AIDS	Almost Ideal Demand System
APC	Average propensity to consume out of income
ARI	Accounting rate of interest
CBA	Cost-benefit analysis
CES	Constant elasticity of substitution
CGE	Computable general equilibrium
CIF	Cost, insurance, and freight
CPI	Consumer price index
CRI	Consumption rate of interest
CV	Coefficient of variation
DRC	Domestic resource cost
DUPS	Directly unproductive profit seeking
EP	Effective protection
EPR	Effective protection rate
EV	Equivalent variation
FAO	Food and Agriculture Organization
FF	Fertilizer fund
FOB	Free on board
FPF	Federal Participation Fund
GDP	Gross domestic product
GMF	Grain Management Fund
GNP	Gross national product
HYV	High-yield variety
IMF	International Monetary Fund
LES	Linear expenditure system
LIFO	Last in, first out
LPG	Liquefied petroleum gas
MANVAT	Value-added tax on manufacturing
MC	Marginal cost
MPC	Marginal propensity to consume out of income
MPL	Marginal product of labor
NSSO	National Sample Survey Organisation (India)
OECD	Organisation for Economic Co-operation and Development
R and D	Research and development

SCBA	Social cost-benefit analysis
SD	Standard deviation
SWF	Social welfare function
TV	Traditional variety
VAT	Value-added tax
WPI	Wholesale price index

The Theory of Taxation
for Developing Countries

1

Introduction

David Newbery and Nicholas Stern

GOVERNMENTS IN DEVELOPING COUNTRIES on the average collect 18 percent of GDP in tax revenue (see chapter 8, table 8-3), a high figure by historical standards yet one that, in many respects, understates the extent of government influence on transactions in the economy. In addition to the traditional tasks of raising revenue to finance public expenditure and managing monetary policy and the exchange rate, governments frequently control or influence the prices of a wide range of goods and services. This control is exercised either directly, through state enterprises, marketing boards, and ration shops, or indirectly, by regulation, licensing, and quotas as well as through the fiscal instruments of taxes, tariffs, and subsidies. The average share of central government revenue in GDP was 14 percent in 1960, 18 percent in 1970, and 24 percent in 1980 for developing countries for which data are available; the average contribution of state-owned nonfinancial enterprises to GDP has risen from 7 percent at the beginning of the 1970s to 10 percent at the end of the decade (World Bank, 1983, pp. 47–51).

The extensive and growing role of the state in economic development did not lack critics in the 1950s and 1960s, but in this period developing countries achieved historically unprecedented rates of growth. Discussions of policy usually centered on identification of the best sectors for investment and promotion and on planning for growth. The 1980s, however, present a very different economic and intellectual environment. Economic performance has been disappointing, the international environment appears hostile, and critics complain of the inefficiency of the public sector. We often find that the emphasis has shifted from planning for growth to increasing efficiency, reducing public expenditure, undertaking structural adjustment, and, in particular, "getting the prices right" (see, for example, *World Development Report 1983*). The extensive government interventions in the economy are being subjected to critical scrutiny, and there is pressure to eliminate distortions, to reform taxes and trade policy, and to reexamine subsidies and the role of state enterprises.

What do we mean when we speak of getting prices right? In the case of imports and exports, an intellectually respectable case may be made for eliminating tariffs and quotas under certain circumstances or for employing them only where more direct instruments, such as consumption taxes, are not available. The same argument cannot be applied, however, to the tax system as a whole—the appropriate tax revenue, however determined, is surely not zero. Hence no comparable case may be made for arguing that there should be no taxes, and price distortions will inevitably remain. We may agree that the present system of taxes, subsidies, public sector prices, and other interventions is unsatisfactory, but we cannot conclude that it would be best to abolish all subsidies and taxes. Instead, proposed reforms must be examined to see whether they are desirable and whether the current policies can be improved. In some cases ways of improving matters may be obvious, but often they are not.

The main aim of this book is to develop, explain, and illustrate methods for analyzing the effects of proposed tax reforms and for identifying those that are desirable. The emphasis falls on the development of formal methods of analysis that can be quantified and applied to policy problems in developing countries. In the United States any serious proposal for tax reform that has been carefully studied by the administration will be presented for discussion, with details of its likely impact on various groups of individuals in the economy and its effect on public revenue. Alternative proposals will have different consequences that can be compared and evaluated. It may appear very natural for us to analyze policies in terms of their consequences for the economy, yet until very recently tax reforms were not discussed in this way. Instead, tax analysts would consider the tax system with various criteria in mind and would suggest ways of reforming taxes that scored poorly by the criteria. Is the tax system horizontally and vertically equitable? Are there anomalies in the treatment of essentially similar categories of income or expenditures? Is the tax base adequately comprehensive, or are there unreasonable exemptions? Is the tax system unnecessarily complex? How do the level and structure of taxation compare in one country with those in others that are comparable? How progressive is the tax system?

We contend that such questions and implied criteria can be very useful in defining the agenda and in identifying taxes that may most advantageously be studied more closely. Still, they either stop short of establishing that certain tax changes would be desirable or raise questions that are not directly relevant. Suppose, for example, that a group of consultants is asked to advise on tax reform in a particular country. After much labor, they produce a table showing the incidence of the present tax system (probably reflecting various assumptions about how to allocate taxes on companies and so forth) together with an estimate of the share of tax revenue that we might expect in a country with the same characteristics (level of income, share of imports, size of extractive sector, and so forth) as the economy under consideration. The table shows that taxes are not very progressive and that the level of "tax effort" is below that predicted. What do we do with this kind of information? Can we conclude that taxes should be more progressive and also that they should raise more revenue?

First, obvious questions must be asked. If the country claims to be concerned with the distribution of income and is anxious to raise additional revenue, then the present tax system scores poorly by comparison with that in other countries, whose example suggests that it should be possible to do better. Second, the table provides some arguments that may be used to counter individuals who claim that reform is impossible or undesirable. Third, closer comparisons may suggest that specific elements of the tax system are mainly responsible for its structural characteristics—maybe income taxation is low, the indirect tax base narrow and regressive, and so forth. We have thus begun to define the agenda for reform. Until specific proposals have been made, however, and until their likely consequences have been assessed, the argument is inconclusive. Revenue, for example, may be low because the only taxes that it is feasible to raise impose a high social cost, one not warranted by the productivity of government revenue. The economy may have important structural features not captured by the estimates of tax effort, nor is there any guarantee that the achievement of "similar" economies carries any moral imperative. Incidence calculations, furthermore, usually implicitly compare the present tax system with a notional and quite irrelevant benchmark of zero taxation.

In order to compare and choose between alternative tax proposals, we need to know more than which groups in society are benefited and which adversely affected by each proposal. The gains and losses must be quantified, which in turn means that the government must collect the relevant data. Over the last few decades the need for systematic data collection has been increasingly recognized, and the ability to collect and analyze data has spread to an ever wider range of countries. The fact that we can now collect and use such data means that it is possible to make formal and quantified contributions to tax analysis, whereas once we had to rely largely on judgment, impression, and hunch. Moreover, if such data are to be used effectively, they must be organized and analyzed systematically: the economist must specify a formal model describing the impact of the policy change. The availability of data provides an incentive for developing tax theory and making it applicable, whereas the theoretical developments in turn identify those data that could usefully be collected and analyzed. Judgments on political acceptability, choice of model, data reliability, and so on can never be eliminated, but we are now able to apply them in a more structured way.

The theory that this book will develop, apply, and discuss reflects and contributes to the modern theory of public economics as summarized, for example, in the textbook by Atkinson and Stiglitz (1980). According to that theory, we first ask about the effects of different sorts of taxes in simple general equilibrium models and then proceed to normative questions. What types of goods should be taxed? What should be the balance between direct and indirect taxation? How progressive should income taxes be?

The essence of the approach lies first in the formal modeling of consequences and second in the use of explicit value judgments to assess the consequences. The methods were initially developed in simple competitive models, and there have been a number of applications to advanced economies (see, for example, those described in the *Journal of Public Economics*). Is this theory applicable to developing countries? More precisely, which parts of the modern theory are applicable and to which problems? How can the theory be extended to deal with important features of developing countries? In examining these questions, the present book has three main objectives. First, it seeks to expound the key concepts of the modern approach that are relevant for our purposes and to sketch their relationship to the remainder of the theory. Second, it aims to identify the structural features of developing countries that constrain and influence the choice of tax policy and to develop suitable models and theories to handle them. Third, it attempts to illustrate the application of the methods set forth here to particular developing countries.

The table of contents suggests the plan of the book. The first part, chapters 1 to 6, addresses basic theory. Chapter 2 surveys modern tax theory in terms of the questions it considers and the kinds of answers it provides. It presents the main results in optimal tax theory and identifies the key features that influence the choice of tax design. It also begins to develop the theory of reform for later application. The theory of reform addresses the identification of desirable changes from a given status quo. In chapter 3 the emphasis falls on the analysis of production and tax incidence. We also develop the general theory according to which shadow prices are used to show how the simple theory of chapter 2 may be extended to a range of more realistic and more complex circumstances. Chapter 4 examines the central question regarding the use of data for the application of the theory and ways of estimating the key parameters of the tax reform formulas. Much of the modern theory is set in a static context, and chapter 5 discusses ways of reinterpreting this theory and extending it to encompass dynamic issues. Finally, chapter 6 relates the approach to techniques already in widespread use—social cost-benefit analysis and the study of effective protection.

Part 2 looks at the structural characteristics of developing countries and their tax systems. These characteristics affect the information available to the tax authorities, which in turn limits the tax instruments that can be used and the policy questions that may usefully be addressed. If information about personal incomes is sparse and unreliable, for example, then income taxes will have limited applicability. It is less important to explore the correct balance between direct and indirect taxes than to ask how best to use indirect taxes. The structure of the economy will also affect the incidence of taxes or, more precisely, the consequences of tax changes. If income taxes have only partial coverage, for example, then increases in income taxes may fall on employers or consumers rather than on the income recipient. In chapter 7 it is argued that the role of agriculture in employment, in food production, and in exports, the existence of labor market dualism, and the extent of market failures and distortions are all, in varying degrees, important features of developing countries that are ignored in the standard model of modern tax theory but can be accommodated in suitably modified theories. Chapter 8 describes the main features of the tax systems of developing countries in a quantitative and systematic way. A leading theorist and adviser to different countries provides, in chapter 9, his view of the important issues in the analysis of reform, drawing on a wealth of practical experience. Chapter 10 outlines the consequences of the special features of labor markets in some developing countries for the analysis of public policy.

Part 3 contains two country case studies of tax reform. The first shows the results of applying the techniques previously discussed for the purpose of identifying desirable tax reforms in India. The emphasis falls on testing the applicability of the methods rather than on making recommendations with regard to the main policy issues facing Indian tax reforms, though many of the calculations should be of direct use. Chapter 12 recounts a substantial tax reform undertaken by Mexico, in which the author was a central participant, and suggests several important lessons. The main one is positive: it *is* possible to reform and improve the tax system, and changes that were said to be administratively impossible or politically infeasible were nevertheless implemented successfully.

It is impractical in a book of this length to analyze completely the potential for tax reform in a single country. The chapter on India mainly emphasized the reform of indirect taxation as it affects consumers (though income taxes are also discussed). The remainder of the book examines the taxation of specific sectors to show how their distinctive features affect the tax options available, the constraints that need to be recognized, and the way in which the incidence of tax changes will depend on the mode of equilibration in the sector. Part 4 discusses the taxation of agriculture in theory (chapters 13 to 16) and part 5 the taxation of agriculture in practice, as illustrated by the reform of agricultural prices in the Republic of Korea (chapters 17 to 19). Part 6 considers some sectoral issues—energy, foreign investment, the pricing of social services, and the subsidization of education. Chapter 20 focuses on energy taxation and pricing and shows how taxes on inputs rather than on final consumption goods feed through the economy and exercise quite different impacts on traded and nontraded goods. Chapter 21 sets forth the theory for the pricing of social services such as health and education, which are frequently subsidized or are provided free and are rationed rather than freely marketed. Chapter 22 examines the issue of raising fees for secondary school students in government-subsidized schools in Kenya. Chapter 23 deals with the optimal tax treatment of foreign private investment, a subject whose importance is growing rapidly with the rise in foreign borrowing.

The final part draws conclusions and discusses directions for future work, asking what the main remaining theoretical and practical problems are and how they might be addressed. Some of these questions are also raised in the present chapter.

The Scope of the Analysis

The book's scope is at once rather limited and very broad. It is limited in the sense that we are investigating and developing methods that are best suited to particular questions and problems; it is very broad in that the methods are applicable to many branches of the large subject of public finance. The broadness accounts in large part for the considerable length of this book. Its breadth also results from the diversity of the views expressed by the more than twenty authors. We do not pretend that a score of economists and more take a common view of the exact way in which tax proposals should be analyzed or of the system and rates that are appropriate. What they do share, in varying degrees, is a willingness to include in their examination of reforms a careful assessment of consequences, involving the study and appraisal of formal methods for carrying out that assessment, drawing on considerable experience with the analysis of taxation in theory and practice.

We shall now offer an informal impression of some of the methods and of the ways in which they can be applied, thereby explaining what is included and what is omitted and how the work relates to some other methods of policy analysis. The most convenient way of describing the scope is through the example, in a simple form, of a concept that will be used extensively in the book—the marginal cost of public funds raised from a particular source.

Consider a reform of the structure of indirect taxes, where good i bears a tax t_i. What happens if t_i is raised? In the simplest case, where t_i falls only on final consumer goods and has no effect on unit production costs, and where markets are sufficiently competitive, the effect will be to raise the price of good i by the increase in the tax, Δt_i. The rise in price will make consumers worse off, and for a small change in tax, the amount by which consumer h is worse off is $x_i^h \Delta t_i$, where x_i^h is the consumption of good i by h. Depending on their consumption levels, different consumers will be differently affected by the tax change. Government revenue will also change. If the total taxable consumption of good j is X_j, then revenue, R, can be written as

$$(1\text{-}1) \qquad\qquad R = R_0 + \sum_j t_j X_j$$

where R_0 is revenue from other sources, which we here suppose is unaffected by indirect taxes. The effect of changing t_i can be found by differentiating R:

$$(1\text{-}2) \qquad\qquad \frac{\partial R}{\partial t_i} = X_i + \sum_j t_j \sum_k \frac{\partial X_j}{\partial q_k} \frac{\partial q_k}{\partial t_i}$$

and the impact on revenue will be $(\partial R/\partial t_i)\,\Delta t_i$. The crucial point to note is that a change in one tax, t_i, will, by affecting the consumer price q_i, also affect the levels of consumption of other taxed goods and will hence affect revenue. (The convention followed in this book is that producer prices are denoted by p and consumer prices by q, where $q = p + t$.) In a systematic treatment of tax reform, these general equilibrium effects must be identified and may be very important. In less simple models the general equilibrium ramifications will obviously be more complex, as we shall see in later chapters.

The data requirements for this simple example are clear. We need consumer expenditure information, from a household budget survey, to identify the x_i^h. We need to know the effective tax rates t_j, that is, the taxes actually collected per additional unit of consumption of each good. Furthermore we require the response of *aggregate* consumption to price changes, $\partial X_j / \partial q_i$, and the effect of taxes on prices, $\partial q_k / \partial t_i$. In this simple example, $\partial q_i / \partial t_i$ will be unity, as the price rises by the same amount that the tax increases, and $\partial q_k / \partial t_i$ will otherwise be zero.

Before we can *value* the consequences of the tax reform, we must weight the changes in household real income and add them to give a measure of social welfare. If β^h is the social marginal utility of consumption of household h, or the social weight on h, then the *fall* in social welfare is

$$(1\text{-}3) \qquad\qquad -\Delta W = \sum_h \beta^h x_i^h \Delta t_i$$

and because the increase in revenue is $\Delta R = (\partial R / \partial t_i) \Delta t_i$, the social marginal cost of raising revenue by changing t_i is the fall in welfare per unit of revenue raised, or $-\Delta W / \Delta R$. If we call this λ_i, then

$$(1\text{-}4) \qquad\qquad \lambda_i = \frac{\Sigma \beta^h x_i^h}{\partial R / \partial t_i}.$$

The social cost on the margin of raising revenue by taxes on good i, λ_i, can be compared with that of raising it via taxing good j, λ_j, and the best (cheapest) way of raising extra revenue identified— or more expensive alternatives can be replaced by cheaper taxes.

The analysis can be taken one step further to address the question of tax design or the selection of the best set of taxes, that is, optimal taxes. If taxes are adjusted until the social marginal costs, λ_i, are all equal, then it is impossible to improve the tax structure, which means that the best set of taxes has been found, subject to the usual qualifications that we have a global maximum.

This example illustrates the theory of marginal tax reform in its simplest form. Notwithstanding its simplicity, it immediately suggests an agenda for applied and theoretical work and indicates the kinds of tax analysis for which the approach is well suited, which are discussed in this book. At the same time, the example will serve to identify the difficulties involved in analyzing other types of taxes in this way. We should emphasize that the example we have given is a very simple one and does not in any sense exhaust the range of methods described in the following chapters. Many or most of the authors are concerned with nonmarginal reforms and with models in which the effects of taxes are more complex than the simple increase in consumer prices described here. We list some of the questions to which the methods illustrated in our simple example are well suited.

The Reform or Design of Indirect Taxes, Including Tariffs

In the simplest case, discussed above, tax changes affect only final consumer prices. Taxes on inputs can be traced through an input-output matrix to find their impact on consumer prices. If producer prices are distorted, then the effects of taxes on production can be evaluated using shadow prices, as discussed in chapter 3. In other complicated cases, taxes will not affect final prices (for example, export prices) but will reduce the incomes of producers and will perhaps reduce prices elsewhere. These and other cases are illustrated in chapters 11, 13, 17, 18, and 20. More generally tax changes affect both consumer prices and incomes of producers.

A Shift to Value-Added Taxes

A value-added tax system is a specific kind of indirect tax system that falls, in principle, only on final consumers and as such is the easiest kind of indirect tax to analyze (see, for example, chapter 11).

Agricultural Pricing and Taxation

Agricultural prices can be influenced by export taxes or can be set directly by marketing boards. They affect consumers in the same way as indirect taxes, but they also affect producers' income, levels of production, and sales to the urban and export sectors. These impacts can be identified and, if we have information about production responses, can be quantified, as discussed in part 4 and as illustrated in chapters 17 and 18.

Subsidies, Transfer Payments, and Personal Income Taxes

Lump-sum taxes or transfers have income effects that affect consumption of taxed goods and welfare but exert no direct effects on relative prices. They are hence easy to analyze and require modest data. Income taxes, however, may affect rewards to labor supply, savings, and possibly investment in human capital. Income taxes with partial coverage may also affect pretax income levels. To the extent that consequential effects can be quantified, they can be analyzed by the same general methods, but the data requirements are formidable. Although income taxes are discussed in chapters 2 and 11, we have not attempted a systematic treatment.

Reform of Quotas, Rations, and Licenses

Although we do not provide explicit empirical illustrations, it is possible to deal with the impact of changing quantitative controls in a relatively straightforward way. An increased import quota, for example, will affect the market price of the imported good, the factor incomes of the quota holders, and the supply and profits of domestic producers. It may have no direct effect on government revenue but only effects that result from changes on demands and supplies of taxed goods. The main difficulties lie in predicting the impacts on production costs, market prices, and quantities—a problem that also arises with tariff changes and that in principle can be captured using the shadow price of the good subject to quota. We discuss some of these difficulties further below.

Public Sector Pricing and Subsidies

For marketed goods such as electricity, changes in price are treated just like changes in tax, except that the public sector enterprise budget is affected rather than the government budget. If funds are fungible between them, the analysis is identical, but if the enterprise is constrained by its budget (in its investment program, for example), then its funds may differ in value from those of the government. For nonmarketed goods such as education, the effect of changing supply and/or price may be a combination of a quota change and a change in transfer. Chapter 21 presents the theory of such changes, and chapter 22 applies it to education.

Company Taxation

Taxes on companies may affect profits, dividends, savings, the allocation and level of investment, and international capital flows as well as the decision to incorporate. The range of effects is wide, the data to identify the impact sparse, and the influence of the legal system, which varies greatly across countries, pervasive. Rather than deal inadequately with the whole topic, we have concentrated on an important example from one country, Mexico (chapter 12), and on one practically important aspect—the taxation of direct foreign investment, which is discussed in chapter 23.

The list of policies that can usefully be analyzed using the approach set forth in this book should suggest the range of applicability and the natural limits imposed by the availability of data and the present state of economic understanding.

In understanding the scope of the methods, it is helpful to compare them with those of social cost-benefit analysis, which may be more familiar. Social cost-benefit analysis identifies the probable consequences for the economy of implementing alternative projects and proposes a method of valuing these consequences in order to rank the projects and to identify those that are best (most socially profitable). In the proposed tax analysis, we identify the probable consequences of alternative reforms and, using the same method of valuing these consequences, rank the proposals in order of desirability, or we identify the most desirable reform. The same set of shadow prices that captures the consequences of demands and supplies generated by a project also captures the consequences of changes in demands and supplies induced by policy reforms, provided the economy is assumed to adjust in a similar manner to the two types of change (as is explained more carefully in chapter 3). In fact, the main difference between project and policy analysis is that a project has direct effects on supplies and demands in the economy, whereas a policy change typically affects prices that in turn induce changes in supplies and demands. An extra step is needed to calculate these induced changes, but otherwise the analysis is conceptually very similar.

Another important link should be borne in mind throughout the book. The analysis of tax reform proceeds by calculating the social marginal cost of raising a dollar of government revenue by changing a particular tax rate and hence identifies the least-cost way of raising revenue, or equivalently, the largest net social gain, if we hold revenue constant and replace the most costly tax by the least costly. The marginal social cost of raising tax revenue should be compared with the marginal social benefit of spending revenue, sometimes called the shadow price of public investible funds in CBA. The revenue and expenditure sides of the budget are thus logically linked. Although this book does not examine direct public expenditure, the techniques of CBA would be precisely analogous to the methods we are proposing.

Some Omissions

Administration and evasion play an important part in the case studies of Mexico and India discussed in part 3. In Mexico, one of the objectives and achievements of the reform was to improve administration and reduce evasion. The chapter on India describes how administration costs can be taken into account in the analysis of the marginal costs of funds from different sources by working in terms of revenue raised net of administration costs. Although these considerations do not readily lend themselves to formal analysis, certain aspects can thus be taken into account in the methods under study. In other examples it will be possible to treat an increase (or decrease) in enforcement as we would an increase (or decrease) in the effective tax. In addition, directly calculated revenue elasticities of tax changes should (and usually would) take into account the response of evasion to changing rates. The consequences of improved collection can thus be handled in a fairly straightforward way. Apart from the important Mexican example, however, we have little to say regarding methods of improving administration and reducing evasion, though the interested reader is referred to Radian (1980).

Although the main emphasis in this book falls on taxation, the analysis applies directly to certain categories of public expenditure. Subsidies often count as items of expenditure but are more sensibly seen as negative taxes and can be analyzed as such. Losses of state-owned enterprises and marketing boards (such as the Grain Fund in Korea; see chapter 18) result when prices are set below cost and can also be interpreted as subsidies. The problem of choosing prices for the outputs of state-owned enterprises is essentially the same as the problem of setting indirect taxes and can be analyzed in the same way.

The book does not directly address questions involving the efficiency of public expenditure. Thus a public enterprise may run at a loss not because its price is too low but because its costs are too high. The main policy question may be how best to improve its operation, whether to transfer it to the private sector or to close it down rather than how to set its price. Similar questions arise with social services such as health and education, though once these questions have been answered, if the activity remains in the public sector, it will still be necessary either to set a price for its output or to choose some other mechanism for allocating output. In either case the techniques developed here will be relevant.

Labor supply, entrepreneurship, risk taking, investment, and savings are all subjects that have been studied in the theoretical literature using the methods described here. The major problem in applying these theories to developing countries lies in the paucity of reliable empirical studies showing how these factors respond to changes in rewards and taxes. The empirical difficulties in measuring labor supply, entrepreneurship, and risk taking are daunting, whereas the incidence of taxes on factor supplies is likely to be more complex in developing countries than in countries with effective and universal tax coverage. In addition, although investment and saving can be measured in some circumstances (although not easily), it has proved very hard using data in developed countries to show how they respond to changing rates of return—see King (1984) for a recent survey. Thus most analyses of taxation and saving merely note that the tax system can introduce very different returns to different forms of investment and saving in a way that has no obvious rationale (see, for example, Kay and King, 1983, and King and Fullerton, 1984). In so doing they make a very valuable contribution, but it does not allow us to calculate the consequences of tax changes for the welfare and behavior of households and for government revenue.

The relation between taxation and growth is discussed in chapter 5. Certain arguments we do not examine in detail, including the suggestion, frequently made, that higher taxes or greater price distortions accompany lower rates of growth. In our judgment, this case has not been clearly argued either in theory or in practice. As we note in chapter 5, there is no general result in theory that higher levels of taxes reduce *rates* of growth—the result can go either way, and long-run effects will often be zero. Furthermore, cross-country comparisons do not clearly indicate the relation asserted. The possibility cannot be dismissed but is very difficult to research in a systematic and coherent way. Such research has not yet been provided and lies beyond the scope of this book.

Most of the book is thoroughly microeconomic, mainly because we are examining either small reforms or equal-yield changes in the tax system that can be expected to have a negligible macroeconomic impact. Chapter 19 is the exception: it explores the likely macroeconomic impacts of a large agricultural price reform in Korea in an econometric model. Tax reforms that lead to a significant impact on real wages (as in Korea), exports, imports, or the sectoral distribution of income would be expected to have such macro impacts, which should obviously be identified and quantified. In principle many of these macro effects should be captured by the set of shadow prices, though in saying so we are merely shifting the problem to the calculation of shadow prices (see chapter 3).

We do not examine the issue of tax reforms directed primarily at restoring macroequilibrium except to observe that, if revenue must be increased or expenditure cut, it is obviously sensible to raise it in the least-cost way or to cut the least valuable expenditure. The calculations reported here would undoubtedly be useful in such exercises, and significant tax reforms may well require the pressure of such external circumstances.

The methods studied are probably best regarded as applying reform in the medium term. They do not concentrate on effective demand, unemployment, and inflation and thus are not short run, and they do not place growth at the center of the stage. As we have noted, however, in judging short-run policy we should take into account the kind of medium-term structure that the government may be seeking.

The book is silent on the positive theory of public finance. The reason is not that we regard the study of the ways in which policies actually are determined as uninteresting (although testable propositions are scarce). Rather we think it is important to discover what would be desirable, even when it may be currently politically infeasible or when prudence cautions against creating an institutional framework to administer proposed taxes. Analysis of the kind we provide can and should make valuable contributions to the process of policy formulation. Thus, for example, if great gains appear to be available from certain policies that may be politically difficult, then a policymaker who was convinced of their value might use the arguments to make his case and, in part, to change what is feasible. Alternatively, we might try to find other, acceptable ways of achieving the same results.

Conclusions

The organizing principle that underlies this book is the systematic and formal development of methods of tax analysis that can be applied quantitatively in developing countries. The distinctive features of such economies account for the emphasis placed on certain kinds of taxes (in particular indirect taxes and taxes on agriculture). The availability of suitable economic theory and data with which to calibrate the models limits the range of tax options that can be fruitfully examined and explains many of the differences between the approach described here and that set out in other books on taxation in developing countries. Thus we largely ignore very general questions such as the overall progressivity of the tax system and issues of balance, fairness, and tax effort, though such questions may be useful in drawing up an agenda of possible reforms.

The approach set forth here has been implemented in India and is currently being applied systematically in Mexico and Pakistan and rather less comprehensively in Thailand, Tunisia, and Indonesia, where the studies are focusing mainly on reforms of the energy price and tax system. (These last results are presented in chapter 20.) What lessons can be drawn from these studies, and what might we learn from further comparative analysis?

Our main conclusion is that the methods set forth here are operational if the relevant data are available. In the Indian case the requirements included cross-section and time-series information on consumer expenditure, an input-output table, and detailed data on the tax system, especially regarding tax revenue actually collected by type of tax. The data requirements are more demanding than those typically used to calculate shadow prices of, for example, the Little-Mirrlees variety, because it is necessary to calculate the response of demands and supplies to price changes.

A second important conclusion is that the approach set forth in this book, because it is systematic, seems to be less prone to important errors of omission. One of the most common errors involves looking at a sector and its taxes in isolation and ignoring the rest of the tax system. Thus when we study the agricultural sector, we run the risk of ignoring nonagricultural taxes. If taxes on agriculture or the prices of inputs and outputs in the sector are changed, however, then in general incomes and expenditures will change, and if nonagricultural goods are taxed, then tax revenues will change. A systematic approach that asks explicitly what the consequences are for government revenue is less likely to overlook taxes and tariffs on consumption goods bought by households in the agricultural sector, though many partial-equilibrium studies do ignore these taxes. Similar errors arise when we argue that agricultural prices should move toward the border price, a contention that is unjustified without further comment on the economy, in particular some statement about the relationship of other prices (of inputs and consumer goods) to the border price.

An important question, and one that is raised at several points in this book, is whether there are robust rules for setting taxes that can be used with some confidence in countries for which data are sparse. One such rule, which is discussed further in chapters 2, 3, and 4, is that indirect taxes should be uniform, with the bulk of the redistribution achieved by lump-sum and uniform transfers to all consumers, rather like the negative income tax proposed in various developed countries. There are three arguments for uniformity. First, some observers might suggest that uniformity restrains the administration from some of its wilder excesses. Second, collection costs may be lower and administration easier when groups of commodities are taxed at the same rate. If, for example, all commodities were taxed at the same rate, then indirect taxes could be abolished and all revenue collected through the direct system (if perfect administration of both systems is assumed). Third, the main analytical argument for uniformity is that it is difficult to estimate the *price* elasticities, on which optimal tax rates depend, using the available data, though it is easy to estimate income (more accurately, expenditure) elasticities from consumer budget data. It is therefore necessary to make assumptions about the price elasticities. If we assume that preferences are additively separable, for example, then price elasticities can be deduced from the expenditure elasticities, and these derived price elasticities can be used to identify the directions of price reform. Additive separability has strong implications, however, of which the most important is that price elasticities will be roughly proportional to (and often about half the absolute size of) the expenditure elasticities. Goods that should be heavily taxed on distributional grounds (luxuries) will have high price elasticities, which on efficiency grounds is a good reason for reducing the tax. On balance, some observers suggest, the two effects tend to cancel out, leaving a presumption that uniformities are best. An alternative approach would be to impose price elasticities (perhaps derived from data in other countries or from prior beliefs) and to proceed directly to the calculation. The danger with this approach is that it involves a temptation to simplify this problem, for example by supposing cross-price elasticities to be zero, in which case goods that are price inelastic *and* luxuries (for example, private motor travel in developing countries) are being implicitly assumed to be strongly substitutable with leisure. In chapter 4 Deaton identifies a central problem: the assumptions that must be imposed in order to extract information from the data may have very strong influences on the answer.

The uniformity results, as we shall see, involve much more than assumptions about the structure of preferences, and they require in addition preferences that are similar across households and an optimal poll subsidy to all households. The argument against uniformity is that the assumptions required to produce the result are implausible, and where they can be satisfactorily tested, they have been rejected. More to the point, the aggregate elasticities that are required to calculate revenue responses to tax changes, however these elasticities are assumed or estimated, provide only part of the information required for tax reform. The remaining information, which becomes relatively more important with increasing aversion to inequality, is the pattern of individual household expenditure levels on particular goods. With these data, we can test the hypothesis of the desirability of moving toward uniformity. Where the hypothesis has been tested on the Indian data (in chapter 11), it is rejected, both in terms of the desirability of a shift toward uniformity and in terms of the optimality of an existing poll subsidy. In other countries, with other, possibly more dispersed tax rates, it may be desirable to move toward uniformity, but it is certainly unwarranted to draw any such general conclusion on the basis of the evidence presented so far.

We would not suggest that very general and robust rules are available. What we hope to have shown is that the application of any such rule in a particular country can be examined in a systematic way. Furthermore, the analysis shows which features, such as consumption patterns, demand responses, and the availability of transfer mechanisms, in the case of uniform taxes, are crucial to deciding the issues.

A valuable feature of comparative studies, in a context where there are many countries for which data are sparse, relates to the transferability of parameter estimates and the sensitivity of results to particular features of the economy. It would be invaluable, for example, to discover similarities in demand patterns across countries, because we would then be able to use estimates derived elsewhere in countries for which the data do not allow the parameters to be estimated.

The other major benefit that should come from systematic tax studies of a number of countries is that we should be able to test the validity of the kinds of prescriptions that are made by tax advisers with limited time and access to data. Is the advice that is currently being given reasonably sound? Can it be improved, subject to the constraints under which it is usually sought (that is, limited time and resources)? How valuable is the extra contribution that a detailed study provides?

Finally, lest it be thought that the methods set out here are unrealistically demanding and hence of little practical use, we should draw some comparisons. The World Bank, in making loans to countries, often makes it a condition of the loan that the country finance a detailed study of some economic issue. A variety of effective protection studies and studies of the impact of energy price changes have been undertaken as a result of these initiatives, sometimes by management consultants or accounting firms and sometimes by research institutes in the developing country. The kind of study we envisage is no more complex or potentially expensive than these studies, and indeed an energy-pricing impact study properly done could have much in common with a tax study, as chapter 20 shows. Furthermore an economywide tax study is arguably the best way to organize and coordinate specific sector studies on energy price impacts and agricultural price interventions, studies of industrial incentives and protection, and shadow-pricing studies. We hope that the methods and illustrations provided in this book will make it relatively straightforward for governments to commission such studies.

PART 1

Theory

THE FIRST PART OF THE BOOK presents the basic theory, providing a foundation for some of the extensions, adaptations, and applications that follow in later parts. Thus we attempt to describe the theory in a way that will make it amenable to empirical work and will illuminate data requirements. At the same time we try to identify the key issues and important assumptions in the posing of questions and the construction of models as well as to describe basic principles of taxation that emerge from the analysis. We also relate the theories to other parts of economic inquiry, such as cost-benefit analysis, trade theory, and demand estimation. The reader should therefore have not only a basis for later chapters but also a survey of the theory of optimal taxation and reform and an introduction to problems of application and research issues. The reader should, in addition, be able to see how the subject fits into economic analysis.

Chapter 2 surveys the theories of optimal commodity and income taxation. It follows these theories in emphasizing consumer welfare and government revenue. Production is pushed into the background by assumptions of constant returns to scale and perfect competition. Thus we see that the government can essentially control private production by using producer prices with minimal impact on the rest of the economy, and we may regard commodity taxes as being entirely shifted forward onto consumers. The central questions, then, are: which final goods should be taxed heavily? which lightly? what should be the structure and progressivity of the income tax? how should the balance be struck between direct and indirect taxes? These are classic questions, involving as central elements the tradeoff between equity, that is, the distribution of welfare across households, and efficiency or incentives, that is, the amounts that are being distributed. We shall see that the answers to these questions are very sensitive to assumptions concerning the form of differences across households, the structure of preferences, and the tax tools available. We also introduce the theory of reform and relate it to that of optimality: the optimum is a state of affairs from which it is impossible to identify a beneficial reform. The chapter identifies certain robust and general principles of taxation from the theories.

The production side of the economy is examined more closely in chapter 3, where we discuss some aspects of the general theory of reform. We then proceed to a discussion of tax incidence, and we shall see the importance of assumptions concerning the coverage of taxes, the openness of the economy, and market structure. Later in the book we shall argue that distinctive features of tax theory for developing countries are the importance of and particular forms taken by these aspects. A brief description is provided of the general theory of marginal reform. We argue that the use of shadow prices allows that theory to cover a very wide range of circumstances. We then judge a reform by asking whether the direct effects on households of a tax change exceed the cost at shadow prices of the extra demands generated by the change.

In chapter 4 Deaton examines the role of econometric analysis in tax design. In so doing he continues the discussion of uniform commodity taxation that began in chapters 2 and 3. It can be shown that, if households have identical and linear Engel curves, and if leisure is separable from commodities, then the optimal structure involves a poll subsidy and uniform commodity taxation. The econometric estimation would not have anything to contribute to the analysis of tax structure. Although the assumptions are not obviously accept-able as descriptions of developing countries, particularly the requirement that the government makes a uniform and optimally chosen poll subsidy to every-one in the economy, the result starkly illuminates the importance of assump-tions concerning preferences and the availability of tax tools. To estimate a linear expenditure system, for example, is very much to prejudge the answer to the problem of tax design. We must also ask whether and in what way the world deviates from these assumptions. Deaton argues that some of the param-eters necessary for the analysis of reform, particularly cross-price elasticities, will be very hard to identify from the data that are likely to be available. Chapter 4, like chapters 2 and 3, suggests that the information and assump-tions on which the analysis of marginal reform is based are, because they are only local, considerably less demanding than those for nonmarginal changes or for the design of an optimal tax system.

The analysis of chapters 2 to 4 is mainly static. In chapter 5 we discuss ways in which the model may be extended to dynamic problems. We are usually forced into a fairly aggregative analysis for any given period, because there will essentially be many commodities arising from the many periods. Although there are problems in describing production possibilities, the behavior of consumers, and constraints on government in dynamic models, it is still possible to show how different assumptions concerning behavior will affect tax policy.

The final chapter of part 1, by Bliss, describes the relationship between the theories of optimal taxation, of cost-benefit analysis, and of effective protec-tion. Policy analysts interested in development are aware of the value of social cost-benefit analysis for investment appraisal, and many countries have been urged to undertake studies of effective protection in order to guide the reform of trade policy and industrial incentives. Both, then, are familiar tools for policy analysts, who will wish to know their relationship to the analysis of policy reform proposed in this book. Theories of optimal taxation and cost-benefit analysis are normative theories in the sense that they ask how taxes should be set or whether a project should be selected. Effective protection is a positive theory, because the measure of effective protection describes the relationship of tariffs to value added in an activity. Before the analysis of effective protection can be made normative, it must, if it is to provide an acceptable indicator of activities that should be promoted or discouraged, be modified so that it becomes a system of shadow prices—that is, so that it becomes identical to cost-benefit analysis. In the course of his discussion, Bliss focuses attention on the difficult question of why tariffs exist in the first place, inasmuch as most trade theory and the analyses under discussion suggest that they should be replaced by alternative policies such as sales taxes, wage subsidies plus profits taxation, and similar measures. Trade taxes, of course, can be administered with greater ease than sales taxes. Although it might be argued that this feature outweighs their other disadvantages, it is hard to accept that all trade taxes can be so defended. Bliss also analyzes shadow prices in a simple model in which tariffs are fixed.

2

The Theory of Optimal Commodity and Income Taxation: An Introduction

Nicholas Stern

WHAT TYPES OF GOODS should be taxed? How progressive should the income tax be? What should be the balance between the taxation of commodities and the taxation of income? These questions are obviously central to public finance and have occupied many of the leading economists of the last two centuries from Smith, Mill, Dupuit, Edgeworth, and Wicksell to Pigou and Ramsey. The period since 1970, however, has seen a tremendous growth in the formal analysis of these problems, and the main purpose of this chapter is to give the reader an introduction to this newer literature. Much of it has been technical, but I shall try here to offer a broad understanding of the methods of approach, the type of arguments used, and the main conclusions reached. An introduction is provided to some of the theories that later chapters will construct and apply to problems of developing countries.

The models to be examined require modifications and extensions before they can be applied to developing countries. Nevertheless, they do provide a number of fairly general and robust lessons, and I shall pay special attention to their identification. The three purposes of the chapter are, therefore, to provide an introduction to the literature on optimal taxation, bringing out the main elements of the approach; to identify general principles; and to establish a point of departure for many of the theories examined in this book.

The next section contains a description of the approach and scope of the modern theories. We shall indicate briefly some historical antecedents, bring out the important elements of the analysis, and underline some of the assumptions that require relaxation before the theories can be applied directly to developing countries.

This chapter is based on my paper "Optimum Taxation and Tax Policy" (Stern, 1984), which was written during a visit to the Fiscal Affairs Department of the International Monetary Fund in the summer of 1983. I am very grateful to the IMF and to Vito Tanzi, director of the department. I received helpful comments from E. Ahmad, A. B. Atkinson, A. S. Deaton, G. Frewer, D. M. G. Newbery, V. Tanzi, and participants at a seminar in the IMF. Special thanks are due to J. A. Mirrlees. All errors are mine.

In the third section I shall set out some of the main results of the theory of optimal taxation. I begin with commodity taxation and the Ramsey rule for the one-consumer economy and then examine its extension to an economy with many consumers. Optimal income taxation, following the approach of Mirrlees (1971), will be presented. I shall examine the appropriate combination of income and commodity taxation, often discussed under the heading of the balance between direct and indirect taxation. The fourth section discusses the specification and use of a social welfare function, an element that is central to the analysis previously described.

Some applications of the theory to discussions of tax policy are presented in the fifth section. It is shown that the simple principles embodied in this section can be used to discriminate among arguments in discussions of public policy. This is, of course, one of the main purposes of theoretical inquiry in economics—to establish which of the many possible intuitive and informal arguments are well founded. Tax reform (that is, the welfare analysis of a small movement from a given initial position) is briefly introduced in the sixth section, and its close relation to the theory of optimality is shown.

The Scope of Modern Theories

Much of the discussion in the nineteenth century was concerned with the enunciation of general principles to guide tax policy. One example was the argument between those who espoused the benefit principle (which states that those who benefit should pay) and those who argued that taxation should be based on ability to pay. This last concept was itself discussed extensively in terms of whether equal absolute or proportional or marginal sacrifice was appropriate where sacrifice was related to utility of (say) income. The argument included a discussion of whether the base should be income, expenditure, or wealth. For an analysis of this discussion and some of the classic statements, the reader may consult Musgrave and Peacock (1967).

The analysis of the questions of public finance in terms of a collection of principles continues and characterizes much of the literature to the present (see, for example, Musgrave and Musgrave, 1980). The modern theories of public economics have much in common with the traditional approach in that they take up two of the important themes of efficiency and equity. A central feature of the modern approach is that efficiency and equity are defined and combined in terms of the criterion of classical welfare economics, a Bergson-Samuelson social welfare function. They are firmly individualistic in that the behavior of consumers is modeled as utility maximization, and the welfare criterion counts as an improvement any change that makes one individual better off without making someone else worse off. The use and role of the social welfare function are discussed further below.

The unifying features of this approach provide substantial clarity and analytic power. There are, however, many interesting ethical economic issues that it leaves out. The approach is essentially "consequentialist," for example, in that policies are evaluated in terms of their consequences. We might argue that, in taxation as with other things, certain principles should be observed irrespective of their consequences. A case in point might be the kind of information the state should be allowed to use. Second, the consequences are evaluated solely in terms of changes in utility of the society's members. Again, this approach might exclude aspects of the consequences of a particular policy—concerning, for example, the rights that it grants individuals. For further discussions of some of these issues, see Sen and Williams (1982). Many of the questions that we are discussing here, however, concern whether a given rate of tax should be increased or decreased, and in this context the difficulties just raised may not be of overwhelming importance. They should not be dismissed, however, and may have considerable relevance for some aspects of social policy, for example, the question of which instruments of policy are admissible.

The analysis of taxation in the modern theory proceeds by first describing the effects of taxation and then applying criteria (usually a social welfare function) to evaluate those effects. This view splits the subject into a logically prior positive side and a subsequent normative side on which value judgments are introduced. In this chapter I shall concentrate on the normative, but it should be recognized that a large part of modern public economics is concerned with the positive: for example, more than half of a major textbook on the subject (Atkinson and Stiglitz, 1980) is devoted to the analysis of the consequences of taxes, and the analysis of normative issues does not begin until page 331. Examples of the positive issues are (1) the analysis of the consequences of income or wealth taxation for risk taking, (2) how different forms of company taxation will affect investment and the distribution of profits, (3) the effects of national debt and taxation on saving and growth, (4) how incomes of different households or groups are affected by a tax change (that is, by the incidence of a change), and so on. The application of careful and formal microeconomic theory to such questions has been a major feature of modern public economics. Questions of incidence will figure prominently in many chapters of the book.

Clearly, if it is difficult simply to calculate the consequences of policies, then the choice of the optimum among all policies may be intractable. After all, we are then searching through a set of options each of which presents analytical difficulties. The normative part of public economics has thus in the main been concerned with models rather simpler than those used for the analysis of positive questions only. For further discussion of the positive models, see Atkinson and Stiglitz (1980), and see Shoven (1983) for a discussion of applied general equilibrium models.

The modern theory of public economics takes as its point of departure the two basic theorems of welfare economics. The first of these states that a competitive equilibrium is Pareto efficient. The second states that a prescribed Pareto-efficient allocation can be achieved as a competitive equilibrium if prices are set appropriately and lump-sum incomes are allocated so that each individual can buy the consumption bundle given in the allocation at the prices that will prevail. The important assumptions for the first theorem are the existence of a complete set of markets and the absence of externalities. For the second theorem we require in addition, for private producers, decreasing or constant returns to scale; for consumers, diminishing marginal rates of substitution; and for the government, the ability to arrange lump-sum transfers and taxes. The prescribed Pareto-efficient allocation is often called "the first best," and we say that the assumptions and policy tools of the second theorem allow us to achieve the first best. With the failure of the assumptions or more limited policy tools, we have a problem of the "second best." Occasionally "first best" and "Pareto efficient" are used interchangeably, but it seems preferable to reserve "first best" for the desired Pareto-efficient allocation (that is, the one selected among all those possible) rather than for any Pareto-efficient point. Obviously, some Pareto-efficient points may involve very unattractive distributions of welfare.

It is common to regard these results as requiring such restrictive assumptions as to be devoid of practical interest, yet it is remarkable that the first of the theorems is an essential part of the argument of those who argue in favor of the virtues of the market mechanism, and the second provides a valuable framework for public economics in that much of the subject is concerned with the investigation of what the government may do, particularly through taxation, when the assumptions required for the second theorem fail to apply. In this chapter we examine the main results of the part of the investigation that concentrates on the inability to achieve a desirable set of lump-sum transfers.

The tax policies that may appropriately be used to deal with externalities have been extensively discussed in the literature (for a classic statement, see Pigou, 1962). The theory of public sector pricing is close to that of commodity taxation in that the difference between price and marginal cost is analogous to a tax (see, for example, Boiteux, 1956), and our discussion of commodity taxation thus essentially includes the important topic of public sector pricing. Valuable and interesting work in public economics has been done on the problem of measuring marginal cost (see, for example, Drèze, 1964).

Recall that a lump-sum tax on an individual is a payment that the individual cannot alter by any action. Thus a tax on cigarettes is not lump sum because an individual can pay less by smoking less; similarly, a wealth tax is not lump sum because one can accumulate less. Clearly we would want to relate our lump-sum transfers and taxes to individual circumstances, yet at the same time the collection of information for those taxes—for example, data on earning power or wealth—will be such as to prevent them from being lump sum. The individual will discover what is being measured and will usually be able to adjust that dimension if it seems desirable to do so. Note that lump-sum taxes are not, in general, impossible. Differential taxation by sex or height is lump sum if it is assumed that no direct action would be taken to change these characteristics and that there would be no emigration. The difficult problem is the achievement of desirable lump-sum taxes.

This conclusion has implications of two sorts. First—a fairly robust general notion—there is an argument in favor of taxing things that individuals or firms cannot easily vary in response to taxation. An important example would be pure rent or monopoly profits, where these can be identified, as we shall shortly see more formally with regard to a case in commodity taxation. Second, we need a theory that addresses the problem of taxation in a world where lump-sum taxes are limited. This consideration leads us directly to the theory of optimal taxation.

In conclusion, it is interesting to note that much of the argument concerning public sector pricing and taxation that we have just been discussing was set forth by Wicksell in a remarkable article in 1896 (see Musgrave and Peacock, 1967). He notes the importance of marginal-cost pricing in the public sector and the importance of financing losses and other government activities by lump-sum taxation, for example, on land. This approach is linked directly to a Pareto improvement through his notion of unanimity.

The Standard Assumptions

As we have indicated, the theories of optimal taxation may be seen as an examination of the principles of taxation when we rule out lump-sum taxation. In order to focus on this question we retain the other assumptions of the standard competitive model that is used in classical welfare economics. Thus we assume that production takes place in firms in competitive conditions, with profits distributed to consumers; that there are no externalities; and that the price-taking consumers maximize utility. Concerning the tax tools to be examined, we usually make the further assumptions that, in the case of income taxation, income can be observed perfectly and, for commodity taxation, that all goods can be taxed. These assumptions are made for (good) reasons of tractability and to allow us to isolate the impact of the absence of lump-sum taxes.

Some of the other assumptions concerning the model and tax tools are relaxed in the next chapter and in other chapters of the book. Thus in chapter 3 we examine the possibility that distortions in the economy give rise to a divergence between shadow prices and producer prices, and we also consider the effects of taxes in noncompetitive markets. In part 4 the limitations on tax tools play an important role in much of the analysis, as does the explicit recognition that households are producing units as well as consuming units. In this chapter, however, we shall keep everything very simple, concentrating on the effects of taxes on consumers and on revenue. We shall see, however, that the extension of the standard theories of externalities and public goods to second-best economies is relatively straightforward. Production is pushed into the background, using the assumptions of competitive markets and fixed producer prices; in a sense we are assuming that the production side can be perfectly controlled, and we concentrate on the consumption side, where we suppose information is weaker, thereby (for example) precluding the full set of lump-sum transfers. Production plays a prominent role in the next chapter.

Optimal Taxation

In this section we examine optimal commodity taxation, optimal income taxation, and the optimal combination, in that order. These topics might be seen as indirect taxation, direct taxation, and the old question of indirect versus direct taxation, which are often discussed rather vaguely and are complicated by different definitions of "direct" and "indirect." Under the optimal taxation approach, we specify the tools that are available in a precise and formal way and then analyze how they should be set. Before examining the analysis in detail, we may usefully consider the balance between direct and indirect taxation in general terms. We shall define a direct tax as one that is personal in that the rate(s) depend on the individual or household (varying, for example, according to income, wealth, age, family structure, and so on).

In standard welfare economics, lump-sum direct taxes may be used to achieve the first-best distribution of income for any set of value judgments, and indirect taxes enter the picture only on efficiency grounds, in particular as a way of dealing with externalities. In the one-consumer economy, furthermore, a poll tax will be the best way of raising revenue. We shall assume (reasonably) that lump-sum taxes are not possible and that there are many consumers. We then examine appropriate taxes on commodities and incomes, and we shall find that both efficiency and equity arguments will be involved in the selection of each type of tax. Furthermore, except in special cases, we would want to use both sorts of tax if both are available.

The question of direct taxation versus indirect does, however, remain interesting, because we can still concern ourselves with the adequacy of uniform commodity taxation. If commodity taxation is at a uniform rate, then the same effects can be achieved by a proportional tax on incomes; thus the indirect taxes could, in principle, be replaced by direct taxes. Whether this is the best way to collect them is, of course, another question. Uniformity is a substantive issue quite apart from the balance beween direct and indirect taxes, because it greatly simplifies administration. In the following discussion uniformity will thus be an important theme.

Commodity Taxation

Economists examining optimal taxation where lump-sum taxes are impossible have concentrated on commodity taxation and income taxation. Analysis of the former problem began with Ramsey (1927). Important papers by Boiteux (1956) and Samuelson (1951) were written shortly after the Second World War, but the subject expanded rapidly in the 1970s, following the Diamond-Mirrlees papers of 1971. The subject of optimal income taxation was created by Mirrlees (1971), discussed below. This has been by far the most influential paper in the area because it both specified the problem precisely and analyzed it in considerable depth; see also Fair (1971).

The Ramsey problem is to raise a given revenue from a consumer through the taxation of the commodities consumed in such a way as to minimize the loss in utility that arises from taxation. Ramsey considered the case of one consumer (or equivalently identical consumers who are treated identically), and so we have a simple efficiency problem in that distributional considerations are ignored (a point to which we shall return). Notice that the one-consumer case is a somewhat artificial vehicle; we could and should raise all the required revenue by a poll tax and have zero commodity taxes. It is best seen as an example with which to develop some intuition and some ways of interpreting the many-consumer case.

In interpreting the results from the Ramsey problem, and for further reference below, we will find it useful to have in front of us a brief description of the partial-equilibrium approach to the question. These two brief analyses will be used to demonstrate the methods and to develop some intuition that we shall call upon in later arguments. They are, however, obviously very simple and unsatisfactory in a number of ways.

The partial-equilibrium assumption here is that the demand for a good or commodity does not depend on the price of other goods, so that we can draw the familiar demand curve DD' (see figure 2-1).[1] We assume producer prices $\mathbf{p}$ are fixed, so that the effect of a tax vector $\mathbf{t}$ is to increase prices $\mathbf{q}$ faced by consumers from $\mathbf{p}$ to $(\mathbf{p} + \mathbf{t})$. The so-called deadweight loss from the taxation of the ith good is measured by the shaded triangle ABC in the figure. The motivation for this definition of deadweight loss is as follows: the state of affairs associated with a given tax, and thus consumer prices and demand, is evaluated by the sum of benefits to the consumers (measured by consumer surplus), to the government (measured by tax revenue), and to producers (measured by profits). Note that the sum is unweighted, so that one dollar to each group is regarded as equally valuable.

Profits here are assumed to be zero (producer prices are fixed, so that competition would drive profits to zero), and we therefore consider only consumer surplus plus government revenue. In the absence of taxation, government revenue is zero, and consumer surplus is the area below the demand curve and above the line GC. With taxation, government revenue is given by the rectangle $ABGH$, and consumer surplus is the area below the demand curve and above AH. The net loss, or deadweight loss, is thus the triangle ABC.

Where taxes are zero, then obviously government revenue is zero. When the tax is GD, so that demand is zero, revenue is also zero. Hence government revenue $ABGH$ has a maximum for some level of tax $\hat{t}$ between zero and GD. It will thus never be optimal to have a tax rate above $\hat{t}$, because lowering the rate to $\hat{t}$ will increase both revenue and welfare. This argument has been standard in public finance since Dupuit first made it in 1844 (see Dupuit in Arrow and

Figure 2-1. *Deadweight Loss in Partial Equilibrium*

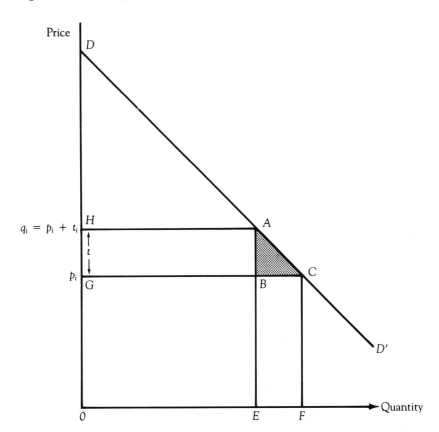

Scitovsky, 1969) and has recently been reemphasized in discussions of the Laffer curve. It also appears in chapters 14 and 16.

We examine the minimization of the sum across goods of triangles ABC (that is, total deadweight loss), subject to the constraint that the sum across goods of the rectangles ABGH (total tax revenue) is not less than a given figure. It is straightforward to show that, following this procedure, the tax as a proportion of the consumer price of each good should be inversely related to the elasticity of demand. Formally, $t_i/q_i = \mu/\varepsilon_i$, where μ is constant across goods and q_i, t_i, and ε_i are, respectively, consumer price, tax, and own-price elasticity of demand (as a positive number) for the ith good.

Following the work of Harberger (1954), who applied this approach to measure the deadweight losses caused by monopoly (the distance of price above marginal cost playing an analogous role to the tax), the empirical literature has included a number of calculations of such triangles. The more modern approach is to use explicit utility functions and "equivalent varia-tions," thus avoiding the unattractive assumption that the demand for a good does not depend on the prices of other goods (see, for example, Hausman, 1981a; King, 1983a; and Rosen, 1978).

We now give a brief mathematical formulation of the central result in optimal commodity taxation, the single-person Ramsey rule. This rule dispenses with the partial-equilibrium assumption concerning demands and uses explicit utility functions. To keep things simple, we retain the assumption that producer prices are fixed, so that an increase in taxes implies an equal increase in consumer prices. Goods may be either bought or sold by consumers. Sales are treated as negative purchases. It is convenient to treat the sale of labor differently from the sale of other goods and to identify it separately as l in the utility function and the budget constraint. If w is the wage faced by the consumer, who has lump-sum income M, $\mathbf{x}$ is the vector of quantities transacted, and $\mathbf{q} \cdot \mathbf{x}$ denotes $\Sigma_i\, q_i\, x_i$, then the individual problem may be written:

(2-1)
$$\begin{array}{c} \text{Maximize} \quad u(\mathbf{x},\, l) \\ \mathbf{x},\, l \\ \text{subject to} \quad \mathbf{q} \cdot \mathbf{x} - w\, l = M. \end{array}$$

Note that if the prices of all goods and labor are raised by taxation in the same proportion, so that $q_i = (1 + \tau)p_i$ and $w = (1 + \tau)w_p$, where w_p is the wage faced by producers (there is a wage subsidy), then we effectively have a lump-sum tax. The reason is that the proportional change in prices is simply equivalent to a reduction of M to $M/(1 + \tau)$, as may be seen by inspection of the budget constraint in problem 2-1. The revenue is $\tau M/(1 + \tau)$. In the one-consumer economy with lump-sum incomes, this form of taxation would be optimal, provided that the revenue requirement R does not exceed M. In this case, the optimal uniform tax rate τ is given by

(2-2)
$$\frac{\tau}{1 + \tau} = \frac{R}{M}.$$

Where there are no lump-sum incomes, proportional taxes (including the wage subsidy) raise no revenue. If the revenue requirement does exceed M, then distortionary taxes (that is, those not equivalent to lump-sum taxes) will be necessary.

If there are no lump-sum incomes (M = 0), then we may choose one good to be untaxed without loss of generality. It is convenient to make that good labor. For a formal discussion of the numeraire, see the appendix to chapter 3. When M = 0, the budget constraint is simply

(2-3)
$$\mathbf{q} \cdot \mathbf{x} = w\, l.$$

Then, for the consumer, a tax rate $\hat{\tau}$ on wage income—reducing the posttax wage to $w(1 - \hat{\tau})$—is equivalent to raising prices to $q/(1 - \hat{\tau})$. We shall assume in what follows in this subsection that there are no lump-sum incomes and that labor is untaxed. Notice that, if we consider leisure L as the argument of the utility function and T as an endowment of time, then equation 2-3 becomes

(2-3a) $$\mathbf{q} \cdot \mathbf{x} + wL = wT.$$

In this sense the individual has an endowment of time that finances the purchase of goods and leisure. A lump-sum tax levied from this endowment would be first best, but we have assumed that this choice is impossible.

We consider, then, just one consumer whose individual demands $\mathbf{x}(\mathbf{q}, w)$ are a function of consumer prices only. The maximum utility an individual can achieve when facing prices $\mathbf{q}$ is written $V(\mathbf{q}, w)$: this is the indirect utility function. The problem then becomes to choose $\mathbf{t}$, or, equivalently, $\mathbf{q}$, to maximize $V(\mathbf{q}, w)$ (and thus to minimize utility loss) subject to the constraint that the tax revenue $\Sigma_k\, t_k\, x_k$ meets the requirement $\bar{R}$. $\bar{R}$ is the value at $\mathbf{p}$ of the bundle of goods and factors required by the government. We need not concern ourselves with the precise form of the bundle required, because the government can transform its revenue at prices $\mathbf{p}$ into whichever goods it desires.

Formally, then, we have the problem

(2-4)
$$\begin{aligned} &\text{Maximize} \quad V(\mathbf{q}, w) \\ &\quad\quad \mathbf{q} \\ &\text{subject to} \quad R(\mathbf{t}) = \Sigma t_k\, x_k \geqq \bar{R}. \end{aligned}$$

Taking a Lagrange multiplier for the constraint, λ, the first-order conditions for maximization are

(2-5) $$\frac{\partial V}{\partial t_i} + \lambda \frac{\partial R}{\partial t_i} = 0.$$

The discussion of optimal commodity taxation has concentrated very heavily on the interpretation and analysis of first-order conditions such as equation 2-5. The satisfaction of these conditions, however, does not guarantee that we have an optimum. Before we can have such a guarantee, generally speaking, the problem must be concave in the sense of maximizing a concave function over a convex set. The revenue constraint, however, is the product of taxes and demands, and furthermore the concavity properties of demands depend on third derivatives of the utility function. Thus the programming problem will not, in general, be concave. We shall in this chapter (and for much of the book) ignore the problem of establishing global optimality, and we do not usually even check for local optimality (through the second-order conditions). In doing so we follow the literature. It seems that little that is both general and interesting concerning the sufficiency of first-order conditions for global optimality has been established or perhaps is to be expected. The analysis of the first-order conditions can, however, yield valuable insights, and as necessary conditions for optimality, they deserve attention. We now investigate them in more detail.

Remembering that producer prices are fixed so that differentiation with respect to t_i and q_i are equivalent, we have

(2-6) $$\frac{\partial V}{\partial q_i} + \lambda\left(x_i + \sum_k t_k \frac{\partial x_k}{\partial q_i}\right) = 0.$$

Using $\partial V/\partial q_i = -\alpha x_i$ where α is the marginal utility of income and the standard decomposition of $\partial x_k/\partial q_i$ into a (symmetric) substitution effect and an income effect ($= s_{ik} - x_i \partial x_k/\partial M$), we have the Ramsey rule

$$(2\text{-}7) \qquad \frac{\sum_k t_k s_{ik}}{x_i} = -\theta$$

where s_{ik} is the utility-compensated change in demand for the ith good when the kth price changes and where θ is a positive number independent of i. It is easy to show that θ is $-\alpha + \lambda(1 - \Sigma_k t_k \partial x_k/\partial M)$, and we explain in the appendix to this chapter that θ may be interpreted in terms of the benefits from a switch to lump-sum finance.

An intuitive interpretation of equation 2-7 is as follows. We can view $\Sigma_k t_k s_{ik}$ as the (compensated) change in demand for the ith good resulting from the imposition of the vector of small taxes $\mathbf{t}$. The typical term in the sum is

$$t_k \, \partial x_i/\partial t_k \Big|_{\text{constant utility}}$$

which is the change in the compensated demand for good i as a result of the increase in consumer price t_k if t_k is small. Summing across k gives the change arising from the vector of taxes. Strictly speaking, of course, the size of the taxes t_k is determined within the problem, and we are not really justified in assuming that taxes t_k are small. With this qualification, however, according to the Ramsey rule, the proportional reduction in compensated demand that results when the set of taxes is imposed should be the same for all goods.

This result is an important one and provides the main insight into tax rules that arise from the theory of optimal commodity taxation. It should be emphasized that proportional changes in *quantity* are equal in this rule. Thus, crudely speaking, quantities that are relatively insensitive to price will be taxed relatively more. It will be important later in our argument that this notion is, in general, very different from the proposition that taxation should be uniform, that is, that all proportional price changes should be equal. The result provides a generalization of the rule that taxes should be inversely related to elasticities of demand, which is familiar from the less rigorous partial-equilibrium treatment that we have just seen. The Ramsey rule offers an example of the general principle that efficient taxation is directed toward goods that cannot be varied by consumers. Note, however, that we need to exercise considerable care with substitutes and complements, a question that is suppressed by the partial-equilibrium approach. If we do take such care, we come directly to the emphasis on the (compensated) quantity reductions.

Given that labor was assumed to be untaxed and that there is an endowment of time, the Ramsey rule can be interpreted in terms of the complementarity with leisure and substitutability for leisure of the taxed consumer goods; a notable early example was the work of Corlett and Hague (1953). Goods that tend, relatively speaking, to complement leisure should bear the higher tax rate. Thus we can show (Deaton, 1981) that, if leisure is quasi-separable from all goods, then the Ramsey rule gives uniform taxation of goods. Intuitively, quasi-separability means that all goods complement leisure equally. Formally, goods i and j are quasi-separable from leisure if the marginal rate of substitution between i and j is independent of leisure at constant utility (where compensation for a change in l occurs via a proportional change in the vector $(\mathbf{x}, l)$. Note that the issues of complementarity, substitutability, and separability with respect to leisure arise because there is an untaxed endowment of time, and in a sense we are trying to levy a tax on this lump-sum income. The conclusions would be expressed in terms of another good if there were a corresponding endowment of that good. The concept of complementarity is, of course, simply another way of considering elasticities. With quasi-separability, furthermore, preferences are such that uniform taxation rather than anything else brings about the equal proportional reductions that we are seeking.

As we have noted, in a sense the one-consumer economy is an awkward vehicle for the development of the argument. The reason is that lump-sum taxation (which we know, in general, is first best) becomes simply a poll tax, which, it might be argued, would be feasible. Alternatively, as we saw above when we dealt with fixed lump-sum incomes, the same result may be achieved equivalently through proportional taxation of *all* goods (including subsidies on factor supplies). The real case of interest is, of course, the many-consumer economy, and here the poll tax is, in general, not *by itself* the best way to raise revenue, and indirect taxation will be required. Indeed, in the many-consumer case the optimal poll tax will often be negative, that is, it will be a poll subsidy. Our discussion of the Ramsey rule should therefore be viewed as a development of the intuition for application in the more general case.

The Ramsey rule would seem to be rather inegalitarian in that it appears to direct commodity taxation toward "necessities," which we usually consider fairly insensitive to price. Still, by formulating the problem in terms of one consumer, we explicitly ignore distributional questions. The result can, however, be generalized to many consumers in a fairly straightforward way. We simply replace $V(\mathbf{q}, w)$ in problem 2-4 with the social welfare function $W(u^1, u^2, \ldots, u^H)$, where u^h is the utility function of the hth individual, which we again consider as a function of consumer prices $\mathbf{q}$ and the wage w^h. The total demand $\mathbf{X}(\mathbf{q}, w)$ is $\Sigma_h \mathbf{x}^h (\mathbf{q}, w^h)$ where $\mathbf{x}^h(\mathbf{q}, w^h)$ is the demand function for individual h. The rule, then, is no longer that the proportional reduction in compensated demand should be the *same* for all goods or commodities; our modification shows how it should vary across goods. The proportional reduction in quantity for a good should now be higher where the share of the rich in its total consumption is higher. Strictly, we are using "the rich" here to designate those people whose social marginal valuation of income is low. Following an argument similar to that used in the derivation of the Ramsey rule equation 2-7, we can show

(2-8)
$$\frac{\sum_h \sum_k t_k s_{ik}^h}{X_i} = -(1 - \overline{b}\, r_i),$$

where s_{ik}^h is the Slutsky term for household h; $\bar{b}$ is the average across households of b^h, the net social marginal valuation of income of household h; and r_i is the normalized covariance between the consumption of the ith commodity and the net social marginal valuation of income plus one (and is defined formally in equation 2-20 below.)[2] By net we mean the value of an extra dollar to individual h as perceived by the government plus any extra indirect tax revenue arising from the expenditure of the dollar (formally $b^h = \beta^h/\lambda + t \cdot \partial x^h/\partial M^h$ where β^h is the social marginal utility of income, M^h is lump-sum income, and λ is the Lagrange multiplier on the revenue constraint). The number r_i is a generalization of the distributional characteristic of a good introduced by Feldstein (1972) and indicates the (relative) extent to which a good is consumed by individuals with a high net social marginal valuation of income—the interpretation as the distributional characteristic is explained when the equation for r_i is presented below (equation 2-20).

Thus the proportional reduction of compensated demand denoted by the left-hand side of equation 2-8 embodies the efficiency arguments for taxing necessities introduced in the Ramsey rule, together with the distributional judgment as associated with the r_i on the right-hand side, which indicates taxation of luxuries. The implication of equation 2-8 for tax rates will depend on the way in which these two effects combine. Much will depend on the structure of preferences and the type of income tax tools available, as we shall see.

Public Goods and Externalities

Where lump-sum taxes are possible, a standard first-order condition for the optimality of the level of public good supply is that the sum across consumers of the marginal willingness to pay should be equal to the marginal cost. A crucial feature is that the sum across consumers is unweighted—because lump-sum taxes have been set optimally, the social marginal utility of income (β^h) is the same for all households. Where lump-sum taxes are not possible, the standard condition is modified in two ways. First, we must weight the willingness-to-pay by the β^h. Second, we must take into account the effect of an extra unit of the public goods on tax revenue. An improvement in the extent or quality of public broadcasting, for example, may produce an increase in the purchase of taxed radios. The first-order condition for the kth public good, level e_k, when revenue is raised by commodity taxes is, therefore,

$$(2\text{-}9) \qquad \sum_h \beta^h \rho_k^h = \lambda p_k - \sum_i t_i \frac{\partial X_i}{\partial e_k}$$

where ρ_k^h is the marginal willingness to pay on the part of the hth household, p_k is the marginal cost at producer prices, and $\partial X_i/\partial e_k$ is the effect on total demand for private good i of a marginal increase in k (see Diamond and Mirrlees, 1971, for a formal derivation).

A similar analysis holds for externalities, as we should expect, inasmuch as public goods are a special case. The standard Pigovian argument for the case where lump-sum taxes are possible is that, for any given private good, each household should face a household-specific tax equal to the marginal diseconomy inflicted on others, measured by their marginal willingness to pay to avoid an increase. Where lump-sum taxes are not possible, the appropriate marginal tax is given by the sum of the marginal willingness to pay weighted by β^h plus any marginal loss to tax revenue associated with demand shifts that follow from an increase in consumption of the private good.

Considered as a whole, the argument underlines two important general principles associated with policy analysis in economies without lump-sum taxes: (1) marginal costs or benefits have to be weighted by social marginal utilities of income and (2) the effect of policy changes on tax revenues through demand shifts must be treated explicitly.

Income Taxation

Both Adam Smith and John Stuart Mill argued that taxation should be linked to ability to pay, with the former stating, "Subjects should contribute in proportion to their respective abilities," and the latter arguing, "Whatever sacrifices the [government] require . . . should be made to bear as nearly as possible with the same pressure upon all."[3] The form that pressure should take was extensively discussed, and conclusions often reflected a notion of cardinal utility, linking income to some utility level. At various points it was suggested that the sacrifice of utility should be equal for everyone or that an equal proportion of utility should be sacrificed. Given a utility function (assumed to be the same for everyone) and one of these principles (say, equal absolute sacrifice), we can calculate a corresponding tax function. If income is Y and the tax payable is $T(Y)$, then, given some total revenue requirement, we can calculate T, assuming that Y is independent of the tax schedule, for each level of Y from

$$(2\text{-}10) \qquad\qquad U(Y) - U(Y - T) = \text{constant},$$

the condition for equal absolute sacrifice. For calculations in this framework, see Stern (1977). We can show, for example, that if $U'(Y) = Y^{-\varepsilon}$, then taxation is progressive (in that the marginal exceeds the average rate) for $\varepsilon > 1$. The logarithmic or Bernoulli form corresponding to $\varepsilon = 1$ gives proportional taxation.

These criteria are adduced, however, without any reference to guiding principles. From this point of view, the notion of "equal marginal sacrifice" set forth by Edgeworth has greater clarity in that it derives from the utilitarian objective of the sum of utilities. If we assume again that pretax income is independent of the tax schedule, and further that everyone has the same strictly concave utility function, then equal marginal utility implies equal posttax incomes. The marginal tax rate is thus 100 percent, casting the question of incentives in a very stark light. This problem of incentives was recognized very early in the discussion: see, for example, McCulloch (1845/ 1975), part 1, chapter 4: "Graduation is not an evil to be paltered with. Adopt and you will effectively paralyze industry. . . . The savages described by Montesquieu, who, to get at the fruit cut down the tree, are about as good financiers as the advocates of this sort of taxes" (p. 146).

The incentive and distribution aspects of the income tax have long been recognized. Perhaps surprisingly, a model that examined the distribution and the size of the cake simultaneously did not appear until 1971 (Mirrlees, 1971). The Mirrlees paper essentially created the subject of optimal income taxation. As we shall see, Mirrlees kept his model as simple as it could possibly be, given the issue at hand, but the problem is nonetheless not easy, and the analysis poses considerable technical difficulties. The reason is that the policy tool is the whole income tax *function*. Thus for each income we must specify the tax payment, and the optimization occurs in a space of all admissible functions. This situation contrasts with that manifested in the problems usually examined in standard microtheory (for example, consumer or producer behavior), where only a finite number of variables—for example, consumption of each type of good—is considered.

We can simplify the income tax problem considerably by confining our attention to a linear tax schedule that combines a lump-sum benefit or tax with a constant marginal tax rate. After the Mirrlees article was published, a number of papers examined the simpler problem (see Atkinson and Stiglitz, 1980, lecture 13, for references). In the discussion of numerical results, I shall concentrate on the linear case but shall begin by setting forth the Mirrlees nonlinear problem, explaining why it takes the form that it does. The main results for the nonlinear problem are then summarized, with numerical calcula-tions for the linear case presented in conclusion to illustrate the sensitivity to the important parameters and in order to compare the computed tax rates with levels we see in practice. Some work has recently been done on an intermedi-ate case with a finite number of individuals—we might interpret them as representative of certain groups—where the optimal tax schedule can be taken as piecewise linear (see Guesnerie and Seade, 1982; and Stern, 1982).

Given that the nonlinear problem will pose difficulties, it is sensible for us to begin by keeping the structure as simple as we can while retaining the question. Considered from this point of view, the model concerned with distribution and incentives must have two features: individuals should not be identical, and there must be an input over which individuals exercise choice. If individuals were identical, then the optimum would be given by a poll tax with zero marginal taxation (this is the standard result of welfare economics); if there were no incentive problem, as we have seen in our discussion of Edgeworth above, the marginal rate would be 100 percent. The Mirrlees model has individuals who differ only in their pretax wage or productivity, and incentives have only one aspect, labor supply. Thus in the model, labor is supplied by individuals, each of whom has an identical utility function in order to maxi-mize the utility of consumption and leisure, in view of the pretax wage and the income tax schedule. The government chooses the income tax schedule so as to maximize a Bergson-Samuelson social welfare function, subject to the raising of some given amount of revenue.

All individuals have the same utility function $u(c, l)$, which depends on consumption c and labor supply l. Individuals differ in their wage rates w, and the distribution of w is described by the density function $f(w)$. We speak of an individual as being of type w. The government knows the distribution of w but cannot identify the w associated with a particular individual. If it *could* do so, then the optimum would be of the standard first-best type, with the lump-sum tax a function of w.

The problem is to choose a function $g()$ that relates posttax to pretax income in order to maximize

(2-11) $\int \phi(u) f(w)dw$

subject to

(2-12) $\int [wl - g(wl)] f(w)dw = R$

where (c, l) is chosen by the individual to maximize $u(c, l)$ subject to

(2-13) $c = g(wl)$

and where $\phi(u)$ is a monotonic transform of utility (we introduce ϕ to provide a way of discussing different attitudes to inequality). The government revenue requirement is R, which is seen as fixed for the problem 2-11–2-13. At a later stage we shall ask how the solution varies with different values of R. The maximand 2-11 is a Bergson-Samuelson social welfare function of additive form; we add $\phi(u)$ across individuals. Equation 2-12 represents the revenue requirement; wl is pretax income, so that $wl - g(wl)$ is the tax payment by individual type w, and this is integrated or added across individuals. The constraint 2-13 represents the second-best nature of the problem, that is, it says individuals make their own choice subject to the budget constraint set by their wage and the government tax function. We can express this idea by saying that no individual would prefer the pretax income of some other individual (pretax income is essentially effort, which individuals select for themselves).

Before proceeding to results, we should note some particular features of the model. First, as specified, the model is static, and there is no saving. This provision keeps the structure as simple as possible. From a broader perspective, we might regard l as representing lifetime labor supply and c as lifetime consumption, but the treatment of l as a vector would take us too far afield at this point. We shall shortly consider a vector of different consumption goods, however. Second, equation 2-12 may be replaced in a general equilibrium framework by a production constraint, namely that total production, a function of total effective labor $\int (lw) f(w) dw$, must equal total consumption $\int cf(w) dw$ plus R. Here we assume that w measures productivity so that wl is effective tasks performed by person type w in hours l. It is then straightforward to show that this general equilibrium model is equivalent to the problem 2-11–2-13. Notice that relative wages and effective hours or tasks per clock hour are exogenous, so that the tasks performed by different individuals are perfect substitutes.

Third, note that the constraint 2-13 gives the model its special structure in that it embodies the incentive constraint. Without this constraint we could go to the first best using lump-sum taxation. It is interesting in this context that the first-best optimum would have utility *decreasing* in ability w if consumption and leisure are normal goods (see Mirrlees, 1979). Intuitively, high lump-sum taxes on people who are able would lead to work concentrated on the most productive people (note that there is no difference between individuals on the consumption side). In the income tax model we assume explicitly that the government *cannot* distinguish between types of individuals and measures only an individual's income (not hours of work or wage). Thus with the constraint embodied in equation 2-13, we must have utility nondecreasing in w—an individual of higher w always has the option of consuming the same amount as an individual of low w while doing less work.

Fourth, we cannot guarantee that at the optimum $l(w) > 0$ for all individuals. Thus it may be optimal for some group of individuals with the lowest productivity to do no work.

We turn now to some results in the Mirrlees model of nonlinear taxation. The number of general results (in the sense that they are independent of functional forms) that are available are rather few. Moreover, these results themselves may not hold if we modify the model, for example to include complementarities between different types of labor (see, for example, Stern, 1982). The important ones in the Mirrlees model are (1) the marginal tax rate should be between zero and one; (2) the marginal tax rate for the person with the highest earnings should be zero; and (3) if the person with the lowest w is working at the optimum, then the marginal tax rate he or she faces should be zero.

I will not offer formal proofs of these propositions here but will give some intuitive arguments (see Mirrlees, 1971, and Seade, 1977, for the formal treatment). Let us consider first whether the marginal tax rate should ever exceed one. The implication would be that the reward for the marginal hour was negative. Hence in the model, no one would choose to work where the marginal tax rate exceeded one, and so we could replace any portion of the $g()$ function that slopes downward with a horizontal section without changing behavior (see figure 2-2), and we can confine our attention to tax schedules with marginal rates that do not exceed one.

We have illustrated the tax function and consumer choice in figure 2-2. For an individual with fixed w, we can draw indifference curves in the pretax-posttax income space, because the former represents work and the latter consumption. Through any point, the indifference curve for a person with higher w will, we suppose, be less steep than that for a person with lower w: at the given consumption level, the person with higher w is doing less work and

Figure 2-2. *The Budget Constraint and Choice of Hours of Work*

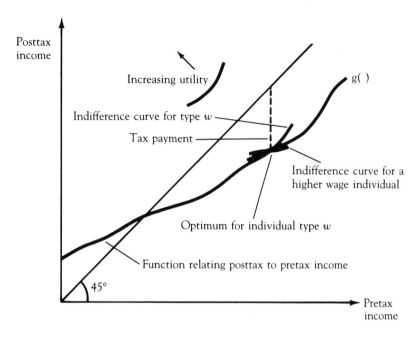

Source: Stern (1984), pp. 339–78.

will thus need less extra consumption to compensate him or her for doing the (lower) amount of extra work required for the extra dollar. In general, then, a person with higher w will locate to the right of (will earn more money than) the person with lower w, because at the optimum for the person with lower w [tangency with $g()$], the indifference curve for the person with higher w will intersect g from above (coming from the left).

The tax payment is given by the vertical distance from $g()$ to the 45 degree line. Note that a movement of an individual parallel to the 45 degree line keeps revenue constant. It is possible to use this feature to show that the marginal tax rate cannot fall below zero. If it were below zero at some income, then $g()$ would be steeper than 45 degrees, as would the indifference curve of any individual choosing that income. In this case, $g()$ would be steeper than 45 degrees and, intuitively, an equal revenue shift of person w in the southwest direction would take that person to a higher indifference curve.

An intuitive argument for the second result would be the following. Suppose, with some given income tax schedule, that the person with highest income earns $Y pretax and the marginal tax rate is positive. Consider the option of lowering the marginal tax rate to zero for all incomes above $Y. The top person may now decide to work more (the reward for the marginal hour has gone up) and, if so, will be better off. The government has lost no revenue, because the tax payment on the income $Y has stayed constant. The utility of the top person has increased, that of others is no lower, government revenue is no lower, and we have therefore found a Pareto-improving change that meets the constraints. Accordingly, the given income tax schedule could not have been optimal, and the schedule that is optimal must have the property that the marginal tax rate at the top is zero. If people near the top elect to work more in response to the change, then they are both better off and pay more tax, so that the argument is reinforced.

We cannot deduce that, where there is no highest income and the distribution of skills includes individuals at or above any positive skill levels, the optimal tax rate tends to zero. There are cases (see Atkinson and Stiglitz, 1980, lecture 13; and Mirrlees, 1971) in which it does not (involving the Pareto distribution). We should remember, too, that the argument assumes that there are no externalities, so that making the top individual better off upsets no one. Furthermore, the "top" may be a very high level of income. Zero may be a poor approximation even within most of the top percentile. Nevertheless, the result is rather striking.

I shall not give the argument for the third result concerning the zero marginal rate at the bottom in any detail. It proceeds along the following lines. Suppose that on a given schedule the marginal rate at the bottom is greater than zero. Consider a change in the lower end of the tax schedule that has the sole effect of inducing the bottom person to do a little more work, thus moving a small amount along the schedule. To the first order in utility, that person is no worse off, because his indifference curve was tangential to the schedule. There is a first-order increase in tax revenue, however, because the marginal rate is positive. Hence, the given schedule is not optimal (for formal discussion of this result and the previous one, see Seade, 1977).

Thus, the general results in this particular model tell us that the marginal rate should be zero at the top and bottom. This finding contrasts strongly with the workings of many tax-cum-social-security systems, and we shall briefly return to this issue later.

Mirrlees (1971) presented a number of numerical calculations of the optimum nonlinear income tax, using the Cobb-Douglas utility function for consumption and leisure and wage distributions based on data for the United Kingdom. From these examples he concluded:

1. The optimal tax structure is approximately linear, that is, a constant marginal tax rate, with an exemption level below which negative tax supplements are payable.

2. The marginal tax rates are rather low ("I must confess that I had expected the rigorous analysis of income taxation in the utilitarian manner to provide arguments for high tax rates. It has not done so" [Mirrlees, 1971, p. 207]).

3. "The income tax is a much less effective tool for reducing inequalities than has often been thought" (Mirrlees, 1971, p. 208).

Ten years ago (Stern, 1976) I investigated a wider class of utility functions and in addition examined sensitivity with respect to the social welfare function and the level of government revenue, confining attention to linear taxation. I used the constant elasticity of substitution utility function

$$(2\text{-}14) \qquad u(c, l) = [\alpha (1 - l)^{-\mu} + (1 - \alpha)c^{-\mu}]^{-1/\mu}$$

with welfare criterion

$$(2\text{-}15) \qquad \frac{1}{(1 - \varepsilon)} \int_0^\infty [u(c, l)]^{1-\varepsilon} f(w) \, dw.$$

The tax function in the model is linear, so that the individual budget constraint is

$$(2\text{-}16) \qquad c = (1 - t)wl + g$$

where t is the marginal tax rate and g the lump-sum grant (the same for everyone). The government budget constraint is

$$(2\text{-}17) \qquad t \int wlf(w)dw = g + R$$

where, as before, R is an exogenous revenue requirement, and where the number of individuals is normalized to 1 so that g is the total payment on lump-sum grants.

The utility function of equation 2-14 has an elasticity of substitution between consumption and leisure of

$$(2\text{-}18) \qquad \sigma = \frac{1}{1 + \mu}.$$

We may use empirical estimates of labor-supply functions to estimate σ, and these suggest a number near 0.4 on the basis of estimates for married males in the United States (Stern, 1976, p. 136). Where the elasticity is less than one, the labor-supply function (for positive g) is forward sloping for low wages and backward sloping for higher wages. Notice that the concept of labor supply in the models is much broader than the simple measure of hours used in the estimation of short-run supply functions. The Mirrlees labor-supply function corresponds to the limit as σ tends to 1 (μ tends to zero), and $\sigma = 0$ gives right angle indifference curves (zero substitution effect). We can show generally that with $\sigma = 0$ the optimal marginal rate is 100 percent. Note that this is zero *compensated* elasticity of labor supply and *not* inelastic labor supply. A selection of the results appears in table 2-1.

We may regard ε as analogous to the elasticity of the social marginal utility of income that is often used in analyses of measures of inequality using the Atkinson index (see Atkinson, 1970), because the utility function is homogeneous degree 1 in consumption and leisure (doubling each would double utility) and is thus itself analogous to income. The specification of ε then completes the statement of distributional value judgments. Note, how-

Table 2-1. *Calculations of Optimal Linear Marginal Tax Rates*

σ	ε = 0		ε = 2		ε = 3		ε = ∞	
	t	g	t	g	t	g	t	g
	R = 0 (purely redistributive tax)							
0.2	36.2	0.096	62.7	0.161	67.0	0.171	92.6	0.212
0.4	22.3	0.057	47.7	0.116	52.7	0.126	83.9	0.167
0.6	17.0	0.042	38.9	0.090	43.8	0.099	75.6	0.135
0.8	14.1	0.034	33.1	0.073	37.6	0.081	68.2	0.111
1.0	12.7	0.029	29.1	0.062	33.4	0.068	62.1	0.094
	R = 0.05 (equivalent to about 20 percent of GDP)							
0.2	40.6	0.063	68.1	0.135	72.0	0.144	93.8	0.182
0.4	25.4	0.019	54.0	0.089	58.8	0.099	86.7	0.139
0.6	18.9	0.000	45.0	0.061	50.1	0.071	79.8	0.107
0.8	19.7	0.000	38.9	0.042	43.8	0.051	73.6	0.082
1.0	20.6	0.000	34.7	0.029	39.5	0.037	68.5	0.064
	R = 0.10 (equivalent to about 45 percent of GDP)							
0.2	45.6	0.034	73.3	0.110	76.7	0.119	95.0+	—
0.4	35.1	0.000	60.5	0.065	65.1	0.076	89.3	0.112
0.6	36.6	0.000	52.0	0.036	57.1	0.047	83.9	0.081
0.8	38.6	0.000	46.0	0.016	51.3	0.026	79.2	0.057
1.0	40.9	0.000	41.7	0.002	47.0	0.011	75.6	0.039

Notes: In each pair of columns, the first entry is the marginal tax rate (percent) and the second is the lump-sum grant. ε = 0 corresponds (roughly) to an absence of aversion to inequality in incomes and ε = ∞ to the Rawlsian maxi-min. In Stern (1976), (1 − ε) is used in place of ε. A central estimate of the elasticity of substitution σ might be 0.4. Total output in these models is about 0.25 (it is endogenous), so that $R = 0.05$ corresponds to government spending (excluding transfer payments) of about 20 percent of gross national product. Where the optimal tax rate is above 95 percent, the precise level and g were not calculated (a dash is shown for g). The level of the uniform grant g was not presented in the Stern (1976) tables. It satisfies the government budget constraint 2-17, that is, $tY = g + R$, where Y is national income per capita. Hence Y can be calculated from the values of t, g, and R presented.

Source: Based on Stern (1976), table 3.

ever, that the social marginal utility of income is independent of g for ε = 0 but does depend on w, so some redistribution is still desirable even in this case. Values of ε between 1 and 2 are quite commonly used. Dalton (1922/1967, pp. 68–69) argued that Bernoulli's law (or utility logarithmic in income and marginal utility, decreasing as the inverse of income), ε = 1, "gives a rather slow rate of diminution of marginal utility," and he saw ε = 2 "as best combining simplicity and plausibility" (although he was working in the context of equal absolute sacrifice). Whether these views of ε helped him when he subsequently became chancellor of the exchequer is a matter for speculation.

National product in the model is endogenous but is mostly near 0.25. Hence a revenue requirement of R of 0.05 corresponds to about 20 percent of GNP. The case ε = 2, R = 0.05, and σ = 0.4 gives a marginal tax rate of 54 percent. The expenditure of the 54 percent of GNP consists of 34 percent for transfer payments and 20 percent for expenditure on goods and services. These results are not wildly out of line with tax rates (taking direct and indirect together) from a number of developed countries. Hence if we consider a wider class of cases than those used by Mirrlees, the computed tax rates may be rather higher.

Generally, the tax rates increase with the aversion to inequality ε and with the revenue requirement R but decrease with σ, the elasticity of substitution. The value of the (uniform) lump-sum grant moves in the same direction as tax rates but much more sharply. Thus, for example, in the case $\varepsilon = 2$, $R = 0.05$, the tax rate is halved as we move from σ of 0.2 to σ of 1.0, but the lump-sum grant is divided by four. For low values ($\varepsilon = 0$) of inequality aversion, the grant becomes very small (for example, zero to three significant figures for $R = 0.05$, $\sigma = 0.8$). The lump-sum grant is the money income of the poorest person (with zero wage). Thus it is never optimal to have negative grants; the poorest individuals could not then survive.

The Combination of Income and Commodity Taxes

The question of the appropriate combination of income and commodity taxation provides fertile ground for confusion. Many economists have claimed that the allocation effects of indirect taxes are inferior to those of direct taxes. The contention in its simple form is mistaken, because there is an excess burden or deadweight loss associated with the divergence between consumer and producer prices for labor and thus with the income tax, just as with other goods. A second example concerns the claim that we often hear, that a switch from income tax to indirect taxes such as a value-added tax would increase work effort. At the simple level, this statement is clearly false: an increase in prices (from the VAT), together with an increase in earnings (from the reduction in income tax), would leave the incentive to work unchanged. Perhaps the argument is intended to be subtler, depending on intertemporal allocations and expectations—on progressivity or on the existence of lump-sum incomes, for example—but it is usually presented in naive forms, such as "taxing spending rather than earning induces work."

As it happens, we can show that, under certain conditions, it would be desirable to tax income rather than goods, but those conditions are very special. The argument depends critically on particular features of the model and involves some difficulty. Furthermore, it is not easy to determine how the obvious divergence of the world from these special conditions should influence our views on the balance between direct taxation and indirect taxation. Thus, at least formally, the subject involves difficulty in analysis, and interpretation is not straightforward. We must beware of simple arguments or contentions such as the ones described.

I shall not present the details of the theorems on the optimal combination of income and commodity taxes but shall instead highlight the importance of the assumptions and give an intuitive feel for the results. There are essentially two theorems: the first deals with the case in which there is a linear income tax, and the second, the case in which there is a nonlinear income tax.

Note that if individuals are identical, then the basic theorem of welfare economics tells us that the first best can be reached with a lump-sum tax to raise the required government revenue and zero marginal taxation of income and goods. With different individuals, then, some combination of income and commodity taxes will be necessary, and each of these is distortionary in that marginal rates of substitution between labor and goods or among goods in consumption will not be equal to marginal rates of transformation in production. Notice that some distortionary taxation will always be optimal in second-best problems, because a marginal imposition of taxes from a position of zero taxation involves zero deadweight loss and will be desirable if it improves distribution.

For the first theorem we assume that a linear income tax is available in the form of a lump-sum grant or tax (the same for everyone) and a constant marginal rate on labor income. As we saw previously, a constant marginal rate on labor is, in this context, equivalent to a proportional tax rate on all goods (and a proportional adjustment to the lump-sum grant/tax), because we assume that there are no sources of income other than the lump-sum grant/tax and wages.

The first-order conditions for the optimal indirect taxes are given, as before, by equation 2-8. The condition for the optimality of the lump-sum grant is that $\bar{b} = 1$, that is, the grant is adjusted to the point where the benefit in terms of social welfare of the marginal dollar (the average of the social marginal utilities of income) is equal to the cost to the government (one dollar). Substituting this condition in equation 2-8 gives us

$$(2\text{-}19) \qquad \sum_h \frac{\sum_k t_k s_{ik}^h}{X_i} = -(1 - r_i)$$

where

$$(2\text{-}20) \qquad r_i = \sum_h \frac{x_i^h}{X_i} \cdot \frac{b^h}{\bar{b}}.$$

Recall that r_i is 1 plus the normalized covariance between consumption of the ith commodity by the hth household and the net social marginal utility of income b^h. From equation 2-20 we think of r_i as the distributional characteristic of good i: it is the weighted average of the x_i^h with weights $b^h/\bar{b}H$), divided by the average (X_i/H), and it measures the extent to which the ith good is consumed by people with a high net social marginal utility of income. If the government is indifferent to distributional considerations in that it sees b^h as equal for all households, then r_i will be equal to 1, and the right-hand side of equation 2-19 will be zero. Indirect taxes are zero and all revenue is raised through the lump-sum grant (tax), as in the case of identical individuals. Thus in this sense indirect taxes are desirable *because* distributional considerations arise: they may be seen as financing reductions in the poll tax (which bears most heavily on the worst off)—although it must be remembered that this consideration applies where the poll tax is feasible, and we are thinking of a combination of poll tax and indirect taxes.

We have seen that indirect taxes appear because we are interested in distribution, but this observation does not tell us what form the indirect taxes should take. The taxation of goods consumed by the rich provides some progressivity, but indirect taxes also have the effect of raising revenue to increase the progressive lump-sum grant (or to reduce the regressive tax), and the taxation of necessities may be an efficient way to raise this revenue (as in the Ramsey case). The way in which these two considerations balance each other depends quite critically on the form of the differences among the population and on the structure of demand functions, as we see from the first of the theorems below.

If we have an optimal linear income tax, individuals have identical preferences but differ in the wage rate, and the direct utility function has the Stone-Geary form, which gives rise to the linear expenditure system

$$(2\text{-}21) \qquad U(\mathbf{x}, l) = \sum_{i=1}^{n} B_i \log (x_i - x_i^0) + B_0 \log (l_0 - l)$$

then the optimal indirect taxes are uniform, that is, the proportion of tax in consumer price (t_i/q_i) is the same for all goods. The result follows from equations 2-19 and 2-20, using $\bar{b} = 1$ and substituting for the specific form of the Slutsky terms derived from equation 2-21. The result was established by Atkinson (1977), and the derivation is provided in an appendix to this chapter.

Deaton (1979 and 1981) shows that it applies in a class of cases somewhat wider than the linear expenditure system. The important conditions are (1) that the Engel curves are linear and identical (that is, for each good everyone has the same constant marginal propensity to consume and the same minimum "requirement" $\mathbf{x}^0$); and (2) weak separability (see equation 2-22) between leisure and goods.[4] The extension allows the B_i and x_i^0 to depend on price and dispenses with the LES labor-supply formulation. Deaton also shows (1979) that, if a subgroup of goods satisfies these two conditions, then taxes should be uniform for the subgroup. These results have recently been extended by Deaton and Stern (1985), who show that differences in intercepts of the Engel curves across households do not disturb the uniformity result provided that they depend only on household characteristics and that there is an optimal system of family grants that depend on household structure.

The second theorem states that, if we have an optimal nonlinear income tax, individuals differ only in the wage rate, and the direct utility function has goods weakly separable from labor in the sense that utility can be written

$$(2\text{-}22) \qquad u(\mathbf{x}, l) = u[\xi(\mathbf{x}), l]$$

where ξ is a scalar function. Optimal indirect taxes are then uniform. Weak separability involves the marginal rate of substitution between goods being independent of labor/leisure. The validity of the separability assumption is not easily judged (similar considerations arise in our discussion of complementarity in the Ramsey problem). Introspection may be as useful as or more useful than econometrics here, because the properties are very hard to determine statistically (and see Deaton's chapter 4 below).

An intuitive argument, due to Mirrlees, would be the following. At the optimum there will be a distribution across households of the pair (ξ, l) where ξ is the subutility. This optimum must have the feature that every ξ is supplied through the goods vectors $\mathbf{x}$ to households at minimum cost, because the separability assumption implies that it is only the level of ξ that affects the incentive problem and not its makeup in terms of goods. By the usual marginal arguments the minimum cost way of supplying the given ξ levels to the different households requires marginal rates of substitution in consumption to equal marginal rates of transformation in production and hence consumer prices proportional to producer prices. That is, we require uniform taxes. We could, presumably, recast this argument as a proof, although the standard discussion uses the calculus of variations (see, for example, Atkinson and Stiglitz, 1980, chap. 14). Intuitively, differences arise only in labor, which itself separates out from the utility function. Indirect taxation, then, cannot improve upon a flexible tax instrument that concentrates on labor income. Note that the more sophisticated income tax in the second theorem allows us to make a weaker assumption regarding preferences.

We shall consider the importance and interpretation of these two theorems shortly, but first we must recognize an important point. The taxes that emerge from optimal tax models depend critically on the combination of three sets of assumptions: (1) the form of differences between households; (2) the range of tax tools assumed to be available; and (3) the structure of preferences. These assumptions are made before specific parameter values, social welfare judgments, and revenue requirements are entered in the model, and the results will also be sensitive to these subsequent selections. The importance of examining the availability of tax tools makes it clear that we must analyze taxation and expenditure together, not separately, because a number of expenditure policies (particularly subsidized rations but also public goods) take the form of a lump-sum grant, and some of these can be differentiated across individuals.

The Social Welfare Function

In the approach just described, judgments concerning the appropriate relationship between efficiency and equity are embodied in the social welfare function. In this section we examine ways of viewing the social welfare function and how examples can be selected.

There are several possible (related) interpretations of the social welfare function. First, we can regard it as representing the views of a commentator with given values who is trying to suggest ways of improving a given tax or policy system. Second, we can see the social welfare function as forming part of a dialogue about policy. Thus it would be possible to imagine a discussion in which an economist calculated that a proposed tax system could be optimal only if the government had certain values. This is the so-called inverse optimum problem examined, for example, by Ahmad and Stern (1984). The government might then respond that either the taxes or the implied values are not what it has in mind. By moving back and forth between values and outcomes, the economist could help the government form a view of what its values are. Third, an analysis may be viewed in terms of interest groups. The social welfare function could be specified so as to reflect mainly or only the welfare of certain groups of individuals. The analysis could then help understand the policies that are proposed or might be proposed by these groups. Fourth, we can see it as arising from a notion of justice in which individuals try to judge what is fair or just from behind a "veil of ignorance," disassociating themselves from knowledge of who they are or will be (see Harsanyi, 1955, or Rawls, 1971). Fifth, the model could be viewed as a positive description of government behavior. There are doubtless further interpretations.

The authors of the various chapters in this book are not committed to a single view and might emphasize different interpretations. I find the first two views of particular interest, and I shall examine them in more detail below in the course of analyzing ways in which the social welfare function might be specified. It should already be clear, however, that the approach cannot sensibly be criticized on the grounds that it presupposes a benevolent and monolithic government. A little careful thought makes plain several different and useful interpretations of the approach. It therefore seems rather odd that this last criticism should surface from time to time.

How, then, might we go about constructing a social welfare function? First, it should be clear that we would not, in general, want to settle on a single social welfare function, because we should expect discussion of values to reveal differences, even after careful analysis has rejected some views as unattractive or inconsistent. Nevertheless, we do want to be able to indicate interesting ranges within which the values could reasonably lie and to grasp the meaning of different specifications.

The approach that I find particularly helpful involves the use of examples and the inverse optimum problem. The simplest course is to think of the following question. Suppose that we can transfer income between individuals without problems of incentives but that some income is lost on the way (perhaps it melts). Consider two individuals A and B. Then let us suppose that we would be prepared to lose as much as a proportion δ of a marginal transfer from A to B and still regard the change as an improvement (but that if the loss were more than δ it would be seen as a deterioration). Then

$$(2\text{-}23) \qquad\qquad \frac{\beta_A}{\beta_B} = (1 - \delta)$$

where β_A and β_B are the welfare weights. In this way we could in principle construct a system of welfare weights for all households. If we take a very simple world where the weights depend only on income M (we can imagine the discussion taking place for a given set of prices), then we can think of a functional form describing the relation between β and M. If, for example, relative β depends only on relative incomes, then we can write

$$(2\text{-}24) \qquad\qquad\qquad \beta = k M^{-\varepsilon}.$$

Then in the above example,

$$(2\text{-}25) \qquad\qquad\qquad \left(\frac{M_B}{M_A}\right)^{\varepsilon} = 1 - \delta.$$

If, therefore, we were prepared to lose as much as half the unit in a transfer from A to B, if A had twice the income of B, then ε would be equal to 1. Similarly, if δ were three-quarters, then ε would be 2.

The dependence of the relative welfare weights only on relative income cannot be accepted without question. In dealing with cases of extreme poverty, for example, we might consider writing $\beta = k(M - \hat{M})^{-\varepsilon}$ where $\hat{M}$ is some minimum subsistence level, so that $\beta \to \infty$ as $M \to \hat{M}$. This procedure again has its drawbacks; in any sample one is likely to find incomes below $\hat{M}$. "Minimum subsistence" does not really mean what it says if many people live with less. The specification of forms such as equation 2-24 requires careful thought and discussion.

The purpose of thinking through our values in a very simple case is that we may find it easy to comment directly on the policy. We can then infer the values in a straightforward way and use them in more complicated contexts. Moreover, experience with the use of optimal tax theory can help us with the problem of inferring values from decided policies. Thus, for example, we showed in the previous section how the optimal marginal tax rate could be related to distributional judgments and the elasticity of substitution between consumption and leisure. If we can estimate or specify the latter and can form some idea of the appropriate marginal income tax rate (and of the uniform lump-sum transfer), then we can infer our distributional values. Similarly, Ahmad and Stern (1984) showed how it is possible to work back from a system of commodity taxation to the underlying values. We therefore now have experience with models that can be of some assistance in a dialogue with policymakers on their preferred ways of specifying the social welfare function.

We should not, however, confine our attention to the second of our interpretations of the social welfare function, which involves government directly. The individual forming a personal judgment of policy will want to examine his (or her) values and should also find such discourse helpful. Thus the models should be considered useful for intelligent political and economic argument as well as in policymaking. Finally, we should note that the social welfare function is only the final step in the consequentialist approach. Most of the work in that approach is associated with calculating the incidence of taxes—that is, how they affect the different households of the economy.

Hence disagreements concerning the specification or use of the social welfare function should not be an excuse for avoiding the major task.

Applications to General Arguments

One of the main purposes of economic theory is to distinguish between correct and incorrect arguments and to help establish reliable rather than unreliable intuition. In this section I shall try to distill from the theory some lessons of this type. I shall begin by setting forth three general principles that emerge from the analysis and shall then turn to the question of uniformity of indirect taxation, commenting briefly on the income tax. The principles will be stated in summary form before their foundation and interpretation are discussed.

1. Tax revenue is raised most efficiently by taxing goods or factors with inelastic demand or supply. Note that this abstracts from distributional questions and that inelasticity refers to compensated demands and supplies. Care should be taken with the pattern of complements and substitutes in that we are looking at the impact on quantities of the whole set of taxes.

2. Taxation concerned with distribution and with externalities or market failures should as much as possible go to the root of the problem. Thus for distribution we should look for the sources of inequality (for example, land endowments or earned incomes) and should concentrate taxation there. In the case of externalities, we should attempt to tax or to subsidize directly the good or activity that produces the externality. Note, however, that it will often be impossible to deal completely with an issue directly, and this limitation will have very important consequences for other policies.

3. We must recognize that it will be impossible to deal perfectly with questions of distribution and market failure directly. The former, for example, require strictly a full set of lump-sum taxes. Thus the target-instrument approach may be treacherous in a second-best world. In this context, a range of policy tools will be required, and we shall need to ask how any particular policy affects all of our objectives—including distribution. The optimal policy for any one tax will often be very sensitive to assumptions concerning the availability and levels of other taxes.

The principles will be discussed in turn and will be related to the preceding analysis. The investigation started with the basic theorems of welfare economics, which clearly establish that the first-best way of raising revenue is a set of lump-sum taxes. The tax payment itself is then completely inelastic in that the behavior of individuals cannot affect the payment. This finding suggests the first principle. The discussion of the Ramsey problem concerning indirect taxes led in the same direction but cautioned us that the compensated demands were relevant. Any system of taxation will have an income effect; we distinguish among them by the "excess burden," or distortions in compensated demands.

The pattern of substitutes and complements will in general be of considerable importance. Away from the optimum, for example, a small increase in indirect taxation may yield a great deal of revenue at little cost if it leads to a sharp switch in demand to goods that are heavily taxed. We must beware of notions of increasing marginal distortion. In a second-best world, for example, we *cannot* assume, even in the one-consumer economy, that a reduction in indirect taxes and an increase in lump-sum taxes will increase welfare (see Atkinson and Stern, 1974). As we show, however, in the appendix to this chapter, in the one-consumer economy a shift away from indirect taxes toward lump-sum taxes, from an initial position, increases welfare, provided that the indirect taxes have been set optimally (given the level of lump-sum finance currently permitted). Even without optimal taxes some indirect tax exists that could beneficially be reduced in a switch to lump-sum taxes. In the many-consumer economy, the welfare effects of a shift between lump-sum taxes or transfers and indirect taxes will depend on the starting point and may be analyzed using the theory of reform described in the next section (this subject is considered in the appendix to this chapter and in chapter 4, by Deaton).

The notion underlying the first principle has been appreciated for a considerable time (by Henry George, Wicksell, Hotelling, and so on), but its application to indirect taxes and income taxes requires care. We saw in our discussion of the income tax, for example, that 100 percent marginal taxation would be indicated where the compensated elasticity of substitution between consumption and leisure is zero. This is *not* the same as a vertical supply curve for labor, which involves simply the balancing of income and substitution effects.

Again, the basic theorem of welfare economics illustrates the second principle in that distribution would be dealt with entirely through lump-sum taxes. It is illustrated, furthermore, by the theorems we have examined, where the optimal income tax was the only policy tool required when differences arose solely in earning capacity. We saw, however, that this result required other very strong assumptions concerning the structure of preferences. Thus although the target-instrument approach can point us to certain taxes, it should never delude us in a second-best world into thinking that we can forget about a target, such as distribution, after mentally allocating some tax to it. Where our instruments are imperfect, we shall have to consider all our objectives in the study of any one instrument.

The third principle is closely linked to the second. We saw that the desirability and structure of a differential system of commodity taxes depended crucially on our assumptions concerning the existence of the income tax and indeed on the type of income tax available. Taxation of necessities may be attractive where the revenue is used to provide a lump-sum grant but unattractive where no such lump-sum grant is possible. A narrow view of targets and instruments or of the policy tools available invites considerable error.

We turn now to the question of whether or not uniform taxation is desirable. We should distinguish sharply at the outset between consumer and producer taxation. The former has been the main subject of this chapter (see chapter 3 for producer taxation). We begin with a discussion of whether the taxes on final goods should be uniform. In general, the results from the many-person Ramsey analysis indicate that there is no bias in favor of uniform taxes. We saw that the rule balances two considerations: on the one hand, we exploit inelasticities in the sense of equal proportional reductions of quantities, but on the other we reduce demand less for those goods consumed by the poor. How these two effects combine will depend on the social values and the structure of demands for different individuals and groups.

The rule is modified in an important way if income taxes are allowed. We saw that in very special circumstances uniformity might be desirable. These circumstances involve, for the optimal linear income tax, for example, differences across individuals arising *only* from the wage rate, or lump-sum income, and not from preferences, a special structure of preferences (based essentially on the linear expenditure system), "minimum quantities," and marginal propensities to spend on each good that are identical across individuals regardless of income. The special nature of the conditions imply, in my judgment, that uniformity is a poor guide for developing countries. Individuals differ in many ways in their preferences, on which religion, caste, and education, for example, may have an important bearing. Furthermore, the underlying expenditure system may be an implausible representation of demands. The income tax is often an instrument of marginal importance and only partial coverage, and so we cannot assume that the poll tax or transfers have been set optimally. On the other hand, subsidized rations, public goods, and some forms of infrastructure allow transfers to certain groups. It is important to link these factors to the analysis of indirect taxation. Thus we may ask whether it is worth raising indirect taxes to finance this form of expenditure.

It is much more difficult to prescribe, however, than to identify the inadequacies of various prescriptions. The derivation of the appropriate set of commodity taxes requires information concerning patterns of complements and substitutes that is very difficult to extract from the data. Our attempts to extract it will require specifications of functional forms, which, as we saw, may have a profound effect on the recommendations. As Deaton (1981) observes: "In consequence, it is likely that empirically calculated tax rates, based on econometric estimates of parameters, will be determined in structure, not by the measurements actually made, but by arbitrary, untested (and even unconscious) hypotheses chosen by the econometrician for practical convenience" (p. 1245). Some of these difficulties are discussed further by Deaton in chapter 4, where he also shows how they relate to the theory of reform—the topic of the next section. Notwithstanding the influence of assumptions concerning functional form, we can still empirically consider the question of whether a move toward uniform taxes will improve welfare.

As we shall see in chapter 3, there is absolutely no reason to assume that uniformity of taxes on intermediate goods is desirable. In general, taxes on intermediate goods lead to inefficiencies, and there is no reason to suppose that uniform taxes lead to any less inefficiency than some arbitrary set. Taxation of intermediate goods should be avoided unless taxing a particular final good is difficult (and *its* inputs might then be taxed) or to improve the distribution of profits where this is not possible by other means.

We saw above how the marginal rate of linear income tax increases with the revenue requirement and the aversion to inequality and decreases with the elasticity of substitution between consumption and leisure. The discussion of the nonlinear tax showed us how the intuition on optimizing *functions* needs to be tutored carefully. There is no presumption, for example, of an increasing marginal rate. Indeed, the optimal schedule will, in general, show first an increasing marginal rate and then a decreasing one. In Mirrlees's calculations (1971), furthermore, the peak of the marginal rate was fairly close to the median. We should be very careful, however, to note that this behavior of the *marginal* rate should not be regarded as conflicting with any notion of the desirability of progression. Such notions should be related to the *average* rate, and it is quite possible for the marginal rate to take the required shape but for the average rate to be increasing much of the way. For this eventuality to occur, it is necessary only for the marginal to exceed the average. Where there is a uniform lump-sum grant, it is quite likely to do so over a big range. We should note, however, that, in any case, a statement concerning the relative desirability of an increasing average rate should itself be derived from a model concerning incentives and distribution and should not immediately be assumed to be obvious.

A marginal rate that at first increases and then decreases contrasts strikingly with the apparent state of affairs in the United Kingdom, where means-tested benefits give high marginal rates at the bottom and the income tax schedule shows increasing marginal rates. The practical issues are no doubt more complicated than our models indicate, but central features in public discussion are the attempt to target transfers to the poor (implying high marginal rates at the bottom) together with incentives (the so-called poverty trap). Thus the considerations of distribution and incentives lie at the heart of the debate.

Tax Reform

By "tax reform" we mean a movement away from some given status quo. We shall concentrate on marginal movements. The method was introduced formally above and will be developed and applied at a number of points in this book. An early empirical application was by Ahmad and Stern (1984)—see also chapter 11 below. We concentrate here on its relationship with calculations of optimality. Let us suppose that we have some vector of tax tools t in operation, the resulting level of social welfare is $V(t)$, and government revenue is $R(t)$. We can regard $V(t)$ as being defined by a Bergson-Samuelson social welfare function as before. We consider an increase in the ith tax t_i sufficient to raise one dollar of extra revenue. The rate of change with respect to the tax is $\partial R/\partial t_i$, hence to raise one extra dollar, we must increase the tax by $(\partial R/\partial t_i)^{-1}$. The rate of change of welfare with respect to the tax is $\partial V/\partial t_i$. We define the *fall* in welfare, λ_i, as the reduction in V consequent upon raising one more dollar by increasing the tax on the ith good.

$$(2\text{-}26) \qquad\qquad \lambda_i = -\frac{\partial V}{\partial t_i} \Big/ \frac{\partial R}{\partial t_i}.$$

We may think of λ_i as the *marginal cost in terms of social welfare of raising one more dollar from the ith tax.* If the marginal cost for tax i exceeds that for tax j, then it would be a beneficial reform to switch taxation on the margin from i to j. Thus, if $\lambda_i > \lambda_j$, we have a gain in welfare of $\lambda_i - \lambda_j$ from raising one more dollar via tax j and one less dollar via tax i. More generally, of any reform Δt, we ask about its consequences for welfare ΔV and for revenue ΔR, and it is beneficial if $\Delta V > 0$ and $\Delta R \geqq 0$. The statistics λ_i guide us in the selection.

There is, in general, a whole collection of beneficial reforms, and we should not expect uniqueness. We will usually choose among beneficial reforms on the basis of criteria that cannot be put directly into the model. Second-best analysis in this case provides a range of desirable options and thus is far from being nihilistic or pessimistic, as it is sometimes portrayed.

The optimum is the state of affairs where no beneficial reform is possible; thus, the theories of optimality and of reform are very close. Here, optimality requires that all the λ_i are equal. Call the common value λ, then

$$(2\text{-}27) \qquad\qquad \frac{\partial V}{\partial t_i} + \frac{\lambda \partial R}{\partial t_i} = 0.$$

This is precisely the first-order condition for optimality that emerges from the problem

$$(2\text{-}28) \qquad \begin{array}{ll} \text{Maximize} & V(t) \\ t & \\ \text{subject to} & R(t) \geqq \bar{R}. \end{array}$$

Notice that away from the optimum there are as many marginal costs of public funds as there are tax tools, and it is misleading to speak of a unique marginal cost of public funds. The Ramsey problem, the many-person Ramsey problem, and the linear income tax are all examples of optimizing models that take the form of expression 2-28.

In work described in Ahmad and Stern (1984, and chapter 11 below), we have applied this framework to the question of tax reform in India. Thus we have approached the question of resource mobilization by asking about the marginal cost in social welfare terms of raising revenue by different means. This approach has included the comparison of taxation of different goods, of state and central taxes, and of indirect taxes and the income tax. For indirect taxes, for example, we have, at fixed producer prices

(2-29)
$$\frac{\partial V}{\partial t_i} = -\sum_h \beta^h x_i^h$$

and

(2-30)
$$\frac{\partial R}{\partial t_i} = \frac{\partial}{\partial t_i}(\mathbf{t} \cdot \mathbf{X}) = X_i + \sum_j t_j \frac{\partial X_j}{\partial t_i}$$

where β^h is the social marginal utility of income for household h and the other notation is as described above (see discussion of equation 2-8). Equation 2-29 may be derived intuitively by noting that an increase in the price of good i hits household h in money terms by the amount of x_i^h that it consumes. The number β^h (a value judgment) converts the money measure into social welfare. They are to be selected by the decisionmaker. Equations 2-29 and 2-30 give us λ_i, as in equation 2-26.

The data requirements then are a consumer expenditure survey for the x_i^h (and thus X_i), knowledge of the tax rates $\mathbf{t}$, and aggregate demand responses $\partial X_j / \partial t_i$. For many countries, some information on all these things is likely to be available. Only *aggregate* demand elasticities are necessary, and they may be estimated from time-series data. Given that tax design, not short-term demand management, is at issue here, we require, in principle, medium- or long-run elasticities. We should subject the value judgments β^h to sensitivity analysis to show how results vary in response to different specifications.

A major effort was required when we applied the theory to India to calculate the tax rates. Notice that the t_j in equation 2-30 are taxes actually levied on final goods. Thus, we need to work with actual tax collections and to calculate the effects that taxing of intermediate goods has on taxes effectively levied on final goods. We call these "effective taxes." Measuring them involves a specification of the input-output process (see chapters 3 and 11). Results are presented in chapter 11. The approach using marginal costs λ is illustrated in the appendix to this chapter in a discussion of a switch between indirect and lump-sum taxes.

Conclusions

The purpose of the chapter has been to develop and explain the main results of the modern theory of optimal taxation, to show how they might be applied to guide our judgment of tax policy, and thus to provide an introduction to some of the arguments and applications set forth in later chapters.

As we saw, the theory implies that a number of simple statements, such as "efficiency requires uniform commodity taxes" or "egalitarianism implies increasing marginal income tax rates," must be approached with great circumspection. On the other hand, we argued that the theory did yield a number of general principles that are useful in guiding the practical decisionmaker. Furthermore, the theory can be applied to the detailed calculation of possible tax reforms, as will be shown in subsequent chapters. We have concentrated on consumers and on government revenue, pushing production into the background. Production will play a more prominent role in the next chapter.

Appendix: Lump-Sum Grants and Indirect Taxes

This appendix addresses some formal aspects of the relation between lump-sum grants and indirect taxes. We know that in the one-consumer economy the best way of raising revenue is a poll tax with zero commodity taxation. In the case of many consumers, we would want differentiated lump-sum taxes or transfers and no commodity taxation. If only a poll tax is allowed, however, we will usually want to combine it with nonzero commodity taxation, and we will often find that the optimal level of a poll tax is negative (that is, it is a transfer). Such would certainly be the case if some consumers could not exist without a transfer. In this appendix we examine two issues. The first is the relationship between the structure of preferences and the indirect tax structure in the presence of a poll tax. Specifically, if we have an optimal poll subsidy, and individuals differ in the wage rate but have identical preferences, as given by the linear expenditure system (equation 2-21), then optimal indirect taxes are uniform. Second, we examine the welfare aspects of a shift toward lump-sum taxation from indirect taxation in an economy with one consumer and toward a poll tax with many consumers.

The Linear Expenditure System and Uniform Taxation

We prove the result just described, which is due to Atkinson (1977). We start from equations 2-19 and 2-20, which give the first-order conditions for optimal taxes on the assumption that the poll tax or transfer is set optimally. The condition for the optimality of the poll tax is, where $b^h = \beta^h/\lambda + \mathbf{t} \cdot (\partial \mathbf{x}^h/\partial M^h)$, and M^h is the lump-sum income of household h,

$$(2\text{-A1}) \qquad \bar{b} \equiv \frac{1}{H} \sum_h b^h = 1.$$

From equations 2-19 and 2-20 we have

$$(2\text{-A2}) \qquad \sum_h \sum_k t_k \frac{s_{ik}^h}{H} = \bar{x}_i - x_i^*$$

where $\bar{x}_i$ is X_i/H, the average consumption of the ith good, and x_i^* is the weighted average using weights $b^h/H\bar{b}$, which sum to one.

The LES demands for the hth consumer, with wage w^h, are (see equation 2-21)

$$(2\text{-A3}) \qquad x_i^h = x_i^0 + \frac{B_i}{q_i}\frac{1}{\alpha^h}$$

where α^h, the private marginal utility of income, is given by

$$(2\text{-A4}) \qquad \frac{1}{\alpha^h} = M^h + w^h l_0 - \mathbf{q}\cdot\mathbf{x}^0$$

and M^h is the lump-sum income of household h, which includes the optimal transfer or tax. The Slutsky terms are given by

$$(2\text{-A5}) \qquad \begin{aligned} s_{ik}^h &= \frac{B_i B_k}{\alpha^h q_i q_k}, \qquad \text{for } i \neq k \\ s_{ii}^h &= \frac{B_i^2}{\alpha^h q_i^2} - \frac{B_i}{\alpha^h q_i^2}. \end{aligned}$$

Substituting into the left-hand side of equation 2-A2, we obtain

$$(2\text{-A6}) \qquad \frac{1}{H}\frac{B_i}{q_i}\sum_h \frac{1}{\alpha^h}\left(B^{\bullet} - \frac{t_i}{q_i}\right)$$

where

$$B^{\bullet} = \sum_{k=1}^{n}\frac{B_k t_k}{q_k}.$$

The right-hand side of equation 2-A2 is

$$(2\text{-A7}) \qquad \frac{B_i}{q_i}(\bar{a} - a^{\bullet})$$

where the macron and asterisk carry the same meaning as for equation 2-A2 and a_i^h is $1/\alpha_i^h$. From equations 2-A6 and 2-A7, we see immediately that t_i/q_i is independent of i, and we have uniform commodity taxation at the rate $B_0^{-1}(a^{\bullet}/\bar{a} - 1)$. This argument is examined for more general preference structures in Deaton (1979) and in chapter 4 of this book.

Marginal Shifts toward Lump-Sum Taxation

We consider first the one-consumer Ramsey problem such that now the government is allowed to levy a lump-sum tax T at a fixed level that is below the revenue requirement. Thus, analogously to equation 2-4 for given T, the problem is

$$(2\text{-A8}) \qquad \begin{aligned} &\text{Maximize by choice of } \mathbf{q}, \quad V(\mathbf{q}, w, -T) \\ &\text{subject to} \quad R(\mathbf{t}, T) = \sum_k t_k X_k + T \geq \bar{R} \end{aligned}$$

where in the indirect utility function V we have lump-sum income $-T$. We continue to assume that wage income is not taxed. Note that if all goods and services could be taxed, we could raise $\bar{R}$ in a lump-sum manner by saying that $t_i = \tau q_i$ for all goods including labor. Indirect tax revenue is then $-\tau T$ (from the budget constraint for the consumer, $q \cdot X - wl = -T$) so that lump-sum plus indirect tax revenue is $(1 - \tau)T$; we can put $\tau = \bar{R}/T - 1$ (< 0) to raise required total revenue. If we assume that one good or service (for example, labor) cannot be taxed, however, then raising $\bar{R}$ will require a combination of indirect taxes and the lump-sum tax.

Taking a Lagrange multiplier λ for the revenue constraint and forming the Lagrangean

$$(2\text{-}A9) \qquad \mathcal{L}(\mathbf{t}, T, \lambda) = V(\mathbf{t}, -T) + \lambda[R(\mathbf{t}, T) - \bar{R}],$$

the first-order conditions (remember T is fixed)

$$(2\text{-}A10) \qquad \frac{\partial \mathcal{L}}{\partial t_i} = 0$$

yield equations 2-6 and 2-7 as before, with

$$(2\text{-}A11) \qquad \theta = -\frac{\alpha}{\lambda} + \left(1 - \sum_k t_k \cdot \frac{\partial X_k}{\partial M}\right)$$

where M is lump-sum income (here equal to $-T$). From equation 2-7 we have

$$(2\text{-}A12) \qquad \sum_k \sum_i t_k s_{ik} t_i = -\theta \sum_i t_i X_i.$$

Hence θ is a positive number, because $\sum_i t_i X_i > 0$ (we have assumed $T < \bar{R}$).

Consider now a shift in the optimization problem brought about by a change in T.

$$(2\text{-}A13) \qquad d\mathcal{L} = \sum_i \frac{\partial \mathcal{L}}{\partial t_i} dt_i + \frac{\partial \mathcal{L}}{\partial T} dT + \frac{\partial \mathcal{L}}{\partial \lambda} d\lambda.$$

But $\partial \mathcal{L}/\partial t_i = 0$ from the first-order conditions 2-A10, and $\partial \mathcal{L}/\partial \lambda$ is zero, because we assume that the budget constraint holds with equality. Hence

$$(2\text{-}A14) \qquad d\mathcal{L} = \frac{\partial \mathcal{L}}{\partial T} dT.$$

Because the budget constraint holds with equality before and after the shift in T, however, we have $d\mathcal{L} = dV$. Thus the gain in welfare from a shift toward lump-sum taxation $(dT > 0)$ from a position with optimal indirect taxes is given by $\partial \mathcal{L}/\partial T$, and from equations 2-A9 and 2-A11 we have

$$(2\text{-}A15) \qquad \frac{\partial \mathcal{L}}{\partial T} = \theta \lambda.$$

Hence θ is a measure, in terms of revenue, of the benefit from a switch to lump-sum taxes, and we have seen that θ is positive. This result was derived in the appendix to Atkinson and Stern (1974).

It is interesting to see how the argument may be expressed in terms of the marginal costs of funds defined earlier in this chapter (see equation 2-6). The result is that the marginal cost of funds raised by lump-sum taxation λ_T is less than that raised by commodity taxation λ_i; the benefit of the switch of a unit of revenue from commodity to lump-sum taxes $\lambda_i - \lambda_T$ is positive. Now

$$(2\text{-}A16) \qquad \lambda_T = -\frac{\partial V}{\partial T} \bigg/ \frac{\partial R}{\partial T} = \frac{\alpha}{1 - \mathbf{t} \cdot (\partial \mathbf{X}/\partial M)}$$

and

$$(2\text{-}A17) \qquad \lambda_i = -\frac{\partial V}{\partial t_i} \bigg/ \frac{\partial R}{\partial t_i} = \frac{\alpha X_i}{X_i + \sum_j t_j (\partial X_j / \partial t_i)}.$$

Then from the optimality of the t_i we have $\lambda_i = \lambda$ for all i, and we may write equation 2-A11, using equations 2-A15 and 2-A16, as

$$(2\text{-}A18) \quad \lambda - \lambda_T = \frac{\theta\lambda}{1 - \mathbf{t} \cdot (\partial \mathbf{X}/\partial M)} = \frac{1}{1 - \mathbf{t} \cdot (\partial \mathbf{X}/\partial M)} \frac{\partial \mathscr{L}}{\partial T}.$$

Hence the benefit as measured by $\lambda - \lambda_T$ is the same as that measured using $\partial \mathscr{L}/\partial T$ where the extra term $1/(1 - \mathbf{t} \cdot \partial \mathbf{X}/\partial M)$ arises, because we have to raise the lump-sum tax by this amount to obtain a unit of revenue (net).

We can now examine generalizations of this analysis (1) to the case where the taxes t_i are not set optimally for given T and (2) to the case where there are many consumers. Where taxes are not set optimally, then we ask whether the marginal cost of funds from i could indeed be lower than that of lump-sum taxes for every i. Thus we ask whether it is possible that

$$(2\text{-}A19) \qquad\qquad \lambda_T > \lambda_i \qquad \text{for every } i.$$

From equations 2-A16 and 2-A17, and the Slutsky decomposition, expression 2-A19 implies

$$(2\text{-}A20) \qquad\qquad 0 < \frac{1}{X_i} \sum_j t_j s_{ji} \qquad \text{for all } i.$$

If we assume that $t_i X_i > 0$ for all i (so that both goods and factors are taxed; a negative t_k for a factor is like a tax because it signifies that the consumer price is below the producer price), then we have, on multiplying by $t_i X_i$ and summing:

$$(2\text{-}A21) \qquad\qquad 0 < \sum_i \sum_j t_j s_{ij} t_i$$

which contradicts the negative definiteness of the Slutsky matrix. Hence equation 2-A19 is not true, and there is a j such that $\lambda_j \geqq \lambda_T$. Thus even if commodity taxes are *not* optimal, there will exist some commodity tax that could be lowered beneficially with a switch to lump-sum taxation.

When there are many consumers, then we restrict attention to a poll tax, so that $R(\mathbf{t}, T) = \mathbf{t} \cdot \mathbf{X} + HT$. We may consider $\lambda_i - \lambda_T$ as before. The expressions for λ_T and λ_i become

$$(2\text{-}A22) \qquad \lambda_T = \frac{\sum\limits_{h} \beta^h}{H - \mathbf{t} \cdot \sum\limits_{h} (\partial \mathbf{x}^h / M^h)}$$

$$(2\text{-}A23) \qquad \lambda_i = \frac{\sum\limits_{h} \beta^h x_i^h}{X_i + \sum\limits_{j} t_j (\partial X_j / \partial t_i)}$$

and

$$(2\text{-}A24) \qquad \frac{\partial \mathcal{L}}{\partial T} = -\sum_{h} \beta^h + \lambda \left(H - \mathbf{t} \cdot \sum_{h} \frac{\partial \mathbf{x}^h}{\partial M^h} \right).$$

When the commodity taxes are optimal, we have $\lambda_i = \lambda$ for all i. Consider as before a marginal increase in T with adjustments in t_i to hold revenue constant from a point where $\partial \mathcal{L} / \partial t_i = 0$, that is, where $\lambda_i = \lambda$ for all i. Then, as before,

$$(2\text{-}A25) \qquad dV = d\mathcal{L} = \frac{\partial \mathcal{L}}{\partial T} dT$$

and

$$(2\text{-}A26) \qquad \frac{1}{1 - \mathbf{t} \cdot \sum\limits_{h} (\partial \mathbf{x}^h / \partial M^h)} \frac{\partial \mathcal{L}}{\partial T} = \lambda - \lambda_T.$$

Notice, however, that we can no longer show that $\partial \mathcal{L} / \partial T = \theta \lambda$ as in the single-consumer case using equation 2-A12, with θ positive, because the proportional reduction in compensated demand (that is, θ for the single consumer) now depends on the good. Hence it is quite possible that $\partial \mathcal{L} / \partial T$ will be negative, so that a switch to lump-sum taxation will reduce welfare. Indeed, from equation 2-A24 we see that if β^h is very high for some h (for example, the very poor) then $\partial \mathcal{L} / \partial T$ will indeed be negative, and starting from, say, zero T, we would want to reduce it—that is, we would want to introduce a lump-sum subsidy. On the other hand, if households are so similar that the one-consumer case is a reasonable approximation, then starting from zero we would wish to increase the lump-sum tax (assuming throughout that $\bar{R} > 0$, so that we are raising rather than distributing revenue).

Notes

1. The presentation of some of the standard theory and of figure 2-1 is taken from Stern (1983a).

2. That is, the covariance of x_i^h and b^h divided by the product of the means of x_i^h and b^h.

3. For references to the early debate, see Atkinson and Stiglitz (1980), lecture 13, and Musgrave (1959), chap. 5.

4. Deaton emphasizes linearity, but the proof also relies on the assumption that they are identical.

3

Aspects of the General Theory of Tax Reform

Nicholas Stern

SOME OF THE GENERAL PRINCIPLES that emerge from the theories of optimal taxation were presented in chapter 2. The purpose was to introduce the theory and to illustrate the approach and some of the results. I therefore explored only a few central themes and did not discuss the main assumptions at length or ask what effect altering them might have—nor did I examine the arguments in detail. This chapter will adopt a broader perspective and will show how the approach can be applied to problems of greater complexity than those discussed earlier. There will also be greater attention paid to some aspects of the detailed formulation in order to demonstrate the importance of certain assumptions and features of the argument. The main purpose of this chapter, therefore, is to examine some of the complex aspects that were suppressed in the simple model of chapter 2. Departures from the simple model may take a number of directions, and this chapter therefore lumps together a number of different points. Of particular prominence, however, are a more careful treatment of the production side of the economy and a fuller examination of tax incidence and imperfect markets. In chapter 2 we worked with constant producer prices and perfect markets so that questions of the impact of tax changes on production and factor incomes could be ignored. The analysis was conducted as if all taxes on goods had been shifted entirely to consumers, with factor incomes left unchanged.

In line with the greater complexity of the models, this chapter involves somewhat more technical detail than its predecessor. This detail reflects the effort to bring into the analysis some issues of practical importance that were neglected in the introductory exposition. The larger dose of theory does not imply that the models are less applicable. Because the sections are fairly disparate, there is no summary of their content here, but one does appear in the concluding section. The standard model of optimal commodity taxation incorporating production is presented first, showing the role of assumptions concerning returns to scale, profits, their taxation, and market structure. I shall consider, in particular, the question of whether certain sectors of the economy should operate efficiently and thus whether they should face the same relative prices in decentralized decisionmaking.

The incidence of indirect taxes in competitive models is examined in the third section, where special attention is paid to the distinction between traded and nontraded goods and to the coverage of taxes across different sectors. Two partial equilibrium topics are subsequently discussed, the incidence of taxes in noncompetitive models and the relationship of the reform analysis introduced in chapters 1 and 2 to standard calculations using familiar deadweight loss triangles. We shall see first that tax shifting in noncompetitive models can be more or less 100 percent and second that our reform approach generalizes the standard triangles in a straightforward way.

A much more general view is embodied in the fifth section, which describes the general theory of reform and shadow prices in models of production and consumption with the possibility of a multitude of constraints. There follows a brief comment on the relations between the theory of optimal taxation and some analyses in trade theory.

The seventh section reviews the general principles in the light of the extended analysis and pays special attention to the case for particular starting points such as uniform taxation. An appendix deals with the choice of normalization and of the untaxed good in tax problems, because it is a feature that may change the appearance of the analysis and thereby seems occasionally to generate confusion.

Production in the Standard Models of Optimal Taxation

The original Diamond-Mirrlees (1971) articles were entitled "Optimal Taxation and Public Production," thus emphasizing the importance of treating together the analysis of prices and quantities. In some of the subsequent literature, production played a minor role and the emphasis was on the detail of tax rules. Here, however, we shall return to the model of Diamond and Mirrlees (1971) to discuss the assumptions about production and in particular their results concerning production efficiency. Thus we examine the conditions under which (1) the public sector should, at the optimum, operate on its production possibility frontier and (2) the economy as a whole should be on its frontier. The former will apply under fairly general conditions, but the latter will generally not hold unless all production is in the public sector, all pure profits are taxed, or there is perfect competition in the private sector, with constant returns to scale.

In its simplest form the model had production taking place entirely in the public sector, and by treating that case first we can see the consequences of introducing private sector production and profits. The government chooses the prices at which goods are sold to or factors are bought from consumers, subject to the constraint that the factors purchased can through the production process produce the goods that are sold. We shall see that in certain circumstances the production choice is equivalent to the government's using a set of prices $\mathbf{p}$ in the public sector to decentralize production decisions so that indirect taxes, $\mathbf{t}$, may be seen as

$$(3\text{-}1) \qquad\qquad\qquad \mathbf{t} = \mathbf{q} - \mathbf{p}$$

where $\mathbf{q}$ is the vector of consumer prices. Household h has a net demand vector $\mathbf{x}^h$ where x_i^h is the amount of the ith good it purchases ($h = 1, 2, \ldots, H$). We follow the usual convention of treating supplies as negative demands, so that if x_i^h is negative, the household sells the ith good and receives q_i per unit. It is a crucial feature of the problem that there are no lump-sum incomes and, in particular, no lump-sum taxes or transfers. Hence if households behave competitively, the demand of household h is a function of $\mathbf{q}$ only and solves the problem of choosing $\mathbf{x}^h(\mathbf{q})$

$$
(3\text{-}2) \qquad
\begin{array}{c}
\text{Maximize} \quad u^h(\mathbf{x}^h) \\
\mathbf{x}^h \\
\text{subject to} \quad \mathbf{q} \cdot \mathbf{x}^h \le 0
\end{array}
$$

where $u^h(\mathbf{x}^h)$ is the direct utility function of household h. We shall assume nonsatiation so that, at the optimum for the consumer, the constraint holds with equality, and we have a unique solution $\mathbf{x}^h(\mathbf{q})$ to problem 3-2. The maximum utility for household h when prices are $\mathbf{q}$ is $v^h(\mathbf{q})$ where v^h is the indirect utility function, which here, like $\mathbf{x}^h(\mathbf{q})$, depends only on prices $\mathbf{q}$, because there are no lump-sum incomes. Thus purchases by the consumer of some goods or services are made possible by the sale of other goods or services.

The government's problem is, then, to choose $\mathbf{q}^*$ to

$$
(3\text{-}3) \qquad
\begin{array}{c}
\text{Maximize} \quad V(\mathbf{q}) \\
\mathbf{q} \\
\text{subject to} \quad \mathbf{X}(\mathbf{q}) \,\epsilon\, G
\end{array}
$$

where

$$(3\text{-}4) \qquad\qquad \mathbf{X}(\mathbf{q}) = \sum_h \mathbf{x}^h(\mathbf{q})$$

and

$$(3\text{-}5) \qquad\qquad V(\mathbf{q}) = W[v^1(\mathbf{q}), v^2(\mathbf{q}), \ldots, v^H(\mathbf{q})]$$

where $W()$ is a Bergson-Samuelson social welfare function and G is the public sector production set. After formulating the problem in this way, Diamond and Mirrlees (1971) showed that, with some fairly weak assumptions, the optimum $\mathbf{X}(\mathbf{q}^*)$ lies on the frontier of the production possibility set G. Hence if G is convex, the government production can be decentralized by using prices $\mathbf{p}$ and asking production sector managers to maximize profits with respect to these prices. The result that optimal production should be on the frontier is important both because it establishes the desirability of production efficiency at the optimum (apart from special cases where the marginal products of factors are zero or negative) and because it allows decentralization of production decisions using prices. Such a proposition in this literature is called an efficiency theorem.

In the present model, the efficiency theorem can be established using only the assumptions that an optimum exists, that $X(q)$ is continuous, and that from the optimum there exists some small price change that would (if feasible) increase social welfare—that is, $V(q)$ is increasing in some q_i or decreasing in some q_j, with $q_j^* > 0$. The proof follows from the argument that, if $X(q^*)$ were not on the frontier, then one could find a price change from q^* that would increase social welfare but would, because of the continuity of $X()$, be sufficiently small to keep $X(q)$ within the production possibility set. Such a price change would violate the optimality of q^* and would yield a contradiction, thus establishing that $X(q^*)$ is on the frontier.

We can use this model to generate the optimal tax rules considered in chapter 2 (for example, equations 2-5 and 2-6) by writing the production set G in the form of a function $g(X) \leq 0$ and introducing the decentralization prices p as the partial derivatives of $g()$ at the optimum. Thus we rewrite expression 3-3 as

$$(3\text{-}6) \quad \begin{array}{c} \text{Maximize} \quad V(q) \\ q \\ \text{subject to} \quad g[X(q)] \leq 0. \end{array}$$

Taking a Lagrange multiplier λ for the constraint 3-6, we have as first-order conditions

$$(3\text{-}7) \quad \frac{\partial V}{\partial q_i} - \lambda \sum_j \frac{\partial g}{\partial X_j} \frac{\partial X_j}{\partial q_i} = 0.$$

The prices, p, that decentralize the optimal production decision must be such that p_i/p_j is equal to the marginal rate of transformation of i into j, that is, $(\partial g/\partial X_i)/(\partial g/\partial X_j)$. Hence we may write

$$(3\text{-}8) \quad p_j = \frac{\partial g}{\partial X_j}$$

and equation 3-7 becomes

$$(3\text{-}9) \quad \frac{\partial V}{\partial q_i} - \lambda \sum_j p_j \frac{\partial X_j}{\partial q_i} = 0$$

or

$$(3\text{-}10) \quad \frac{\partial V}{\partial q_i} - \lambda \frac{\partial}{\partial q_i}\bigg|_p (p \cdot X) = 0$$

where the derivative is to be understood at constant p (we have written it as

$$\frac{\partial}{\partial q_i}\bigg|_p$$

in the second term to emphasize the point). From $\mathbf{q} = \mathbf{p} - \mathbf{t}$ and summing $\mathbf{q} \cdot \mathbf{x}^h = 0$ over h, however, we have

(3-11) $$0 = \mathbf{q} \cdot \mathbf{X} = \mathbf{p} \cdot \mathbf{X} - \mathbf{t} \cdot \mathbf{X}.$$

From equations 3-10 and 3-11

(3-12) $$\frac{\partial V}{\partial q_i} + \lambda \frac{\partial}{\partial q_i}\bigg|_{\mathbf{p}} (\mathbf{t} \cdot \mathbf{X}) = 0.$$

Now equation 3-12 is in the form of equations 2-5 and 2-6, so we have established that it is possible to analyze the problem of optimal taxation in this general equilibrium model *as if* it were simply a problem of maximizing social welfare subject to a revenue constraint. In so doing we have shown the desirability at the optimum of aggregate production efficiency. In addition, as we now see, it is unnecessary to assume that producer prices are actually fixed. We simply carry out the differentiation in equation 3-12, using producer prices at the levels associated with optimal production. This procedure is rather satisfactory in a number of respects. First, the problem with the revenue constraint allows us to focus on the problem of tax rules on the consumption or demand side only. Second, the production efficiency theorems illuminate a class of cases suggesting that for the analysis of projects we may be able to use a system of shadow prices that remains the same throughout the public sector. Similarly, as we shall see below, the theorems indicate the desirability of avoiding the taxation of intermediate goods for private production. Third, we would not want to be confined to models in which producer prices are independent of demand, because we would then be essentially forced to make the assumptions of the nonsubstitution theorem (constant returns to scale, no joint production, and only one nonproduced input) in order to justify the fixed producer prices.

Our analysis of optimal tax rules in chapter 2 was rather more general than the simple assumptions made there might suggest. The model we used in equation 3-3, however, with all production in the public sector, is itself restrictive. Is it possible to introduce private production into this framework?

Two special cases allow competitive private production to be encapsulated in the above analysis: (1) constant returns to scale in the private sector and (2) the ability to tax the profits of each firm at 100 percent. In these two cases we can continue to write the problem as in equation 3-3, supposing that the government can act as if it had full control of the private sector. The production that emerges at the optimum is then decentralized, using prices $\mathbf{p}$ as before except that now some of the enterprises are in the private sector. This difference does not affect the solution because, in the case of constant returns to scale, profits are zero, whereas in the second case they can all be taxed away. The essential difference between private and public production in this type of model is the generation of household incomes through profits in the former. This distinguishing feature has been suppressed directly by each of the two assumptions described above.

The production efficiency theorem tells us that intermediate goods should not be taxed. The whole production sector must be efficient, and thus all enterprises should buy and sell at the same prices. This is an important result where fiscal policy is concerned and suggests the desirability of systems such as VAT that allow the rebating of taxes on inputs so that indirect taxation falls only on final goods. We have seen, however, that the assumptions required for such a result are rather strong. In addition to the optimality of taxes, we require the following. First, there must be no pure private sector profits, or they must be fully taxed away. Second, it must be possible to tax all final goods and factors. Third, there must be perfect competition. Such restrictions do not mean that the results are uninteresting; on the contrary, they direct us immediately to some principles that are very useful in the guidance of practical policy. We can conjecture from this discussion, for example, that intermediate goods should be taxed only if the taxation of final goods is very costly or impossible. Thus effort should concentrate on taxing particular intermediate goods that appear as inputs into those final goods that cannot be taxed although it would be desirable to do so. Similarly, departures from efficiency can be justified in order to improve the distribution of income, for example through the subsidization of inputs to particular "deserving" groups (perhaps "cottage" industries). We would want to be convinced, however, that this was the best method of increasing the income of these groups (and that they were deserving).

Like other applications of perfectly competitive theory, this argument has confined attention to diminishing and constant returns to scale. If property rights to pure profits are marketable, then constant returns become the central case, with each kind of property taxed at different rates. Two problems then arise. First, can we discriminate perfectly between different kinds of property, and second, can we distinguish property from entrepreneurial or management services? If we fail to make the last distinction, then we may encounter important disincentive problems. The treatment of increasing returns raises serious modeling problems, because we must depart from perfect competition. In this area economic theory has recently made substantial progress—see, for example, Hart (1979)—and applications of some of the positive theories that have been developed may soon be feasible. Some simple partial-equilibrium models are discussed below.

Our discussion of efficiency theorems has thus far dealt with production in the economy as a whole or with "aggregate production efficiency." As we saw, rather strong assumptions were required to establish the desirability of this type of efficiency. It can be shown much more generally that public sector efficiency is a feature of optimal policy. We must suppose only that it is possible to dispose beneficially of extra output. If so, then we have no reason for failing to produce extra output from given inputs in the public sector—that is, there would be no argument in these models in favor of public sector inefficiency. With public sector efficiency we should then use the same set of shadow prices for all public sector enterprises—an important result. These prices may, however, differ from private sector production prices if the conditions for aggregate production efficiency do not apply.

Thus far we have assumed that production takes place in firms, either public or private. Nothing in the theory, however, prevents production from taking place in households. Indeed it is standard in general equilibrium theory to regard a household net demand function $\mathbf{x}^h(.)$ as being net of any production that takes place within the household. This possibility was noted in the original Diamond and Mirrlees papers. The relevant demand elasticities or derivatives in the tax rules described in chapter 2 then become those that relate to net sales and purchases, for example, to marketed surplus in the case of a peasant household that sells grain and buys other goods. This example demonstrates that two crucial aspects of the distinction between the production and consumption side in these models are the government's ability to observe firms and to set different prices for different agents. Hence, for example, we have assumed that profits can be observed for private producers but not for peasant households. In addition we have just supposed that the peasant households trade at consumer prices rather than at producer prices. In other models observability and control of private production, and government influence on peasant households and the prices they face, might be described differently. Some of these issues call for further research, and others are treated in part 4, on agriculture.

It should not be forgotten that the reasons for taxation of intermediate goods discussed here supplement, where they are relevant, the familiar arguments for taxation concerning externalities and market power.

Our discussion of production in this section has shown that the simple analysis of chapter 2 can be firmly embedded in a general equilibrium context. We have seen further that a number of valuable lessons concerning shadow prices and taxation in models with differing assumptions were evident along the way. The models discussed, however, were still fairly simple. We now turn to a more general framework.

Incidence of Indirect Taxes

Our previous discussion of tax rules has been conducted as if there were a 100 percent shift of indirect taxes. As the previous section explained, this reasoning involves the assumption not that producer prices actually are fixed but simply that optimal tax rules can be written as if they were. In this section I shall briefly discuss some positive aspects of the incidence of indirect taxes, without assuming optimality in any sense but instead asking what effect a tax change would have on prices. This consideration would be a crucial element in an analysis of tax reform, because price changes will affect changes in demand, supply, revenue, and welfare. We concentrate on changes from a given state of affairs rather than comparing equilibria with and without taxes, because it is the former that is practically relevant. We concentrate on perfectly competitive models—imperfect competition and oligopoly are considered in the next subsection.

In many respects the positive analysis of incidence is the most important and difficult part of the analysis of reform. Once the effects of taxes have been determined, and provided that we are willing to make value judgments, it is a relatively straightforward matter to evaluate those changes. Much of the effort in later chapters in this book is directed precisely toward the calculation of incidence. We shall see that the answers will depend critically on the structure of the model. Notice that more than half of the standard textbook on modern public economics (Atkinson and Stiglitz, 1980) addresses positive issues before normative questions are reached. In this section we simply characterize some of the important ingredients of the models and emphasize the role of assumptions concerning the openness of the economy and the coverage across sectors in determining the incidence of tax changes.

We consider three cases of general equilibrium: (1) in a closed economy where all goods may be taxed and a given good is taxed at the same rate wherever it is used; (2) the same situation in an open economy; and (3) a closed economy where there is only partial coverage, so that the same good or factor is treated differently in different parts of the economy. The fourth case of partial coverage in an open economy can be investigated along similar lines.

In a closed economy where all goods may be taxed we should distinguish between cases in which taxes are rebated on inputs (through, for example, a VAT) and cases in which they are not. The former case is relatively straightforward. To keep things simple, we suppose competitive conditions, no joint production, and constant returns to scale. We separate goods and factors and suppose that all the former are subject to indirect taxation, which is rebated on inputs. Thus we may write:

$$(3\text{-}13) \qquad\qquad \mathbf{q} - \mathbf{t} = \mathbf{p} = \mathbf{c}\,(\mathbf{p}, \mathbf{w})$$

where $\mathbf{q}$ is the vector of consumer, or final good, prices, $\mathbf{p}$ that of producer prices, $\mathbf{w}$ that of factor prices, and $\mathbf{t}$ that of tax rates, with $\mathbf{c}(.)$ the per unit cost function (in vector form). Differentiating, where δ_{ij} is 1 if $i = j$ and 0 otherwise,

$$(3\text{-}14) \qquad\qquad \frac{\partial q_j}{\partial t_i} = \delta_{ij} + \frac{\partial p_j}{\partial t_i}$$

and

$$(3\text{-}15) \qquad\qquad \frac{\partial p_j}{\partial t_i} = \sum_k \frac{\partial c_j}{\partial p_k}\frac{\partial p_k}{\partial t_i} + \sum_m \frac{\partial c_j}{\partial w_m}\frac{\partial w_m}{\partial t_i}$$

or, in matrix form,

$$(3\text{-}16) \qquad\qquad \frac{\partial \mathbf{p}}{\partial t} = \frac{\partial \mathbf{p}}{\partial t}A + \frac{\partial \mathbf{w}}{\partial t}B$$

where $(\partial p/\partial t)_{ij}$ is $\partial p_j/\partial t_i$, $(A)_{kj}$ is $\partial c_j/\partial p_k$, $(\partial w/\partial t)_{im}$ is $\partial w_m/\partial t_i$, and $(B)_{mj}$ is $\partial c_j/\partial w_m$. Note that A is the familiar input-output matrix. Thus

$$(3\text{-}17) \qquad\qquad \frac{\partial \mathbf{p}}{\partial t} = \frac{\partial \mathbf{w}}{\partial t} B(I - A)^{-1}$$

and the effect of taxes on producer prices works entirely through changes in factor prices.

If there is only one factor (so that the nonsubstitution theorem applies), and it is taken as numeraire, then $\partial w_m/\partial t_i$ is zero, and $\partial p/\partial t = 0$. Thus producer prices are fixed, the change in tax has no effect on producer prices,

$$(3\text{-}18) \qquad\qquad \frac{\partial q_i}{\partial t_i} = \delta_{ij}$$

and we can regard a tax on good i as having been entirely shifted to consumers, with no effect on any other price. In general, however, factor prices will change and by an amount that depends on the demand side of the economy. The tax change might, for example, induce a change in demand toward land-intensive goods, thus pushing the rent on land upward. These effects on factor prices clearly involve the solution of the general equilibrium and will depend, among other things, on the functioning of factor markets. Some examples are provided in the discussion of agriculture in part 4.

Where the taxes on inputs are not rebated, then producers pay $\mathbf{q}$ for inputs but receive $\mathbf{p}$ for their outputs and equation 3-13 becomes:

$$(3\text{-}19) \qquad\qquad \mathbf{p} = \mathbf{c}(\mathbf{q}, \mathbf{w}).$$

If we differentiate,

$$(3\text{-}20) \qquad\qquad \frac{\partial \mathbf{p}}{\partial t} = \left(I + \frac{\partial \mathbf{p}}{\partial t}\right)A + \frac{\partial \mathbf{w}}{\partial t}B$$

or

$$(3\text{-}21) \qquad\qquad \frac{\partial \mathbf{p}}{\partial t} = A(I - A)^{-1} + \frac{\partial \mathbf{w}}{\partial t}B(I - A)^{-1}$$

and

$$(3\text{-}22) \qquad\qquad \frac{\partial \mathbf{q}}{\partial t} = \frac{\partial \mathbf{p}}{\partial t} + I = (I - A)^{-1} + \frac{\partial \mathbf{w}}{\partial t}B(I - A)^{-1}.$$

Thus the effect of taxes on consumer prices involves the effect that occurs through factor prices as before but now has $(I - A)^{-1}$ in place of I (compare equations 3-22 and 3-18). The former, being larger, reflects the way in which taxes on inputs, inputs into inputs, and so on feed into final prices. In chapter 11, Ahmad and Stern consider a fixed-coefficients model and suppress factor price effects so that they can define the effective tax, $\mathbf{t}^e$, or the component of tax in price as

(3-23) $$\mathbf{t}^e = (I - A)^{-1}\mathbf{t}.$$

The above analysis identifies the data requirements for the analysis of incidence in these models: (1) we must know how the tax system treats inputs, in particular whether rebates are available, (2) we need the input-output matrixes A and B, and (3) we must have the general equilibrium derivatives $\partial w_m / \partial t_i$. For this last piece of information we may use a computable general equilibrium model or intelligent guesswork guided by small-scale general equilibrium models that are analytically tractable. Either method would require supplementation using sensitivity analysis.

In an open economy some prices may be fixed on the world market. Let us take an extreme case, assume that all consumer prices are exogenous, and regard $\mathbf{q}$ as fixed so that $\partial \mathbf{q} / \partial \mathbf{t} = 0$ and $\partial \mathbf{p} / \partial \mathbf{t} = -I$. Then from equation 3-17 we have

(3-24) $$\frac{\partial \mathbf{w}}{\partial \mathbf{t}} = -B^{-1}(I - A).$$

Changes in taxes $\mathbf{t}$ on domestic production translate directly into changes in factor prices. The only information required is the input-output matrixes A and B. In these circumstances the standard considerations of the factor price equalization theorem mean that there would be as many goods as factors, so that B would be square and in general invertible so that equation 3-24 could be solved.

Many combinations of assumptions can readily be assembled as to which goods are traded, which factors are fixed, which taxes are rebated, the relative tax treatment of imported and domestic production, and so on. We should consider also whether imports are really perfect substitutes for the domestic goods of the same name. Another polar case involves regarding them as perfect complements (see Ahmad and Stern, chapter 11), with intermediate cases treated in terms of elasticities of substitution—in these cases, of course, the prices of domestic and imported goods may differ. I hope the above simple examples indicate the sorts of issues that arise and the effects of different assumptions. Two of the extreme cases mentioned above highlight the possibilities: when producer prices are fixed, the effect of taxes is wholly passed onto the customer, but where market prices are fixed (for example, via imports that are perfect substitutes for domestic production), the effect is wholly transferred onto factor incomes. Some empirical examples are provided in chapter 11 (Ahmad and Stern) and in chapter 20 (Hughes).

The question of coverage arises when the same good or factor is treated differently in different parts of the economy. To be specific, we pick a factor. If sellers of the factor are free to sell it where they like, then competition will establish a single sellers' price. The different tax treatment will thus imply that the buyer's price is different in different sectors. The marginal product of the factor would then differ with different uses, and we would have productive inefficiency. This was a central point in Harberger's famous treatment of

corporation tax, which, he argued, led to different costs of capital in incorporated and unincorporated enterprises and thus caused inefficiency (for a discussion of the Harberger model and references, see Atkinson and Stiglitz, 1980,
chap. 6).

The variation in coverage may be deliberate government policy, for example
to encourage small-scale industries, or may be dictated by costs of administration, where coverage of very small establishments may be too costly, or
through evasion, where some individuals or enterprises may be more willing to
evade or may find it easier to do so. These variations are probably rather
common in developing countries and may have important effects. In an
extreme case the differential coverage may lead to zero revenue if, for example,
producers that are liable or are not evading are driven out of business by those
who do not pay taxes. Both theoretical and applied research for developing
countries could be fruitful in this area.

Some Partial-Equilibrium Issues

We now consider two rather different issues in partial equilibrium. The first
concerns the shifting of taxes in noncompetitive models; this is set in partial
equilibrium for simplicity. The second provides a link between the standard
analysis in terms of consumer surplus together with triangles of deadweight loss
and the approach using indirect utility functions, which is used for much of this
book.

The Effects of Taxes in Noncompetitive Models

In our discussion of noncompetitive models, we confine ourselves to partial
equilibrium. Noncompetitive behavior in models of general equilibrium poses
difficult conceptual and analytic problems, and the analysis of tax shifting can
become intractable. As Hart (1979) has shown, however, many of the effects
of noncompetitive behavior in general equilibrium are captured in partial
models. For purposes of comparison it is useful to recall the standard competitive analysis of tax shifting in partial equilibrium. The shifting of an indirect
tax will always be between 0 and 100 percent. We shall see that in noncompetitive models shifting can be well over 100 percent. The degree of shifting
will depend sensitively on how the elasticity of demand varies along the
demand curve and on market structure. In the standard competitive model in
partial equilibrium, we divide the effect of a specific tax t per unit of output into
a portion that falls on consumers and a portion that falls on producers. Thus if q
is the consumer price, $q - t$ the producer price, and $D(q)$ and $S(q - t)$ the
demand and supply functions, we can calculate the effects of taxes on prices by
differentiating the equilibrium condition

$$(3\text{-}25) \qquad\qquad D(q) = S(q - t)$$

with respect to t. The immediate result is

$$(3\text{-}26a) \qquad \frac{dq}{dt} = \frac{\eta}{\eta + \varepsilon p/q}$$

and

$$(3\text{-}26b) \qquad \frac{dp}{dt} = \frac{d}{dt}(q - t) = \frac{-\varepsilon}{\varepsilon + q\eta/p}$$

where η is the elasticity of supply and ε the elasticity of demand, both defined as positive numbers. The rise (per unit tax) in consumer price plus the fall in producer price is one (see figure 3-1). For small taxes, $q/p \simeq 1$, and the proportion that is shifted to consumers becomes $\eta/(\varepsilon + \eta)$.

The conclusion from this theory is that the proportion that is shifted to consumers is in general between 0 and 100 percent, with 100 percent shifting only if η is infinite (fixed supply price or horizontal supply curve), or ε is zero (completely inelastic demand or vertical demand curve). Note that in this partial-equilibrium framework, free entry would in general lead to infinitely elastic supply and thus a 100 percent shift. The competitive model, however, with or without free entry is only one of the market structures that we would want to consider, and it transpires that conclusions concerning tax shifts are rather sensitive to the differences between models.

In Stern (1985) the effect of indirect taxes on prices was examined for a

Figure 3-1. *The Effect of Tax on Price in Partial Equilibrium in the Competitive Model*

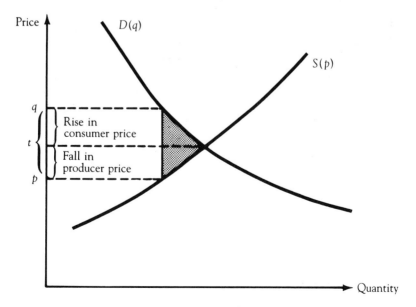

number of different market structures: monopoly, oligopoly, and monopolistic competition as well as perfect competition. I shall not repeat the analysis here but shall give examples from table 1 of that paper, which summarizes the results concerning tax shifting. The oligopoly model considered was of conjectural variation, where each firm supposes that the other firms will respond to a 1 percent change in output by adjusting their output by α percent. With n identical firms and constant marginal costs, we can show that the consequence for market price q of a tax change is given by

(3-27)
$$\frac{\partial q}{\partial t} = \left(1 - \frac{\gamma}{\varepsilon} + \frac{F\gamma}{\varepsilon}\right)^{-1}$$

where $\gamma = \alpha + (1 - \alpha)/n$, ε is the elasticity of demand, and F is the elasticity with respect to price of the elasticity of demand ($F = \partial \log \varepsilon/\partial \log q$). As a check, note that if $n = 1$ and $F = 0$ (constant elasticity), we have $\partial q/\partial t$ equal to $1/[1 - (1/\varepsilon)]$, which is the familiar markup on marginal cost from the simple monopoly pricing model. Equation 3-27 serves to illustrate the many possibilities as F, α, and n vary. For the linear demand (where $F = 1 + \varepsilon$), for example, we have

(3-28)
$$\frac{\partial q}{\partial t} = \frac{1}{1 + \gamma} < 1$$

and for the isoelastic case ($F = 0$) we have

(3-29)
$$\frac{\partial q}{\partial t} = \left(1 - \frac{\gamma}{\varepsilon}\right)^{-1} > 1.$$

Intuitively, with higher F the price-increasing effect of a tax will be less, because the rise in price is dampened by the increase in elasticity. Thus with oligopoly, the tax shifting can be on either side of 100 percent.

Note that the importance of functional form of demand functions in tax analysis has been illustrated once again. We would congratulate an econometrician on giving us a reliable estimate of the price elasticity, but here the elasticity of the elasticity is crucial. That would, unless we take some care, usually be dictated by the shape of the demand function we choose to estimate, for example, the linear or log-linear/constant elasticity. A functional form that allows F to be estimated is

(3-30)
$$\log X = B - Aq^F.$$

The resulting equation 3-27 can be generalized in a fairly straightforward way to monopolistic competition, for example, where free entry yields zero profits. The analysis underlying equation 3-27 also generates the effect of a tax change on profits. If the increase in tax decreases profits (as it will if $F > 1 - \varepsilon$), then it will lower the number of firms. This consequence will tend to increase the price so that equation 3-27 will understate the price-increasing effect of the tax.

We must therefore see the usual analysis of tax shifting in perfect competition, which is embodied in figure 3-1, as a rather special case. It is quite
possible, for example, that 100 percent shifting is a reasonable intermediate
assumption and not the polar case that the simple theory would make it appear.

Welfare Analysis in Partial Equilibrium

In the welfare analysis of reform introduced in chapters 1 and 2, I examined
changes in household welfare ΔV and government revenue ΔR (ΔZ is the
change in Z): changes in profits were assumed to be zero (in a broader analysis
they feed into ΔV, and in addition ΔR must be examined at shadow prices). In
partial-equilibrium models we consider the change in consumer surplus, in
producer surplus (or profit), and in government revenue. As an example we
take the case of the monopolist.

$$(3\text{-}31) \quad \begin{array}{ll} \Delta \text{ Consumer surplus} & = -X\Delta q, \ \Delta \text{ Profit} = -X\Delta t \\ \Delta \text{ Government revenue} & = \Delta(tX) \end{array}$$

where X is output (note that we have used profit maximization in calculating Δ
profit). Consumer surplus, profit, and government revenue are illustrated in
figure 3-2. If the changes in these items are all weighted equally in forming the
change in welfare ΔW, we have

$$(3\text{-}32) \qquad \Delta W = -X\Delta q - X\Delta t + X\Delta t + tX'\Delta q$$

$$(3\text{-}33) \qquad = (-X + tX')\,\Delta q.$$

We realize immediately that, because $dq/dt > 0$, welfare is increased by a
subsidy to the monopolist, because if $t > 0$, we have $(-X + tX' < 0)$. The
optimal subsidy is given by $-X + tX' = 0$ or

$$(3\text{-}34) \qquad\qquad \frac{t}{q} = -\frac{1}{\varepsilon}.$$

The result should be intuitively clear, because it involves a subsidy of the
excess of price over marginal revenue so that profit maximization by the
monopolist in fact results in market prices equal to marginal cost. Although
the result is obvious here, the argument illustrates how welfare calculations
can be made in the noncompetitive model, using the standard techniques of
welfare economics. For more complicated models the main difficulty lies in
calculating the response of prices and quantities to the tax change. The result
that the derivative of the profit is simply minus the output would not extend to
the oligopolistic model, where the equilibrium reaction of other firms would
have to be incorporated. This subject calls for further research, but see in
particular Seade (1985) and Stern (1985) for an indication of the types of
result that are possible.

We can use the same partial-equilibrium criterion (change in consumer
surplus plus government revenue plus profit) to illustrate the relation between

Figure 3-2. *Welfare Analysis in Partial Equilibrium*

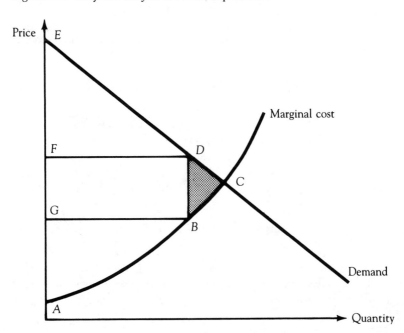

Note: ABG, profit (excluding fixed cost); BDFG, government revenue; FDE, consumer surplus; BCD, deadweight loss.

our approach and the traditional triangles denoting deadweight loss. For simplicity we consider the case of constant marginal cost, so that the MC curve in figure 3-2 is horizontal. The deadweight loss, the triangle BCD, has area $kt^2/2$ for a linear demand curve (or a linear approximation) with gradient $-k$. The rate of change with respect to t is then simply kt, hence for a small change Δt the change in deadweight loss is $kt\Delta t$ or $-t\Delta X$.

In the reform approach described in chapters 1 and 2 we have, for one consumer, $\Delta V = -\alpha X \Delta t$, where α is the marginal utility of income and $\Delta R = \Delta(tX) = t\Delta X + X\Delta t$. If the marginal utility is specified as one (consumer surplus and government revenue are of equal value), the marginal loss from a change is then $(-\Delta V + \Delta R)$ or $-t\Delta X$, which is precisely the expression derived in the preceding paragraph.

The General Theory of Reform and Shadow Prices

Earlier in this chapter we saw how the analysis of tax rules could be set in a simple model with production, and in chapter 2 a discussion of tax reform was set in a similar context. The particular form of optimal tax rules and the direction of beneficial reform will usually depend on the special features of the model under consideration, but the approach is rather general, as are certain results and principles. We shall now examine the general theory of reform and shadow prices, showing how the earlier discussion embodies these general principles. A tax should be increased if the direct impact on households of making the change exceeds the cost at shadow prices of the extra demands generated. The shadow price of a good embodies the welfare consequences of the general equilibrium adjustments that flow from an extra demand for that good, and thus the shadow price obviously depends on the way in which the economy adjusts.

We take a fairly general model first and then consider some special cases. The treatment here is based on Drèze and Stern (1985). The government is concerned with the selection of certain policy variables, for example, taxes, quotas, or rations. At the initial position some of these are chosen optimally and the remainder are fixed at predetermined positions—the vector describing the former group is s and the latter group ω. Social welfare $V(s, \omega)$ and excess demands $E(s, \omega)$ are both functions of the vector (s, ω). The choice of the (s, ω) may then be described by the solution of the problem (P) in expression 3-35, which is

$$(3\text{-}35) \qquad (P) \qquad \begin{array}{ll} \text{Maximize} & V(s, \omega) \\ \quad s \\ \text{subject to} & E(s, \omega) = z \end{array}$$

where the vector z describes the availability of publicly supplied goods. The components of z may be positive, zero, or negative (corresponding to public demands). We are supposing that the problem (P) is feasible, so that we shall usually require the dimension of s to be greater than or equal to that of E and z (that is, there are at least as many policy variables to be chosen as constraints). If the two dimensions are exactly equal, then if the function E is invertible, s will be defined as a function of z, and there will be essentially no choice. Thus the case that we call fully determined, in which policies are determined entirely by constraints, is included. Further constraints, in addition to those arising through $E(s, \omega) = z$, may be added to the analysis, although they will add extra terms to the Lagrangean (see below). Notice that we are writing $E(s, \omega) = z$ to hold with equality, because we are describing through s whatever rationing process may be involved if the equilibrium is not of the standard Walrasian type. It should be emphasized that the assumption that the dimension of s is greater than or equal to z is not a strong one. It simply involves the assertion that there is a process by which the equilibrium can be established, that is, there are at least as many equilibrium instruments as there are goods. These instruments may be the prices, but of course they do not have to be (there could be adjustments in rations). Where there are more instruments than goods, then the government will usually have a choice.

The Lagrangean for expression 3-35 is

$$(3\text{-}36) \qquad \mathcal{L}(s) = V(s, \omega) - v[E(s, \omega) - z]$$

where v is the vector of shadow prices. The shadow price of a good is the increase in the value of the social welfare function when an extra unit of public supplies is made available. Thus

(3-37) $$v = \frac{\partial V^*}{\partial z}(\omega, z),$$

where V^* is the maximum value for the problem (P), given ω and z. It follows (as a deduction, not a definition) that the shadow prices will be equal to the Lagrange multipliers for (P) if s is chosen optimally. Notice that the definition of the shadow price also covers the case in which s is determined entirely by the constraints. In that case the shadow prices are simply $(\partial V/\partial s) \cdot (\partial s/\partial z)$ where $\partial s/\partial z$ is the Jacobean of the function relating s to z, that is, a shift in z changes the s in a way given by the constraints, and this change in s yields a change in welfare that is the vector v.

The shadow prices refer to the constraints as written in expression 3-35 and not to some generalized availability in the economy as a whole. Thus, for example, if there is unemployment of some type of labor, it does *not* follow that its shadow price is automatically zero. There will be some repercussion of a change in government demand for that type of labor, and the general equilibrium effect of this repercussion, incorporating the various rationing processes that may be relevant, will, together with the social welfare function, determine the shadow prices.

The first-order conditions for a maximum in (P) are

(3-38) $$\frac{\partial \mathcal{L}}{\partial s} = 0$$

or

$$\frac{\partial V}{\partial s} - v\frac{\partial E}{\partial s} = 0.$$

A reform is a change in $d\omega$ in the variables ω, which had previously been seen as predetermined. In order to satisfy the scarcity constraints, we must have

(3-39) $$\frac{\partial E}{\partial \omega}d\omega + \frac{\partial E}{\partial s}ds = 0.$$

The consequent change in social welfare is

(3-40) $$dV = \frac{\partial V}{\partial \omega}d\omega + \frac{\partial V}{\partial s}ds$$

$$= \left(\frac{\partial V}{\partial \omega} - v\frac{\partial E}{\partial \omega}\right)d\omega$$

using equations 3-38 and 3-39. This is, essentially, an envelope theorem. It tells us that the welfare impact of a reform is given by the direct effect on social welfare $\partial V/\partial \omega$ less the cost of the extra net demands at shadow prices $v\,\partial E/\partial \omega$; this approach to reform makes the argument intuitively rather obvious. The directness of the argument and the very general structure of the model also make it clear that the principle has great generality.

The first-order condition for optimality of the variable ω is the equality of $\partial V/\partial \omega$ and $v\,\partial E/\partial \omega$. This reflects the obvious but important general principle that the optimum is the position from which no beneficial reform is possible. In this sense the theory of optimality is a special case of the theory of reform.

It should be clear that the above analysis rests on the idea that the government chooses optimally those instruments that it can influence. We should again emphasize, however, that the fully determined case in which the government has no choice of instruments, so that there is no optimization, is included throughout as a special case. People who claim that governments do not optimize, I would suggest, are often thinking of this fully determined case. Notice also that the shadow price v depends crucially on the way in which equilibrium is reestablished after some change in z and therefore that we must consider very carefully which variables are classified in $\mathbf{s}$ (endogenous) and which in ω (predetermined). In the analysis of marginal reform it is tempting to regard the status quo as emerging from a fully determined model. In that case we must describe the variables in terms of $\mathbf{s}$ and ω. The answer, then, to the question of whether a tax should be increased will depend on which other variables (for example, other taxes) are assumed to adjust to restore equilibrium. The above discussion is rather general, and we turn now to a more particular model structure.

Let us suppose now that prices faced by producers are $\mathbf{p}$ and by consumers are $\mathbf{q}$, that $\mathbf{Y}(\mathbf{s}, \omega)$ is the vector of net supplies (positive entries in $\mathbf{Y}$ are outputs and negative entries inputs) by producers and $\mathbf{X}(\mathbf{s}, \omega)$ is the vector of net demands by households (positive entries in $\mathbf{X}$ are demands and negative entries supplies). We assume for the moment that intermediate goods are not taxed and return to the issue below. Then $\mathbf{E} = \mathbf{X} - \mathbf{Y}$ and

$$(3\text{-}41) \qquad -v\cdot \mathbf{E} = v\cdot(\mathbf{Y} - \mathbf{X})$$
$$= (v - \mathbf{p})\cdot \mathbf{Y} + (\mathbf{q} - v)\cdot \mathbf{X} + \mathbf{p}\cdot \mathbf{Y} - \mathbf{q}\cdot \mathbf{X}.$$

But $\mathbf{p}\cdot \mathbf{Y} - \mathbf{q}\cdot \mathbf{X}$ is the profits of firms less the expenditure of households and is therefore the direct tax revenue of the government. Hence we can write

$$(3\text{-}42) \qquad\qquad -v\cdot \mathbf{E} = R_v$$

where R_v is the government revenue at shadow prices, because we may interpret $(\mathbf{q} - v)$ as "shadow consumption taxes" and $(v - \mathbf{p})$ as "shadow producer taxes" (so that $v\cdot \mathbf{Y}$ is "shadow profit" and $\mathbf{p}\cdot \mathbf{Y}$ actual profit). The change in welfare from the reform $d\omega$ is

$$(3\text{-}43) \qquad\qquad dV = \left(\frac{\partial V}{\partial \omega} + \frac{\partial R_v}{\partial \omega} \bigg|_v \right) d\omega$$

which is the direct increase in welfare $\partial V/\partial \omega$ plus the change in shadow revenue; this formula generalizes the discussion of reform that appeared above (see equations 2-5 and 2-6). At an optimum

$$(3\text{-}44) \qquad \left. \frac{\partial V}{\partial \omega} + \frac{\partial R_v}{\partial \omega} \right|_v = 0$$

which generalizes equations 3-12, 2-5, and 2-6. Consideration of shadow revenue has expositional advantages for policymakers. The importance of the part of shadow revenue that is actual revenue can be grasped immediately without great insight into general equilibrium or knowledge of welfare economics. The second part can then be explained as an adjustment to take into account the differences between shadow and market prices. This topic is explored further below.

Suppose now that the taxes, t, are considered as predetermined variables with producer prices, p, as equilibrating or endogenous variables (with p and t determining consumer prices through the relation $q = p + t$). Alternatively we could consider some of the p_i as predetermined, with an endogenous rationing system bringing about equilibrium. To keep things simple, we consider a fully determined model. Because the taxes t are among the predetermined variables, ω, and the p among the endogenous, s, in expressions 4-17 and 4-20, the derivatives of E and R_v hold p constant (as well as v). Thus, from equations 3-40 we have the change in welfare as

$$(3\text{-}45) \qquad dV = \left(\frac{\partial V}{\partial t} - v \frac{\partial X}{\partial t} \right) dt.$$

Because the p are held constant in the differentiation, the change in net demands E comes about on the consumption side only. The ith component of the vector in parentheses in equation 3-45 may be seen as the marginal social value of increasing the tax rate and represents the direct effect $\partial V/\partial t_i$ less the marginal cost of supplying the extra consumer demand $v(\partial X/\partial t_i)$. Changing t_i by itself and holding production constant is, of course, not feasible. The role of the shadow price, however, is precisely to take into account the change in welfare arising from the general equilibrium consequences of restoring feasibility.

Expression 3-45 may be rewritten, where consumer prices are q,

$$(3\text{-}46) \qquad dV = \left[\frac{\partial V}{\partial t} + \frac{\partial}{\partial t} (q \cdot X) - p \frac{\partial X}{\partial t} + (p - v) \frac{\partial X}{\partial t} \right] dt$$

since the change holds consumer (lump-sum) incomes, and thus $q \cdot X$, constant (lump-sum incomes in the model come from firms or government, and these are being held constant in the partial differentiation). Because

$$(3\text{-}47) \qquad q = p + t$$

however, and we are holding p constant, we may rewrite equation 3-46 as

$$(3\text{-}48) \qquad dV = \left[\frac{\partial V}{\partial \mathbf{t}} + \frac{\partial}{\partial \mathbf{t}} (\mathbf{t} \cdot \mathbf{X}) + (\mathbf{p} - v) \cdot \frac{\partial \mathbf{X}}{\partial \mathbf{t}} \right] d\mathbf{t}.$$

This equation gives a more explicit generalization of equations 2-6 and 3-12 than that provided in equations 3-43 and 3-44.

Where producer prices $\mathbf{p}$ are proportional to shadow prices v, the marginal social value of increasing the ith tax is, where $v = \lambda \mathbf{p}$,

$$(3\text{-}49) \qquad \frac{\partial V}{\partial t_i} - \lambda \mathbf{p} \cdot \frac{\partial \mathbf{X}}{\partial t_i}.$$

Because in this special case $\mathbf{q} = \mathbf{p} + \mathbf{t}$ and $\mathbf{q} \cdot \mathbf{X}$ is constant,

$$(3\text{-}50) \qquad \frac{\partial}{\partial t_i} (\mathbf{p} \cdot \mathbf{X}) = - \frac{\partial}{\partial t_i} (\mathbf{t} \cdot \mathbf{X}).$$

The marginal social value is

$$(3\text{-}51) \qquad \frac{\partial V}{\partial t_i} + \lambda \frac{\partial}{\partial t_i} (\mathbf{t} \cdot \mathbf{X})$$

which corresponds to the special case of equations 3-12 and 2-5.

An alternative and convenient way to express the issues that arise in this last case is, as we saw in equation 2-26, to use the statistic

$$(3\text{-}52) \qquad \lambda_i = - \frac{\partial V}{\partial t_i} \bigg/ \frac{\partial R}{\partial t_i}$$

where R is $\mathbf{t} \cdot \mathbf{X}$. Then λ_i is the marginal cost in terms of social welfare of an extra unit of government revenue. Thus if $\lambda_i < \lambda$, increasing the ith tax imposes a social cost lower in value than the revenue raised (assuming $\partial R / \partial t_i$ is positive). If $\lambda_i > \lambda_j$, then we can increase social welfare at constant revenue by switching a unit of revenue on the margin from good i to good j (chapter 11 and other chapters have examples of the application of this concept).

Where $\mathbf{p}$ is not proportional to v, then the reform rule using λ_i as in equation 3-52 must be modified to take into account the difference between (relative) shadow prices and market prices. The modification can be expressed in a number of ways. First we can define

$$(3\text{-}53) \qquad \lambda_i^v = - \frac{\partial V}{\partial t_i} \bigg/ \frac{\partial R_v}{\partial t_i}.$$

Then, in line with the earlier reform rule (when $\mathbf{p} = v$) that a switch in revenue from i to j increases welfare at constant tax revenue if $\lambda_i > \lambda_j$, we now see that a switch in *shadow* revenue from i to j increases welfare if $\lambda_i^v > \lambda_j^v$. This relation follows immediately from equations 3-53 and 3-43. An alternative way of expressing the previous reform rule is that an increase in the ith tax will increase social welfare if

(3-54)
$$\phi_i > \frac{1}{\lambda}$$

where ϕ_i is the reciprocal of λ_i. The expression ϕ_i is generalized as follows.

Given that policymakers might find it useful to see the role of actual revenue in the calculation, it is helpful to decompose the change in shadow revenue $\partial R_\nu/\partial t_i$ into one in actual revenue and the remainder corresponding to the difference between $\mathbf{p}$ and ν. Because $\partial R_\nu/\partial t_i$ appears in the denominator, we work in terms of the reciprocal of λ_i^ν, which we call ϕ_i^ν. Then

(3-55)
$$\phi_i^\nu \equiv \phi_i + \psi_i^\nu$$

where ψ_i^ν is minus $\partial S/\partial t_i$ divided by $\partial V/\partial t_i$, where $\partial S/\partial t_i$ is $(\mathbf{p} - \nu)\,\partial X/\partial t_i$. The term ϕ_i^ν is the cost in terms of shadow revenue of a unit of social welfare arising from a reduction in the ith tax and ϕ_i the corresponding loss in actual revenue. Similarly, ψ_i^ν is the necessary adjustment to actual tax revenue (per unit of welfare) associated with the excess of the shadow value of meeting extra demands over the value at producer prices. Policymakers may find the second term esoteric or suspect, so that it may be an advantage to express it separately. If the second term is small, then we may be able to express the analysis in terms that are readily understandable without being misleading. We should not do so, however, without checking the magnitude of the second term.

The consideration of ϕ_i rather than λ_i permits a useful decomposition:

(3-56)
$$\phi_i = \frac{1}{\lambda_i} = \frac{X_i}{\sum_h \beta^h x_i^h} + \frac{\sum_j t_j (\partial X_j/\partial t_i)}{\sum_h \beta^h x_i^h}$$

where the first term on the right-hand side of equation 3-56 involves only the levels of individual demands and the welfare weights β^h and not the demand derivatives. It is sometimes termed the distributional characteristic, or rather its inverse—see, for example, Feldstein (1972). Equation 3-56 is useful in isolating the contribution of the demand effects on ϕ_i in one term, and we sometimes find that the distributional characteristic plays the dominant role in determining the ranking of λ_i or ϕ_i (see, for example, Drèze, 1983). Taking expressions 3-55 and 3-56, we have a three-way additive decomposition of the term ϕ_i^ν into a distributional term, a tax revenue term that arises from demand changes, and a shadow tax revenue term from demand changes, where the latter two terms have the welfare-weighted sum $\sum_h \beta^h x_i^h$ in the denominator.

A multiplicative decomposition of ϕ_i^ν is

(3-57)
$$\phi_i^\nu = \frac{1}{D_i}\left[1 + \frac{1}{X_i}\mathbf{t}\cdot\frac{\partial \mathbf{X}}{\partial t_i} + \frac{1}{X_i}(\mathbf{p} - \nu)\frac{\partial \mathbf{X}}{\partial t_i}\right]$$

where D_i is $(\sum_h \beta^h x_i^h)/X_i$, the distributional characteristic. The first and second terms together constitute a tax elasticity and the third a shadow tax elasticity. Where $\mathbf{p} = \nu$, ϕ_i^ν is a product of a distributional term, $1/D_i$, and a nondistributional tax revenue term. Where $\mathbf{p} \neq \nu$, it should be remembered that shadow prices depend on distributional judgments and thus enter the shadow tax elasticity.

We saw earlier in this chapter that the analysis in chapter 2 of optimality and reform could be set in a simple model with production. We have seen in this section how that model could in turn be generalized to reflect a more complicated world. This last step has depended heavily on the notion of shadow prices, and we may reasonably ask how, in practice, these would be calculated.

From the definition of shadow prices (see expressions 3-35 and 3-36) we can see that their calculation essentially involves combining the general equilibrium consequences of a unit increase in the availability of a good from the public sector with a welfare judgment of these consequences. Thus, in principle, we need a full, computable general equilibrium model to calculate them. We might argue, furthermore, that if we had such a model, we would not need to use shadow prices to make judgments, because the consequences would be calculated explicitly. This reasoning, however, overlooks a number of important points. First, we may wish to use the shadow prices in a more detailed context than the CGE model, for example to appraise individual investment decisions at the level of the enterprise—a level of detail absent from the CGE model. Second, we would often want to examine the consequences of a policy for individual households, or at least for a sample of several thousands. It would be impossible to include such a sample in most CGE models, yet it would be of great importance to know the gainers and losers. If we are to concentrate on this type of question on the consumption side, then it may be necessary to sacrifice detail on the production side. Often such detail can best be summarized through shadow prices. Third, it is often desirable to investigate the policy reform under a number of different assumptions about the model. Although some parameter changes can be examined fairly easily in CGE models, certain radical changes may be much more difficult. Altering shadow prices, however, is generally easy, and shadow prices can usefully summarize model variation.

This last point raises some difficult questions concerning judgment about the useful performance of different models. If we are unsure about the elasticity of substitution between certain factors in a CGE model, then it would usually be straightforward to vary that parameter and see how the policy evaluation is affected. On the other hand, our worries about the model usually include some that are rather deeper. We may, for example, be unsure about the way the labor market works, say, in terms of the net effects on the agricultural sector of withdrawing a unit of labor. Should we be assuming that certain parts of the industrial sector are oligopolistic? If so, what kind of oligopoly? Will trade unions in other sectors attempt to insist on a given real wage? How much will the production of electricity depend on coal and how much on hydroelectric or nuclear fuels? All of these major questions could have substantial implications for policy, and the model builder could rarely be confident of the answers. It is generally impossible to adapt the CGE model so that it can address these questions explicitly. The models are usually complicated enough to make it difficult to see the consequences of a fairly radical change in assumptions. Indeed, in some respects the raison d'être (and disadvantage) of such a model is that we cannot always see through the structure to discover or intuit the main elements in determining the results.

It is often possible, however, to guess at the consequences of some of these questions for shadow prices. If potential migrants from agriculture can seek work without joining the ranks of the urban unemployed, for example, then the shadow wage rate will be lower. If an industry is believed to work under oligopolistic conditions (and profits can be taxed), then the shadow price of its output may be lower than if we assume the price to have been determined competitively. In many cases some simple economic theory can help us answer these questions. Shadow prices provide a flexible tool that allows us to examine fairly readily the guesses of economists and politicians.

We do not, in general, have much experience with comparing the ability of different models and approaches to handle such questions concerning flexibility. In view of the nature of the issue, it would not be straightforward to be formal about comparisons. The problems raised, however, are of considerable importance and deserve further work. It should be clear that shadow prices constitute a valuable and powerful tool that is complementary to the CGE model. Furthermore, we need techniques for computing shadow prices in a context less formal than the CGE model. A number of these CGE models are available and have been the subject of much discussion in the literature over the last two decades. This is not the place to debate the merits of the various models and methods. My purpose here has been to show how the shadow prices can be used in the analysis of policy reform in general and not just in project appraisal.

Trade, Optimal Taxation, and Reform

Many of the results discussed in the earlier sections of this chapter apply directly to trade. We simply think of trade as being one production sector that, through the world market, transforms one good into another. Where the country is small, so that it cannot affect world prices, then the marginal rates of transformation through the trade activity will be determined by relative prices on the world market. If the trading quantities of the country do affect world prices, then the ratio of marginal revenues indicates the marginal rates of transformation.

The production efficiency theorems, in the cases where they apply (see above) now give us quite strong results. Where aggregate production efficiency is desirable, then in the small economy there should be no tariffs on inputs into production. Taxation of final goods should be the same regardless of whether the source is domestic or foreign; the possibilities include a tax on sales to final consumers or domestic excises on final goods matched by tariffs on imports of final goods. As in the standard theorems of welfare economics (see chapter 2), the first-best approach is to organize distributional policy through lump-sum taxes. Where these are not possible, the next best method is through optimal commodity taxes, leaving the production side efficient (where profits are zero or are taxed away). Tariffs on intermediate goods would be desirable in this context only (1) to compensate for some other distortion (which is there for some exogenous reasons), (2) to improve distribution through pure profits where these exist and cannot be taxed, (3) to allow for imperfect foreign markets (the familiar optimal tariff argument), or (4) where final goods are not taxable.

Where aggregate efficiency cannot be established, we saw earlier that public sector efficiency would usually still be desirable. The implication is that relative public sector shadow prices should be equal to relative world prices for goods that are (optimally) traded by a small country.

We see therefore that the standard welfare analysis of trade theory is firmly within the framework discussed here. From this point of view the theory of optimal taxation simply makes more formal and generalizes some of the standard propositions of trade theory. Both can be seen as part of second-best welfare economics, that is, the study of policy when there are many constraints and a number of objectives that must be traded off one against the other. The general theory of reform and the theory of trade reform, therefore, can embody similar principles and methods. For further discussion of the relationship between the welfare theory of trade and the approach taken here, the reader may consult Dixit and Norman (1980), particularly chapter 6, and chapter 6 by Bliss in this book.

A Review of the General Principles

Our discussion of the role of production in models of optimal taxation and tax reform has provided an important extension of the analysis of chapter 2. First, we have been able to discover further guiding principles concerning production efficiency. Second, we have shown how the simple theory of reform considered in chapter 2 can be made more powerful by introducing shadow prices. In this section we shall begin by assessing some of the lessons that arise from these two further steps. We then discuss whether the theories point to specific tax rules such as uniform taxation or inverse-elasticity formulas. We shall suggest that, although the theories provide valuable and important lessons for practical tax policy, they do not in general provide direct results on tax rates. Finally, we shall argue that the theory of reform does provide a useful contribution to the assessment of particular proposals for tax changes.

The most robust of the efficiency results is the desirability of public sector efficiency—that is, if it is possible to produce more of some good with the same inputs and no reduction of output of other goods, then we should do so. We require only that there be a beneficial way of disposing of extra output. When enterprises make decisions using shadow prices, all the relative shadow prices should be the same for all enterprises. In other words, we can think in terms of a project appraisal division in a planning commission that would, for example, set economywide prices for certain important public sector inputs. Aggregate production efficiency is desirable under stronger assumptions, the implication being that relative public sector shadow prices and private producer prices should be equal and that there should be no taxation of intermediate goods. Thus in a small economy there should be no tariffs, and commodity taxes should be on final goods only, irrespective of origin. These are very strong implications and require the possibility of taxation of *all* final goods and the ability to tax the pure profits of individual firms at any rate that seems desirable. Thus it is a much less firm guide to policy, and the lesson should be of a different type. The appropriate conclusions from this result should be that care should be taken to justify departures from aggregate efficiency in terms of specific and well-defined arguments. Thus we may point directly to final goods that are difficult to tax or to profits that cannot be taxed in ways other than through inputs. Tariffs on imports in excess of the rates levied on domestic production would have to be justified in a similar fashion or in terms of specific dynamic considerations involving learning and other matters.

The main lessons from our extension of the theory of reform are, first, that, if shadow prices are introduced, then we have a workable and fairly general procedure for analyzing reform. The problems involved in calculating the shadow prices are no more or less severe than they are in other contexts. Second, we have seen that the analysis becomes extremely simple when producer and shadow prices are the same. This equality raises issues similar to those involved in aggregate production efficiency, and the arguments we have just considered indicate that we cannot in general assert that producer and shadow prices should be equal. Nevertheless, as we saw, the (reciprocal of the) cost of an extra unit of social welfare as a result of a consumer price change can be decomposed into the product of the distributional characteristic and the sum of two revenue elasticities, one for actual tax revenue and the other for shadow revenue (this last term representing the difference between the market cost and shadow cost of extra consumer demands).

The reasons why shadow prices fail to be equal to producer prices will depend on the model or implicit model of the economy that is being considered. In some circumstances the assumption of private constant returns will be acceptable, but full taxation of final goods will not be. In other cases it may be unreasonable to assume that certain markets, for example factor markets, operate perfectly. As before, we may see producer prices as a useful benchmark for shadow prices, with deviations being justified by particular considerations. This suggestion is partially supported by the result that shadow prices should, in certain circumstances, be such that competitive private sector industries with constant returns to scale break even with respect to these prices. The intuitive reason is the following. Imagine a hypothetical reform that replaces an element of private production in these industries with equal public production using the same inputs (it is immaterial whether or not such a reform is actually possible). Then, because there are no profits, there is absolutely no effect on social welfare. Because shadow prices indicate changes in social welfare from public sector production changes, taking into account the general equilibrium consequences, the value of the public sector changes at shadow prices must be zero (Diamond and Mirrlees, 1976). The result should be sharply distinguished from the *equality* of shadow prices and producer prices, which requires much stronger assumptions.

We have used the theories of optimal taxation to draw general lessons about practical policy and have pointed to the theory of reform as a way of evaluating or generating possible changes. Still, do the lessons indicate particular rules for calculating taxes such as inverse elasticity formulas or uniform taxes? In my judgment they do not. My arguments in chapter 2 are reinforced by the discussion in this chapter. Thus the possible divergence between shadow prices and producer prices adds an extra and important element to the analysis of commodity taxation in terms of price and income elasticities and in terms of distributional judgments.

Our decomposition of $1/\lambda_i$ in equation 3-56 into an income distributional term and a term involving taxes can be used to show that uniform taxes will *not* in general be optimal even if shadow prices are equal to producer prices. Suppose in equation 3-56 that taxes were at a uniform proportional rate, so that

$$(3\text{-}58) \qquad \mathbf{t} = k\mathbf{p}, \qquad \mathbf{q} = (1 + k)\mathbf{p}, \qquad \text{and} \qquad \mathbf{t} = \frac{k}{1 + k}\mathbf{q}.$$

Then for fixed producer prices (so that derivatives with respect to t_i and q_i are the same), we have

$$(3\text{-}59) \qquad \sum_j t_j \frac{\partial X_j}{\partial t_i} = \frac{k}{1 + k} \sum_j q_j \frac{\partial X_j}{\partial q_i} = \frac{k}{1 + k}(-X_i)$$

because, for each h, $\mathbf{q} \cdot \mathbf{x}^h$ is constant if there is no change in lump-sum incomes so that

$$(3\text{-}60) \qquad \sum_j q_j \frac{\partial x_j^h}{\partial q_i} = -x_i^h.$$

Equation 3-59 then follows from equation 3-60, when we use $X_i = \sum_h x_i^h$. From equations 3-56, 3-58, and 3-59 we have

$$(3\text{-}61) \qquad \frac{1}{\lambda_i} = \frac{1}{1 + k} \frac{X_i}{\sum_h \beta^h x_i^h}.$$

Thus λ_i is proportional to the distributional characteristics $\sum_h (\beta^h x_i^h)/X_i$, and the λ_i will be equal for different i only if the distributional characteristics are equal. Thus *from* uniform taxes we would in general want to increase taxes on goods with low distributional characteristics and decrease them on goods with high distributional characteristics. If we are not concerned about distribution, or if we have levied optimal lump-sum taxes (or see Deaton's argument below) so that β^h is the same for all h, then from equation 3-61 we have that λ_i is independent of i so that it would not be desirable to move from uniform taxes.

In chapter 4 Deaton shows that, where income and commodity taxes can be combined, there emerges a theorem for reform corresponding to that for the optimality of uniform proportional commodity taxes. With (1) an optimal uniform lump-sum benefit, (2) *identical* linear Engel curves, (3) additive separability, and (4) income differences arising *only* through wage rates, then the tax reform analysis implies that we would want to move toward uniform proportional taxes. Considered collectively, these are very strong and implausible assumptions. In rural communities, for example, the endowment of land will be a crucial determinant of income. If the endowment correlates with certain net demands, then we may wish to take into account the correlation in designing taxes. In most developing countries, the coverage and administration of transfer payments would be such that it would be absurd to suppose that an optimal uniform lump-sum benefit was even an approximation. Religious differences often imply substantial differences in consumption patterns and so on. Thus we require detailed empirical analysis to determine which directions reform should take, and we have no reason to assume that uniformity is best. An important part of such analysis would be an expenditure survey, because it means that we do not have to used fitted values for *current*, prereform, consumption levels. Thus although price elasticities may involve estimation difficulties, we know quite a lot about the relationship between consumption of goods, income, and other household characteristics, and we would be negligent in making distributional judgments if we suppressed or ignored this information.

In the above discussion I do not mean to deny the importance of the results and arguments presented by Deaton in chapter 4. They clearly indicate the key roles of consumption patterns, demand responses, sources of differences between households, and the availability of other taxes in determining appropriate directions of reform. These factors are all emphasized in the previous discussion, but the uniformity results cast their importance in a very stark light. In particular we should emphasize one aspect that may have received insufficient attention, namely the role of other taxes that operate through the side usually classified as expenditure. These have to do with food rations in many developing countries, for example, or with household support systems such as the child benefit in the United Kingdom. These are transfers to households that depend on their demographic structure. "Expenditure" on such items would often be included in the desired tax revenue, which is usually held constant in the tax analysis. Whether or not these are set optimally crucially affects the structure of taxes. Deaton and Stern (1985), for example, show that if Engel curves are linear and parallel, if differences between households arise only from household characteristics (or are otherwise uncorrelated with welfare weights), if leisure is separable, and if the grants based on the demographic structure of households are set optimally, then optimal commodity taxes are uniform.

The point is, again, that a person's view of the distributive role of commodity taxes should be influenced by the distributive pattern of government policies as a whole. Although there is no way of avoiding the empirical examination of possible reforms in terms of their consequences, we must take care to keep the questions open. Thus, for example, we would not want to confine attention to the structure of commodity taxation without asking about the possibility of using revenue from commodity taxation in other ways. Given that other instruments are fixed, for example, it may be desirable to adjust the way in which commodity tax revenue is raised. On the other hand, it may be desirable to increase revenue from commodity taxation in order to finance lump-sum subsidies to particular kinds of households. In chapter 11 Ahmad and Stern give examples of some calculations for India.

We have argued then that the general theories indicate principles, tax tools, and important assumptions but not specific rules. Proposed changes must be formulated and evaluated, and we have discussed at length procedures for examining marginal reform. Many proposed or actual reforms, however, are not small or local, and we need methods for examining nonmarginal reforms, too. Broadly speaking, these methods have, in the modern taxation literature, been of two kinds: the analysis of household survey data and computable general equilibrium models. The former have been widely used in the literature on the reform of direct and indirect taxation, particularly concerning labor supply. Examples concerning direct taxation and labor supply include Hausman (1981b); on housing, King (1983a); and on the balance between direct and indirect taxation, Atkinson, Stern, and Gomulka (1980). These applications have focused on the family or household, on which survey data are often available. To use this detailed information on households, we make the simple assumption concerning production, namely that producer prices are fixed.

The standard procedure is then to examine the change in welfare of each household from a proposed change using an estimated demand/supply response and an associated utility function. The change in utility is generally calibrated in money terms, using the equivalent variation or some analogue. We consider revenue changes simultaneously using the demand/supply responses. We also have the option of finding (using iterative procedures) constant revenue changes. More generally, we can put the revenue change side by side with utility changes and ask, for example, whether utility changes in the sample are judged to compensate for the revenue loss. The approach using a sample of households has the great advantage of being able to describe the characteristics of gainers and losers in the population. There is such heterogeneity in populations of households that, for any reform that is remotely revenue neutral, there will be many losers and many gainers. It will often be crucial for the policymakers to know who they are, and this information is suppressed if we work only with a few (or even thirty or forty) "typical" households. It should be emphasized that the information provided in large samples involves the kind of detail that populations and governments find both important and easy to understand. A sample of 5,000 households, for example, might represent a population of 25 million households. A reform of benefits that makes fifty households in the sample considerably worse off would exert the same effect on a quarter of a million households in the total population. Such a feature would surely be important, and we would want to know the particular characteristics of this group. Such information cannot be captured by specifying a few typical households.

The computable general equilibrium approach generally uses much less detail on the household side but pays more attention to production assumptions. They will not be discussed in detail here, because a valuable survey (Shoven, 1983) is available, and recent books illustrate their application to the problems of developing countries (see Dervis, DeMelo, and Robinson, 1982). Some dynamic simulation models are discussed in chapter 5.

A particular advantage of these applied nonmarginal methods is that they can indicate the magnitude of welfare gains and their distribution in the population. Thus, for example, we can empirically examine the suggestion that the redistributional power of indirect taxes is small (see, for example, Gandhi, 1979, or Sah, 1983a). In this case it is easy to produce examples of indirect tax changes under discussion (for example, a proportional VAT in India) that make some of the poor much worse off than they presently are (see, for example, Ahmad and Stern, chapter 11).

The marginal and nonmarginal approaches are complementary. For example, we have seen that the marginal analysis does not require the specification of individual utility functions, because the welfare impact of price changes is given in that method by current demands. Responses are required only in the aggregate to determine the revenue consequences of changes. Many changes can be considered at the same time, because we are presenting a set of welfare-improving reforms. Still, although it is less demanding in assumptions and parameter estimates, its marginality limits its scope. Hence, ideally, we should carry out both methods and check one against the other. If, for example, a nonmarginal analysis indicated an improvement from reforms in a direction that the marginal analysis had shown to be unattractive, we might want to be a little circumspect and to examine the source of the discrepancy.

In comparing marginal and nonmarginal analyses, we are considering a number of distinctions each of which requires careful analysis and which should not be confused. First, there is the small/large issue. Should we make a series of small changes based on fairly good information, or if we are far from the optimum, should we make a large reform to a fairly good position (notwithstanding that a full optimum may be hard to identify)? Second, there is the issue of certainty versus uncertainty. If we are more uncertain about responses at points some distance from where we now stand, then how should our uncertainty affect our actions? This consideration does not necessarily militate in favor of small movements. Third, marginal reform is easier to analyze than nonmarginal reform. Although from one point of view it is better to do what we can do well than make a mess by undertaking something more difficult, we should not duck the more difficult questions: improvements in understanding and techniques might have substantial payoffs.

The emphasis on marginal reform in some chapters of this book should not therefore be construed as implying that actual changes should be small. To suggest a direction and not a magnitude of change is not to imply that the movement should be small. The conclusion must be that marginal and non-marginal analysis are complementary and should be carried out side by side.

Conclusions

We have examined in this chapter a number of difficulties that were suppressed in the simple models of chapter 2. There the competitive assumption together with constant returns to scale and the absence of profits allowed us to focus attention on consumers and on government revenue rather than on the production side. This chapter has therefore examined production and market structure in greater detail.

Early in this chapter we examined results—the production efficiency theorems—on the question of whether production should be efficient at the optimum. We saw that efficient production would generally be desirable for the public sector taken separately but would apply to the economy as a whole only if there were competitive conditions in the private sector together with constant returns to scale or the full taxation of profits.

The positive analysis of the incidence of indirect taxes in competitive models was also discussed. The role of two key assumptions was emphasized: the openness of the economy and the coverage of taxes. If prices of some goods are fixed on the world market, then taxation is shifted back to factors. If some taxes apply to certain sectors but not to others, then if consumer prices of final goods are uniform, some producers will be paying different prices for inputs, with consequences for factor incomes and efficiency.

In the subsequent discussion of noncompetitive models we concentrated on partial equilibrium. We saw that tax shifting in oligopolistic models and in models of monopolistic competition could be above or below 100 percent, so that 100 percent was not the polar case it might appear to be from simple models of perfect competition.

In treating the general theory of reform and its relationship with shadow prices, we saw that much of the previous analysis in chapter 2 was applicable if producer prices were replaced by shadow prices. Thus, for example, the net effect on welfare of a tax change is given by its direct impact on households less the cost at shadow prices of meeting the extra demands generated. The discussion of the relationship between the tax analysis presented in this book and policy analysis in trade models showed that the former carried over in a direct way to the latter, with many of the standard trade results fitting directly into the framework.

The review of some general principles presented in chapter 2 emphasized the role of shadow prices as embodiments of some of the more complex general equilibrium adjustments. If the shadow prices are combined with the tax analysis, then the results of chapter 2 can be generalized in a direct way, which makes these results much more powerful. I also argued that marginal reforms and nonmarginal or optimal changes should be analyzed side by side. The two are complementary in that we would want to check the directions of nonmarginal change using local information and to ask how big a movement in a suggested direction should be. Together they provide governments with a sensible and useful structure for the analysis of policy.

Appendix: Normalization and the Choice of Untaxed Goods

The role of normalizations in tax models deserves special attention because failure to understand it often leads to mistakes and can mislead in the interpretation of results. We make just two simple points. First, if there are positive profits (which are not fully taxed), we can place only one linear restriction on the full vector of producer and consumer prices in the system. Thus we cannot simultaneously choose a price to be unity and choose an untaxed good. Second, the choice of numeraire can sometimes alter the appearance of optimal tax rules, but it would be a mistake to interpret this change as significant.

The first point may be seen as follows. If consumer prices are q, producer prices are p, and there are no lump-sum incomes other than through the profits of privately owned enterprises, then the general equilibrium system is homogeneous degree one in the vector (p, q). If the whole vector is multiplied by λ, then consumers have their incomes raised by a factor through the profits of firms that increase by a factor λ, but the prices they face are increased by the same proportion. Hence their behavior and welfare are unchanged, as are those of firms. Tax revenue is also scaled up by λ. Thus it is possible to choose one linear normalization for the vector (p, q).

Notice that we cannot in general normalize p and q separately (for example, by writing $p_1 = q_1 = 1$) without imposing a real restriction on the system. Normalization is possible only if producer prices do *not* affect household decisions via the profits of firms. Constant returns to scale or 100 percent profits taxation would usually be involved. Where lump-sum transfers r are possible, then the vectors (p, q, r) replace (p, q) in the above discussion, and we are allowed one linear normalization on (p, q, r). It is easy to show in general that the difference across goods of the proportion of tax in the price $(t_j/q_j) - (t_i/q_i)$ is numeraire free, and thus it is often convenient to discuss which goods i and j should be the more heavily taxed in terms of this measure.

The second point concerns the choice of untaxed goods in models where producer prices are treated as fixed. Then it is easy to show that, if lump-sum incomes are zero, the Ramsey rule (see equation 2-3) for $(n - 1)$ goods implies the Ramsey rule for the nth—that if the "proportional reductions in compensated demand" for $(n - 1)$ goods are equal, then the proportional reduction for the nth good is identical. This statement is not true if the model is specified so that lump-sum incomes are not zero. An example arises if leisure rather than labor is treated as a good so that there is a lump-sum income wT where T is total time and w is the wage. Then the proportional reduction in the supply of labor (not the demand for leisure) is equal to the proportional reductions in the compensated demands for other goods. If lump-sum incomes are zero, the Ramsey rule is symmetrically interpreted across goods.

If, however, lump-sum incomes are not zero, then complementarity and substitutability with the endowments, for example, leisure, become important. It is common in these models to choose labor or leisure as untaxed, and thus the good that is the endowment is also the good that is the numeraire. It is important to understand that the results derive their real structure from the aspect concerning the endowment.

4

Econometric Issues for Tax Design in Developing Countries

Angus Deaton

EMPIRICAL WELFARE ECONOMICS attempts to use data on individual or aggregate behavior to infer the consequences for behavior and for welfare of various actual or contemplated policy changes. The examples discussed here relate to the calculation of optimal taxes and of welfare-improving tax changes, but essentially the same tools apply to the analysis of projects, to cost-benefit analysis, or to any other policy measure. In principle, the procedure is straightforward. A model is developed linking prices, taxes, quantities, and welfare, and tax rules or shadow prices are characterized in terms of unknown but potentially observable empirical magnitudes. Econometric analysis then provides estimates of these magnitudes, allowing calculation of the desired tax rates, shadow prices, or directions of reform. In practice, severe problems arise. In particular, tax rules are rarely explicit; they do not yield formulas with tax rates on the left-hand side and empirically determinable quantities on the right-hand side. Instead, conditions are provided that must be satisfied by the configuration of prices and quantities when taxes are at their appropriate levels. This feature complicates the computations, but the real difficulty is that it becomes unclear which empirical magnitudes are important and which are not. Data collection is expensive, econometric estimation is rarely straightforward, and efforts should concentrate on areas in which they can do the most good. Most seriously, however, there is the risk that supplementary assumptions in the econometric work, made for convenience or even unconsciously, can exert a very large effect on the final results. Separability assumptions in particular are widely used in empirical work and tend to have dramatic consequences for the structure of optimal tax or pricing systems.

To fix ideas, I begin with a specific and fairly standard model of taxation. It is not necessarily the most appropriate model for poor countries (indeed, an important task is to develop specific models of public finance to match specific institutional constraints), but by making simple assumptions about produc-

I am grateful to Jerry Hausman, Mark Gersovitz, James Mirrlees, David Newbery, Nicholas Stern, and participants at the National Bureau of Economic Research taxation workshop for their helpful comments on earlier versions.

tion, I am able to focus on the relationship between tax policy and consumer behavior. In my first section, rules for optimal taxation and for tax reform are derived. In the second, I discuss alternative ways of specifying demand functions for estimation and examine the ways in which the specification interacts with the tax rules to determine the answers. I argue that a very delicate balance must be struck between measurement on the one hand and prior assumption on the other if the small amount of existing empirical evidence is to have more than a decorative effect on the results. A final subsection deals briefly with some of the issues that arise in the estimation of the production side, and I discuss ways of using engineering and farm management data to supplement econometric estimation of supply parameters. A third section deals with the availability of relevant data for developing countries and with the econometric problems that arise in using them. I also consider the sort of feasible econometric research program that would make a significant contribution.

A Simple Model of Taxes and Tax Reforms

I use a standard model of commodity taxation in an economy with many consumers (see, for example, Atkinson and Stiglitz, 1980, chap. 14). There are assumed to be constant returns in production (or 100 percent profits taxation), and I treat producer prices as fixed. Not all goods can necessarily be taxed, but the government can pay a uniform cash benefit (positive or negative) to some subset of the population. The government, for example, may be able in urban areas to provide quota amounts of food at below-market prices. If such quotas are lower than actual consumption levels, or if any excess can be sold at the market price, such schemes are equivalent to cash subsidies. Some consumers cannot be reached in this way, however—for example those outside the urban areas or those without fixed addresses.

The government social welfare function is written

$$(4\text{-}1) \qquad W = W(u^1, u^2, \ldots, u^h, \ldots, u^H)$$

for household utility levels u^h. Household preferences are defined by indirect utility functions:

$$(4\text{-}2) \qquad u^h = V^h(w^h T + g, w^h, \mathbf{q})$$

for indirect utility function V^h, wage rate w^h, time endowment T, benefit level (grant) g, and commodity price vector $\mathbf{q}$. Prices are in part fixed producer (or border) prices $\mathbf{p}$ and in part taxes $\mathbf{t}$, that is,

$$(4\text{-}3) \qquad \mathbf{q} = \mathbf{p} + \mathbf{t}$$

where t_i is zero for goods that cannot be taxed. The government must meet a revenue requirement R and must finance the benefits so that

$$(4\text{-}4) \qquad \sum_h \mathbf{t} \cdot \mathbf{x}^h = R + H_u g$$

for vector $\mathbf{x}^h$ of household h's consumption levels, with H_u the number of households covered by the benefit scheme (u = urban, for example). Note that the model has no income tax; in the somewhat unlikely event that all goods are taxable, and all households are covered by the benefits, a linear income tax can be replicated by a suitable combination of benefit level and uniform commodity taxes. Nonlinear income taxes are rarely important for more than a small segment of the population in developing countries.

In any given economy at any given time, taxes are likely to be an accretion of ill-fitting parts accumulated over time by the uncoordinated actions of overlapping fiscal authorities. It is therefore sensible to begin by looking at welfare-improving reforms. Increasing the tax on good i will alter social welfare by the amount

(4-5)
$$\frac{\partial W}{\partial t_i} = \sum_h \frac{\partial W}{\partial u^h} \cdot \frac{\partial V^h}{\partial q_i} = -\sum_h \beta^h x_i^h$$

with

(4-6)
$$\beta^h = \frac{\partial W}{\partial u^h} \bigg/ \frac{\partial V^h}{\partial g}$$

so that β^h is the social marginal utility of money to h, and the last equality in equation 4-5 follows from Roy's theorem. Equation 4-5 gives the costs of an increase in t_i. The benefits derive from increased government revenue, and this must be accorded a social welfare "price." Away from a welfare optimum, there is no reason to suppose that all government revenue, however raised or spent, has the same marginal value. Even so, I work with a single social welfare price of government revenue, λ; the problems thereby ignored are not of central concern here. Given λ, the marginal benefits of an increase in t_i are given by

(4-7)
$$B_i = \lambda \sum_h (x_i^h + \mathbf{t} \cdot \partial \mathbf{x}^h / \partial q_i).$$

For the benefit g, the corresponding expressions are

(4-8)
$$\partial W / \partial g = \sum_{h \in u} \beta^h$$

and

(4-9)
$$B_g = -\lambda \left(H_u - \sum_{h \in u} \mathbf{t} \cdot \frac{\partial \mathbf{x}^h}{\partial g} \right).$$

Consequently, social welfare is increased by a small increase in t_i if the following condition holds

(4-10)
$$\mathbf{t} \cdot \left(-\frac{\partial \mathbf{X}}{\partial q_i} \right) < X_i - X_i^*,$$

where $\mathbf{X}$ is the vector of aggregate demands, whereas $\mathbf{X}^*$ is the vector of demands weighted by β^h / λ, that is,

(4-11) $$X_i^* = \sum_h \beta^h x_i^h / \lambda.$$

Similarly, benefits should be increased if

(4-12) $$\bar{\beta}_u + \bar{\rho}_u \lambda > \lambda$$

where $\bar{\beta}_u$ is the mean of β^h in the covered sector and $\bar{\rho}_u$ is the mean of $\rho^h = \mathbf{t} \cdot \partial \mathbf{x}^h / \partial g$, the propensity to pay tax from additional benefit.

The rules 4-10 and 4-12 are those that I shall use to illustrate econometric and data requirements. They serve also to characterize *optimal* tax and benefit rates if the inequalities are replaced by equalities. Note, however, that expression 4-10 does not give conditions on the taxes themselves. One possible way to obtain such conditions is to invert the matrix $-\partial \mathbf{X}/\partial \mathbf{q}$ through the inequality in order to obtain welfare-improving conditions on the tax rates themselves. In general, of course, it is not legitimate to (pre- or post-) multiply a matrix through a set of inequalities such as expression 4-10. If the inverse of $-\partial \mathbf{X}/\partial \mathbf{q}$ is a positive matrix, however, the inversion is legitimate, and this will be guaranteed, for example, by restricting cross-price elasticities so that, for each good, the absolute value of one minus the good's own-price elasticity is greater than the sum of the absolute values of the cross-price elasticities. Although this condition would seem to be worth pursuing further, I have not been able to find natural assumptions about preferences that would yield exactly these restrictions. It seems better to pursue preference restrictions directly, and I do so in the next section.

These formulas are sufficient to show what is required of the empirical analysis. It must be possible to obtain data on aggregate quantities and on consumer and producer prices. Disaggregated data on quantities are also required so that the social weighting schemes can be applied to yield all X_i^*. The procedure is relatively straightforward. It is more difficult to obtain information on the price and income responses $\partial \mathbf{X}/\partial \mathbf{q}$ and $\partial \mathbf{X}/\partial g$, the latter being required for calculating the benefit levels via expression 4-12. As is emphasized in other chapters of this book, especially chapters 2 and 11, and by Ahmad and Stern (1984), and provided that only small reforms are considered, the reform approach asks much less of the econometric analysis than does the calculation of optimal taxes. In the formulas above, the tax rates, benefits, price responses, and quantities are actual, observed quantities (or transformations of observed quantities) as they actually exist. In contrast, the inequalities will become equalities only if taxes differ from their current values and if quantities, responses, and so on all adjust. The calculation of the optimum therefore requires that price and income responses be calculated at points possibly quite different from either the current position or anything else previously observed. Tax reform requires knowledge only of the current position and current values of the derivatives of the demand functions. Tax optimization requires knowledge of the demand function over a large range of its arguments. I shall argue in the next sections that even the former is an ambitious requirement relative to the data and techniques actually available.

The Specification of Preferences and Technology

Estimation of price and income responses is accomplished through specification of a system of demand functions. We can choose from many possibilities, and the guiding principle is to select a functional form that allows the data to be used to the best effect in narrowing down good tax reforms. There is no guarantee, of course, that all the parameters required will even be estimable on the best available data. Nature may not be kind enough to perform crucial experiments on our behalf. Consequently, the calculations will always contain a judicious blend of prior restriction and of measurement, and the weaker the data, the stronger the restrictions must be. In the next section I shall discuss data availability in more detail, but here I consider two stylized cases, the first, in which data are scarce (the normal case), and the second, in which data are plentiful and measurement can dominate assumption.

Demand Functions When Data Are Scarce

For many countries, household survey data can be used to provide estimates of total consumption of various commodities as well as of how these consumption levels vary with income and with household socioeconomic characteristics. Measurement of price responses, however, requires data from several time periods, and there will rarely be enough such observations to allow estimation of more than a few price elasticities at best. Restrictions that link the various responses are therefore required, and it is natural to look for reasonable assumptions about consumer preferences that will provide them.

One relatively unrestrictive case, but one commonly used, involves the assumption that goods are separable from leisure and that, within the goods branch of preferences, the demand for each good is a linear function of total commodity expenditures. The linear expenditure system, first estimated by Stone (1954), is such a model, although it also imposes separability between each and every good. It has also been widely estimated for many developing countries; see particularly the volume by Lluch, Powell, and Williams (1977). Consequently, the linear expenditure system is a good benchmark from which to start. Its estimation is known to be feasible with very limited computing technology, and for many countries parameter estimates already exist. Such parameter estimates, however, prove to be of limited usefulness in tax reform or optimal tax calculations. Atkinson (1977) showed, in the model of section 1, with tastes represented by the linear expenditure system, with *all* consumers receiving an *optimal* benefit level, and with *all* goods taxable, that the optimum tax rate is uniform across all goods. (Atkinson discusses this model in chapter 14 below.) In Deaton (1979), I extended this result and weakened the assumptions. In particular, only linear Engel curves and separability of goods from leisure are required, and not all goods need be taxable. Indeed, given an optimal benefit level, any group of taxable goods that is separable (that is, the marginal rates of substitution within the group are independent of consumption levels outside the group) and has within-group linear Engel curves should optimally be taxed at the same rate. In these cases, estimation is not required for optimal tax calculation. There is no point in going to the trouble of estimating the linear expenditure system, because the outcome is determined as soon as the specification has been decided.

It is important to note that the optimality of uniform commodity taxation does not imply that any *movement* toward uniformity will improve social welfare. If the conditions given above about linear Engel curves and separability are true, for example, then it does not follow that a "reform" in which the lowest tax rate is raised to equal the second lowest and the highest tax rate is lowered to equal the second highest will necessarily be an improvement, unless of course this alteration produces uniformity. To extend the uniform optimal tax rule to a "move to uniformity" tax *reform* rule requires further assumptions. Consider the (very restrictive) case of linear Engel curves, separability between each and every good (additive separability), and optimal benefit levels with complete coverage. In this case, which includes the linear expenditure system, the tax reform rule 4-10 takes the form: increase τ_i, the tax *rate* on good i, t_i/q_i, if

$$(4\text{-}13) \qquad \tau_i < \mathbf{b} \cdot \mathbf{t} + \alpha(\bar{m} - m^*)/\bar{m}$$

where $\mathbf{b}$ is the vector of marginal propensities to spend, α is a positive constant, $\bar{m}$ is mean expenditure on taxable goods, and m^* is a weighted average of expenditures on taxable goods, the weights for each household being $\beta^h + \rho^h$ normalized to sum to unity. Because the right-hand side of inequality 4-13 is independent of i, the tax reform rule approves of anything that brings commodity taxes closer to uniformity. Once again, there is little need for econometric analysis, and the optimality of uniform taxation extends to the tax reform program. The assumptions required for expression 4-13 are stronger, however, than for the results at the optimum, and in particular the additive separability among goods plays a crucial role.

How does the tax reform program change if additive separability is maintained but linearity and optimal benefits assumptions are dropped? Under additivity, the substitution matrix for household h, S^h, must satisfy

$$(4\text{-}14) \qquad \begin{aligned} q_i q_j S^h_{ij} &= \phi^h m^h b^h_i b^h_j && \text{for } i \neq j \\ q_i^2 S^h_{ii} &= -\phi^h m^h b^h_i (1 - b^h_i) && \text{for } i = j \end{aligned}$$

where ϕ^h is a positive scalar, and b^h_i is household h's marginal propensity to spend on good i; see Frisch (1959) or Deaton and Muellbauer (1980a, pp. 138–40). Equation 4-14 gives an expression for $\partial x^h_i/\partial q_j$ for each household and thus for $\partial X_i/\partial q_j$ in total. If this is substituted into the tax reform rule, and the algebra is worked out, it can be shown to be desirable to raise τ_i if the following holds

(4-15) $\qquad \frac{1}{H}\sum_h [\phi^h m^h b_i^h(\tau_i - \rho^h)] < q_i \bar{x}_i - \frac{1}{H\lambda}\sum_h (\beta^h + \lambda\rho^h)q_i x_i^h.$

With parallel linear Engel curves and identical tastes, b_i^h, ϕ^h, and ρ^h are independent of h, $\rho^h = \mathbf{b} \cdot \mathbf{\tau}$, so that if the benefits are optimal, formula 4-12 holds as an equality, the right-hand side of expression 4-15 is proportional to $(\bar{m} - m^*)$, and the rule reduces to expression 4-13. With nonoptimal benefits, and other things being equal, a benefit level that is too low (deserving consumers cannot be reached) leads to a tendency to leave tax rates on necessities relatively low and to make it less likely to be beneficial to raise them. In the possibly more usual case where revenue in the hands of the government is at a premium, the benefit level is too high, and there will be pressure to raise taxes on necessities above a uniform rate. Condition 4-15 will also differ from the uniformity prescription because of taste differences and nonlinear Engel curves and therefore offers scope for the incorporation of household budget information about differences among households in consumption patterns and in propensities to consume. From this point of view, the rule is very satisfactory; information that is available is used, and different social weights for different income levels, socioeconomic groups, or regions can be incorporated, whereas information that is not available, that on price responses, is covered by the additivity assumption.

The difficulty here is the suspicion that the rules are not robust to changes in the supplementary assumptions. Additivity is far from being the only way of restricting preferences, and alternative specifications may yield quite different rules for reform. In Deaton (1981), I showed that *optimal* tax rates can be very sensitive to "small" variations in separability assumptions. In particular, it is possible to move from progressive commodity taxation (luxuries taxed at higher rates) to regressive taxation by a small change in assumptions that is unlikely to be detectable with even good, plentiful data. It may, however, be the case that tax reform rules are more robust than optimal tax rates, and this possibility can be examined by deriving rules corresponding to expression 4-15 for alternative preference structures and comparing results. As an example, take a representative consumer with *indirectly* additive preferences (Houthakker, 1960), for whom cross-price elasticities are independent of the good affected. Such a restriction gives

(4-16) $\qquad \begin{aligned} \epsilon_{ij} &= -\omega_j(1 - e_j + \xi) & \text{for } i \neq j \\ \epsilon_{ii} &= -1 + (1 - \omega_i)(1 - e_i + \xi) & \text{for } i = j \end{aligned}$

where ϵ_{ij} is the cross-price elasticity of good i with respect to q_j, e_j is good j's expenditure elasticity, $\xi > 0$ is a scalar with $e_i > \xi$, and w_j is the budget share of good j. If equation 4-16 is inserted into the tax formula, the reform rule is: increase τ_i if

(4-17) $\qquad \tau_i < \mathbf{\tau} \cdot \mathbf{w} + (e_i - \xi)^{-1}[\mathbf{\tau} \cdot \mathbf{w} + (X_i - X_i^*)/X_i].$

This expression is not the same as that obtained under the assumption of direct additivity and does not in general imply that moves toward uniformity are always desirable. Since, however, $(X_i - X_i^*)/X_i$ is, like e_i, a measure of the expenditure elasticity of good i, the second term on the right-hand side of expression 4-17 has the elasticity in both numerator and denominator. In consequence, for some preferences and configurations of taxes, the rule may not deviate too much from the uniformity prescription. In general, the right-hand side of expression 4-17 will vary from good to good, so that there will be moves toward a uniform tax structure that will *decrease* social welfare. It is of course no good either to assume direct additivity and to prescribe uniformity or to assume indirect additivity and to prescribe something else. Before we can make a sensible recommendation, we must be able to tell which, if either of them, is correct in a particular context.

Separability assumptions are not the only way in which prior information can be used to supplement data insufficiency. Most practitioners would express their priors not in terms of preferences but more directly in terms of the elasticities themselves. My impression is that many people will hazard informed guesses about expenditure and own-price elasticities but rarely about cross-price effects, presumably on the grounds that such effects are of second-order importance. Such ideas can be formalized by asserting that changes in the tax on good i have a negligible effect on the total revenue collected from other goods, so that the reform rule 4-10 becomes: increase τ_i if

$$(4\text{-}18) \qquad\qquad \tau_i < (-\bar{\epsilon}_{ii})^{-1}(X_i - X_i^*)/X_i$$

where $\bar{\epsilon}_{ii}$ is the mean own-price elasticity. At first sight, this seems quite different from the previous rules in that the divisor on the right-hand side is a *price* elasticity and not a *total expenditure* elasticity. Commodities that are both luxuries *and* price inelastic, if they exist, will tend to be penalized by expression 4-18, whereas in the previous rules the income elasticity term always tended to offset the inequality of distribution of the good so as to bring the tax rate more or less into line with those on other goods. Consider, for example, the implications of expression 4-18 for the relative tax rates on gasoline and food. Gasoline tends to be purchased directly only by relatively wealthy individuals in developing countries, so that the numerator on the right-hand side of expression 4-18 will be large. The opposite will be true for food. Food, as a necessity, is supposed to be relatively price inelastic, and in spite of its luxury nature, the same is often thought to be true of gasoline demand, either because rich people once they possess vehicles will stop at nothing to use them or because gasoline is only a component of running costs so that, even if the elasticity with respect to total cost is quite high, the elasticity with respect to the gasoline price alone can be expected to be small. If this chain of informal empiricism is correct, and if indeed cross-price effects are small, then it is clearly desirable to tax gasoline more heavily than food. As was the case when I considered direct versus indirect additivity, an alternative and more or less plausible specification of demand behavior has led to quite different tax and tax reform rules.

My essential point here is that, within the class of models considered in this and the previous section, the data typically available in developing countries are simply not adequate to indicate what the tax rates ought to be or how they ought to be reformed. Tax rules depend in an essential way on parameters that we can hope to measure only with the help of good and plentiful data. Calculated optimal tax rates for developing countries or calculated directions of reform should therefore be viewed with great circumspection. Although their derivation involves parameter estimation and the use of actual data, it remains true that variation in essentially untestable prior assumptions is capable of radically changing the numbers.

Such a conclusion has positive as well as negative aspects. No recommendation can be fully supported with the available data. Still, we can reasonably consider which positions it might be reasonable to occupy for the time being and which, by contrast, can readily be dismissed as implausible. Within the current class of models, my own personal position would be to opt for a lump-sum subsidy together with uniform tax rates. I believe that such a prescription cannot be shown to be incorrect, given current knowledge. First, I do not think that it is even possible in most developing countries to disprove the linear Engel curve and additivity assumptions that formally give rise to the proposition, at least for broad categories of goods. Engel curves from cross-section data are typically not linear, but the curvature is typically not supported by such time-series evidence as exists, and at a conceptual level, the comparison of different households with different income levels cannot tell us what will be the effects of increasing income for a given household or group of households. The latter effect enters into the calculations, and the long-standing contradictions between cross-section and time-series estimates suggests that the distinction is an important one (see, for example, Kuznets, 1962). Second, my interpretation of the alternative formulas 4-15 and 4-17 is that they are not in gross violation of the lump-sum subsidy/uniformity result. Clearly, further work is required to support or to disprove this contention, but the deviations of these formulas from this result seem to me to be second-order effects. We are left with formula 4-18 and the example involving food and gasoline. We should note, however, that this is a very special case. It is a common example that is produced in response to the uniformity claim but one that is remarkably difficult to replicate. The words "necessity" (something that is hard to do without) and "luxury" (something that one can easily forgo) by their very meaning suggest that price and income elasticities are generally believed to be directly related across goods. This notion is formalized by separability. I find this as good a source of casual empiricism as any, and it leads to the lump-sum subsidy/uniformity results. Although there undoubtedly do exist informal estimates and beliefs about price and income elasticities, it seems incorrect to accord them much weight without tracing their sources. In the gasoline example, there is "technical" information about the share of gasoline in running costs, and this is obviously relevant, but such information is the exception rather than the rule for consumer behavior, though, as I shall argue below, there is much more scope for such devices in estimating supply responses. In many cases, however, a widely believed price elasticity proves to have come from an earlier empirical study, and that study has to be evaluated directly, not given enhanced status because of its priority in time.

A further positive feature of the focus on lump-sum subsidies and uniform rates is the prominence given to the lump-sum subsidies themselves. Their role in the analysis and conclusion, together with the widespread use in developing countries of policies that in important respects resemble lump-sum subsidies, suggests that the evaluation of changes in these subsidies should be a central part of reform analysis. Thus, for example, when the marginal cost of funds is calculated for a number of different goods, we should ask how these compare with the marginal benefit of increasing a lump-sum subsidy. Such subsidies occur, for example when commodities such as foodstuffs are publicly supplied and with some forms of public goods (but should not be confused with subsidies to prices without rationing). Once again we have seen in tax analysis the importance of carefully examining the tools that are available to the government and of considering taxes and expenditures simultaneously. A narrow view of the tax problem and options available may be very misleading.

I should end this section with some disclaimers about cases in which lump-sum subsidy/uniformity clearly does not apply. The framework used here assumes that *all* goods are taxable, and that is clearly not true in most developing countries. Given additive separability, as well as the linearity assumption, of course, goods that can be taxed ought to be taxed uniformly. If very narrowly defined goods are being considered, however, and sometimes nothing else is administratively feasible, then both additivity and the linearity of Engel curves become implausible, and there is no predisposition in favor of uniformity. An important theoretical issue for tax design in developing countries is how the conflicting demands of feasibility and separability should be reconciled. If it is possible to tax only goods produced in the formal sector, or only goods that are traded, and yet these goods are companions in separable groups with untaxable goods, then it is far from clear what tax rates should be.

Demand Functions with Plentiful Data

Provided that data are plentiful and of the right type, the difficulties of the previous section can be avoided by estimating sufficiently *general* systems of demand functions. The crucial property required is that preferences be represented by a *flexible functional form*. The basic idea is that the specification of preferences, whether by means of a utility function, an indirect utility function, a cost function, or whatever, should have sufficient parameters so configured that, at any given point in price and income space, the derivatives of the demand functions can take on any values consistent with the theory. Such specifications ensure at least the possibility of a local approximation to whatever the demand functions happen to be, and they guarantee that, at least as far as income and the matrix of price elasticities are concerned, our measurements are indeed measurements and not prior assumptions in disguise. This order of approximation, a second-order flexible functional form, is probably sufficient for evaluating tax reform proposals but is not accurate enough to calculate optimal taxes. For the latter, we need to know how elasticities change with changes in taxes and with redistribution, so knowledge of at least the second derivatives of demands is required. This in turn would require third- or higher-order flexible functional forms for the preference representation functions.

There currently exists a fair selection of second-order flexible functional forms that could be used in this context. Best known is perhaps the *translog*— see, for example, Christensen, Jorgenson, and Lau (1975)—in which the indirect utility function is expressed as a quadratic in the logarithms of price-to-income ratios, namely

$$(4\text{-}19) \qquad V(m, \mathbf{p}) = \alpha_0 + \Sigma\ \alpha_k\ \log \frac{p_k}{m}$$

$$+ \tfrac{1}{2} \Sigma_k \Sigma_j\ \beta_{kj}\ \log \frac{p_k}{m}\ \log \frac{p_j}{m}$$

where α_0, α_k, and β_{kj} are parameters with $\beta_{kj} = \beta_{jk}$ and m denotes household "full income," $wT + g$. By Roy's identity, the demand functions are

$$(4\text{-}20) \qquad \frac{p_i x_i}{m} = \frac{\alpha_i + \Sigma_j \beta_{ij}\ \log \dfrac{p_j}{m}}{\Sigma_k \alpha_k + \Sigma_k \Sigma_j \beta_{kj}\ \log \dfrac{p_j}{m}}$$

which can be estimated subject to an arbitrary (and harmless) identifying restriction such as $\Sigma\alpha_i = -1$. An alternative second-order flexible functional form is provided by Deaton and Muellbauer's (1980b) Almost Ideal Demand System (AIDS), which specifies the cost function as

$$(4\text{-}21) \qquad \log c(u, \mathbf{p}) = \mu_0 + \Sigma\mu_k\ \log p_k$$

$$+ \tfrac{1}{2}\Sigma_k\Sigma_j\gamma_{kj}\ \log p_k\ \log p_j + u\ \Pi_k p_k^{\theta_k}$$

where μ_0, μ_k, θ_k, and γ_{kj} are parameters. Shepherd's lemma yields the demands

$$(4\text{-}22) \qquad \frac{p_i x_i}{m} = (\mu_i - \theta_i \mu_0) + \Sigma_j \gamma_{ij}\ \log p_j + \theta_i\ \log (m/P)$$

where $\log P$ is given by

$$(4\text{-}23) \qquad \log P = \mu_0 + \Sigma\mu_k\ \log p_k + \tfrac{1}{2} \Sigma_k\Sigma_j\gamma_{jk}\ \log p_k\ \log p_j.$$

Under favorable data conditions, P can be accurately approximated by a parameter-independent price index, so that equation 4-23 becomes an effectively linear system with consequent benefits for estimation. Otherwise, both AIDS and translog models are equally flexible and are equally suited (or unsuited) to the estimation of the required responses.

Both translog and AIDS provide integrated models of demand and prefer-ences so that the welfare and empirical analyses are properly tied together. It is notable, however, that the tax reform formulas as presented in the previous section involve only aggregate price responses. There is therefore no obvious need for a utility-consistent analysis. In consequence, we might even consider estimating demand functions using a constant-elasticity, or Rotterdam, de-mand system (see Theil, 1965), neither of which is utility consistent except in trivial cases. As long as tax reform alone is being considered, such models may be adequate; they are flexible functional forms, and both are capable of providing consistent estimates of income and price elasticities at a point. Their use to calculate optimal taxes, however, is inadvisable. The theory of optimal taxation makes sense only in a world where consumers have well-behaved preferences and demand functions, so that taxes can be set to accomplish the social purpose of raising revenue and redistributing income at minimum cost in terms of distortion. If the estimated demand functions are preference inconsis-tent, calculated "optimal" tax rates are likely to make no sense whatever. In contrast, optimal taxes from the AIDS or the translog may be wrongly calculated because true preferences may be globally representable by neither one, but the calculations will at least be internally consistent.

A number of other points should be noted about systems such as the translog and AIDS. Estimation on time series by nonlinear least squares or by full-information maximum likelihood does not automatically lead to estimates that are fully consistent with the theory. The demand systems must be zero-degree homogeneous in prices and income. This feature is automatic for the translog in equation 4-20 but for the AIDS requires imposition of $\Sigma_j \gamma_{ij} = 0$ for all i. Symmetry of the substitution matrix (a property used by all the usual optimal tax results) is ensured by the symmetry of β_{ij} in the translog and of γ_{ij} in the AIDS. This symmetry can be achieved by standard linear restrictions within a nonlinear regression procedure. There is another, more awkward property, however. If equation 4-19 is to represent preferences legitimately, it must be quasi-convex in prices, and similarly the AIDS cost function 4-21 must be both concave and strictly quasi-concave in prices. In general, it is not possible to impose these restrictions globally. Instead, it is possible to estimate the models subject to the restriction that the estimated Slutsky matrix be negative semi-definite at a point, say the sample mean or, more usefully, at the point from which tax reform is to be considered. Note once again that this procedure works satisfactorily for the analysis of tax reform but is not really sufficient for optimal tax calculation. At nonrestricted points, we risk a nonconcave esti-mated cost function with attendant absurdities such as *negative* deadweight loss or positive responses to compensated price increases.

Some Issues in the Estimation of Supply Responses

The model that I have used so far, with the assumption of constant producer prices, essentially removes production from consideration. Developing countries have many tax and price reform problems, however, with regard to which this assumption is quite inappropriate. Many developing countries have agricultural procurement schemes of one kind or another, so that assessment of the effects of price reforms depends heavily on knowledge of own- and cross-price supply responses for the agricultural produce under consideration. Models of this type are discussed elsewhere in this volume (see chapters 13–18), and I shall confine myself to a brief discussion of the similarities and differences between modeling supply and demand.

The same general techniques apply to both. Demands are modeled using consumer cost or utility functions, whereas supplies are modeled with the aid of profit or cost functions. Both provide representations of technology that are particularly convenient for modeling price changes, because factor demands and commodity supplies and their derivatives can be obtained quickly and easily by straightforward differentiation. The translog profit function, for example, takes the same form as equation 4-19, with "profit" replacing "utility" and with the price-to-income ratios representing the prices of inputs and outputs relative to one of the inputs/outputs that is chosen as numeraire. Data are probably less scarce on the production side than on the demand side, though with regard to the latter, long time series with relative price variation are rarely available. Good data are, however, available from farm management surveys on the operation of individual farms, and there is information of an "engineering" or technical variety relating inputs and outputs. It is not difficult to obtain rough orders of magnitude on yields, on feed costs per animal, and so forth. It is more difficult to know how to incorporate these data into the representations of technology that are useful for the analysis, that is, the cost and profit functions. These "dual" representations are immensely convenient for market analysis, because they focus immediately on *prices*. The technical information, however, is typically about *quantities* and the relationships between them. To illustrate the issues, I discuss a model of land allocation that is loosely based on the work of Braverman, Hammer, and Jorgenson (1984) on agriculture in Cyprus. The model shows how restrictions similar to additivity on the demand side can arise in the analysis of production, so that, as for demand, cross-price effects can be simply and effectively restricted.

Consider an agricultural economy where three agricultural crops compete for a limited supply of land. I assume that all inputs *other* than land are available in infinitely elastic supply at fixed prices, so that, given the allocation of land to each crop, efficient production is attained by having each sector independently efficient without regard to the others. If land, like the other inputs, were also available in unlimited quantities at fixed price and quality, then the three sectors would be independent, and the profit function for the crop sector as a whole would be simply the sum of the three separate profit functions for the three sectors. Because the output price of each crop would appear only in the profit function for its own sector, the cross-price supply responses, for example the effect of a change in the wheat price on the output of barley, would all be zero. The presence of land in fixed supply, however, means that this is no longer the case. If the output price of barley is increased, land will be reallocated from other crops to barley production, so that the output of the other crops will fall. If this is the only effect, and I shall assume that it is, then although the cross-supply responses are not now zero, they are still heavily restricted.

I work with restricted profit functions for each sector in which the amount of land a_i is taken as fixed. Let p_i be the output price for crop i, and $\mathbf{w}$ be the vector of input prices taken to be common across sectors. The sector i restricted-profit function is then written $\pi\,(p_i, \mathbf{w}, a_i)$ and the profit function for the entire crop sector as $\Pi\,(\mathbf{p}, \mathbf{w}, A)$, where A is the (fixed) total amount of land available and we have

$$(4\text{-}24) \qquad \Pi\,(\mathbf{p}, \mathbf{w}, A) = \max_{a}\,[\Sigma\pi_i(p_i, w, a_i);\, \Sigma a_i = A]$$

so that $\Pi(.\,,.\,,.)$ embodies an efficient allocation of land between crops. If the rental price of land, either actual or shadow, is r, then equation 4-24 can be rewritten as

$$(4\text{-}25) \qquad \Pi\,(\mathbf{p}, \mathbf{w}, A) = \Sigma\,\pi_i^{*}(p_i, w, r)$$

where π_i^{*} is the *un*restricted profit function for sector i. The restrictions on output responses can be seen straightforwardly from equation 4-25. Given the additive structure, the output y_i of crop i depends only on its own price, on the input prices, and on the rental rate r. Hence changes in the output prices of other crops work only through their effects on r, which in turn adjusts so that the land market clears. Because y_i is the partial derivative of Π and thus π_i^{*} with respect to p_i, the derivative of y_i with respect to p_j for i not equal to j is given by

$$(4\text{-}26) \qquad \frac{\partial y_i}{\partial p_j} = \frac{\partial^2\pi_i^{*}}{\partial p_i\,\partial r}\cdot\frac{\partial r}{\partial p_j} = \frac{\partial^2\pi_j^{*}}{\partial p_j\,\partial r}\cdot\frac{\partial r}{\partial p_i}$$

where the last equality follows by the symmetry of the cross-price derivatives. Rearranging the last two terms gives

$$(4\text{-}27) \qquad \frac{\partial^2\pi_i^{*}}{\partial p_i\,\partial r}\div\frac{\partial r}{\partial p_i} = \frac{\partial^2\pi_j^{*}}{\partial p_j\,\partial r}\div\frac{\partial r}{\partial p_j}.$$

Because the left-hand side is independent of j, and the right-hand side is independent of i, both are independent of either and of all indexes. Hence for some scalar ψ that is independent of i, we have

$$(4\text{-}28) \qquad \frac{\partial^2\pi_i^{*}}{\partial p_i\,\partial r} = \psi\,\frac{\partial r}{\partial p_i}.$$

Hence, substituting back in the original expression for the cross-price derivative 4-26, for i not equal to j,

$$(4\text{-}29) \qquad \frac{\partial y_i}{\partial p_j} = \psi \frac{\partial r}{\partial p_i} \cdot \frac{\partial r}{\partial p_j}.$$

The quantity ψ can readily be determined from the market-clearing condition for land. Because a_i is minus the partial derivative of π_i^* with respect to r, the market-clearing condition is

$$(4\text{-}30) \qquad \sum_k \frac{\partial \pi_k^* (p_k, \mathbf{w}, r)}{\partial r} = -A.$$

Differentiating with respect to p_j gives

$$(4\text{-}31) \qquad \left(\sum \frac{\partial^2 \pi_k}{\partial r^2} \right) \cdot \frac{\partial r}{\partial p_j} = - \frac{\partial^2 \pi_j}{\partial r \, \partial p_j}.$$

Comparison of equations 4-31 and 4-28 shows that ψ is the bracketed expression on the left-hand side of equation 4-31. It is minus the sum of the derivatives of acreage for each crop, with respect to the rental, and it can be regarded as the total additional land that would be made available in response to a change in the rental price.

Note first that, if the responses of rent to each of the output prices are known, and if the total response of land use to rent changes is known, then all the cross-price supply elasticities can be directly calculated. I think it unlikely that such things *would* be known in practice, but even without any such knowledge, the restrictions embodied in equation 4-29 are likely to be useful if there are a large number of outputs. Note that without such restrictions, there are $n(n-1)$ cross-price responses when there are n crops, and half of these can be inferred by symmetry. Given equation 4-29, only $(n+1)$ responses are required. Hence, if $\frac{1}{2}n(n-1)$ is greater than $n+1$, equation 4-29 is helpful even without knowledge of the quantities on the right-hand side.

In cases where there are fewer than four crops, so that the restrictions themselves are not useful, it is nevertheless possible to rewrite equation 4-29 in a form that uses quantities that might more realistically be available. The trick, as usual, is to try to convert information about prices, for example, the response of land rent to an increase in the support price of a crop, into information about quantities, for example the marginal productivity of land in growing that crop. Some of this conversion can be accomplished using the *restricted* profit function with which I started and which I have not yet really used. The link between the restricted and unrestricted profit functions is the first-order condition for the allocation of land, that is,

$$(4\text{-}32) \qquad \frac{\partial \pi_i (p_i, \mathbf{w}, a_i)}{\partial a_i} = r.$$

From this the derivatives of a_i with respect to both r and p_i can be obtained in terms of the derivatives of the restricted profit functions π_i. The derivatives of a_i, however, are the double derivatives of the *un*restricted profit functions π_i^*;

which, via equation 4-31 above, yield the rent price derivatives that appear in equation 4-29. Hence if we differentiate equation 4-32 with respect to r and p_i in turn, equate the derivatives of each a_i to the double derivatives of the π_i^*s, and finally use equation 4-31 to substitute in equation 4-29, we have

$$(4\text{-}33) \qquad \frac{\partial y_i}{\partial p_j} = \frac{\partial y_i / \partial a_i}{\partial^2 \pi_i / \partial a_i^2} \cdot \frac{\partial y_j / \partial a_j}{\partial^2 \pi_j / \partial a_j^2} \div \left(\Sigma\, 1 \middle/ \frac{\partial^2 \pi_k}{\partial a_k^2} \right).$$

This may or may not be easier to evaluate than equation 4-29, but there seems to be a better chance. The marginal productivities of land are taken with output and other input prices considered fixed, so the complementary or substitutable inputs are allowed to adjust. The double derivatives of profit with respect to acreage are, of course, the reciprocals of the derivatives of acreage with respect to the rental price and provide another way of evaluating that quantity.

Data and Estimation

The most important source of data in developing countries is the *household expenditure survey*. The commonest type of survey is a general-purpose household inquiry, with a sampling proportion of perhaps 1 in 2,000 and containing (among other things) questions on household characteristics, demographic structure, and expenditures on a typically lengthy list of consumption items. Income and labor supply may or may not be included, but it is relatively uncommon for a single survey to contain both detailed expenditure information and data on sources of income, including hours and wage rates. Many expenditure surveys also collect data on quantities purchased as well as on expenditures, at least for goods that come in well-defined units. Hence we find numbers of eggs or kilos of fruit together with expenditures on them, but only expenditures on clothing or entertainment. I discuss below what use, if any, we can make of this sort of information.

Household expenditure surveys are widely available around the world, and few countries have not carried one out at least occasionally. Only a relatively small proportion of these are publicly available—household budget surveys have always been politically sensitive—and are in a form that permits use. Still, a number of developing countries (India, Indonesia, Malaysia, Sri Lanka, and Thailand, for example) have the ability to conduct high-quality surveys and have considerable experience in doing so. Moreover, the countries listed undertake surveys on a more or less regular basis, not every year, but at variable intervals. Although the design of the questionnaire changes (usually gradually) over time, such repeated surveys allow the integration of cross-section and time-series evidence. These regular surveys draw new random samples each time, so that the households are not the same from survey to survey, as would be the case with panel data. Genuine panel data are even scarcer in the developing world than in the developed countries and for good reason. It is difficult to track any given household over an extended period of time, so that the panel, through attrition, becomes seriously unrepresentative over time. Second, if the quality of responses is poor, then with panel data, where the main interest lies in changes between one response and the next, the ratio of noise to signal may become unacceptably high. This is not a disadvantage if the purpose is only to measure the changes themselves, because reporting errors are common across panels and cross sections, but it becomes a serious issue in econometric estimation (see Ashenfelter, Deaton, and Solon, 1985). Even so, there is scope for experimentation with relatively short-lived "rolling" panels, in which each household is interviewed on four or five occasions and is then replaced, with one-quarter or one-fifth of the respondents dropping out and being replaced at each round.

The second major source of relevant data is information on aggregate consumption of various items and on prices over time. Some of these data are not independent of the household survey data, because for some items the only method of estimating aggregate consumption is to "blow up" the survey estimate. For many items, however, there are other sources of information, usually import and export returns from ports and border posts together with returns from large-scale enterprises, sources that are either controlled by the state or large enough to be willing to cooperate with state data collection. Although coverage from these sources is at best partial, especially in largely rural subsistence economies, such data are likely to be particularly useful for tax purposes because the goods that are covered by these data overlap significantly with the goods that are actually or potentially taxable. If it is possible to collect data on production and distribution of a product, it is usually also possible to tax it. The *price* data in the aggregate time series are likely to be genuinely independent of the survey evidence. Prices are calculated from separate surveys, from standardized items at various locations, or, where data permit, by repricing the volume of consumption at base prices and then deriving an implicit price deflator by comparison with the expenditure series. Note that such prices, like the consumption figures, are averaged over the whole population; they provide no information on who gets what or on who pays what.

These sources are likely to be adequate for tax reform calculations as described in our discussion of demand functions when data are scarce, although not for estimating the flexible functional forms that were subsequently discussed. Consider the tax reform condition 4-15, that is,

$$\frac{1}{H}\sum_h [\phi^h m^h b_i^h(\tau_i - \rho^h)] < q_i \bar{x}_i - \frac{1}{H\lambda}\sum_h (\beta^h + \lambda\rho^h)q_i x_i^h.$$

On the right-hand side, the β^h weights are likely to vary with income [for example, in the Atkinson, 1970, version $\beta^h = (m^h)^{-\epsilon}$ for total expenditure m^h and some number $\epsilon > 0$] but also with region and with family size and/or composition. Given ρ^h (see below), the whole can be evaluated either by direct computation from the household survey or by parametrizing $q_i x_i^h$ as a function of the factors determining the weights and estimating from the survey data. The quantities ρ^h are the tax rates weighted by household h's vector of marginal propensities to consume and can be estimated in a number of ways. One possibility is to fit a nonlinear flexible Engel curve. For example, the form

$$(4\text{-}34) \qquad q_i x_i = \beta_{i0} \, m + \beta_{i1} \, m \log m + \beta_{i2} \, m \, (\log m)^2$$

often fits the data well and is utility consistent. An alternative much used in studies in India is to fit separate Engel curves for consumers in different income groups; this procedure certainly allows a wide range of b_i^h values, though it is unclear why the marginal propensities should be discontinuous at arbitrary income boundaries. Whenever possible, estimates of the slopes of Engel curves should be compared with similar results from time-series data. Ever since Kuznets's (1962) work it has been clear that estimates of income elasticities based on time series and household surveys tend to differ, with the latter tending to be much more dispersed from unity than the former. The root cause is presumably the inability to control completely in the cross section for those factors that are correlated with income and vary from household to household but are relatively constant over time, education and *relative* incomes being the obvious examples. The ρ^h parameters of the theory are those revealed from time series, ideally panel data. Nevertheless, judicious use of cross-section estimates, modified by such time series as are available, should be adequate. The parameter ϕ^h in expression 4-15 links price elasticities to income elasticities for household h; for goods whose budget share is small, it is the ratio of the (absolute values of) price elasticity to income elasticity. For broad groups of goods, a household-invariant number of about one-half is reasonable, whereas for more narrowly defined commodities, larger figures should be used. If estimates of price elasticities are available, their comparison with income elasticities yields values for ϕ using expressions such as 4-14.

The procedure is straightforward, certainly more so than the estimation of the fully flexible functional forms discussed earlier in this chapter. The standard data for estimating such models are aggregate time series, though it is also possible to use disaggregated data from several different household surveys. If prices are the same for all households in the cross section, then an n good demand system requires *at least* $(n - 1)$ time periods to estimate a matrix of price elasticities that is unrestricted (except in the case of homogeneity). Many more periods are required if the estimates are to be at all precise. India through the National Sample Survey has been collecting consumers' expenditure data for longer than any other developing country. Of the nearly forty "rounds" so far completed, some two dozen contain consumer expenditure data. If all of these were available for analysis (as they most certainly are not), a flexible system could be estimated with some confidence for perhaps six or eight commodity groups. If such limitations are accepted, there is no reason to suppose that the results would not be useful. Many important issues about the general balance of taxation, and such matters as food subsidy policy, depend on the split of consumers' expenditure into food and nonfood or on the distinction between cereals and meat. For some developing countries, at least, flexible function forms can be estimated to illuminate these issues.

An apparently attractive alternative is to recognize that, within a survey, prices vary from location to location and to use this spatial variation in prices to estimate price elasticities. Because prices are not directly measured, the temptation is to take the expenditure and quantity information and to derive a price by division. Quantities can then be regressed on incomes and prices in the usual way, and apparently sensible results are usually obtained. Unfortunately, I do not believe that this technique is satisfactory, because the estimates that it produces are not estimates of price elasticities. The root of the problem is that expenditure divided by physical quantity yields, not price, but unit value. For some commodities—for example, gasoline—prices and unit values may be very close to one another over a household survey. For most commodities and virtually all foodstuffs, however, unit values reflect quality variations as much as price variations. Rich households, for example, buy more expensive cereals, fruits, vegetables, and meats than do poor households, and unit values so calculated are systematically and positively related to household income. This characteristic, it turns out, can be dealt with. The insuperable problem comes with the likelihood that quality is also likely to be negatively related to price, so that in times of high price, or in areas of high price, quality will tend to be lower. In such circumstances, it is not possible to identify both the price elasticity of demand and the price elasticity of quality.

The algebra is simplest in a constant-elasticity model. Such models are not theoretically satisfactory, but the issues are clear in this case and carry through to better models, albeit in a more complicated form. Imagine a commodity for which quantity is well defined and readily measured and to which quality can be added variably. Purity is the obvious example; sugar can vary from a rough substance full of impurities through an infinitely variable spectrum to 100 percent pure refined sugar. Schematically, imagine the following true model

$$(4\text{-}35) \qquad y_h = \beta_0 + \beta_1 x_{1h} + \beta_2 x_{2h} + u_h$$

$$(4\text{-}36) \qquad x_{3h} = \gamma_0 + \gamma_1 x_{1h} + \gamma_2 x_{2h} + w_h$$

where all variables are measured in logarithms, y_h is quantity purchased by household h, x_{1h} is income, x_{2h} is price, and x_{3h} is quality. β_1 and β_2 are the income and price elasticities of demand, γ_1 and γ_2 the income and price elasticities of quality, and both γ_2 and $\beta_2 < 0$. The terms u_h and w_h are random errors. Quality is measured in such a way that unit values are the product of a quality and price, so that, in logs, unit value z_h is given by

$$(4\text{-}37) \qquad z_h = x_{3h} + x_{2h}.$$

Price is not observed, only unit value z_h. By substitution of equations 4-37 and 4-36 and rearrangement,

$$(4\text{-}38) \qquad x_{2h} = (1 + \gamma_2)^{-1}(z_h - \gamma_0 - \gamma_1 x_{1h} - w_h)$$

so that we have the following correct equation

$$(4\text{-}39) \quad \begin{aligned} y_h &= [\beta_0 - \beta_2\gamma_0/(1 + \gamma_2)] + [\beta_1 - \beta_2\gamma_1/(1 + \gamma_2)]\, x_{1h} \\ &\quad + \beta_2 z_h/(1 + \gamma_2) + u_h - w_h/(1 + \gamma_2). \end{aligned}$$

Hence, if we mistakenly interpret unit value as price, and regress quantity on income and unit value, we estimate, not the price elasticity β_2, but the quantity $\beta_2/(1 + \gamma_2)$. Because γ_2 plausibly lies between 0 and -1, we would expect this procedure to yield "price elasticities" that are correct in sign but much too large in magnitude. This expectation seems to me to be consistent with the evidence that I have seen. Note also that, under the same conditions, income elasticities will also be severely overestimated if γ_1 is at all large.

Quality variations are of course not explicitly recognized in the optimal tax model, and the quantities in the latter are probably most sensibly interpreted as physical quantities *plus* the quality. If so, then the elasticity we require is that of ($y_h + x_{3h}$) with respect to x_{2h}. Substitution in the above equations shows that this is $\beta_2 + \gamma_2$, which is only equal to $\beta_2/(1 + \gamma_2)$ in the entirely fortuitous situation when the sum of the price elasticities is unity, that is, $1 + \beta_2 + \gamma_2 = 0$. Once again, $(\beta_2 + \gamma_2)/(1 + \gamma_2)$ is the parameter that is identified, not $(\beta_2 + \gamma_2)$ itself.

Consistent estimation of the price elasticity requires some means of splitting z_h into its price and quality components. One possibility is to gather genuine price data on homogeneous commodities. Because most countries do so by separate surveys for the purpose of calculating general price levels, it is unclear why such data could not be collected in a way that is integrated with the household surveys themselves. Unfortunately, the fact is that the information is not gathered in this way, perhaps because of the difficulty of identifying homogeneous commodities in different locations. The other possibility, an econometric one, involves finding an instrumental variable (or set of variables) that is orthogonal to quality variations but not to price variations. Regressing z_h on these instruments will "purge" the x_3 component, allowing consistent estimation of the effect of x_2 on y_h. If equation 4-36 is really correct, however, such instruments do not exist. Consider dividing the sample into regions, and assume that prices are the same within regions but vary across regions. A possible "between-regions" estimator is that formed by a regression involving regional averages of quantities on incomes and unit values. This device does not work, however, because the interregional price variation induces interregional quality variation, which is therefore present in the averaged regression just as it was in the original micro version. In contrast, we might look at the *within*-regions estimator. Because prices are constant within the region, a regression of z on x_1 yields an estimate of γ_1, the income elasticity of quality, which can be used to construct a consistent estimate of the income elasticity β_1. γ_2 cannot be estimated on a sample where prices do not vary, however, and so consistent estimation of β_2 is not possible. It seems therefore that only genuine price information can allow estimation of price elasticities from cross sections.

Conclusions

I have examined the possibilities of calibrating a simple model of tax reform and optimal taxation in the context of the data typically available in developing countries. Many such countries have rich data in the form of household surveys. These are excellent sources for the documentation of all kinds of distributional issues, for measuring consumption expenditures and their distribution over households of differing socioeconomic characteristics. They are poor sources, however, for the measurement of the ways in which quantities respond to price changes, and most developing countries do not have adequate time-series data to permit the estimation of own- and cross-price elasticities for more than a small number of interacting goods. Assumptions about preference structure, however, can be used to link price with income elasticities so as to allow essentially complete evaluation of tax reform proposals using only survey data. Perhaps not surprisingly, different assumptions about preferences lead to different rules for tax reform, and data are unlikely to be sufficient to let us distinguish between the different assumptions. I have argued in favor of uniform commodity taxation together with lump-sum subsidies and have advocated reforms that move in this direction but other positions could also be argued. More empirical work needs to be done to discover whether the lump-sum subsidy/uniformity prescription can seriously be threatened as a broad guide to policy. Price data, unlike survey data, are scarce and must be used sparingly. They are perhaps best used to estimate price elasticities for very broad groups so that, in conjunction with the survey evidence, broad sectoral tax policies can be assessed, for example on cereals versus meat or food versus manufactured goods. It is also possible that, within subsectors, price elasticities can be estimated, for example for a group of travel modes. The separability needed to validate the method, however, correspondingly limits the usefulness of the results, because it is frequently desirable to tax goods within separable groups at the same rate.

All of this discussion applies to *tax reform*. The global knowledge of demands and of preferences required for optimal taxation is simply not obtainable in developing countries nor probably in developed countries. It might be argued that, in an uncertain world, a gradualist approach is desirable in any case, so that the identification of desirable directions of reform is all that a policymaker can reasonably expect. Real reforms always involve finite, not infinitesimal changes, however; there are costs to the *process* of tax reform, so that it is not obviously desirable to change taxes a little every year, and governments often phrase their reform objectives in terms of the elimination of deficits, so that analysis should concentrate on minimizing the social costs of raising substantial amounts of extra revenue. Nevertheless, the quality of our empirical knowledge clearly decreases as we move the economy away from previous experience, and advisers would be wise to recognize that fact when they tender advice. I do not say that brave and visionary economists should not offer "optimal" solutions to fiscal problems, but they should always make clear that these solutions are based on untested deductive reasoning and that, without the relevant empirical evidence, it will be even more than usually hazardous to follow such advice.

5

Dynamic Issues

David Newbery and Nicholas Stern

MOST FORMAL MODELS used in modern public economics are static. In addition they usually involve the assumption of competitive equilibrium with prices, known to all agents, which ensure market clearing. A great advantage of this type of model is that it forces the analyst to take general equilibrium responses into account. On the other hand it is frequently criticized for its failure to capture dynamic issues. This criticism has some force but needs to be examined carefully. We shall first examine the intertemporal reinterpretation of the standard model, using dated commodities, to determine its adequacy for the analysis of policy issues in dynamic economies. Although this type of model can be very useful for examining, for example, the medium-term balance of taxation across different types of goods and the medium-term balance between direct and indirect taxation, there are important dynamic issues concerning growth and industrial change for which we need models with a different focus. In the remainder of this chapter we shall examine other possible ways of analyzing these issues in the spirit of the rest of our inquiry. Where any policy is concerned, we need first to calculate its likely effects (in this case stretching over time) and then to assess those effects to judge whether they constitute an improvement.

We begin with more aggregated questions concerning the level of saving, investment, and government revenue. Thus we consider levels of savings and investment and their relations to investment policy. We consider tax policy in growth models more explicitly, afterward discussing the interrelationships between revenue, expenditure, and growth. Would we want or expect revenue and expenditure, for example, to increase over time, and does high government expenditure impede or enhance growth?

More disaggregated problems are then examined, when we consider the more firmly microeconomic questions of the dynamic effects of taxes on the structure of production. What effect will taxes have on innovation, production costs, and market structure? The final section assesses the state of dynamic theory. This theory has been studied by many of the same people who have developed the static techniques but is still in a less satisfactory state. Part of the explanation is that it is technically more demanding, but the main reason is

We are grateful to Pradeep Mitra and Sweder van Wijnbergen for very helpful comments on this chapter.

that for a number of problems it is difficult to produce models that capture the issues involved. Nevertheless, much has been accomplished, and a number of aspects look promising for further research.

The Arrow-Debreu Model and Some Problems

The standard Arrow-Debreu model of general equilibrium can be interpreted as a full intertemporal model provided that goods are distinguished not just by their physical characteristics (and location) but also by their date of availability (and the state of the world). Thus umbrellas delivered on January 1, 1990, if the weather is wet are distinguished from umbrellas now or from umbrellas on that date if the weather is dry. In the strong form of the model, there are markets for every commodity (that is, for every good-date-state). Thus if there are T dates, and S states at each date, and N physically different goods, there are NTS Arrow-Debreu commodities, and there would be NTS markets. There are, however, less demanding conditions in which fewer markets are needed. If agents have rational expectations about the future market-clearing prices of goods in each state of the world, for example, and if they can transfer wealth through time by borrowing or lending on perfect capital markets, and if they can buy insurance that pays one dollar in any particular state of the world, then the equilibrium will be the same as that involving a complete set of markets but will only require $(NT + TS)$ markets (NT markets for dated goods and TS for dated insurance contracts). If, in addition to holding rational expectations, agents either are risk neutral or face no risk, then the original equilibrium can be supported with spot markets at each date, together with a perfect capital market.

This trick of interpreting a model of the economy that is seemingly purely static as an intertemporal model has advantages and obvious limitations. The main advantage is that under strong assumptions (among other things rational expectations, competitive behavior, and no market failures) the economy will be on an efficient growth path, and government intervention will be associated with efficient revenue raising and redistribution rather than with direct concern with the rate of growth. (In addition we need an assumption to rule out "oversaving.") Put another way, the claim that an economy is not on an efficient growth path is usually a claim that there is some market failure and that, before devising some policy response, it is important to identify the source of the market failure. It may be better to address the market failure directly rather than to attempt to change the rate of growth by some other policy.

In the context of taxation, the model allows, for example, the production efficiency results to be interpreted in an intertemporal context. The Diamond-Mirrlees result is that, with constant returns to scale in private production (or 100 percent profits taxes) and no constraints on commodity taxation, it is desirable to preserve production efficiency. In the intertemporal context this situation would imply that all producers should face the same interest rate when making investment decisions, though it will in general be desirable to tax (or subsidize) savings (Diamond and Mirrlees, 1971, p. 277). This statement has direct implications for the design of corporation taxes, and it immediately focuses attention on the reasons for taxes on savings, which should be to improve the intertemporal and interpersonal distribution of consumption.

It is doubtful that the Arrow-Debreu model is adequate for thinking about intertemporal tax issues even in a developed market economy with a value-added tax system (that is, one that permits production efficiency), though it remains a useful point of reference. It is even more unlikely to be satisfactory in a developing country, for the following reasons.

Let us take the Diamond-Mirrlees model, in which indirect taxes imply a difference between producer and consumer prices, as the simplest model of taxation in the Arrow-Debreu framework. Producer prices are those that affect only production decisions and (with zero profits or full taxation) need have no effect on the distribution of income, because any change in producer prices can be offset by changes in tax rates, leaving consumer prices unchanged. Consumer prices can be altered by changing tax rates. Producers whose sales to consumers cannot be taxed are treated as consumers, whose net trades with the taxable sector are treated like the net trades of normal consuming households and are taxed accordingly. The smaller the proportion of production that takes place in this "household" sector, the more useful is the production efficiency result and the easier it is to calculate the right set of consumer taxes. The calculations in turn rest on the assumption that consumers maximize their welfare when they are faced with these consumer prices.

There are several reasons why the Diamond-Mirrlees model is not well suited to intertemporal choices. First, there is the standard objection to the Arrow-Debreu model, whether or not it is applied to taxation, that the full set of markets that it supposes does not exist. Second, it is particularly hard to separate savings and investment decisions for a large fraction of the private sector, and hence it is hard to separate consumption decisions from intertemporal production decisions. A similar feature arises when we consider the taxation of peasant agriculture when taxes can be placed on net trades only and not on production and consumption separately (see chapters 13, 15, and 16). Third, it is difficult to believe that consumers can or do make the rational intertemporal decisions, of the type specified in the model, that are intended to maximize their lifetime welfare (and that of their offspring). Let us consider each objection in turn.

The Existence of Markets

There can be little doubt that the full set of markets embodied in the Arrow-Debreu theory is absent. On the other hand, intertemporal transactions do take place very generally, and spot markets are widely available. We must therefore ask whether the assumptions concerning markets are seriously misleading for the questions under discussion. In the present state of knowledge, we should probably leave open the answer to this question. The sensible thing is to proceed with the analyses that are possible while being continually aware of the problem. Thus we can, for example, suppose that certain markets (for example, crop insurance) do not exist, and we may ask what effect their absence should have on other tax and pricing policies in other markets. Alternatively, we may be willing to suggest that a key issue for peasants is whether they have access to certain forms of credit and that whether or not there is a forward market for flashlight batteries in cloudy weather is relatively unimportant for peasants' production and savings decisions. On the other hand, the absence of a forward market for flashlight batteries may imply that investment in this sector is more risky than it would otherwise be. These are matters of judgment in model building and call for further research.

Separating Savings and Investment

The second reason why the Diamond-Mirrlees model may not be appropriate for intertemporal choice is that in developing countries it is difficult to face producers and consumers with different prices. If all investment took place in formal sector firms that were subject to close tax auditing and had access to a well-functioning capital market, then individuals would lend their savings to the capital market, which would in turn lend them to the most profitable private (and public) firms. These funds would be efficiently allocated and would earn the same (risk-adjusted) rate of return. These returns would be taxed at rates specific to the lender. Standard optimum tax theory could readily be applied.

In most developing countries this description is unlikely to be reasonable for any but the larger incorporated firms in the modern sector, and even these may have predominantly foreign owners. Most enterprises are financed from the savings of the owners (and their close relatives) and have limited access to bank borrowing. In particular, startups are overwhelmingly financed from savings, not just in developing countries, but in most economies (Little, Mazumdar, and Page, 1984, chap. 7). Size gives access to formal credit markets, and the distinctive feature of most developing countries is that a large fraction of production takes place in small firms. Although it is difficult to obtain reliable statistics, Little, Mazumdar, and Page estimate that firms with fewer than five employees account for between one-half and two-thirds of manufacturing employment in low-income Southeast Asia. In some countries and industries there is a bimodal distribution of firm size, reflecting two distinct modes of production—cottage industry and larger-scale formal manufacturing enterprises.

It is not difficult to account for the difficulties experienced by small firms in raising funds from the formal credit market, for they are unproven, often have little collateral, and impose high information and transaction costs on the lender. They have high failure rates and thus threaten high default rates. Adverse selection makes it unattractive to compensate for these default rates by high interest rates, and hence credit markets invariably quantity ration credit—often offering zero amounts to small firms.

If firms find it difficult to borrow, they also often find it easy to evade or avoid taxes on their profits. Often their accounts are sketchy at best or nonexistent, and it is hard to distinguish business costs from their private consumption. Indeed, it is often argued that, where the government attempts to meet the unfulfilled demand for credit by small businesses, it should in exchange require the successful applicants to provide accounts that not only demonstrate the viability and creditworthiness of the business but also form the basis for profits taxation (in countries with profits taxes, that is). The fact that tax advisers feel the need to stress this point suggests that even firms with access to formal credit markets are frequently untaxed.

Intertemporal Rationality

Consumers making rational savings decisions (or adjusting them in the light of changed circumstances) require forecasts of future returns to saving and an idea of the value of additional future consumption. Returns are remarkably difficult to forecast, however, even in a well-functioning capital market, let alone in the fragmented capital markets characteristic of developing countries. Unforeseen inflation, financial crises, changes in asset values, and business failures (and unexpected successes) make even short-run predictions hard, whereas the relevant time periods for lifetime decisions may average fifteen to twenty years. Even if life expectancies can be insured, a person's own health and likely demands at retirement, as well as those of a family, are matters of conjecture, not experience. In theory these uncertainties and information problems might lead individuals to save more or less than they would in a certain or perfectly insured world, but the fact that governments in most developed countries feel the need to require certain levels of life insurance and minimum pension provisions suggests a skepticism as to whether individuals would provide adequately for the future if left to their own decisions. The role of expectations concerning future income, needs, tax policy, and so on is clearly crucial.

For a number of reasons in addition to the possible effects of uncertainty, a government may judge that private individuals in private markets may save too little. Individuals may have a "defective telescopic faculty," for example, which prevents them from considering themselves in T years' time as they would consider themselves now. In such circumstances they may (eventually) welcome government intervention to bolster "their higher self." One should always be wary of this type of paternalistic argument, but it may have some substance in this context.

The government may believe that individuals perceive the price of future goods relative to goods now to be higher than the relative shadow prices (see below). They might do so, for example, if they incorrectly perceive the degree to which future costs will be lowered by current infrastructural investment. Alternatively, market imperfections such as limited access to financial institutions may mean that the private returns to saving are very low. If for any reason the future price that individuals perceive is thought to be too high, then what are the consequences? Other things being equal, this perception will raise the social weight on incomes of high savers, because they have a high propensity to spend on future goods with low shadow prices. In this sense there is a premium on saving. Notice that a similar argument would apply to people with a preference for bananas if the shadow price of bananas were low. The argument concerns market failure rather than uncertainty.

Alternatively, saving may in some respect resemble public goods or positive externalities. If some part of the social returns to my saving accrue to others (for example, through taxation), then my private incentive to save may be insufficient in the absence of some subsidy or tax privilege. Thus as Sen (1967) has argued, individuals may be prepared to make a joint commitment to saving that they would not be prepared to make in isolation.

The sense in which saving has positive externalities must be considered rather carefully. One argument involves taxation and is essentially familiar in that if savings are heavily taxed, for example, through the taxation of companies, then the government may want to encourage savings by other means in part to correct a distortion elsewhere. It is sometimes also suggested that individuals who save for bequests may fear that their children will spend part of their inheritance on others (through marriage, for example); in other words the private benefit the parents perceive from saving is lower than the social benefit. Although the argument has some superficial plausibility, it is not obviously valid without further specification of the precise way in which the utility of descendants affects the utility of parents and the ways in which the descendants interact with each other.

These arguments suggest that, for saving and investment, relying solely on analogies with Arrow-Debreu choices and markets may be unsatisfactory in terms of both models and policy. In the next three sections we examine some aggregative aspects of savings, investment, and government revenue and pose policy questions that take into account some of the problems we have mentioned.

Investment Policy

In competitive intertemporal equilibrium, the government would choose its public investments using the same rate of discount as the private sector and would borrow from the same capital market (supposing that the Diamond-Mirrlees assumptions concerning taxes and prices apply in an Arrow-Debreu intertemporal world). The aggregate rate of saving and investment would be "right," or at its second-best optimal level, given the unavoidable distortions introduced to finance government activities and to improve the distribution of income over time and between individuals. For the reasons we have described, however, this model may be inappropriate, and the government may believe that the rate of investment and hence the rate of growth is too low and that special efforts are needed to improve resource mobilization for investment.

Concern for investment and growth has been a major distinguishing feature of public policy in developing countries. Indeed, in one of the most influential papers to be published on economic development, Sir Arthur Lewis stated, "The central problem in the theory of economic development is to understand the process by which a community which was previously saving and investing 4 or 5% of its national income or less, converts itself into an economy where voluntary saving is running at about 12 to 15% of national income or more" (Lewis, 1954, p. 155). Developed countries may worry about their growth rate, but there has not been the same emphasis on increasing the rate of savings and investment. Instead the emphasis has been on the rate of technical progress, which, in conventional growth accounting calculations, typically accounts for more than half of increases in per capita income. Hence the focus in developed countries is on research and development, policies that affect industrial performance, education, policy toward high technology, and the like. Although critics of public policy have paid particular attention to the structure of taxes on investment and capital income, arguing that they may have undesirable effects on the allocation of investment (see, for example, King and Fullerton, 1984), there have been fewer questions raised about its level.

In developing countries it has been argued that physical capital formation is more important than technical progress in raising the rate of growth. Similar growth accounting exercises suggest that increases in capital per worker account for perhaps as much as 80–90 percent of increases in output per head, in contrast to 40–50 percent in developed countries (Nafziger, 1984, pp. 275–80; Sen, 1983). We do not mean to underplay the importance of human capital formation or education, though the relatively high rates of unemployment of secondary-school leavers in many countries suggests that standard schooling alone may not be the best solution to the scarcity of human capital. We do not mean that technical progress is unimportant, only that in most developing countries new technology in the modern sector is likely to be acquired from abroad, embodied in new physical capital, rather than developed at home. Put another way, developing countries are attempting to catch up with developed countries, which are in turn expanding the frontiers of technical knowledge.

The hypothesis that the productivity of capital in developing countries is high should not be accepted without further inquiry, and the recent experience of some developing countries raises some serious questions about it (see below). Let us for the moment, however, maintain the hypothesis and discuss how it might be taken into account in public policy. If the returns to investment are high in developing countries, then what does it matter if domestic savings are low, provided that the countries can borrow on the international capital market? This question has several answers, though it should be said immediately that there was a dramatic change in the availability of private foreign capital for developing countries in the 1970s. The debt problem of the early 1980s in part reflects the sudden increase in this availability of credit, which stood in marked contrast to the situation in earlier periods.

First, if, as we argued, a substantial fraction of private investment takes place in small firms with little access to *domestic* credit markets, then foreign borrowing will be irrelevant to the finance of such investment. Foreign credit is likely to be available to public enterprises and the foreign multinationals, and to domestic capital only via domestic financial institutions. Public enterprises may not have access to the most productive areas for investment or may make inefficient use of such opportunities, whereas multinationals tend to restrict their activities to specific industries and may, in any case, be limited by the government's concern about the extent to which foreign interests control the economy. Foreign loans to governments are rationed for much the same reasons that loans to small businesses are rationed—foreign bankers are concerned with expropriation, repudiation, or liquidity constraints that force default. All these perceived limitations restrict debt to some fraction of ability to pay, typically measured by exports. Once this limit is approached, it becomes harder and increasingly costly for the country to borrow more.

If foreign savings are limited, then why are domestic savings inadequate? Part of the reason is the fragmentation of the domestic credit market that makes it hard for savers (as opposed to investors) to earn a reasonable real return on their savings. (Their problems are frequently compounded by government restrictions on credit institutions and inadequate money rates of return in periods of high inflation.) Second, although developed countries can institutionalize savings for retirement by compulsory pension plans or social security levies, governments in developing countries can effectively do so only for the salaried formal sector, which may amount to less than 20 percent of the labor force. No doubt there are other reasons as well—for example, some observers might argue that the extended family solves the pension problem by making transfers from young to old, by supporting the elderly. If so, there is no need to save for retirement, but there will be two adverse consequences. First, in a growing economy with funded pensions (that is, pensions paid from accumulated savings), there will be an excess of savings over dissavings, or positive net savings. With intergenerational transfers, however, there need be no net savings. Second, if the only way to ensure support in old age is by having an adequately large family, population growth rates may be excessive, especially if there are lags in adjusting to changes in mortality.

The view that the rate of investment is too low in developing countries is a central feature of some of the approaches to social cost-benefit analysis (see Dasgupta, Marglin, and Sen, 1972; or Little and Mirrlees, 1974) that were developed in the late 1960s, when raising the rate of saving was viewed as the central problem of development. There are now substantial reservations concerning this view. Many developing countries have been remarkably successful at raising the rate of saving from a very low level to levels comparable with those in developed countries. Thus the World Bank's *World Development Report 1984* reveals that sixteen of the seventy-two developing countries for which there were data increased their share of gross domestic savings by more than 5 percent of GDP between 1960 and 1982, though six of these were middle-income oil exporters, which might be expected to have greatly in-creased domestic savings. Table 5-1 presents weighted-average data by country group and shows that private consumption has fallen as a share of GDP in all developing country groups except for "other low-income economies." Gross domestic savings has risen in both low- and middle-income economies by about 3 percent of GDP, and gross domestic investment has risen by about 5 percent. Savings rates are now close to those of industrial market economies, with investment rates even higher. Savings rates for "other low-income economies" have fallen by 4 percent, however, though investment rates have remained essentially unchanged. In these economies, savings and investment rates are well below those in developed countries.

Two points emerge clearly from these data. First, high savings rates do not guarantee increased rates of growth (though it is hard to know what might have happened without the increases). In some countries the productivity of invest-ment (as measured by the inverse of the incremental capital-output ratio) has been disappointingly low (*World Development Report 1983*). There are many possible reasons for this, including capacity utilization, especially during the post–oil shock recession, management, infrastructure, mismeasurement of output or investment, and so on. It is an area of considerable interest for future

Table 5-1. *Savings and Investment Rates*

Economy	Private consumption[a]		Gross domestic saving[b]		Gross domestic investment[b]	
	1960	1980–82[c]	1960	1980–82[c]	1960	1980–82[c]
Low income	78	70	18	21	19	25
India	79	69	14	21	17	24
Other[d]	82	85	10	6	13	14
Middle income	70	66	19	23	20	25
Oil exporters[e]	70	61	19	27	18	26
Oil importers	70	70	19	20	20	25
Industrial market	63	61	22	21	21	21

a. Public consumption = 100 − private consumption − gross domestic savings.
b. Percentage of gross domestic product.
c. Average of 1980 and 1982.
d. Excluding India and China.
e. Excludes high-income oil exporters.
Sources: World Bank (1982, 1984), table 5.

research. Second, poor countries with the exception of India and China have experienced falling savings rates.

To summarize, it appears that, in many developing countries, but probably not in all, it is arguably desirable to increase rates of investment. With reasonably efficient project selection and project management, it may be, too, that some of the increase in investment should take place in the public sector. In some cases public investment may be ill chosen and may earn low rates of return, in which case mobilizing extra resources for public investment may not be advised.

The implications for policy analysis and for policy are as follows. Where it is desirable to increase the rate of investment and therefore also savings if foreign borrowing is constrained, then we should investigate policies that are likely to stimulate saving. These may include favorable tax treatment of saving, promotion of reliable financial institutions, or changes in interest rate policy. At the same time we should incorporate premiums on government revenue and private savings into the system of shadow prices to be used in the appraisal of public projects and in the analysis of tax reform. (The role of shadow prices in the analysis was described in chapter 3.) The treatment of these premiums and shadow prices is described, for example, in Little and Mirrlees (1974).

Similarly, we could justify tax incentives for investment, for example, in the treatment of depreciation allowances. We would then need to know the elasticity of response to these incentives so that we could check whether the value of the extra investment stimulated would be likely to exceed the opportunity cost of the tax revenue (and correspondingly with the evaluation of savings incentives). Thus the methods we have described, including the prediction of responses using estimated elasticities, can in principle be applied in this area too. Reliable estimates of these responses would not be easy to find, although some implicit judgments would be present in current policies toward savings or investment incentives.

In countries where the profitability of projects appears to be low, then research and public action should be concentrated on the reasons. Thus, for example, capacity utilization may be low because of an unreliable supply of electricity or water, in which case this should be taken into account in evaluating projects in public utilities. Correction of these unreliabilities may then yield an extremely high social rate of return. If the cause is subsidized prices, leading to excess demand and load shedding, the return from raising the price and eliminating the excess demand will be not only the increase in production efficiency but also the gain in government revenue. Alternatively, it may be low through lack of availability of spare parts because of import quotas. In this case some liberalization of import policy might be indicated.

It appears, therefore, that the methods we have described can usefully be applied to important aspects of savings, investment, and growth, in large part through the system of shadow prices used in reform analysis and in the evaluation of fiscal incentives for savings and investment. We shall consider tax policy and savings more closely in the next section before discussing some effects on investment and production.

Tax Policy in Growth Models

If we knew how savings and profits responded to tax changes in a dynamic model of general equilibrium, then we would be able to evaluate the dynamic consequences of these tax changes. The simplest model to analyze is one in which savings and investment depend only on current variables, such as net profits or net income (and possibly on the marginal tax rates). (The strength of this assumption is discussed below.) In this case, the tax change would change net profits and/or net income, which would affect the flow of private savings and investment. The benefit of the tax change would be the present value of the time pattern of extra tax receipts, and the social cost would be the present value of the social cost of the fall in consumption in each period (including all the repercussions through changes in saving).[1] If the tax falls mainly on the rich, the social cost of the drop in their consumption is likely to be small, but the social value of the change is not necessarily positive, because the fall in their savings may well affect future tax revenue or the future consumption of groups with higher welfare weights. For taxes that reduce private profits, the argument may apply more strongly, because we would expect the savings or retention rate from profits to be higher than that from normal income.

A highly simplified example may be helpful. Suppose that the profits of a firm are taxed, saved, or consumed and that the social value of consumption by the owners of the firm is zero (an approximation designed to simplify). The rate of profit is r, the rate of saving from after-tax profits is s, and the rate of profits tax is τ. Initial capital is K_0, and its rate of growth, g, is given by

$$(5\text{-}1) \qquad\qquad g = sr(1 - \tau)$$

so that capital stock at date t is

$$(5\text{-}2) \qquad\qquad K_t = K_0 e^{gt}.$$

The sole social value of private investment in this simple model lies in its capacity to generate tax revenue. Then

$$(5\text{-}3) \qquad\qquad \psi_0 = \int_0^\infty \tau r\, e^{-(i-g)t} dt$$

where ψ_0 is the relative value of private capital to public funds and i is the discount rate (or the accounting rate of interest, when public funds are the unit of account in each period); ψ_0 is simply the present value of the profits tax revenue arising from a unit of capital. The social value of a unit of profits is then simply $s\psi_0$. If i, r, s, and τ are constant (again we simplify drastically), then

$$(5\text{-}4) \qquad\qquad \psi_0 = \frac{r\tau}{i - g}$$

provided that $i > g$. $K_0 \psi_0$ is just the present value of the private sector capital stock. Increases in taxes will be desirable if $\partial \psi_0 / \partial \tau$ is positive, that is, if

$$(5\text{-}5) \qquad \frac{r}{(i-g)^2}(i - rs) > 0$$

where we have assumed (implausibly) that r and s are independent of τ and have used equation 5-1 to find $\partial g / \partial \tau$. Expression 5-5 would be positive if $i > rs$. Put another way, if $1 > s\psi_0$, profits taxes should be raised, because public income is more valuable than private income and the profits tax transfers from the latter to the former (it is easy to check from equation 5-1 and expression 5-5 that this condition becomes $i > rs$). As taxes increase, however, so the reinvestment rate (s) in taxable domestic activities would surely eventually fall and the model would cease to apply.

It is also instructive to consider the effect on the time path of tax receipts of a change in the tax rate. Tax revenue at date t is

$$(5\text{-}6) \qquad R_t = r\tau K_t = r\tau K_0 e^{gt}$$

and

$$(5\text{-}7) \qquad \frac{\partial R_t}{\partial \tau} = r K_t \left(1 + \tau t \frac{\partial g}{\partial \tau}\right)$$

$$= r K_t (1 - rs\tau t),$$

assuming constant r and s, using equation 5-1. Tax receipts would be higher until date T, where $T = 1/rs\tau$, and would thereafter be lower. Raising taxes on private profits is thus eventually a self-destructive enterprise, though one that may have a positive present value, provided that the government can make adequate use of the revenue collected.

We have introduced this highly simplified example simply to indicate some of the issues involved and some possible types of analysis. As we have seen, we can in principle in this case follow the procedure, which should now be familiar, of first predicting the effects of tax changes and then evaluating them. In this case prediction of the relevant effects is very simple and is embodied in equations 5-1, 5-2, and 5-6. The evaluation was based on the drastic but simple assumption underlying equation 5-3 that the social value of consumption by the taxed group is zero. The reader is directed below in this chapter to some models in which the dynamic consequences of taxes may be more complex. Notice, furthermore, that the shadow value of a unit of profits $s\psi_0$ in this model represents a special case of the expression (where h denotes the household, j the good, and t the time period and where v_t and q_t are shadow and market prices for consumption in period t in terms of present values)

$$(5\text{-}8) \qquad b^h = \beta^h - \sum_j \sum_t \frac{v_{jt}}{q_{jt}} \frac{\partial (q_j x_{jt}^h)}{\partial m^h}$$

for the net marginal social value, b^h, of extra income to household h (the welfare weight, β^h, less the value at shadow prices of extra demands; see Drèze and Stern, 1985). If first-period commodities are relatively more valuable socially than future commodities (in terms of v/q), then, other things being equal, b^h will be positively related to marginal propensities to save (that is, higher propensities to spend on future commodities). In this case the market prices of future commodities q_t facing the profit earner are particularly high because his income in each period is taxed. Thus the ratio of shadow prices to market prices is relatively higher for first-period consumption.

Problems in Determining the Dynamic Effects of Taxes

There are three kinds of difficulty with the approach sketched above. The first is the issue of whether it is reasonable to model intertemporal decisions in terms of rules of thumb (such as constant savings rate) rather than engage in an explicit exercise in optimization. Such rules of thumb should be interpreted not as irrational behavior but simply as an individual's attempt to find a reasonably good policy in face of complexities and uncertainties that cannot be described or modeled perfectly. It is possible to show that such rules are utility maximizing if the individual has a certain (possibly misspecified) view of the environment. Consider, for example, the classic Ramsey optimal savings model in which the consumer chooses the time path of consumption to maximize the undiscounted present value of his or her utility:

$$(5\text{-}9) \qquad \text{Max} \int_0^\infty u(c)dt \qquad \text{s.t.} \qquad c = f(k) - \dot{k}$$

where k is capital, $\dot{k}$ is investment (dots refer to time derivatives), and $f(k)$ is output.

We assume that the utility function is isoelastic, that is,

$$(5\text{-}10) \qquad\qquad\qquad u'(c) = c^{-\eta}$$

where η is the elasticity of the marginal utility of consumption, and furthermore that $\eta > 1$. The first-order conditions for the optimal growth path are

$$(5\text{-}11) \qquad\qquad\qquad \eta \frac{\dot{c}}{c} = f'(k)$$

(that is, the rate of fall of the marginal utility of consumption is equal to the rate of return on investment, or in the language that we shall use below, the consumption rate of interest is equal to the rate of return on investment). Now we ask whether equation 5-11 can be satisfied for a constant savings rate, that is, for

$$(5\text{-}12) \qquad\qquad\qquad c = (1 - s)f(k).$$

Differentiate equation 5-12 with respect to time:

$$(5\text{-}13) \qquad\qquad\qquad \frac{\dot{c}}{c} = \frac{f'(k)}{f(k)} \dot{k} = sf'(k)$$

[using $\dot{k} = sf(k)$], and substitute in equation 5-11 to solve for s:[2]

(5-14) $$s = \frac{1}{\eta}.$$

Thus, for any constant savings rate, there is a utility function (isoelastic with elasticity $1/s$) for which the constant savings rule is intertemporally optimal. More generally, Goldman (1968) shows that for any strictly increasing consumption function $c = c(y) = c\{f(k)\}$, there is a utility function for which that consumption function is optimal. The key assumption is that income is a stable function of capital. Note that taxes on income or profits that are constant over time will not affect this result. In the present case someone with an isoelastic utility function whose income derives entirely from capital will save the same fraction of income for any (constant) tax rate. The assumption of constant future tax rates, of course, may be unreasonable.

The great advantage of such simple rules as models of behavior is that they typically allow the positive model to be solved more easily. We must take care, however, with the normative models, because we may have to specify social welfare in the absence of a formal model of utility maximization by the individuals. Nevertheless, if we take the rule of thumb as being broadly consistent with an attempt by the individual to improve utility in a complex environment, then it is reasonable to write down a social welfare function that formalizes the utility accruing to the consumption stream for the individual that arises in part from the individual's own behavior.

The second and related difficulty lies in describing the rules of thumb, of which the most difficult is to predict the impact of tax changes on private savings, investment, and marginal (as opposed to average) rates of return. We do not want to make the rules of thumb overly rigid, because we are thinking of them as a rough and ready kind of optimization. The difficulty lies in trying to find the right balance between the extremes, between rigid rules of thumb and full-blooded perfect-foresight dynamic optimization.

If the rule of thumb is not rigid, then it is clear that expectations concerning the future will be crucial. The important assumptions will concern the movement of income and taxes over time and of household requirements. We should deal with distributions of these random variables, rather than with point estimates, together with a model of how the household reacts to uncertainty. Predictions regarding the effects of taxes on saving will be rather different depending on whether a household believes a tax change to be temporary or permanent. Thus a tax on consumption that is thought to be temporary might increase savings substantially, whereas one considered permanent would have a smaller effect because it will also be incurred when the savings are subsequently spent.

Recent empirical work on savings in developed countries has been much concerned with whether dynamic behavior is optimizing. It has concentrated on whether the life-cycle model fits the data in terms of stochastic behavior and the role of surprises or wealth-age profile and the like. This question has been examined using both cross-section and time-series data, and the recent studies have been reviewed by King (1984), who concludes: "In fact, there is a remarkable conformity in the findings using cross-section data, panel data and aggregate time-series data that about twenty or twenty-five percent of the population behaves in a way which may well be inconsistent with the life-cycle model, whereas for the rest of the population observed behavior is not inconsistent with the model" (p. 92).

For people whose behavior is inconsistent with the model, he suggests that borrowing constraints may be the reason. This finding is important for policy toward credit in that it indicates that there may be gains to easing the constraints for certain groups. The design of policy in such circumstances is a delicate matter because the constraints faced by these groups may be associated with genuine worries about default. If the government treats default lightly, it may exacerbate its difficulties. The problem is not straightforward. Furthermore, it is noteworthy that in the studies reviewed by King the effects of interest rates on saving are very hard to establish (King, 1984, p. 71), which makes analysis of tax policy in relation to the general level of savings very difficult. It should also be emphasized that the data sets available in the studies reviewed by King are of a far higher quality than those to which researchers working on developing countries would have access.

With regard to developing countries, a number of writers have recently argued that the supply of savings would be very responsive to higher interest rates and the provision and reform of financial institutions (see, for example, McKinnon, 1973, or Shaw, 1973). Correspondingly, gains from encouraging savings by fiscal means could, if the argument is valid, be substantial. Unfortunately the evidence that is available on the interest elasticity of savings in developing countries is not such as to allow any confident conclusions.

A further difficulty lies in predicting the response of the government to increased revenues. If, for example, the government finds it hard to resist increasing low-value public consumption when it receives profits from its investment, or if it prices the output of public sector projects too low or operates them inefficiently so that they earn low rates of profit, then the shadow value of private investment relative to public funds may be high, and the case for taxing savings and profits will diminish. Unfortunately, this type of analysis involves some difficult judgments about future government behavior, although such judgments are necessary for much of cost-benefit analysis.

Formal Models in the Literature

There is a substantial literature on formal models of taxation in dynamic economies. We shall not attempt a survey in this brief subsection but shall merely direct the reader to some of the important contributions and lines of inquiry. In providing this introduction, we have drawn heavily on the extensive survey papers by Chalmley (1983) and Kotlikoff (1984).

One identifiable group of studies examines the public policy and the value of savings in simple neoclassical growth models with fixed savings ratios (examples are Arrow and Kurz, 1969; Boadway, 1978; Bradford, 1975; Feldstein,

1972; and Marglin, 1963). Given that private savings decisions do not embody intertemporal optimization, there is no reason to suppose that they lead to solutions with any optimality properties. If a government welfare function were based on consumption streams, we would expect government intervention to be able to improve on any equilibrium path established in the absence of government policy. The value of savings as described in our simple example plays a central role. Models of dual economies in which similar questions are examined have been analyzed by Newbery (1972) and Stern (1972).

A second class of model has intertemporal optimization by consumers. A critical feature, however, is that future individuals do not transact in the current marketplace and that we do not necessarily assume that they are properly represented by their ancestors. As a result, if the government welfare function takes into account the well-being of all future individuals, it may be possible to improve on the market equilibrium. The absence of future generations in current markets plays a role analogous to that of externalities (which we may regard as the absence of a market) in modifying Ramsey-like rules for optimal commodity taxation applied to the intertemporal model (see, for example, Atkinson and Sandmo, 1980; Diamond, 1973; and King, 1980).

In these models we can again consider the question of the uniformity of taxation across commodities, in this case consumption of goods in different periods. The proposition that taxes should be uniform then becomes the statement that an appropriate tax base is expenditure, because a tax on expenditure at the same rate in each period has the uniformity property in this context. Not surprisingly, separability between leisure and goods is again crucial, and we can show in special models—for example, those in steady state, with individuals working for only one period and consuming in two (see, for example, Atkinson and Sandmo, 1980; and King 1980)—that uniformity is optimal. As should be clear from the discussion in chapters 2 to 4, this result is very sensitive to assumptions and would not usually hold if individuals work for two periods rather than one (recall that the uniformity results depend on there being a single factor that is supplied). In this context, a proportional income tax is possibly superior to a proportional consumption tax. We cannot, therefore, settle the issue between expenditure and income taxation on theoretical grounds (for further discussion, see Atkinson and Sandmo, 1980; Auerbach, Kotlikoff, and Skinner, 1983; and King, 1980). This theoretical ambiguity has led to two rather different approaches to the question of the appropriate tax base in a dynamic economy. The first (see Kay and King, 1983; Meade, 1978) notes the advantages of an expenditure tax on practical grounds—its main attraction is that it does not require a distinction between capital and income, a distinction that lies at the source of many administrative difficulties and tax dodges. Second, the absence of clear-cut analytical rankings has stimulated a number of economists to simulate (see below).

In the third group of models, money and inflation are central. These models introduce a financial asset or assets, and savings may be held either in that asset or in physical capital. Typically savers are assumed to allocate their wealth between assets to equalize rates of return. We can then study the inflation tax and the optimal rate of inflation. In the long run the inflation rate is equal to the growth rate of the nominal quantity of money per unit of output, although the short-run relations are less clear. The inflation tax creates revenue for the government (which may be used, for example, to decrease other taxes) and shifts portfolios in favor of physical assets. The latter effect may be valuable if the savings rate is (thought to be) too low. For further reading, see Sidrauski (1967); Phelps (1973a); Calvo and Fernandez (1983); and Chalmley (1983). For an empirical discussion of the incidence of the inflation tax in Mexico, see chapter 11.

Fourth, there has been a lively discussion following Feldstein (1974) on the effects of social security, and it has been suggested that the provision of unfunded social security benefits can imply a substantial reduction in private saving. It seems that an assessment of the evidence for this suggestion depends quite sensitively on the model, the data, and the investigator.

Finally a recent collection of papers attempts to extend the models of static reform analysis to a dynamic context (see, for example, the survey by Kotli-koff, 1984, for detailed references). The papers are based firmly on the same set of principles as the static models in that they use optimizing behavior for individuals, first deriving the consequences of tax changes and then evaluating them. The optimizing choices of individual households concern the allocation of consumption over time in response to relative intertemporal prices in an analogous manner to the allocation of prices across goods. We can then ask how a tax reform that changes the intertemporal prices will affect revenue and welfare. The most popular type of exercise has been the replacement of the income tax by a consumption or wage tax (see, for example, Auerbach, Kotlikoff, and Skinner, 1983; Fullerton, Shoven, and Whalley, 1983; and Summers, 1981). The additional complications of the dynamic models usually entail simulation exercises, and analytic results are not easily obtained. The simulation studies differ in their focus, but the introduction of dynamics usually involves the sacrifice of some of the detail of static studies, in particular distribution within a generation. Thus, for example, Auerbach, Kotlikoff, and Skinner (1983) deal with an infinite horizon, perfect-foresight, overlap-ping-generations model with endogenous labor supply. Each generation forms a fifty-five-year lifetime plan for consumption and labor, but there is no technical progress and only a single consumption good. On the other hand, Fullerton, Shoven, and Whalley (1983) have myopic foresight and a simple allocation between current and future consumption but fifteen current com-modities together with leisure. In each case movements from an income tax to a consumption tax generate annual gains averaged over the path of two or so percentage points of GNP. The main determinant of these gains is the increase in capital stock brought about by the big response of savings to the higher posttax interest rates arising from the switch to consumption taxation—the interest elasticity of savings is crucial.

In suggesting that the interest elasticity was high, Summers (1981, who also found high gains to a similar switch) drew attention to the important point that we must take into account the effect of changes in interest rates on the perceived value of lifetime wealth. Thus, for example, if we consider a two-period model with given income W_1 in period 1 and zero in period 2, then the budget constraint is

$$(5\text{-}15) \qquad\qquad C_1 + \frac{C_2}{1+r} = W$$

where the interest rate is r and consumption in the two periods is C_1 and C_2. A change in r then has an income and substitution effect that may cancel [for example, $U(C_1, C_2) = C_1^{\alpha} C_2^{1-\alpha}$] or may even indicate an interest rate elasticity that is negative. Suppose, however, that the income accrues in both period 1 and period 2. Then the constraint is

$$(5\text{-}16) \qquad\qquad C_1 + \frac{C_2}{1+r} = W_1 + \frac{W_2}{1+r}.$$

An increase in the interest rate now lowers $W_2/(1 + r)$, and if W_2 is large relative to W_1, then C_1 will go down and savings $(W_1 - C_1)$ will increase. This effect is crucial in obtaining the high positive elasticities of the savings rate with respect to the rate of interest derived by Summers (1981)—elasticities as high as 2 or 3. His model had wages growing at a constant rate, with savings allocated only for retirement, which took place after a given number of years. It is clear from the example that the forecast behavior of income is the key issue.

There is no doubt that other aspects of the models used involve simplifications that are important from the standpoint of exerting a strong influence on tax reform analyses—for example, constant elasticity of substitution utility and production functions, with output being produced in a single sector. These problems are familiar from the static analysis, however, and the main extra difficulty is in specifying savings behavior. As Kotlikoff (1984) concludes, "There is as yet no convincing empirical evidence and certainly no professional consensus that households make savings decisions in accordance with the dictates of neoclassical optimisation" (p. 92). Fullerton, Shoven, and Whalley (1983) remark at the end of their paper, "Additional analysis with the model indicates considerable sensitivity to the elasticity of savings with respect to the real after-tax rate of return. Further efforts to narrow the professional consensus on the value of this elasticity would clearly aid policy evaluation" (p. 22).

Notwithstanding the strong reservations concerning the unknown savings response, these models do show that the static theory can be developed and applied in a dynamic context at the expense of some simplifications, notably concerning within-generations distribution. It is likely that they could be usefully applied to developing countries, although the previous results clearly indicate that a high priority should be attached to learning more about savings responses. The treatment of expectations about future income and taxes will be crucial. It will be particularly important to examine how the responses vary across sectors and with different financial arrangements for the channeling of savings.

The Dynamics of Government Revenue Requirements

For much of the discussion of taxation in this book, the required level of government revenue is taken as given. As noted in chapters 2 and 3, the appropriate level can be analyzed using much the same cost-benefit techniques as are employed for taxation. Some important dynamic features of the expenditure side, however, should be discussed. First, the desired level of development expenditure will depend on the social need for and productivity of investment, which in turn depend on the growth prospects. Thus, for example, rapid industrial growth is likely to demand a rapid increase in capital-intensive public sector electricity generation. Infrastructural investments such as electricity supply and communications are likely to complement private investment, but if private capital or entrepreneurship is particularly scarce, then public investment may have to substitute for private investment. Either way, the growth prospects of the economy will have a direct effect on the development budget.

The Movement of Expenditure over Time

A related issue is that the budget is not static but will change over time and with it the revenue needs of the economy. As a result, we will be interested in the elasticity and buoyancy of the tax system. The elasticity of tax revenue measures the percentage by which tax revenues will rise in response to a 1 percent increase in GDP, if we assume no change in the tax structure. It thus measures, roughly speaking, the progressivity of the tax system, for with progressive taxes, the proportion of tax revenue will rise with an increase in incomes. As the share of the modern sector increases, so will the revenue share, assuming that the modern sector is taxed more heavily than the traditional sector.

The buoyancy of the tax system measures, in addition to the elasticity, the extent to which revenue can be increased by raising the rates in the tax structure. The distinction is useful, for revenue gained by increasing the tax rate might raise the marginal cost of public revenue, whereas increases resulting from an elastic tax system might not raise the marginal cost. In fact elasticity and buoyancy are usually defined after the fact, so that we attempt to measure the former by netting out discretionary changes in taxes and the latter simply by relating actual tax revenue to income (see, for example, Goode, 1984, pp. 71ff., or Toye, 1978).

For most of this book we ignore not only dynamic issues but also the whole expenditure side of the budget, and it is therefore necessary to say briefly how they could be included. As noted in chapters 1, 2, and 3, the relationship between the revenue and expenditures sides of the budget is captured by the marginal cost of revenue and the social value of public expenditure. Specifically, if the social value of public funds is designated λ, then at an optimum this should be equal to the marginal costs of raising revenue (λ_i by changes in tax rate i) and the social value of other public expenditure.

The role of the development plan now becomes clear, for if the plan is properly done, it should forecast the future evolution of the economy, identify the public investment requirements, and, most important, estimate the return to the marginal investment project at each date. The revenue target should be the level of revenue required to finance all projects whose social value exceeds the marginal social cost of the tax revenue.

Can we say anything about the way this revenue requirement is likely to vary with the level of development? Is the tax system likely to be adequately elastic, or are increases in tax rates to raise its buoyancy likely to be required? Even more interesting, is the tradeoff between equity and efficiency likely to change systematically over time?

It must be admitted that, although these are important and interesting questions, there are no clear-cut answers. Nevertheless, the approach under study offers both a coherent framework within which to ask these questions and rather different insights from more conventional approaches. The coherent framework is, as mentioned above, that of social cost-benefit analysis and in particular the evolution over time of the social value of government revenue.

We can identify some of the issues using a discussion drawn from Little and Mirrlees (1974). Let us define $\lambda(t)$ as the value of government funds in a given period relative to the marginal value of private consumption in *that* period, using, for example, a reference consumer. Then

$$(5\text{-}17) \qquad\qquad \lambda(t) = \frac{\nu(t)}{\mu(t)}$$

where $\nu(t)$ is the present value of a marginal unit of government funds in year t (that is, relative to a numeraire now) and $\mu(t)$ is the present value of a marginal unit of private consumption. Then

$$(5\text{-}18) \qquad\qquad -\frac{\dot{\lambda}}{\lambda} = -\frac{\dot{\nu}}{\nu} - \left(-\frac{\dot{\mu}}{\mu}\right).$$

Yet $-\dot{\nu}/\nu$ is the ARI, because Little and Mirrlees take government funds as the numeraire, and $-\dot{\mu}/\mu$ is the rate of fall of a marginal unit of consumption or a CRI. If we can guess at the ARI and CRI, then we have from formula 5-9 the rate of change of λ.

Little and Mirrlees plot the logarithms of the weights of public and private income over time, so that their slopes measure (minus) the ARI and CRI,

Figure 5-1. *Shadow Price of Government Revenue*

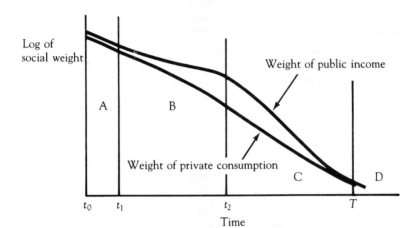

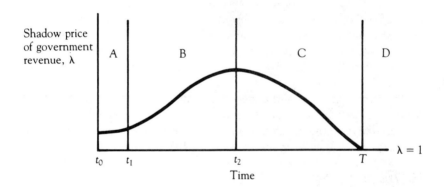

respectively, whereas their distance apart is log λ. Figure 5-1 (top panel) is taken from their second example (Little and Mirrlees, 1974, fig. 5, p. 284) and shows an economy in which consumption is growing (and hence the marginal utility of consumption is falling at a rate CRI). Suppose that the marginal use of public funds is for investment, but, before t_1, good public sector investment projects are scarce (because of a shortage of skills or absorptive capacity generally) and the ARI and CRI are close, so that λ is approximately constant. Investment is expanded steadily from t_1 to t_2, and as a result the (own) rate of return, or the ARI, is driven *below* the CRI. Eventually, as public sector skills improve, foreign markets are established, and absorptive capacity increases, so the productivity of investment rises, and from t_2 onward, the ARI exceeds the

CRI, and the government cannot raise enough revenue to invest to the point at which the ARI is driven down to the CRI. In period C, then, public funds are particularly tight, investment is constrained by savings, taxable capacity, and foreign borrowing limits, and so the shadow price λ is high but falling. If the ARI is never less than the CRI, however, then λ will always be decreasing, as in phase C, and its initial value will therefore be quite high. If investment is the marginal use of public funds, λ will be low, as shown in period A of figure 5-1, only for countries that face very unproductive investment alternatives, either because of great poverty and shortage of complementary inputs or because of temporary income (for example, oil revenue) that is high relative to absorptive capacity.

The shadow price, λ, when compared with the marginal cost of revenue λ_i, is intended to balance the supply of and demand for government revenue. We can regard λ as the demand price and λ_i as the supply price, using a language analogous to Marshallian demand theory. As the country develops, it seems plausible that the marginal cost of raising a given fraction of GNP in tax revenue will fall, for a variety of reasons. First, the range of goods and services that can effectively be taxed is likely to increase as the tax administration improves and as standards of bookkeeping rise. Any reduction in administration costs will itself reduce the marginal cost of funds for a given range of taxes.

Second, and closely related, as the economy develops, so the relative size of the modern sector increases. Because it is easier to tax incomes and profits in the modern sector, the range of administratively feasible tax instruments will increase. Again, the relative size of the taxed and untaxed sectors directly affects the elasticity of supply or demand of the taxed goods: the wider the range of untaxed alternatives, the higher those elasticities will be and the lower the taxable capacity of the taxed sector (or the higher the marginal cost of revenue). Labor will thus allocate itself to equalize after-tax incomes, and if the range of untaxed occupations is high, then the income tax will be relatively ineffective because it will be shifted onto profits or increases in goods prices. The supply schedule of government revenue is thus likely to shift to the right as development occurs, as shown in figure 5-2. Notice that we are assuming that the government takes advantage of the opportunities that arise to exploit the possibility of lower social marginal costs of funds.

The relationship between the level of public expenditure and its marginal value is given by a demand schedule, which will also shift. If the shadow price λ is rising, as in period B of figure 5-1, then demand must be increasing faster than supply, and the share of revenue in GNP will also be rising, as shown by the shift from A to C in figure 5-2. If, as will typically be the case, the shadow price is falling, then demand could still be increasing, but clearly taxes as a fraction of revenue would not be rising so rapidly and might even be falling, as shown in the shift from A to D. They could not do so, however, without a rather dramatic fall in the productivity of public expenditure.

These arguments suggest that taxes should rise as a proportion of GNP as income per head rises. Progressive income taxes will achieve this goal auto-

Figure 5-2. *Marginal Costs and Benefits of Government Revenue*

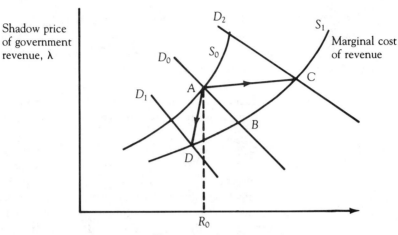

Tax revenue/GNP (percent)

matically, as will increasing the range of goods subject to taxation, though in the latter case, the structure of taxation should almost certainly change in response to the improvements in the instruments available.

The Effects of Taxes on Growth

In this subsection we very briefly discuss a suggestion that has risen to prominence recently in public discussion: that the level of taxes adversely affects the rate of growth. It has been argued empirically that countries with higher rates of taxes have lower rates of growth. It should be clear that as a theoretical generalization this statement cannot be correct. The answer will depend on the model. Let us take a simple aggregated model and concentrate on the level and productivity of investment. If the government's marginal propensity to invest is one, public and private investments are equally productive, and deadweight losses from taxation are low, then increased taxation will increase the level of investment and the level of growth in the short run. Long-run effects on the growth rate will be zero in models where this rate is determined by exogenous factors, such as the growth of the labor force. On the other hand, if the marginal propensity to invest by the government or the productivity of investment is very low, or if deadweight losses are very high, then we reach the opposite conclusion. Note that the level of taxation may affect the level of labor supply but will probably not affect the rate of growth of that labor supply.

The empirical evidence is very hard to assess. On the one hand, a simple comparison of growth rates and tax rates across countries reduces the process of growth to a single-equation model, with growth dependent on a single variable, the aggregate tax rate. On the other hand, a model that dealt with the structure in a more detailed way would be hard to specify and to estimate in a plausible form.

Costs, Innovation, and Market Structure

In the models we have discussed so far, the social productivity of investment as measured using shadow prices both guides the process of structural change and influences tax policy through the shadow value of changing outputs in different sectors. In this section we first examine the role of taxes in changing production costs and then discuss some alternative views of the effects of tax policy on innovation and the production structure.

It seems useful to consider the specific example of a change in tariff or quota and then to consider different types of possible response. First, a socially unprofitable industry may close down, or a socially profitable industry may now set up, if the reform corrects previous distortions. Second, the degree of competition may change and may affect the extent to which economies of scale are realized as well as the size of monopolistic inefficiencies. Third, the extent of rent seeking (Krueger, 1974) may change. Fourth, other things, such as learning by doing, may change.

The first factor will be captured by the methods discussed in this book and may well be large if the change in output level and the difference between market and shadow prices are large, as is quite possible. The second can be captured in a suitably well specified model of production and market equilibrium. In a small protected market, import-competing firms subject to scale economies are likely to be few in number, oligopolistic, and suboptimum in scale. Lowering tariffs or relaxing quotas will increase competition, lower prices, increase demand, and possibly lead to rationalization, in which fewer domestic firms producing larger quantities at lower unit cost survive. Harris (with Case, 1984) calculates the effect of tariff reductions for Canada in a model that drops the conventional assumptions of perfect competition and constant returns. He finds gains between five and twenty times as large as those derived on the conventional assumptions of constant returns and perfect competition. These mostly resulted from increased specialization, increased lengths of production run in industries that specialize, and hence lower costs as a result of scale economies. The problem facing such modelers should not be underestimated, as Whalley (1984) shows. It is necessary to have not only a formal model of oligopolistic equilibrium but also estimates of the elasticity of the cost functions, that is, of the extent of scale economies. Nevertheless, for trade policy reform, modeling of scale economies and imperfect competition should obviously take high priority. Although we have no empirical examples yet to offer (indeed, Harris's work is really the only available example), some of the theoretical issues are discussed further in chapter 3, and we view this as a high-priority area for development and application.

The third kind of impact of liberalization on production costs occurs via reductions in the level of rent seeking or in the extent of "directly unproductive profit-seeking" activities (Bhagwati and Srinivasan, 1980). Some might argue that allowing for these changes in DUPS activities significantly increases the welfare gain to liberalization. The problem is first to construct a satisfactory model of rent seeking, second to distinguish between the pure cost and the transfer elements involved, and last to estimate their relative magnitudes. Present developments in the theory of entry deterrence may throw further light on the problem, but for the moment relatively crude estimates and much sensitivity analysis are all that can realistically be offered.

The final category of impacts on cost is a residual, reflecting current theoretical and empirical ignorance, for which the only satisfactory remedy is careful research on the consequences at the firm and industry level of trade liberalization. Is the rate of technical progress affected? (See Krueger and Tuncer, 1982.) Are the industries better placed to respond to export opportunities (Morawetz, 1981)?

At a fairly superficial level, all these aspects come under the heading of measuring the elasticity of response to policy change and thus fall within the scope of the discussion in chapters 2 and 3. It should be clear, however, that the responses involved are much more difficult to capture than conventional demand and supply functions. If we confined our attention to those functions narrowly interpreted, furthermore, we would still face the difficult question of the difference between short- and long-run elasticities in the analysis of reform. In principle we require the full intertemporal analysis of responses, but in practice we are likely to have a fairly unsatisfactory mixture of estimates of responses for periods that may differ for different industries or for different goods. The accuracy of approximations using this type of data is an interesting topic for empirical and theoretical research.

One approach to taxation that differs rather sharply from the arguments we have presented so far is based on a Kaldorian view of the process of growth (see Kaldor, 1964). In his "Memorandum on the Value-Added Tax," Kaldor considers the replacement of the taxation of profits by taxation of value added and attempts to calculate the effects through an ambitious though only partially articulated model that involves increasing returns to scale and imperfect competition, a vintage model of production and uncertainty about the future.

Kaldor (1964) then starts the discussion of this "model" by saying, "By far the most important question in connection with a value-added tax consists of its effects on economic efficiency" (p. 270), and he summarizes his argument:"If a value-added tax of a uniform rate of 10% were substituted for the existing profits tax and the income tax on undistributed profits (as well as for the purchase tax), the 'supply price' of manufactured goods (excluding the tax) relative to money wages would tend to fall, partly as a result of a reduction in the margin of profit on sales, and partly of a consequential increase in average efficiency" (p. 287). He suggests that the efficiency gains arise because of the replacement of the profits tax, which he says increases the average age of machines. Unfortunately the argument is a little hard to follow, because the model and tax scheme are not described explicitly. Kaldor argues elsewhere (for example, Kaldor, 1966) that the increasing returns and vintage effects he has in mind are more important for manufacturing than, say, for services. Although the argument is unsatisfactory, it is a noteworthy attempt to blend a rather complicated dynamic theory of firm behavior with public discussion of practical policy.

Our main purpose in discussing this view of value-added taxes is twofold: to show, first, that there have been broad-based taxes in recent times whose advocates have been influenced by theories that have been concerned explicitly with notions of efficiency involving dynamic aspects, and second, that we can try to build, and apply to taxation, theories of firm behavior that look rather different from the competitive model used hitherto.

An approach that has some similarities in spirit but is directed toward the analysis of monopoly and any associated social costs is that of Littlechild (1981). He attacks measures based on deadweight loss calculations on the grounds that profits form an essential part of the dynamic structure of capitalist growth. Thus new products or techniques are introduced in the hope of gaining some profits before competitors have time to catch up. It is misleading, Littlechild argues, to present profits as costs arising from monopoly, for without them many of the benefits to consumers of new products and growth would be lost. This picture of growth and competition is an old one in economics and is perhaps most eloquently expressed in Schumpeter (1954).

Littlechild does not provide a formal model of the process he has in mind and confines his attention to attacking standard deadweight loss measures in equilibrium models. It would be fascinating, although possibly very difficult, to develop a model of the effects of taxation on efficiency in the kind of environment described by Littlechild and Schumpeter.

Conclusions

We have seen in this chapter that many of the techniques and models developed in a static context can be interpreted in or adapted to a dynamic framework. The extra difficulty of that framework implies, however, that we must be more modest in the level of detail. Thus in much of our discussion of dynamics in this chapter we spoke in terms of aggregative models in which the issues were the value of consumption, investment, and government revenue. This part of the theory is perhaps at a point where it could usefully be combined with estimates of the marginal cost of funds to see whether expenditure should be expanded or contracted.

Overall, however, we would judge that the role of dynamic theory has been the useful but limited one of clarifying concepts and providing insights. In this area we may expect and hope for further research. We would not, however, expect that research to be necessarily straightforward. It is not simply that the technical aspects of dynamic analysis are more demanding. There are many problems, such as the effects of taxation on innovation and on the productivity of innovation, for which we do not have models that are sufficiently plausible to form the basis of policy analysis. Advances in the specification and estimation of predictive dynamic models will be required. Notwithstanding these difficulties, the models do provide helpful guidance on such crucial issues as the taxation of savings, and in this area we would expect further empirical and theoretical work to be fruitful. The models do also show how methods developed in a static context can be extended and applied to dynamic problems.

Notes

1. Boadway (1979) gives a good example of a neoclassical growth model in which the tax change contemplated is a small increase in the profits tax rate and a corresponding reduction in labor taxes, with government expenditure held constant at each moment. Savings are a constant but differing fraction of after-tax wage or profit income, and they finance investment. Boadway shows how to calculate the time path of the effect on consumption from wages and profits, from which it is a simple step to calculate their social value, given a social welfare function or set of social weights.

2. Existence of an optimal savings rate is guaranteed if $\text{Lim}_{t \to \infty} ku'(c)$ is finite (Mirrlees, 1967). We assume that the present problem satisfies this condition; if $f(k) = k^{\alpha}$, for example, $\eta > 1/\alpha$ will be sufficient.

6

Taxation, Cost-Benefit Analysis, and Effective Protection

Christopher Bliss

ALL THREE FIELDS of the title represent substantial branches of theoretical and applied economics. To survey any one, let alone all three together, would require more work and space than a short chapter can encompass. Instead the present chapter attempts to elucidate the relationship between the three approaches. This undertaking sounds more straightforward, but even so it is not free of difficulties. Briefly, taxation, cost-benefit analysis, and effective protection represent approaches that were developed to deal with somewhat different problems, and for this reason they cannot simply be compared according to their performance in one specific area. On the other hand, although they are distinct, they are not wholly unconnected. Moreover, in trying to elucidate the connection between them, we are led to consider an issue that is difficult to resolve satisfactorily: how to deal with nonoptimal tariffs—tariffs that are there and ideally should not be.

That this last problem is inescapable will shortly become clear. Indeed, it could be said that the literature has sometimes suffered from a failure to consider it directly and explicitly. The problem arises in connection with effective protection and cost-benefit analysis. In certain applications, both of these approaches involve a negative evaluation of tariffs. If tariffs do harm, it seems only reasonable to ask why they should not be removed. Why bother with measuring the effective protection entailed by a tariff structure when it should be swept away? If tariffs should go, furthermore, what is the point of relating effective protection theory to tax theory or cost-benefit analysis?

The issue raised by these embarrassingly pointed questions will be discussed at length below. We may anticipate the findings of that investigation by saying that no clear and convincing conclusion emerges. Tariffs can be shown, under theoretical assumptions that seem quite relevant to reality, to be an inferior form of intervention. This finding is one of the oldest in international trade theory, and it has been refined by modern writers and freed from a dependence on the unnecessarily restrictive assumptions that were used to support it in the past. Regardless of the recommendations of economic theory, however, tariffs are frequently encountered. So we cannot evade the question of whether the effective protection concept says anything useful about them, nor can we avoid deciding how to deal with them in cost-benefit analysis. Finally, tariffs can be considered as taxes, and we need to decide how they compare with other taxes.

Because I shall take for granted in the following discussion that tariffs are theoretically inappropriate, I should briefly mention the kind of reasoning that underlies the conclusion.[1] A primitive argument asserts that tariffs are "distorting," which means that they interfere with the ideal operation of prices as signals of social scarcity. This conclusion is most easily demonstrated for an economy that is undistorted in any respect apart from the possible presence of tariffs. This demonstration, however, is not satisfactory, as such additional distortions undoubtedly exist, and a recognition of their importance explains the development of the important theory of "domestic distortions."[2] The literature has established that a tariff is the best intervention only in precisely defined and perhaps unusual circumstances; otherwise domestic distortions (including problems of income distribution) are best dealt with by taxation that does not discriminate against international trade. This line of reasoning supposes the possibility of alternative instruments. It is sometimes argued that tariffs are, for some countries at least, the only feasible instrument or, administratively, the least-cost way of collecting revenue.

The following discussion underlines the distinction between positive and normative economics and discusses how the various theories relate to those two types of theory. I subsequently examine at length the issue of the explanation of tariffs, effective protection, and taxation theory and cost-benefit analysis. The theory of cost-benefit analysis in a tariff-distorted economy is developed in a later section and in the appendix. Finally, my conclusion refers to the particular problems of developing countries.

Positive and Normative Economics

Before proceeding further, we should note the important distinction between positive and normative theory. Taxation theory as we shall discuss it and cost-benefit analysis both derive from normative welfare economics. They are concerned with the making of recommendations that aim to increase the sum of utilities, to bring about a Pareto improvement, or to augment some other measure of welfare. This is less obviously the case where effective protection is concerned. EP analysis was originally developed to provide a description of the effects that a tariff structure has on production. A typical statement of EP theory would be: "A tariff on an intermediate input to an activity will decrease the effective protection of the value added generated in that activity." This is not as such a normative statement. We could make it one by adding sufficient clauses, but the same could be said of almost any descriptive statement. Nonetheless, the boundary between the descriptive and the normative is quickly traversed. One important reason why the EP concept attracted attention was that it seemed to offer a guide as to how the allocation of resources in the economy might be improved.

Consider the following line of reasoning. Under the simple assumptions of classical welfare economics, where income distribution can be handled by means of discriminating lump-sum transfers and there are no externalities that have not been optimally taxed or subsidized, we can remedy any unfavorable consequences that might otherwise follow from the pursuit of efficiency as an objective. It can then be shown that the economy should be as far as possible "undistorted." This statement will usually imply that there should be no tariffs, and indeed, the demonstration that tariffs are not an optimal instrument of intervention can be carried further into many cases of trade theory (the so-called second-best trade theory) in which the pure assumptions of classical welfare economics are not all required.

If we now observe an economy with tariffs, and if it is not one of the cases in which theory shows that a tariff is an optimal intervention, we may conclude that the economy is distorted. Distortion is a question not directly of prices, however, but of real allocations and the resulting welfare levels. How are we to translate our observation on the side of prices into statements about real distortions, notably the over- or underexpansion of particular sectors? Some of the appeal of the EP approach is that it seems to offer answers to this type of question.

Furthermore, some of the answers, theoretical and empirical, are exceedingly interesting. There is the clear lesson that we must consider a tariff structure as a whole to see its effects and that inspection of nominal rates of protection of particular sectors could be misleading. Empirical studies have revealed that activities generating negative value added at world prices are sometimes encountered in developing countries (see Krueger, 1984, and Little, Scitovsky, and Scott, 1970). In other cases, sectors nominally protected were shown to be hampered by the tariff structure more than they were assisted, because their input costs were inflated by the effects of other tariffs.

It emerged therefore that EP theory, although originally formulated as a positive theory of the effects of tariffs, has been much employed as a guide to the reform of trade regimes and a guide to the allocation of resources. It is difficult to see how matters could have been otherwise. In any case, this chapter will consider EP theory almost exclusively in its aspect as a system for guiding resource allocation. When we proceed in this way, a certain amount of bias is introduced, as the positive theory of effective protection is underemphasized. This approach, however, is the one that brings EP, TAX, and CBA theory immediately to bear on one another, and for that reason it recommends itself.

As EP theory was developing, TAX theory was undergoing a renaissance involving the revival of Ramsey's theory of optimal indirect taxation, new developments in the theory of optimal income taxation, and the integration of TAX theory and the welfare economics of production in the paper of Diamond and Mirrlees (1971).

Finally, CBA theory, particularly in its applications, has seen many new developments. Diamond and Mirrlees had established the important result that, if optimal indirect taxation is employed, then the public sector should use world prices to evaluate projects, thus identifying a critical link between TAX theory and CBA theory. This last link was greatly expanded and refined in a work strongly oriented toward empirical application, the manual of Little and Mirrlees (1974). In using world prices where possible to evaluate projects, the Little-Mirrlees system had a certain affinity to the EP approach. The two were not identical, however, and Little and Mirrlees explicitly rejected the EP measure as a generally valid index of a project's social net benefit. Their argument will be considered below.

The Explanation of Tariffs

Although the achievements of the new theory have been impressive, it has tended to aggravate some problems in the course of resolving others. Notably, its negative evaluation of tariffs—that is, apart from a small number of precisely delineated cases—has somewhat handicapped it in making recommendations for a world replete with tariffs and other trade restrictions. These restrictions cannot usually be explained by the particular reasons recognized by the theory. A theoretically purist view would hold that the first priority, as dictated by the theory, is to press for the removal of nonoptimal tariffs. Still, this position is not easy to maintain if it does not meet with immediate success. In the meantime some quite important questions call for answers: for example, should a certain project be implemented or not?

More basically, is the purist position even right? If the prevalence of tariffs in a world with other instruments of intervention, such as taxes and subsidies, is not to be explained by their efficiency, what does explain that prevalence? Without an answer to this question, the theorist cannot be said to understand the world for which he offers recommendations—an unsatisfactory position at best and one that might well call into question the value of the advice being offered.

These inescapable problems have led to attempts to develop positive theories of tariffs, theories that would explain tariffs and why they persist rather than answering the normative question of whether they do good. Once again, the positive and the normative, although distinct, are closely connected. One of the great problems that a positive theory of tariffs must face is how it will explain the existence of an institution—inefficient protection— without predicting that efficient interventions, such as subsidies, will be chosen instead.

As there is little finished theory to report, we confine ourselves to considering what form such a theory would have to take.[3] The idea is to consider the nation as a set of interest groups engaged in a power struggle to further their own interests. The policies that result will be the outcome of such a game, which is what a power struggle is. A competitive equilibrium is an example of a game in which the players are all small agents who choose their net demands and the rules of the game adjust prices to clear markets. More generally, the specification of the game must include the definition of the moves that are available to the various players or groups or the variables that they control, how allocations result from their choices, what coalitions are possible, and which side payments are feasible. The possibilities are clearly endless. Received trade theory, however, already includes examples that can be applied to show how a power struggle game may lead to tariffs. Stolper and Samuelson (1940) showed how the removal of a tariff in a simple trade model would always harm one factor. We may make that example into a game of the form described: factors form the groups; they control only votes, which determine policy; policy cannot include subsidies or side payments favoring one factor; and, finally, the factor that would lose from the removal of the tariff controls more votes. The outcome of the game is now a tariff on the import of the good that intensively uses the majority factor.

Formally this example is clear. The only issue is how well it describes the world. Why, for example, does labor vote for tariffs and not for subsidies for labor-intensive industry financed by profits taxation? In fact tariffs are used in this example because they are the only instrument available that will achieve the end that, it is claimed, explains their use. Many arguments for tariffs, positive and normative, on examination prove to take this form. The argument is so convenient that it deserves close scrutiny.

It often happens, however, that tariffs are established because they are administratively feasible and because low collection costs attach to them. Once these tariffs are in place, interest groups that benefit from them develop their political awareness and organization, and these cannot simply be transferred to the support of some other instrument. Thus more than simple administrative feasibility may often explain the presence of a tariff; other means of raising revenue are often underexploited. Even countries with primitive administrations do in fact collect considerable sales taxes, notably on sales from the public sector (often by charging above marginal social cost), whereas tariffs can be, and are, evaded by smugglers. It is perilous to generalize. Income taxes are difficult to collect in many developing countries, of course, but the existence of income taxes is not needed to show the inefficiency of tariffs.

In one version of the power struggle model, politicians and bureaucrats play a central role. They prefer protection to less interventionist measures because it gives them more scope to grant and receive favors. A favor could even be the pleasure that certain people derive from the exercise of power over others.

These are important considerations, but they are not really explanations of protection at all. Rather they indicate a tendency for certain kinds of political systems to exhibit a preference for discretion over rules. The principles of rational economic policy are complex, but given sufficient information they reduce to rules to be applied without favor. Tariff barriers have never been erected according to such formulas. They often go up in response to a crisis plus some pressure-group politicking and political pleading. They leave the legislator with a great deal of room for maneuver, that is, a chance to exercise power of his own. Tariffs are not, however, the most appealing instrument in this category. Subsidies can be, and have been, used to favor particular regions, even particular firms. Tariffs can sometimes achieve the same end—only one region or firm may be involved—but often they cannot. The argument from self-serving politicians would not lead us to expect tariffs. Indeed, this line of argument can be turned around to say that some tariffs derive their appeal from their resemblance to honest nationalist measures, whereas nothing makes an assembly cry foul as much as a proposal for a subsidy.

Beneath many of these arguments lies an idea that we might call "the principle of concentrated effect." Not infrequently the costs of a tariff, including its excess burden, are widely dispersed, and no individual or small group feels these costs as a large imposition worth making a fuss about. The benefits, however, are often concentrated and, for those who are concerned, well worth lobbying and fighting for. This principle may go so far that the adversely affected individuals may not even be aware that they will pay part of the cost. Ask ordinary consumers whether they think that the national textile industry should be protected from competition from Asian imports. Now translate the tariff or quota proposal into an addition to their clothing costs, and ask them again. The most important question in the present context is whether such economic myopia applies more strongly in the case of tariffs than it does, say, in that of subsidies.

With this last case we have trespassed into another area. The positive theory of tariffs is intended above all to be a rational economic model of political choice in which the players understand the game and make rational decisions subject to the constraints that they face. Even the principle of concentrated effect comes under that heading; not to bother about something because it is not worth the trouble is a rational economic decision, unfortunate though its consequences may be. Sometimes, however, people really do not seem to understand that tariffs are not the only form of intervention, that tariffs impose an excess burden, that the arguments against tariffs do not depend upon assuming that other nations are "playing fair," that protection is not the best way of dealing with unemployment, and so on. Such misunderstandings create a certain bias in favor of protection and encourage the accumulation of numerous, sometimes complex tariffs that may be harder to remove than they were to establish. The fact of their inefficiency, furthermore, may not motivate any party to seek an improvement. The individuals who gain may not wish the fact of their benefit to be brought too much into the open. The consequence is that we must sometimes consider tariffs whose only real rationale may be historical.

Let us return to general theoretical considerations. It has not proved easy to provide arguments that really explain tariffs; there are inherent difficulties in doing so. Nevertheless, we must bear in mind the possibility that the tariffs we encounter are protecting a sectional interest or a power group. This will have very important implications. In TAX theory, for example, it is no use to propose that tariffs be circumvented by taxation designed to offset their effects if the same sectional interests that established the tariffs are going to defeat our proposals. If we build into our CBA system the principle of evaluation at world prices, and if this principle offends the same interests, then the point again applies. If, on the other hand, the tariffs that we encounter are largely historical hangovers, or have not served the interests that established them, they must be taken as given and not treated as reflections of the power in the hands of lobbies. So important is the possibility that tariffs are to some extent accidents of history or mistaken policy that we develop later a theory of optimal cost-benefit analysis rules for an economy subject to such tariffs.

Effective Protection

Effective protection theory centers on the activity or on the project, and this focus has made the possibility of a connection with CBA theory readily apparent, whereas its relation to TAX theory is less obvious. Its focus on the activity has appealed to policymakers, who must deal with questions having to do with activities (that is, industries, sectors, and projects) rather frequently. Indeed, the question of whether EP theory provides a guide to policy is central in evaluating its use. The relation of EP theory to general economic theory is made difficult by the same concentration on activities. The reason is that most economic theory has concentrated on goods as the basis of, for example, welfare evaluation, to the exclusion of value-added activities.

We consider, as is usual, a fixed-coefficient constant-returns activity. The fixity of coefficients will rule out the substitution of some inputs for others that takes place as the result of the imposition of tariffs. It has been argued that the inability of EP analysis to take such substitution into account is a serious defect of the measure. There are indeed problems with the concept, but this one is arguably not the worst. Insofar as substitution introduces an ambiguity into the *definition* of the rate of effective protection, the difficulty has the character of an index number problem. As with other examples of index numbers, the ambiguity may not appear in some applications, as will be seen.

Effective protection is usually defined as:

$$(6\text{-}1) \qquad EP = \frac{\text{Value added at domestic prices}}{\text{Value added at world prices}} - 1.$$

We are assuming that all goods are tradable and therefore have world prices, an assumption that we shall relax later. The allocation problem has little interest, however, if all goods and factors are tradable, and we assume that there is one nontradable input, labor. Value added is measured, in conformity with usual practice, without the inclusion of a charge for wages. Now,

$$(6\text{-}2) \qquad \text{Value added at domestic prices}$$

$$= \text{Value added at world prices}$$

$$+ \text{Value added due to tariffs}$$

so that equation 6-1 becomes

(6-3) $$EP = \frac{\text{Value added due to tariffs}}{\text{Value added at world prices}}.$$

For equilibrium in the domestic economy, only the allocation of labor is at issue. Were there to be no tariffs, the best wage offers that the various activities would be able to make to labor would be their various values added at world prices for unit employment. Naturally, it is not activities that attract labor but the people who control them—their managers—but I shall freely employ the useful shorthand of referring to activities as if they were managers. The wage would be bid up until it equaled the highest value added per unit of labor available to the economy, and all activities unable to offer that much would be unused. This, of course, is the efficient solution for the whole economy. The index of effective protection as shown in equation 6-3 now has a nice, meaningful interpretation. It indicates the extent to which tariffs have pro- portionately assisted a particular activity in bidding for labor. Labor in this interpretation stands for nontraded factors, so we could say, more generally, that the index of effective protection measures the extent to which an activ- ity's ability to bid for factors of production has been augmented by the tariff structure, this ability being expressed as a proportionate increase. It may well be that the assistance provided is negative, because value added due to tariffs might be negative. When the denominator of equation 6-3 is negative, we cannot use this interpretation, and equation 6-3 is undefined if its denomina- tor is zero, but these cases need not concern us.

The interpretation that we have offered also indicates at once why the index of effective protection cannot generally be used as a guide to optimal resource allocation. Consider an auction in which various parties send in sealed bids. The auction is being manipulated, and the auctioneer increases some of the bids received by various percentages, for whatever reason. If the auction interested us, we would obviously be much concerned with the percentages by which various bids were being marked up; we would want to know these values.

Knowing these values, however, we would not be able to predict the outcome of the auction. To do so we would need to know the original bids. An analogous point applies to effective protection. If we know the values of indexes of effective protection for various activities, then we know by what percentage tariffs have enabled them to increase their bids for resources. We also need, however, to know value added at world prices per unit input to know what will happen and what should happen. Expression 6-3 is simply a ratio and remains the same whether value added per unit of labor is $100 or $10,000. This last point corresponds to the objection that Little and Mirrlees voiced to the use of the index of effective protection in project evaluation. The produc- tivity of the project in the relevant sense, value added per unit of resources used, is not taken into account.

The argument elaborated above may be taken further. Suppose we have an economy with a price system that has been distorted by tariffs. Again we set aside the question: why not remove the tariffs? We want to know, however, whether a small shift of resources from one activity to another would be an improvement. This question raises quite complicated issues, some of which we shall examine later, but for the time being we take a simple view. As all goods except labor are tradables, we may suppose that any changes that we make will be absorbed by trade and, if they show a surplus, will help the balance of payments position, which would be unambiguously a good thing.

We are considering activities that have succeeded in the competitive bid for labor, admittedly under a distorted price system, but their success still tells us something about value added per person. Given the extra piece of information, that all the activities we are considering are in equilibrium under the distorted price system, we can determine which activity best utilizes labor to the social advantage, and we can express that property in terms of effective protection.

Denote by the following acronyms the various quantities that will figure in our calculation. All are assumed to be measured for unit input of labor.

$VADP$ = Value added at domestic prices.

$VAWP$ = Value added at world prices.

$VADT$ = Value added due to tariffs.

EP = Index of effective protection.

Subscripts will denote specific activities, so that EP_i, for example, is the index of effective protection of activity i.

Consider two activities, activities 1 and 2, both in use in an equilibrium with a tariff-distorted price system. As both successfully bid for labor, they must have the same value added at domestic prices. Thus

$$(6\text{-}4) \qquad\qquad VADP_1 = VADP_2$$

or

$$(6\text{-}5) \qquad\qquad VAWP_1 + VADT_1 = VAWP_2 + VADT_2.$$

Our criterion for allocating scarce labor in the socially optimal manner will be that it should be employed where the value added at world prices that it generates is maximal. We can express 6-5 as

$$(6\text{-}6) \qquad\qquad VAWP_1(1 + EP_1) = VAWP_2(1 + EP_2).$$

It follows from equation 6-6 that to choose the value added at world prices per unit of labor employed is equivalent to choosing the activity with the lowest index of effective protection. The two criteria are the same. Now, suppose that activity 3 is an entirely new activity, a project, an activity not previously undertaken in the domestic economy. Let activity 1 be among those with the highest $VAWP$ per unit of labor employed. It is clear that activity 3 should be introduced and allowed to take labor away from activity 1, or from equally productive activities, only if

(6-7) $VAWP_3 > VAWP_1$.

We cannot say what $VADP_3$ will be, whether it will be lower or higher than other rates in the economy, so we cannot establish the vital link 6-6, which was necessary to allow us to translate a resource allocation rule into an effective protection rule (that is, it does not follow that $EP_3 < EP_1$).

The foregoing discussion should have made clear why such divergent opinions have been able to coexist concerning the usefulness of EP measures as guides to resource allocation. Thus the point made by Little and Mirrlees—and the same point has been made by others—appears to be quite decisive against the use of the EP index. On the other hand, these indexes are widely advocated and frequently employed. It is clear, however, that different problems are involved. For rearrangements of activities within a given equilibrium, the EP rule is valid but only because it measures $VAWP$ indirectly. For introducing new activities, changing the basis, we must use the $VAWP$ measure to obtain sensible and valid answers. No indirect route is likely to be valid.

A few generalizations may quickly be noted. Labor in the above discussion can stand for any nontradable resource. If, however, there are many distinct nontradable inputs, the problem is much more complicated. The domestic resource cost approach, briefly treated at the end of this section, was developed as a response to this problem. If linearity, or constant returns, is not satisfied, the same analysis can be applied at the margin, and equation 6-6 in particular will be valid for marginal value added and a marginal definition of effective protection. Empirical implementation is, of course, greatly hindered if input-output tables cannot be employed to obtain the estimates required.

What happens when we introduce substitutability into the model? If we want to use EP indexes as guides to resource allocation, they must satisfy (6-6), as they will only if they are measured in equilibrium, including the effects of substitution due to tariffs. If activity 3 has a lower EP index than activity 1, then it would be a good idea to take resources from 1 and give them to 3 if both activities were going to keep to their tariff-distorted input coefficients.

It does not follow, however, that there cannot exist some set of input coefficients feasible for activity 1 at which its unit value added at world prices would be higher than any that activity 3 could show, however it altered its input coefficients. This point has been used as an argument against the effective protection index. It is not decisive, however, to argue against a measure that it provides only a sufficient condition for an improvement that is not necessary, and it would be reasonable to doubt the feasibility of a measure that depends upon knowing the unobservable input coefficients that would be observed were prices different.

In discussing effective protection, we have placed much of the emphasis on the issue of the welfare evaluation of resource allocation changes. This emphasis fits the central concerns of this chapter, which include the elucidation of the relation between EP and CBA theory. Effective protection theory, however, has often been considered as a positive framework for evaluating the effects of tariffs on activities, and some problems with the measure refer to that application. Thus the Ramaswami and Srinivasan (1971) example shows how the pull of protection depends upon factor endowments. This area is well reviewed by Ethier (1977). We might say that effective protection rates are to activities as tariffs are to goods. Considerable difficulties stand in the way of rewriting trade theory, let alone welfare or tax theory, in the language of effective protection. The demand side must be expressed in terms of goods, because the demand for a value-added activity is not, for the consumer, a natural concept. Effective protection theory as a descriptive model must therefore be confined to the production side, where in fact it has made its contributions.

We have argued that effective protection measures the extent to which the tariff structure has exerted a pull on resources toward a particular sector. What is measured, to be precise, is resource pull after the fact—the pull that arises, given the prices of a general equilibrium that itself reflects the existence of tariffs. Unfortunately from the standpoint of neatness, the general equilibrium effects of a tariff structure do not necessarily imply that a high resource pull will lead to the relative expansion of a sector. This simple point does not discredit the concept, but it reminds us that resource pull measured away from the full optimum is not the same as overexpansion relative to that optimum. TAX theory offers an analogy. If it can be shown that the rate of taxation on a certain good is higher than the optimum would require, it does not necessarily follow that less of the good is being consumed than would be consumed in the optimum.

The links between EP theory and TAX theory remain to be explored. The concept of the taxation of an activity is quite natural and has obviously been much discussed in such applications as the taxation or subsidy of investment. The direct taxation or subsidy of producers' goods and services would be the closest analogue to tariffs. We may imagine such instruments changing the prices faced by producers from p to $p + t$. As with tariffs, so with such taxation, we must consider the whole price structure to see how a particular activity is affected, and a concept of effective taxation could clearly be developed (see chapter 11 by Ahmad and Stern for some theory and empirical applications). Still, why should the authorities wish to tax or subsidize a particular activity? Optimal tax theory usually teaches that no taxes should be levied on transactions between producers. Three cases come to mind. There might be an external cost or benefit from an activity the extent of which it seems desirable to influence, or there could be rents that cannot be directly taxed but could be partly captured by indirect sales taxation, or it may be infeasible to tax the final good.

A tariff involves direct taxation of producers' sales and purchases, but it falls on consumers as well. By considering extensions of the concept of effective protection to sales taxation, we raise again the question of the motivation that underlies tariffs. Looking at activities rather than the net production of final goods does not help us to understand that awkward question.

The notion of domestic resource cost comes into play when there is more than one nontraded input in use. This situation introduces the possibility of a different kind of resource pull—a pull away from ideal free-trade equilibrium, that is—but not because of tariffs. If various factors operating in the markets for inputs cause the prices that rule to diverge from the optimal shadow prices, or from social opportunity costs, of those inputs, this creates another pull. DRC may be defined:

$$(6\text{-}8) \qquad DRC = \frac{\text{Social opportunity cost of resources employed}}{\text{Value added at world prices}}.$$

The DRC approach is very close to CBA and should be considered in conjunction with that method. Note that if we have constant returns to scale, or are calculating at the margin, all activities in use would generate one unit of domestic value added for each unit of domestic resources valued at market prices. In an economy in which market prices measured social opportunity costs (that is, with no domestic distortions of any kind), equation 6-8 would be equal to $VADP/VAWP$, which is the same as the effective protection measure plus one.

Taxation Theory

The literature on taxation is very extensive. If we exclude all except that which lies within the purview of the present chapter—connections with cost-benefit theory, or effective protection—much still remains within our scope. The survey by Dixit (1984a) provides a good synthetic overview of this field. There is quite an old tradition of looking at tariffs as a kind of taxation (see Corden, 1974). Excess burden theory has been applied to show that tariffs are inefficient taxes compared with other forms of taxation, while Pigou (1947) applied optimal tax theory to tariffs after its investigation by Ramsey.

In classical welfare economics, the government was assumed to command the possibility of levying discriminating lump-sum taxes. By "lump sum" we mean that the payment is independent of the actions that the agent may subsequently decide to carry out. The term "discriminating" implies that the amount due to or from each agent can be tailored to that agent's particular position, including true wealth-earning ability. The chief and basic result of classical welfare economics is that lump-sum taxation is superior to all other forms of taxation. Furthermore, if optimal lump-sum taxation is levied, any inefficient position can be dominated by an efficient position in which no one is worse off and some people gain. See Atkinson and Stiglitz (1980, chap. 11).

The difficulties with lump-sum taxation are obvious. The government does not have access to the information that it would require to discriminate perfectly between individuals, nor could it obtain this information, as not all agents' interests would be served by revealing it. Classical welfare theory therefore apparently rested on an insecure foundation, and much of the history of welfare economics was taken up with more or less ingenious attempts to surmount the difficulty. Developments in the theory of economic policy since World War II, however, have largely bypassed the problem by basing the theory of economic policy on a more realistic specification of the instruments available to the government—specifically, on real world tax instruments. This type of approach is often called the theory of the second best, but it is really the theory of the best based on realistic assumptions. Modern tax theory is founded on second-best assumptions.

The theory is reviewed in chapters 2 and 3. Here we concentrate on the overlap with our main concerns. The old and the new theory share quite a wide range of conclusions. Thus the second best has not made it possible to establish that tariffs are good instruments of intervention. They should probably be used only where a social cost attaches to trading as such. This is the case with the optimal tariff model with its variable terms of trade or where autarky is valued for its own sake. In these cases both producers and consumers should be taxed at the same rate for engaging in international trade, an activity to which a social cost attaches. Apart from such cases, taxes or subsidies directed specifically at consumers or producers are superior to tariffs. This conclusion can be drawn from an extensive literature that has applied the second-best approach to the analysis of various distortions and is summarized in Corden (1984, sec. 6). See also Bhagwati and Ramaswami (1963). The conclusion that taxes and subsidies are best directed accurately toward the source of the distortion that they are designed to offset has been as great a unifying principle as was the old classical one, that all distortions should be removed, in its day.

The important Diamond-Mirrlees theorem already mentioned can be placed in context as an example of the foregoing type of result. The theorem shows that public sector production should be of maximum value at world prices (we take the application of the result to an open economy with only tradable goods, the one particularly relevant to our present concerns) even if the government can levy only indirect taxes that do not discriminate between consumers. Moreover, if no pure profits arise in the private sector, as they would not with constant returns to scale, the whole of production, public plus private, should maximize at world prices. Here the second-best nature of the problem arises from the fact that there can be no lump-sum taxes to adjust consumer incomes. The intervention is thus directed as closely as possible to the source of the difficulty and is applied to the prices that consumers face. Producers should not face indirect taxes. For this result we require that it be feasible to tax all final goods (see chapter 3).

In fact the assumption that no taxation is allowable except indirect taxation is not needed to obtain the result. We can allow general income taxation not restricted to linear income tax schedules provided that all consumers face the same income tax schedule. With this provision, if consumers are not all identical, we are still left short of the perfectly discriminating lump-sum transfers required by classical theory, but we have enough for the Diamond-

Mirrlees result. Indirect taxes in this case still conform to the Ramsey rules, but their values may of course be radically altered by the fact that alternative revenue-raising instruments are present.

As has been remarked, the Diamond-Mirrlees framework has immediate implications for social cost-benefit analysis, as is seen most simply with the full (general equilibrium) Diamond-Mirrlees solution for an open economy that is supported by the following prices. Public sector producers, and private producers, if we add the appropriate assumptions, face world prices. Households face world prices modified by optimal indirect taxes and subsidies, and they also face an optimal income tax schedule if we permit that form of taxation. A new idea for a public sector project can be evaluated using world prices for tradables.

It will be seen that there are no tariffs as such. A consumer good that is only imported can carry a tariff, because in that case a tariff and a consumption tax are the same. Only if a certain commodity is to be untaxed at the optimum will consumers and producers face the same price, but it would be a no-tariff price. The distinguishing feature of tariffs is that they raise prices for both consumers and producers and by the same amount.

As a result, if we try to apply the cost-benefit aspects of the Diamond-Mirrlees theory to an economy that includes many tariffs, we encounter the problem discussed above, namely we start from an economy that, according to the theory, is unnecessarily distorted. We need, then, to develop a different theory for evaluating partial changes when these take place in an economy far from its optimum. I do not say that the description of the optimum provided by second-best theory will be irrelevant to our task but only note that we will be doing something rather different. This theory is the subject of the next section.

Optimal Taxation and Cost-Benefit Analysis with Tariffs

The argument has made clear how tariffs should be treated ideally. If they are historical hangovers or the products of misunderstanding, it would benefit everyone if they were removed and if parallel adjustments were made in taxation to protect those who would otherwise lose. If they are there to protect an interest group that has not been able to protect its interests by other means, and if that interest is immovable and cannot be accommodated by more efficient means, we must clearly take them as given. Still, we must do more as well. We must write into our model that the said interest exists and that it must not be harmed by policy changes. Our model so written will lead to the natural conclusion that a tariff is not the most efficient way of buying off an interest group. Put simply, the most efficient way of buying off an interest group is to weight the welfare of the members of that group in the social valuation function more than they would be if we considered only equality and fairness. In the outcome the theory will look much the same, but the numbers that emerge will be different.

The argument expressed above is valid only for prespecified interest groups, meaning those whose membership does not itself depend upon the solution to the model. When city dwellers, or doctors, command a special power that enables them to insist on certain income levels, then we cannot deal with the problem by writing the valuation function in a different form, and the desirability of aggregate productive efficiency can be undermined. See Anand and Joshi (1979). This important argument shows that aggregate efficiency may not be the appropriate objective in an economy in which the distribution of income is inseparably linked to the allocation of labor. Public sector efficiency may still be desirable.

Although some tariffs clearly protect visible and powerful interest groups, much economic research proceeds on the assumption that tariffs can be circumvented. The reason may be that some tariffs are viewed as historical hangovers, or it may be that the economist is recommending a reform that would have been attractive to the interest group had it commanded its instruments. This point applies to TAX reform and to the use of EP analysis as a guide to resource allocation as much as it does to tariff reform.

We shall now examine one case in detail. Tariffs are in place and affect the private sector, and they cannot be removed. Indirect taxation, however, can alter the prices faced by consumers, and the public sector can be instructed to ignore tariffs in its own decisions. We can think of the reform of private sector tariffs as something too complex and full of political traps to be undertaken, or we can regard it as something that could be done but that remains to be done when a cost-benefit decision must be made. This last philosophy underlies much EP analysis and CBA theory. Thus, while Ramaswami and Srinivasan (1971) have argued that we should remove removable tariffs rather than develop methods to calculate around them, Little and Mirrlees take a more circumspect view.

> The rationale of the system described is that of estimating those prices which would prevail in the economy if it were to operate so as to maximize society's ends, this maximization being constrained by the available resources, and by the possibilities of the tax system. But the maximization may also be constrained by the fact that certain indicated reforms are very unlikely to be made. [Little and Mirrlees, 1974, p. 72]

To lend meaning to the assumption that tariffs are given and we have to act with them as they are, we must prohibit direct taxes and subsidies on producers' sales and purchases, for if these were to be allowed, they would be used simply to cancel out the effects of the tariffs. This point, however, can apply only where tradables are concerned, for policy influencing producers through the prices that they pay and receive for nontradables is allowable within the spirit of our approach. In our previous discussion, particularly of EP theory, we neglected nontradables, or rather we aggregated them and called them "labor," but we did so only for the sake of simplicity. The treatment of nontradables, their pricing, and the measurement of their opportunity costs, are at the heart of our problem.

The formal model behind the argument is presented in my appendix, but now we consider the various components of the model, particularly the variables that the government will choose and the constraints to which the choice will be subject. First comes the *social valuation function*, considered to be a sum of welfare indicators for various individuals or groups in the economy. Its form, naturally, involves many value judgments, but it may also, as I have explained, reflect some brute political facts. What is interesting to note is that the only arguments of the aggregate welfare function will be the prices that consumers pay and receive for the goods and services for which they engage in exchange, plus the income tax schedule, which must be the same for all individuals by assumption.

Next we come to *constraints*. First, there are overall supply-demand constraints in the various markets of the economy. Where tradables are concerned, this is not a good-by-good balance but an overall balance of value at world prices. Where nontradables are concerned, the markets, of course, must balance good by good. The supplies and demands to be taken into account are as follows. Households supply and demand goods. The levels of these demands depend upon the prices that they face and on the income tax schedule. Next, firms demand some goods as inputs and supply others as outputs. The prices that firms face for tradables are given, as world prices plus the given tariffs, but the government may choose the prices of producers' nontradables, and these need not be the same as the consumers' prices. Equally, consumers need not face the given tradables' prices that are predetermined for firms. Last, the government itself contributes to supply and demand through its own productive economic activity, both with regard to tradables and to nontradables, and these production levels must be chosen, of course, in conformity with the production possibility set of the public sector.

This is the constrained-maximization problem from which come all the results about to be quoted in summary. This type of analysis establishes the way in which the best equilibrium for the case concerned can be supported by prices. Such support assumes a general application of the method to CBA analysis. The evaluation of a one-off project, without any implication that the method will be generally applied, can be difficult; for an analysis and for more general results, see Drèze and Stern (1985).

We may conclude:

- Despite the fact that private production decisions are distorted by the presence of tariffs, and even if there is an optimal income tax, indirect consumer taxes should still accord with the modified Ramsey tax rule. Naturally, the fact that the same necessary condition applies should not be taken as an indication that these taxes will have the same magnitudes that they would without the considerations mentioned.

- These indirect consumer taxes should be measured as departures of consumer prices from public sector shadow prices. Where tradables are concerned, the latter are proportional to world prices (they make no allowance for the tariffs that the private sector faces), and they are not necessarily the same as private sector prices even for nontradables.

- Public sector production should maximize net value at public sector shadow prices. For tradables these shadow prices are obtained by converting world prices at the shadow price of foreign exchange. For nontradables they are equal to the rates at which the private sector translates tradables into nontradables when the prices of the nontradables that it faces are changed, these rates being weighted by world prices.

The last condition may be elucidated by an example. Suppose that the private sector imports steel, paying a tariff, and converts it into nontradable bridges using nontradable labor. The labor could otherwise be employed producing nontradable haircuts or tradable wheat. Given the model as formulated, the only instrument that the government can wield to influence the actions of the private sector is to change nontradable prices, here the price of a bridge and the price of a haircut. Holding consumer prices constant, it changes producer prices for nontradables and, as the private sector substitutes in production, this substitution can be used to price a bridge in terms of foreign exchange.

As the price of a bridge is increased, labor is drawn from cutting hair and planting wheat. The price of haircuts is increased along with the rise in the price of bridges, so that the only output reduction involves tradable wheat. We thus derive a measure of the opportunity cost of a bridge in terms of wheat, and this wheat in turn is priced at the world price to give a shadow price of the bridge in terms of foreign exchange. This account shows how in principle the shadow price of a nontradable good would be computed. Naturally, once we have the optimal prices, it makes no difference to social cost whether we withdraw resources from haircuts or from wheat production.

The example is simple. In reality we will be involved in a complex input-output calculation as nontradables used as inputs to nontradables are chased back through the production system to dissolve to tradables.

Further Implications for Cost-Benefit Analysis

We have seen in the previous section what shadow prices for the evaluation of public projects should be in principle. It is very helpful for practical application that tradables are priced proportionately to world prices, although it may not always be easy to determine exactly what value to use for the world price. The computation of shadow prices for nontradables, however, is rather complicated. If project evaluation were to be organized on a large scale, with many projects evaluated on the same lines, it would be worth making the accurate evaluation of shadow prices for major nontradables, notably labor, a research project in itself. In practice such large-scale evaluation may not happen, however desirable it may be.

Several approximations suggest themselves. The influential Little-Mirrlees manual incorporates the view that the individual project evaluator will be able to do quite a lot of the work of translating the costs of major nontradable items into implicit tradables cost. Large items would have to be traced part of the way through the input-output structure. Small items could be evaluated at market prices and converted to international value using the shadow exchange rate. This is not a theoretically ideal measure, but it may be good enough in a field where much will have to be approximate.

Another approach to the pricing of nontradables is to use transformation rates from the existing public sector technology. This procedure provides an upper-bound estimate of the social costs involved and could be seriously misleading. Finally, market prices—that is, producer prices—could be used to value nontradables and not simply for small values, as mentioned above in connection with Little-Mirrlees. Again, it is not theoretically correct to do so. These prices measure the rates at which the private sector can transform one good into another while having its production structure distorted by the effects of tariffs on tradables. The overall value of a unit of resources is, other things being equal, higher when that unit is under the control of the public sector, because of the distortionary effects of tariffs.

The Developing Country

Nearly all the theory discussed in this paper is, it seems, as applicable to the advanced economy as to the developing country. It is not true that only developing countries suffer from income inequalities, and it is not the case that the imports of developing countries alone are subject to tariffs. The highest tariffs in the world are to be found in developing countries, but not generally in the poorest developing countries. True, income taxes are hard to collect in developing countries, but they are in some rich countries as well. In any case, income taxes figure in our analysis only as an optional extra.

It could be argued that some characteristic features of developing countries militate against the application of this theory to that case. The sharpness of the urban-rural division in some developing countries, for example, helps make a political economy in which equality may have to take a back seat. Suppose that communicable disease is a more serious problem when people are crowded close together in large numbers. Efficiency will then require more provision of public health and medical facilities in towns than in the countryside. Equity argues for equal provision, or even for favoring the countryside, but in the compromise between efficiency and equity, the town may do better than the countryside. This example illustrates the point that some of the stark differences between rich and poor countries involve issues that are not centrally considered by any of our three theoretical models.

Such considerations, then, are not in opposition to the theory that has been discussed but stand outside it. We should never forget, however, that the prevalence of such problems in developing countries makes rational economic planning a peculiarly difficult exercise.

Appendix: Mathematical Details

This appendix presents the model of the tariff-bound economy in a simple form. It embodies a crucial simplifying assumption, that private sector producer prices do not matter for household welfare. This is the implication of the constant-returns assumption, which has been widely employed. The reader may check which conditions are altered if this assumption is not made.

Notation

Lowercase Roman letters denote vectors of appropriate dimension, and Greek letters denote scalars. The partial derivatives of a scalar-valued function, which form a vector, however, are denoted by the appropriate Greek letter subscripted. This occurs in only one instance: so, specifically, Ω_T and Ω_{NT} are vectors of partial derivatives of the public sector production constraint, measured by Ω, with respect to tradable and nontradable goods. The partial derivatives of supplies, or of unweighted demands, with respect to prices are not-necessarily-square matrixes. Thus $\partial x^{NT}/\partial q^T$ is the matrix of the partial derivative of unweighted demands for nontradables with respect to the tradables prices faced by consumers. Finally, $\Gamma()$ denotes the amount of tax payable on the income that is its argument.

$V^h[q^T, q^{NT}, \Gamma(.)]$ = household h's indirect utility function/functional.

β^h = marginal utility of income of household h.

$x^T(q^T, q^{NT})$ = unweighted demands for tradables summed over households.

$x^{NT}(q^T, q^{NT})$ = unweighted demands for nontradables summed over households.

$x_w^T(q^T, q^{NT})$ = demands for tradables summed over households weighted by β^h.

$x_w^{NT}(q^T, q^{NT})$ = demands for nontradables summed over households weighted by β^h.

The weights mentioned above are the β^h values computed at the optimum. The demand functions depend upon $\Gamma(.)$, as well as upon the prices, but this is not explicitly indicated.

q^T = household prices for tradables

q^{NT} = household prices for nontradables

$\hat{p}$ = world prices for tradable goods

p^{NT} = private sector producer prices for nontradables

$\hat{t}$ = predetermined tariffs

$y^T(\hat{p} + \hat{t}, p^{NT})$ = private sector net supply of tradable goods

$y^{NT}(\hat{p} + \hat{t}, p^{NT})$ = private sector net supply of nontradable goods.

z^T	= public sector production of tradables
z^{NT}	= public sector production of nontradables
$\Omega(z^T, z^{NT})$	= public sector production function
σ	= shadow price of foreign exchange
v	= shadow prices of nontradables
μ	= shadow price of public sector production

Constrained Maximization

The variables to be chosen are q^T, q^{NT}, p^{NT}, z^T, and z^{NT}. The maximand is the sum of household indirect utilities.

$$(6\text{-}A1) \qquad \text{Maximize} \ \sum_h V^h[q^T, q^{NT}, \Gamma(\cdot)]$$

subject to

$$(6\text{-}A2) \qquad \hat{p} \cdot [y^T(\hat{p} + \hat{t}, p^{NT}) + z^T - x^T(q^T, q^{NT})] \geqq 0$$

$$(6\text{-}A3) \qquad y^{NT}(\hat{p} + \hat{t}, p^{NT}) + z^{NT} - x^{NT}(q^T, q^{NT}) \geqq 0$$

$$(6\text{-}A4) \qquad \qquad \qquad \qquad \Omega(z^T, z^{NT}) \geqq 0$$

The constraints represent, respectively: the balance of trade condition for tradables evaluated at prices $\hat{p}$, the condition that the demand must not exceed the supply for any nontradable, and the production feasibility constraint for public production. The shadow prices of these constraints are σ, v, and μ, respectively.

We are not going to derive conditions for the optimal income tax schedule $\Gamma(.)$. As is well known, this derivation is exceedingly complicated. Our results will be true for any Γ, however, and hence true for the optimal Γ. It is interesting to note that income tax revenue does not explicitly enter into the problem. The problem says that income may be transferred at will between individuals, provided that the transfers can be implemented through an income tax system common to all consumers. The technical supply-demand constraints, however, make themselves felt should such transfers become infeasible. The income tax schedule affects demands, and rates must be set such that the balance of payments constraint, and the availability of nontradables to meet demands, are not violated.

Necessary Conditions

We assume an internal solution. Necessary conditions are obtained for each of the choice variables. They are all vectors, so the conditions in each case take the form of a vector equation. We present the conditions in a useful shorthand: arguments of functions are dropped whenever there is no ambiguity.

$$(6\text{-}A5) \qquad q^T: \quad -x_w^T - \sigma\hat{p} \cdot (\partial x^T/\partial q^T) - v \cdot (\partial x^{NT}/\partial q^T) = 0$$

$$(6\text{-}A6) \qquad q^{NT}: \quad -x_w^{NT} - \sigma\hat{p} \cdot (\partial x^T/\partial q^{NT}) - v \cdot (\partial x^{NT}/\partial q^{NT}) = 0$$

$$(6\text{-}A7) \qquad p^{NT}: \quad \sigma\hat{p} \cdot (\partial y^T/\partial p^{NT}) + v \cdot (\partial y^{NT}/\partial p^{NT}) = 0$$

$$(6\text{-}A8) \qquad z^T: \quad \sigma\hat{p} + \mu\Omega_T = 0$$

$$(6\text{-}A9) \qquad z^{NT}: v + \mu\Omega_{NT} = 0$$

Interpretations

Conditions 6-A5 and 6-A6 add up to a kind of Ramsey rule for optimum indirect taxation. Upon making small changes in consumer prices, we compare the changes in the levels of demands, weighted by prices ($\sigma\hat{p}$, v) but not by the β^h values, with the weighted levels of total demands. Condition 6-A7 justifies the interpretation that has been offered of the prices that should be used in CBA analysis. Thus:

$$(6\text{-}A10) \qquad v/\sigma = \hat{p} \cdot (\partial y^T/\partial p^{NT}) \cdot (\partial y^{NT}/\partial p^{NT})^{-1}$$

so that **v** translated to world prices measures the rate at which, by altering nontradables prices faced by private producers, nontradable net outputs may be substituted, through changes in the outputs of tradables, to international value. Finally, 6-A8 and 6-A9 show what prices public sector planners should use. They must be proportional to $\sigma\hat{p}$ and **v** for tradables and nontradables, respectively.

Notes

1. The theory does note the existence of a number of cases in which a tariff is the optimal intervention, notably the "optimal tariff" that is imposed when the terms of trade faced by a country vary with the extent of its trade. On this argument for a tariff, and on the wide-ranging arguments against it, see Corden (1984).

2. See Bhagwati and Srinivasan (1973), Corden (1974), and Johnson (1965). A particular case of a "distortion" is an imperfection of income distribution in the home economy.

3. See Baldwin (1982) and Findlay and Wellisz (1982). Also see Krueger (1974).

PART 2

Structural Issues
and Taxation

THE GENERAL PRINCIPLES of optimal taxation on the theory of tax reform were set out in part 1. This part is intended to identify the features of developing countries that are likely to influence the analysis. The standard model used to express the theory of part 1 may require modification in two important ways. First, the range of instruments available is likely to be more limited, and second, the incidence of the taxes that are available may be quite different. Optimal tax theory stresses that the design of any one part of the tax optimum, such as commodity taxation, depends sensitively on the other instruments that are available. It is therefore important to identify the instruments that are likely to be available and the features of developing countries that restrict the range of feasible taxes.

The incidence of taxes is central to any study of their redistributive impact and is affected by the coverage of the tax, whether it is sector specific and whether it falls on inputs or outputs. Most standard tax models assume that only outputs or factor incomes are taxed and that any taxes are universal, not sector specific. If it is impossible to tax agricultural income directly, then income or wage taxes that are confined to the nonagricultural sector may have a quite different incidence from a universal income tax. If the urban labor market operates to equilibrate the after-tax level of utility in the rural and urban sectors, urban income taxes may increase the cost of labor without reducing the after-tax wage. Taxes on agricultural output may reduce the rural wage and may also lower the urban wage. Subsidies to the urban poor but not to the rural poor may merely increase the number of migrants or may lower alternative income without reducing poverty.

Input taxes are considered to be undesirable in optimal tax models if all rents and outputs can be taxed. If it is not possible to tax all commodities, then input taxes will often be desirable, and their incidence will depend on the structure of production and demand. Taxes on inputs into the production of traded goods, whose prices are given by the international market, will be shifted back and will lower the pretax price of the input and will hence lower various factor incomes. Taxes on inputs into nontraded goods may merely increase the price of the nontraded output. Chapter 7 examines some characteristic features of developing countries to clarify the restrictions on the choice and coverage of tax instruments. The incidence of taxes will depend on the way in which the urban and rural labor markets work, whether the tax is sector specific, and how the market price of the taxed commodity is determined.

Chapter 8 quantitatively describes the main features of the tax structures of eighty-six developing countries and hence provides evidence on the relative importance of various types of tax. The features that mold and constrain the choice of tax instruments receive their visible expression in the pattern of taxation to be observed in countries at various levels of income. In chapter 9 Musgrave draws lessons, on the basis of his practical experience in developing countries, regarding the reforms that are feasible and desirable and with respect to the constraints that are of greatest practical importance. He shows how a tax adviser might respond to the evidence discussed in the previous two chapters. As mentioned above, the incidence of taxes on the urban and rural sectors depends on the ways in which labor markets equilibrate, and chapter 10 provides a survey of labor markets in relation to public policy in developing countries.

7

Taxation and Development

David Newbery

THE MAIN AIM of this book is to explain the techniques of modern tax theory and to show how they may be applied to the analysis of tax reform and policy changes in developing countries. Public economics has advanced rapidly since 1970, and we may identify three main reasons. First, economists became willing once again to describe society's objectives by a social welfare function that could evaluate the consequences of alternative policies. This device allows us to deal systematically with the conflict between equity and efficiency that was resolutely avoided as unscientific in the post-Robbins age of "new welfare economics." Second, the coherence that this approach provided meant that it was possible to construct simple but powerful models of the economy that could be used to answer many of the standard questions of public finance in a rigorous way, as is shown in more detail in chapter 2. Finally, computers, developments in econometrics, and the growing availability of large sets of survey data on consumer budgets meant that the new theory could be applied. The distinctive feature of the new approach is that it is consequentialist—the desirability of any policy is to be judged solely by its consequences for members of the community, not by abstract descriptions of the policy (such as fairness). The theoretical models usually go further and restrict attention to a small number of consequences judged to be relevant—typically changes in consumption and wealth (that is, future consumption). These consequences can in principle be measured, and the approach strongly suggests that they should be measured in order to evaluate proposed policy changes.

The standard model developed for modern tax analysis is perfectly competitive and, in the absence of distortionary taxes, would yield an efficient equilibrium. The government is concerned to raise revenue and to improve the distribution of income but does not have enough information about the preferences and endowments of its citizens to do so by means of individual lump-sum taxes. Consequently, it can achieve its aims only by using taxes that give rise to distortions. The optimum tax structure balances the gain in equity (measured by the social welfare function) against the cost of the fall in efficiency. As such the model seems more appropriate for a market economy with few uncorrected market failures in long-run equilibrium at full employment. It may appear to be quite inappropriate for a developing economy, where the problems seem quite different. Some development economists argue that the main role of the government is to combat the impediments to development, to mobilize resources in order to raise the growth rate, not to balance static efficiency costs delicately against improvements in the distribution of income between contemporaries. Instead of worrying about static redistribution, government should aim to raise future consumption levels. In the standard model, the only constraint limiting the choice of the tax system is information about preferences and endowments, whereas in developing countries institutional, political, administrative, structural, and cultural constraints may drastically limit the range of tax instruments that are effectively available. How suitable, then, is this modern approach for tax analysis in developing countries?

I would argue that the basic model does indeed need to be modified to include important features of developing countries, and this is one of the main reasons for the present book. I would also claim that, despite the obvious differences between developing countries and the textbook competitive model, the same basic techniques can usefully be applied to the analysis of tax reform. In short, although the differences justify this book, the similarities justify the method. It is notable that the original articles by Diamond and Mirrlees (1971) were in part motivated by the attempt to develop a satisfactory method of social cost-benefit analysis for use in developing countries. In the final chapter of their book on project appraisal for developing countries, Little and Mirrlees (1974) show the close relationship between their method and the results of the Diamond-Mirrlees model. It could also be argued that adaptation of the model to developing countries will make tax theory more useful for developed countries, which also deviate from the competitive textbook model. Just as studies of distorted labor markets in developing countries led to the development of more satisfactory theories of the behavior of developed country labor markets, so a study of tax theory in an economy with limited information, limited tax instruments, and widespread distortions should throw light on similar if less extreme problems facing policymakers in developed countries.

One of the main conclusions of modern tax theory is that the design of the tax system depends sensitively on the tax instruments that it is feasible to use, and these in turn depend on the information that is available to the tax authorities. If we had complete information about preferences, attributes, and endowments, differentiated lump-sum taxes would be best, but there would be strong incentives for taxpayers to conceal this information, making lump-sum taxes unattractive. If income taxes are feasible, then the role of indirect taxation is reduced, but if income taxes are infeasible, then indirect taxes are obviously crucial. Their impact will in turn depend on whether lump-sum subsidies or transfers can be made to consumers. The choice of taxes will thus depend on the objectives of the government, on the set of tax instruments that it is feasible to employ, and on the way these taxes affect consumers' welfare and government revenue. Developing countries may differ from the standard models of modern tax theory in these three respects. Because the structure of taxation depends so sensitively on the range of instruments available, it is clearly important to ask what limits the choice rather than to accept current practice as defining the limits of the possible.

The Special Characteristics of Developing Countries

The object of this chapter is to describe the features of developing countries that are likely to influence tax analysis and require modifications to the standard model either because they restrict the set of instruments or because they alter the instruments' impact. The first part therefore lists those characteristics of developing countries that appear relevant to tax analysis. Few developing countries exhibit all the features listed below, and their relative importance will vary widely from country to country. The list therefore exaggerates the differences between developing and developed countries. I shall review this list systematically and shall discuss the ways in which the features affect tax analysis. The list suggests the constraints that may influence the choice of tax structure. I shall subsequently single out the public sector, which frequently accounts for a significant fraction of nonagricultural production, for special discussion, afterward briefly examining the tax structures observed in developing countries to see how far these constraints appear to be important in molding tax choices. The evidence suggests that tax structures and levels of taxation vary between countries far more widely than any simplistic structural analysis might suggest. This variation indicates that governments may differ in their objectives, in the power structure that constrains what is politically feasible, and in their administrative capacity, which in turn is heavily influenced by the balance of political power. I shall also consider the objectives and political constraints that affect tax policy, administrative capacity, and the problem of tax evasion.

Some of the themes of this chapter receive more extensive treatment in later chapters. Tanzi in chapter 8 provides the evidence on the structure of taxation; Musgrave in chapter 9 draws lessons, based on his practical experience in developing countries, of what tax reforms are feasible. I mentioned above that the standard tax models appear to be static in their emphasis on the balancing of static efficiency costs against redistribution among contemporaries. This important and far-reaching criticism was discussed in chapter 5. At a number of points in this chapter I discuss some of the reasons why dynamic issues are likely to be more important in developing countries.

The Importance of the Primary Sector

The share of agriculture in GDP in low-income countries was 37 percent in 1981, and its share of the labor force was 70 percent (45 percent and 73 percent, respectively, if India and China are excluded).[1] Thus the agricultural sector accounts for a large fraction of employment and a significant fraction of income but has a level of productivity apparently only one-quarter that of the nonagricultural sector.[2] The coexistence of two sectors of radically different levels of labor productivity is a classic symptom of dualism but needs to be interpreted carefully. The main reason is that workers may be classified as belonging to the agricultural sector on the basis of their main occupation even though a significant fraction of their time is spent on nonagricultural activities. If the income from these nonagricultural activities is correctly attributed, then productivity differences between the sectors narrow dramatically, though they do not disappear. Thus Bertrand and Squire observe that average labor productivity in Thai agriculture in 1970 was only 12 percent of that in nonagriculture, as indicated by national accounts data (Bertrand and Squire, 1980, p. 507). Nonagricultural activities account for one-third of labor time in the rainy season and two-thirds in the dry season and represent between a quarter and half of total income (p. 491). The average income differential between rural and urban households was about 37 percent in money terms, but the cost of living was 16 percent lower in rural areas, so although there remains a significant income difference between urban and rural areas, it is far lower than superficial estimates of per capita product might suggest.

The primary sector also includes minerals extraction, and together with agricultural products, fuels, minerals, and metals account for a significant fraction of export earnings, especially in poor countries, as table 7-1 shows. Poor countries thus depend heavily on primary products for their export earnings, and these are notorious for their price instability. Although the share of agricultural products in exports falls as income levels rise, the openness of the economy also rises, so that most developing countries are exposed to substantial export risk.

Dualism

A dual economy is one with a significant difference in the economic and social organization of the traditional, rural sector and the modern capitalist sector. Different writers have chosen to emphasize different features of the two sectors, and dual-economy models have proven both flexible and popular in analyzing the development process.[3] For some, the important distinction lies in the products produced—food versus nonfood. For others it is the supposed difference in social organization (semisubsistence or capitalist) or location (urban or rural).

For tax analysis two aspects of dualism are of central importance. The first is the extent to which transactions within the traditional sector can be taxed, and the second is the extent to which dualism is evidence of market failure and particularly market segmentation. If the two sectors are characterized only by their location, by the goods they produce, by the degree of capital intensity, or by the extent to which they can be taxed but there is no market segmentation, then, as we shall show below, the simple competitive tax model can be reinterpreted in a way that makes it directly applicable. If markets are segmented, then the model needs more radical changes. The issue of market

Table 7-1. *Percentage Share of Merchandise Exports, 1982*

Economy	Fuels, minerals, and metals	Other primary commodities	Total primary commodities	Exports of goods and non-factor services in GDP
Low-income economies	20	30	50	9
Low-income economies, excluding India and China	15	55	80	11
Middle-income oil exporters	79	12	91	24
Middle-income oil importers	13	27	40	22
Industrial market economies	12	14	26	19

Sources: World Bank (1984, 1985).

segmentation is easiest to study in the labor market, and indeed, labor market segmentation has been the critical defining characteristic of dualism for many writers.

Segmentation of the Labor Market

In a segmented labor market, the marginal products of the same kind of labor differ significantly between sectors. (A dual labor market is segmented into just two sectors.) Squire (1981, chap. 5) distinguishes two main models of dualism, which he labels "traditional sector dualism" and "modern sector dualism." In both versions, the marginal product of labor in the modern sector exceeds that of the traditional sector, but the reasons for the gaps differ. The central concept in both models is the supply price of labor from the traditional to the modern sector. The supply price of potential migrants is the lowest wage they would need to be paid in the modern sector in order to induce them to migrate. In money terms it may be substantially higher than their income in the rural sector because of the higher cost of urban living (especially shelter and transport). Where differences in purchasing power exist, it is important to distinguish between the supply price of labor *to* the urban sector (measured as the equivalent *urban* wage) and the supply price *from* the rural sector (measured by the equivalent *rural* income). These differences are to be understood and, where they need emphasis, will be distinguished by the urban and rural supply prices.

Traditional sector dualism has the modern sector wage equal to the urban supply price of labor. The rural supply price, however, exceeds the MPL in the traditional sector. Labor supply and demand are in equilibrium in the modern sector, and there is therefore no unemployment in that sector. Modern sector dualism has the modern sector wage above the urban supply price of labor. If the modern sector wage is fixed independently of the supply price, then the two parts of the dual labor market are rigidly segmented, and agricultural taxes do not affect urban wages. If the modern wage is some markup on the supply price, then wage levels are still linked in the two sectors even though they are not equated. In either case the gap between the modern wage and the supply price will result in an excess supply of labor and possibly in open urban unemployment.

Early dual-economy models of development placed the labor market failure in the traditional sector. Thus in the important early models of Lewis (1954) and Fei and Ranis (1961), the rural wage was set at the subsistence level, which, if it were above the rural MPL, would imply the existence of "surplus labor" and a misallocation of labor. In other models, the rural supply price of labor is equal to the average product of labor, which exceeds the marginal product, because the migrant worker moving to the modern sector would forfeit a claim on family income. Jorgenson (1961, 1967) produced an early model with this feature, and chapter 15 by Heady and Mitra explores the consequence of this assumption. Most of these models appear to have been developed with densely populated Southeast Asian economies in mind and seem not to fit the facts in newly independent East African economies, for which Harris and Todaro (1970) developed the alternative model of modern sector dualism. In this the modern sector wage is kept above the urban supply price of labor, because of minimum-wage laws (which were important in East Africa), trade union pressure (often exercised on governments and hence important in setting the minimum wage), or the hiring practices of modern sector firms, particularly those in the public sector, which often accounted for the larger part of formal employment.

One implication of this view of dualism is that the wage differential will attract migrants from the rural sector until it equilibrates *expected* utility in the two sectors. Migrants forgo a known rural income as part of a gamble on obtaining a higher-paid job in the formal sector; if the job does not materialize, they will be forced into the urban informal sector at a real income below that in the rural sector and will perhaps also experience intermittent open unemployment.

The implications of these alternative views of dualism for tax analysis will be considered below, but it is worth asking whether the available evidence supports the view that labor markets are segmented. This evidence is reviewed in Berry and Sabot (1978) and more extensively in Squire (1981), and the following summary draws heavily on the latter source.

Two important distinctions must be drawn, between unskilled labor and educated labor on the one hand, and between short- and long-run equilibria on the other. The evidence suggests that, for unskilled labor, rural labor markets appear competitive, labor is highly mobile both geographically and occupationally, and unemployment rates are low. Although minimum-wage legislation has distorted the low-paid labor markets in some countries, this feature should not be exaggerated, as this legislation is frequently limited in coverage and effectiveness. Trade union activity may be a more important distortion but has little effect on unemployment, because of the heterogeneity of labor, because of employment opportunities, and because the poor cannot afford the luxury of search unemployment.

Educated labor, in contrast, is often wealthy enough to endure relatively long periods of search unemployment, and unemployment rates for this category are high in many countries. Here the Harris-Todaro explanation of unemployment is more convincing; salary structures for educated workers are frequently inflexible or slow to adapt, as are the expectations of the educated job seekers.

The policy implications of educated unemployment are twofold. Not only would greater flexibility in salary structures be desirable, but the policy of widespread educational subsidy also needs to be reexamined. In chapter 22 Armitage and Sabot examine the case for reducing government subsidies to secondary education in Kenya.

The distinction between the short run and the long run is also important for several reasons. The extreme form of modern sector dualism that occurred in newly independent countries may have been a disequilibrium phenomenon. Over time, real minimum-wage levels, which have been eroded by inflation, have largely eliminated what might now be seen as a temporary aberration. It may also be true that the educated labor market will eventually equilibrate once salary structures and expectations adapt. Certainly the dramatic change in supply and the long lags in the production of educated labor make disequilibrium, perhaps for long periods, understandable. The other reason for attention to the time scale is that the short-run and long-run impacts of tax changes may be quite different, especially on unemployment and in the incidence of the tax. This possibility is explored further below.

An assessment of the nature of labor market dualism is rather difficult. Fields, in chapter 10 below, argues strongly for the applicability of a suitably modified Harris-Todaro view, that is, for modern sector dualism. Heady and Mitra show in chapter 15 that whether or not there is traditional sector dualism may have important consequences for tax design. Squire's (1981) assessment is that there is little evidence for traditional sector dualism, though it may just be hard to observe. It therefore seems appropriate to discuss the tax implications of both views.

Dualism, Capital Market Fragmentation, and the Rate of Savings

In the Lewis model of dualistic development, capital formation and savings take place only in the modern sector, and there only out of profits. Lewis (1954) was interested in answering "the central problem in the theory of economic development," which he stated as understanding the process by which a community that was previously saving and investing 4 or 5 percent or less of its national income turns into an economy in which voluntary saving amounts to about 12–15 percent of national income or more. If the supply of labor is constant at a subsistence-determined real wage, the profit-maximizing capitalists will, in the absence of technical progress, invest some fraction of profits so that the modern sector grows at a steady rate $g = rs$, where r is the net rate of return and s is the fraction of profits saved.[4] The modern sector will grow faster than the traditional sector, its share in GDP will grow, and hence the share of profits and savings will also grow.

The key element in this story is that the traditional sector either does not save or cannot transfer its savings to the modern sector. The lack of financial intermediaries explains the latter (though landlords might save from rental income and transfer this to the modern sector, as Fei and Ranis, 1961, argue). The lack of net saving in the traditional sector is explained by poverty, the shortage of investment opportunities, and/or the institutional structure of the extended family, which makes saving for retirement unnecessary, as the old are supported by their offspring. In this story, the rate of growth of the economy is severely limited by the supply of savings from the initially small modern sector. The fragmented capital market, together with "nonrational" savings behavior in the traditional sector (and of urban workers) gives rise to a serious market failure, for the rate of investment will be inefficiently low. Economists have therefore argued that the government should use its tax power, particularly its ability to tax agriculture by turning the internal terms of trade against them, to raise the rate of investment and growth. This dynamic argument for taxation has been discussed at greater length in chapter 5, which also discusses the statistical evidence on savings and investment.

Income Distribution

It is sometimes argued that, as the level of economic development rises, so income inequality first rises and then falls (as measured, for example, by the Gini coefficient), though the proportion living in absolute poverty (less than some fixed level of purchasing power) falls steadily with increasing per capita income. (See, for example, Nafziger, 1984, chaps. 3 and 5 and the references therein). Other economists have claimed that a characteristic feature of many developing countries is that the mass of the population is fairly uniformly poor, the middle class is very small, and the rich have levels of income comparable to those of people who are reasonably well off in developed countries.

The facts, however, preclude any simple generalization. Some very poor countries have highly unequal income distributions; others exhibit low inequality. If anything, the description given above fits Latin America more than other countries. Thus of the forty-seven low- and middle-income countries for which Ahluwalia (1974) was able to obtain income distribution data, twenty-two are classified as exhibiting high inequality, whereas ten of the fifteen Latin American countries exhibit high inequality (in which the bottom 40 percent receive 10 percent or less of total income while the top 20 percent receive 60 percent or more).

On the other hand, a number of countries have pursued active income redistribution policies and have managed substantially to improve the standard of living of the bottom 40 percent. Several of these, such as Sri Lanka and

Egypt, have done so by issuing food rations that account for a significant fraction of imputed income of the poorest. Also, Asian countries appear to have less inequality at the upper end of the income distribution. Thus of the eight Asian countries listed by Ahluwalia, the highest share of income received by the top 20 percent, was Malaysia (1970) with 56 percent, and the unweighted average was 47 percent.

Size Distribution of Firms

Small-scale enterprises are a characteristic feature of most developing countries, with a large fraction of manufacturing employees (perhaps half or more) employed in firms of fewer than five employees (Little, Mazumdar, and Page, 1984). In some countries, the size distribution of firms is consequently bimodal, with two characteristic types of firms—small, cottage industry workshops, often in the rural or urban informal sector, coexisting with much larger formal sector firms. In many countries a significant fraction of modern firms are foreign owned, especially in the extraction and plantation sectors. In others, the fear of foreign domination severely restricts the inflow of foreign private investment. Designing the correct structure of incentives and taxes on foreign firms is a delicate matter that is considered in greater length by Gersovitz in chapter 23. Similarly, in many countries a large fraction of the modern sector is in the public sector—as much as half in the case of India, for example. Often the size of the public sector is a response to an unwillingness to admit foreign firms and to the small financial base of domestic capital. The public sector thus makes profits (maybe negative) as well as raising tax revenue; it invests in directly productive activities as well as in infrastructure; and as its range of activities widen, so do the problems of coordination and decisionmaking. The size of the public sector sharply raises the question of the proper behavior of public enterprises, their investment and pricing criteria, and the logic for their continued existence in the public sector.

Population Growth, Demographic Structure, and Education Levels

The rate of population growth in poor countries between 1973 and 1983 was 2.0 percent a year and 2.6 percent if India and China are excluded. It was 2.4 percent for middle-income countries and 0.7 percent for industrial market economies (*World Development Report 1985*, table 19). The consequence is a rapidly growing labor force, a high dependency ratio, and a high proportion of the population that is of school age. Furthermore, education, which has expanded until 30 percent of the relevant age group in poor countries are enrolled in secondary education in poor countries (42 percent in middle-income countries), places a heavy burden on public expenditure. On the other hand, high population growth rates imply a low proportion of the population retired and hence a lower burden of support for the old.

Low-income countries have an adult literacy rate of 50 percent, though for sub-Saharan Africa it is only 26 percent, for Latin America 79 percent, and for East Asia 84 percent. These rates can be expected to rise in response to the recent expansion in education.

Imperfect Competition, Trade Distortions, and the Scarcity of Foreign Exchange

Developing countries include some of the most distorted economies, though not all developing countries suffer from these problems, nor are they confined to developing countries. The prevalence of market imperfection is important when judging the applicability of standard competitive tax models and may substantially alter the consequences of tax changes. Although imperfectly competitive behavior is not limited to developing countries, it may be more important than in developed countries for several reasons. First, the scale of the manufacturing sector and the size of the market generally will often be much smaller in developing countries. A process may have a minimum economic scale that is small relative to that of a typical market in a developed country but large relative to that in most developing countries. Its size would not matter for traded goods in the absence of trade barriers, but developing countries in their anxiety to attract foreign investment often provide sufficient protection to ensure profitable domestic production of one, or at most a few, foreign firms, which will then clearly be imperfect competitors.

The other important difference in the nature or degree of distortion in developing countries is that quotas, licenses, and tariff barriers are more prevalent than in developed countries. Often the tariff structure is such as to encourage domestic production of final consumer goods while permitting relatively free imports of capital or intermediate goods. The consequences may perversely generate high rates of effective protection, raise the cost of domestic production, and create a bias against exports (Little, Scitovsky, and Scott, 1970). Instead of reducing the dependence of the country on imports, the tariff structure frequently makes it more vulnerable to fluctuations in export earnings, as the few remaining imports are essential for a significant fraction of production, which must be severely curtailed if the imports cannot be financed. Foreign exchange is frequently perceived as being peculiarly scarce or in excess demand at official exchange rates. It appears so usually because of the inappropriate level of the exchange rate, because of speculative fears about future devaluation caused by rapid domestic inflation, or even because of fears of future currency inconvertibility. Low real rates of interest, a frequent consequence of rapid inflation, may also provoke capital flight and hence excess demand for foreign exchange.

Planning, Public Capital Formation, and the Importance of State-Owned Enterprises

Developing countries appear to attach greater importance to planning than do industrial market economies, and the public sector is often directly responsible for a significant fraction of capital formation. Thus for developing countries for which data are available, the average contribution of state-owned nonfinancial enterprises to GDP has risen from 7 percent at the beginning of the 1970s to 10 percent at the end of the decade, and they now account for at least a quarter of total capital formation (World Bank, 1983, pp. 49–51). Developing countries are not, of course, alone in exhibiting this increase; the centrally planned economies are an extreme case (and historically an important model for planning in developing countries), whereas many European countries plan and have extensive public ownership of the means of production and a large share of public investment in total capital formation.

The standard explanation for planning and the heavy involvement of the public sector in economic activity is market failure, which is argued to be especially acute at low levels of development. Social overhead capital, or infrastructure, typically enjoys substantial economies of scale, is lumpy, must be coordinated with other location-specific investments, and may be difficult or inefficient to supply through the market. Roads are the leading example, but other components of the transport system may share some of these features. Other investments may be too large for private finance—dams, power stations, electricity grids, and ports. They may generate benefits that are hard to capture except through the tax system—roads, irrigation, sanitation, and urban development.

If planning is to be consistent, it will typically attempt to influence private decisions, and many of the distortions noted in the previous sections may be traced to attempts to control or direct private sector decisions in directions favored by the plan.

Consequences of the Special Features of Developing Economies for Tax Design

The modern approach to public finance starts from the assumption that the government (or the decisionmaker) wishes to maximize an individualistic social welfare function in which social welfare is an increasing function of individual utilities, as discussed in chapter 2. If the government had full information about each individual's abilities, endowments, and preferences, and about production possibilities, then it would achieve the social optimum by ensuring efficiency in production and choosing the best distribution of wealth among individuals. Under favorable assumptions (no economies of scale and no other sources of market failure), this goal could be achieved as a competitive equilibrium in a market economy with a suitable set of individually tailored lump-sum taxes and transfers. Governments do not have full information, however, and even if they were successful in eliminating market failures in production and in ensuring competitive behavior and hence production efficiency, they would be faced with an inevitable conflict between equity and efficiency in allocating output among consumers. The government can make redistributive taxes depend only on information revealed by consumers in the course of choosing their hours of work, their occupation, and their income and consumption pattern, and when taxes paid are made to depend on these behavioral responses, they will influence and distort these responses with some loss in efficiency. Taxes may also depend on family size, age, and possibly disabilities, which may in large part be unalterable characteristics.

Optimal tax theory asks how observed market behavior can be used to design the best set of taxes, which, subject to the information available, maximizes social welfare. The crucial question is, what information is available, or rather, what information is both available and admissible. (For a variety of reasons it may be agreed, and possibly constitutionally decreed, that certain information, such as race, sex, religion, credit rating, and so on, may not be used in the design of government policy.) As Stern shows in chapter 2, the design of the tax system may depend sensitively on the information assumed to be available or, equivalently, on the tax instruments that it is feasible to use. The simplest assumption is that taxes depend linearly on purchases (and sales) of goods (and labor). This linearity can be achieved by constant unit purchase taxes, and an income tax (proportional and uniform) would then be unnecessary, as it could be replaced by additional commodity taxes. These restrictions lead to the study of optimal commodity taxation. If the government is free to make uniform lump-sum transfers to individuals, the constraints, and hence the nature of the solution (the design of the tax system), change dramatically. If the government can in addition make income tax rates nonlinear, so that the marginal tax rate depends on the level of income, then again, the solution changes radically, perhaps to the point where commodity taxation is not needed at all. Indeed, the distinctive difference between direct and indirect taxes is not so much on *what* is taxed (personal income or commodity purchases), but on *how* it is taxed and whether the tax rate is individually specific, and hence direct, or not individually specific, and hence indirect. Linear taxes are thus logically seen as indirect taxes, whereas nonlinear taxes, where the rate varies with the individual's consumption level, can act as direct taxes.

Apparently small changes in the information available to the government thus have profound implications for the tax instruments that can be used and for the design of the tax system. The key question to ask in adapting modern tax theory for application in developing countries is what information is available to the tax authorities or could reasonably be collected. With that question in mind, we can examine the list of distinctive characteristics of developing countries. We start on the assumption that we, and the government, are interested in maximizing social welfare. Later we can return to the obviously important question of whether this is a reasonable or plausible assumption.

The Importance of Agriculture

The distinctive features of agriculture for tax purposes are that production requires immobile and inelastically supplied land, that it typically takes place on a large number of separately owned farms, whose size distribution is often very skewed, and that one of its main outputs is food, which is the major consumption item for the poor. In addition, a large fraction of wealth in developing countries consists of land ownership, and the inequality in land ownership thus correlates well with inequality in wealth. Both because the agricultural sector is so important in developing countries and because of these special features, a significant fraction of this book addresses the analysis of agricultural taxation, and the subject is considered extensively in chapters 13 to 19. Thus we can be fairly brief in this chapter.

If land ownership and its productivity were known, then a land tax would be attractive both because taxes on inelastically supplied goods (land services) are nondistortionary and because the tax would fall relatively more heavily on the wealthy, who own disproportionately more land than the poor, many of whom are indeed landless. Clearly this information is locally available, and when the main centers of power were both local and heavily dependent on land, as in feudal societies, land taxes, notably tithes, were a major source of revenue, as Hinrichs (1966) and Wald (1959) both show. With the centralization and urbanization of government, this detailed and local information is no longer so readily available to the central government, though two alternatives remain. The first is to decentralize the tax-collecting power to the local level, where the information remains. The British in India did so by "tax farming" (the title is doubly appropriate). They appointed Zamindars, frequently from the local aristocracy, and paid them a percentage of the land taxes collected. In some cases this right to tax appears to have been auctioned off to the highest bidder (Taylor and others, 1965, pp. 129–30), and the Zamindars typically subcontracted these tax powers. The final result was a system of taxation that extracted most of the agricultural surplus, leaving the peasants at a subsistence level, though only a fraction of the surplus found its way to the central government. Alternatively, land tax revenues can be collected by and for the lowest level of government and can be allocated to expenditure that generates purely local benefits (such as local roads, health, and education).

The second alternative is to collect the necessary information by a land register and cadastral survey (that is, a survey of land value, location, and ownership), as discussed in chapter 13. Clearly, this alternative is likely to be expensive and slow and is likely to require a fairly high level of professional skill and management. Implementation will also be difficult if it is politically opposed by powerful local groups. Because land ownership conveys local political power in agrarian societies, the prospects for a centrally imposed land tax do not look good. Yet in earlier periods land taxes provided a significant fraction of tax revenue, and it is interesting to ask why this is now no longer the case. One possible reason is that the very inelasticity of supply and specificity of the land may make it a potentially very exploitative tax instrument. In decentralized semifeudal societies, where taxes are chosen by the powerful to advance their own objectives, this aspect poses no objection, and land taxes are then attractive. In more centralized societies, however, where the government may wish to alienate neither the local power groups nor the local population, land taxes either will be opposed, if equitable, or will lose their potentially attractive equity features. Hence the relevant question to ask is not whether the information about land value and ownership is potentially available but whether it could be made available in an unbiased form to the central government and whether it could be used to collect a just tax.

The next question to ask is whether rural income can be measured for tax purposes. Three considerable obstacles stand in the way. First, rural income derives from a wide variety of disparate sources, and most rural inhabitants are self-employed for a substantial fraction of time. It is hard to imagine collecting this widely dispersed information and verifying it. Second, much of the income may be in kind (as subsistence consumption, free rations, rights to grazing, and so forth), and many of the expenses needed to produce the income may not be accurately known, let alone recorded, by the taxpayer. Finally, written records are few, literacy cannot be assumed, and income levels are frequently so low that the administrative costs of assessing income could make the enterprise pointless.

If income cannot be taxed, can gross agricultural production be taxed? If so, such a tax might be a reasonable proxy for a land tax (assuming that input costs for a given crop do not vary too much across farms). Again, because food is a major output, and because much of it is either consumed on the farm or marketed locally and informally, the usual answer is that only cash crops marketed through formal channels (coffee, tea, and so on) can be readily taxed on the basis of gross output. In other cases, it is only realistic to imagine taxing the *marketed surplus*, that is, output less local consumption, or even only *exports* (that is, output less domestic consumption). Often this result may be achieved by taxing rural purchases from the modern sector.

The fact that it may be possible only to tax the marketed surplus of the agricultural sector is central to tax design and is considered at length in chapters 13–17. It requires an important change in the standard tax model, because it now becomes necessary to consider rural production as taking place within a producing *and* consuming household, which for many purposes is best considered as a consumer who supplies agricultural goods in exchange for nonagricultural goods. The choice of taxes will also depend on whether it is possible to tax agricultural goods consumed by urban workers at different rates from those imposed in the rural sector, as Heady and Mitra and Sah and Stiglitz show in chapters 15 and 16.

Other Features of the Primary Sector

Extractive industries are typically easier to tax and often generate sizable rents that can be transferred to the public sector. The main problem facing the government is that of measuring the rental element in gross production without distorting the incentive to explore for new deposits or providing opportunities for the concealed transfer of profit through transfer pricing.

Often the industry is foreign owned, and the taxation of foreign profits raises special issues that are considered further below in chapter 23. In many other cases the industry is publicly owned, and rental transfers are then simplified. Because the design of resource taxes is a specialized field not peculiar to developing countries (though arguably more important there), we do not discuss the issue further and instead refer the reader to two recent studies—Garnaut and Clunies-Ross (1983) and Pearce, Sibert, and Walter (1984).

Both agricultural commodities and minerals face unstable and unpredictable world prices, and taxes on primary commodities are likely to yield revenues that fluctuate even more strongly than these commodity prices for the following reasons. For mineral resources, the tax base is effectively profit, which, if production costs are reasonably stable, will be more unstable than prices unless prices and output are negatively correlated—an outcome that is unlikely except for dominant producers or cartel members. For agricultural commodities the government may well feel that the farmer should be shielded from the full effects of world market price instability, in which case the tax, being the difference between a volatile external price and a less volatile internal price, will be more unstable than the international price. This characteristic has several consequences, some rather unexpected. First, the problem of tax design is often changed to one of pricing policy—what price should be guaranteed to agricultural producers, when the export price is unknown, rather than what the export tax rate (or schedule) should be. This reformulation of the question prejudges the issue of how best to deal with commodity price instability. As argued in chapter 18 below, as well as in Newbery and Stiglitz (1981), this is often not the best solution. It also means that tax rates are not only unstable but unpredictable, which complicates the analysis of pricing reform, as chapter 18 shows. Finally, of course, it destabilizes tax revenue. Commodity export revenue will also fluctuate in phase with this tax revenue, and the government will effectively have to decide what to do with these fluctuations in foreign exchange availability, as well as choosing how much of the volatility to accept itself and how much to leave facing the primary producers.

In principle, the answer to both questions is fairly straightforward, and the main problem appears to be the practical one of managing public expenditure effectively. First, the government takes into account international income-averaging facilities, such as the Compensatory Financing Facility of the IMF or Stabex for signatories to the Lomé Convention and calculates the residual fluctuation in its revenue not covered by such schemes. The choice is then to balance the costs and benefits of varying the level of public expenditure and varying the size of foreign exchange reserves (or international debt). Roughly one-third of Papua New Guinea's tax revenue, for example, came from copper in the 1970s and was subject to larger fluctuations than the considerable instability in the price of copper. The government operated a buffer fund, and transferred only a moving average of past tax revenues to the budget, so that most of the fluctuations in tax revenue were absorbed in fluctuations in the reserve level of this fund. The main advantage of making explicit this two-stage procedure was the practical one of containing public expenditure during periods of optimism when tax revenues are high. Other countries, such as Morocco in the mid 1970s, have interpreted sudden price increases of their main mineral export as permanent shifts in level rather than temporary fluctuations and have raised expenditure swiftly only to discover that tax revenues fell as the price boom ended. Because it is typically harder to reduce expenditure than to increase it, this strategy imposes higher adjustment costs than the buffer fund alternative.

Dualism

As I noted above, two aspects of dualism are important for tax analysis: the extent to which transactions within the traditional sector can be taxed and the extent of market segmentation. Market segmentation is discussed below. Here I concentrate on tax constraints. These have already been discussed above and will be examined extensively in chapters 14 and 15. For the present it will be enough to consider one important constraint—the difficulty of taxing labor in the traditional sector. There is, in principle, little difficulty in taxing labor in the modern (or formal) sector. For this purpose the urban informal sector can be considered as a part of the traditional sector. What effect does the restriction on tax powers have on the design of taxes and on their incidence?

In order to examine the sectoral aspect of dualism, as opposed to the market segmentation aspect, suppose that labor markets in each sector are competitive, with wages equal to the marginal product of labor and labor freely mobile between sectors. If labor migrates from the traditional to the modern sector when it is advantageous to do so, then taxes on unskilled labor in the modern sector will effectively increase the cost of employment without reducing the after-tax wage. It is important to stress that the argument does not apply to skilled labor, which would be most unlikely to migrate to the rural sector in response to a small fall in its after-tax income. The incidence of the tax will thus fall almost entirely on profits. In figure 7-1, the marginal product of labor gives the demand for labor in each sector, equal to the after-tax wage. If there are no labor taxes, equilibrium will occur at C, with a wage AC and modern sector employment AL. If labor is taxed in the modern sector but taxes on the rural sector do not change, the equilibrium occurs at D, the after-tax wage falls slightly to DB, modern sector employment declines by ΔL to BL, and profits fall from CFH to DEG. The more elastic the supply of rural labor, the more the tax is shifted to modern sector profits. Such a tax is clearly inefficient, as it encourages inefficiently capital-intensive production in the modern sector and reduces the modern sector investible surplus. Even if the government believes that this fall in private savings can be more than matched by increased public sector saving, it would still be preferable to tax pure profits rather than labor to avoid the distortion (though taxes on foreign investment need careful design, as noted in chapter 23).

Conversely, if the government taxes the rural sector (for example, by

Figure 7-1. *Incidence of a Modern Sector Wage Tax on Unskilled Labor*

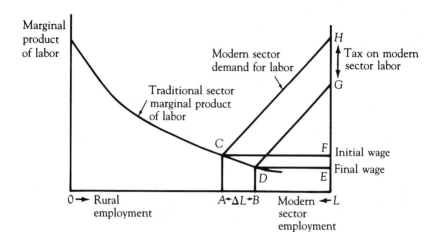

imposing an export tax on the main agricultural product, such as the rice export tax in Thailand), then the supply price of rural labor will be reduced, and there is then a case for taxing urban labor to offset this discrepancy between the supply price of labor and the social opportunity cost of labor. In short, a key feature of dualism is that sector-specific taxes (taxes on agriculture; taxes on urban labor) have repercussions for the other sector that must be carefully traced. Heady and Mitra in chapter 15 show how to modify the standard tax model to accommodate dualism and confirm that dualism has very important consequences for tax design.

Segmentation of the Labor Market

The distinctive feature of labor market segmentation or dualism is the implied market segmentation and consequent sectoral misallocation of labor. Whether or not labor market segmentation is a serious problem in developing countries has been vigorously disputed, and the simplest conclusion is that, although it may not be important in many countries, as Squire (1981) argues, in other countries or periods it may be or may have been important, as Fields claims in chapter 10. Our present purpose is not to resolve the dispute but to discuss how labor market segmentation, if it exists, affects tax analysis apart from the features of dualism just discussed. Market segmentation implies market inefficiency, which in turn implies that public intervention may be able to improve resource allocation. If labor market dualism implies an inefficient allocation of labor, can the government improve this allocation, and if so, how? What are the implications for taxes on labor and for employment policy?

There are, as already mentioned, two polar types of labor market dualism. Traditional sector dualism implies that the inefficiency lies in the rural labor market and that the modern sector labor market is competitive. The wage in the modern sector is equal to the MPL and to the urban supply price. The rural supply price, however, exceeds the rural MPL. Modern sector dualism has the modern sector wage, equal to the MPL, above the urban supply price of labor. (It is also possible to have both types of dualism, with inefficiencies in both labor markets, though for analytical purposes this will usually be equivalent to one polar extreme or the other.)

Traditional Sector Dualism

If the rural supply price of unskilled labor exceeds the rural MPL, and it is not possible to eliminate this inefficiency by direct policies, then the opportunity cost of labor will be below the modern sector wage, with too little modern sector employment. The obvious implication is that unskilled modern sector employment should be subsidized, though because the marginal cost of raising the revenue to pay the subsidies will typically exceed the value of consumption resulting from the extra employment, it will not be desirable to reduce the net cost of modern sector employment to the rural MPL. This issue is central to social cost-benefit analysis in developing countries, and the determination of the accounting or shadow-wage rate, to be used in public sector project appraisal, is one of the distinctive features of the Little and Mirrlees method. Their argument is, briefly, that the shadow wage is likely to be close to the actual wage because the relative value of public funds is likely to be high compared with its value as a subsidy to consumption. (I assume that all other prices are undistorted. Otherwise, care must be taken in measuring the MPL and the extra consumption at accounting prices.) If, in addition, as seems to be the case, rural labor markets are thought to be fairly efficient, then the case for a subsidy is further reduced. If agriculture is heavily taxed on its output, then, as argued above, it may in fact be desirable to tax urban unskilled labor.

Heady and Mitra examine the consequences of traditional sector dualism for tax design in chapter 15 and show that it does indeed imply subsidizing modern sector employment, though this may best be achieved in rather indirect ways, by varying tax rates on sector-specific consumption goods, such as rural and urban services.

Modern Sector Dualism

For the purposes of tax analysis, we must ask several questions about the way the labor market works and equilibrates. First, what determines the modern wage—why is it above the urban supply price of labor, and what relation does it bear to this supply price? Second, how do taxes affect the before- and after-tax modern wage? Third, how does the labor market equilibrate? Is there open unemployment of unsuccessful migrants, who continue to flow into the urban labor pool until the *expected* wage, allowing for the probability of unemployment, is equated with the supply price? Alternatively, does this less attractive alternative take the form of disguised unemployment or employment in the informal urban sector at a wage below the supply price? Yet again, does a failure to find a modern sector job force the migrant to return quickly, so that there is little open unemployment, as seems to be the case in many countries? If the urban informal and rural sectors pay essentially subsistence wages, for example, and if migrants cannot afford to finance spells of unemployment, then there may be little open unemployment despite a considerable wage gap. If access to modern jobs is rationed, according to some characteristic (education, relationship to existing employees, and so forth), rather than randomly allocated to those in the labor pool, then there may be no advantage to unemployment and, again, little open unemployment.

Some of these issues are discussed by Fields in chapter 10, who gives extensive references to the various reformulations of the original Harris-Todaro model. Stiglitz (1974b, 1982b) addresses these questions directly, and the following analysis builds on his models. For the present, all we can do is note how the answers to these questions bear on the question of tax analysis. Again, there are two types of question: what is the incidence of urban labor taxes and agricultural taxes, and how might the inefficiency be reduced by tax policy?

The first requirement is for a clear model or explanation of the wage gap. At least three different explanations have been offered—that the gap is set by institutional factors (trade union pressure, minimum-wage legislation, and so on), that firms optimally set the wage to reduce labor turnover costs (Stiglitz, 1974b), or that firms again optimally set the wage but this time recognize that wages affect labor productivity—the so-called efficiency wage hypothesis (Bliss and Stern, 1978; Mirrlees, 1976; Stiglitz, 1976, 1982b). The least well articulated of these is the institutional explanation. If, for example, the wage is set by minimum-wage legislation, then an urban wage tax may leave the wage unchanged and may reduce the after-tax wage, though the same effect could be achieved more directly by lowering the real value of the minimum wage (perhaps by not raising its nominal value in line with inflation). If the minimum-wage legislation results from effective political pressure or from conscious government preference, then neither course of action may be feasible, though circumstances (and governments) do change, and the real unskilled wage fell dramatically in some Latin American countries during the "debt crisis" of the early 1980s. Similar issues arise if the modern sector wage is set by trade union pressure, though here a wage tax that reduces labor demand may be partly borne by labor if the union is concerned about employment prospects (though not if the union is concerned only with the welfare of the remaining or original members).

In the labor turnover model, there are fixed costs incurred by the modern sector firm when a new worker is hired, and hence labor turnover, which necessitates extra hiring, is costly. The quit rate is argued to decrease as the firm's wage relative to alternative opportunities increases, either elsewhere in the modern sector or in the traditional sector, and as the risk of unemployment when quitting rises. Hence it pays firms to offer a wage above the supply price in order to obtain a "committed," or stable, workforce. In this case the wage gap will either be fixed or will depend on the rural wage rate, and taxes on agriculture will again lower both the supply price of labor and the modern sector equilibrium wage.

Taxes on modern labor have different effects, depending on their form. Let the training cost per worker hired be T, the quit rate r, the firm's after-tax wage w, the rural wage w_a, the average modern sector wage paid by other firms $\bar{w}$, and the rate of unemployment u. Then the total wage cost per worker to the firm is

$$(7\text{-}1) \qquad w^* = \operatorname*{Min}_{w} [w + Tr(w/\bar{w}, w/w_a, u)]$$

where the firm's quit rate depends on the relative attractiveness of alternatives, as argued above. (In equilibrium, $w = \bar{w}$ if firms are similar, and both $\bar{w}$ and u will be endogenously determined. Each firm, behaving competitively, treats $\bar{w}$ and u as exogenous.) A specific tax on employment of τ per worker (for example, for social security) will clearly have no effect on the after-tax wage, w, because for fixed $\bar{w}$, u, the solution to equation 7-1 for w is the same as the solution to

$$(7\text{-}2) \qquad \operatorname{Min} [w + \tau + Tr(w/\bar{w}, w/w_a, u)].$$

It will reduce modern sector employment, however, and therefore ultimately the level of unemployment and may thus have repercussions on w_a and u, in turn affecting $\bar{w}$, but these effects are likely to be small if labor supply is fairly elastic, and the main impact will thus be on profits, as in the earlier models.

Still, an ad valorem wage tax (or tax on urban wage income) will alter the wage chosen by the firm. If the tax rate is t, so the cost of labor is $w(1 + t)$ when the after-tax wage is w, then the firm's problem is

$$(7\text{-}3) \qquad \operatorname*{Min}_{w} [w(1 + t) + Tr(w/\bar{w}, w/w_a, u)]$$

and the firm must now balance a reduction in w in order to lower the tax bill against the cost of losing workers to the rural sector, though it need not worry about the relative attractiveness of other modern sector wage offers. Stiglitz (1974b, pp. 220–21) shows that the effect is likely to be a fall in urban unemployment, an increase in rural output, and possibly, but not necessarily, an increase in total output. The tax on labor will thus be borne partly by labor and partly by profits and may, by reducing unemployment, improve labor allocation.

In the efficiency wage model, the productivity of workers is a function of their wage, as shown in figure 7-2 below. As the wage rate increases, output per man-hour initially rises faster, and wage costs per unit output fall until they are minimized at a wage w^*. Bliss and Stern (1978) have cast considerable doubt

Figure 7-2. *Labor Productivity in the Efficiency Wage Model*

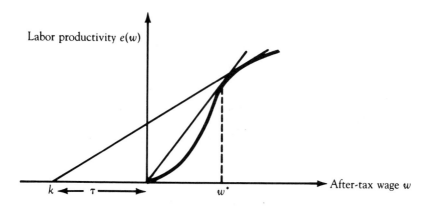

on this approach as a theory of how wages are actually determined if it is interpreted as a nutritional explanation, and it is not clear how other factors would affect the relationship $e(w)$ if alternative explanations were proposed (such as worker morale, adverse selection, and so forth). The main point, however, is that in this simple model the impacts of labor taxes are quite different from those in the turnover model and make plain the importance of explaining the determination of the modern sector wage.

In the efficiency model, let w be the after-tax wage, and suppose that the firm wishes to minimize wage costs per unit output or, in the absence of taxes,

$$(7\text{-}4) \qquad \underset{w}{\text{Min}}\left[\frac{w}{e(w)}\right] = w^*.$$

An ad valorem employment tax at rate t will alter the firm's problem to

$$(7\text{-}5) \qquad \underset{w}{\text{Min}}\left[\frac{w(1+t)}{e(w)}\right] = (1+t)\,\underset{w}{\text{Min}}\left[\frac{w}{e(w)}\right] = (1+t)\,w^*$$

and the after-tax wage, w, will not be changed. The tax will fall entirely on profits. A specific tax, τ, on the other hand, will have an effect on w, for the firm's problem is now

$$(7\text{-}6) \qquad \underset{w}{\text{Min}}\left[\frac{w+\tau}{e(w)}\right]$$

and the solution, shown in figure 7-2, is for the firm to *increase* the after-tax wage in order to increase output per worker and reduce the specific tax per unit of output. Hence the specific tax is more than 100 percent shifted (in terms of unit labor costs) to profits. Finally, taxes on agriculture will have no effect on the modern sector wage (unless there are transfers by modern sector employees to/from rural areas), though they may affect the level of unemployment.

The conclusion to be drawn from these models is that sector-specific taxes may have very different impacts on the cost of employment and the return to employment and migration, depending on the reason for the wage gap. In all these models, labor is inefficiently allocated, and though the level of modern sector employment could in theory be too high or too low, depending on the model and the strength of the various effects, it seems likely that employment is too low. It follows that the shadow wage will differ from (and be lower than) the market wage, though the design of appropriate taxes is complex, as the consequences of the taxes or subsidies depend very sensitively on the reason for the wage gap. Rather than discuss the various cases, we refer the reader to the extensive analysis in Stiglitz (1982b). Some of these issues are also reviewed in chapter 10 by Fields, and others are discussed in chapter 16 by Sah and Stiglitz.

Income Distribution

A highly unequal income distribution has two obvious implications for taxation. First, the significant excess of the income of the rich above mean income suggests that it is desirable to collect substantive tax revenues from the rich. Thus the top decile households in those poor and lower-middle-income countries for which there are data receive 37.5 percent of household income ($SD = 5.6$ percent), whereas in industrial countries the share is 25 percent ($SD = 4$ percent; source: *World Development Report 1984*, table 28). A hypothetical tax of 50 percent on the excess of income above the average and restricted to the top decile would yield revenue of 14 percent of household income in such a developing country, compared with only 7½ percent in an industrial country. These calculations are of course illustrative and do not clinch the case for higher tax rates in the presence of greater before-tax income inequality, which should properly balance the advantages of raising revenue against the disincentive effects. Thus stated, the problem concerns the design of the optimal income tax, first formulated by Mirrlees (1971) and reviewed by Stern in chapter 2 (see also Stern, 1976). Mirrlees and Stern show that, in the models considered, greater inequality in income-earning ability did indeed result in higher optimal tax rates, and their findings support these crude calculations.

The second implication is closely related but raises different problems. If a significant fraction of the population is very poor, then on redistributive grounds there may be a good case for income transfers or subsidies. This statement must be qualified in two ways. First, the value of revenue for investment purposes may be very high in a tightly savings-constrained economy, providing that it has attractive investment possibilities available. Revenue for investment and growth may therefore take priority over current redistribution, or put another way, there may be a better case for redistributing from the rich today to consumers in the future via investment rather than to the poor today at the expense of investment. This important issue is discussed at greater length in chapter 5 and is usually described as the tradeoff between equity and growth. Cline (1972) attempted to quantify this tradeoff for four

Latin American countries. He assumed that income taxes would be used to redistribute income to the poor and estimated the likely fall in savings, investment, and growth rates, making assumptions favorable to the hypothesis that these effects would be most adverse. He found a large fall in the predicted growth rates of three countries but observed that the absolute income levels of the poorest 70 percent of the population would be higher under these redistributive policies for between thirty and sixty years. In his later survey of other simulation studies, he concluded that the impact of redistribution on growth was likely to be very slight (Cline, 1975). The second qualification is that, the larger the fraction of the population in poverty and the more uniform the distribution of income among members of this group, the more costly it will be to improve their standards of living, and the more attractive the option of redistribution over time by growth appears.

Thus great inequality provides a motive for higher taxes on the rich, and possibly transfers to the poor, but are either of these options feasible? Musgrave in chapter 9 notes some of the problems involved in taxing the rich, and they revolve around three important features of developing countries. The first is that a substantial fraction of their income may come from capital, which is often internationally mobile. High taxes on capital income may thus encourage capital flight. Income derived from internationally marketable skills is likewise in potentially elastic supply, which again limits their taxability. Second, much of the income is entrepreneurial income, which is hard to measure and thus hard to tax. Finally, the rich are powerful and are often the final arbiters of the design of the tax system, which will frequently be sprinkled with loopholes that favor tax avoidance by the rich. It is notable that the theory of optimum income taxation both assumes a closed economy and observable income and applies better to immobile employees than to entrepreneurs. It also ignores the whole issue of savings, which, as chapter 5 shows, further complicates the desirability of taxing entrepreneurial and capital income.

The other side of the income distribution question is the feasibility of making transfers to the poor. Whether or not such transfers are feasible makes a considerable difference to the design of indirect taxes, as Stern argues in chapter 2. Deaton discusses the subject further in chapter 4. If it is feasible to transfer income to the poor (or to everyone), then it may be desirable to collect (indirect) taxes as efficiently as possible, largely ignoring distributional considerations, as these are better met by the expenditure side of the budget or by income transfers and specific subsidies. Goode (1984, pp. 288–95) argues that the expenditure side of the budget is potentially important for redistribution in developing countries. If it is not possible to make lump-sum transfers to individuals, then the taxes must take into account the distributional consequences and the tradeoff between equity and efficiency in the collection of revenue.

Why might it be difficult to make lump-sum subsidies? According to one argument, it is difficult to check that claimants have not registered under a variety of names. Where countries have good records of births and deaths, or a system of identity cards, then there is less of a problem than elsewhere, especially where literacy rates are not high. Nevertheless, as mentioned above, several countries operate ration schemes of various types (Sri Lanka, India, Bangladesh, and Egypt), and their experience suggests that it may be possible to offer lump-sum subsidies in some form, if it is considered desirable to do so. Often the subsidies take the form of food rations or kerosene rations (Sri Lanka), and in some cases (notably in Sri Lanka in the late 1970s) these rations are freely marketable and hence are essentially equivalent to income transfers (Gavan and Chandrasekara, 1979; Goode, 1984, pp. 289–90). Where the rations are not resalable and are restricted to income-inferior foodstuffs, they may be an effective way of targeting the subsidies to the poorest group (Timmer, Falcon, and Pearson, 1983, pp. 65–76 and references therein).

A crucial question to ask of income transfers is whether they are truly lump sum and universal or are contingent upon some economic choice, such as urban residence. If the transfers have only partial coverage and are allocated on the basis of income or location, then their incidence may be quite different. In an extreme case, subsidies to the urban poor may only lower the cost of urban employment, without raising urban consumption levels. Whether or not the transfers are truly lump sum also bears directly on the argument for uniform commodity taxation made by Deaton in chapter 4.

Size Distribution of Firms

The main consequence of the relative importance of small, informal, and often transient firms is that they are hard to tax by comparison with the large formal sector firms. It may be possible to tax them on a presumptive basis, as Musgrave notes in chapter 9, but if not, then the presence of firms producing untaxed substitutes for taxed goods limits the desirability of taxing these goods. The difficulty of tracing small firms also argues for a value-added tax structure, which makes it feasible at least to tax inputs into these small firms and also increases compliance by these firms, inasmuch as their existence can now be inferred from the VAT returns of other firms. Gil Díaz in chapter 12 notes that one of the main effects of the 1977 Mexican tax reform, in which cascaded sales taxes were replaced by VAT, was the increase in compliance. (His analysis raises the important question as to whether this increased compliance resulted from the tax reform itself or from the increased interest in and energy devoted to fiscal matters, which also led to the tax reform.)

Population Growth, Demographic Structure, and Education Levels

Rapid population growth has consequences for saving and public expenditure (on education, social security, and so forth) that have already been mentioned. It affects the labor market in a variety of ways. A rapid expansion of secondary education often leads to disequilibrium in the market for educated labor, as remarked above and as discussed by Fields in chapter 10. The frequently high level of subsidy for secondary education is not only costly but often inequitable and hence a good candidate for reduction, as Armitage and Sabot argue below in chapter 22. Low levels of past education in turn mean low levels of literacy, so that certain kinds of income and profits taxation become problematic (though literacy itself does not guarantee their feasibility). If educated labor is in scarce supply, then, because tax collectors need to be educated and the educated wage may be relatively much higher compared with the unskilled wage than in developed countries, it follows that administrative costs per unit of revenue will in general be higher in developing countries. This in turn limits the range of taxes that are administratively cost effective and helps explain the differences in tax structures between developed and developing countries.

The higher cost of administrative expertise is amplified by the greater inequality in income and wealth distribution, for the top few percent of taxpayers are likely to have incomes that are a very large multiple of standard civil service salaries and can afford to offer relatively more tempting bribes than the rich in a more egalitarian society. When the British imposed a tax-collecting service on the defeated Chinese nation in the nineteenth century to collect reparations, they replaced the inefficient local bureaucracy with a highly paid, high-prestige meritocratic civil service. In return for the high pay, its officials were subject to close audit and, if they were discovered accepting bribes, were dismissed and returned in disgrace, having lost their favored station in society. This penalty was sufficient to ensure honesty and integrity, and the tax collection was a model of efficiency rarely matched. Probably its collection costs were not very high per unit of revenue raised, though its salary levels may have made the system look expensive.

Imperfect Competition, Trade Distortions, and the Scarcity of Foreign Exchange

The standard tax model assumes perfect competition and nonincreasing returns, yet imperfectly competitive behavior (and economies of scale) may be relatively more important in developing countries than in developed countries. The assumption of perfectly competitive behavior plays two roles in the theory of optimum taxation. First, if producers take prices as given, and if the prices they face are undistorted, then they will produce efficiently. Second, competitive bidding for the (privately or publicly owned) factors and constant returns will eliminate (supernormal) profits, and hence changes in prices that induce changes in patterns of production will not have any effect on profits. Together these consequences imply that, if producers and consumers can be confronted with different prices, then the issues of equity and efficiency can be separated when policies directed at producers are chosen. It is desirable to confront producers with efficient—that is, undistorted—prices, because doing so will result in efficient production without adversely affecting the government's ability to redistribute income by direct and indirect taxes. Taxes on producers are therefore unnecessary and undesirable.

Imperfectly competitive producers, on the other hand, produce inefficiently and in some models make profits. Taxes on inputs and outputs may affect this inefficiency and if so offer the prospect of improving efficiency. Changes in trading possibilities that lead producers to change their pattern of production may be expected to change profits and hence the distribution of income, and so the government can no longer separate equity and efficiency considerations when choosing its production tax policies. In order to determine the effect of taxes on production choices and profits, however, we need a theory of the imperfectly competitive firm, and there is as yet no single satisfactory model available. Different models of the firm lead to different predictions of the effects of taxes. The problem is complicated because imperfect competition presupposes barriers to entry, notably economies of scale, and much may hinge on the effect of taxes on these barriers. As already noted in chapter 1, tariff or quota reductions may, by lowering entry barriers to foreign competition, greatly alter the domestic competitive structure, increasing efficiency, lowering prices, and lowering profits.

The other feature of imperfect competition that is important for the analysis of tax reform is the incidence of various taxes (or, more precisely and less ambitiously, the incidence of tax changes). In perfect competition with constant returns, taxes affect output or factor prices (or both) in relatively simple ways. In the simplest case of one nonproduced factor and a closed economy, the impact of output (consumption) taxes falls entirely on consumer prices, as shown in chapter 2. In a small open economy, output taxes on exportable goods have no effect on the export price and are shifted backward onto the fixed factors, with important distributional and price consequences, as Hughes shows in chapter 20.

Taxes on imperfectly competitive firms may be shifted forward in part, in whole, or by more than 100 percent, depending on the curvature of demand curves, the nature of competition, the mode of behavior of the firms in the industry, and the conditions of entry (see Seade, 1985, and Stern, 1985). It is therefore more complicated to trace through the consequence of tax changes on prices, though Stern argues in chapter 3 that the assumption of 100 percent shifting of output taxes represents a plausible compromise between the predictions of alternative models.

Trade distortions, such as import tariffs, quotas, export taxes, differential exchange rates, and foreign exchange rationing, are much more important in developing countries than in developed countries and raise the following critical question. Because most developing countries are too small to affect import prices, there is no case on optimal tariff grounds for anything except an export tax on those (few) goods for which the country has some monopoly power (Brazilian coffee, Ghanaian cocoa, Indian tea, and so forth). For such countries, it is a standard result of modern trade theory that trade taxes (except for these optimal export taxes) are inferior to consumption taxes for redistributive purposes and are inferior to more direct instruments for correcting domestic distortions.[5] Why, then, are trade distortions so prevalent, and does their prevalence suggest that tax policy is shaped in important ways by factors other than those considered in this book?

An explanation for the prevalence of these trade distortions might include the following components. First, it is usually easier to tax goods at their point of entry into a country than at their point of consumption (or sale to final consumer). Hence trade taxes are administratively preferred to consumption taxes and would be equivalent to consumption taxes if domestic producers were also subject to the same tax and the good was not used as an intermediate input (or was eligible for a rebate if so used). It may therefore be preferable to reform taxes by introducing these domestic producer taxes and rebates rather than switching to consumption taxes (provided that it is possible to administer a system of rebates without extensive fraud).[6] Second, the trade taxes may have been chosen as a response to a balance of payments crisis. If so, then the issue of reform consists in finding the appropriate exchange rate and fiscal balance at which the tariffs are no longer necessary, and the problem is one of "structural adjustment" in the language of the World Bank and the IMF. Third, the tariffs may have been designed to encourage foreign firms to set up domestic production, which generates profits that can be taxed locally rather than by the foreign government. This issue is discussed in more detail in chapter 23, where the conclusion that these tariffs are inferior to more direct instruments is confirmed. Similarly, tariffs designed to encourage domestic producers to set up, and designed to ensure that they have adequate profits to finance their investment, are again inferior to alternative solutions to capital market imperfections and the "infant industry" problem, as discussed by Baldwin (1969) and in chapter 5 on dynamic tax issues.

Finally, local producers may be successful in lobbying for protection that raises their profits. If so, then again the standard argument is that protection is an inefficient instrument to use, either to offset the distortions that provide their legitimate case for corrective action or to provide transfers where no such corrective action is needed. This argument, however, ignores an important issue, that of credibility or permanence. If a firm lobbies successfully for some assistance, then it would prefer such assistance to be long lasting and dependable. Straight subsidies will be repeatedly questioned every time public expenditure is under scrutiny, because it will show up as an outflow from the budget. Tariff protection, on the other hand, apparently generates revenue, and the subsidy (the difference between the revenues that an equal-rate consumption tax would yield and the actual tariff revenue) is concealed and hence is less vulnerable to scrutiny. Moreover, the more complex the tariff structure, the less obvious it will be how best to make gradual reforms. Hence there is a positive advantage to such complexity from the viewpoint of the protected firm (assuming that in fact it is effectively protected).

The practical issue of tariff reform then resolves into a series of questions.

First, is it practically feasible to remove unwarranted protection or to replace it by less costly alternatives? If so, is it administratively feasible to replace tariffs by consumption taxes (or their equivalent)? If so, then consider eliminating production distortions by switching to consumption taxes and then ask whether the implied consumption taxes could not be further reformed. If the answer to either question is no, then the problem is the more difficult one of choosing the direction of reform, given the feasibility constraints.

Planning, the Public Sector, and the Problem of Coordination

I noted above the greater importance of state-owned enterprises, public capital formation, and planning in developing countries. Their importance may be a cause of many of the distortions encountered in developing countries. What are the implications of these features for tax analysis? In the case of public capital formation or production by state-owned enterprises, there are two direct implications for tax analysis. First, the difference between the market price and the social marginal cost of a publicly supplied good or service is probably best treated as a tax, because it accrues as public revenue. (The alternative is to treat the revenue received by different public enterprises as distinct categories of income with different shadow values. Although this procedure would imply inefficiency in the organization of the public sector, it may be a more realistic description. Earmarked taxes, such as road fund taxes, share the same characteristics.) As such, public sector pricing policy can be analyzed in the same way as tax reform, using the techniques set out and illustrated in this book. Thus it would be desirable to distinguish between the prices charged to other producers and to final consumers. If the modern sector faces undistorted prices, then it will be desirable to set public sector prices to producers at marginal cost, but it may also be desirable to charge higher prices to final consumers (that is, to levy positive taxes on these goods). For goods such as electricity or gas, such price discrimination may take place in the absence of explicit taxes, though it may be preferable for both accountability and control to require uniform prices and explicit taxes on purchases by final consumers. In some countries public sector prices are clearly well below efficient levels even for consumers and may be a major source of revenue problems for the public sector. Increasing these prices and levying taxes on consumption may be a very low-cost source of additional revenue.

The other main implication of the presence of a large public sector for tax analysis is that funds will be required for public investment. Part of this will come from public sector profits, but the higher the rate of growth of demand for public sector outputs, the more pressing the demands for public investment will be. The result will be an increase in the shadow price of government revenue and an increase in the need for tax revenue.

Most developing countries are mixed economies, and planning, if it is to be consistent, will need to influence private decisions. In principle this causes no problem, since the objectives that guide the choice of tax policy should be the same as those guiding the planners and should require the same market prices and taxes. In practice there is likely to be a real problem of coordinating the policies used to guide the private sector in the planned direction and to guide the tax system, which also influences the private sector. Again, this problem is not confined to developing countries.

The Relationship between Tax Structure and the Level of Development

One obvious way to see whether these various characteristics of developing countries affect the way in which taxes can be raised is to study the structure of taxation and its relation to the level of development. Since the work of Hinrichs (1966) and Musgrave (1969), there have been a large number of such studies (recently surveyed and updated by Tait, Grätz, and Eichengreen, 1979). Tanzi, in chapter 8, presents the best available statistical information on the tax structure of eighty-six developing countries, drawing on the IMF's published and unpublished data.

Musgrave's argument was that lack of availability of "tax handles," that is, administratively simple ways of collecting revenue, might limit revenue collection at low levels of income, but he noted that these limitations should become less severe as the economy develops. Most attempts to account for the share of tax revenue in GDP regress this share on proxies for possible tax handles. The evidence in Tait and others (1979) suggests that the tax share is positively correlated with the share of mining in GDP and also with the share of nonmineral exports to GNP. Perhaps surprisingly, the tax share is not significantly correlated with per capita income nor with the share of agriculture in GDP. Moreover, even these relationships are significant only for countries with GNP of less than $10 billion (fifty-one of the sixty-three countries studied, period 1972–76), and with income per capita less than $750 (fifty-six of the sixty-three countries, same period). Changes in the tax share could be explained by three main factors: changes in the price of primary exports, changes in their volume, and changes in the tax regime on these exports. The evidence thus (weakly) supports the tax-handle explanation and points to the importance of mineral taxation and trade taxation.

Tanzi finds that the structure of taxation also depends (weakly) on the level of development. Thus income taxes are weakly correlated with GNP/head, though personal income taxes are a very small fraction of GNP in developing countries, averaging less than 2 percent of GNP, or 11 percent of tax revenue, and less than 5 percent of GNP in all but three countries. Corporate income taxes are relatively more important, though, yielding 18 percent of tax revenue. Export taxes appear to be an alternative to corporate taxes in that those countries with high export taxes have very low corporate tax revenues and vice

versa. This finding suggests that mineral exports are typically taxed by corporation taxes, whereas agricultural exports, not surprisingly, are easiest to tax by
export taxes. Indirect taxes are relatively more important, with domestic sales
taxes accounting for 26 percent of taxes, and taxes on foreign trade (mainly
import duties) yielding 33 percent. Foreign trade taxes are negatively correlated with income per capita and the share of domestic sales taxes, which is
consistent with the view that, as development proceeds and domestic production of import substitutes becomes more important, domestic sales taxes will
account for a larger share of indirect tax revenue.

The implication of these findings is that corporation taxes, and particularly
taxes on minerals, are important in developing countries, though, as we
remarked above, the taxation of minerals is a specialized topic on which we
defer to existing studies. Personal income taxes are relatively unimportant, and
we have relatively little to say about them. Indirect taxes are of overwhelming
importance, and much of the book is devoted to their study. This dependence
on indirect taxes may explain why neither the share of agriculture nor the level
of income per capita has a statistically significant effect on the tax share, for it
is as easy (or as hard) to tax the agricultural sector using indirect taxes on their
purchases as it is to tax the nonagricultural sector. The dependence on indirect
taxes suggests also that it may be difficult to tax rural and urban consumers at
different rates, though even if it were possible to do so, the *level* of taxes on
each sector might not be very different, especially given the link between them
created by labor migration. Because indirect taxes are likely to be less progressive than income taxes, it is not so surprising to find little association between
the tax share and the level of per capita income, though the tax share notably
varies widely across countries of similar income levels, suggesting that other
factors must be quite important as well.

It is also worth noting that the "structure of taxation" is itself an elusive
concept, because the same economic and fiscal consequences may often be
achieved in apparently very different ways. Thus a tax structure consisting of a
proportional income tax and no indirect taxes would be equivalent to an
alternative structure in which there is no direct taxation but uniform indirect
taxes. Thus the apparently crucial distinction between direct and indirect
taxes is not clear-cut, and it may be more useful instead to distinguish between
taxes that are nonlinear functions of personal variables such as income or
expenditure (true direct taxes) and those that are linear and potentially
equivalent to indirect taxes. Even the tax share in GDP is an ambiguous measure
of fiscal impact, for taxes that are used to finance transfers or subsidies are
equivalent to (perhaps more complex) income taxes with exemptions that
yield lower gross revenue. Nontax instruments that lower the market price of
factors (such as overvalued exchange rates) will lower the apparent cost of
government expenditure and may be equivalent to higher levels of taxation
and expenditure in a less distorted economy. Indeed, the close connection
between distortions, which generate discrepancies between market and

shadow prices, and taxes, is further illuminated in chapters 3 and 15. This
equivalence is stressed by the notion of a "shadow tax," defined and discussed
above.

Thus part of the unexplained variation in tax rates and tax structures across
countries of similar economic structure may be explained by the ambiguity in
measuring these concepts. Another obvious explanation is that governments
differ either in their objectives or in the strength of the political constraints
that limit their pursuit of these objectives. If so, are these features relevant
when we apply the modern approach to tax analysis?

Differences in Objectives and Political Constraints

The modern approach assumes that the objective is to maximize social
welfare, which is taken to be an increasing function of individual welfare.
Furthermore, an individual's welfare is assumed to depend on that individual's
consumption (and effort expended in working), and for most purposes it is
assumed that the individual chooses consumption and work to maximize this
utility.[7] Optimal tax theory draws a sharp distinction between cases in which it
is desirable to promote efficiency (because to do so does not compromise the
prospect of improving equity) and cases in which efficiency must be sacrificed
in the pursuit of equity. Thus trade taxes and taxes on intermediate goods that
introduce inefficiencies into production will be undesirable unless they provide
additional leverage over the distribution of welfare, which they will not,
provided that production is competitive and consumers can be taxed on their
consumption. These efficiency results only require social welfare to be increasing in individual welfare, and it is not necessary to be more specific about the
form of the social welfare function. In cases where equity and efficiency must
be balanced, as in the design of direct and indirect taxes on consumers, the tax
rates will obviously depend on the exact form of the social welfare function.

The analysis of tax reform makes less stringent demands on the specification
of the form of the social welfare function for two reasons. First, if the object is
to identify directions in which to change various taxes that will improve social
welfare, the answer may often be fairly insensitive to the exact specification of
the social welfare function. Second, the evaluation of a tax reform consists in
predicting the consequences and then in valuing them. There is nothing in
principle to limit the set of consequences to just the changes in individual
consumption levels, though this would be the natural strategy when evaluating
the change in social welfare. Thus in studying agricultural price reform in
Korea in chapter 17, Braverman and his coauthors claim that the Korean
government is interested not only in consumer welfare but also in the degree of
self-sufficiency of the country in cereal production. Because consumer welfare
depends on production and consumption levels of cereals, among other things,
it is straightforward to calculate the effect on aggregate production, consump-

tion, and hence self-sufficiency in the course of calculating the welfare impact. The obvious problem is that of weighing an objective such as self-sufficiency against consumer welfare.

The main question we need to ask when examining the economic objectives of developing countries is how far they can be accommodated within the individualistic welfare-based approach of modern tax analysis. The view taken in this book is that most of the apparent differences between stated objectives and those embodied in the standard social welfare function arise from two sources. First, many of the stated objectives are proximate rather than ultimate objectives, useful for organizing the tasks of government but not inconsistent with the ultimate objective of increasing social welfare. Second, government is the art of the possible, and the distribution of political power may severely restrict possibilities. Let us consider the first argument in more detail.

Many countries argue that their overriding economic objective is to raise the rate of growth by encouraging investment. This goal is quite consistent with the ultimate objective of trying to improve the intertemporal distribution of consumption in circumstances where it is believed that the market-determined levels of savings and investment are too low. Social cost-benefit analysis has developed techniques to appraise investment projects that take into account this savings constraint while exhibiting the same social welfare foundation as modern tax theory.

Similarly, developing countries (and developed countries) are frequently concerned with employment creation, apparently as a separate objective. Again, the cost-benefit response is to argue that unemployment is undesirable because it leads to low consumption, and on social welfare grounds it is desirable to raise the consumption levels of the unemployed. Often the most efficient way to do this is by creating a demand for labor, recognizing that the social opportunity cost of employment (or the *shadow-wage rate*) may, for various reasons, be below the market wage. Thus the government's objective of raising the level of employment may reflect its desire to improve the distribution of income, given the existence of various labor market imperfections. If unemployment results in a deterioration of skills and self-respect, then these are aspects of intertemporal productivity and preferences.

Similarly, most proximate goals encountered in development plans or policy statements can be seen as summarizing in tangible form the consequences of pursuing social welfare in a distorted economy facing particular constraints. The advantage of listing these proximate objectives such as raising the rate of investment, increasing employment, increasing exports, reducing the rate of inflation, and so forth, is that they are concrete and recognizable objectives in a way that raising social welfare is not. The disadvantage is that the desirability of these objectives depends on their effects on individuals, which can only be satisfactorily measured through the ultimate objective of raising social welfare.

The most problematic proximate objective that quite clearly has a profound influence on the choice of taxes is the objective of raising domestic *production*, as opposed to raising consumption levels. Tariffs, quotas, import licenses, and the whole structure of trade protection are often defended as the means by which the objective of encouraging domestic production is best achieved, but why is domestic production to be encouraged, and is trade protection the best way to do it? Here we need only summarize the arguments explained above in connection with trade protection. Briefly, trade protection is normally inferior to more direct policies that address the relevant market failure but may be defended on grounds of administrative cost or credibility if the alternative policies are either administratively cumbersome or if durable guarantees are required. The proximate goal of encouraging domestic production is consistent with the view that market failures of various sorts impede the pursuit of efficiency, but this proximate goal is a very poor guide to policy by itself.

A closely related proximate goal already mentioned is the desire for self-sufficiency. Here the argument appears to be that domestic production may reduce the level of risk facing the economy compared with reliance on the uncertainties of foreign trade, and in the absence of a complete set of insurance markets, there is no guarantee that the unaided market will choose the right portfolio of domestic production and imports. Once more, the standard argument is that specific intervention is preferable to general and inefficient intervention. If domestic production of a particular good provides insurance to the economy, then there is a case for subsidizing its production directly where the market fails to reward such activities adequately. Thus grain merchants will store grain in the expectation of selling at a profit during periods of scarcity, and their storage provides some insurance against such scarcity. They may store too little, however, because the social value of grain during scarcity (avoiding starvation) may greatly exceed the market value of the grain, which is limited by the ability to pay of those who are starving (see Newbery and Stiglitz, 1981, chaps. 29 and 30, and 1982).

This last defense of protection—of reducing risk, or vulnerability to external shocks—effectively illustrates the importance of clarifying the ultimate objective (social welfare) rather than relying on a proximate objective (reduced dependence on imports). It forces one to ask about the *cost* of risk or the benefit of reducing risk and also about the most cost-effective way of reducing the risk. There are many examples where domestic production reduces the economy's dependence on final consumption goods but greatly increases its dependence on intermediate imports, thus reducing the economy's flexibility. The costs of external shocks may considerably increase as a result.

One final argument for encouraging the domestic production of apparently comparatively disadvantageous goods is peculiarly difficult to evaluate—the argument of national pride, or self-respect. In part the argument may reflect the belief that useful skills will be learned, that useful information about production possibilities will be acquired, or that the vulnerability of the economy will be reduced. In part it may ultimately be a pure collective consumption good, a feeling of well-being enjoyed by the citizenry when contemplating their national achievements. Both types of benefits can in principle be accommodated within the individualistic social welfare approach with the same advantages as before. The argument that some category of production has some of these listed benefits is no longer enough to justify its protection or subsidy, for what matters is whether this particular activity generates more benefits, or benefits that are more valuable, than those of the activities that it might displace. In short, it should compel its advocates to quantify and compare when making their case.

It is obviously impossible to examine the whole range of objectives that governments have advanced at various times and places, but this partial list suggests two conclusions. First, all the proximate goals considered above could be reinterpreted in terms of their effect on the level and/or distribution of consumption, and the reasons for identifying the specific goals can be traced to possible market failures. As such, they will automatically be included in any comprehensive social welfare–based approach. Second, if any proximate goal cannot be so reinterpreted, then we would have grave doubts about accepting it.

To summarize, the advantage of the social welfare–based approach is that it is, in principle, comprehensive; it provides a natural way of comparing and combining various proximate objectives; and it reminds us that policies have costs as well as benefits and that what matters is the size of the net benefit. Proximate goals may be more concrete and may lend themselves to administrative decentralization but too frequently ignore the cost side of the policies. As a result, policymakers may fail to quantify the benefits or may fail to search out and choose between alternative ways of achieving the benefits.

Clearly, however, countries adopt policies that do not appear to advance their stated objectives and that it would be hard to defend as increasing social welfare. In many cases the simplest interpretation is that the policies were chosen to advance the special interests of unrepresentative coalitions. The existence of such coalitions pursuing their own interest rather than that of the nation is a fact of life and imposes possibly severe political constraints on the kinds of reforms that it might be possible to persuade the government to undertake. Although political constraints are clearly important, most economists feel uneasy about taking them into account. Part of the reason is that they are not well understood—by economists, at least. Particular constraints may persist over quite long periods yet may suddenly change. They may be more apparent than real, for there are success stories involving tax reforms that have been achieved despite the opposition of apparently strong interests. The Mexican example discussed in chapter 12 exhibits some of these features. More worrying, policy decisions now—to create a structure of licenses and quotas, for example—may lead to the emergence of new interest groups, which constrain future choices. Nevertheless, as Bird (1974) has persuasively argued, it can be highly counterproductive to ignore the political feasibility of a given proposal. If one tax is theoretically superior to another but is politically less feasible, then to recommend it may mean that the chance to improve the tax system is lost. Bird was interested in the apparent paradox that, although land taxes appear ideal for developing countries, their importance as revenue sources has steadily declined as they shifted from being a dominant source of government revenue, in some countries at least, to being a universally negligible source, as they are at present. This paradox was also noted by Wald in his earlier book on the taxation of agricultural land (Wald, 1959). Their diagnoses and recommendations, however, diverge sharply, for Wald ascribes the decline to a failure to index the land tax and a mistaken switch to other modes of agricultural taxation. He concludes by recommending an "ideal" land tax that would tax land on its presumptive net income at a rate related to the income or wealth of its owner. This presumptive net income, or rent, would be deduced from the fertility of the land and its proximity to markets (that is, its productive potential and the farm-gate prices for its products).

Bird (1974, chap. 13) takes issue with both the diagnosis and the conclusion. In his view, political opposition is crucial for understanding the reluctance of governments to restore land taxes to their earlier role and is arguably responsible for the apparent administrative inability to collect the necessary information and enforce collection, which is usually held to be the proximate reason for the poor performance of land taxes. Moreover, Wald's ideal tax is particularly ill suited to developing countries, because its progressive intent will be the more strongly resisted by large landed interests and the complexity of the information it requires makes it easy for such interests to delay its introduction, usually indefinitely. Bird's ideal is, in contrast, to aim for relatively simple taxes, based on simple, even crude valuation techniques, supplemented by as many benefit taxes and user charges as possible. We shall return to this issue of land taxation in chapter 13, but for the moment let us consider several important lessons suggested by Bird's careful and well-documented study.

First and most obviously, a tax that adversely affects the ruling elite is likely to be resisted where alternative taxes are less adverse for this group. If the tax is enacted, it may be accompanied by a variety of exemptions and loopholes that substantially alter its distributive impact and may make it undesirable.

The second point is that if a proposed tax reform has a potentially significant perceived impact on a small and well-defined group, then the group may find it cheaper to dissuade the government from the reform than to acquiesce and pay the tax. The conditions under which an interest group will form and devote resources to influencing the government's decision have been set forth by Olson (1965) and others and have been found to be empirically relevant in various studies of lobbying for protective tariffs. A corollary of this approach is that reforms may become feasible if circumstances change, and as the balance of power shifts with changes in economic structure, different taxes become feasible.

The last lesson is that one of the basic arguments of welfare economics may have to be reversed in certain circumstances. The argument is that, if an inefficient tax can be replaced by an equal-yield but more efficient tax, then it should be unanimously supported as an example of a Pareto-improving change. If we take this view, it is very difficult to understand why relatively inefficient taxes such as taxes on agricultural marketed surplus or exports are not replaced by nondistortionary land taxes. Why cannot the interest groups be bought off by the gain in efficiency released by the reform?

The answer is that the taxpayer views the results quite differently. From the taxpayer's point of view, the attraction of a highly inefficient tax is that it limits the extent to which the government can reduce the individual's welfare, whereas there may be no such limit with an efficient tax. In short, the taxpayer mistrusts the statement that the reform will be an equal-yield reform and may believe (quite logically) that, if the reform reduces the inefficiency or social cost of raising more revenue, then the government will wish to increase taxes.

Administrative Capacity and the Problem of Tax Evasion

One of the most important constraints limiting the choice of taxes is the administrative capacity of the tax authorities. There is little we can add to the recent and very thorough discussion of the problem presented by Radian (1980), but a number of points are worth remarking. Tax theory emphasizes the importance of information for the design of taxes, but this information must be collected, the tax liability calculated, and payment enforced. Two of the most difficult problems are to collect and process the information efficiently and to audit, assess, and enforce the taxes in such a way that compliance is increased and evasion reduced. These problems can be greatly reduced by attracting high-quality staff in sufficient numbers, with the right facilities (essentially a good institutional memory) and a well-defined tax law with the means for enforcement. As I noted earlier, these facilities are likely to be relatively scarcer in developing countries than in rich countries and thus more expensive, so that the range of cost-effective taxes is narrower. Because fewer skilled personnel are required to implement a routinized and stable tax system than one in a state of flux, tax reforms are likely to be administratively more expensive in developing countries, and the case for stability and simplicity is relatively stronger.

Several points emerge strongly from Radian's study. Revenue departments often lack the flexibility and the funds to attract and keep the right caliber of personnel, even though it would be highly cost effective to do so. The tax structure is typically complex and in a state of flux. As a result information is processed slowly, audits are rare, and hence enforcement is lax and compliance low. There is, on the one hand, great scope for increasing the administrative efficiency of tax collection, though on the other hand we have considerable evidence that attempts to do so are often ineffective. A large part of the explanation must be that the political will to improve the system is lacking, though the role of bureaucratic inertia (uniform salary scales, security of tenure, and so forth) should not be underestimated.

The implications for tax analysis are threefold. First, it may be difficult to increase the efficiency with which taxes are in fact collected in the short run, although there are counterexamples of which the Mexican case of chapter 12 may be one. It is therefore important to examine the effective tax system rather than the nominal or legally defined system. How much revenue is in fact collected per unit of commodity or income? Is evasion systematically related to income, location, line of business, and so on? Second, it is harder to predict the consequences of introducing new taxes, because it is also necessary to predict the effectiveness of collection. It is easier to predict the consequences of small changes in existing taxes. Again, small tax reforms are easier to analyze than issues of tax design. On the other hand, if changes in taxes are administratively expensive (and whether or not they will be depends on the nature of the change), then a sequence of small changes in the tax system may be more costly than a single more fundamental reform.

Third, administrative costs will typically make it undesirable and/or infeasible to tax all goods, and it will be desirable only to extend taxation to an additional commodity if the benefits of doing so exceed the extra administrative costs. (In some cases it may be very costly to exempt certain items, for example if goods are subject to a retail-level value-added tax at a uniform rate, then it may be harder to monitor exemptions or goods subject to lower rates.) As the country develops, or the tax administration is improved, so the benefits of adding extra taxes are likely to rise relative to the costs, and one practically important type of reform to analyze is the extension of tax coverage. A new and interesting question arises—which good is it most desirable to add to the existing system? Two factors are now relevant—which untaxed good has the lowest social marginal cost, λ_i, of increasing the tax rate (from zero), and which good has the most favorable ratio of extra revenue to the administrative cost of introducing it? The value of λ_i for good i is, from equations 2-26–2-30 of chapter 2,

(7-7)
$$\lambda_i = \frac{d_i}{1 + \dfrac{1}{X_i} \sum_j t_j \dfrac{\partial X_j}{\partial t_i}}$$

where

$$X_i = \sum_h x_i^h$$

and

$$d_i = \sum_h \beta^h x_i^h / X_i$$

are, respectively, aggregate consumption of good i and the distributional characteristic of good i, which will be high for goods consumed relatively by the socially deserving (those with high social weight β^h). It is thus desirable to add goods that are income elastic (low d_i) and substitutable with goods currently heavily taxed (high $t_j \, \partial X_j / \partial t_i$).

The extra revenue generated will depend on the size of the new tax base, X_i, the desired level of the new tax, t_i, and the extent to which the good is substitutable for highly taxed goods. These considerations illustrate the importance of closing loopholes (cases where close substitutes of taxed goods are untaxed) as well as the potential conflict between equity and cost effectiveness—goods with a broad base are likely to have adverse distributional characteristics (that is, high d_i).

Administrative capacity bears obvious similarities to (and has logical connections with) political constraints, and both limit the range of feasible changes that it is sensible to study. Administrative reform, provided that it is effective (an important proviso), increases the range of taxes that it is feasible to collect and should lower the variance in the effective rate at which any particular tax is collected from different individuals. Both effects are likely to be socially desirable, whereas well-designed reforms are likely to lower the collection cost per unit of revenue raised. Increasing the effectiveness with which undesirable taxes (undesirable on equity and efficiency grounds, that is) are collected may of course make matters worse.

Conclusions

Modern tax analysis starts with social objectives, specifies the tax instruments that it is feasible to impose or alter, and models their impact on the economy, on revenue, and on consumption levels. This approach can be applied in developing countries, but the details of the analysis will typically differ from the standard models in two ways—the range of instruments will be more limited, and the impacts on the economy may be different. Apparently no compelling case can be made for assuming that social objectives should be very different in developing countries, though the political constraints on feasible changes may be more pervasive and harder to analyze, as they typically affect the administration of the tax system in addition to shaping its design. These constraints may also be influenced by the tax system, which in allocating rents may create new interest groups or may affect the strength of existing groups.

A great merit of the modern approach to tax analysis is that it emphasizes the importance of the information available (or potentially available) to the tax authorities, because this will determine the effectiveness of various tax instruments. It demonstrates that the form of the optimal tax system depends sensitively on the availability of tax instruments (and on the information required to impose them).

For developing countries, several important characteristics limit the range of feasible taxes and modify their incidence. The main distinguishing feature is the importance of the agricultural sector. Transactions within the sector are hard to observe and are therefore hard to tax. Land is a theoretically ideal tax base, and land taxes were a major source of revenue in earlier times. The information required to levy the taxes is, however, only readily available at the local level, and substantial political impediments block transferring the information to the central government and implementing a central land tax or using the information locally. Nevertheless, if these impediments can be overcome, land taxes are potentially very attractive. In their absence, agricultural taxation will be limited to taxes on inputs and on marketed surplus or on the export surplus. In choosing such taxes it will be necessary to accept a tradeoff between equity and efficiency not only in consumption (all non-lump-sum taxes involve the tradeoff) but also in production.

The agricultural sector is also important as a source of labor, and taxes on agriculture will typically affect its supply price. Taxes on urban labor may or may not fall on urban wages, depending on the relationship between the urban after-tax wage and the supply price of rural labor. Where tax coverage is sector-specific (to urban labor or to agricultural producers), then its incidence depends critically on the way the two sectors interact and on the way the markets for their inputs and outputs equilibrate.

Indeed, one of the most important features of developing countries is that many taxes have only a partial or sector-specific coverage, and this may significantly alter their incidence. Deaton in chapter 4 argues, for example, that, if governments make optimal uniform lump-sum transfers to households, then it would be hard to find evidence to argue against uniform commodity taxation. If the government is only able to make lump-sum transfers to an economically defined subgroup of the population (such as urban residents), however, then the transfer will cease to be truly lump-sum subsidies, and the argument for uniformity will collapse. As noted above, an urban subsidy may be shifted forward entirely to firms and may not affect urban consumption levels, which might be set by the rural standard of living.

Another important conclusion, which may change with development and with improvements in tax administration, is that personal income taxes are relatively ineffective tax instruments, covering a small proportion of the population. Although it may still be very desirable to use income taxes where possible, it is doubtful that they can replace indirect taxes, which will continue to be a major source of tax revenue (together with various rent taxes on minerals and profits taxes on corporations). In early stages of development, trade taxes (tariffs) may be the most cost-effective way of raising revenue, despite the unattractive ways in which they tax production. As domestic production expands and the ability to administer more complex tax structures improves, it is likely to become desirable to replace these trade taxes with taxes that fall on final consumers, thereby avoiding unnecessary distortions to production. Trade taxes create rents to domestic producers that may be hard to remove though not necessarily impossible to reform. Thus as the process of development changes the set of feasible tax instruments, we would anticipate the desirability of reforming the structure of indirect taxes. It is not presumed either that taxes are currently optimal or that they are incapable of reform because they represent the unique equilibrium to the present balance of power in the economy.

In designing the structure of indirect taxes, we must consider the extent to which the government can meet its redistributive objectives through the expenditure side of the budget (by subsidies or by transfers in kind). If lump-sum transfers are feasible, then the efficiency questions become more prominent—broadening the tax base, moving tax rates toward uniformity (as Deaton argues), and taxing inelastically supplied goods. If such transfers are not feasible, then the structure of indirect taxes may appear very different and will reflect the conflict between equity (lower taxes on mass consumption goods with low-income elasticities) and efficiency (in which these features tend to be associated with low price elasticities and hence with higher taxes).

Finally—a point that may be very important in some developing countries—the profits of state-owned enterprises are akin to tax revenues, and setting their prices poses essentially the same problem as setting indirect tax rates. Yet many state-owned enterprises run at a loss (or fail to earn a normal return on their capital) and may thus be selling at subsidized prices rather than generating positive tax revenues. Reforming public sector prices may be the least costly way of raising extra revenue and would permit reduction of some of the most costly taxes (perhaps trade taxes).

Notes

1. World Bank (1983). Other figures are:

Economy	Percentage of GDP	Percentage of employment
Developing countries		
Lower middle income	22	55
Upper middle income	10	30
Industrial market economy	3	6

2. Productivity is measured as sectoral GDP divided by sectoral employment. This level of productivity holds for all developing countries and is slightly higher for the poorest countries apart from China and India. The statistics are, however, shaky and affected by the substantial price distortions encountered in developing countries. Other points are raised below.

3. See Fei and Ranis (1964), Lewis (1954), and the survey by Dixit (1971) as well as chapters 13, 15, and 16 below.

4. Dixit (1971, p. 337) shows how to accommodate technical progress, which does not alter the story substantially.

5. Only if the constraints that limit the choice of policy directly concern trade flows are trade taxes warranted (Bhagwati, 1971; Dixit and Norman, 1980, chap. 6; and see chapter 6 of the present book).

6. Tax authorities in some countries are very skeptical that it would be possible to verify the legitimacy of the invoices that entitle the recipient to a rebate.

7. This assumption seems reasonable if the individuals are well informed about the consequences of their choice but less so if they are not. Where there is evidence that individuals are not well informed about the consequences of various choices, for example in the choice of education, health, or pension provision, it may be sensible to distinguish between the individual's utility function, which describes the benefits that will actually result from alternative choices, and the choice function, which predicts what the individual would choose.

8

Quantitative Characteristics of the Tax Systems of Developing Countries

Vito Tanzi

THIS CHAPTER DISCUSSES the existing tax systems of the developing countries and uses data on total tax revenue for eighty-six nations. I briefly discuss the relationship between total tax revenue and gross domestic product, the empirical importance of various tax sources at different levels of per capita income, and the factors that may lead a country to prefer one type of tax rather than another. The last section is somewhat different from the two preceding ones, as it shifts the emphasis from quantitative to qualitative aspects of the developing countries' tax systems. It briefly considers some aspects of the tax system that are necessary if taxes are to be used as instruments of economic policy. (A detailed discussion is provided in Tanzi, 1983.)

The eighty-six country sample is quite comprehensive; it includes most developing countries with per capita incomes ranging from about $100 to about $6,000 (in 1981 prices). The information comes from both published and unpublished data collected by the IMF's Bureau of Statistics. The data have been collected in accordance with consistent definitions and methods, so that they are likely to be more reliable than those from other sources. One statistical problem remains, however. For thirty-one countries the data are comprehensive in the sense that they refer to all levels of government. These are mostly countries in which noncentral (that is, state and local) tax revenues are important. For the remaining countries, the data refer to central government tax revenue only. This limitation should be kept in mind.

The basic data are shown in two tables. Table 8-1 gives total tax revenue, as well as tax revenue by type of tax, as a percentage of GDP. Table 8-2 gives tax revenue by type of tax as a percentage of total taxes. The tables also indicate the years over which the revenue data have been averaged in order to reduce, whenever possible, the effect of transitory events. In most cases the data have been averaged around 1981. Per capita incomes in U.S. dollars are also provided for 1981. Tables 8-3 and 8-4 summarize the two basic tables. They average the information by four income ranges. (Appendix tables 8-A1 and 8-A2 provide the same information organized by region.)

(Text continues on page 218.)

Table 8-1. *Tax Revenue, by Type of Tax*
(percent of GDP)

Country	Ab-bre-via-tion	Years	GNP per capita (1981 dollars)	Total taxes	Income taxes			
					Total	Indi-vid-ual	Corpo-rate	Other
Chad	CH	1974–76	110	9.33	1.67	0.97	0.70	n.a.
Bangladesh	BA	1977–79	140	8.07	1.23	1.10	0.13	n.a.
Ethiopia[a]	ET	1975–77	140	11.51	2.84	1.18	1.35	0.32
Nepal	NE	1980–82	150	7.12	0.53	0.38	0.15	n.a.
Burma	BU	1980–82	190	9.82	0.48	n.a.	n.a.	n.a.
Mali	MA	1981–83	190	13.90	2.48	0.72	1.56	0.20
Malawi[a]	MU	1979–81	200	15.79	5.80	2.30	3.50	n.a.
Zaire	ZA	1980–82	210	18.27	6.82	3.01	3.81	n.a.
Uganda	UG	1981–83	220	2.64	0.21	0.15	0.05	0.01
Burundi	BR	1979–81	230	12.86	2.70	1.18	1.34	0.18
Burkina Faso	BK	1981–83	240	12.85	2.44	1.49	0.54	0.41
Rwanda	RW	1978–80	250	11.13	2.17	0.82	1.24	0.11
India[a]	IN	1979–81	260	15.93	2.43	1.14	1.22	0.08
Somalia[a]	SO	1975–77	280	16.88	1.46	1.32	0.13	n.a.
Tanzania	TA	1979–81	280	17.78	5.68	1.73	3.52	0.42
Haiti	HA	1981–83	300	10.46	2.05	0.64	1.50	n.a.
Sri Lanka[a]	SL	1979–81	300	19.60	2.70	0.66	2.05	n.a.
Benin	BE	1977–79	320	16.33	2.82	0.53	1.72	0.57
Central African Republic	CA	1981–83	320	14.96	2.65	1.27	1.38	0.01
Sierra Leone	SE	1981–83	320	11.80	3.15	1.31	1.82	0.03
Madagascar[a]	MD	1980–82	330	15.09	2.58	1.39	1.19	n.a.
Niger	NI	1978–80	330	11.72	3.62	0.71	2.54	0.37
Pakistan	PA	1980–82	350	13.07	2.43	0.76	0.48	n.a.
Gambia[a]	GA	1976–78	370	15.04	2.23	0.84	1.27	0.12
Sudan	SU	1980–82	380	9.70	1.67	0.67	0.85	0.15
Togo	TO	1981–83	380	24.40	9.17	1.72	6.82	0.62
Ghana	GH	1981–83	400	5.50	1.45	0.75	0.65	0.05
Kenya[a]	KE	1979–81	420	21.40	6.98	n.a.	n.a.	n.a.

| Domestic taxes on goods and services | | | | Foreign trade | | | | So-cial secu-rity | Wealth and prop-erty | Other |
Total	General sales, turn-over, VAT	Ex-cises	Other	Total	Im-port duties	Ex-port duties	Other			
1.47	0.92	0.29	0.27	5.27	4.50	0.77	n.a.	0.19	0.15	0.57
3.31	1.37	1.84	0.10	3.09	2.82	0.17	0.09	n.a.	0.25	0.19
3.24	0.92	2.22	0.10	4.90	3.02	1.88	n.a.	n.a.	0.24	0.29
3.15	1.89	0.94	0.32	2.77	2.55	0.22	n.a.	n.a.	0.63	0.05
6.57	5.91	0.02	0.65	2.76	2.76	n.a.	n.a.	n.a.	n.a.	n.a.
5.70	3.02	2.45	0.22	3.02	2.61	0.37	0.04	0.82	0.58	1.31
5.58	4.51	0.70	0.38	3.82	3.82	n.a.	n.a.	n.a.	0.53	0.06
3.47	2.46	0.98	0.03	6.58	4.64	1.93	0.01	0.68	0.01	0.70
0.80	0.56	0.18	0.06	1.63	0.47	0.93	0.23	n.a.	n.a.	n.a.
3.59	n.a.	3.43	0.16	5.10	3.58	1.51	0.01	0.43	0.96	0.07
2.43	1.12	0.86	0.44	5.96	5.30	0.26	0.40	1.39	0.17	0.48
2.12	n.a.	2.11	0.01	6.06	3.18	2.88	n.a.	0.51	0.12	0.15
10.01	0.13	5.26	4.61	2.81	2.68	0.08	0.05	n.a.	0.20	0.48
4.53	n.a.	2.49	2.04	7.67	7.30	0.37	n.a.	n.a.	0.36	2.87
8.69	8.29	0.22	0.18	3.16	2.12	1.00	0.03	0.05	0.12	0.09
2.85	0.38	1.89	0.58	3.75	3.02	0.73	n.a.	0.12	0.17	1.52
5.79	2.70	2.95	0.13	10.44	4.18	6.25	0.01	n.a.	0.10	0.57
2.30	0.75	1.10	0.45	9.34	8.58	0.29	0.47	1.57	0.04	0.25
3.42	0.99	1.23	1.21	6.55	4.97	1.56	0.02	1.68	0.07	0.58
2.84	n.a.	2.72	0.12	5.57	4.67	0.78	0.12	0.05	n.a.	0.18
6.01	3.44	1.43	1.13	3.64	3.17	0.47	n.a.	1.88	0.32	0.67
2.60	1.69	0.81	0.10	4.69	4.04	0.55	0.11	0.62	0.35	−0.17
5.31	1.02	4.29	n.a.	5.29	4.82	0.19	0.29	n.a.	0.04	n.a.
0.62	n.a.	0.13	0.42	11.80	10.28	1.50	0.02	0.09	0.51	0.06
3.02	n.a.	2.47	0.55	4.93	4.73	0.20	n.a.	n.a.	0.01	0.06
4.14	3.09	0.40	0.66	8.88	7.30	0.21	1.37	1.77	0.37	0.06
1.92	0.22	1.56	0.14	2.13	0.95	0.81	0.37	n.a.	n.a.	n.a.
8.79	5.75	2.30	0.75	4.84	4.66	0.18	n.a.	n.a.	0.48	0.30

(Table continues on the following page.)

Table 8-1 (*continued*)

Country	Ab-bre-via-tion	Years	GNP per capita (1981 dollars)	Total taxes	Income taxes			
					Total	Indiv-id-ual	Corpo-rate	Other
Senegal	SN	1980–82	430	20.54	4.99	2.78	1.31	0.89
Mauritania	MU	1977–79	460	16.66	5.19	4.26	0.80	0.13
Yemen Arab Republic	YA	1981–83	460	19.81	2.53	1.54	0.92	0.07
Liberia	LI	1981–83	520	25.35	8.85	6.29	2.44	0.12
Indonesia[a]	ID	1980–82	530	20.85	16.94	0.39	15.59	0.95
Lesotho	LE	1975–77	540	19.92	3.19	1.96	1.07	0.17
Bolivia	BO	1980–82	600	6.30	1.11	0.67	0.42	0.02
Honduras	HO	1979–81	600	13.48	3.80	1.32	2.45	0.03
Zambia[a]	ZM	1978–80	600	22.96	8.88	4.50	3.92	0.47
Egypt	EG	1981–83	650	29.77	8.32	2.24	6.00	0.08
El Salvador	ES	1981–83	650	11.20	2.52	1.10	1.12	0.31
Swaziland[a]	SW	1977–79	760	28.38	8.46	3.26	4.65	0.55
Thailand[a]	TH	1980–82	770	13.48	2.79	1.20	1.59	n.a.
Philippines[a]	PH	1980–82	790	11.21	2.55	1.22	1.35	n.a.
Papua New Guinea	PN	1980–82	840	18.56	11.37	5.60	5.77	n.a.
Grenada	GR	1975–77	850	19.68	4.18	2.96	1.22	n.a.
Morocco	MO	1980–82	860	21.66	4.60	2.15	2.18	0.28
Nicaragua	NC	1981–83	860	23.62	2.93	n.a.	n.a.	n.a.
Nigeria	NG	1976–78	870	18.89	14.72	0.01	14.71	n.a.
Zimbabwe	ZI	1980–82	870	23.13	12.53	6.59	5.37	0.58
Cameroon	CM	1981–83	880	16.78	6.33	2.49	3.84	n.a.
Botswana	BT	1980–82	1,010	25.87	11.93	n.a.	n.a.	11.93
Congo	CO	1978–80	1,110	26.87	17.13	2.95	14.15	0.01
Guatemala[a]	GU	1980–82	1,140	9.75	1.23	0.27	0.95	0.01
Peru	PE	1980–82	1,170	16.98	3.60	0.41	3.62	0.06
Ecuador[a]	EC	1978–80	1,180	12.15	3.65	n.a.	2.34	1.32
Jamaica	JA	1976–78	1,180	24.28	6.80	4.43	2.37	n.a.
Côte d'Ivoire	CT	1980–82	1,200	20.44	2.87	1.39	1.35	0.14
Dominican Republic[a]	DR	1980–82	1,260	10.29	2.52	0.86	1.65	0.01
Mauritius[a]	MR	1981–83	1,270	18.71	3.64	1.95	1.70	n.a.

Domestic taxes on goods and services				Foreign trade				Social security	Wealth and property	Other
Total	General sales, turn-over, VAT	Excises	Other	Total	Import duties	Export duties	Other			
5.68	2.89	2.37	0.42	7.93	7.58	0.34	0.01	1.14	0.55	0.26
3.21	2.09	0.73	0.39	6.55	6.44	0.11	0.01	1.45	0.17	0.09
1.93	n.a.	1.38	0.55	12.17	12.17	n.a.	n.a.	n.a.	0.18	3.00
7.06	0.72	3.38	2.96	8.76	8.58	0.13	0.06	n.a.	0.22	0.44
2.22	1.02	0.96	0.24	1.25	0.91	0.33	n.a.	n.a.	0.31	0.13
0.87	n.a.	n.a.	0.87	14.47	14.30	0.16	n.a.	n.a.	0.06	1.33
2.65	0.34	2.18	0.12	2.19	1.80	0.04	0.34	n.a.	0.13	0.23
3.61	1.00	2.35	0.26	5.80	3.38	2.42	0.01	n.a.	0.12	0.15
10.71	2.66	7.83	0.22	1.77	1.74	n.a.	0.03	0.73	0.76	0.10
5.23	n.a.	n.a.	n.a.	8.21	8.21	n.a.	n.a.	5.13	0.58	2.30
4.59	2.01	2.16	0.42	3.24	0.94	2.30	n.a.	n.a.	0.81	0.02
0.79	n.a.	n.a.	0.79	18.65	16.29	2.36	n.a.	n.a.	0.34	0.15
6.60	2.70	3.07	0.83	3.11	2.72	0.38	n.a.	n.a.	0.18	0.80
5.20	1.65	2.26	1.29	2.78	2.65	0.12	0.02	n.a.	0.47	0.21
2.81	n.a.	2.70	0.11	4.18	3.77	0.36	0.05	n.a.	n.a.	0.20
4.20	1.53	0.22	2.45	8.97	5.41	3.29	0.27	n.a.	0.57	1.76
8.48	5.51	2.25	0.72	5.36	5.03	0.30	0.02	1.37	0.55	1.30
11.47	2.63	5.95	2.89	4.32	2.36	0.34	1.61	3.10	1.40	0.40
0.60	n.a.	0.60	n.a.	3.56	3.55	0.01	n.a.	n.a.	n.a.	0.01
8.04	5.57	2.36	0.11	2.26	2.26	n.a.	n.a.	n.a.	0.07	0.23
2.87	1.23	1.35	0.29	5.63	4.34	1.29	n.a.	1.17	0.47	0.31
0.40	0.11	n.a.	0.30	13.46	13.40	0.06	n.a.	n.a.	0.08	n.a.
2.69	2.45	0.17	0.02	4.56	4.44	0.07	0.02	0.69	0.02	0.14
3.12	1.81	1.11	0.21	2.32	1.18	1.08	0.06	1.20	0.09	1.79
7.68	5.43	2.08	0.16	5.11	3.45	1.64	0.02	0.74	1.07	−1.21
2.24	1.45	0.70	0.11	4.00	3.21	0.64	0.15	n.a.	0.43	1.83
13.01	5.29	6.60	1.13	1.23	1.23	n.a.	n.a.	1.66	0.76	0.82
5.48	2.18	1.85	1.45	9.47	7.17	2.30	n.a.	2.08	0.48	0.06
3.31	n.a.	2.79	0.52	3.60	2.72	0.75	0.12	0.51	0.10	0.26
3.80	n.a.	2.45	1.35	10.13	6.89	3.14	0.11	n.a.	0.76	0.38

(Table continues on the following page.)

Table 8-1 (*continued*)

Country	Ab-bre-via-tion	Years	GNP per capita (1981 dollars)	Total taxes	Income taxes			
					Total	Indi-vid-ual	Corpo-rate	Other
Colombia[a]	CL	1979–81	1,380	12.21	2.93	1.34	1.57	0.03
Tunisia[a]	TU	1980–82	1,420	25.13	4.85	2.17	2.26	0.42
Costa Rica[a]	CR	1978–80	1,430	17.51	2.71	2.70	0.02	n.a.
Turkey	TR	1979–81	1,540	16.60	10.03	8.11	1.13	0.80
Syrian Arab Republic	SA	1979–81	1,570	9.96	2.47	n.a.	n.a.	n.a.
Jordan	JO	1980–82	1,620	17.86	3.13	n.a.	n.a.	n.a.
Paraguay[a]	PA	1978–80	1,630	11.09	1.65	0.04	1.39	0.32
Korea, Rep. of	KO	1981–83	1,700	16.33	4.34	2.29	2.05	n.a.
Malaysia	ML	1979–81	1,840	22.82	9.57	2.11	7.45	n.a.
Panama[a]	PM	1979–81	1,910	21.54	5.94	n.a.	n.a.	5.94
Brazil[a]	BR	1980–82	2,220	23.47	3.07	0.14	1.08	1.84
Mexico[a]	MX	1978–80	2,250	16.55	5.84	2.59	3.13	0.13
Portugal	PG	1980–82	2,520	28.23	5.68	2.18	1.50	2.00
Argentina[a]	AR	1980–82	2,560	19.88	2.82	0.04	0.01	2.77
Chile[a]	CI	1981–83	2,560	24.79	5.44	3.11	2.30	0.03
South Africa[a]	SF	1979–81	2,770	20.71	11.96	4.19	7.33	0.44
Yugoslavia[a]	YU	1979–81	2,790	32.64	2.63	1.14	n.a.	1.50
Uruguay	UR	1981–83	2,820	20.43	1.60	0.17	1.36	0.06
Barbados	BD	1980–82	3,500	24.95	9.22	4.37	4.42	0.42
Bahamas	BM	1977–79	3,620	16.33	n.a.	n.a.	n.a.	n.a.
Cyprus	CY	1981–83	3,740	19.32	4.67	2.92	1.00	0.75
Gabon	GB	1974–76	3,810	20.69	10.55	0.59	9.78	0.18
Venezuela[a]	VE	1977–79	4,220	20.00	14.89	0.81	14.08	n.a.
Greece[a]	GE	1979–81	4,420	27.33	4.93	3.59	1.13	0.21
Israel[a]	IS	1979–81	5,160	36.53	16.90	12.16	4.06	0.68
Singapore	SG	1980–82	5,240	18.45	9.19	n.a.	n.a.	n.a.
Trinidad and Tobago[a]	TT	1979–81	5,670	33.83	28.39	4.59	22.34	1.46
Oman	OM	1981–83	5,920	12.91	12.07	n.a.	12.03	0.03

n.a. Not available.

Note: Countries are listed in ascending order of per capita GNP.

| | Domestic taxes on goods and services | | | Foreign trade | | | | So-cial secu-rity | Wealth and prop-erty | Other |
| | General sales, turn-over, VAT | Ex-cises | Other | | Im-port duties | Ex-port duties | Other | | | |
Total				Total						
4.01	1.96	0.78	1.27	2.30	1.50	0.77	0.02	1.90	0.30	0.78
7.39	1.63	2.64	3.11	8.42	8.14	0.27	n.a.	3.08	0.69	0.71
5.61	1.64	3.62	0.35	3.57	2.11	1.46	n.a.	4.96	0.43	0.23
3.99	0.59	1.45	1.96	1.49	1.39	n.a.	0.10	n.a.	0.38	0.71
1.47	n.a.	0.11	1.36	3.62	3.31	0.28	0.02	0.51	0.53	1.37
1.90	n.a.	1.55	0.35	10.41	10.41	n.a.	n.a.	n.a.	1.67	0.75
2.22	0.65	1.36	0.21	3.08	2.23	0.09	0.76	1.58	0.74	1.82
8.41	4.04	2.53	1.84	2.68	2.68	n.a.	n.a.	0.20	0.18	0.52
4.50	1.28	1.91	1.31	8.19	3.79	4.40	n.a.	0.12	0.12	0.33
4.58	1.90	1.96	0.72	2.88	2.45	0.40	0.03	6.12	0.52	1.50
11.33	0.09	4.30	6.93	0.83	0.57	0.27	n.a.	7.60	0.42	0.22
5.29	2.44	1.77	1.08	2.65	0.92	1.73	n.a.	2.42	0.27	0.07
10.27	4.70	4.61	0.97	1.54	1.54	n.a.	n.a.	8.83	0.36	1.55
8.77	2.60	3.66	2.51	1.85	1.26	0.34	0.25	3.35	1.37	1.71
13.26	10.88	1.70	0.68	1.36	1.36	n.a.	n.a.	3.28	0.03	1.43
5.91	2.72	2.72	0.46	0.93	0.86	0.06	0.01	0.29	1.34	0.29
8.85	5.77	n.a.	3.08	3.34	3.34	n.a.	n.a.	17.67	0.13	0.01
9.41	5.38	3.79	0.23	2.51	2.16	0.34	n.a.	5.60	0.97	0.35
6.26	3.29	1.46	1.52	5.07	4.99	n.a.	0.08	2.75	1.36	0.29
1.70	n.a.	n.a.	1.70	11.50	10.60	0.32	0.58	1.82	0.56	0.75
4.61	n.a.	3.66	0.95	4.73	4.73	n.a.	n.a.	4.40	0.63	0.27
1.64	1.46	0.08	0.09	7.16	6.06	0.99	0.12	0.85	n.a.	0.49
1.35	n.a.	0.88	0.47	1.95	1.95	n.a.	n.a.	1.12	0.28	0.40
10.08	5.60	3.32	1.16	1.41	1.41	n.a.	n.a.	8.31	0.96	1.64
10.38	9.10	1.08	0.20	1.60	1.60	n.a.	n.a.	5.94	1.17	0.54
3.85	n.a.	1.35	2.49	1.56	1.56	n.a.	n.a.	0.47	2.56	0.83
1.73	0.71	0.28	0.74	2.76	2.75	n.a.	0.01	0.62	0.11	0.22
0.17	n.a.	n.a.	0.17	0.55	0.53	n.a.	0.02	0.12	n.a.	n.a.

a. State and local tax revenues are included.
Sources: International Monetary Fund (1984); World Bank (1983).

Table 8-2. Tax Revenue, by Type of Tax
(percent of total tax revenue)

Country	Years	GNP per capita (1981 dollars)	Income taxes Total	Individual	Corporate	Other	Domestic taxes on goods and services Total	General sales, turnover, VAT	Excises	Other	Foreign trade Total	Import duties	Export duties	Other	Social security	Wealth and property	Other
Chad	1974–76	110	18.16	10.60	7.57	n.a.	15.72	9.79	3.12	2.81	56.66	48.29	8.37	n.a.	2.08	1.51	5.87
Bangladesh	1977–79	140	15.19	13.51	1.67	n.a.	41.15	16.90	23.04	1.21	38.20	34.92	2.15	1.12	n.a.	3.17	2.30
Ethiopia[a]	1975–77	140	24.88	10.32	11.78	2.77	28.47	8.05	19.53	0.89	42.00	26.22	15.78	n.a.	n.a.	2.07	2.57
Nepal	1980–82	150	7.40	5.31	2.09	n.a.	44.18	26.48	13.23	4.48	38.94	35.81	3.13	n.a.	n.a.	8.83	0.65
Burma	1980–82	190	4.89	n.a.	n.a.	n.a.	67.00	60.21	0.18	6.60	28.11	28.11	n.a.	n.a.	n.a.	n.a.	n.a.
Mali	1981–83	190	17.89	5.24	11.21	1.44	40.96	21.82	17.54	1.61	21.77	18.81	2.68	0.28	5.84	4.13	9.40
Malawi[a]	1979–81	200	36.67	14.58	22.09	n.a.	35.36	28.55	4.43	2.38	24.28	24.28	n.a.	0.05	n.a.	3.34	0.35
Zaire	1980–82	210	37.44	16.52	20.90	0.03	19.14	13.57	5.41	0.16	35.79	25.50	10.23	0.05	3.68	0.08	3.88
Uganda	1981–83	220	11.61	5.99	4.96	0.65	32.51	21.90	6.45	4.16	55.76	20.15	29.63	5.98	n.a.	n.a.	0.12
Burundi	1979–81	230	21.23	9.31	10.51	1.41	28.18	n.a.	26.92	1.26	39.01	27.77	11.19	0.06	3.44	7.58	0.55
Burkina Faso	1981–83	240	19.02	11.65	4.21	3.16	18.90	8.71	6.79	3.41	46.26	41.18	1.99	3.09	10.78	1.30	3.74
Rwanda	1978–80	250	19.52	7.34	11.20	0.97	19.21	n.a.	19.07	0.14	54.23	28.81	25.42	n.a.	4.61	1.10	1.34
India[a]	1979–81	260	15.27	7.17	7.63	0.48	62.81	0.82	33.03	28.96	17.65	16.83	0.53	0.29	n.a.	1.26	3.01
Somalia[a]	1975–77	280	8.58	7.78	0.80	n.a.	26.88	n.a.	15.01	11.87	45.41	43.12	2.29	n.a.	n.a.	2.09	17.04
Tanzania	1979–81	280	31.80	9.57	19.75	2.48	48.71	46.38	1.33	1.01	18.02	12.11	5.73	0.18	0.28	0.68	0.31
Haiti	1981–83	300	19.67	6.06	14.15	0.05	27.69	3.78	18.16	5.75	36.84	29.75	7.09	n.a.	1.19	1.69	12.91
Sri Lanka[a]	1979–81	300	13.88	3.38	10.50	n.a.	29.75	14.14	14.94	0.68	52.91	21.39	31.44	0.07	n.a.	0.52	2.94
Benin	1977–79	320	17.19	3.24	10.47	3.48	14.03	4.52	6.74	2.77	57.33	52.68	1.77	2.88	9.67	0.25	1.54
Central African Republic	1981–83	320	17.73	8.47	9.21	0.05	22.87	6.61	8.20	8.07	43.79	33.21	10.45	0.12	11.24	0.48	3.89
Sierra Leone	1981–83	320	26.95	11.68	15.04	0.23	24.43	n.a.	23.42	1.01	46.51	39.09	6.33	1.09	0.47	n.a.	1.63
Madagascar[a]	1980–82	330	17.01	9.19	7.82	n.a.	40.01	23.03	9.50	7.49	23.92	20.75	3.17	n.a.	12.59	2.11	4.36

Country	Year																
Niger	1978–80	330	30.97	6.09	21.72	3.16	22.26	14.43	6.96	0.87	40.01	34.38	4.70	0.92	5.26	2.98	-1.47
Pakistan	1980–82	350	18.61	5.77	3.68	n.a.	40.61	7.77	32.84	n.a.	40.45	36.85	1.42	2.18	n.a.	0.32	0.01
Gambia[a]	1976–78	370	14.66	5.58	8.36	0.73	3.91	n.a.	0.83	2.67	78.83	68.60	10.12	0.11	0.59	3.23	0.35
Sudan	1980–82	380	18.44	6.96	10.62	0.87	24.35	n.a.	21.50	2.85	56.38	52.85	3.53	n.a.	n.a.	0.21	0.62
Togo	1981–83	380	37.54	7.05	27.94	2.54	16.97	12.65	1.65	2.68	36.44	29.96	0.86	5.62	7.28	1.51	0.26
Ghana	1981–83	400	26.81	13.83	12.06	0.93	36.01	4.16	29.20	2.65	37.11	16.90	13.29	6.93	0.04	n.a.	0.02
Kenya[a]	1979–81	420	32.70	n.a.	n.a.	n.a.	40.98	26.73	10.75	3.50	22.66	21.85	0.81	n.a.	n.a.	2.23	1.43
Senegal	1980–82	430	24.67	13.71	6.12	4.83	27.79	15.07	10.79	1.94	38.51	37.10	1.38	0.03	5.37	2.56	1.07
Mauritania	1977–79	460	31.06	25.51	4.80	0.75	19.25	12.56	4.43	2.25	39.44	38.73	0.67	0.04	8.71	1.00	0.54
Yemen Arab Republic	1981–83	460	13.01	8.03	4.62	0.37	9.01	n.a.	6.12	2.89	61.24	61.24	n.a.	n.a.	n.a.	0.93	15.81
Liberia	1981–83	520	36.84	27.65	8.68	0.52	27.73	2.83	12.64	12.26	32.83	32.10	0.49	0.24	n.a.	0.97	1.63
Indonesia[a]	1980–82	530	81.20	1.90	74.70	4.60	10.69	4.92	4.64	1.13	5.97	4.38	1.59	n.a.	n.a.	1.48	0.65
Lesotho	1975–77	540	15.88	10.05	4.98	0.86	4.80	n.a.	n.a.	4.80	71.85	71.03	0.82	n.a.	n.a.	0.31	7.16
Bolivia	1980–82	600	17.82	10.70	6.86	0.26	42.46	5.52	35.02	1.91	33.90	28.21	0.62	5.06	n.a.	2.09	3.73
Honduras	1979–81	600	28.08	9.79	18.11	0.19	26.82	7.44	17.42	1.96	43.12	25.13	17.94	0.05	n.a.	0.87	1.10
Zambia[a]	1978–80	600	38.58	19.63	16.91	2.05	46.73	11.59	34.17	0.96	7.69	7.55	n.a.	0.14	3.19	3.35	0.46
Egypt	1981–83	650	27.93	7.57	20.09	0.27	17.55	n.a.	n.a.	n.a.	27.62	27.62	n.a.	n.a.	17.24	1.93	7.72
El Salvador	1981–83	650	22.55	9.81	9.97	2.77	41.03	17.98	19.30	3.76	28.93	8.37	20.51	0.04	n.a.	7.27	0.21
Swaziland[a]	1977–79	760	29.66	11.42	16.21	2.03	2.75	n.a.	n.a.	2.75	65.86	57.68	8.18	n.a.	n.a.	1.20	0.53
Thailand[a]	1980–82	770	20.70	8.91	11.79	n.a.	49.00	20.06	22.81	6.12	23.04	20.18	2.84	0.03	n.a.	1.30	5.96
Philippines[a]	1980–82	790	22.75	10.94	12.04	n.a.	46.38	14.69	20.15	11.54	24.77	23.60	1.02	0.14	n.a.	4.19	1.92
Papua New Guinea	1980–82	840	61.11	30.25	30.86	n.a.	15.21	n.a.	14.59	0.62	22.58	20.36	1.97	0.25	n.a.	n.a.	1.10
Grenada	1975–77	850	21.40	15.09	6.31	n.a.	21.20	7.78	1.24	12.18	46.03	27.81	17.00	1.22	n.a.	2.92	8.44
Morocco	1980–82	860	21.25	9.91	10.06	1.29	39.13	25.42	10.37	3.33	24.74	23.21	1.41	0.11	6.35	2.54	6.00
Nicaragua	1981–83	860	12.34	n.a.	n.a.	n.a.	48.60	11.24	25.35	12.02	18.21	10.23	1.63	6.35	13.22	5.92	1.71
Nigeria	1976–78	870	77.20	0.07	77.13	n.a.	3.33	n.a.	3.33	n.a.	19.41	19.37	0.04	n.a.	n.a.	n.a.	0.05
Zimbabwe	1981–82	870	54.53	28.68	23.38	2.48	34.77	24.19	10.10	0.48	9.38	9.38	n.a.	n.a.	n.a.	0.30	1.01
Cameroon	1981–83	880	45.53	12.08	33.45	n.a.	15.01	6.49	6.87	1.64	29.04	22.89	6.12	0.03	6.66	2.45	1.31
Botswana	1980–82	1,010	46.00	n.a.	n.a.	46.00	1.60	0.45	n.a.	1.15	52.10	51.85	0.25	n.a.	n.a.	0.30	n.a.
Congo	1978–80	1,110	63.75	10.96	52.67	0.11	9.99	9.12	0.62	0.25	16.96	16.52	0.27	0.17	7.69	0.09	1.53
Guatemala[a]	1980–82	1,140	12.63	2.72	9.78	0.13	32.22	18.77	11.33	2.12	23.42	12.00	10.81	0.61	12.31	0.95	18.47

(Table continues on the following page.)

Table 8-2 (continued)

Country	Years	GNP per capita (1981 dollars)	Income taxes				Domestic taxes on goods and services				Foreign trade				Social security	Wealth and property	Other
			Total	Individual	Corporate	Other	Total	General sales, turnover, VAT	Excises	Other	Total	Import duties	Export duties	Other			
Peru	1980–82	1,170	20.77	2.37	20.15	0.35	45.50	32.10	12.46	0.94	30.06	20.48	9.44	0.15	4.39	6.30	−7.02
Ecuador[a]	1978–80	1,180	29.17	n.a.	18.14	11.03	18.17	12.08	5.80	0.91	33.67	26.88	5.54	1.25	n.a.	3.52	4.65
Jamaica	1976–78	1,180	28.20	18.47	9.73	n.a.	53.38	21.55	27.17	4.66	5.06	5.06	n.a.	n.a.	6.94	3.18	3.25
Côte d'Ivoire	1980–82	1,200	14.05	6.79	6.59	0.67	26.82	10.64	9.07	7.11	46.32	35.09	11.23	n.a.	10.18	2.33	0.29
Dominican Republic[a]	1980–82	1,260	24.57	8.39	16.06	0.12	32.52	n.a.	27.45	5.06	34.48	26.32	6.93	1.22	5.02	1.03	2.38
Mauritius[a]	1981–83	1,270	18.30	10.29	8.01	n.a.	20.66	1.12	12.45	7.10	55.22	37.83	16.85	0.54	n.a.	3.84	1.98
Colombia[a]	1979–81	1,380	23.97	10.95	12.80	0.22	32.85	16.08	6.41	10.37	18.84	12.32	6.33	0.19	15.53	2.45	6.36
Tunisia[a]	1980–82	1,420	19.28	8.64	8.97	1.67	29.45	6.50	10.51	12.44	33.45	32.35	1.10	n.a.	12.27	2.76	2.78
Costa Rica[a]	1978–80	1,430	15.49	15.39	0.10	n.a.	32.06	9.39	20.69	1.98	20.37	12.05	8.32	n.a.	28.32	2.44	1.31
Turkey	1979–81	1,540	60.38	48.88	6.66	4.84	24.06	3.53	8.78	11.75	9.07	8.46	n.a.	0.62	n.a.	2.28	4.21
Syrian Arab Republic	1979–81	1,570	25.19	n.a.	n.a.	n.a.	14.80	n.a.	1.01	13.79	36.33	33.32	2.76	0.25	5.15	5.23	13.29
Jordan	1980–82	1,620	17.54	n.a.	n.a.	n.a.	10.58	n.a.	8.65	1.94	58.40	58.40	n.a.	n.a.	n.a.	9.33	4.13
Paraguay[a]	1978–80	1,630	14.89	0.31	12.59	2.74	20.00	5.89	12.25	1.86	27.74	20.10	0.78	6.86	14.27	6.63	16.47
Korea, Rep. of	1981–83	1,700	26.60	14.03	12.57	n.a.	51.49	24.71	15.50	11.28	16.40	16.40	n.a.	n.a.	1.25	1.11	3.16

214

Malaysia	1979–81	1,840	41.82	9.37	32.43	0.02	19.83	5.63	8.44	5.77	35.89	16.58	19.32	n.a.	0.51	0.52	1.43
Panama[a]	1979–81	1,910	27.55	n.a.	n.a.	27.55	21.29	8.84	9.12	3.32	13.35	11.40	1.84	0.12	28.44	2.43	6.94
Brazil[a]	1980–82	2,220	13.06	0.61	4.61	7.84	48.29	0.37	18.36	29.56	3.57	2.42	1.15	n.a.	32.33	1.80	0.95
Mexico[a]	1978–80	2,250	35.45	15.77	18.91	0.77	32.25	14.75	10.92	6.58	15.59	5.49	10.10	n.a.	14.74	1.64	0.34
Portugal	1980–82	2,520	20.08	7.71	5.33	7.04	36.41	16.64	16.35	3.43	5.47	5.46	0.01	n.a.	31.27	1.27	5.49
Argentina[a]	1980–82	2,560	14.18	0.22	0.05	13.92	44.45	13.37	18.61	12.48	9.36	6.34	1.80	1.22	16.42	6.94	8.64
Chile[a]	1981–83	2,560	20.46	11.36	9.01	0.09	53.03	41.22	8.54	3.28	6.45	6.06	n.a.	0.38	12.15	2.33	5.58
South Africa[a]	1979–81	2,770	57.72	20.27	35.35	2.10	28.53	13.14	13.17	2.22	4.50	4.15	0.29	0.07	1.39	6.48	1.38
Yugoslavia[a]	1979–81	2,790	8.05	3.46	n.a.	4.59	27.20	17.78	n.a.	9.41	10.15	10.15	n.a.	n.a.	54.16	0.41	0.03
Uruguay	1981–83	2,820	7.82	0.87	6.64	0.31	45.98	26.28	18.58	1.12	12.25	10.49	1.77	n.a.	27.48	4.78	1.68
Barbados	1980–82	3,500	37.01	16.08	19.16	1.78	24.66	13.96	4.37	6.33	18.75	18.17	0.16	0.43	12.33	5.34	1.90
Bahamas	1977–79	3,620	n.a.	n.a.	n.a.	n.a.	10.32	n.a.	n.a.	10.32	70.50	65.00	1.95	3.55	11.20	3.44	4.54
Cyprus	1981–83	3,740	24.14	15.06	5.18	3.89	23.87	n.a.	18.95	4.92	24.49	24.47	n.a.	0.02	22.82	3.28	1.30
Gabon	1974–76	3,810	49.81	2.90	46.03	0.89	8.11	7.19	0.46	0.46	35.55	29.69	5.34	0.52	4.16	0.01	2.35
Venezuela[a]	1977–79	4,220	74.37	4.07	70.30	n.a.	6.75	n.a.	4.41	2.34	9.78	9.78	n.a.	n.a.	5.63	1.45	2.02
Greece[a]	1979–81	4,420	18.04	13.14	4.15	0.75	36.89	20.50	12.14	4.24	5.13	5.12	0.01	n.a.	30.44	3.51	5.98
Israel[a]	1979–81	5,160	46.28	33.32	11.10	1.86	28.42	24.90	2.95	0.56	4.37	4.37	n.a.	n.a.	16.29	3.19	1.42
Singapore	1980–82	5,240	49.71	n.a.	n.a.	n.a.	20.91	n.a.	7.36	13.55	8.48	8.48	n.a.	n.a.	2.57	13.84	1.49
Trinidad and Tobago[a]	1979–81	5,670	83.82	13.60	66.05	4.18	5.16	2.12	0.84	2.20	8.18	8.16	n.a.	0.03	1.85	0.32	0.66
Oman	1981–83	5,920	92.20	n.a.	91.91	0.30	1.59	n.a.	n.a.	1.59	5.16	5.08	n.a.	0.09	1.05	n.a.	n.a.

n.a. Not available.

Note: Countries are listed in ascending order of per capita GNP.

a. State and local taxes are included.

Sources: International Monetary Fund (1984); World Bank (1983).

Table 8-3. Tax Revenue, by Type of Tax and by Country Group
(percent of GDP)

Per capita income (dollars)		Total taxes	Income taxes				Domestic taxes on goods and services				Foreign trade				Social security	Wealth and property	Other
Range	Average		Total	Individual	Corporate	Other	Total	General sales, turnover, VAT	Excises	Other	Total	Import duties	Export duties	Other			
0–349	241	12.90	2.66	1.14	1.50	0.13	4.11	1.87	1.64	0.60	4.94	3.82	1.05	0.07	0.48	0.24	0.50
350–849	548	12.50	5.50	2.15	2.97	0.23	4.14	1.43	2.24	0.60	6.62	5.92	0.58	0.12	0.49	0.30	0.47
850–1,699	1,195	18.16	5.75	2.15	3.25	0.84	4.73	1.89	1.91	0.92	5.31	4.35	0.81	0.15	1.12	0.53	0.66
1,700 or more	3,392	22.75	8.08	2.35	5.00	0.92	6.30	3.10	2.16	1.40	3.19	2.72	0.42	0.05	3.90	0.64	0.64
All countries	1,330	17.77	5.60	1.94	3.14	0.52	4.81	2.07	1.97	0.88	5.02	4.20	0.72	0.10	1.49	0.43	0.57

Sources: International Monetary Fund (1984); World Bank (1983).

216

Table 8-4. Tax Revenue, by Type of Tax and by Country Group
(percent of total taxes)

Per capita income (dollars)		Income taxes				Domestic taxes on goods and services				Foreign trade				Social security	Wealth and property	Other
		Total	Individual	Corporate	Other	Total	General sales, turnover, VAT	Excises	Other	Total	Import duties	Export duties	Other			
Range	Average															
0–349	241	19.68	8.71	10.73	0.97	32.28	14.98	12.86	4.44	39.25	30.14	8.37	0.73	3.23	2.05	3.51
350–849	548	29.55	12.25	15.47	1.22	26.19	8.63	15.73	3.46	38.06	32.87	4.19	0.99	2.02	1.76	2.49
850–1,699	1,195	30.29	11.05	17.50	3.77	25.76	10.11	10.54	5.14	29.47	23.72	4.85	0.89	6.74	3.04	4.66
1,700 or more	3,392	35.63	9.09	23.09	3.89	27.40	12.57	9.95	6.43	15.40	13.01	2.08	0.31	15.64	3.05	2.88
All countries	1,330	28.70	10.25	16.53	2.43	27.93	11.66	12.23	4.88	30.63	24.98	4.91	0.73	6.86	2.48	3.40

Sources: International Monetary Fund (1984); World Bank (1983).

Of the eighty-six countries considered, twenty-two had (in 1981) per capita incomes of less than $350; forty-three had per capita incomes less than $850; and sixty-five had incomes less than $1,700. The median income was about $850. The tables allocate total tax revenue among the following categories: income taxes (individual and corporation), domestic taxes on goods and services (general sales taxes and excises), taxes on foreign trade (import and export duties), social security taxes, taxes on wealth and property, and other taxes (poll and stamp taxes, for example).[1]

The Level of Taxation

The lowest ratio of total tax revenue to GDP is found in Uganda, at 2.6 percent; Ghana, at 5.5 percent; and Bolivia, at 6.3 percent. Ten countries have tax ratios of less than 10 percent. Most of these have very low per capita incomes. At the other extreme, eleven countries have tax ratios exceeding 25 percent. Of these ten, six have relatively high per capita incomes (Tunisia, Portugal, Yugoslavia, Greece, Israel, and Trinidad and Tobago), whereas the other five (Liberia, Egypt, Swaziland, Botswana, and Congo) are closer to the median income (their incomes range from $500 to $1,100). No country with a really low income appears in this group.

These results suggest a relationship between per capita income and the tax ratio. Such a relationship would conform with an expectation, supported by various authors, that, as countries develop, tax bases grow more than proportionately to the growth of income. In other words, the capacity to tax grows with the growth of income. (See especially Musgrave, 1969.) In addition to this supply-side argument, there is also the consideration that, as income grows, countries generally become more urbanized. Urbanization per se brings about a greater demand for public services while at the same time facilitating tax collection. Thus it increases the need for tax revenue and the capacity to tax. It is a fact of life that in the majority of countries a large proportion of total domestic taxes originate in the capital city or in the large urban centers, whereas much of the public expenditure also takes place there.

The correlation of the above tax ratios against the logarithm of per capita GDP supports the above expectation. This correlation is shown below for the eighty-six countries combined, for the forty-three countries with per capita incomes of less than $850, and for the forty-three countries with per capita incomes of $850 or more. Figures 8-1 to 8-3 show the relevant scatter diagrams. The coefficients in parentheses are t values, two asterisks implying significance at the 1 percent level and one asterisk significance at the 5 percent level.

For eighty-six countries:

$$(8\text{-}1) \quad \frac{\text{Total tax revenue}}{\text{GDP}} = -4.8586 + 3.3792 \log (\text{GNP per capita}).$$
$$(1.19) \quad (5.61)^{**}$$
$$\bar{R}^2 = 0.264$$

Figure 8-1. *Share of Total Tax Revenue, and GNP Per Capita*

Share of tax in GDP (percent)

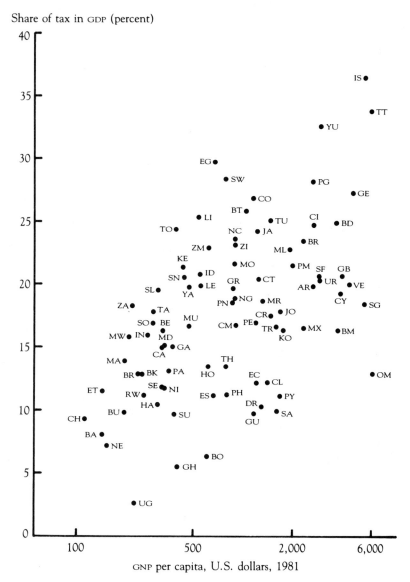

GNP per capita, U.S. dollars, 1981

Note: The x-axis represents a natural log scale.

Figure 8-2. *Share of Total Tax Revenue,*
GNP Per Capita Less Than $850

Share of tax in GDP (percent)

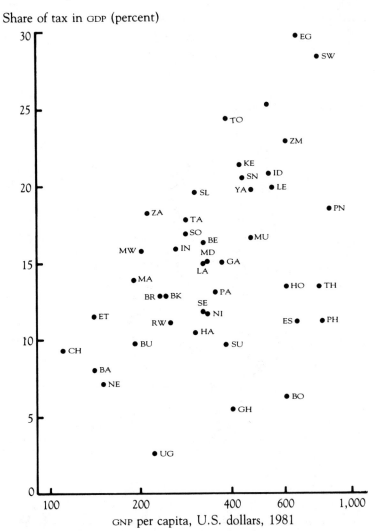

GNP per capita, U.S. dollars, 1981

Note: The x-axis represents a natural log scale.

Figure 8-3. *Share of Total Tax Revenue,*
GNP Per Capita of $850 or More

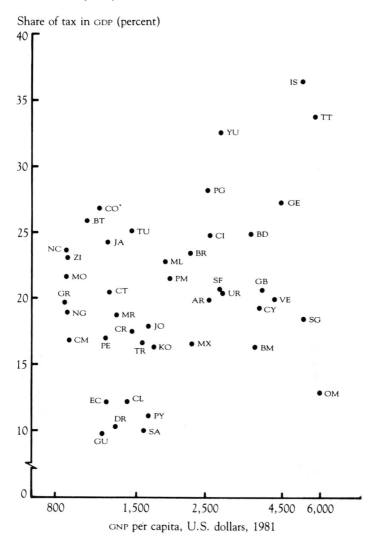

Share of tax in GDP (percent)

Note: The x-axis represents a natural log scale.

For forty-three countries with per capita income of less than $850:

$$(8\text{-}2) \quad \frac{\text{Total tax revenue}}{\text{GDP}} = -16.0983 + 5.3453 \log (\text{GNP per capita}).$$
$$\phantom{(8\text{-}2)} \qquad\qquad (1.69) \quad (3.30)^{**}$$
$$\bar{R}^2 = 0.191$$

For forty-three countries with per capita income equal to or more than $850:

$$(8\text{-}3) \quad \frac{\text{Total tax revenue}}{\text{GDP}} = -3.5262 + 3.1691 \log (\text{GNP per capita}).$$
$$\phantom{(8\text{-}3)} \qquad\qquad (0.30) \quad (2.04)^{*}$$
$$\bar{R}^2 = 0.07$$

Figure 8-4 shows these equations in graphic form.

Some theoretical arguments lend support to a causal relationship between per capita income and tax level (for example, Musgrave's tax-base, or tax-handle, theory), but it would be naive to accept a purely deterministic or mechanical relationship, as many historical, political, or social factors play a role.

Tables 8-3 and 8-4 provide in a summary fashion the same information as tables 8-1 and 8-2. For all eighty-six countries combined, the (unweighted) average ratio of tax revenue to GDP was 17.8 percent around 1981. That ratio was 12.9 percent for the twenty-two countries with per capita income of less than $350, however, and 22.8 percent for the twenty-one countries with per capita income of $1,700 or more. For the forty-three countries in between, it was about 18 percent, showing no significant difference between the group of countries with per capita incomes between $350 and $850 and those with per capita incomes between $850 and $1,700. Table 8-A1 shows that, if we ignore Europe (represented by only four countries), then Africa and the Western Hemisphere regions have similar tax ratios (about 17–18 percent), whereas Asia has a considerably lower tax ratio (about 15 percent) and the Middle East a considerably higher tax ratio (about 21 percent), very much the result of oil taxation.

Several studies (Chelliah, Baas, and Kelly, 1975; Tait, Grätz, and Eichengreen, 1979; Tanzi, 1981) have shown that the total tax ratio may be influenced by other factors in addition to per capita income. Such factors may include the monetization and openness of the economy, the share of mining in GDP, an export ratio that excludes mineral exports, the literacy rate, and the urbanization rate. Also, of course, the desired level of public expenditure is likely to play a role in determining the extent to which countries take advantage of their "taxable capacity." Rather than duplicating the results of some of these studies in explaining the total tax ratio, I shall consider some of these factors in the analysis of the tax structure.

The Structure of Taxation

Although many studies have analyzed the level of taxation in developing countries, few have paid particular attention to its structure. Yet it may be

Figure 8-4. *Regression Equations of Tax Ratios in Groups of Developing Countries*

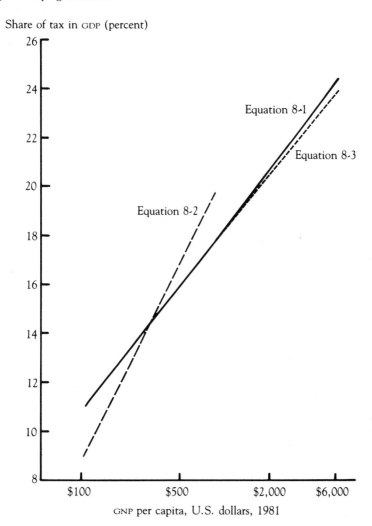

Share of tax in GDP (percent)

Equation 8-1

Equation 8-3

Equation 8-2

GNP per capita, U.S. dollars, 1981

Note: The x-axis represents a natural log scale.

fruitful to analyze structure, as there must be specific reasons why, say, one country ends up with a very large share of revenue from taxes on corporate income, whereas another may end up with a tax structure biased toward export duties. Historical or cultural factors clearly play a large role, but more must surely be involved. I shall deal separately with income taxes, domestic taxes on goods and services, taxes on foreign trade, and other taxes.

Income Taxes

For the eighty-six countries combined, the unweighted ratio of income taxes from all sources was 5.5 percent of GDP and 28.7 percent of total tax revenue. Tables 8-1 and 8-2 show the very wide range of importance of income taxes in the tax systems of developing countries. Income taxes vary from less than 1 percent of GDP in Nepal, Burma, and Uganda, for example, to 28 percent in Trinidad and Tobago (see table 8-1), or from 5 percent to 92 percent of total tax revenue (see table 8-2). The two tables indicate that the wide range results largely from taxes on corporations rather than from taxes on the incomes of individuals.

Individual income taxes account for 1.9 percent of GDP and for 10.3 percent of total tax revenue for the whole eighty-six countries. In only five countries (Liberia, Papua New Guinea, Zimbabwe, Turkey, and Israel) do they exceed 5 percent of GDP. Israel and Turkey have by far the highest ratios at more than 8 percent of GDP. The revenue from taxes on the incomes of individuals exceeds 4 percent of GDP in only eleven countries. Thus it can be concluded that these taxes are much less important (in terms of actual collection) in developing countries than they are in developed countries, where in 1981 the share of individual income taxes to GDP in OECD countries was 12 percent. The share of these taxes in total tax revenue was 32.8 percent. This low level is almost surely due to the combination of high tax avoidance and high levels of exemptions, as the marginal rates are often as high in developing countries as in developed countries. In only six countries (Mauritania, Liberia, Papua New Guinea, Zimbabwe, Turkey, and Israel) do individual income taxes account for more than one-fourth of total tax revenue, and in only seven countries do they exceed one-fifth of total tax revenue. On the other hand, in more than half of the countries considered, these taxes account for less than one-tenth of total taxes.

Economic development, as measured by per capita income, seems to correlate with a growing importance of these taxes; however, the correlation is not strong. The correlation coefficient is .26, significant at the 5 percent level. Individual income taxes account for only 1.1 percent of GDP in countries with per capita income of less than $350 but represent 2.4 percent of GDP in countries with per capita income of $1,700 or more. Their share of total tax revenue rises from 8.7 percent in the poorest group of countries to about 12 percent in the next income group. It declines to about 9 percent for the group with the highest income (see table 8-4). In addition, tables 8-A1 and 8-A2 show the relative importance of these taxes "by regions." If we eliminate Europe and the Middle East, the variation among regions is not very high.

The relative unimportance of taxes on individual incomes is disappointing, as these taxes have traditionally been considered the major instrument for pursuing (through fiscal tools) the objective of income redistribution.[2] Although this result is disappointing, it should not surprise experts who have worked intimately with these countries. The requirements for an effective system of personal income taxation are many and are satisfied, if at all, only when the level of development is high. When the agricultural sector is large, accounting standards are poor, the level of literacy is low, and most economic activity takes place in small establishments, the effective taxation of personal income is difficult (Goode, 1962) even though the greater concentration of income in developing countries as compared with industrial ones reduces the need to impose a mass-based income tax to raise a significant level of revenue (Tanzi, 1966). In developing countries far more than in developed countries, the personal income tax is often a tax on the wages of public sector employees and of the employees of large, and often foreign, corporations.[3] As the proportion of total personal income derived from work in large establishments and in the public sector rises, so does the possibility of taxing personal income.

For fourteen developing countries, it was possible to obtain the proportion of revenue from individual income taxes derived from wages and salaries. These data indicate that for the whole group that proportion was 71 percent, whereas it surpassed 90 percent in four countries (see table 8-5).

Corporate income taxes are somewhat more important than the taxes on the incomes of individuals. This is the reverse of the situation in industrial countries. These taxes account for 3.1 percent of GDP and for 16.5 percent of total tax revenue for the eighty-six countries combined. In six countries (Indonesia, Nigeria, Congo, Venezuela, Trinidad and Tobago, and Oman) the share of these taxes as a proportion of GDP exceeds 10 percent; in thirteen countries it exceeds 5 percent. These countries all depend heavily on oil or

Table 8-5. *Share of Individual Income Taxes Derived from Wages and Salaries, Selected Countries*
(percent)

Country	Share	Country	Share
Benin	88.60	Mexico	76.18
Burkina Faso	58.24	Morocco	77.54
Cameroon	16.11	Niger	66.51
Chad	64.25	Rwanda	100.00
Gabon	92.91	Togo	93.49
Mali	28.23	Zaire	95.57
Mauritania	50.35	Zambia	88.96
		Average	71.21

Note: Years are the same as in table 8-1.
Source: International Monetary Fund (1984).

other mineral exports. These exports are carried out by a few large corporations that make sizable profits and thus provide the government with a source of revenue that is easy to tap. (Mineral production could be taxed through export taxes; but as we shall see below, export taxes are generally applied to *agricultural* exports.) The importance of corporate income taxes can also be assessed by the fact that, in at least twelve countries, they account for more than one-fourth of total tax revenue and in six countries for more than one-half.

The impact of economic development on corporate income tax is greater than on individual income taxes. The correlation coefficient between the share of corporate income taxes in GDP and per capita income is .43 (significant at the 1 percent level). Table 8-3 shows that the share of these taxes in GDP rises from 1.5 percent for the group of countries with per capita incomes lower than $350, to 5.0 percent for countries with per capita incomes of $1,700 or more. As a share of total tax revenue, these taxes rise from 11 percent for the lowest income group to 23 percent for the highest income group. These results are somewhat surprising, as corporate income taxes have been falling over time and have become relatively unimportant for OECD countries. For these countries, in 1981, corporate income taxes accounted for only 2.8 percent of GDP and 7.8 percent of total tax revenue. We thus observe an unusual bell-shaped relationship whereby higher per capita income leads first to an increase in corporate income tax revenue and then to a decline. One explanation of this pattern may be that mineral exports raise the per capita incomes of developing countries and at the same time provide them with an important tax handle. By the time countries move into the OECD group, the importance of mineral exports in determining per capita incomes has been somewhat reduced, whereas other tax handles have become available.[4]

Tables 8-3 and 8-4 and appendix tables 8-A1 and 8-A2 cast additional light on *total income taxes*. Tables 8-3 and 8-4 show their growing importance in the tax systems of the developing countries as per capita income rises.[5] Whereas the poorest group (with per capita incomes less than $350) collects only 2.7 percent of GDP from total income taxes, and about 20 percent of total tax revenue, countries with per capita incomes of $1,700 or more collect about 8 percent of GDP and about 36 percent of total tax revenue. The relative importance of income taxes on individuals as compared with those on corporations is also shown. The importance of oil (and other mineral exports) and of per capita income is evident from tables 8-A1 and 8-A2. As oil exports become less important and per capita income rises, individual income taxes gain in importance, whereas the corporate income taxes become far less important. (Compare Europe with the Middle East in tables 8-A1 and 8-A2.)

Domestic Taxes on Goods and Services

Domestic taxes on goods and services account for 4.8 percent of GDP and for 28 percent of total tax revenue for the whole group. The importance of these taxes in generating revenue varies considerably among the eighty-six countries. In seven countries (Uganda, The Gambia, Lesotho, Swaziland, Nigeria, Botswana, and Oman) the ratio of domestic taxes on goods and services in GDP is less than 1 percent. It is not obvious what these countries have in common except that they do not have general sales taxes, though most of these countries make heavy use of import duties. (See below for more details.) Nine countries (India, Zambia, Nicaragua, Jamaica, Brazil, Portugal, Chile, Greece, and Israel) collect more than 10 percent of GDP from these taxes, while twenty-two countries collect from them more than 40 percent of total tax revenue. There is no correlation between the share of these taxes in GDP and per capita income. This statement is true for all domestic taxes on goods and services combined and also for general sales taxes and excises considered separately.

There are relatively few countries without some sort of "general" sales tax. Twenty-two countries have value-added taxes, whereas the rest have other forms of general sales taxes. Here the adjective "general" must be read as if it stood between quotation marks, as these taxes are often anything but general. In most countries the value that is added at the retail level, and often even at the wholesale level, is exempt; services are exempt; and so are many categories of goods. Furthermore, in some countries, goods produced under particular conditions (for example, by the cottage industry in Pakistan) are also exempt. These legal exemptions must of course be augmented by the illegal ones owing to tax evasion. The result is that for many countries the tax base consists predominantly of imports subject to these taxes. For several countries for which the information is available, the share of total general sales tax revenue collected from imports often exceeds 50 percent. It is unlikely that in many countries more than 20 percent of *domestic* value added is subject to this form of taxation. (This conclusion is supported by unpublished data for several countries.) The high rate of base erosion explains why in many countries relatively high legal rates generate low tax revenue. Because of these factors, the distinction between a general sales tax (often imposed with multiple rates) and excises is at times more a legal distinction than an economic one.

In twelve countries general sales taxes generate revenue greater than 5 percent of GDP. By far the largest percentage (10.9) is obtained by Chile, where the sales tax accounts for 41 percent of total tax revenue. For all countries combined, general sales taxes account for 2.1 percent of GDP and 11.7 percent of total tax revenue. These taxes are thus slightly more important than the taxes on individual income.

The contribution of *excises* to total revenue is about the same as that of the general sales taxes: 2 percent of GDP and 12.0 percent of total tax revenue. Only four countries generate more than 5 percent of GDP from excises (India, Zambia, Nicaragua, and Jamaica), with the first place going to Zambia—where excises amount to an extraordinary 7.8 percent of GDP. In nine countries excise taxes account for more than one-fourth of total tax revenue. Bolivia shows the highest percentage with a share of 35 percent.

Excises are imposed on many products and for many reasons. Three products, however—alcohol, tobacco, and petroleum—are known to play a very important role in excise taxation. To determine just how important this role is, information has been gathered and shown in table 8-6. The table refers to fifty

Table 8-6. Excises on Alcohol, Tobacco, and Petroleum

Country	Percent of total tax revenue				Percentage of GDP				Percentage of excises			
	Alcohol	Tobacco	Petroleum	Total	Alcohol	Tobacco	Petroleum	Total	Alcohol	Tobacco	Petroleum	Total
Chad	n.a.	n.a.	2.29	2.29	n.a.	n.a.	0.21	0.21	n.a.	n.a.	71.55	71.55
Ethiopia	5.17	0.70	5.27	11.13	0.59	0.08	0.59	1.26	27.25	3.86	25.37	56.48
Nepal	n.a.	5.33	n.a.	5.33	n.a.	0.38	n.a.	0.38	n.a.	40.29	n.a.	40.29
Mali	0.48	0.88	14.53	15.90	0.07	0.12	2.03	2.22	2.75	5.21	82.36	90.32
Zaire	0.62	4.04	n.a.	4.66	0.11	0.73	n.a.	0.84	11.36	74.19	n.a.	85.56
Burundi	26.54	n.a.	n.a.	26.54	3.38	n.a.	n.a.	3.38	98.57	n.a.	n.a.	98.57
Burkina Faso	n.a.	n.a.	3.79	3.79	n.a.	n.a.	0.48	0.48	n.a.	n.a.	54.98	54.98
Rwanda	19.07	n.a.	n.a.	19.07	2.11	n.a.	n.a.	2.11	100.00	n.a.	n.a.	100.00
India	n.a.	3.81	6.45	10.26	n.a.	0.56	0.88	1.44	n.a.	10.92	17.37	28.29
Tanzania	n.a.	0.26	n.a.	0.26	n.a.	0.05	n.a.	0.05	n.a.	71.30	n.a.	71.30
Benin	n.a.	n.a.	3.34	3.34	n.a.	n.a.	0.55	0.55	n.a.	n.a.	49.65	49.65
Central African Republic	5.42	n.a.	2.77	8.20	0.81	n.a.	0.42	1.23	66.16	n.a.	33.84	100.00
Sierra Leone	3.31	10.63	7.08	21.02	0.39	1.24	0.82	2.46	14.18	45.46	30.23	89.87
Niger	1.21	0.71	5.00	6.92	0.14	0.08	0.58	0.81	17.45	10.29	71.67	99.42
Sudan	1.83	1.96	1.83	5.61	0.18	0.19	0.18	0.54	7.19	7.70	7.19	22.07
Togo	n.a.	n.a.	1.65	1.65	n.a.	n.a.	0.40	0.40	n.a.	n.a.	100.00	100.00
Senegal	1.33	1.97	5.88	9.18	0.28	0.42	1.30	1.99	12.32	18.41	54.38	85.10
Mauritania	0.27	0.20	3.58	4.05	0.05	0.03	0.59	0.67	6.33	4.69	81.13	92.14
Liberia	1.73	n.a.	n.a.	1.73	0.07	n.a.	n.a.	0.07	15.19	n.a.	n.a.	15.19
Indonesia	0.11	4.19	n.a.	4.30	0.02	0.87	n.a.	0.89	2.48	90.21	0.01	92.70
Bolivia	4.30	3.53	26.51	34.34	0.26	0.21	1.66	2.14	12.60	10.10	75.29	97.99
Honduras	8.76	3.20	2.29	14.24	1.18	0.43	0.31	1.92	50.28	18.39	13.06	81.73
Zambia	16.15	4.15	11.65	31.95	3.70	0.95	2.66	7.32	47.28	12.15	34.07	93.49
Thailand	5.35	6.00	10.01	21.37	0.72	0.81	1.35	2.88	23.48	26.22	43.98	93.68
Grenada	0.85	0.39	n.a.	1.24	0.16	0.06	n.a.	0.22	83.78	16.22	n.a.	100.00

Morocco	0.92	5.20	3.02	9.13	0.20	1.13	0.65	1.98	8.89	50.15	28.97	88.01
Guatemala	5.37	2.61	2.62	10.59	0.52	0.25	0.26	1.03	47.36	23.05	23.07	93.49
Peru	0.79	1.91	6.95	9.64	0.14	0.33	1.21	1.69	7.81	18.72	68.03	94.57
Ecuador	1.22	0.80	3.12	5.14	0.14	0.09	0.38	0.62	20.80	13.90	54.10	88.80
Côte d'Ivoire	n.a.	1.48	5.77	7.25	n.a.	0.30	1.18	1.48	n.a.	16.36	63.59	79.95
Dominican Republic	11.04	3.58	12.30	26.91	1.13	0.37	1.24	2.73	40.61	13.15	44.21	97.97
Mauritius	7.87	3.15	n.a.	11.02	1.55	0.62	n.a.	2.17	63.18	25.35	n.a.	88.53
Colombia	0.11	n.a.	6.30	6.41	0.01	n.a.	0.77	0.78	1.88	n.a.	98.12	100.00
Costa Rica	2.80	0.56	1.77	5.14	0.49	0.10	0.31	0.90	13.59	2.73	8.54	24.86
Turkey	n.a.	n.a.	0.27	0.27	n.a.	n.a.	0.04	0.04	n.a.	n.a.	3.09	3.09
Paraguay	3.24	1.54	n.a.	4.78	0.36	0.17	n.a.	0.53	26.46	12.58	n.a.	39.04
Korea, Rep. of	6.03	n.a.	n.a.	6.03	0.98	n.a.	n.a.	0.98	38.91	n.a.	n.a.	38.91
Malaysia	1.26	0.53	3.02	4.80	0.29	0.12	0.68	1.08	15.07	6.31	34.95	56.33
Panama	2.42	n.a.	5.32	7.74	0.52	n.a.	1.14	1.67	26.54	n.a.	58.23	84.77
Brazil	0.07	n.a.	8.30	8.37	0.02	n.a.	1.94	1.96	0.36	n.a.	45.14	45.49
Mexico	1.03	1.46	3.35	5.85	0.17	0.24	0.53	0.94	9.49	13.53	25.69	48.71
Portugal	n.a.	3.75	8.57	12.33	n.a.	1.06	2.41	3.47	n.a.	23.05	52.26	75.32
Argentina	0.02	0.50	11.64	12.15	n.a.	0.10	2.28	2.39	0.12	2.72	62.09	64.92
South Africa	4.00	2.40	5.05	11.46	0.83	0.50	1.04	2.37	30.39	18.22	38.34	86.95
Cyprus	1.54	4.87	5.45	11.87	0.30	0.94	1.05	2.29	8.15	25.71	28.77	62.63
Venezuela	1.90	1.32	1.17	4.39	0.38	0.26	0.23	0.88	43.44	29.61	26.42	99.48
Greece	0.54	3.38	5.42	9.34	0.15	0.92	1.48	2.55	4.43	27.89	44.61	76.94
Israel	n.a.	0.76	2.16	2.91	n.a.	0.28	0.79	1.07	n.a.	25.12	73.67	98.79
Singapore	1.25	0.52	2.99	4.77	0.23	0.10	0.55	0.88	17.01	7.03	40.68	64.71
Trinidad and Tobago	0.47	n.a.	0.37	0.84	0.16	n.a.	0.12	0.28	55.92	n.a.	44.00	99.92
Average, 50 countries	3.91	2.55	5.15	9.34	0.57	0.42	0.84	1.44	26.98	22.80	43.16	72.80

n.a. Not available.

Note: Years are the same as in table 8-1. Countries are listed in ascending order of per capita GNP.

Source: International Monetary Fund (1984).

229

countries and shows excise tax revenues from those three products as shares of total tax revenue, GDP, and total excises. The total columns understate the importance of these taxes, as for several countries some of the information needed is unavailable.

By and large petroleum is the most important, followed by alcohol and by tobacco. Forty-three percent of total excise tax revenue comes from petroleum. Alcohol accounts for another 27 percent, whereas tobacco's share is about 23 percent. Overall, these three products account for 73 percent of total excises shown in table 8-6. (The actual percentage is much higher because data for some countries and for some of these excises are lacking, thus biasing the total downward.) In nineteen of the countries shown in table 8-6, they account for more than 90 percent of total excise tax revenue. In fourteen of the countries shown, excises on these three products account for more than 2 percent of GDP, and in seventeen countries they account for more than 10 percent of total tax revenue.

Alcohol is a very important tax base in several countries. It accounts for an extraordinary share of total tax revenue, for example, in Burundi and Rwanda (26.5 percent and 19.1 percent, respectively). In Zambia and the Dominican Republic, it accounts for more than 10 percent of total tax revenue. Tobacco is most important in the tax systems of Nepal, India, Sierra Leone, Thailand, Cyprus, and a few other countries, but its highest share is never as high as that of alcohol. Petroleum accounts for more than 25 percent of Bolivia's total tax revenue and for relatively high shares in Mali, India, Zambia, Thailand, Dominican Republic, Argentina, and a few other countries. (The importance of petroleum is often somewhat higher than these figures indicate, as in many countries it is also taxed with export or import taxes.)

Foreign Trade Taxes

Foreign trade taxes account for a little over 5.0 percent of GDP and for 30.6 percent of the total tax revenue of developing countries. These taxes are thus more important than the taxes on income. The factors that lead a country to rely on export taxes are somewhat different from those that lead it to rely on import taxes. As a consequence, I shall consider these two taxes separately.

Import duties are by far the single most important revenue source: they contribute 4.2 percent of GDP and 25 percent of total tax revenue. Import duties generate more than one-fourth of total tax revenue in almost half of the eighty-six countries. As with other revenue sources, the importance of import duties varies considerably among countries. As a percentage of GDP, import duties are most important in the group of twenty-two countries with per capita incomes below $350. They are least important for the countries with incomes of $1,700 or more (see table 8-3). (This statement does not mean that, in these higher-income countries, imports can come in freely. Quotas and other restrictions may take the place of the duties. In such cases the government is transferring the power of taxation to importers.) By region, they are most important in the Middle East and in Africa, where they generate about twice as much revenue as in other regions.

Total tax ratios rise with per capita income, whereas the ratio of import duties to GDP is negatively related to the level of income. There is thus a significant fall in the contribution of import duties to total tax revenue (see table 8-4). That share is 30 percent for countries with incomes less than $350 and 13 percent for countries with incomes of $1,700 or more. The declining importance of import duties cannot be explained in terms of a tax-handle theory; the ratio of imports to GDP (the presumed tax base) is much higher in the countries with per capita incomes of $1,700 or more than in the countries with per capita incomes of less than $350.[6] Explicit policy choices must thus be involved.

We would expect revenue from import duties to be higher in countries that are open and that do not rely much on domestic taxes on goods and services.[7] To provide some support for these conjectures, table 8-7 has isolated the eight countries with the highest ratios of revenue from import duties to GDP and the eight countries with the highest ratios of revenue from domestic transaction taxes to GDP. Table 8-7 shows also the share of imports in GDP. The striking feature of this table is the degree to which import duties substitute for domestic taxes on goods and services and vice versa. All the great users of taxes on

Table 8-7. *Indirect Taxes*
(percent of GDP)

Country	Import duties	Domestic taxes on goods and services	Total indirect taxes	Imports
Countries with highest import duties				
Swaziland	16.29	0.79	17.08	81.10
Lesotho	14.30	0.87	15.17	112.63
Botswana	13.40	0.40	13.80	79.40
Yemen Arab Republic	12.17	1.93	14.10	52.61
Bahamas	10.60	1.70	12.30	321.68
Jordan	10.41	1.90	12.31	82.25
Gambia	10.28	0.62	10.90	55.75
Benin	8.58	2.30	10.88	40.11
Countries with highest domestic taxes on goods and services				
Chile	1.36	13.26	14.62	16.94
Jamaica	1.23	13.01	14.24	29.17
Nicaragua	2.36	11.47	13.83	28.97
Brazil	0.57	11.33	11.90	8.73
Zambia	1.74	10.71	12.45	29.25
Israel	1.60	10.38	11.98	35.54
Portugal	1.54	10.27	11.81	39.58
Greece	1.41	10.08	11.49	25.24

Sources: Table 8-1 for revenue data and, for import data, IMF, *International Financial Statistics.*

imports make little use of taxes on domestic transactions, and all the great users of domestic taxes on goods and services make little use of import duties.

A more formal test of the above relationship can be made by regressing the share of import duties in GDP (ID/GDP) against (a) per capita income ($\bar{Y}$), (b) the share of imports in GDP (IM/GDP), and (c) the share of domestic taxes on goods and services in GDP (DOM/GDP). The estimated equation is the following:

$$(8\text{-}4) \qquad ID/GDP = 4.8482 - 0.0008\bar{Y} + 0.0434\ IM/GDP$$
$$\phantom{(8\text{-}4) \qquad ID/GDP = }(8.03)^{**}\ (4.02)^{**}\quad (5.90)^{**}$$

$$- 0.2239\ DOM/GDP.$$
$$(2.48)^{*} \qquad\qquad\qquad \bar{R}^{2} = 0.39$$

where the numbers in parenthesis are t values. Two asterisks indicate significance at the 1 percent level, whereas one asterisk indicates significance at the 5 percent level.

The equation strongly backs our hypothesis. Import duties are positively influenced by the openness of the economy and negatively influenced by the level of per capita income and by the country's reliance on domestic taxes on goods and services. (Incidentally, openness does not play any role in determining a country's total tax ratio. It was not significant in a test that regressed the tax ratio against per capita income and the ratio of imports to GDP.)

Table 8-8 summarizes some relevant relationships for these taxes. It shows that, in spite of the fact that imports as a share of GDP rise rather sharply as income rises (see column 3), the share of import duties in total tax revenue falls considerably (column 4). That the importance of imports as a tax base is inversely related to the level of income can be seen most clearly from column 5: the effective tax rate on imports averages about 21 percent for the low-income countries and about 8.5 percent for the high-income countries.

Table 8-8. *Basic Relationships for Import Taxation*

Per capita income ($\bar{Y}$) (dollars)	Percentage of GDP			Import duties as percentage of total tax revenue (4)	Import duties as percentage of imports (5)
	Total tax revenue (1)	Import duties (2)	Imports (3)		
0–349	12.90	3.82	20.75	30.57	21.11
350–849	17.50	5.92	38.13	32.87	15.54
850–1,699	18.16	4.35	31.93	23.72	14.05
1,700 or more	22.75	2.72	51.74	13.01	8.50
All countries	17.77	4.20	35.42	25.09	14.87

Sources: Table 8-1 for revenue and data and, for import data, IMF, *International Financial Statistics.*

The behavior of the effective tax rate on import values can result either from a systematic reduction of the statutory levels of import duties as per capita income rises, or from progressively more generous exemptions and exonerations from customs duties without any necessary change in the statutory rates. I am not aware of any study that has assessed whether the level of *statutory* rates falls as income rises. It would require too much effort to make the assessment here, even though the needed information is available. The second possibility would be much harder to check, as the required data are not readily available, and in fact they may not be available at all for most countries.

Table 8-9 contains whatever information could be found on this issue. The table covers eighteen countries and shows that the proportion of exempted imports ranges from 12 percent in The Gambia to 75 percent in Malaysia. The average for the group is 45 percent. The reasons for this erosion of the import tax base are several. The most important are (a) duty-free imports by the public sector; (b) duty-free imports by embassies and by other agents with diplomatic status; (c) duty-free imports by private enterprises benefiting from incentive legislation; (d) zero rating of imports for social reasons. Table 8-9, although interesting, does not allow us to make any statement about a possible relationship between this form of tax-base erosion and the level of per capita income.

Export taxes continue to play a significant role in many countries but have a

Table 8-9. *Exempted Imports as Percentage of Total Imports*

Country	Year	Exempted imports
Antigua and Barbuda	1981	50
Burundi	1983	40
Cameroon	1979	52
Côte d'Ivoire	1979	32
Egypt	1983	70
Fiji	1981	29
Gambia	1977	12
Grenada	1983	57
Haiti	1977	41
Malaysia	1981	75
Mauritius	1978	25
Morocco	1978	35
Pakistan	1980	34
Sierra Leone	1980	54
Somalia	1978	60
St. Lucia	1983	50
Trinidad and Tobago	1981	62
Western Samoa	1979	39
Average		45

Source: Estimates based on unpublished national sources.

much more limited importance than import duties. For the whole group they account for 1.1 percent of GDP and 7 percent of total tax revenue. Their importance falls with the rise of per capita income. They generate 11 percent of total tax revenue (1.62 percent of GDP) for the group of countries with per capita income less than $350 but less than 3 percent of total tax revenue (0.44 percent of GDP) for the countries with per capita income of $1,700 or more (see tables 8-3 and 8-4).[8] The ratio of export duties to exports is 11 percent for the lowest income group and falls respectively to 5.1 percent, 4.4 percent, and 3.3 percent for the other three income groups. The ratio is 6.1 percent for the eighty-six countries combined. It is highest in Africa (7.3 percent) and in the Western Hemisphere (5.8 percent), lower in Asia (5.2 percent), and much lower in the Middle East (2.4 percent) and in the few European countries (0.1 percent).

Sri Lanka has by far the highest ratio of revenue from export taxes to GDP (6.2 percent). Export taxes are also very important in Malaysia, Grenada, Rwanda, El Salvador, and a few other countries. In the discussion of corporate income taxes, I argued that those taxes were particularly important in countries that export *mineral* products, as these exports are normally carried out by large enterprises. Following the same line of reasoning, we would expect export taxes to be particularly important in countries that export *agricultural* products, as agricultural production is far less concentrated and the information required to tax agricultural incomes *as incomes* is normally not available. Countries thus often have little alternative but to tax agricultural production through export taxes. If this line of reasoning is correct, the countries that use corporate income taxes extensively should use export taxes very little and vice versa unless of course they are important exporters of both mineral and agricultural products. Table 8-10 casts some light on this hypothesis.

Table 8-10 shows the eight countries with the highest revenue from export taxes (as percentages of GDP) and the eight countries with the highest revenue from corporate income taxes. The relationship is obvious: the heavy users of corporate income taxes make almost no use of export taxes, whereas the heavy users of export taxes make little use of corporate income taxes. The major exceptions—Malaysia and Swaziland—export not just agricultural products but also mineral products, so that they can make heavy use of both taxes. It thus appears that the structure of production and exports is a major determinant of the tax structure at least insofar as the choice between corporate income taxes and export taxes is concerned.

Other Taxes

We can be very brief with the remaining taxes. *Social security taxes* generate revenues on the same order of magnitude as the taxes on the incomes of individuals—1.15 percent of GDP and 7 percent of total tax revenue. As their base is wages, and as the share of wages in national income rises with per capita income, it is not surprising to find some relationship between these taxes and

Table 8-10. *Export Duties and Corporate Income Taxes*
(percent of GDP)

Country	Export duties	Corporate income taxes
Countries with highest export duties		
Sri Lanka	6.25	2.05
Malaysia	4.40	7.45
Grenada	3.29	1.22
Mauritius	3.14	1.70
Rwanda	2.88	1.24
Honduras	2.42	2.45
Swaziland	2.36	4.65
El Salvador	2.30	1.12
Countries with highest corporate income taxes		
Trinidad and Tobago	n.a.	22.34
Indonesia	0.33	15.59
Nigeria	0.01	14.71
Congo	0.07	14.15
Venezuela	n.a.	14.08
Oman	n.a.	12.03
Gabon	0.99	9.78
Malaysia	4.40	7.45

n.a. Not available.
Source: Table 8-1.

per capita income.[9] Tables 8-3 and 8-4 show that these taxes grow in importance as income rises. Per capita income, however, is not the sole determinant of these taxes' importance. Sociopolitical factors are perhaps equally important; many of the countries with the highest share of GDP coming from this source are Latin countries (Costa Rica, Panama, Brazil, Portugal, and Uruguay). In these countries social security taxes account for 5–8 percent of GDP.

Of the three theoretical tax bases—income, consumption, and wealth—wealth is by far the least important. *Wealth taxes* account for only 0.4 percent of GDP and 2.5 percent of total tax revenue for the eighty-six countries taken together. They are very important in Singapore, where they account for 2.6 percent of GDP and for about 14 percent of total tax revenue. Singapore is essentially a city-state, so that a large share of wealth is in the form of buildings. In only six other countries do wealth taxes account for more than 1 percent of GDP. This low yield on the part of these taxes is surprising in view of the fact that they used to be a major revenue source in earlier times (Adams, 1982; Hinrichs, 1966).[10] In recent times administrative constraints have usually made these taxes both unproductive and inequitable in developing countries. Their most sophisticated version—the net wealth tax—has proved a costly mistake in developing countries that have attempted to implement it. These taxes show some relationship to per capita income (see tables 8-3 and 8-4).

The correlation coefficient between the ratio of wealth and property taxes to GDP and per capita income was 0.37, significant at the 1 percent level.

Table 8-11 has isolated for the last three years for which the information is available the recurrent taxes on immovable property (property taxes on building and land) for forty-nine countries.[11] Singapore again emerges as the only country where these taxes are truly important, although they also contribute significant revenues in Nepal, El Salvador, Jamaica, Bahamas, Barbados, and a few other countries. These taxes are also correlated with per capita income. The coefficient of correlation between their share in GDP and per capita income is .38, significant at the 1 percent level.

Other Aspects

This chapter has sought to give the reader a feel for the quantitative aspects of the developing countries' tax systems. If I were now to conclude, however, readers who know little about these tax systems might form the impression that they have learned more from the chapter than they have. The fact is that tax systems differ in more than the statistical aspects described above.[12] Each tax system has its own characteristics and peculiarities, and these cannot be captured by purely statistical summaries. To give a more comprehensive picture of the tax systems of developing countries we would need the *statutory* description in addition to the statistical and what, for lack of better words, we shall call the *real* or *effective* description. The correlation between these three descriptions can be low indeed.

The statutory tax system could be outlined in part by presenting the relevant information about rates, taxable bases, methods of payments, and so on, as described in the laws. This information is generally available for many countries and for most taxes, although absence of codification often makes it difficult to trace. In some countries, locating a given tax law can be a major and frustrating enterprise. Locating the regulations that accompany the law may be even more difficult. If readers were provided with the statutory information, in addition to statistical information, their knowledge would undoubtedly increase but not by as much as they might believe and certainly not by as much as it would increase if we were dealing with advanced countries. The reason is that in developing countries the gap between the statutory tax system and the effective or real tax system may be wide indeed. This gap also affects the quality or the meaning of the statistical description. Two countries could conceivably have similar statistics but totally different statutory systems. They could have similar laws and end up with highly different statistics. How do these differences come about? I outline some of the reasons below. (A more extensive discussion can be found in Tanzi, 1983.)

First, there is the wedge introduced by explicit and intentional tax evasion. The individual who earns an income equal to x or sells an amount equal to y but declares only half of these amounts has, in an effective sense, reduced the burden of taxation, thus changing the relationship between the statutory system and the statistical description.

Table 8-11. *Recurrent Taxes on Immovable Property*

Country	Percentage of total tax revenue	Percentage of GDP
Chad	0.48	0.05
Bangladesh	1.84	0.15
Ethiopia	1.84	0.21
Nepal	4.82	0.34
Mali	1.17	0.16
Zaire	0.08	0.01
Burundi	0.18	0.02
Rwanda	0.50	0.06
Tanzania	0.66	0.12
Haiti	0.48	0.05
Central African Republic	0.11	0.02
Madagascar	0.05	0.01
Niger	0.09	0.01
Sudan	0.21	0.01
Togo	0.44	0.11
Senegal	0.99	0.21
Mauritania	0.16	0.03
Yemen Arab Republic	0.66	0.13
Liberia	0.97	0.22
Indonesia	0.84	0.17
Lesotho	0.09	0.02
Bolivia	0.16	0.01
Egypt	1.08	0.32
El Salvador	3.90	0.44
Philippines	0.42	0.05
Grenada	0.95	0.18
Morocco	0.18	0.04
Nicaragua	1.21	0.27
Guatemala	0.71	0.07
Ecuador	0.26	0.03
Jamaica	3.03	0.72
Côte d'Ivoire	0.75	0.15
Colombia	0.24	0.03
Tunisia	0.11	0.03
Costa Rica	0.15	0.03
Turkey	0.49	0.08
Syrian Arab Republic	2.67	0.27
Jordan	0.30	0.05
Paraguay	2.82	0.31
Panama	2.18	0.47
Brazil	0.10	0.02
Uruguay	0.34	0.07
Barbados	3.30	0.75
Bahamas	3.44	0.56
Cyprus	0.68	0.13
Greece	0.21	0.06
Israel	0.98	0.36
Singapore	13.03	2.41
Trinidad and Tobago	0.18	0.06

Note: Years are the same as in table 8-1. Countries are listed in ascending order of per capita GNP.
Source: International Monetary Fund (1984).

Second, a wedge is introduced by poor, or more often nonexistent, accounting. Again, the unwary observer may believe that what shows up in the statistics as an "income" tax was actually imposed on a clear-cut concept of income and that what shows up as a sales tax was imposed on an objectively measured concept of sale. The reality is, however, far different. It is not uncommon for the government to form some idea of income from the volume of the turnover and some idea of sales from, say, the size of the establishment. (Several countries, for example, collect a minimum tax on corporate income. This tax is assessed as a given percentage—often 1 percent—of the turnover. It is generally shown as an income tax, but is it one? See Mutén, 1982.) In these cases, the theoretical distinction between, say, an income tax and a sales tax has no real-life counterpart. It would thus be naive to apply the public finance theories related to specific taxes to these statistical concepts.

Third, the wedge can be introduced by the timing of the payment. Suppose, for example, that a tax on corporate income is paid with a two-year delay, so that this year's collection is determined by the corporate income of two years ago. Suppose, as is frequently the case, that there is a significant and variable rate of inflation. In such a case, this year's revenue from the tax on corporate income might bear no relationship to this year's corporate income. Unfortunately, information about these lags is not readily available and is generally unknown, so that when we compare statistics between countries such information cannot be taken into account.

If tax evasion, accounting standards, lags, and other factors were unchanging, they could, perhaps, be taken into account in an analysis of the tax systems. To complicate matters even more, however, they keep changing, being influenced by factors such as the rate of inflation, the personality of the tax administrators, the political mood, the means available to the tax administration, the rigidity with which the courts are applying the penalties to tax evaders, the degree of corruptibility of the tax inspectors, and the variability in the exchange rate. An intimate knowledge of a tax system is thus necessary before theoretical prescriptions for tax reform are made. In taxation, perhaps more than in any other area, perfection may be the enemy of the good. What looks just right in theory may be quite wrong in practice. The basic truth to remember is that control over the statutory system (over the tax laws) may at times be accompanied by very little control over the effective system. If such is the case, changing the laws may mean far less than we believe.

Appendix: Supplementary Tables

Table 8-A1. *Tax Revenue, by Region*
(percent of GDP)

Country	Average income (dollars)	Total taxes	Income taxes				Domestic taxes on goods and services				Foreign trade				Social security	Wealth and property	Other
			Total	Individual	Corporate	Other	Total	General sales, turnover, VAT	Excises	Other	Total	Import duties	Export duties	Other			
Africa	666	17.41	5.56	1.93	3.05	0.54	4.02	1.86	1.64	0.60	6.44	5.55	0.79	0.09	0.65	0.31	0.39
Asia	1,008	15.02	5.12	1.53	3.44	0.09	5.21	1.82	2.31	1.07	3.92	2.91	0.96	0.04	0.07	0.39	0.33
Europe	3,002	24.82	5.59	3.59	1.19	1.05	7.56	3.33	3.26	1.62	2.50	2.48	n.a.	0.02	7.84	0.49	0.83
Middle East	2,984	21.40	8.58	4.80	7.36	0.27	3.83	3.03	0.91	0.52	4.88	4.81	0.06	0.01	2.34	0.79	0.99
Western hemisphere	1,841	17.62	4.86	1.42	2.93	0.62	5.45	2.14	2.20	1.11	3.96	3.03	0.76	0.17	2.02	0.53	0.81
All countries	1,330	17.77	5.47	1.94	3.14	0.52	4.81	2.07	1.97	0.88	5.02	4.20	0.72	0.10	1.49	0.43	0.57

n.a. Not available.

Sources: International Monetary Fund (1984); World Bank (1983).

Table 8-A2. *Tax Revenue, by Region*
(percent of total tax revenue)

Country	Average income (dollars)	Income taxes				Domestic taxes on goods and services				Foreign trade				Social security	Wealth and property	Other
		Total	Individual	Corporate	Other	Total	General sales, turnover, VAT	Excises	Other	Total	Import duties	Export duties	Other			
Africa	666	29.76	10.80	16.42	2.46	23.85	10.73	10.36	3.30	38.55	31.92	5.86	0.77	3.78	1.77	2.32
Asia	1,008	29.16	10.05	18.18	0.44	38.39	15.10	16.21	7.07	27.18	21.84	5.03	0.31	0.33	2.81	2.12
Europe	3,002	26.14	17.65	5.33	4.22	29.69	11.69	14.06	6.75	10.86	10.73	n.a.	0.13	27.74	2.15	3.42
Middle East	2,984	41.83	13.63	41.03	0.81	14.59	8.30	4.20	4.47	26.38	25.76	0.55	0.07	7.95	3.94	5.32
Western hemisphere	1,841	24.73	7.53	14.75	3.11	31.03	11.62	13.60	5.84	25.19	18.77	5.27	1.15	10.55	3.15	5.32
All countries	1,330	28.70	10.25	16.53	2.43	27.93	11.66	12.23	4.88	30.63	24.98	4.91	0.73	6.86	2.48	3.40

n.a. Not available.

Sources: International Monetary Fund (1984); World Bank (1983).

240

Notes

1. The major categories also contain a column called "other." This refers to taxes that could not be allocated to the specific subcategories. Some income taxes, for example, cannot clearly be allocated to individuals or corporations.

2. It is disappointing from an equity point of view, but it may be welcome from an efficiency point of view.

3. The share of wages and salaries in national income is generally much lower in developing countries than in developed. Therefore the need for taxing nonwage incomes is far greater.

4. The statutory rates at which profits are taxed in the developing countries are *grosso modo* of the same order of magnitude as in the OECD countries (Lent, 1977). The use of investment incentives (in the form of tax holidays, allowances, etc.) in the developing countries is at least as widespread as in the OECD countries. The greater importance of these taxes in the former group of countries is therefore probably accounted for by a higher share of profits in GDP.

5. The correlation coefficient for total income taxes (including individual and corporate as well as "other") of .47 is significant at the 1 percent level.

6. The imports/GDP ratios are, respectively, 23.3 percent for the low-income group and 56.3 percent for the high-income group.

7. The theory of tax structure change argues that, as countries develop, foreign trade taxes are progressively replaced by domestic taxes on goods and services (see Tanzi, 1973 and 1978).

8. The correlation coefficient ($-.22$) between the ratio of export duties to GDP and per capita income is negative and significant at the 5 percent level.

9. The correlation coefficient between the ratio of social security taxes to GDP and per capita income was .39, significant at the 1 percent level.

10. The noninclusion of local taxes for many countries, however, may have biased the contribution of these taxes downward.

11. The data in tables 8-1 and 8-2 include all taxes on wealth ownership as well as on wealth transfer.

12. At this point, Disraeli's well-known observation—that there are three kinds of lies: lies, damned lies, and statistics—appears highly pertinent.

9

Tax Reform in Developing Countries

Richard Musgrave

TAX REFORM IN DEVELOPING COUNTRIES involves broad issues of economic policy as well as specific problems of tax structure design and administration. All these aspects are important, and none can be neglected. First, there are the central problems of revenue requirement and of how to fit the revenue structure into development policy. This area of concern includes the impact of alternative taxes on saving and investment and their implications for the macro balance (domestic and foreign) of the economy. There is also the important goal of securing a fair distribution of the tax burden. Among more specific tax issues, attention needs to be given to the composition of the tax structure as well as to the design of its major components. The problem throughout is not simply to determine what would be desirable but also to assess what is administratively practicable and (as all tax reformers well know) within the ballpark of political feasibility.

Although the key problems are encountered in most situations, what needs to be done and what can be done depend on the geography, institutions, politics, and developmental stage of the particular country under investigation. Tax reform, like other aspects of public policy in developing countries, does not lend itself readily to generalization. Markets tend to be more segregated and imperfect than in industrialized countries, mobility tends to be lower, dependence on foreign markets and markets for particular products is greater, and political and administrative constraints are more powerful. We must allow for these factors to produce policy proposals that offer not only sound economic policy but also a chance of implementation.

I thus address the basic issues that must be faced in building a sound tax structure rather than emergency situations of fiscal imbalance or breakdown that may require immediate attention. In this area I follow the general approach taken by a generation of tax reform studies, beginning with the World Bank Mission to Colombia in 1949. Working under the direction of Laughlin Curry, I then took part in the Bank's first major report on tax reform, seen in the broader context of economic development, a report that has become something of a prototype.

Tax Reform and Development Policy

I begin with the broader issues relating tax to development policy and subsequently consider more specific aspects of tax design.

The Revenue Target and Tax Effort

Tax policy, and what is to be done about particular taxes, cannot be determined without reference to a revenue target. It is therefore well to begin by examining the budgetary implications of the development plan or, if there is none, of the expected pattern of economic growth. What will revenue requirements be, and what is the prevailing revenue system expected to yield? Are revenue estimates consistent with the projected rate of growth? How do they compare with projected expenditure levels? What additional revenue is required to maintain internal and external balance? The revenue assumptions and requirements of the development plan must thus be made explicit and consistent.

It does not follow, however, that the revenue target is the dependent variable in the system. Revenue requirements implicit in the economic plan may be unrealistically high, in which case other variables must be adjusted and rendered consistent with a feasible revenue goal. This point may seem obvious, but only too frequently there is no such consistency in the overall plan. One reason is that the finance ministry typically deals with tax policy and current expenditures, whereas capital expenditures and general planning are part of the planning ministry. With inadequate communication between the two— and planning ministries are usually supported by a superior technical staff—tax policy tends to receive inadequate attention and dangles outside the core of policy thinking.

I have noted that the economic plan (or policy thinking even in the absence of a formal plan) has to involve revenue targets but that these cannot simply be viewed as a target that "must" be met. As a result we must consider the level of taxation that a country can afford and the minimum level for which it should aim. Obviously, the purpose of tax policy should not be to maximize revenue, much less to push rates beyond that level. Economic development in a mixed economy requires appropriate contributions by both the private sector and the public sector; excessive levels of taxation are to be avoided. It is also well, however, to observe that tax missions will frequently encounter complaints of overtaxation, even where the charge is far from appropriate. Some operational criteria of tax effort must thus be developed. A tax-to-GNP ratio of at least, say, 18 percent seems called for in most cases, yet prevailing ratios in developing countries are frequently much below that level (see chapter 8). Ratios for Latin American countries are typically about 14 percent, whereas those for Asian countries are somewhat higher.

Still, generalizations are again difficult. If we consider the taxable capacity of a particular country, some obvious features demand attention. One is the level of per capita income as it indicates the slack for diversion of resources from private sector consumption. The poorer the country, the more burdensome is such diversion. At the same time, the scope for diversion becomes larger if the distribution of income is highly unequal, as it frequently is. Next, the availability of "tax handles" enters as a limiting factor. Depending upon the institutional setting of the private sector, the administrative task of diverting tax revenue may be more or less feasible. The existence of sizable retail establishments, large manufacturing units, and a substantial share of the labor force working as employees thus all furnish tax handles that facilitate administration, as does an open economy with a small number of import points. Small agriculture, small retail establishments, and a large share of the labor force in self-employment in turn complicate tax collection. The availability of administrative staff also poses an important constraint. Next, there is the willingness of the political system to apply taxes broadly and, last but not least, the willingness of the judiciary to enforce tax rules, applying adequate penalties where they are needed.

Nevertheless, it remains helpful to compare the tax effort of a particular country with that of others in the same region and subject to more or less similar circumstances. As a result we now have a substantial literature (see chapter 8) regarding techniques of measuring and comparing tax effort. If countries were similar in per capita income and in economic structure, a simple comparison of tax revenue-to-GNP ratios might do. Countries differ, however, and we must allow for such differences. A country's tax effort may thus be measured by comparing its actual-revenue-to-GNP ratio (or revenue-to-GDP ratio) with that which would result if it had responded in an average fashion to a set of relevant economic characteristics. These responses are obtained by considering a sample of countries and fitting an equation to predict the tax-to-GNP ratio (or tax-to-GDP ratio) from such characteristics. In various studies of this sort, export, import, mining, and agricultural shares in GNP performed best as explanatory variables, with per capita income relatively unimportant. We then obtain a measure of average tax effort by applying the estimated coefficients to the variables of the particular country and comparing the estimated ratio with the actual ratio. Although "average" behavior with regard to relevant characteristics is not necessarily desirable, this approach nevertheless provides a more meaningful standard of comparison than that given by reference to unadjusted actual-tax-to-GNP ratios only.

Levels of Saving and Investment

We must next consider the relationship of taxation effects to economic development goals. Among these, the impact of taxation on consumption and saving is of prime importance.

The rate of household saving in developing countries is typically very low and of near negligible importance in the overall savings rate. To the extent that such saving occurs, it originates almost entirely in the top decile (or less) of the income scale. Progressive income taxation at the upper end of the scale thus threatens what little household saving there is. Yet to exclude the upper-income households or to tax them inadequately means to bypass the luxury consumption of high-income receivers. Because we shall find this to be the major pocket of transferable "surplus," tax policy confronts a dilemma. Ideally, the dilemma would be resolved by a progressive expenditure tax, but there are severe administrative limitations on its feasibility in developing country settings. The use of specific savings incentives (such as credits for income that is saved or exclusion of capital earnings) under the income tax may offer a partial solution but is also problematic. Typically, such incentives do more harm in decimating the tax base and in creating horizontal inequities than they do good in securing a higher rate of net saving. In all, the problem of generating a higher rate of household saving is more a matter of checking inflation and creating adequate savings institutions than a concern of tax policy.

There is, however, a more direct link of tax policy to business saving. Business saving, especially on the part of larger companies, is typically an important source of saving. Profits taxes, it appears, are the form of taxation that falls most heavily on saving. This aspect must be considered in determining the level of company taxation as well as its structure. Favorable treatment of retentions may be in order even though such treatment runs counter to the usual (developed country) argument for integration of corporate and personal income taxes.

Nevertheless, the taxation of private sector saving is only part of the problem. The other and potentially more important part is the role of public sector saving. This role is not measured adequately by reference to the state of budget surplus or deficit alone. The composition of the tax and expenditure structure also matters. Thus public investment, financed by taxes drawn from consumption, also adds to capital formation, whereas public consumption outlays, financed by taxes drawn from saving, will reduce it. Clearly the relevant concept of public investment is not in terms of public acquisition of assets or construction projects. "Current" outlays on health or education may contribute as much or more to economic growth.

Because capital is mobile, at least in the absence of exchange controls, the level of net returns available abroad sets a clear limit on domestic taxation of capital income (see chapters 8 and 12). It follows that the level of corporate taxation must be modest if domestic capital is to be kept at home and if foreign capital is to be attracted. Also, moderation in the rate of tax is preferable to extensive use of investment incentives, pressure for which is as lively in developing countries as elsewhere. Reason for skepticism regarding the beneficial effects of such incentives is equally strong, if not stronger, especially because, as noted below, such incentives are frequently used very selectively, with selection criteria vague and inadequately related to the development plan.

A major question is whether special incentives should be given to foreign capital (see chapter 23). Preferential treatment of such capital may attract inflow without at the same time surrendering the tax base provided by domestic capital. Special allowances are thus tempting, but two provisos should be noted. First, nothing is gained (and valuable revenue is lost) if such incentives are offset by stricter taxation of repatriated earnings in the source country. Second, competition among developing countries for bigger and better tax incentives generates tax relief above that needed to attract foreign capital. Finally, it is to the advantage of developing countries to design incentives so as to induce capital to stay for a substantial period and to flow into investments that generate local value added.

Foreign and Domestic Balance

From the standpoint of domestic balance, the important consideration is whether taxes fall on consumption or on saving. From the standpoint of foreign balance, the important question is to what extent taxes will fall on domestic production or on imports. Income taxation will differ in its effect, depending on the spending patterns of taxpayers (that is, spending on imports versus spending on domestic output). To the extent that consumption out of high incomes is more import intensive, progressive taxes will be more favorable to the balance of trade. Effects of profit taxation will depend on the weight of associated capital imports in affected types of investment. A general sales tax will be spread equally, whereas manufacturing excises and import duties will curtail domestic production and imports, respectively. Subsidies to exports improve the balance of trade, whereas taxes on domestic output affect it adversely. Combining considerations of both domestic and foreign balance, the choice of tax mix is thus an important factor in economic policy. Frequently the domestic tax base is developed insufficiently, whereas imports offer a more accessible tax handle. The necessity of maintaining domestic balance thus tends to generate excessive protection and a level of import duties higher than that required by considerations of foreign balance.

The Pattern of Distribution

The distribution of the tax burden is an important issue in developing countries no less than in industrialized countries. To be sure, the setting differs. The basic solution to poverty in developing countries must involve the growth of per capita income. This growth requires capital formation, both public and private. Taxation is needed to finance the former, but progressive taxation interferes with the latter. This statement may seem to suggest that a fair distribution of the tax burden is a luxury that poor countries cannot afford. Yet it also seems evident that fairness in taxation is especially important where the level of income is low and its distribution is highly skewed. Moreover, a perception that gains and burdens of growth are distributed fairly is essential to the advance of democratic institutions, with fairness in taxation an important part thereof. For these and other reasons, the issue of burden distribution must be faced.

Distribution of Income

Available data on the distribution of income in developing countries are typically incomplete and of questionable quality. The usual picture, however, shows highly unequal, indeed kinked, distribution. It begins with a large bottom group, encompassing, say, two-thirds of the population and receiving a rather uniformly low income. This group includes the traditional agricultural sector and recent immigrants to urban centers. The next decile or two reflect a small "middle class" with incomes substantially above subsistence but still quite low compared with middle-class incomes in developed countries. At the top, there is a small segment of the population with high incomes comparable to those in developed countries. The top decile of the population may receive as much as 50 percent of total income, as compared with 30 percent or less in industrialized countries. The significance of this kinked pattern for distribution of the tax burden will be noted presently.

Although the general picture is as I have just described it, information on income distribution for the particular country under consideration may be lacking or wholly inadequate. Yet some such information is needed as a point of departure for judging the distribution of the tax burden. The analysis may thus have to begin with the modeling of income distribution. Modeling is not too difficult for some sectors of the economy, such as the income of government employees and of employees of the larger manufacturing establishments. For other sectors, estimates may have to be based on indirect evidence. Levels of income for major groups in the traditional sector may have to be estimated from living standards, including home-grown food and other nonpecuniary sources. The income of self-employed people may also have to be derived from indirect evidence. Capital income is especially difficult to obtain, although sample information from tax returns and reference to national income data are of some help. Having estimated distributive patterns by sector, we may then obtain a national picture by attaching weights based on labor force, employment, and national income data. Caution is again necessary, however, as the latter might not offer a reliable anchor, and income tax data may not be available in convenient form. In all, estimating the distribution of income is a precarious task. The derivation of at least rough patterns of distribution is facilitated, however, by the fact that the high degree of overall inequality stems from sharp differences in the average levels of income between various sectors (for example, employees in traditional agriculture and in the developed sector). In all, the distribution is substantially more skewed toward the top, and the pattern is flatter below than in high-income countries.

Distribution of the Tax Burden

Estimating the distribution of the tax burden involves allocation of total tax collections by income brackets. Given this information, taxes allocated to each bracket may then be expressed as a percentage of income in that bracket.

The most critical step in the analysis involves the choice of incidence assumptions. General practice has been to assign personal income taxes to the taxpayer and product and sales taxes as well as import duties to the consumer of the taxed product, whereas property taxes and land taxes are charged to the owners. Taxes on company profits are usually assigned to the shareholder or owner of the equity, or they are assumed in part to be shifted to consumers. Tariffs on capital goods, finally, are allocated to the consumers of the output into which such goods enter. Taxes on public enterprise profits are usually excluded from the analysis.

The basic data required for such tax allocation involves the distribution of income by types of earning, expenditure patterns by income levels, and the distribution of property. With data on income distribution typically incomplete, data on consumer expenditure patterns are even more scarce. Yet such data are needed if commodity taxes are to be allocated among consumers. For the case of broadly based consumption taxes, such as value-added taxes or retail sales taxes, the necessary information relates to the distribution of a fairly inclusive concept of consumption expenditures, whereas for particular excises or import duties, selective consumption patterns (for example, on liquor, cigarettes, and cars) are required. This picture is complicated by the fact that the consumption patterns may differ sharply not only with regard to income but also with regard to sectors of the economy. The collection of data from household budget surveys is not prohibitively difficult to carry out and yields information that is of great value, not only in the context of tax burden analysis, but also for broader purposes of development policy.

Data on the distribution of property and wealth are even more scarce than data on the distribution of expenditure patterns. This difficulty is less serious, however, because holdings of taxable property are highly concentrated in the upper-income and wealth groups, with only a small part of capital income accruing to property held below the top decile or 5 percent of the population.

An alternative and less ambitious approach to the estimation of tax burdens involves a comparison of burdens on families of specified composition, size, and location. This permits allowance for family circumstances and regional tax differences. It also does not require estimation of an income distribution. The role of incidence assumptions, however, is the same as under the previous approach. Information regarding expenditure patterns is again required but may now be used with reference to particular locations and types of households rather than on an overall basis. This is a major advantage, because consumption patterns, especially in developing countries, may differ sharply by region. Thus it is desirable to pursue both methodologies.

In either case, the estimating procedure involves methodological difficulties, difficulties that may well be more serious than are weaknesses in the underlying distributive data. Most important, the resulting distribution of tax burden depends on the incidence assumptions that are used. In this sense, the estimated distribution is not an empirically derived result but simply shows the quantitative implications of the underlying hypotheses. Another limitation of this procedure lies in its partial nature. The burden distribution of taxes on earnings is viewed as affecting households from the *sources*, or earnings, side of the budget only, whereas that of product taxes is taken to affect households from the consumption, or *uses*, side only. Thus "second-round" effects of earnings taxes on product prices and of factor taxes on earning patterns are disregarded. Because the distribution of earnings generated in the production of X may well differ from that generated in the production of Y, product taxes that change the output mix between X and Y may also affect the distribution of earnings. Similarly, taxes on income may affect relative product prices and thus the real income of consumers and so forth. A further shortcoming of the analysis is that deadweight losses are overlooked, so that the total burden is understated. Moreover, such losses are not the same for all tax dollars, so that a potential bias is added to the estimated burden distribution.

Ideally, we should allow for second-round effects and deadweight losses, as recent models that estimate incidence in the context of a general equilibrium analysis attempt to do (Shoven, 1983; Whalley, 1984). Such studies, however, are still in an early stage and are not easily applied to developing countries in which the required data are hardly available. Moreover, methodology rests on an assumption, particularly questionable for developing countries, that the economy responds in a purely competitive fashion. That is to say, incidence is estimated not on the basis of observation of the economy's actual responses to past tax changes but on the basis of what the hypothetical response would be if markets were assumed to be perfectly competitive. Whatever the merits of this assumption for industrialized countries, it would surely be of doubtful realism in the context of most developing countries.

Nevertheless, thought should be given to the extension of general equilibrium models to such a setting; and short thereof, allowance may be made for particular instances in which differences in product mix have a direct bearing on the distribution of factor earnings. There is also the question of whether the partial-equilibrium assumptions traditionally applied to the incidences of particular taxes in the United States and the United Kingdom are equally valid if they are applied to developing countries. Important structural differences exist, such as the higher degree of sectoral separation, the isolation of some sectors from market transactions, the position of the developing countries as price takers in world markets, their openness, and the paramount importance of capital inflow. These differences suggest that appropriate assumptions may differ as well.

Income versus Consumption Base

I now turn to selected aspects of tax structure design, beginning with the choice between income and consumption as a tax base. Although tax literature has traditionally featured a broad-based income tax as the best form of taxation, recent writing has veered toward consumption as the preferred base. This literature stresses the deadweight loss or efficiency cost that arises because an income tax discriminates in favor of present consumption over future consumption, whereas a consumption tax is neutral in that respect. In addition, it is argued that a consumption tax is more favorable to saving and hence to economic growth.

Whatever the merits of the consumption base for countries such as the United Kingdom or the United States, consumption offers an especially attractive tax base for developing countries. There are various reasons why this is the case. To begin with, developing countries are in urgent need of capital formation, and saving is needed to sustain it. Thus taxation should draw on consumption rather than on saving. At the same time, the level of consumption for the larger part of the population is very low, leaving little or no "surplus" that can be transferred to the budget. Given the highly unequal distribution of income and the low rate of private sector saving, there exists, however, a substantial surplus in the form of "luxury consumption" at the upper end of the income scale. This sector of the population, however, is also the source of private sector saving, whether as household savers or as shareholders in companies. Income taxation sufficiently progressive to absorb a large part of surplus consumption, therefore, would also threaten most of private sector saving, this problem being worse in cases where effective taxation of capital income is limited by what capital can earn abroad. The obvious answer, therefore, is to focus directly on the taxation of consumption out of high incomes.

Ideally, such taxes would take the form of a progressive expenditure tax. Such a tax could be imposed as a personal tax, with progressive rates applicable to taxpayers' global consumption expenditures. There has been much discussion in recent literature of how such a tax would be administered. Some of the difficulties that arise with income tax (for example, measuring depreciation and the treatment of capital gains) would be avoided, which of course is a great advantage, especially under conditions of inflation. Other and new difficulties would arise, however. The modern concern with an expenditure tax dates to Nicholas Kaldor (1956), who in fact attempted to apply it in India, but the experiment proved a failure. This outcome may not be surprising, because the administration of such a tax requires accurate accounting for financial transactions. Moreover, less reliance can be placed on withholding at source than under the income tax.

I therefore do not believe that a personal expenditure tax is a feasible solution for developing countries. A sales tax in turn reaches the consumption base but does so in an inequitable fashion. Rather, emphasis needs to be placed on taxing luxury consumption by taxing "luxury goods." The identification of "luxury goods," it must be noted, does not entail rendering moral judgment as to what form of consumption is necessary or desirable. Rather, the determination is based on the weight of such goods in consumer outlays at various levels of household income, that is, in line with income elasticities. To determine the degree of "luxuriousness" involved in various goods again requires data on expenditure patterns, a point to which we shall return below.

As a substitute for a full-fledged expenditure tax, such taxation may take the form of a "purchase tax," that is, a multiple system of commodity taxes, or it may be built into the rate structure of a value-added tax, although this involves a more difficult task. Moreover, an important contribution may be made by various forms of wealth taxation, including a graduated property tax. These possibilities suggest an important area of research, more promising than heavy reliance on progressive income tax rates.

Because luxury consumption carries a heavy import component, and because scarce foreign exchange is of vital importance for development, the use of luxury taxes gains additional importance. It will be noted below, however, that there exists a substantial difference between taxation of imported luxuries as an integral part of a scheme designed to reach luxury consumption (whether imported or home produced) and a system of differentiated tariffs on imported luxuries only. The latter interferes with efficient allocation and should not be justified as necessary for progressive consumption taxation. Note also that the categories of taxed items have to be defined sufficiently broadly so as to preclude substitution of essentially similar goods.

Personal Income Tax

The personal income tax, for obvious reasons, does not occupy the central position in the tax structure of developing countries that it holds in industrial nations. Yet it is an important part of the tax system, especially as it applies to the modern sector of the economy. Pending the development of a comprehensive system of luxury excises, the income tax is the major part of the tax structure that permits introduction of even a moderate progression into burden distribution. Progression in the rate structure, however, is not our primary concern. The primary concern is the fact that typically there are large holes in the tax base, with certain sectors of the economy escaping income tax coverage. This characteristic offends the premise that uniform coverage is desirable. Tax liabilities should be assessed on total income, independent of source or use, in order to avoid horizontal inequities and inefficiencies that otherwise result.

Full Base Coverage

Deficient base coverage is not limited to developing countries but appears there in accentuated form. Still, the entire GNP should not be reflected in taxable income. After all, the tax base aims at net income only and in the context of the national accounts is part of the national income rather than part of GNP. Depreciation and indirect taxes are thus excluded. Moreover, some components of national income, such as the corporation tax, do not enter the base, whereas other items (mainly transfers) that are not part of national income should be included. It is thus not surprising that taxable income, even if defined comprehensively, might account for not more than, say, one-third of GNP. We should object not to this feature, however, but only to the shortfall that results because taxable income actually reached is only a fraction, frequently less than 50 percent, of the properly determined amount. This loss of base occurs because (1) income accruing in some sectors of the economy is not accounted for or is accounted for only very imperfectly and (2) the law permits certain forms of income to be excluded that should in fact be part of the tax base.

To derive the magnitude of the shortfall, we begin by estimating total personal income received in various sectors of the economy. Next, we deduct amounts of income that are not taxable because they fall below the exemption limit, so that we determine what "full" taxable income for various sectors should be. We then deduct that part of income which remains tax free because of various exclusions and deductions permitted by the law. Such exclusions with little justification include bonuses, holiday pay, and so forth. Other exclusions result from incentive provisions of the law. Deducting all these, we determine what taxable income would be if the law was fully applied. Comparing this figure with actual taxable income, we then calculate the base deficiency by sectors. Note that this gap does not include the reduction in base due to exemptions and statutory exclusions or deductions. It measures only the deficiency that arises because the prevailing law is not fully enforced. An even larger gap arises if we allow for preferences and loopholes in the tax law and compare the actual and the "correct" "comprehensive" base.

The extent of revenue loss due to ineffective enforcement in various sectors depends on how large a share of the sector's income would remain outside taxable income even under full enforcement. Thus the loss of revenue from ineffective enforcement in agriculture is reduced because much of agricultural income (at least in the traditional sector) would fall below the exemption limits even if it were covered.

There are substantial difficulties in obtaining this information. Data on earnings of employees in the public sector and in larger private establishments are widely available, but data for the self-employed are not. The self-employed include small traders and farmers but also groups with substantial income in both the professions and trade. By the nature of the problem, data are most scarce precisely where the gap in taxable income is largest. Because the information cannot be derived from the tax data with which the figures are to be compared, earnings must be estimated in the context of population, employment, and national income data. Moreover, some information on the distribution of earnings is needed in order to determine a rough breakdown of the sectoral totals into taxable and nontaxable components. Estimation of loss of tax base due to exclusions and deductions is somewhat simpler, because at least rudimentary data should be available from tax statistics. To be sure, the availability of such data depends on how tax files are kept and on the extent to which computerized information is available.

Although not all the necessary information can be obtained, an analysis of this sort will be useful, even if it is imperfect, to identify the sectors of the economy in which major base deficiencies exist and to determine where efforts at improved administration and enforcement are most needed.

Hard-to-Tax Groups

This discussion immediately draws attention to the treatment of certain problem groups that show the greatest deficiency in coverage. The hard-to-tax groups—typically including small retail establishments, professionals, and farmers—are of particular importance in developing countries. They require treatment other than that provided by refined methods of tax administration and provisions in the revenue code, provisions that are drawn from and are appropriate to industrialized countries. A more realistic approach is needed, using presumptive taxation, applied outside and in lieu of the regular framework of income and sales taxation, as well as estimated tax bases, applied within the context of the regular tax system.

Small taxpayers, involving five employees or fewer, may be reached most effectively by a *presumptive tax*, imposed in lieu of the regular income and sales tax. The presumptive approach determines the level of income and sales that may be imputed to a particular category of taxpayer and then imposes a tax on that basis. The presumptive tax is computed conservatively so as not to exceed the amount that would be payable under the regular tax, and it leaves the taxpayer free to demonstrate that a lesser liability is called for.

By its simplicity the system aims to minimize administrative cost while providing a reasonable minimum level of yield. To implement the scheme, amounts of tax must be determined from a matrix table, with type of activity listed vertically and level of sales horizontally. To compute the income tax, a profit margin, typically applicable for each line of activity, is estimated and then applied to presumptive sales. Although classification by type of activity and determination of a representative profit margin are relatively simple, the effectiveness of the approach (for estimating both presumptive income and sales tax liabilities) hinges on classification by level of sales. As the small establishments covered by the presumptive approach typically do not have adequate sales accounting, physical indicators such as floor space, location, and so forth must be used. Such indicators must obviously be developed on a trade-by-trade basis.

Although the presumptive approach will be appropriate for very small taxpayers, a somewhat more refined procedure is desirable for the group of slightly larger taxpayers, for whom use of an *estimated tax* may be viewed as transition to normal treatment. Here the tax may be imposed within the context of the regular income and sales tax, but the tax administrator should assess liabilities on the basis of a specified estimating procedure. The taxpayer again remains free to demonstrate "true" liability on the basis of adequate documentation and accounting records. Use of specified estimating procedures has the further advantage of avoiding bargaining between assessor and tax-payer, a practice that invites collusion.

The estimating procedure might be based on three steps, involving estima-tion of (1) gross sales from specified indicators, (2) gross income by the deduction of nonaccountable expenses from gross sales, and (3) net income by the further deduction of accountable expenses. The estimation of gross sales under (1) might be based on indicators such as number and skill level of employees, installed equipment, level of activity, size of inventory, material purchases, and so forth. The deduction of nonaccountable expenses under (2), including mostly minor items, would be based on presumptive amounts appropriate to particular categories of activity. Further deductions under (3) would be allowable only on the basis of proper documentation. The latter would include items involving larger outlays such as wages, material purchases, interest, and depreciation.

Application of these approaches, especially at the presumptive level, poses different problems for different branches of types of activity and must be addressed category by category. For somewhat larger taxpayers, dealt with under the estimated tax, small manufacturers, retailers, and service establish-ments are of major importance. Special problems arise in connection with professionals and larger agricultural establishments, cattle raisers in particular. Because of widespread underreporting, the latter two groups frequently remain largely outside the regular income tax system. Relatively high incomes may be involved, so that there is an especially serious defect in tax coverage. More adequate inclusion of these groups is not only a technical problem and cannot be solved unless enforcement is firmly supported by the judiciary and by the political system. Typically, prosecution is ineffective, fines are small, and penalties for late payment (especially under conditions of inflation) are minimal.

Inflation

The difficulties that inflation poses for income tax administration are of particular importance for developing countries, given their propensity to suffer high rates of inflation and their long administrative lag in settling accounts. Although the problem of bracket creep can be handled to some degree by indexing procedures, the distorting impact upon the tax base, especially with regard to changes in the real value of assets, is a more difficult problem.

Control of inflation accordingly not only requires adequate taxation but also in turn becomes a prerequisite for constructing a tax system that runs smoothly.

Personal Savings Incentives

With increased saving a major concern of development policy, tax incentives to stimulate saving are frequently given by exempting interest income from government securities or savings institutions as well as by exclusion of earnings that are added to savings accounts. Most tax analysts have taken a critical view of such provisions and hold that the resulting damage to tax equity outweighs the possible gain in additional saving that is thereby stimulated. This is the case especially with regard to small savers, either those who are below the exemption level of income tax or those whose marginal rate is very low. Moreover, the value of tax reduction given by the exemption of interest, which rises with income and is determined by the taxpayer's marginal rate, raises additional problems of tax equity. These problems might be avoided by using a credit rather than a deduction, but the alternative approach of encouraging saving via taxation of luxury consumption is much to be preferred.

Perhaps the best that can be expected from income tax incentives to saving is the redirection of (rather than the increase in) savings from informal or curb markets to organized savings institutions. But with typically lagging responses of interest rates on savings deposits, the impact of inflation upon the real rate of return on saving is likely to outweigh the tax factor. Thus interest rate adjustments and the availability of indexed bonds are of greater importance than tax policy.

Further Issues

A host of other issues arise upon which I cannot elaborate here. They include problems of rate structure, of low-income relief, and of deductions, exclusions, and other technical aspects of income taxation that must be addressed in developing countries as well as in industrial settings. There are also important problems of tax administration, including issuance of taxpayer numbers, the availability of tax files that permit cross-checking between districts, centralized treatment of larger returns, and computerization. A serious defect results from the frequently lengthy delay with which returns are audited and final assessments are made. The need for more expeditious handling of returns is of particular importance in inflationary settings where delay in settlement and payment reduces the real value of liabilities on which no adequate interest charge has been placed, as is typically the case. In dealing with these issues, training facilities and adequate salary scales for tax officials are of strategic importance, especially because the private sector tends to bid away competent administrators who have gained experience. These problems are not primarily a matter of economic analysis yet are of major importance in creating an effective tax system.

Company Taxation

The structure of company taxation in developing countries is complicated by the variety of legal forms in which business units operate. Small units, operating as proprietorships, have much greater importance than they do in developed countries, and large corporations occupy a much smaller position. In between there are a variety of entities, including partnerships and various types of companies with limited liability, all of which pose special problems of taxation.

Structure

First, there is the question of how the large corporations should be treated, that is, whether there should be an absolute corporation tax, independent of the individual income tax (the so-called classical method), or whether the two forms of taxation should be integrated, with corporate-source earnings taxed at the shareholder level only. There are various reasons why the case for integration is weaker in the developing country setting than it is for industrialized countries. Saving in the form of retained earnings is the major source of private sector saving and should be encouraged. The "double taxation" of dividends that results under the classical system does precisely that, as it discourages distribution. To be sure, the same would apply if there was no taxation at the corporate level, but then foreign-owned capital would not be reached at all. Allowing for both factors, the classical system with a moderate rate of corporation tax is usually appropriate for developing countries.

Below the level of the larger corporations, there are a variety of limited liability and partnership forms of organization. Here the problem is where to draw the line above which a separate profits tax is to apply and how to do so without discrimination and without discouraging use of the more efficient form of limited liability organization. Below this level, there is a typically large sector of small proprietorships. Here taxation must be in the context of the individual income tax, supported by the previously noted procedures of esti-mated and presumptive taxation as well as by a licensing system. Although taxation can be approximate only, the development of reasonably effective approximation procedures may well be more important than concern with technical refinement of corporation tax law, refinements that will apply only to a relatively small sector of business.

Inflation

Inflation, as noted before, interferes with the definition of the income tax base but does so even more where the company tax is concerned. This is the case especially with regard to depreciation. Although reliance is based frequently on periodic revaluation of old capital, an orderly provision for continuing inflation adjustment is much to be preferred. The development of an indexing procedure for depreciation reserves, which is not without difficulty, offers the most feasible solution while permitting depreciation schedules to be set in line with economic depreciation.

Foreign-Owned Business

Large corporations in developing countries are frequently subsidiaries of foreign corporations, so that the corporation tax applies largely to the taxation of foreign investment income. The problem is to obtain a reasonable share in earnings for the host country, especially where the value added in the form of domestic labor is relatively small. At the same time, taxation must be such as not to discourage the desired capital inflow. As noted above, the presence of such companies requires a classical corporation tax rather than an integrated system. Next there is the question of how the host country can participate in the taxation of distributions at the shareholder level. This participation has to be arranged via a withholding tax, a form of taxation that is also helpful in discouraging repatriation, thus retaining capital in the host country. Finally, difficult problems arise in identifying the tax base, that is, the share in the subsidiary's profits that are to be assigned to the host country. Complex problems of arm's-length pricing and treatment of goodwill arise, problems that must frequently be resolved by negotiation.

A special set of problems arises where foreign investment is involved in the exportation of natural resources, with the host country participating in the form of royalties and thus standing more or less outside the regular tax system. Determination of appropriate levels of royalty poses further questions of entitlement to a national resource and profit sharing between developer and host country.

Public Enterprise

The role of public enterprises is of major importance in developing countries. Such enterprises frequently remain outside the regular tax regime and are afforded exemptions or special treatment. This situation is clearly undesirable. Preferential treatment places public enterprises at an unfair advantage where competition with private firms is concerned, obscures their comparative profitability, and protects them against the rigors of accounting requirements imposed by the regular tax regime. This treatment is unfortunate, as it promotes poor accounting practices and protects such enterprises from public scrutiny. Auditing by the fiscal authorities is needed, if only to offset the tendency for public enterprises in developing countries to act as independent agents.

For all these reasons, public enterprises should be subject to a regular enterprise tax. The further question of how after-tax profits should be dealt with—whether they should remain within the enterprise or should be transferred to the government's capital budget for reallocation—is a separate issue and should be dealt with as such. The same applies to whether and to what extent public enterprise pricing should be used as a mechanism by which product taxes are imposed or subsidies are passed to consumers. Domestically produced fuel is thus made available frequently at below-export prices, or tax exemption granted to public enterprises permits lower prices to consumers. Here, as in other instances of "tax expenditures," more efficient policy decisions will emerge if the public enterprise is instructed to engage in marginal-cost pricing. Consumer support rather than tax relief is best given in the form of price subsidies where it is needed.

Investment Incentives

Investment incentives may take various forms, including accelerated depreciation and investment credits. Both raise the net rate of return, and neither is neutral. The former favors long investments, the latter short ones. A more neutral technique takes the form of permitting part of the cost to be expensed, with the remainder depreciated in line with economic life. Another approach frequently used in developing countries takes the form of tax holidays for the early years of the investment.

As I noted earlier, investment incentives in developing countries are frequently given in selective form, so as to direct capital toward tax-favored industries and regions (see chapter 23). Interindustry differentiation may be based on characteristics that are relevant for development strategy, including capital/labor ratios, the degree of import substitution, foreign exchange needs, domestic value added, the continuity of output, and so forth. Weights must thus be attached to these features in line with the establishment of priorities within a meaningful policy design. Otherwise selection becomes a matter of politics, and loose definition invites corruption in the assignment of tax-favored status. In opposition to the incentive approach, it is argued that market forces are best suited to make efficient choices and that selective interference should be avoided. The role of tax policy and of differential incentives in particular thus depends on the extent to which the structure of capital formation is to be directed by economic planning and the extent to which it is to be left to the play of the market. Still, if differentiation is applied, it should be based on firm, well-defined, and meaningful categories and should not be left to the discretion of individual officials.

The use of regional incentives poses similar problems. From the economist's point of view, a good case can be made against regional differentiation. Economic development will be served best, so the argument goes, by permitting backward regions to decline while advancing regions are allowed to spurt ahead. Yet labor mobility may be limited, and there may be historical, political, social, and strategic reasons for regional balance. The question, then, is how regional incentives should be applied. To achieve the desired goal, employment-based incentives may be more appropriate than capital-based incentives. This is the case especially in the context of regional policy but also in the context of more general application. Where labor is overpriced and capital is underpriced, employment-based incentives may help to encourage more labor-intensive types of technology.

Returning once more to the treatment of foreign capital, we must distinguish between incentives directed at attracting new capital (such as tax holidays for the first years of operation) or at the retention of old capital (such as preferential treatment of retentions or a penalty on repatriation via withholding tax). Throughout, and especially in the latter context, the effectiveness of such incentives depends on the tax treatment by the country of origin and on the extent to which similar or even larger incentives are offered by competing developing countries.

Product Taxes

Commodity taxes invariably play a major part in the tax structure of developing countries. The reason, simply, is that product taxes are easier to impose than income taxes. Fewer points of tax collection are needed, and taxation may be concentrated on products that afford convenient handles, whether at the point of import or at the stage of domestic manufacture. There is also the previously noted case for taxing luxury products. Thus there frequently develops a hodgepodge of product taxes imposed in a pragmatic fashion and without internal consistency. Unit as well as ad valorem taxes are used, and taxation is imposed at various stages of production.

A General Consumption Tax

Following the income tax argument for broad-based taxation, tax reformers have favored transformation of the ad hoc system into a general consumption tax assessed on a broad base and at a uniform rate. In industrialized countries, such a tax may be imposed as either a retail sales tax on consumption or a value-added tax of the consumption type, that is, a value-added tax that exempts capital goods from the base. Where both options are available, the choice between them is a matter of administrative convenience. The identical base is covered, and the burden distribution will be the same. In developing countries, however, the retail option is typically not available, because retail establishments tend to be small, informal, and unstable. Thus sales cannot be determined readily, and enforcement at the retail level is difficult. The trend, therefore, has been toward a value-added approach. This technique is more readily feasible, especially because the invoice method facilitates the collection process and introduces an element of self-enforcement.

If we take a pragmatic approach, the value-added methodology may also be combined with taxation at the manufacturing level. Thus in the case of products for which sizable manufacturing establishments exist, the first tax may be imposed at that level, with whatever value-added taxation above that level proves feasible. Obviously the point of import also provides a convenient handle at which to tax.

Distributive Aspects

The disadvantage of this general approach is that a broad-based, uniform-rate consumption tax does not place sufficient emphasis on the consumption of high-income groups. As I noted before, at this point the major slack, with resources available for transfer to the public sector, can be found. The magnitude of this potential may be seen by the following illustration. Suppose that the top decile of the income distribution receives 50 percent of the income and that 90 percent thereof is consumed. Suppose also that in the nine lower deciles all income is consumed. If we define "excess consumption" as per capita consumption above, say, twice its average level, excess consumption thus defined will absorb 26 percent of total income.[1] This statement is only an illustration, of course, but it suffices to show the magnitudes involved. A general consumption tax does not draw upon this prime source of potential revenue to an adequate degree.

The question is how this difficulty can be remedied. In industrialized countries, a large part of the population is covered by income tax, so that lower-level relief from a general consumption tax can be given via an income tax credit. This remedy is helpful but is not available in developing countries. Another possibility is to combine a higher rate of consumption tax with exclusions of certain consumption items that draw a large share of low-income budgets. This approach helps at the lower end of the scale, but it also greatly reduces the tax base. Most important, it does not offer a way of taxing high-income households at adequate rates. As I noted earlier, the best solution would be in the form of a personalized and progressive expenditure tax, a tax almost ideally suited to the needs of developing countries. Unfortunately, however, its use (in particular, the required auditing of financial transactions) seems hardly feasible in that setting, where even the simpler aspects of income tax administration meet with substantial difficulty.

The only feasible remedy, it appears, is to supplement the broad-based consumption tax with a set of ad valorem excises imposed on items that weigh heavily on high-income budgets. This approach may involve imports, where the tax is imposed conveniently at the point of entry, or home production, where it may best be placed at the manufacturing level. In other instances, where luxury services are involved, taxation at retail is required.

Integration with Tariff Structure

Finally, we note the importance of integrating commodity taxation into the tariff structure. The basic principle is that sales and excise taxes should apply equally to imports and domestic products. In addition to a basic and uniform rate of tariff (which will tend to equalize effective protection), surcharges should be applied only where they are deemed necessary because of infant industry but not in order to tax luxury imports in particular. Taxation of luxury consumption is properly performed through the imposition of excises on such goods, including domestically produced products as well as imports in the base. Otherwise, undesirable shelters of protection are provided for the domestic production of such goods.

Taxes on Property and Land

It remains to consider the taxation of wealth in its three major forms, that is, the taxation of real estate, a possible wealth or net worth tax, and, most important, the taxation of land.

Real Estate

Taxation of real estate, in developing countries as anywhere else, is usually a matter of local, frequently city, government. Nevertheless, it is very much part of the overall tax problem, the more so because cities, as a result of the immigration of rural population, are typically short of funds. Moreover, the taxation of residential real estate is a convenient way of reaching consumption of high-income households. Real estate is visible and may be attached and regarded as an indicator of wealth. A classified and moderately progressive property tax is thus an attractive objective of tax reform. Problems of implementation are substantial, however, as they involve introduction of a viable assessment procedure and one that, once applied, can be updated periodically to adjust for inflation.

Wealth

The idea of a general wealth tax, imposed in the form of a tax on net wealth, is attractive, especially as it can be integrated with the administration of the income tax. In practice, however, such a tax usually reduces to the taxation of real estate, because intangible wealth (as its counterpart of capital income) is difficult to reach.

Land

Because the agricultural sector in most developing countries is large, land revenue is of great potential (if usually not actual) importance. This is the case especially because income from land tends to be reached only imperfectly under the income tax. Large landholders and cattle raisers frequently fall into the hard-to-tax category, whereas the taxation of peasants poses its own social and political problems.

In a perfectly competitive system, it would make little difference whether land was assessed in line with its market value, its actual income, or its potential income under full utilization. In practice, however, the three bases differ substantially. Land is frequently underutilized and held for speculation. It is clearly desirable in principle to tax income from land in line with capacity utilization, as doing so increases the cost of underutilization. For this purpose, however, adequate land surveys and their maintenance on an up-to-date basis are needed. As in the case of property taxation, reform of the cadastral system is a first step toward tax reform and one that is costly and (with the cadastral system frequently under army control) difficult to carry out.

Another aspect of land taxation should be noted. This is the possibility of using the fiscal system to integrate the traditional sector of small landownership into the modern economy and into the sociopolitical system. A modest degree of land taxation may encourage peasants to become engaged in market activity, and local use of the funds thus raised (for example, in supplying fertilizer or farm equipment to local cooperatives) can serve to render this process acceptable.

Conclusions

The image that I hope emerges from the preceding observations on tax policy in developing countries is one of a large number of specific issues of tax design, to be dealt with in the context of the economic, institutional, and political setting of the particular country. Though this is basically a piecemeal approach, the pieces are held together by establishing and then achieving the feasible revenue requirement. They are also held together by their relationship to the objectives of economic development policy. This involves their impact on domestic and foreign balance (saving, investment, and foreign exchange) as well as on structural objectives, such as the advance of certain industries or sectors of the economy. Finally, the pieces must fit together in providing a burden distribution appropriate to the limited capacity of resource release from the private sector, and a typically highly unequal distribution of income.

In order to secure these objectives, we have seen that differentiation in taxation may be called for where specific policy needs require it. Yet we have proceeded on the general premise that, as a point of departure, equal and broad-based taxation is desirable, that is, that the income tax base should include all sources of income and that the sales tax base should give comprehensive coverage over all products. Only by adherence to such a rule is it possible to eliminate arbitrary and distorting differentiation and to fend off the ever-continuing pressures for their expansion. This has been the experience of tax reform, applicable no less to developing countries than to industrialized countries.

The premise of broad-based tax design may be considered to conflict with the methodology of optimal taxation, a perspective pursued in other essays in this volume. (See especially chapters 2 and 3 above.) The conflict would seem to be a matter of practicability and emphasis rather than analysis. Other things being equal, it is of course desirable to minimize deadweight loss and to distribute the burden in line with the weights prescribed in the accepted social welfare function. In other words, it is desirable to apply a system of taxation that minimizes welfare losses as weighted by a social welfare function. Such a solution, as shown in the theoretical work of the last decade, involves a complex set of differential rates for both income and product taxation. If such sets of rates could be determined and applied, the outcome would, by definition, be optimal indeed. The question, however, is one of emphasis and feasibility.

As a matter of practical policy, there appears to be a good case for beginning with a move toward broad-based and uniform taxation, thereby eliminating the arbitrary array of existing differentials—differentials that were created by the politics of tax evasion rather than in pursuit of efficiency objectives. The presumption underlying much of the traditional work on tax reform is that substitution of comprehensive base and horizontally uniform coverage will improve both efficiency and equity. More specifically, the presumption is (1) that uniform taxation is likely to be more efficient than taxation based on random differentiation and (2) that the existing pattern of differentiation, reached on grounds quite unrelated to optimal tax considerations, will not be superior to the random pattern. Once a framework of broad-based taxation has been established, differentials may then be introduced to minimize deadweight losses where it is feasible to do so and compatible with other policy objectives. Differentiation to minimize deadweight losses, however, cannot furnish the primary point of departure. This is the case especially because priority needs to be given to viewing taxation as an instrument of development policy. Here the dynamic aspects of taxation effects, and their operation within the specific structure of the economies of developing countries, are of crucial importance.

Note

1. If Y = total income and N = population, the top decile consumes $0.9 (Y/2)$, which is $(9/2) (Y/N)$ per capita. Similarly, the other nine deciles consume $(Y/2)$ in total and $(5/9) (Y/N)$ per capita. Therefore, average per capita consumption is $0.95 (Y/N)$. If the top decile is taxed on its consumption above twice the average per capita, the tax base is $[(4.5) (Y/N) - (1.9) (Y/N)]N/10 = 0.26Y$, which is 26 percent of total income.

10

Public Policy and the Labor Market in Developing Countries

Gary Fields

WHEN PUBLIC ECONOMISTS formulate models of tax policy and other economic interventions in developing countries, they seek to capture the salient features of relevant markets. The market of interest in this chapter is the labor market. Labor markets in developing countries are typically characterized by wage dualism.[1] This chapter examines the consequences of wage dualism for analysis of the workings of labor markets in developing countries and for the design of public policy. Although the discussion concentrates on developing countries, it is equally applicable to dualistic labor markets elsewhere, for instance when we analyze the economics of minimum wages in the United States, where some jobs are covered by minimum-wage legislation and some are not.

I formulate a labor market model characterized by wage dualism, intersectoral migration, and search unemployment heuristically in my second section below. There is now widespread agreement on the analytical utility and empirical relevance of this class of models; see, for example, Sabot (1982), Stiglitz (1982b), Krueger (1983), Fields (1984), and the references cited therein. I then consider various aspects of public policy in the light of this labor market model. The policies examined include urban employment creation, rural development, incomes policies, migration restriction, tax-subsidy policy, improvements in labor market functioning, and education policy. It is shown that the wage dualism model has implications for public policy that differ from those of the standard textbook model.

Before proceeding, I should note what we will *not* be studying. In a developed country context, one of the chief applications of public economics to labor economics (and vice versa) has been in the area of labor supply. Abundant research has been conducted on the effects of taxes on labor supply in advanced economies; this literature is reviewed by Rosen (1980), Hausman (1981b, 1983), Heckman and MaCurdy (1981), and Killingsworth (1983). Also, recent years have witnessed numerous studies of the ways in which public income maintenance programs influence labor supply in those economies; see,

I am grateful to Ronald Ehrenberg, Olivia Mitchell, David Newbery, Nicholas Stern, and anonymous referees for helpful comments on a draft.

for instance, Cain and Watts (1973), Pencavel (1982), and Burdett and others (1983). In developing countries, these issues are quite unimportant. Taxes are presumed to have little effect on labor supply for the simple reason that most workers do not pay taxes, at least not direct ones; see, for instance, Ebrill (1984), and Newbery (chapter 13 of this volume). Probably much more important are the effects of taxes on labor demand, which are reviewed in this chapter and others. Public income maintenance programs are all but absent in developing countries and for that reason are not treated here.

Let us turn, then, to a characterization of labor market conditions in a "typical" developing country and a framework for analyzing public policy in light of these labor market conditions.

The Analytical Framework and Its Empirical Foundations

The literature on labor markets in developing countries is now vast, but the following features are widely regarded as descriptively realistic.[2]

- *Wage dualism.* The same labor is often paid a different wage, depending on the sector of the economy in which it is employed. Institutional and/or market forces may be responsible; for further discussion, see below. Simple tabular data on differentials in pay have been presented by many authors—for instance, Kannappan (1983). Pay differentials across sectors of employment for observationally equivalent labor have been confirmed in a multivariate framework using earnings function analysis; for summaries, see Berry and Sabot (1978) and Fields (1980).

- *Persistent open unemployment.* According to international convention, an individual is classified as openly unemployed who lacks a job and is actively looking for one. Various studies (Squire, 1981; Turnham, 1971) reveal persistently high rates of open unemployment in developing countries, even though few people in poor countries can afford to be openly unemployed for very long. On average, open unemployment rates of developing countries exceed those found in developed countries. This rate omits hidden unemployment (or underemployment), which is found to exceed open unemployment (Sabot, 1977; Yotopoulos and Nugent, 1976).

- *Migration into high-wage labor markets.* The evidence shows that high-wage labor markets attract disproportionately large numbers of migrants (Sabot, 1982; Todaro, 1976). This phenomenon reflects purposeful migration behavior: people choose a place to live in part on the basis of the economic opportunities offered.

- *High-wage labor markets exhibit high open unemployment rates.* Average incomes in developing countries are higher in urban than in rural areas (World Bank data). Also, open unemployment rates are higher in urban than in rural areas (Squire, 1981; Turnham, 1971). Thus, urban labor markets have both high wages and high open unemployment rates compared with rural labor markets. Further regional disaggregation reinforces the high-wage–high-unemployment pattern (Fields, 1979, 1982, has evidence from Colombia, for example).

- *Tendency toward expected wage equalization.* The wages paid to workers in different sectors have not equalized. Rather, it is *expected* wages (the wage if employed weighted by the probability of being employed) that tend to equalize. They do so because high-wage labor markets attract large numbers of migrants, which raises unemployment and results in a relatively low probability of employment.

A suitable analytical framework for studying public policy and the labor market must incorporate these stylized facts. Some models are better suited to this purpose than others.

Labor Market Characterization in Dualistic Development Models

For the last three decades, a dominant theme in development economics has been the postulate of dualistic economic development. Development economists have emphasized the technological differences between the two sectors and accordingly have often labeled them "modern" and "traditional." International trade economists have stressed the production of two different goods and have adopted corresponding terminology: "manufacturing" and "agricultural" products.

Wage dualism is a feature of the dualistic models of development economists (Fei and Ranis, 1964; Jorgenson, 1961; Lewis, 1954) and of international economists (for example, Bhagwati and Ramaswami, 1963, and Jones, 1971; see Magee, 1976, for a survey). Despite the many attractive features of these models, they share a common problem for our purposes: in both types of models, everybody is assumed to be employed in one of the two sectors. This assumption of full employment is inconsistent with the stylized facts presented above. To make these models suitable for labor market analysis, they must be amended to permit open unemployment as an outcome.

To allow for open unemployment, some authors have built models with economywide minimum wages set above market-clearing levels; for example, see Brecher (1974). Although such models yield persistent unemployment on account of the minimum wage, they do not permit wage dualism; all employed workers receive the minimum wage. The economywide minimum-wage models do not capture all the stylized facts either.

These problems are overcome in models with sector-specific minimum wages in which labor force migration and unemployment result from wage dualism. Such models have been constructed by Todaro (1969), Harris and Todaro (1970), Tidrick (1975), and others. The key features of this class of models are detailed below.

Why Is There Wage Dualism?

Before considering models that have wage dualism, we may well ask why wage dualism might be found. The reasons offered for the apparent differentials fall into two categories—institutional and market—of which the institutional dominate thinking and discussion. The institutional theories stress public pay policy. Governments are believed to encourage wages that are higher than market clearing by some or all of the following devices: passing minimum-wage laws; encouraging the formation of trade unions and lending government support to their bargaining strength; establishing the public sector as a relatively high-wage employer; and encouraging multinational firms to establish pay parity between expatriate labor and nationals. These nonmarket determinants of wages have been discussed widely; see, for instance, Reynolds (1965), Berg (1969), Frank (1968), Kannappan (1977), Starr (1981), and Fields (1984). Market reasons for wages that are higher than market clearing have been offered by other analysts. Stiglitz (1974a, 1976, 1982a), for example, suggests that firms may find it profitable to raise wages by x percent if doing so will lead to an increase in worker productivity greater than x percent as a result of better nutrition, improved morale, or lower labor turnover. Not all wages are affected identically, however, either for market reasons (for example, a more experienced labor force is more valuable in some industries than in others) or for institutional reasons (for example, trade unions exert differential influence in different industries; certain industries or occupations are exempted from minimum-wage laws). The result is a structure of wage differentials. Whether the institutional class of explanations or the market accounts for observed wage differentials in any given country, and to what extent, is an empirical question that has not as yet been answered definitively in the literature; most observers give greater weight to the institutionalist explanation for wage differentials in developing countries.

Wage Dualism in the Harris-Todaro Model

The existence of persistent wage differentials matters a great deal for the analysis of the workings of labor markets and for the formulation of other public policies. In the standard case, the wage, the quantity of labor supplied, and the quantity of labor demanded are jointly determined on the basis of labor supply and labor demand curves. In contrast, persistent wage differentials imply a causal structure running *from* the wage in the high-income sector *to* the quantity of labor demanded *to* the quantity of labor supplied. (For simplicity, I shall refer to this as "the institutional causal structure" in "a wage dualism model.")

The wage dualism model and the associated causal structure gained attention and widespread acceptance among economists through the insightful work of Harris and Todaro (1970); this work is summarized in Todaro (1976). The core features of this model are:

- A *dualistic economy*, consisting of a modern urban sector and a traditional agricultural sector
- *Wage dualism*, resulting from a rigid wage above market-clearing levels in the modern sector together with market-clearing wages in agriculture
- *Migration* on the basis of differences in *expected* wages (the wage if employed multiplied by the probability of employment)
- Persistent *urban unemployment*
- Tendency toward *expected wage equalization*.

Let M and A denote the modern sector and agriculture respectively, N employment, L labor force, and $E(W_i)$ the expected wage in sector i. The Harris-Todaro model posits that people migrate from rural to urban areas if the expected urban wage exceeds the rural wage and that they continue to do so until the two expected wages are equal. Thus the Harris-Todaro equilibrium condition is $E(W_A) = E(W_M) \leftrightarrow W_A = W_M N_M/L_M$. This expression says that the labor force allocates itself between sectors so that in equilibrium the agricultural wage is equated to the modern sector wage multiplied by the ratio of modern sector employment to modern sector labor force (employed plus unemployed).

The presentation above follows the original Harris-Todaro formulation in suppressing consideration of labor force heterogeneity. With heterogeneity, all variables in the model should be subscripted i; the core features would then pertain to labor of any given type. Linkages between the markets for different types of workers would have to be carefully specified. For alternative formulations of such interlinkages between markets for workers who differ in educational qualifications, see Fields (1974) as well as the discussion below.

Critiques and Responses

I believe that the Harris-Todaro model possesses great analytical usefulness. Others think differently. It is well to address their concerns before proceeding.

Some authors have taken exception to the Harris-Todaro model (and by implication, to the entire class of models with wage dualism, labor force migration, and unemployment). The Harris-Todaro model has been accused by various critics of being both incomplete and incorrect. Of these criticisms, some attack core features of the model; others accept the core features but are concerned with Harris and Todaro's specific formulation of certain relationships.

One really fundamental criticism of the Harris-Todaro framework concerns the nature of migration itself. In their model, migration is a "pull" phenomenon, the pulling force being the lure of high urban wages. This notion contrasts with a "push" view of migration, whereby landless individuals and others are forced off the land and have no choice but to seek jobs in the city. The Harris-Todaro model treats migration as a choice. In those instances where the marginal potential migrant in an economy has no possibility of self-employment or wage employment in agriculture, the Harris-Todaro model does not apply.

Another criticism of the Harris-Todaro model concerns its assumption of probabilistic hiring. Migration exists in the model to enhance the probability that workers will be hired for high-paying modern sector employment. Indeed, in their formulation, the nonmigrant has no chance whatever of getting a job in the modern sector. Hiring through word of mouth and other informal channels often takes place. The Harris-Todaro model has been extended to allow for it in Fields (1975b). This phenomenon does not invalidate the model unless the payoff of the probabilistic job search falls to zero. No one, I think, would seriously maintain that this last assumption would find much empirical support.

A third objection relates to an assumption implicit in the Harris-Todaro model concerning capital markets. By not considering them, Harris and Todaro are implicitly denying them a role. Still, capital markets in developing countries are imperfect at best. Typically, workers would not be able to finance a spell of job search in the city from their own resources, nor could they borrow reasonably. They must often take up employment in the urban traditional sector and search for a job in the modern sector; I have extended the Harris-Todaro model to allow for this possibility in Fields (1975b). Alternatively, they might have to save money in the village before being able to depart for the city; I am working on this problem now.

Other criticisms are also handled by expanding the Harris-Todaro model to accommodate alleged deficiencies. Banerjee's (1983) examination of the Delhi labor market, for instance, showed that migrants who took jobs in the urban informal sector were less likely to obtain jobs in the formal sector than those who never entered the informal sector. This finding in no way invalidates the Harris-Todaro model. In fact, it is exactly what would be implied by a model with an urban informal sector in which the urban unemployed (who are available for full-time job search) have better chances of finding modern sector employment than do urban informal sector workers (who have less time available for job search). Besides allowing for the existence of an urban traditional sector and on-the-job-search, the Harris-Todaro model has also been extended to include family migration, job fixity, favoritism and discrimination in hiring, labor force heterogeneity, and many other aspects of labor market reality.[3]

Some observers see the Harris-Todaro model as having been so fundamentally qualified that it no longer possesses the same essential core. Others, myself included, see it as alive, well, and embellished. I consider below some of the ways in which the model has been used for policy purposes.

Public Policy in Models with Wage Dualism

The Harris-Todaro analysis and models derived from it have served as the basis for extensive policy discussion. The issue is how to promote economic growth, to increase productive employment, and to achieve desired distributional goals. More specifically, given wage dualism and the migration response to such differentials, what should be done? There are a number of policy options.

Urban Employment Creation

The Harris-Todaro model explicated a policy puzzle that was confronting developing country planners in the 1960s: growing urban unemployment. Not only were urban unemployment rates disturbingly high, but they appeared resistant to policy. Policymakers in developing countries and in development agencies perceived that the urban unemployed constituted a potentially productive but unutilized resource. Because this labor was unemployed, its shadow price was thought to be low, possibly even zero. Accordingly, policymakers endeavored to create additional urban jobs that would employ the same labor pool. ("Promoting industrial sector labor absorption" was a phrase in common use at the time.) Try as they might, however, governments and aid agencies striving to diminish unemployment in the cities through urban job creation were confronted with worsening urban unemployment as migrants from the rural areas streamed into the cities.

Harris and Todaro's analysis showed that this situation was entirely understandable, once wage dualism had been recognized. The point is evident if we take the Harris-Todaro equilibrium condition stated above and perform comparative statics with respect to modern sector employment. The explanation is the following. When developing countries offered more urban jobs at a relatively high wage, they raised the *expected* income in the city above that in the countryside and thereby created a disequilibrium situation that could not persist. Because the wage of employed labor could not fall to clear the market as in the textbook labor market model, the gap in expected incomes could be eliminated only if the probability of urban employment were to fall, that is, by rural-urban migration with a consequent rise in urban unemployment. The creation of more jobs would thus be expected to lead to more unemployment, as in fact it did.

Various analysts (for example, Harberger, 1971; Stiglitz, 1982b) have investigated the shadow pricing of labor in circumstances of the sort envisioned by Harris and Todaro. The conclusion emerges that, when additional urban jobs are created, so much migration is induced that the shadow price of labor is approximately the urban modern sector wage. The reason is that the creation of urban employment raises modern sector output, lowers agricultural output, and leaves total GNP effectively unchanged. A shadow price of labor approximately equal to the urban modern sector wage is much higher than the agricultural wage (the shadow price of labor in Lewis-type models) or zero (the shadow price in income-sharing models in which leisure is not valued).

In sum, one of the primary contributions of the Harris-Todaro framework is to show that the creation of urban jobs in the modern sector within the existing institutional structure is not compatible with the goals of higher GNP, lower unemployment, and reduced poverty. Other policy options have been sought.

Rural Development

The Harris-Todaro model implies that the solution to *urban* unemployment is *rural* development. The reason is that rural development raises rural incomes and narrows rural-urban income disparities; this phenomenon stems migration and lessens urban unemployment. Thus, if there is something akin to a development fund (for example, the availability of a given amount of foreign aid or concessionary loans), a preferred use is to channel the funds into capital or infrastructure for rural production rather than into urban job creation (it must of course be verified that development resources can effectively be utilized in the rural economy).

Thinking on development policy shifted in the 1970s in favor of rural development, in part because of the intellectual impetus provided by the Harris-Todaro model. Other factors were also responsible, for example the growing concern for channeling development resources toward the poor, who in most countries are disproportionately rural. Nevertheless, the general equilibrium feature of the Harris-Todaro model showing the *behavioral* connections between urban and rural development had an important influence.

Incomes Policies

Neoclassical economics might suggest that the most direct policy to pursue in an economy with wage dualism would be to eliminate the gap between the urban (or modern sector) wage and the rural (or agricultural) wage. Standard arguments might be evoked to condemn the inefficiency and other undesirable features of minimum wages or other forms of nonmarket wage determination.[4] Indeed, incomes policies aimed at reducing or eliminating wage dualism by lowering artificially high wages have been prescribed for many developing countries.[5]

The main question about incomes policy is feasibility: can real modern sector wages be reduced to rural sector levels? Under conditions of rapid inflation, which many developing countries are experiencing, real wages can be made to fall simply by not raising nominal wages as much as prices. Such a policy, however, runs counter to one of the key features of Harris-Todaro-type models, namely, wage *rigidity* in the modern sector. Models of wage dualism are premised on the assumption that no instruments are available to reduce real modern sector wages to market-clearing levels; wage rigidity is a stylized representation of this assumption. Harris and Todaro (1970) put it aptly: "In the final analysis, however, the basic issue at stake is really one of political feasibility, and it is not at all clear that an incomes policy is any more feasible than the alternatives" (p. 138). Once it had been concluded that the urban wage probably could not be lowered directly, other policy options were therefore considered instead.

Migration Restraint

Harris and Todaro recommended a two-pronged strategy consisting of urban employment creation and migration restrictions. The migration restriction policy would prevent unemployment from rising in response to job creation. They wrote (1970): "Therefore, if the optimum position is to be achieved, a combination of both instruments will have to be used" (p. 138). (The word "optimum" is used here in the usual aggregate way; distributional considerations are absent.) Harris and Todaro were clearly uneasy about advocating migration restrictions, even though such policies had been instituted in nearby Tanzania. (Harris and Todaro were writing in Kenya.) In fact, they voiced their reservations about "interference with individual mobility attendant to the policy package just discussed."

They were not alone. Bhagwati and Srinivasan (1974) were also uncomfortable on ethical grounds and responded by demonstrating that, in the Harris-Todaro model, a first-best solution could be attained by fiscal means, as discussed below. Migration restrictions were shown not to be needed to attain the optimum, and the associated ethical issues were thereby put to rest.

Tax-Subsidy Policy

A number of papers have demonstrated the attainability of a first-best outcome using just taxes and subsidies, provided that the fiscal authorities possess sufficient control over the postulated policy instruments. Whether or not they do so is another matter. A negative view is taken by a number of the authors in this volume, especially in chapters 6, 7, 12, and 13.

Bhagwati and Srinivasan (1974) pioneered in the theoretical analysis of tax-subsidy policy in the Harris-Todaro model by showing that the first-best solution could be attained by *either* an across-the-board wage subsidy regardless of the sector of employment *or* a wage subsidy in manufacturing accompanied by a production subsidy in agriculture. The first policy works by equating the consumption and production prices with the domestic rates of transformation in production and substitution in consumption. The second policy equates the two rates of substitution in consumption and transformation in production with each other and with the consumption price. Similar results showing that tax-subsidy policy can be used to bring about a first-best allocation have been derived in other variants of the Harris-Todaro model; see Stiglitz (1982b).

One feature of the Harris-Todaro model, including Bhagwati and Srinivasan's and Stiglitz's extended analysis of it, is that, though it assumes labor mobility between sectors, it precludes capital mobility. A number of authors (Corden, 1974; Corden and Findlay, 1975; Khan, 1980; McCool, 1982;

Neary, 1981) have modified the Harris-Todaro model to allow for capital mobility, producing a framework very much like that used in the international trade literature. These models, like the Bhagwati-Srinivasan analysis before them, yield the result that a first-best allocation is attainable through an across-the-board employment subsidy.

The tax-subsidy analyses described thus far share a common feature: taxes and subsidies function as indirect instruments of incomes policy, the direct instrument (lowering modern sector wages) having been ruled out. By employing taxes and subsidies, the fiscal authorities are able to eliminate duality in net after-tax wages.[6] When taxes and subsidies equalize net wages, the resultant full-employment allocation lies on the economy's production possibilities frontier.

As regards tax and subsidy policy, a cautionary note in Bhagwati and Srinivasan (1974) should be borne in mind: "Since taxes must be collected to disburse subsidies, the question arises whether those who ask for minimum real wages will not, even when such taxes are imposed on them in a lump sum fashion, seek to revise the real minimum wage that is demanded. We have assumed, of course, that the minimum real wage is independent of the tax policy chosen" (p. 507).[7] This is one of the few times that the dependence of the minimum wage on tax-subsidy policy has received attention in the literature.

Another possible constraint concerns the range of available policy instruments. All of the preceding models assume that the required subsidy could be financed by nondistortive lump-sum taxation. This assumption was relaxed in a paper by McCool (1982), who examined two alternative funding sources: a tariff and a tax on manufacturing profits only. Under either financing scheme, attainment of the first-best optimum is no longer assured, because both build in a tax bias against the manufacturing sector. Moreover, McCool showed that a subsidy to manufacturing employment alone will assuredly be the worst use of any given revenue. The reason is that an increase in manufacturing employment increases the return to capital in that sector, which induces an inflow of capital, thereby further lowering the agricultural wage and increasing unemployment. He concluded that it would be preferable to use the tax revenues for agricultural wage subsidies.

Anand and Joshi (1979) questioned the attainability of the first best on different grounds. Noting that "'a crucial assumption underlying the 'generalized theory of distortions and welfare' . . . is that the government has complete control over the distribution of income" (p. 336), they investigated the implications of dropping this assumption in a number of dual-economy models with factor price distortions, including the Harris-Todaro model. To do so, they took as their income distribution constraint that the wage in the manufacturing sector must equal the minimum net income of workers. (The fate of workers who are unemployed and who hence do not get the "minimum net income" remained unspecified.) Anand and Joshi found that such a model could yield *either* attainability of the first best by an across-the-board wage subsidy *or* an efficiency-equity tradeoff. The first best is attainable if taxable profits are sufficient to cover the required labor subsidy. If they are not, manufacturing sector workers have higher incomes than agricultural workers, migration occurs, and unemployment results, thereby precluding the first best. Whether or not a first best is attainable thus depends on the parameter values in a given situation.

In conclusion, tax and subsidy policy may enable a Harris-Todaro-type economy to achieve a first-best optimum, *provided* that the policy instruments are unconstrained. These policy options may well be unfeasible, however, in which case constraints on the range of instruments may condemn a developing economy to a second-best situation.

Labor Market Functioning

A policy suggestion may be made in very different areas. All of the models cited thus far embody a particular assumption about the nature of job search: that an individual who aspires to a relatively high-paying urban job must leave the agricultural sector and migrate to the city in search of the better-paying alternative. This may be an accurate characterization of job search in most institutional circumstances, but other arrangements are possible in which on-the-job search becomes the norm.[8] Consider a policy according to which a network of employment exchanges around the country is established and employers are required to fill all vacancies through the employment exchange. (Sweden does something very similar [see, for instance, OECD, 1963]). This would considerably reduce the payoff to a job aspirant who migrated in search of a job, in turn retarding rural-urban migration, diminishing urban unemployment, and increasing rural production. This option is a fitting subject for cost-benefit analysis but has not yet been considered in the literature.

Education and Human Resource Policy

The features of labor markets in developing countries that are captured by the Harris-Todaro model—wage dualism, migration into high-wage areas, and persistently high unemployment in high-wage labor markets—also have important implications for public sector education policy. In developing countries, the public sector is the main provider of education, and the education sector is a large user of public resources; see, for instance, World Bank (1980b). In the 1960s, education seemed to be in short supply. Studies were undertaken of human resource needs (or, as they were then called, of "manpower requirements"), and the call went out for educational expansion. The public sector was urged to build enough schools, to supply enough teachers, and to award enough student fellowships to meet the "needs" of the economy and the "social demands" of the people.

Public economists and others came to see the manpower requirements approach to educational planning as deficient. Although it sought to gauge the

economy's ability to employ educated labor productively, this approach completely ignored the cost side. The correct criterion, said public economists, is
the balance between marginal social costs of education and marginal social
benefits. Social benefit-cost analyses appeared in the path-breaking studies of
Becker (1964), Hansen and Weisbrod (1970), and others for the United
States, and these were followed by a spate of social cost-benefit studies for other
countries, developed and developing; see Psacharopoulos and Hinchliffe
(1973) for a valuable summary of the literature up to that time.

At present, the standard method for conducting social benefit-cost analysis
is so well established that it has become part of the standard tool kit offered in
courses on the economics of education.[9] I shall first describe the standard
method, then criticize it. The social costs in the standard method include
(1) the direct monetary cost of educating a student (teachers' salaries, books,
and so forth), plus (2) the student's forgone earnings while in school, measured
as the labor market earnings of an individual without the education in question. The social benefits of education are measured by the difference in
earnings streams between persons with the education level and persons who
lack it. Sometimes the comparison entails simple tabulations of average
earnings by schooling level; at other times it involves more sophisticated
earnings function analysis. On occasion, the earnings differential is multiplied
by an adjustment factor, reflecting the presumed unmeasured greater ability of
persons with more schooling. The magnitude of the adjustment factor in such
instances is assumed, not derived. The social rate of return is the internal rate
that equates the benefit and cost streams.

Despite widespread agreement regarding the way to do cost-benefit analysis,
the conventional method does not fully capture the social costs and benefits of
education, particularly in economies with wage dualism and the other Harris-
Todaro features described above. My critique is at two levels.

At one level, the established method is narrow in what it includes. The
benefits are generally defined to be earnings gains (assumed to measure productivity increases attributable to schooling); as such, only economic efficiency is
considered, and education's contribution to social welfare through facilitation
of equity objectives is omitted.[10] Also omitted are such other social benefits of
education as a well-informed populace, better maternal care, reduced fertility,
enhanced social mobility, and the like.[11] Presumably these omitted factors
enhance social well-being, and consequently the more narrowly defined benefits (that is, economic efficiency) are regarded as *understating* the true social
benefit of education. Accordingly, when social benefit-cost analysis is conducted in practice, the internal rate of return or benefit-cost ratio is taken as a
lower limit on education's contribution to welfare.

Regarding the outcome of standard calculations as the lower limit presupposes that education's contribution to efficiency is correctly measured. My
second criticism of conventional cost-benefit analysis of education is that, in
the labor market circumstances typical of developing countries, the standard
way of measuring the social benefit of education (earnings differentials be-

tween persons with different levels of education) would ordinarily be expected to *overstate* the marginal social benefit of education. The reason is that wages in key sectors of developing countries are frequently set above market levels (see above) and because unemployment of educated labor is widespread (Blaug, 1973; Blaug, Layard, and Woodhall, 1969; Psacharopoulos and Hinchliffe, 1973; Turnham, 1971). Under such circumstances, we cannot assume, as does the standard method, that more education will result in more *employed* educated labor. The additional educated labor may be underemployed, displacing less educated labor in relatively unskilled jobs, or it may be openly unemployed; see Fields (1974). To evaluate the social benefit of education, we must determine the kind of work that the marginal educated worker is likely to get, if any; the extent to which he or she displaces less educated laborers; the extent to which educated workers are more productive than uneducated workers in the jobs they take; and what the uneducated workers will do instead. It is not a simple matter to find the answers to these questions. Instead, some authors multiply the educated-uneducated earnings differential by the employment rate for educated labor. In so doing, they implicitly assume that if 90 percent of the educated labor force is currently employed, employers would create 90 new jobs in response to an extra 100 newly educated persons in the work force. There is no reason whatever for believing that employers would act in this way; the easy computation is unwarranted.

I conclude, therefore, that public economics has led investigators to conduct social benefit-cost analysis of educational programs and, in so doing, to ask the right questions about the value of educational expansion. Application of this tool of public economics is preferable to previous methods of educational planning such as manpower planning, in which the cost side was omitted altogether. The manpower requirements approach, however, was well directed in asking about the needs of the economy and about the kinds of work that the newly educated are likely to find. The possibility of unemployment and underemployment among the educated is very real in a Harris-Todaro-type economy with wages that are greater than market clearing. In such circumstances, which probably are the typical ones, the social benefit-cost tool must be wielded with greater sensitivity. That it has not yet been handled in this way may reflect insufficient communication among education economists, labor economists, and public economists as well as the difficulty of doing the correct analysis.

Conclusions

Developing countries' labor markets typically exhibit large wage differentials across sectors, in part because of public pay policy. In addition to wage dualism, the salient features of labor markets in developing countries include high unemployment rates in high-wage (typically urban) labor markets and substantial migration from low-wage areas to high-wage ones. These wage differentials, unemployment patterns, and migration responses have implications for the formulation of public sector tax, subsidy, and hiring policy.

Public policy in developing countries should be analyzed using labor market models with these features. Such analysis shows that the first-best optimum may be attainable even in an economy with intersectoral wage differentials and consequent labor force migration. First, however, the tax and subsidy instruments at the government's disposal must be sufficiently far-reaching. Restrictions on available instruments, such as the ability to tax profits in only one sector of the economy but not the other, or the necessity of meeting an income distribution constraint, or minimum wages rising as workers are taxed to pay subsidies, may condemn the economy to a second-best situation.

A number of other policy conclusions also emerge. One is that the solution to *urban* unemployment may be *rural* development. Another is that creating better labor market information may reduce the incentive to migrate to high-wage labor markets in search of employment; this would lower unemployment and raise national product. Furthermore, investments in education and human resources are now harder to evaluate, because the possibility that the educated may become unemployed or underemployed must be taken into account. In each area, public policies must be based on careful social cost-benefit analysis.

Notes

1. The term "dualism" connotes a high-wage–low-wage dichotomy. The term "segmentation" is used to generalize this notion to a multiplicity of wages.

2. Good places for newcomers to this field to start would be Reynolds (1973), Berry and Sabot (1978), Squire (1981), Mazumdar (1983), and Kannappan (1983). The classic reference—still very useful today—is Turnham (1971).

3. For a summary, see Todaro (1976). See also Mincer (1976) and Hall (1972) for similar extensions in a developed country context.

4. For a review of such arguments, see Mincer (1976), Welch (1978), and Ehrenberg and Smith (1982).

5. See, for instance, Todaro (1971) and the references cited therein.

6. Another possibility, of course, is that the government *creates* dualism, for example by providing subsidized public services to urban but not rural residents. In this case, the migration consequences of such subsidies should enter into any evaluation of the subsidy scheme.

7. Similar assumptions are very common in the literature on taxes and subsidies in the presence of distortions; the distortion is taken as exogenous and unresponsive to policies aimed at removing it.

8. See Fields (1975b) for a formulation of on-the-job search in a Harris-Todaro context.

9. Readers are referred to Psacharopoulos (1982) for a description of such methods; also see Yotopoulos and Nugent (1976, chap. 11) for an overview in the context of developing countries.

10. Equity is occasionally the focal point of analyses of educational systems. As examples, see Fields (1975a) and chapter 22 in this volume.

11. A number of such aspects are discussed in Anderson and Bowman (1966) and in Anderson and Windham (1982).

PART 3

Case Studies
in Tax Reform

THIS PART DESCRIBES two substantial but contrasting empirical studies. The chapter on India by Ahmad and Stern deals with an attempt to develop and apply the theory of reform set forth in part 1. The authors consider the identification of suggestions for directions of reform as well as analyzing proposals being discussed by the Indian government. The chapter by Gil Díaz considers a major reform of the Mexican tax system that has already taken place. Gil Díaz describes its effects in a quantitative and systematic way but without attempting to fit it into a single theoretical framework.

The chapters are also complementary in that they focus on different sorts of taxes and different constraints facing the government. Thus Ahmad and Stern place their emphasis on indirect taxes, which are the predominant source of revenue, and pay little attention to the corporation tax, whereas for Mexico this tax is a major source of revenue (it is examined closely by Gil Díaz). The chapters share a concern with tracing the consequences of reform for government revenue and for households in different circumstances.

The first problem for Ahmad and Stern was to identify the effects of input taxes on prices. Such taxes are prevalent in India and make it quite difficult to say just how much each good is taxed. This task of calculating "effective taxes" is carried out using an input-output model based on information assembled for the Sixth Plan. The exercise in itself can be of help to the government in understanding the impact of its policies—for example, some apparently subsidized goods are, in fact, taxed through their inputs, and it would appear to be possible to justify substantial export rebates in terms of returning taxes paid on inputs if the government were anxious to stop discouraging exports.

Ahmad and Stern then calculate the social marginal costs of raising revenue from different goods using aggregate demand responses and the effective taxes following the theory described in part 1 and using a variety of different distributional assumptions. These social marginal costs are then compared with the social marginal costs that would arise from raising extra revenue through income and poll taxation. Groups of taxes such as import tariffs and sales taxes are also examined, and state and central taxes are compared. An increase in a poll transfer (for example, via food rations) financed by income taxation or sales taxation would appear to be desirable (if it were feasible) on all but the least egalitarian values. The authors show how the comparison between social marginal costs may be adjusted to take into account the costs of tax collection and administration. A shift to a uniform value-added tax is unattractive on distributional grounds, although a differentiated VAT could take distribution into account somewhat while avoiding the taxation of inputs.

Gil Díaz shows that the recent Mexican tax reform was designed in part to remove many of the complexities of the previous system and to improve enforcement. He emphasizes the need to take into account the proximity and openness of the economy to the United States, which prevents the after-tax rates of return to mobile factors from falling below certain levels. Major elements of the reform were the substitution of a VAT for a cascading system of sales taxation and substantial changes to the corporation tax system to simplify, widen the base, and take into account inflation. It seems that the reforms were largely successful in simplifying administration and improving compliance. Gil Díaz also examines the distributional consequences and finds that they were not adverse. One tax that appears to be particularly regressive in the Mexican context is the inflationary tax on money holdings.

The studies therefore show that systematic and quantitative analysis of tax reform in the consequentialist manner is possible both before and after the event. Their different coverages and emphases show too that a very broad range of tax questions is amenable to this kind of approach. Because the studies were both conducted at a fairly aggregative level, however, they were forced to ignore some important sectoral detail. Thus neither one pays close attention to agriculture or public sector pricing, though in both countries they are very important policy issues. These topics and others are taken up in later parts of the book.

11

Alternative Sources of Government Revenue: Examples from India, 1979-80

Ehtisham Ahmad and Nicholas Stern

GOVERNMENTS IN MOST COUNTRIES have a variety of tax tools at their disposal. In part 1 of this volume we saw how the choice of the source for extra tax revenue can be guided by simple theory. We first use a simple model to predict the consequences of changing particular taxes and then use value judgments that characterize social improvements to evaluate these consequences. In this chapter we show how these techniques can be applied using the example of the Indian economy. Through this case study, some of the theory and techniques were developed and tested. Thus we shall concentrate on showing what the methods can and cannot do, on how practical difficulties can be overcome, and on how they may be developed and extended, rather than on drawing immediate policy conclusions for India.

The existing set of tax instruments in a country reflects its general level of development (see chapters 7 and 8), its history and constitutional structure, and numerous ad hoc decisions taken in the past. It may nevertheless be difficult or costly to change the instruments, and it is therefore of interest to investigate the consequences of marginal adjustments to the existing structure. Thus our first task is to trace the effects of marginal changes of existing taxes on prices. In so doing we calculate in a simple model the tax component in the price, or the "effective tax." This allocation of effective taxes to goods is a major undertaking when taxes on inputs are pervasive and involves an explicit model of the production structure. Second, we calculate the social marginal cost of public funds from different sources, show how administrative costs can

This chapter is part of a program of research on the Indian fiscal system that was carried out at the Development Economics Research Centre, University of Warwick, with the help of grants from the Economic and Social Research Council, the Overseas Development Administration, and the Nuffield Foundation. The research is being continued at the London School of Economics. We are grateful to Avinash Dixit, Geoffrey Frewer, John Holsen, David Newbery, Kevin Roberts, Zmarak Shalizi, and Armondo Pinell-Siles for comments and encouragement and to Julie Richardson for assistance. The results should be treated as preliminary and are subject to revision. A full report on our work will be provided in Ahmad and Stern (forthcoming).

be incorporated, and discuss ways of using the estimates to guide policy. Third, we consider more radical changes in the existing structure. Fourth, we examine a number of possible extensions to our simple production model to determine the potential for extensions of the theory, particularly that relating tax changes to price changes. Finally, we consider directions for further research.

Many developing countries rely very heavily on indirect taxes and, within these, particularly on trade taxes. Thus tariffs have been an important source of revenue, and because of the pattern of imports, intermediate and capital goods have often been seen as natural targets. This has been true to some extent in India, although excises on domestic production have played an increasing role as the productive structure of the economy expanded. In India, trade taxes and excises are determined by the central government, whereas sales taxes are within the jurisdiction of state governments. Similarly, the personal income tax is determined by the central government, although the bulk of the proceeds must be distributed to the states. The taxation of agriculture is a matter for the states, and agricultural income does not attract the personal income tax. Thus the central government's choice of sources for extra revenue is constrained not only by administrative and political costs and difficulties but also by the constitution. The main existing tax instruments are therefore excises, tariffs, and the personal and corporate income taxes from the center and the sales tax from the states. We shall examine all of these as potential sources of extra revenue except for the corporate income tax, the legal complications of which precluded study in the time available.

The investigation of each of these sources for India involved a considerable amount of work. We shall not present all the calculations in full here, because our main objective is to indicate how results can be obtained and used and to comment on extensions. A more detailed treatment is available in a series of discussion papers that have been widely circulated and in our book (Ahmad and Stern, forthcoming). In the book we take into account a number of complications that are not examined here, and thus the numerical values presented here should be regarded as tentative and subject to revision.

The plan of the paper is as follows. In the next section the model for the effective tax calculations is set out, and theoretical aspects of the taxation of inputs are discussed. We then summarize results based on the latest estimates of the production structure available to us—the input-output table for eighty-nine sectors from the technical note to the Sixth Indian Plan. Also explicitly considered are the different sources of the taxation of inputs and how far export subsidies could be seen as the rebate of domestic taxes. The fourth section examines the balance of commodity taxation between the "center" and the "states," showing how taxes interact and how the theory of marginal reform may be extended to cover the case where a group of taxes has to be changed simultaneously.

There follows a brief review of the elements of the theory of marginal reform (see chapters 2 and 3) that are necessary for our comparison of the costs of revenue from different sources, and it is shown how administrative feasibility and costs of collection could be incorporated into the analysis. We summarize calculations of the social welfare loss from raising a marginal rupee from the income tax and assemble the calculations of the marginal costs of revenue from different sources in order to compare their attractiveness. Income taxes and the various indirect taxes are considered, but we do not discuss company taxation, which raises rather complicated theoretical and legal issues as well as posing serious data problems.

The sixth section considers nonmarginal reforms that are of relevance in the Indian context. A comprehensive treatment would place much greater de-mands on modeling and would require more data than are necessary for marginal reforms. Nevertheless it suggests that a move toward a value-added tax at a uniform rate would adversely affect the poorer sections of Indian society. Given the nondistortionary effects of the VAT on production, how-ever, there may well be advantages in considering a nonuniform VAT, or a uniform VAT supplemented by selective excises or tariffs, such that the effec-tive or overall tax system reflects distributional considerations. As with all reform, including the marginal variants, administrative feasibility and costs of collection will play an important role in the adoption of any particular line of action.

The seventh section of the chapter contains a discussion of some theoretical features of the model of "effective taxes" and possible extensions. In particular we relax the assumptions of a single factor and fixed coefficients in production.

The final section includes suggestions for further work and a commentary on the relationship between the analysis and practical policy.

The Composition of Indirect Taxes: Theory

Economists often argue that the tax system should be designed to avoid the taxation of intermediate goods. The reason is that it may lead to inefficiencies in that different industries will face different relative prices, so that the marginal rate of transformation between inputs, or between an input and an output, would be unequal across industries. Thus it would in principle, follow-ing the standard microeconomic argument, be possible, by a reallocation of inputs, to have strictly more of one good while having no less of another. Below we discuss different methods of reducing the taxation of commodity inputs while maintaining the same revenue. We examine first the replacement of existing indirect taxes by new types that avoid the taxation of inputs. Second, we discuss how the extent of taxation of inputs may be measured, evaluated, and adjusted. We then examine the balance between different types of indirect tax and between the taxes allocated to the states in the constitution and those allocated to the center. This first section is thus devoted to theoret-ical issues.

Avoiding Taxes on Inputs: Purchase Tax and Value-Added Tax

Two widely used systems of indirect taxes avoid the taxation of inputs: a purchase tax or tax on final sales and a value-added tax, or VAT, in which taxes paid on inputs are rebated or offset against the taxes collected on outputs. Each has advantages and disadvantages. An advantage of the purchase tax is that producers are left out of the indirect tax system altogether, and only outlets to final consumers are included. An obvious disadvantage, however, is the difficulty of identifying the final point of sale. Each person in the chain might try to claim that all sales were to other wholesalers or retailers, and doubtless a little ingenuity would lead to the production of receipts from some other agent not classified as a final consumer. The difficulty is particularly severe where there are a large number of small final outlets, as is the case with many goods in India.

It would be wrong, however, to dismiss the purchase tax immediately. Some states (for example, Karnataka) have a predominantly single-point sales tax such that a good is taxed only once in the distribution chain, usually at the wholesale stage. There is indeed the difficulty that agents claim the tax has already been paid, with false documents being produced in support, but nevertheless many collections are quite successful (see India, Karnataka Taxation Review Committee, 1982, pp. 30–32). A purchase tax could operate in a similar manner but with exemption if it could be proved that the sale was to a bona fide producer. Wherever exemptions are allowed in the tax system, abuse is possible, and no doubt it would often be falsely claimed that sales were to producers. Nevertheless, there can be some control over who has the right to be viewed as a producer and some checks on the buyer's claimed purchases. Thus the purchase tax is a system that merits careful consideration.

The rates of purchase tax across different goods would, we assume, differ according to elasticities of demand, distributional considerations, and so on. One way of raising the same revenue that is provided by the existing system would, in principle, be to make the purchase tax rates equal to the calculated effective tax rates on final goods.

Such a change would involve different systems of revenue sharing between the center and the states than those at present in existence. Currently the revenue from certain taxes (for example, the union excise) goes to the center and that from others (for example, state sales tax) goes to the states; the taxes under the two headings are, in general, specified in the constitution. With a unified purchase tax, we could have a system of proportional sharing of total revenue or the allocation of purchase tax on certain goods to the states and others to the center. The latter method might involve a minimum of constitutional adjustment but would have the disadvantage that taxes on different goods might be difficult to harmonize. Where there are close substitutes or complements, it is important for indirect taxes to take account of the connections. Further incentive considerations suggest that taxes might best be collected through that part of government that will receive the revenue.

The VAT has the advantage of making it unnecessary to identify the final consumer. The final consumer is self-determined as one who does not claim, or does not have the right to claim, a rebate for taxes paid on purchases. A major disadvantage is that, in principle, every producer, wholesaler, and retailer is brought into the tax system, so that there is a substantial administrative burden. Where large companies are involved, this burden may not be too problematic—they would already be required to keep accounts and relationships with authorities—but with many small concerns, as in India, the administrative problems would be substantial.

Administrative considerations led the Jha committee (Ministry of Finance, 1978) to recommend a VAT on manufacturing, or MANVAT. It would be interesting to estimate how far different definitions of a MANVAT would avoid taxation of inputs.[1] We would want to know, furthermore, whether the particular taxation of inputs that was alleviated corresponded to areas where substitution possibilities were the greatest, for losses from taxation of intermediate goods may be substantial where elasticities of substitution are high.

The self-policing aspect of VAT has often been cited as an advantage (for example, in Kaldor, 1964). Sellers have an incentive to conceal in their records the tax collection on their sales (because this must be paid to the authorities), whereas the purchasers will want to include in their records all the taxes paid on their inputs (because these can be offset against their payments to the authorities).[2] Thus we can cross-check claims. Given that the VAT is a tax on wages plus profits, such records can provide valuable information on profits. Indeed, Kaldor (1964) argued for the United Kingdom that the VAT could act in part as a substitute for a corporation tax.

VAT is often seen as a uniform tax, and this aspect has sometimes been treated as a virtue. This argument in favor of uniformity is often quite mistaken (see chapter 2; it requires, among other things, an optimal uniform poll transfer), and the distinguishing feature of a VAT should be seen as the rebating of taxes on inputs. We could, in principle, design a VAT to raise the same revenue that we see at present, basing the rates for each good on the appropriate effective taxes. Considerations similar to those for the purchase tax concerning the allocation of revenues between the states and the center, and associated constitutional problems, apply.

Measuring Taxes on Inputs: Effective Taxes

We now discuss the measurement, evaluation, and adjustment of taxes on inputs. To keep things simple, we begin with the simple, static closed-economy Leontief model, and we then consider an open economy, dynamic aspects, flexible coefficients, and multiple factors. These last provide examples of the incidence analysis discussed in chapter 3.

All purchasers of a good pay a price inclusive of tax. The purchasers' price vector **q** is defined as the price paid by consumers and also that paid by producers for purchase of inputs. The producers' price vector **p** represents the price received by producers for sales. We consider the simple input-output model of production with fixed input-output matrix A, gross output vector $\mathbf{Y}$, and net output vector $\mathbf{Z}$. Then inputs are $A\mathbf{Y}$, and

$$(11\text{-}1) \qquad \mathbf{Z} = \mathbf{Y} - A\mathbf{Y} = (I - A)\mathbf{Y}.$$

Competitive pricing conditions for this model are

$$(11\text{-}2) \qquad \mathbf{p}' = \mathbf{q}'A + \mathbf{v}'$$

where primes denote row vectors and $\mathbf{v}$ is the vector of value added by industry (which we assume for the moment to be fixed). If $\mathbf{t}$ is the tax vector, then

$$(11\text{-}3) \qquad \mathbf{q} = \mathbf{p} + \mathbf{t}$$

and from equations 11-2 and 11-3 we have

$$(11\text{-}4) \qquad \mathbf{q}' = \mathbf{t}'(I - A)^{-1} + \mathbf{v}'(I - A)^{-1}.$$

In this model we define the effective tax vector $\mathbf{t}^e$ as

$$(11\text{-}5) \qquad \mathbf{t}^{e'} = \mathbf{t}'(I - A)^{-1}$$

and prices in the absence of taxes, the "basic" price vector $\mathbf{p}^b$, as

$$(11\text{-}6) \qquad \mathbf{p}^{b'} = \mathbf{v}'(I - A)^{-1}.$$

The ith component of $\mathbf{t}^e$ is the amount by which government revenue would increase if there was a unit increase in final demand for a good. This is our formal definition of the effective tax: if the final demand vector is z and government revenue R, we have $t_i^e = \partial R / \partial z_i$. We may also define $\mathbf{t}^{\text{diff}}$, where

$$(11\text{-}7) \qquad \mathbf{t}^{\text{diff}} = \mathbf{t}^e - \mathbf{t}$$

which measures the difference between the effective tax, $\mathbf{t}^e$, and the nominal tax, $\mathbf{t}$. Thus $\mathbf{t}^{\text{diff}}$ tells us the extent to which inputs are taxed. The overall level of taxation of inputs in the economy is given by $\mathbf{t}^{\text{diff}}$ times the final demand vector $\mathbf{Z}$, or

$$(11\text{-}8) \qquad \begin{aligned} \mathbf{t}^{\text{diff}} \cdot \mathbf{Z} &= \mathbf{t}^{\text{diff}'}(I - A)\mathbf{Y} \\ &= \mathbf{t}^{e'}(I - A)\mathbf{Y} - \mathbf{t}'(I - A)\mathbf{Y} \\ &= \mathbf{t}'(I - A)^{-1}(I - A)\mathbf{Y} - \mathbf{t}'\mathbf{Y} + \mathbf{t}'A\mathbf{Y} \\ &= \mathbf{t}'A\mathbf{Y}. \end{aligned}$$

Alternatively, we can see this last measure of the taxation of inputs as simply a decomposition of the total tax payment

$$(11\text{-}9) \qquad \begin{aligned} \mathbf{t} \cdot \mathbf{Y} &= \mathbf{t}'(I - A)\mathbf{Y} + \mathbf{t}'A\mathbf{Y} \\ &= \mathbf{t} \cdot \mathbf{Z} + \mathbf{t}'A\mathbf{Y} \end{aligned}$$

into a tax on final demand, $\mathbf{t} \cdot \mathbf{Z}$ and a tax on intermediate goods, $\mathbf{t}'A\mathbf{Y}$.

Although $\mathbf{t}^{\text{diff}}$ measures the extent to which inputs are taxed in the above model, it does not indicate any costs associated with distortions of choice of technique resulting from the taxation of inputs, because all coefficients are fixed. Further changes in factor prices and pure profits have been assumed away, because we have a single factor and zero profits. The relaxation of some of these assumptions is discussed below. Here we concentrate on the effect of taxation on the composition of inputs and relax only the assumption of fixed coefficients (thus retaining a single factor and zero profits).

We assume as before that each industry has a single output (no joint production). We may then write $c_i(\mathbf{q}, w)$ as the minimum unit cost of producing good i when input prices are $\mathbf{q}$ and the single factor has price w. If we choose the single factor as numeraire, we may write the vector of costs as a function $\mathbf{c}(\mathbf{q})$ of $\mathbf{q}$ only. The most efficient way of producing each good can be defined simply in terms of the technique that gives the minimum quantity of the factor directly and indirectly required in production. These minimum unit costs, γ, as is well known (for example, Bliss, 1975, chap. 11), are the prices of the nonsubstitution theorem satisfying

$$(11\text{-}10) \qquad\qquad \gamma = \mathbf{c}(\gamma)$$

so that

$$(11\text{-}11) \qquad\qquad \gamma' = \mathbf{v}'(\gamma) [I - A(\gamma)]^{-1}$$

where $\mathbf{v}(\gamma)$ is the vector of factor requirements per unit of output for each industry and $A(\gamma)$ the input-output matrix at prices γ. Notice that $\mathbf{v}$ and A now depend on prices, whereas they were previously fixed, and that

$$(11\text{-}12) \qquad\qquad [A(\mathbf{q})]_{ij} = \frac{\partial c_i}{\partial q_j}$$

from the standard properties of the cost function.

Where we have taxation of sales, producers receive a price $\mathbf{p}$ but pay $\mathbf{q}$ for inputs. Thus in equilibrium, if we generalize equation 11-2 above,

$$(11\text{-}13) \qquad\qquad \mathbf{p} = \mathbf{c}(\mathbf{q}).$$

The difference between prices with and without taxation is $(\mathbf{q} - \gamma)$, which may be written, by means of equations 11-3, 11-10, and 11-13, as

$$(11\text{-}14) \qquad\qquad \mathbf{q} - \gamma = \mathbf{c}(\mathbf{q}) - \mathbf{c}(\gamma) + \mathbf{t}$$
$$\geqq A'(\mathbf{q}) (\mathbf{q} - \gamma) + \mathbf{t}$$

using the concavity of the cost function and equation 11-12. Thus

$$(11\text{-}15) \qquad\qquad \mathbf{q}' - \gamma' \geqq \mathbf{t}' [I - A(\mathbf{q})]^{-1}$$

because $[I - A(\mathbf{q})]^{-1}$ is assumed to be a nonnegative matrix. The implication of equation 11-15 is that the effective tax calculated in our empirical work, which is based on the input-output matrix as measured at the ruling prices, *underestimates* the price-raising effect of the taxes. The reason is that the fixed coefficients assumption ignores the rise in price associated with the reorganization of inputs from those associated with $A(\gamma)$, which minimize resource costs, to $A(\mathbf{q})$.

We can illuminate this point by writing a decomposition of the overall price rise as

$$(11\text{-}16) \qquad \mathbf{q}' - \boldsymbol{\gamma}' = \mathbf{t}'\,[I - A(\mathbf{q})]^{-1} + (\mathbf{p}^{b'} - \boldsymbol{\gamma}')$$

which comes from equations 11-4, 11-5, and 11-6. We must remember that A is now a function of $\mathbf{q}$. Thus the price rise is made up from the effective taxes and the increase in the vector of resource costs of production, $(\mathbf{p}^b - \boldsymbol{\gamma})$. We know that $(\mathbf{p}^b - \boldsymbol{\gamma})$ is nonnegative from inequality 11-15 or from the property that $\boldsymbol{\gamma}$ is the vector of minimum resource costs. Similarly, the increase in the costs of production at market prices associated with the tax is

$$(11\text{-}17) \qquad \mathbf{p} - \boldsymbol{\gamma} = \mathbf{t}^{\text{diff}} + (\mathbf{p}^b - \boldsymbol{\gamma}).$$

An obvious measure of the resource cost of the input taxation per unit of output is simply $(\mathbf{p}^b - \boldsymbol{\gamma})$, where

$$(11\text{-}18) \qquad \mathbf{p}^b = \mathbf{v}'(\mathbf{q})\,[I - A(\mathbf{q})]^{-1}$$

and $\boldsymbol{\gamma}$ is given by equation 11-11. This statement would be combined with a measure of output shifts in a calculation of overall losses. For marginal changes, we would be interested in the rate of change of $\mathbf{p}^b$ with respect to taxes, which may be derived as follows. From equations 11-4, 11-5, and 11-6, we have

$$(11\text{-}19) \qquad \mathbf{p}^b = \mathbf{q} - \mathbf{t}^e.$$

Thus

$$(11\text{-}20) \qquad \frac{\partial \mathbf{p}^{b'}}{\partial \mathbf{t}} = \frac{\partial \mathbf{q}'}{\partial \mathbf{t}} - \frac{\partial \mathbf{t}^{e'}}{\partial \mathbf{t}}$$

where $\partial \mathbf{q}'/\partial \mathbf{t}$ is the matrix with ijth element $\partial q_j / \partial t_i$. From equations 11-3, 11-12, and 11-13, we have

$$(11\text{-}21) \qquad \frac{\partial \mathbf{q}'}{\partial \mathbf{t}} = (I - A)^{-1}$$

a condition that is discussed further below. From equations 11-5, 11-20, and 11-21, we have

$$(11\text{-}22) \qquad \frac{\partial \mathbf{p}^{b'}}{\partial \mathbf{t}} = -\mathbf{t}'\,(\partial \bar{A})\,\bar{A}'$$

where $\bar{A}$ is $(I - A)^{-1}$ with the ijth element $\bar{a}_{ij}$, ∂A is the derivative of $\bar{A}$ with respect to prices $\mathbf{q}$—it is a tensor with kjlth element α_{kjl} equal to $\partial \bar{a}_{kj} / \partial q_l$—and the ijth element of the right side of equation 11-22 is $-\Sigma_{k,l}\, t_k\, \alpha_{kjl}\, \bar{a}_{il}$. Notice that both $(\mathbf{p}^b - \boldsymbol{\gamma})$ and its marginal version 11-22 depend on the *change* in input-output coefficients because the shift in these causes the resource cost. We know that the total loss $(\mathbf{p}^b - \boldsymbol{\gamma})$ is positive for each good, although this will not necessarily be true for the marginal loss. The calculation of these losses poses problems, however, because we observe $A(\mathbf{q})$ and not the input-output matrix $A(\gamma)$ and do not know the rate of change of A with respect to prices. We could compute $A(\gamma)$ or the derivative of A with a general equilibrium model of the production side that involved flexible coefficients. The answer, however, would be largely prejudged by the choice of the functional forms and the invention of parameters that would not, in general, be available at the level of disaggregation of the standard input-output matrixes. (Similar problems arise on the demand side; see chapter 4, by Deaton.)

So far we have considered the case of a closed economy. Let us now allow for imports. Unless otherwise stated, all imports are assumed to be complementary; that is, production of good j at unit level requires a_{ij}^d of good i produced domestically and a_{ij}^m of imported good i. The assumption is relaxed in equations 11-81 and 11-82, where we show that the analysis of price effects is correct for marginal changes even where we allow some substitutability. The restrictive import policies in operation at the time may have implied that complementarity had to be established before imports were allowed. In the absence of taxes, the competitive pricing conditions for domestically produced goods become

$$(11\text{-}23) \qquad\qquad \mathbf{q}' = \mathbf{q}'A^d + \mathbf{v}'$$

where A^d is a matrix of input-output coefficients for domestic flows. The foreign exchange costs ($\mathbf{p}^{m'}A^m$ if $\mathbf{p}^m$ are import prices) of imported inputs have been included in the vector of value added, $\mathbf{v}$, and there are assumed to be no import quotas. If we allow for the imposition of excise taxes on domestic production $\mathbf{t}^d$, and for import duties $\mathbf{t}^m$ (both expressed per unit), the pricing equation becomes

$$(11\text{-}24) \quad \mathbf{q}' = \mathbf{t}^{d'}(I - A^d)^{-1} + \mathbf{t}^{m'}A^m(I - A^d)^{-1} + \mathbf{v}'(I - A^d)^{-1}$$

where A^m is the matrix with ijth element a_{ij}^m. Thus the effective taxes, $\mathbf{t}^{e'}$, are given by

$$(11\text{-}25) \qquad \mathbf{t}^{e'} = \mathbf{t}^{d'}(I - A^d)^{-1} + \mathbf{t}^{m'}A^m(I - A^d)^{-1}.$$

This expression provides an example of the incidence analysis discussed in chapter 3.

In this formulation the contribution of excise taxes, which fall only on domestic production, to effective taxes is given by $\mathbf{t}^{d'}(I - A^d)^{-1}$ and that of import duties is $\mathbf{t}^{m'}A^m(I - A^d)^{-1}$. Note that in this model the tax effects are additive (the imported and domestic inputs are different goods, and we cannot add A^d and A^m to get an aggregate input-output matrix). The effects of sales taxes levied on total commodity flows, regardless of the origin of the commodity, are given by equation 11-25, because we can see these (sales taxes) as in part affecting prices of domestically produced goods through imported inputs and in part through domestic inputs.

Notice that we have confined attention here to the effect of taxes on the prices of domestically produced goods in a fixed-coefficients linear model with only one domestic factor and a fixed exchange rate (domestic factors and foreign inputs are added to form **v** using a relative price, the exchange rate, which we assume is constant). More general models are discussed below. Tariffs will also directly affect the prices of imported consumption goods; this feature will be examined in subsequent work. A more detailed discussion of agriculture is provided in parts 4 and 5 of this book. For the calculations in this chapter, we assume that all increments in consumption bear the effective tax, and therefore it is simplest to assume that the consumption of imported goods is regulated by quotas (see next subsection).

The effective taxes will be important ingredients for our marginal reform calculations in that they will tell us the effects on government revenue of output increases in domestic production. They are, however, of substantial interest in their own right as descriptions of the tax system. Governments will often find it difficult to judge the consequences of taxes in a complicated production and fiscal structure. In this context the t^e will be a very useful summary statistic of the fiscal system that may well influence policy directly if it reveals, for example, that the government is, in fact, taxing heavily goods that it meant to subsidize or to tax only lightly.

So far we have assumed a static model. Much of the input taxation, however, arises through the taxation of capital goods. In principle, we would need a fully articulated dynamic model to determine the effect of taxes imposed in one period on prices in all other periods (this type of model is discussed in chapter 5). To keep things simple, we may attempt to capture the effects of taxes on capital goods by including a term in equation 11-2 that is $r\mathbf{p}'B$, where B is a capital stock matrix and r a rate of interest—thus we charge an implicit rental for the equipment. This formulation would be correct in steady state and is, we hope, an adequate approximation out of steady state. In equations 11-4 to 11-6, we would therefore simply replace A by $(A + rB)$.

To give an aggregative indication of the orders of magnitude involved, suppose that the real rate of interest is 5 percent and the capital-output ratio is 5. Then capital represents 25 percent of cost, and an effective tax rate of 20 percent on capital goods will contribute 5 percent to effective tax rates. Given effective rates of 10 percent or so, this effect is not small. It is clear that the theoretical and empirical aspects of the dynamic effects of taxes or prices deserve further research.

Marginal Reform and Effective Taxes

The discussion of the social marginal cost of public revenue in part 1 of this book dealt with taxes on final goods. When there are taxes on intermediate goods we can translate these, using certain assumptions, into "effective taxes" on final goods, as we have just seen. Using the calculations described above, we can thus put the theory set forth in part 1 into practice. In this subsection we show how and clarify the assumptions involved.

The expression for the social marginal cost, λ_i, of revenue derived in chapter 2 is

$$(11\text{-}26) \qquad\qquad \lambda_i = \frac{\displaystyle\sum_h \beta^h x_i^h}{X_i + \displaystyle\sum_j t_j \frac{\partial X_j}{\partial t_i}}$$

where t_j are taxes on final goods, x_i^h are household demands, X_i are the aggregate demands $(\Sigma_h x_i^h)$, and β^h are welfare weights. We can apply this concept to the model described below as follows. Recall that the denominator in equation 11-26 is simply $\partial R/\partial t_i$ and the numerator $-\partial V/\partial t_i$. Thus if we replace the vector **t** by the vector of effective tax rates, we can see equation 11-26 as giving the cost in social welfare from a small (unit) increase in the *effective tax* on the *i*th good. Thus we raise the price of the *i*th good, holding constant all other prices. Then the effect on revenue $\partial R/\partial t_i$ is calculated using *effective taxes*, because the demand shifts will change revenue through taxes on both inputs and outputs. The calculations of the preceding section allowed us to switch from the space of nominal taxes $(\mathbf{t}^m, \mathbf{t}^d)$ to effective taxes, thus preserving the simplicity of equation 11-26.

The treatment of imports implicit in using equation 11-26 in its simple form, after substituting $\mathbf{t}^e$ for **t**, is as follows. We suppose that imports of consumer goods are rationed so that demand changes fall entirely onto domestic production. Imports are perfect substitutes for domestically produced goods in consumption. We suppose that taxes on imports rise by the amount of the price increase in domestically produced goods, so that the increase in effective tax applies to imported consumer goods as well. This situation would occur if the effective tax was increased by increasing the sales tax. Then the numerator of equation 11-26 accurately measures $-\partial V/\partial t_i$, and the denominator $\partial R/\partial t_i$, if we use total consumption (imported and domestic) x_i^h of good i by household h. The procedure is convenient if the data do not split consumption by origin. In subsequent work we shall be disaggregating, so that we may simply treat domestic consumption and foreign consumption as different goods.

The simplicity obtained using these assumptions allows us, for our illustration of the method, to confine our data requirements to t_i^e, x_i^h, $\partial X_j/\partial t_i$, and β^h, where x_i^h comes from a consumer demand survey, $\partial X_j/\partial t_i$ from aggregate demand responses, and β^h from value judgments. Thus the method can be put into practice using data that would be available in many countries. For effective taxes, we need tax collections by commodity and input-output tables. We need a household expenditure survey and estimates of demand responses for x_i^h and $\partial X_j/\partial t_i$. We also require value judgments β^h. All of these matters are discussed below.

In work currently under way and to be published in Ahmad and Stern (forthcoming), we break down consumption of good i into cash and kind as well as domestic and imported components. This exercise obviously involves a considerable increase in the burden of calculations, but much of the extra information of this sort that is required can nevertheless be constructed from consumption surveys and other sources.

It should be noted that a simple reformulation of equation 11-26 is

$$(11\text{-}27) \qquad \lambda_i = \frac{\sum\limits_h \beta^h q_i x_i^h}{q_i X_i + \sum\limits_j (t_j^e/q_j) q_j X_j \epsilon_{ji}}$$

where ϵ_{ji} is $q_i \, \partial X_j / \partial q_i \, X_j$, the uncompensated elasticity of good j with respect to the ith price. This is a convenient form to apply to the data, because $q_i \, x_i^h$ represents expenditure by the hth household on the ith good, and consumer demand information often comes in the form of the ϵ_{ji}. Notice that t_j^e/q_j is simply the effective tax as a proportion of the market price; expressing taxes in this way allows us to calculate on the consumption side using expenditures and elasticities (although our results for effective taxes that concentrate on production will be expressed as a proportion of producer prices; see table 11-1).

$$(11\text{-}28) \qquad \beta^h = k \, (I^h)^{-\epsilon}$$

where I^h is the expenditure per capita of the hth group and ϵ may be considered an index of inequality aversion (see, for example, Atkinson, 1970). For $\epsilon = 0$, we have all β^h equal to one, or no aversion to inequality, and $\epsilon = 5$ begins to approach concern only with the poorest group. In the examples that follow, the "welfare weights" have been normalized by choice of k such that $\Sigma_h f^h \beta^h \equiv \bar{\beta} = 1$ for each of $\epsilon = 0, 0.1, 1, 2,$ and 5, where f^h is the proportion of households in the hth group.

As explained in chapters 2 and 4, it is interesting and important to compare the social marginal costs λ_i from raising revenue by indirect taxation with the social marginal cost λ^{PT} of raising revenue by a poll tax. This is given by

$$(11\text{-}29a) \qquad \lambda^{PT} = \frac{1}{1 - \bar{\delta}}$$

where

$$(11\text{-}29b) \qquad \bar{\delta} = \sum\limits_h f^h \delta^h$$

and

$$(11\text{-}29c) \qquad \delta^h = \mathbf{t} \cdot \frac{\partial \mathbf{x}^h}{\partial M^h}$$

where δ^h is the marginal propensity to spend on indirect taxes out of lump-sum income (M^h), and we have used $\bar{\beta} = 1$. The cost $(-\Delta V)$ to households of a unit increase in a poll tax is $H\beta$ and the extra revenue is $H - H\bar{\delta}$, because the loss in indirect tax payments must be subtracted from the revenue H. The ratio $(-\Delta V/\Delta R)$ is λ^{PT} and yields equation 11-29a. If $\lambda_i < \lambda^{PT}$, then we would want to increase the ith tax to finance a reduction in the poll tax, or an increase in the poll transfer.

Marginal Reform: The Center and the States

The theory developed can also tell us about the balance between state and federal taxes. If good i is allocated to the state and good j to the center, then we can compare λ_i and λ_j, the social losses from a marginal rupee raised on goods i and j. The issue is a little more complicated than this statement in at least three respects. First, we must consider the taxation of inputs. Second, there will often be both state and federal taxes on the same good; in fact this will usually be the case if we speak of effective taxes. Third, we may have to take into account separate budget constraints for the states and the center.

The comparison between state and center with respect to the taxation of inputs is relatively straightforward. We saw above that with fixed coefficients the taxation of inputs would be measured by $\mathbf{t}^{\text{diff}}$, which is effective taxes less nominal taxes. Where there are taxes from different sources, their effects in this model are additive. Hence we add $\mathbf{t}^{\text{diff}C}$ and $\mathbf{t}^{\text{diff}S}$, the taxes on inputs arising from central taxes and state taxes, to arrive at the overall $\mathbf{t}^{\text{diff}}$.[3] The contributions $\mathbf{t}^{\text{diff}C}$ and $\mathbf{t}^{\text{diff}S}$ may therefore be compared directly, component by component.

Second, where there are both central and state taxes on a good, then we cannot compare the marginal losses, λ_i, by separating out "central goods" and "state goods" for tax purposes. Because we shall be speaking of effective taxes much of the time, this problem is pervasive. We shall write the two effective tax vectors arising from central and state sources as $\mathbf{t}^{eC}$ and $\mathbf{t}^{eS}$. With our assumptions on the production structure, the vector of total effective taxes, $\mathbf{t}^e$, is $\mathbf{t}^{eC} + \mathbf{t}^{eS}$, and we can examine marginal reforms by specifying an increase in state and central taxes as involving an increase $\Delta\mathbf{t}^{eS}$ and $\Delta\mathbf{t}^{eC}$, respectively. The $\Delta\mathbf{t}^{eS}$ and $\Delta\mathbf{t}^{eC}$ may be chosen in a number of ways, which we shall discuss below. The marginal loss from raising one rupee in state taxes then is

$$(11\text{-}30) \qquad \lambda^S = \frac{\sum\limits_{h}\sum\limits_{i}\beta^h x_i^h \Delta t_i^{eS}}{\sum\limits_{i}\left(X_i + \sum\limits_{j} t_j^e \frac{\partial X_j}{\partial t_i^e}\right)\Delta t_i^{eS}}$$

(with a similar expression for λ^C). This expression may be written as a weighted average of the λ_i using weights θ_i^S that sum to one:

$$(11\text{-}31) \qquad \lambda^S = \sum_i \theta_i^S \lambda_i,$$

where

$$(11\text{-}32) \qquad \theta_i^S = \frac{\Delta t_i^{eS}\left(X_i + \sum\limits_{j} t_j^e \frac{\partial X_j}{\partial t_i^e}\right)}{\sum\limits_{i}\left(X_i + \sum\limits_{j} t_j^e \frac{\partial X_j}{\partial t_i^e}\right)\Delta t_i^{eS}}.$$

Table 11-1. *The Taxation of Inputs*

Commodity	t^e	t^{diff}	t^{diffC}	t^{diffS}	Proportion of domestic gross output
1. Rice and products	−0.035	−0.009	−0.014	0.006	0.0445
2. Wheat and products	0.069	−0.018	−0.027	0.008	0.0226
3. Jowar and products	0.012	0.002	0.001	0.002	0.0075
4. Bajra and products	0.003	0.004	0.002	0.005	0.0025
5. Other cereals	0.009	0.013	0.002	0.011	0.0066
6. Pulses	0.048	0.038	0.022	0.016	0.0108
7. Sugarcane	0.003	−0.010	−0.015	0.005	0.0135
8. Jute	−0.001	−0.003	−0.004	0.001	0.0010
9. Cotton	−0.005	0.005	0.000	0.005	0.0077
10. Plantations	−0.014	−0.016	−0.043	0.027	0.0060
11. Other crops	0.005	−0.001	−0.003	0.002	0.0617
12. Milk and products	0.009	0.008	−0.003	0.011	0.0308
13. Other animal husbandry	0.014	0.014	−0.004	0.018	0.0157
14. Forestry and logging	0.051	0.012	0.007	0.005	0.0070
15. Fishing	0.012	0.012	0.007	0.005	0.0042
16. Coal and lignite	0.065	0.018	0.009	0.008	0.0060
17. Petroleum and natural gas	0.201	0.036	0.027	0.009	0.0023
18. Iron ore	0.233	0.134	0.104	0.030	0.0006
19. Other minerals	0.058	0.073	0.056	0.017	0.0020
20. Miscellaneous food products	0.067	0.047	0.021	0.026	0.0178
21. Sugar	0.202	0.038	0.016	0.022	0.0088
22. Gur and khandsari	0.059	0.042	0.004	0.038	0.0107
23. Vanaspati	0.191	0.075	0.038	0.036	0.0064
24. Other edible oils	0.074	0.015	−0.009	0.024	0.0062
25. Tea and coffee	0.221	0.050	0.020	0.030	0.0044
26. Other beverages	3.590	0.074	0.049	0.025	0.0012
27. Tobacco manufacture	0.939	0.115	0.097	0.018	0.0047
28. Cotton textiles excluding (29)	0.108	0.051	0.034	0.017	0.0248
29. Cotton textiles, handloom and khadi	0.070	0.082	0.056	0.026	0.0122
30. Woolen and silk textiles	0.411	0.325	0.297	0.028	0.0026
31. Artificial silk fabrics	0.598	0.442	0.432	0.010	0.0035
32. Jute textiles	0.142	0.069	0.053	0.016	0.0045
33. Ready-made garments	0.093	0.081	0.067	0.013	0.0084
34. Miscellaneous textile products	0.132	0.114	0.091	0.023	0.0065
35. Carpet weaving	0.052	0.048	0.038	0.011	0.0015
36. Wood products	0.093	0.078	0.057	0.021	0.0066
37. Paper, paper products and newsprint	0.275	0.106	0.075	0.031	0.0061
38. Printing and publishing	0.090	0.090	0.068	0.022	0.0046
39. Leather and products	0.053	0.054	0.027	0.027	0.0033
40. Leather footwear	0.183	0.122	0.101	0.021	0.0023
41. Rubber products	0.408	0.161	0.124	0.037	0.0065

Table 11-1 (*continued*)

Commodity	t^e	t^{diff}	t^{diffC}	t^{diffS}	Proportion of domestic gross output
42. Plastics and synthetic rubber	0.480	0.248	0.216	0.032	0.0036
43. Petroleum products	0.548	0.013	0.009	0.004	0.0153
44. Miscellaneous coal and petroleum produce	0.518	0.087	0.065	0.022	0.0029
45. Inorganic heavy chemicals	0.262	0.079	0.060	0.019	0.0039
46. Organic heavy chemicals	0.362	0.127	0.103	0.024	0.0010
47. Chemical fertilizers	−0.235	0.042	0.017	0.025	0.0102
48. Insecticides, fungicides, etc.	0.241	0.173	0.119	0.053	0.0010
49. Drugs and pharmaceuticals	0.300	0.166	0.116	0.050	0.0096
50. Soaps and glycerines	0.267	0.119	0.072	0.047	0.0024
51. Cosmetics	0.260	0.086	0.050	0.036	0.0020
52. Synthetic rubber and fibers	1.029	0.131	0.099	0.031	0.0029
53. Other chemicals	0.388	0.174	0.142	0.032	0.0047
54. Refractories	0.102	0.049	0.035	0.013	0.0037
55. Cement	0.457	0.079	0.058	0.022	0.0024
56. Other nonmetallic products	0.148	0.096	0.074	0.022	0.0101
57. Iron and steel, ferroalloys	0.134	0.113	0.093	0.027	0.0157
58. Castings and forgings	0.110	0.110	0.093	0.017	0.0013
59. Iron and steel structures	0.557	0.141	0.123	0.018	0.0035
60. Nonferrous metals, alloys	0.171	0.101	0.084	0.017	0.0106
61. Metal products	0.170	0.114	0.098	0.017	0.0147
62. Tractors and agricultural implements	0.220	0.089	0.056	0.034	0.0024
63. Machine tools	0.228	0.125	0.099	0.026	0.0015
64. Office, domestic, commercial equipment	0.228	0.073	0.055	0.018	0.0007
65. Other nonelectric machinery	0.163	0.134	0.120	0.014	0.0151
66. Electric motors	0.267	0.125	0.100	0.025	0.0024
67. Electric cables and wires	0.331	0.151	0.129	0.022	0.0033
68. Batteries	0.337	0.087	0.072	0.015	0.0010
69. Electrical household goods	0.357	0.112	0.091	0.021	0.0011
70. Communications and electronic equipment	0.239	0.137	0.115	0.022	0.0022
71. Other electrical machinery	0.219	0.129	0.106	0.023	0.0065
72. Ships and boats	0.070	0.070	0.054	0.016	0.0008
73. Rail equipment	0.107	0.107	0.079	0.028	0.0046
74. Motor vehicles	0.376	0.118	0.089	0.029	0.0088
75. Motorcycles and bicycles	0.157	0.114	0.093	0.021	0.0035

(*Table continues on the following page.*)

Table 11-1 (continued)

Commodity	t^e	t^{diff}	t^{diffC}	t^{diffS}	Proportion of domestic gross output
76. Other transport equipment	0.130	0.086	0.062	0.024	0.0005
77. Watches and clocks	0.358	0.151	0.115	0.036	0.0004
78. Miscellaneous mfg. industries	0.360	0.111	0.094	0.017	0.0121
79. Construction	0.065	0.065	0.043	0.022	0.0695
80. Electricity, gas, water supply	0.113	0.073	0.055	0.018	0.0202
81. Railways	0.052	0.052	0.037	0.015	0.0127
82. Other transport	0.150	0.115	0.081	0.034	0.0438
83. Communications	0.011	0.011	0.007	0.004	0.0048
84. Trade, storage, warehouses	0.010	0.018	0.010	0.008	0.0907
85. Banking and insurance	0.004	0.006	0.003	0.002	0.0184
86. Real estate, owner dwellings	0.007	0.008	0.005	0.003	0.0216
87. Education	0.092	0.093	0.066	0.027	0.0451
88. Medical health	0.210	0.210	0.117	0.093	0.0186
89. Other services	0.046	0.040	0.026	0.014	0.0593

Notes: t^e = effective taxes from all sources as a proportion of the producer price; $t^{diff} = t^e - t$, where t^e is the overall effective tax vector and t is the nominal vector of commodity taxes. $t^{diffC} = t^{eC} - t^C$, where t^{eC} is the effective tax from union taxes: excises, import duties and subsidies, and t^C the corresponding nominal tax vector. $t^{diffS} = t^e - t^S$, where t^e is the effective state tax vector, comprising sales tax, state excise, and other taxes, and t^S the equivalent nominal tax vector. The proportion of sectoral gross value of output in total domestic output is shown in column 5.

This has the natural interpretation of being the proportion of the extra rupee arising from the increase in taxes on the *i*th good. From equations 11-31 and 11-32, it is clear that only the relative values of the components of t_i^{eS} come into the calculation of λ^S.

We may now compare λ^C and λ^S, which correspond to different ways by which the states and center can raise revenue. Δt^{eC} and Δt^{eS} may be specified in a number of ways. For the center, for example, we could increase all import tariffs by one percentage point—that is, from t^m to $(t^m \times 1.01)$—and could calculate the effect on t^{eC}; or we could do the same thing for excise taxes. For the states, we could increase all state sales taxes by one percentage point and ask about the effect on t^{eS}. Some examples appear below.

Third, we consider separate budget constraints for the state and center. To ease notation, we drop the superscript e here and concentrate only on effective taxes, or taxes on final goods. It may help to define issues if we deal first with the optimization problem and then with that of reform.

We write the optimization problem as

$$\underset{t^C, t^S}{\text{Maximize}} \quad V(t^C + t^S)$$

subject to

$$(11\text{-}33) \qquad \begin{aligned} t^C . \mathbf{X} &\geq R^C \\ t^S . \mathbf{X} &\geq R^S \end{aligned}$$

where R^C and R^S are the revenue requirements of the center and states. Demand $\mathbf{X}$ and social welfare V are functions of the consumer price vector given by producer prices (assumed fixed) plus $t^C + t^S$. Thus the taxes from the two sources are additive. Taking Lagrange multipliers for the two constraints, we have as first-order conditions

$$(11\text{-}34a) \qquad \frac{\partial V}{\partial t_i^C} + \lambda^C \frac{\partial}{\partial t_i^C} (t^C . \mathbf{X}) + \lambda^S \frac{\partial}{\partial t_i^C} (t^S . \mathbf{X}) = 0$$

$$(11\text{-}34b) \qquad \frac{\partial V}{\partial t_i^S} + \lambda^C \frac{\partial}{\partial t_i^S} (t^C . \mathbf{X}) + \lambda^S \frac{\partial}{\partial t_i^S} (t^S . \mathbf{X}) = 0.$$

Given that the derivatives of V with respect to t_i^C and t_i^S are equal (and similarly for $\mathbf{X}$), we have, on subtracting equation 11-34b from equation 11-34a,

$$(11\text{-}35) \qquad \lambda^C = \lambda^S.$$

This expression tells us that, at the optimum, the marginal cost of the two sources should be the same even though there are two budget constraints. This situation is intuitively obvious, because we can consider the standard problem with the one budget constraint, $R^C + R^S$, and one overall tax vector, t, solve this, and then divide the optimal tax vector t into portions t^C and t^S, a procedure that yields R^C and R^S as required. Note that the argument depends on there being agreement between center and state on the objective and on there being additive taxes.

Away from the optimum, we cannot suppose that λ^C and λ^S are equal. If there are separate budget constraints, we should consider the effect of raising a unit of state revenue on the revenue of the center. Thus we can calculate

$$(11\text{-}36) \qquad -\frac{\Delta R^C}{\Delta R^S} \equiv \mu_S^C.$$

The number μ_S^C tells us the loss in central revenue if state taxes are increased by an amount sufficient to raise one rupee. As before in our discussion of equations 11-31 and 11-32, we may consider the extra revenue being raised through some vector Δt^S. Then

$$(11\text{-}37) \qquad \mu_S^C = \frac{- \sum_i t^C . \dfrac{\partial \mathbf{X}}{\partial t_i} \Delta t_i^S}{\sum_i \left(X_i + t^S . \dfrac{\partial \mathbf{X}}{\partial t_i} \right) \Delta t_i^S}$$

and we can compare μ_S^C and μ_C^S.

In the next two subsections we give empirical estimates of some of the measures suggested here.

The Taxation of Inputs

We examine in this subsection the extent and sources of input taxation and, as a basis for possible subsidies, the level of taxation of production for exports. The simplest indicator of the extent to which indirect taxation of all intermediates affects the producer price of a given commodity is given by t^{diff}, where $t^{\text{diff}} = t^e - t$, as described above. We concentrate on data for India for 1979–80 as the base year of the Sixth Five Year Plan. The vector t^e is the total effective tax arising from the main central taxes, excises on production, import duties and subsidies, and state-level taxes such as sales taxes, excises on liquor, and other taxes levied or collected by state governments. The difference between the effective tax and the nominal tax on a given commodity, arising from central taxes, is indicated by $t^{\text{diff}C}$, and the corresponding state-level difference is $t^{\text{diff}S}$. In table 11-1 we present the overall level of taxes t^e and t^{diff}, together with $t^{\text{diff}C}$ and $t^{\text{diff}S}$.

The calculations involve the careful assembly of actual tax collections by commodity and the input-output tables. At present they ignore taxes on capital inputs. Further details on these calculations and extensions are described in Ahmad and Stern (forthcoming).

There are four commodity groups for which $t^{\text{diff}} > 20$ percent, and these are (30) "woolen and silk textiles," (31) "artificial silk fabrics," (42) "plastics and synthetic rubber," and (88) "medical health." These are all final goods with the exception of (42), which is also partly an intermediate good. There are, however, thirty commodity groups for which t^{diff} is 10–20 percent. Of these, sixteen are clearly intermediate goods, and one, (18), is a raw material. It is significant that this category includes commodity groups such as (57) "iron and steel ferroalloys," (58) "castings and forgings," (66) "electric motors," and (71) "other electrical machinery." These are mainly capital goods, and the effects on prices of taxing them would operate through stocks, as described above, as well as through the input-output matrix.

It is also clear that a large proportion of t^{diff} on intermediate goods and final manufactures is due to $t^{\text{diff}C}$, or union taxes, a major component of which is due to the element of union excises on manufacturing.

Thus table 11-1 shows that there is very considerable taxation of intermediate goods in India. From column 1 it may be seen that, although there are some particularly high effective taxes, t^e, most of these "outliers" were caused by high nominal rates. On average, effective taxes range between 10 percent and 15 percent, with t^{diff} about 6 percent or 7 percent. Thus in the cases indicated above, indirect effects of taxation often add as much as 100 percent to nominal rates. The effect would be amplified if we included taxes on capital inputs (see above).

The heavy taxation of intermediate goods in India provides the government with a possible basis for remission of domestic taxation on the production of export goods under international agreements. Using our estimates of the effective taxes on domestic production, and the Government of India Planning Commission (1981) estimate of exports for 1979–80 given in the input-output table, the total domestic taxation of exports would be $t^{e'} X^{exp} =$ Rs.9,775 millions, or 6 percent of the value of exports where $t^{e'}$ is the effective tax vector and X^{exp} is the vector of exports. Some relief may already be allowed to production for export, however (and may not be declared against export subsidies or export promotion as such). If, for example, all nominal taxes on production for export were rebated, but not nominal taxes on inputs purchased for that production, then domestic taxation of exports would be given by $t^{diff'} X^{exp} =$ Rs.4,680.26 million. This is probably a lower bound to the level of subsidy that would be permissible as a remission of domestic taxes. India's Ministry of Finance (1981, p. 9) mentions a figure of Rs.3,788.9 million under the heading of "Foreign Trade and Export Promotion" in the combined revenue expenditure accounts of the center, states, and union territories. Presumably not all of this figure would go toward subsidies to the exporters, as some would be spent on maintaining Indian missions abroad and so on. A level of Rs.3,000 million for subsidies would imply that the permissible export subsidies could have been between one and one-half and three times the levels obtained in 1979–80.

We should note a number of points concerning this argument. That a subsidy may be permissible under international agreements does not imply that it is desirable. It would be hard, however, to imagine why a country short of foreign exchange and probably facing elastic demands for much of its exports would want to tax exports. Hence there is a prima facie argument that the rebate through export subsidies may be sensible. We may also ask where the extra revenue for the subsidy would come from. If we turn to trade policy, one method of raising the revenue would be to replace licensing of commodities by import tariffs, thus transferring income from individual importers and traders to the exchequer. This approach would not affect the domestic price of imported goods. We do not, however, have sufficient information on licensing at present to attempt such an exercise. More generally we could examine the social marginal costs for extra revenue, choose the lowest, and compare this marginal cost with gains from export subsidies. This last set of calculations would require estimates of shadow marginal costs of production.

Federal and State Taxes

We begin the comparison with input taxation. The major element in the taxation of commodities via inputs, t^{diff}, as noted in the previous section, is the federal taxation of intermediate goods and manufactures, t^{diffC}. Thus t^{diff} is primarily due to the structure of the excise tax that is levied mainly on production and in particular on domestic manufacturing activities. In general, $t^{\text{diff} C} > t^{\text{diff} S}$ for manufacturing and services, $t^{\text{diff} S}$ being of the order of 2 percent on average. In the case of food items, however—sugarcane, milk, and animal husbandry as well as processed foods, such as sugar, vanaspati, tea, and coffee—$t^{\text{diff} S} > t^{\text{diff} C}$. Federal taxes do not bear heavily on such food items; indeed there are effective federal subsidies on several food items (although, as we remarked above, the model we have used for effective taxes is limited by the level of aggregation and needs to be supplemented by detailed sectoral analyses—for example, for agriculture). State taxes, and in particular the sales tax, are levied largely on items of final consumption; also, given the tax base available to the states, food items are quite often subject to tax.

Second, we evaluate marginal across-the-board increases in two major central taxes—in excises and import duties, on the one hand, and in the sales taxes, on the other. Each reform represents a nominal tax increase, and in order to apply the theory embodied in equations 11-30–11-32, 11-36, and 11-37, these must be translated into increases in effective taxes. The effective taxes associated with excises, the sales tax, and the import duty are given by

(11-38)   excises: $t^{eC'}_{(\text{ex})} = t^{C'} (I - A^d)^{-1}$

(11-39)   sales: $t^{eS'} = t^{S'} (I - A^d)^{-1} + t^{S'} A^m (I - A^d)^{-1}$

(11-40)   imports: $t^{eC'}_{(\text{m})} = t^{m'} A^m (I - A^d)^{-1}$

where t^C, t^S, and t^m represent per unit (nominal) rates of excise duty, sales tax, and import duty, respectively; A^d is the coefficient matrix for domestic inputs into domestic production; and A^m is the coefficient matrix for imported inputs into domestic production. It is assumed that imported inputs are strict complements to domestic inputs and there are fixed coefficients throughout (we discuss this assumption elsewhere in this chapter).

We then calculate $\Delta t^{eC}_{(\text{ex})}$, Δt^{eS}, and $\Delta t^{eC}_{(\text{m})}$—the increases corresponding to a 1 percent across-the-board increase in excise, sales tax, and import duties, respectively—by considering the changes in effective rates through equations 11-38–11-40. These are then substituted into equation 11-30 (in the case of sales tax) to give the corresponding welfare losses per rupee of revenue 11-41–11-43 associated with each tax change,

(11-41)
$$\lambda^{ex} = \frac{\sum_h \sum_i \beta^h x_i^h \Delta t^{eC}_{i(\text{ex})}}{\sum_i \left(X_i + \sum_j t_j^e \frac{\partial X_j}{\partial t_i^e} \right) \Delta t^{eC}_{i(\text{ex})}}$$

for excises,

(11-42)
$$\lambda^{sa} = \frac{\sum_h \sum_i \beta^h x_i^h \Delta t^{eS}_i}{\sum_i \left(X_i + \sum_j t_j^e \frac{\partial X_j}{\partial t_i^e} \right) \Delta t^{eS}_i}$$

for sales taxes, and

$$(11\text{-}43) \qquad \lambda^m = \frac{\sum_h \sum_i \beta^h x_i^h \Delta t_{i(m)}^{eC}}{\sum_i \left(X_i + \sum_j t_j^e \frac{\partial X_j}{\partial t_i^e} \right) \Delta t_{i(m)}^{eC}}$$

for imports.

These are presented in table 11-2, below. The data sources and estimates we have used are discussed in detail in Ahmad and Stern (1983a and forthcoming). Briefly, the β^h were presented in equation 11-28; the household expenditures are based on the Twenty-eighth Round (1973–74) estimates of household expenditures published by the National Sample Survey Organisation for fourteen urban and fourteen rural groups updated to 1979–80. The aggregate demand responses are based on the work of Radhakrishna and Murty (1981), who used the Nasse modification of the linear expenditure system to provide separate estimates for eight household groups (four rural and four urban) and for nine commodity groups. Thus the effective taxes that were calculated for the eighty-nine-good classifications of table 11-1 have to be merged to nine goods (see Ahmad and Stern, 1983a, and forthcoming). The effective tax rates appear in table 11-4, below.

Although the demand responses used in this paper have been based on estimates from Radhakrishna and Murty (1981), and standard errors for these are not available, experiments with similar data sets have shown that the parameters of the modified LES are very tightly defined, with low standard errors (see Ahmad and Stern, forthcoming). Translating these into standard errors for the λ_i, we find that they are very small. Even if these standard errors are not small, however, we can still argue that the estimated $\lambda_i, \hat{\lambda}_i$ is above $\hat{\lambda}_j$. Then the expected change in welfare from a switch into j is positive, and if the distribution is symmetric, the probability of an increase in welfare is above 50 percent. Note that a test of the null hypothesis that λ_i is equal to λ_j at a conventional 5 percent level is not particularly interesting.

It is clear that, at low levels of inequality aversion (see equation 11-28), ϵ, say 0 or 0.1, $\lambda^m > \lambda^{ex} > \lambda^{sa}$, and we might regard an increase in sales taxes as causing less social loss per marginal rupee of revenue than an increase in excise duties, which would, in turn, cause less social loss than an extra rupee generated through import duties. For $0.1 < \epsilon < 1$, however, the ranking of the welfare loss associated with excises and import duties changes, and $\lambda^{ex} > \lambda^m$. The initial ranking is completely reversed at moderate levels of inequality aversion, say $\epsilon = 1$, and $\lambda^{sa} > \lambda^{ex} > \lambda^m$, with relative differences widening at higher levels of ϵ. This rather intriguing result reflects the relative pattern of Indian state and central taxes, with sales taxes bearing rather heavily on final consumption goods consumed by the lower-income groups, and excises and import duties falling relatively more on intermediate goods and ultimately on manufactures.

Thus any suggestion from the previous subsection that the government might move away from the heavy taxation of intermediate goods to the taxation of final goods on efficiency grounds would be tempered by a note of caution concerning the type of final good that should be taxed more heavily. A 1 percent increase in sales taxes, it has been seen above at moderate levels of inequality aversion, leads to a greater welfare loss per rupee of revenue than a similar increase in excise duties and import tariffs, which are the main sources of taxation on intermediate goods. A selection of particular goods for sales tax increases rather than across-the-board changes could avoid this apparent conflict—see table 11-4.

The welfare loss from each type of tax may also be compared with that from a poll tax, λ^{PT}. On the assumption that the marginal propensity to pay tax is on average 10.5 percent, we find $\lambda^{PT} = 1.1173$. From table 11-2 we observe that $\lambda_i < \lambda^{PT}$ for $\epsilon > 0.1$ for all types of tax. Thus with only a moderate amount of aversion to inequality, we would suggest that indirect taxes should be raised to finance an increase in a poll subsidy, if this were feasible. The poll subsidy is therefore *not* optimal in the sense required for the discussion of uniformity of indirect taxes in chapters 2–4. Note first that this type of result might be expected in general, because, roughly speaking, indirect taxes relieve individuals of revenue in proportion to their expenditure, whereas lump-sum poll transfers give it back in equal amounts to all (although this abstracts from demand responses). Second, it must be remembered that uniform poll subsidies would be very hard to administer. There would be a strong possibility that the transfers would end up in the hands of those whose social marginal utility of income was not at all low.

India is a federal country in which some tax revenues accrue to the center and some to the states, so that the effects of taxes levied by the states (or by the center) on the revenue of the center (or the states) are of considerable interest. If an increase in state taxation causes a shift of consumption into commodities taxed by the center, for instance, then the state increase could result in an increase in central tax revenues. On the other hand, there may be few or neutral substitution effects, and the state tax increase may have mainly an income effect, which may imply a reduction of central tax revenues. We

Table 11-2. *Welfare Losses per Marginal Rupee Associated with a 1 Percent Tax Increase*

Change	$\epsilon = 0$	$\epsilon = 0.1$	$\epsilon = 1$	$\epsilon = 2$
λ^{ex}	1.1459	1.1084	0.8497	0.6605
λ^{sa}	1.1204	1.0867	0.8509	0.5867
λ^{m}	1.1722	1.1205	0.7729	0.5375

Notes: λ is defined in equations 11-41–11-43, and the role of ϵ in equation 11-28. $\lambda^{PT} = 1.1173$, where $\lambda^{PT} = 1/(1 - \bar{\delta})$ and $\bar{\delta} = 10.5$ percent. The value λ^{PT} is the social marginal cost of raising extra revenue through a poll tax—see equations 11-29a–11-29c—and $\bar{\delta}$ is the average across households of the marginal propensity to spend on taxes.

consider here a 1 percent increase in the level of all central taxes and a 1 percent increase in the level of all state taxes which lead to effective tax increase Δt^S and Δt^C. The loss in central revenue (per rupee of state revenue) consequent on Δt^S is given by equation 11-37. There is an analogous expression for μ_C^S, or the loss in state tax revenues per rupee of central revenue consequent on Δt^C. In India, state tax revenue consists largely of sales taxes, and we also consider a 1 percent increase in the level of sales taxes that gives an effective tax increase Δt^{sa}. The loss in central tax revenue (per rupee of state revenue) consequent on a 1 percent increase in sales taxes is given by the expression μ_{sa}^C.

$$(11\text{-}44) \qquad \mu_{sa}^C = \frac{-\sum_i t^C \cdot \dfrac{\partial X}{\partial t_i} \Delta t_i^{sa}}{\sum_i \left(X_i + t^S \cdot \dfrac{\partial X}{\partial t_i} \right) \Delta t_i^{sa}}.$$

In similar fashion, we can consider increases in central taxes emanating from small increases in effective import duties or excise taxes, which are the major sources of central tax receipts. Thus Δt^{ex} and Δt^m are the effective tax changes associated with a 1 percent increase in excise taxes and import duties, respectively. The consequent losses in state tax revenues (per rupee of central revenue) are given by μ_{ex}^S and μ_m^S, where

$$(11\text{-}45) \qquad \mu_{ex}^S = \frac{-\sum_i t^S \cdot \dfrac{\partial X}{\partial t_i} \Delta t_i^{ex}}{\sum_i \left(X_i + t^C \cdot \dfrac{\partial X}{\partial t_i} \right) \Delta t_i^{ex}}$$

and

$$(11\text{-}46) \qquad \mu_m^S = \frac{-\sum_i t^S \cdot \dfrac{\partial X}{\partial t_i} \Delta t_i^m}{\sum_i \left(X_i + t^C \cdot \dfrac{\partial X}{\partial t_i} \right) \Delta t_i^m}.$$

The values of μ are presented in table 11-3.

We see from table 11-3 that raising Rs. 1 from all state taxes results in a loss of approximately 7 paise in central government tax revenue, but raising Rs. 1 from all central taxes results in a loss of 5 paise in state tax revenue. A comparison with the marginal propensity to pay all indirect taxes from extra income of approximately 10.5 paise per rupee suggests that an increase in either central or state taxes has primarily income effects, given the demand system we have used.

This finding is confirmed by an examination of the individual taxes, where we discover only small differences when we alter the source of the marginal rupee. Raising Rs. 1 from the sales tax, for instance, would also cost approx-

Table 11-3. *The Loss in Revenue from Changes in Taxes Sufficient to Raise One Rupee*

Tax increase	Rupees
Loss in central tax revenue	
In all state taxes, μ_S^C	0.0686
In all sales taxes, μ_{sa}^C	0.0688
Loss in state tax revenue	
In central taxes, μ_C^S	0.0511
In excise taxes, μ_{ex}^S	0.0459
In import duties, μ_m^S	0.0411

Note: μ is defined in equations 11-37 and 11-44–11-46 and represents, for example, the loss in terms of rupees of central revenue (μ_S^C) from an increase in state tax revenue of one rupee.

imately Rs.0.07 in central tax revenue. Raising Rs.1 from either the excise tax or import duties, however, would cost Rs.0.046 or Rs.0.041, respectively, in terms of state tax revenue. Central and state taxes thus do interact, although, given the demand system we have used, the substitution effects do not appear strong. This absence of substitution effects, we presume, is in part a consequence of the level of aggregation across goods, and with a finer classification the interactions may appear as more important.

A Comparison of Alternative Sources of Revenue

In this section we draw together some of the analysis and calculations of our earlier papers (Ahmad and Stern 1983a, and 1984, collected and revised in Ahmad and Stern, forthcoming), and of the preceding section and juxtapose the evaluation of commodity taxes and income tax reforms to provide a view of possible sources of additional revenue. We discuss in this subsection theoretical aspects of the comparison of different sources. We then examine the integration of administrative costs and provide a brief description of our treatment of the income tax in Ahmad and Stern (1983b) as background to the results on different sources of revenue for India for the year 1979–80, which are then presented.

General Theory

Our comparison of different sources of extra revenue will draw on four criteria: (1) the marginal social loss to households as evaluated through λ; (2) the effects on production choices through the taxation of inputs; (3) relations between state and center; and (4) administration and evasion. Simple versions of the theory associated with the first three criteria have been presented above, and some complications will be discussed below. In this subsection we concentrate on the method of application and on integration of the criteria.

A unifying feature of our approach to reform has been the calculation of the loss in social welfare (λ) from the marginal rupee raised from each source: we derived λ_i for the taxation of good i, λ^T for various reforms of the income tax, λ^C for central taxes, and λ^S for state taxes. A comparison between taxes on the basis of λ would in general involve the suggestion that, other things being equal, we would shift from sources with high λ or high social losses from the marginal rupee to sources with low λ. Thus if λ_i for good i is greater than λ_j, then we would want to shift on the margin from commodity i to commodity j. If λ^T is lower than all the λ_i, we would want to shift from indirect to direct taxation. If λ^C is bigger than λ^S, then the marginal rupee from state taxes causes less social loss than that from central taxes—and so on.

The use of λ for different instruments involves considering the rate of change of household welfare and social welfare with respect to government revenue. The idea may therefore be illustrated graphically by plotting social welfare (W) against R—see figure 11-1. In the figure we have drawn three curves passing through the point (R^0, W^0)—the status quo described by the existing tax structure and associated level of social welfare W^0 and government revenue R^0. The curve labeled T shows the relationship between W and R if all movement from R^0 is through income taxes, with all other taxes constant; that labeled S shows movement in welfare if all taxes except state taxes are held constant, and, similarly, C is for movements in central taxes. The gradients of

Figure 11-1. *The Choice among Taxes with Differing Marginal Social Costs*

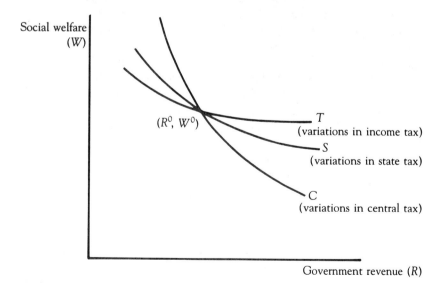

Notes: The graphs represent the rate of change of social welfare with respect to different sources: T represents the income tax, S, state taxes, and C, central taxes. The marginal social losses λ^C, λ^S, and λ^T are (minus) the gradients of the curves.
Source: Ahmad and Stern (1984).

the curves are $-\lambda^T$, $-\lambda^S$, and $-\lambda^C$, respectively. As we have drawn it, we have $\lambda^T < \lambda^S < \lambda^C$.

The best the government can do for movements from R^0 using a single instrument is to follow the highest curve, that is, to maximize welfare at each level of R. Thus, in figure 11-1, for increases in government revenue we would follow the T curve—that is, we would increase revenue through income taxation—and for decreases in revenue we would follow the C curve. The rule is: for increases in R, raise the taxes that do least marginal damage, and for reductions in R, lower the taxes that do greatest marginal damage.

If the values of λ are unequal (as above), we can improve W at given R^0 by raising a marginal rupee through income tax and reducing central taxes by the same amount; the gain is $\lambda^C - \lambda^T$. At the optimal combination of taxes for given R^0, the three curves would be tangential, corresponding to $\lambda^T = \lambda^S = \lambda^C$.

The empirical analysis of the marginal losses has worked with a model with fixed producer prices and constant factor incomes. Thus deadweight losses or distortions arising from indirect taxes and income taxes are not those that disturb production efficiency. We began the theoretical discussion of departures from production efficiency in the second section of this chapter and will continue it below. We should emphasize at this stage, however, that from the theoretical point of view it cannot generally be asserted that direct taxation is more or less distortionary than indirect taxation; income taxation has its own distortion in imposing a wedge between marginal products and marginal rates of substitution between labor and goods, just as indirect taxes in general prevent the equality between marginal rates of substitution in consumption and marginal rates of transformation in production. Chapter 2 showed that a switch to lump-sum taxes from commodity taxes would increase efficiency (in the sense of utility in a one-consumer economy) if the commodity taxes were optimal, but otherwise even this outcome is not guaranteed (although there would exist at least one commodity tax from which a switch to lump-sum taxes would be improving; see the appendix to chapter 2). The appropriate combinations of direct and indirect taxation depend quite sensitively on circumstances, as we saw in chapters 2 to 4.

Costs of Administration

An estimate of the administrative costs could be incorporated into our analysis in the following way. Suppose that raising an extra rupee via income tax (including effects on other tax revenues of the income tax change) involves an administrative cost θ^T. Then to raise one rupee net of administrative costs, we will have to have an increment in the gross revenues of $1/(1 - \theta^T)$, and thus the welfare cost to households will be $\lambda^T/(1 - \theta^T)$. Similarly, the welfare cost of an extra rupee, *net*, via the taxation of good i will be $[\lambda_i/(1 - \theta_i)]$, where θ_i is the administrative cost of a rupee via the ith good.

Then a reform that raises one rupee net via the income tax and loses one rupee net via taxation of the ith good is beneficial if

$$(11\text{-}47) \qquad \frac{\lambda^T}{(1 - \theta^T)} > \frac{\lambda_i}{(1 - \theta_i)}$$

where we have assumed that administrative savings of θ_i arise if the tax is reduced.

Our empirical analysis deals entirely with actual collections, and in this sense evasion is taken into account. Furthermore, our analysis of marginal reforms is in terms of an extra rupee actually collected from consumers rather than in terms of some notional expected revenue. There may be difficulties in predicting who will pay the extra tax, and this ambiguity will cause problems in evaluating the distributional consequences of reform. A judgment of the severity of these difficulties must depend on the case being considered (for further discussion, see Ahmad and Stern, 1983b).

The effective taxes reflect revenue collections and not entirely the rate structures of the various constituent taxes. Thus in cases where there is significant evasion or inefficiency of collection, effective taxes can be increased through better enforcement without changing statutory rates.

The Theory of Income Tax Reform

The analysis of the reform of the income tax proceeds as does that of indirect taxes, which is summarized in equation 11-27. We review the analysis briefly here as an explanation of the empirical results to be presented in the next section (see Ahmad and Stern, 1983b, for further details). For a given marginal reform, we consider the effects on revenue ΔR and on social welfare ΔW, aggregating across households using welfare weights. A beneficial reform is available if $\Delta W > 0$ and $\Delta R < 0$. Where extra revenue involves a loss in social welfare, we calculated $\lambda = -\Delta W / \Delta R$ as the social loss per marginal rupee of revenue associated with the reform. A beneficial reform at constant revenue is then achieved by switching a marginal rupee from a source with a higher social loss to one with a lower social loss.

In the absence of estimates of factor supply responses to tax changes, we have assumed that pretax incomes are unchanged, although we discuss ways in which the results might be affected by relaxing this assumption. A reform of the income tax system will then imply changes in ΔM^h in posttax incomes M^h.

Suppose for the moment that all individuals face the same consumer prices $\mathbf{q}$, that the indirect utility function of household h is $V^h(\mathbf{q}, M^h)$, and that purchases are $\mathbf{x}^h(\mathbf{q}, M^h)$. We express social welfare through a Bergson-Samuelson social welfare function $W(V^1, \ldots, V^H)$. An income tax reform represented by $(\Delta M^1, \ldots, \Delta M^H)$, then, yields a change in social welfare

$$(11\text{-}48) \qquad \Delta W = \sum_h \beta^h \Delta M^h$$

where $\beta^h = \partial W / \partial M^h$ and is the social marginal utility of income for household h.

The change in government revenue ΔR from household h involves $-\Delta M^h$, but in addition we must take into account the change in indirect tax revenue from the adjustment in purchases consequent upon ΔM^h. Suppose the vector of per unit tax rates is t (the same for all households). The change in indirect tax payment by households is then

$$(11\text{-}49) \qquad \sum_h t \cdot \frac{\partial x^h}{\partial M^h} \Delta M^h.$$

Thus

$$(11\text{-}50) \qquad \Delta R = -\sum_h \Delta M^h + \sum_h t \cdot \frac{\partial x^h}{\partial M^h} \Delta M^h.$$

The quantities ΔW and ΔR give us the marginal social loss and the marginal tax revenue from the reform associated with $(\Delta M^1, \Delta M^2, \ldots, \Delta M^H)$ and defined by the income tax change under consideration. A number of possibilities were considered, and the results are summarized in the next subsection. For comparisons with other possible reforms, it is convenient to define the marginal loss per rupee raised by an income tax reform as

$$(11\text{-}51) \qquad \lambda^T = \frac{-\Delta W}{\Delta R}.$$

The β^h, or welfare weights, are, as above, value judgments, specified exogenously, and we experiment with a number of possibilities. The $\partial x^h / \partial M^h$ will be based on the demand studies mentioned earlier (see Radhakrishna and Murty, 1981) and the effective taxes are as described earlier for the nine commodities of the demand system. In using the demand information, it is helpful to rewrite the second term in ΔR (see equation 11-49) using

$$(11\text{-}52) \qquad \delta^h \equiv t \cdot \frac{\partial x^h}{\partial M^h} = \frac{t_i}{q_i} \frac{\partial (q_i x_i^h)}{\partial M^h}.$$

Thus we use the marginal budget share $\partial (q_i x_i^h)/\partial M^h$ and the proportion of tax in price t_i/q_i. The quantity δ^h is itself a feature of the hth household and the tax system that is useful to policymakers: it is the marginal propensity to pay indirect taxes by household h.

The two types of income tax reform we shall consider are changes in the tables describing tax liabilities for those above the exemption limit and changes in the exemption limit itself. For a given set of taxpayers—and we must remember that we are, so far, assuming pretax incomes to be fixed—it is a straightforward matter to calculate the ΔM^h from changes in the tax tables. The effect of a change in exemption limit for given tax tables is, in principle, particularly simple, because it involves changes in disposable income only for those who move in or out of the tax net. It should be noted that, in the sense that the income tax tables define taxes to be paid on the whole of income (subject to being above the limit) and are not based on the difference between income and the exemption limit, the tables are defined independently of the exemption limit. For a marginal change in the exemption limit, we may suppose that the effect applies to one household type only. In this case we label λ^T as λ^h to remind us that we are dealing with a change in the income of one household type only, and we have

$$(11\text{-}53) \qquad\qquad \lambda^h = \frac{\beta^h}{1 - \delta^h}.$$

Again λ^h (like δ^h) is an interesting feature of household h, whether or not household h is at the exemption limit, because it tells us, for fixed gross incomes, the impact on welfare from reducing government revenue by one rupee in the form of transfers to household h. The transfer $1/(1 - \delta^h)$ would be more than one rupee because the government recoups δ^h per rupee transferred via indirect tax revenue. The net change in government revenue is

$$(11\text{-}54) \qquad\qquad -\frac{1}{1 - \delta^h} + \frac{\delta^h}{1 - \delta^h} = -1.$$

In interpreting our results, we should keep in mind two important facts. First, in our examples we have been concerned with the collection of the additional rupee from the income tax and the distribution of this revenue burden across households, given the information available as to who actually pays income tax. These examples may be poor approximations of the distribution of extra burdens that would arise from an attempt to raise an extra rupee. Second, in India it is largely the fixed-salaried government servants and employees of large firms who pay the income tax. Consequently, statutory changes in income tax rates may well lead to changes in pretax incomes, leaving income tax payers relatively unaffected. Thus the incidence of the extra rupee may be largely on firms or on government salary bills.

We have so far supposed that pretax incomes are fixed. The analysis in the case where factor supplies respond to tax changes was described in Ahmad and Stern (1983b) for the case of labor supply. It is broadly similar to that for indirect taxes, but for data reasons, we are unable to put this analysis into practice for India, as estimates of a commodity demand and labor supply system would be required, and we know of no such information for India.

The modification in the analysis of marginal reform comes in the prediction of the effects on revenue of a tax change. The effects on household welfare of a marginal change are given simply by the change in pretax income at zero supply response, just as the marginal effects on household welfare of price changes are given by the consumptions of the goods whose prices have changed, and we do not need estimates of household responses. If factor supplies are reduced as the result of an income tax increase, then the increase in revenue ΔR as described above has been overestimated, and the marginal damage $-\Delta W/\Delta R$ per rupee of revenue has been underestimated. We may therefore focus a discussion of the effects of incentives in this analysis by asking how much extra revenue will be raised by the tax increase. We should also consider, in principle, general equilibrium effects on pretax wages and other prices (see below).

Estimates

The analyses in Ahmad and Stern (1983a and b) and in the previous sections of this chapter provide estimates of the welfare losses associated with different sources of government revenue. These are assembled for commodity taxes and for the personal income tax.

Commodity Taxes

The welfare losses associated with raising Rs. 1 of government revenue from indirect taxes on different goods, appear in table 11-4. The λ_i are calculated as explained at the start of this chapter and in equation 11-27. The data were described briefly in the discussion of table 11-2. Effective taxes t^e are used in the expression based on the eighty-nine-good classification of table 11-1. Because the demand responses we are using have a nine-good classification, the effective taxes on the eighty-nine goods are merged to nine (as previously explained).

These results show considerable sensitivity to the level of inequality aversion, ϵ. The λ_i for "cereals," for instance, is less than those for "other foods,"

Table 11-4. *Welfare Loss for Indirect Taxes*

| | Effective | Levels of inequality aversion ϵ | | | | | | | | |
Commodity	tax	0	r	0.1	r	1	r	2	r	5	r
Cereals	−0.052	1.0340	8	1.0310	7	0.9862	2	0.9095	2	0.5898	2
Milk and dairy products	0.009	1.0037	9	0.9698	9	0.7065	9	0.4828	9	0.1004	9
Edible oils	0.083	1.0672	6	1.0493	6	0.8974	4	0.7413	4	0.3388	5
Meat, fish, eggs	0.014	1.0532	7	1.0309	8	0.8538	6	0.6948	5	0.3514	4
Sugar and gur	0.069	1.0892	5	1.0673	5	0.8812	5	0.6948	5	0.2635	6
Other foods	0.114	1.1352	4	1.1145	3	0.9513	3	0.8042	3	0.4643	3
Clothing	0.242	1.2450	1	1.1894	1	0.7966	7	0.5170	7	0.1255	8
Fuel and light	0.274	1.1632	2	1.1525	2	1.0629	1	0.9683	1	0.6777	1
Other nonfood	0.133	1.1450	3	1.0873	4	0.7173	8	0.4869	8	0.1757	7

Notes: The welfare loss for commodity i, λ_i, represents the effects on all households (using the β^h corresponding to various levels of inequality aversion ϵ) of an increase in the tax on the ith good sufficient to raise a rupee of government revenue. r denotes the rank of the good by λ_i. A good ranked 1 would be such that a switch of taxation from it to any other good would increase welfare at constant revenue. The effective taxes from table 11-1 are merged to nine commodity groups using the gross value of domestic output as weights.

Source: Ahmad and Stern (1983b); revised version published as Ahmad and Stern (1984).

"clothing," and "other nonfood" at low levels of ϵ, but at moderate ($\epsilon = 1$) or higher levels, the welfare loss from taxing cereals exceeds those of all other commodity groups other than "fuel and light." Recall that, in India, these two commodity groups figure predominantly in the consumption of the groups with low expenditure. Intuitively, when efficiency considerations dominate (ϵ close to zero), then the low price elasticities of demand for cereals and fuel make them attractive targets for taxation. When distribution becomes a major issue (higher levels of ϵ), however, the importance of these items in the budgets of the poor (low-income elasticity of demand) leads to their being less attractive than other goods.

Given the role of price (both own price and cross-price) and income elasticities in our conclusions, the level of aggregation across commodities is clearly important. Here we are restricted to the aggregation level at which demand estimates are available. This restriction usually implies only a few and highly aggregated commodity groups because time series are, in general, required for the price variability necessary for estimation, and these series are usually too short to provide enough degrees of freedom for more than a few parameters. It is possible that the high level of aggregation we are using means that we are missing important deadweight losses associated with high elasticities of substitution among finer classifications of goods.

The level of aggregation is also important for the specification of tax rates. Thus the item "fuel and light" contains a mixture of items from cow dung to firewood to coal, kerosene, and electricity. These should be treated very differently; for example coal can bear tax rates of about 50 percent, kerosene has a subsidized ration together with an open market, electricity is supplied from the public sector at a price that should be compared with social marginal cost (to find implicit tax rates), and cow dung bears very little effective tax (there may be some through agricultural inputs). The different goods are consumed by very different household groups. It is therefore important to supplement analysis at our level of aggregation with detailed sectoral studies. Examples are provided in part 6. Some further discussion of the Indian case will appear in Ahmad and Stern (forthcoming), where we shall also closely examine the balance between cash-and-kind purchases.

The results of table 11-4 refer to effective taxes on particular goods. These can be varied one by one, however, only by introducing taxes operating at the final stage (and thus not affecting prices of other goods) or by varying a number of taxes at once to produce the result that only one effective tax is changed. As we showed earlier, however, the methods can be adapted to more obvious policy instruments, such as an increase in all state taxes or an increase in all import duties. Similarly, we can examine the λ associated with changing a given excise tax. We need merely calculate the associated marginal social losses per rupee of revenue raised. The results of some possible reforms were presented in earlier text and in table 11-2, and the effects of reforms in state taxes on government revenue (and vice versa) were presented in table 11-3.

The marginal costs of revenue raised through commodity taxation are now compared with those associated with reforms in the income tax.

The Personal Income Tax and Comparisons with Indirect Taxes

The three reforms concerning the personal income tax are summarized in table 11-5. These are (1) a marginal change in the exemption limit; (2) a 1 percent increase in the marginal income tax rates with the existing exemption limits; and (3) existing exemption limits and marginal tax rates kept, with the exception of the two upper tax bands, each of which is increased by 5 percent. Except for the first case, we assume that the revenue comes from existing taxpayers, and we use data from official sources on collections. We do *not* assume that there is full enforcement of legal rates—we suppose simply that the revenue is distributed across existing taxpayers in the manner described. In the first case, we keep the old rates constant and move an individual at the exemption limit into the system. For further details, see Ahmad and Stern (1983c).

The marginal social losses per rupee of revenue associated with reform 1 appear in table 11-5. These are measured by λ^h, as defined in equation 11-53. Reforms 2 and 3, λ^T, are defined by equations 11-48, 11-50, and 11-51.

The β^h appearing in the formulas used in the calculations for table 11-5 are based on per capita disposable expenditure for urban households so that we may compare these results with those from the earlier analysis. The income tax data, however, are based on taxable income, and we must therefore work back to expenditure. Expenditure is calculated from official data on gross nonagricultural taxable income, by assuming deductions for the purpose of income tax at 15 percent of the gross income and an average savings rate of 25 percent (this is a little above the average rate for the economy as a whole—income tax payers are richer than average). This procedure provides a comparison with λ_i, calculated for indirect taxes, which are based on NSSO data on expenditures. The household expenditure per capita of income-tax-paying households falls entirely within the highest NSSO expenditure category.

Table 11-5. *Welfare Losses Associated with Income Tax Reforms*

Reform	$\epsilon = 0$	$\epsilon = 0.1$	$\epsilon = 1$	$\epsilon = 2$	$\epsilon = 5$
1. λ^h	1.1431	1.0825	0.5941	0.2448	0.0044
2. λ^T	1.1431	0.9624	0.2199	0.0424	0.0000
3. λ^T	1.1431	0.8339	0.0448	0.0005	0.0000

Notes: Reform 1: Marginal changes in exemption limits $\lambda^h = \beta^h/(1 - \delta^h)$. The household per capita expenditure figures for the calculations of β^h and δ^h (see equations 11-28 and 11-52) were based on income data for tax-paying urban households from official sources (see Ahmad and Stern, 1983c). Reform 2: Increase in all marginal income tax rates of 1 percent. For λ^T, see equations 11-48, 11-50, and 11-51. Reform 3: Increase in top two marginal income tax rates: 55 percent → 60 percent, 60 percent → 65 percent for reforms 2 and 3. For λ^T, see equations 11-48, 11-50, and 11-51.

Sources: Ahmad and Stern (1983a, 1983c).

For $\epsilon = 0$, or no aversion to inequality, the policymaker would be indifferent between the three methods of raising Rs.1 from the personal income tax. With no labor supply responses and welfare weights all equal to unity, λ^T becomes simply $1/(1 - \delta)$, where δ is the marginal propensity to pay indirect taxes for this group: for $\delta = 12.5$ percent we have $\lambda^T = 1.143$. $\lambda^h > \lambda^T$ (reform 2) $> \lambda^T$ (reform 3) for positive levels of ϵ. The first inequality follows from the lower weight on the expenditure of richer households that are brought into reform 2. Analogously, only the two groups with the highest per capita expenditure are affected in reform 3. This argument abstracts from incentive and incidence effects and assumes that the administrative costs of each reform are the same: we explained above how these considerations could be introduced into the analysis.

A comparison of the corresponding columns of tables 11-4 and 11-5 suggests that, at moderate and high levels of inequality aversion ϵ, say $\epsilon \geq 1$, it would be preferable to raise an extra rupee from the personal income tax rather than to use commodity taxes. At very low but positive levels of ϵ, say $\epsilon = 0.1$, in comparing λ^T with λ_i, we see that there would be a lower welfare loss from raising the extra rupee in government revenue either through increasing all marginal income tax rates (reform 2) or increasing the marginal income tax rates for the highest two expenditure groups (reform 3). For some commodities, however, $\lambda^h > \lambda_i$ at $\epsilon = 0.1$; see, for example, the λ_i for food items 1–5 in table 11-4. At $\epsilon = 0$, $\lambda_i > \lambda^h$ ($= \lambda^T$) only for commodity groups (7) "clothing," (8) "fuel and light," and (9) "other nonfood," and for other commodities $\lambda_i < \lambda^h$ or λ^T. This result shows the importance of the distributional considerations and demonstrates that, at very low levels of ϵ, extra tax on some commodities might be preferable to additional income taxes, which are the reforms that are preferred at higher levels of aversion to inequality.

If there are differences in administration costs, then, as we have seen, we should compare $\lambda^h/(1 - \theta^h)$ and $\lambda_i/(1 - \theta_i)$, where θ^h and θ_i are the respective administrative costs of raising one rupee from adjusting the exemption limit and the tax on the ith good. Thus, for example, if we compare the columns for $\epsilon = 2$ in tables 11-4 and 11-5, we see λ^h at about 0.245 and λ_i at about 0.68, giving λ^h/λ_i equal to 0.36. Hence if θ_i is zero, a marginal switch from commodity taxes to the income tax (by lowering the exemption limit) would be attractive, provided that θ^h does not exceed 0.64—in other words provided that the administration cost of raising an extra rupee from lowering the exemption limit does not exceed 64 paise. The corresponding borderline administration cost per rupee at $\epsilon = 1$ (less aversion to inequality) would be lower—about 34 paise. Where aversion to inequality is substantial, it seems most unlikely that administration costs could be sufficiently high to reverse the attractiveness of a switch to income taxation by lowering the exemption limit.

The discussion is entirely in terms of actual revenue collections, hence the analysis includes the possibility of evasion, at least where pretax incomes are fixed.

The analysis here would be modified by disincentive effects, as was discussed in Ahmad and Stern (1983c). We cannot rule out the possibility that the effects on revenue could be strong: an extreme case would be where reducing rates actually increased revenue, although the absence of examples contrasts strikingly with the frequency of the suggestion. We cannot treat the issue numerically without explicit factor supply functions, and these are not available for India. We should also stress that the analysis is marginal. If substantial extra revenue is sought, it may be impossible to find it among the higher-income tax groups.

If we combine the calculations presented earlier with those discussed in this section, the position is the following (see tables 11-2, 11-4, and 11-5). With no aversion to inequality and fixed-factor incomes, we would be indifferent among various ways of raising an extra rupee by the income tax and between these and a general increase in commodity taxes. Among commodity taxes we would, broadly speaking, concentrate extra revenue on goods with low demand elasticities. These are primarily foods (see table 11-4) and thus are goods subject to state taxes (see table 11-2). The position changes sharply, however, as soon as we bring in distributional considerations. For moderate levels of inequality aversion (for example, $\epsilon = 1$), an extra rupee from the income tax becomes attractive, the marginal social costs from an extra rupee from cereals becomes relatively high, and state taxes are no more attractive than central taxes. With strong aversion to inequality ($\epsilon = 5$), the argument for the income tax is very strong, cereals become very unattractive as a source of revenue, and import duties represent the most desirable general source of extra indirect tax revenue. Among the sources of indirect tax, we saw in tables 11-1 and 11-3 that central taxes (particularly the excise) are least attractive from the standpoint of taxation of inputs. Extra state indirect tax revenue has a slightly higher cost, however, in terms of central indirect tax revenue than vice versa.

There are of course many directions that empirical research should take: disaggregation across commodities, a closer examination of agriculture, separate treatment of cash-and-kind incomes, administration and evasion, the role of rationing, factor supply responses, nonmarginal changes, and a more detailed account of the production side, including intertemporal aspects, substitution among inputs, monopoly, and oligopoly. This obviously amounts to a formidable research agenda, including in principle a detailed, long-term analysis of the entire Indian economy. It should take place after a number of theoretical advances have been made. This type of consideration, however, applies to any policy analysis, and we must cut through the complications with reasonable simplifying assumptions. We hope to make modest steps toward analyzing some of the problems mentioned (see Ahmad and Stern, forthcoming). Some of the theoretical questions have been examined in chapter 3, and others will be analyzed below in this chapter. Some priorities for further research are indicated in conclusion.

Nonmarginal Reforms

The marginal approach we have adopted is robust in a number of respects (as we saw in chapters 2 and 3). It is fairly economical on assumptions and data in that it leans heavily on the result that the extent of current purchases of a good reflects the cost to a household of a price increase resulting from a tax change. Thus behavioral responses arise only in predicting the change in revenue.

These advantages flow from the consideration only of marginal reforms, but therein lies the disadvantage. The approach in its simple form rules out the analysis of substantial changes. It is, therefore, highly complementary to nonmarginal analysis in a number of ways. First, it allows greater detail in that consumption and production response are required only locally and not in a tax environment that is very different from the current one. Second, much, but not all, of the data for the nonmarginal analysis could be collected simultaneously. Third, we can use a marginal analysis to check on a nonmarginal one not only in terms of possible directions of reform at the beginning and end of the change but also to provide extra, supplementary detail. Thus we would like to see the two approaches carried out simultaneously and have illustrated this plan of action in our analysis of the possible introduction of a VAT in India, which is summarized briefly in this section (see also Ahmad and Stern, 1983a and forthcoming).

An alternative view of the marginal approach could refer to the problem of collecting extra revenue using existing tax tools as opposed to a nonmarginal problem of replacing the existing system with entirely different instruments. Strictly speaking, the distinction between existing and new instruments, on the one hand, and marginal and nonmarginal analysis, on the other, are not the same, but the dividing line will often be similar.

We shall outline first a method for assessing some of the nonmarginal reforms that have been proposed for India. Next we present some estimates for a proportional VAT and for proportional VAT with zero rates for cereals. Policy implications are subsequently examined.

Method

For substantial reforms, we can no longer work with the differentials of welfare and revenue, and we must compare welfare and revenue before and after reform. The same kind of approach, however, continues to apply. If we write q^1 and q^0 for the post- and prereform prices, t^{e1} and t^{e0} for the effective tax rates, and similarly W^1, W^0 and R^1, R^0 for post- and prereform social welfare and revenue, we are looking for changes from t^{e0} to t^{e1} that yield $W^1 > W^0$ and $R^1 \geqq R^0$. The calculation of W^1 now involves a full specification of the social welfare function $W(U^1, \ldots, U^H)$ and the individual utility functions U^h or the indirect utility functions V^h, and we can no longer work simply with the β^h evaluated at the initial position. These in turn will yield the demand functions $\mathbf{x}^h(\mathbf{q}, M^h)$ and thus $\mathbf{X}^1$, which is required for the calculation of R^1.

An analysis might then proceed as follows: we first find a $\mathbf{q}^1$ that satisfies $R^1 \geqq R^0$. We might be interested in equal revenue reforms and could then solve $R^1 = R^0$. Thus we could express the reform in terms that involve one degree of freedom, which is then settled by the equal revenue condition. We might, for example, consider an increase in certain taxes and a reduction in one particular tax, or we could consider changing all taxes and distributing the extra revenue as a uniform lump-sum handout. More generally, however, we would simply want to establish what happens to government revenue and, if necessary, to demonstrate that $R^1 \geqq R^0$.

As before we can drop any reference to the social welfare function and calculate V^{h1} and V^{h0} for each household and thus who gains and who loses. A natural way of expressing $V^{h1} - V^{h0}$, or the utility increase for household h, is using the equivalent variation E_{01} defined in the standard way by the implicit equation

$$(11\text{-}55) \qquad\qquad V^{h1} = V^h(\mathbf{q}^0, M^{h0} + E_{01}^h).$$

Thus E_{01}^h is simply the amount of money we would have to give to household h, if the original prices were ruling, to allow it to reach the postreform utility level. If we define E_{01}^h explicitly using the expenditure function $e^h(\mathbf{q}, U^h)$

$$(11\text{-}56) \qquad\qquad E_{01}^h = e^h(\mathbf{q}^0, V^{h1}) - M^{h0}.$$

Thus E_{01}^h is a money measure of the benefit of the reform to household h; it is positive for a utility increase and negative for a decrease. For small changes in effective taxes, it is simply $-\Sigma_i x_i^h \Delta t_i^e$. For larger reforms it is still of interest to compute $-\Sigma_i x_i^h(q_i^1 - q_i^0)$, as this represents the cash gain if quantities were the same before and after the reform. It has the advantage of working with actual quantities x_i^h rather than the implicit fitted quantities in the equivalent variation approach. It has the major disadvantage, however, that we know that quantities would not stay the same or indeed could not in cases where this would involve violation of the budget constraint. Possible compromises are a subject for further research (we can, for example, use household-specific "random" terms that are held constant across the reform).

We must emphasize strongly that the data requirements and assumptions for nonmarginal reforms are much more stringent than for marginal reforms. The utility function and related demand function must be specified for each household, and we cannot simply use the *existing* consumer expenditure and aggregate demand functions as before. In the marginal case, we may be able to provide a reasonable guess at the aggregate functions without specifying in detail the constituent elements from different households. Similarly, for aggregating utility changes, we need the social welfare *function* W and not simply the marginal social welfare weights β^h, although, if real income changes are not large, the β^h may not vary a great deal with the price and income changes under consideration.

We shall consider two nonmarginal reforms corresponding to proposals that have been discussed in the Indian context. The first is for a value-added tax at a uniform rate, and the second is for a VAT at a uniform rate but applying only to a subset of goods. For the purpose of this analysis, we shall define the VAT as a tax system that involves no taxation of inputs. A uniform VAT makes the proportion of effective tax in the price of final goods the same for all goods. We also consider below the case of differential rates. In the uniform case if the rate is τ, we have

$$(11\text{-}57) \qquad \tau = \frac{t_i^{e1}}{q_i^1}$$

for all i. The rate τ will be determined by the revenue requirement. Thus if $\bar{R}$ is the amount that must be raised from consumer expenditure, we have

$$(11\text{-}58) \qquad \tau \sum_i q_i^1 X_i^1 = R^1 = \bar{R}.$$

For unchanged revenue, $R^1 = R^0 = \bar{R}$. If we assume total consumer expenditure to be unchanged by the reform, τ may be calculated by dividing $\bar{R}$ by total prereform consumer expenditure.

A VAT, as defined, involves no taxation of inputs, hence under such a system producer prices and basic prices (see above) will be the same. Basic prices $\mathbf{p}^b$ have been taken as representing the real resource costs, and we shall assume that these are unchanged by the reform.

$$(11\text{-}59) \qquad \mathbf{p}^b = \mathbf{p}^{b1} = \mathbf{p}^{b0} \equiv \mathbf{q}^0 - \mathbf{t}^{e0}$$

$$(11\text{-}60) \qquad \mathbf{q}^1 = \mathbf{t}^{e1} + \mathbf{p}^{b1}.$$

With a uniform VAT,

$$(11\text{-}61) \qquad \mathbf{t}^{e1} = \tau \mathbf{q}^1$$

and we have

$$(11\text{-}62) \qquad \mathbf{q}^1 = \frac{1}{1-\tau}(\mathbf{q}^0 - \mathbf{t}^{e0}) = \frac{1}{1-\tau}\mathbf{p}^b.$$

The reform considered here would require an administrative system to collect VAT that might differ considerably from the old. We have considered it as replacing all indirect taxes, and thus the reform would be substantial administratively as well as from the economic point of view. We might therefore also ask whether the same net result could be achieved by readjusting rates within the existing system, for example, by making nominal rates uniform. There are two important respects in which this approach would not work. First, uniform nominal rates do not imply uniform effective rates: if $\mathbf{t}'$ is a vector with equal components, $\mathbf{t}'(I - A)^{-1}$ will not be, in general. Second, an essential element of a VAT is the reimbursement of tax paid on inputs, and this is not part of the existing system.

We can think of a nonuniform VAT simply as a tax system that involves no taxation of inputs and thus has producer prices equal to basic prices, with nominal and effective tax rates the same. Thus there is a huge array of possibilities that we could examine. At this stage we merely draw attention to this large number and indicate that we have in some respects already presented one of them that is of interest, namely the existing system of effective tax rates. We can imagine a nonuniform VAT that sets the rate on each commodity equal to the effective rate. Because at each stage in production the taxes on inputs are essentially reimbursed, the rate on each commodity will be the effective rate. With a fixed-coefficients technology, this would be identical to the existing system, but from a wider viewpoint it would avoid taxation of inputs and thus production inefficiencies.

Proportional Value-Added Tax

In India net indirect taxes averaged approximately 8.3 percent of total consumer expenditure for the year 1979–80.[4] One might consider replacing all taxes and subsidies with a proportional value-added tax of 8.3 percent of the tax-inclusive price of all goods. This is a nonmarginal reform in prices, and we would expect changes through demand responses in commodities consumed. A proportional tax, however, enables us to estimate revenue from total expenditure, and we do not at this point need specific assumptions on commodities consumed. If total expenditure is unchanged, then the given VAT raises the required revenue.

We have estimated the equivalent variation E_{01}^h, for each per capita expenditure group where

$$(11\text{-}63) \qquad E_{01}^h = (M^h - \mathbf{q}^1 \cdot \mathbf{a}) \prod_i \left(\frac{q_i^0}{q_i^1}\right)^{\alpha_i} - (M^h - \mathbf{q}^0 \cdot \mathbf{a}).$$

Here M^h is the per capita expenditure level, the $\mathbf{q}^0$ and $\mathbf{q}^1$ are the pre- and posttax prices, α_i is marginal budget share and, along with $\mathbf{a}$, is determined by the Stone-Geary utility function. The parameters α_i and $\mathbf{a}$ are taken from Radhakrishna and Murty (1981), from their extended LES estimates (which are not the same throughout the population). The E_{01}^h for rural and urban areas, associated with a proportional VAT, is presented in table 11-6.

The example suggests that the proportional VAT would be equivalent to reducing the expenditures of the poorest rural households by as much as 6.8 percent and *increasing* those of the richest rural households by more than 3 percent. For urban groups, again, the poorest are most affected, though not as severely as in the rural areas, with the two poorest urban groups suffering a loss equivalent to a decline by approximately 5 percent. The richest urban groups

Table 11-6. *Equivalent Variations, E_{01}^h, for Proportional Value-Added Tax*

Group	Percentage of population	Per capita expenditure (M^h) (rupees per month)	E_{01}^h (rupees per month)	E_{01}^h / M^h
Rural				
1	0.28	17.09	−1.142	−0.067
2	0.30	22.63	−1.531	−0.068
3	0.92	27.19	−1.851	−0.068
4	1.68	31.81	−1.674	−0.053
5	2.42	35.14	−1.843	−0.052
6	4.63	42.10	−2.196	−0.052
7	9.34	49.94	−1.002	−0.020
8	15.07	62.07	−1.850	−0.030
9	15.84	78.53	−0.393	−0.005
10	14.60	102.84	−0.247	−0.002
11	7.01	137.93	3.166	0.023
12	3.68	192.92	5.249	0.027
13	0.71	274.69	8.348	0.030
14	0.43	460.15	15.932	0.035
Urban				
15	0.01	13.70	−0.663	−0.048
16	0.03	22.25	−1.094	−0.049
17	0.07	27.51	−0.945	−0.034
18	0.12	31.63	−1.071	−0.034
19	0.30	36.82	−1.229	−0.033
20	0.69	42.36	−0.645	−0.015
21	1.64	50.43	−0.708	−0.014
22	3.45	62.28	−0.800	−0.013
23	4.46	79.08	0.819	0.010
24	5.23	103.50	1.318	0.013
25	3.34	138.84	4.621	0.033
26	2.32	195.10	7.167	0.036
27	0.76	277.15	10.879	0.039
28	0.57	464.00	19.334	0.042

Note: $E_{01}^h = (M^h - \mathbf{q}^1 \cdot \mathbf{a}) \, \Pi_i \, (q_i^0 / q_i^1)^{\alpha_i} - (M^h - \mathbf{q}^0 \cdot \mathbf{a})$. See equation 11-63.
Source: Ahmad and Stern (1983a).

gain most, however—equivalent to an increase in expenditure of approximately 4 percent. A number of important refinements of this analysis are under way and will no doubt modify the figures. An explicit treatment of cash-and-kind consumption would probably lead to a lower estimate of losses to poorer rural households, although no doubt there would still be a loss. If the VAT replaced tariffs, benefits to richer urban households might be magnified. Uniformity, however, would probably continue to benefit richer groups and to penalize the poorer.

Proportional Value-Added Tax with Zero Rates for Cereals

In this subsection we examine a reform that is often recommended—a proportional VAT with exemptions or zero rates on certain items to allow for "distributional" considerations. Some of the problems in implementing a partial VAT have been discussed earlier. Here we will confine our attention to a discussion of effective taxes and will assume that one group, cereals, has a zero effective rate, which would be equivalent to zero-rated VAT on this group. We abstract also from the problems of administration and payments of rebates that would be necessary to make such a system operational.[5] The hypothetical reform thus maintains revenue constant, sets a zero rate on cereals, and applies a proportional VAT at an enhanced rate on the remaining commodities.

The consumption of cereals was approximately 20 percent of the total private consumption expenditure for the year 1979–80.[6] Setting the tax on the cereals group to zero, we have approximated equal revenue. There is fixed total expenditure on commodities, with a proportional VAT at 10 percent on all other commodities.

The equivalent variations E_{01}^h for this reform are presented in table 11-7. Again, it is apparent that the poor lose and the rich gain in both rural and urban areas, so that this sort of reform is not likely to appeal to many policymakers. It needs to be said, however, that the poor lose less and the rich gain less than in the proportional VAT case. The distribution of losses is different in rural and urban areas. In the proportional VAT case, ten of the rural groups and eight urban groups suffer losses. In the selective proportional VAT case, six of the rural groups suffer lower losses, but now ten urban groups lose. The reason is the higher tax on noncereals, which form a greater part of the urban budgets.

Thus, although the selective VAT is to be preferred to the proportional VAT, neither of the cases considered would qualify if distributional considerations were at all important. It would be interesting, however, to study a system with, for example, a selective VAT, plus food subsidies, plus special taxation of selected items such as gasoline and some luxury items. We could very probably produce a package that would lose no revenue and would look attractive in terms of the above analysis.

Policy

The analysis set forth in the previous subsections was based on published NSSO consumer expenditure data for various household groups classified in terms of per capita expenditure. These data did not distinguish between purchases and expenditure out of home-grown stock, a phenomenon that is likely to be important for rural households operating farms. Thus the equivalent variation exercise would overstate the losses or gains to such households arising from a major reform. These households are likely to be relatively better off, however, than the households that rely on wage incomes and form part of a

Table 11-7. *Equivalent Variations,* E_{01}^h, *for Proportional Value-Added Tax with Zero-Rated Commodities*

Group	Per capita expenditure (M^h) (rupees per month)	E_{01}^h (rupees per month)	E_{01}^h/M^h
Rural			
1	17.09	−0.387	−0.023
2	22.62	−0.533	−0.024
3	27.19	−0.652	−0.024
4	31.81	−0.769	−0.024
5	35.14	−0.699	−0.020
6	42.10	−0.847	−0.020
7	49.94	0.673	0.013
8	62.07	0.567	0.009
9	78.53	0.262	0.033
10	102.84	0.430	0.004
11	137.93	2.823	0.020
12	192.92	4.344	0.025
13	274.69	6.605	0.024
14	460.15	11.734	0.026
Urban			
15	13.70	−0.198	−0.014
16	22.25	−0.359	−0.016
17	27.51	−0.416	−0.015
18	31.63	−0.471	−0.015
19	36.82	−0.539	−0.015
20	42.36	−0.732	−0.017
21	50.43	−0.801	−0.016
22	62.28	−0.901	−0.015
23	79.08	−0.613	−0.008
24	103.50	−0.401	−0.004
25	138.84	2.904	0.021
26	195.10	4.443	0.023
27	277.15	6.686	0.024
28	464.00	11.795	0.025

Note: See table 11-6 for a definition of E_{01}^h.

growing number of landless laborers, who for the most part depend on seasonal cash income and direct purchases of grain and other items. Thus the overall pattern, with a move to uniformity being regressive, is unlikely to be overturned by a more detailed analysis, although in principle we should take into account general equilibrium effects on wages (see, for example, parts 4 and 5 of this book).

The estimates of nonmarginal reform in the previous subsections have indicated the "undesirability" of "uniformity" in taxation, echoing our results above and our previous work relating to marginal directions of reform in cases where distributional considerations are of importance. As we saw also, it cannot be argued that an optimal lump-sum poll tax was in operation as required in the theoretical results that show uniform commodity taxes to be optimal in certain circumstances.

Although a uniform VAT on all final goods might be undesirable, a nonuniform VAT would not be subject to the same objections and would avoid the distortionary effects of the existing set of effective taxes. A nonuniform VAT, however, could create administrative difficulty unless there were just a few categories, although the current tax structures themselves encompass considerable differentiation. Constitutional difficulties in India, furthermore, might rule out replacing all taxes with a VAT, whether uniform or otherwise. Nevertheless, a nonuniform VAT, supplemented by some subsidies and special taxes on selected items, may provide an attractive package and one that deserves further analysis.

A feasible alternative for major reform for the central government, which would involve the least adjustment to existing constitutional arrangements, is to replace the present system of (central) excises with a MANVAT, as recommended by India's Ministry of Finance (1978). This tax could be nonuniform to preserve some of the progressivity of the present system. If a uniform VAT is more practical, then it might need to be supplemented by a set of specific taxes or subsidies such that the overall set of "effective" taxes reflects the distributional preferences of the government.

The short-run costs of administration for a nonmarginal reform are likely to be very large if it involves new types of taxes. For certain new taxes, it might be argued that long-run administrative costs and evasion would be reduced, and the intertemporal cost-benefit calculation could be quite complex. In this respect, as in others, the analysis of nonmarginal reform is more difficult than that of marginal reform, in which administrative costs could be introduced in a more straightforward manner.

Extensions of the Model: The Supply Side

For most of the calculations in this chapter, we have assumed a very simple model of production with competitive markets, fixed coefficients, no joint production, and only one nonproduced factor. This situation provides a special case of the nonsubstitution theorem, which implies that prices are independent of demand. Thus producer and consumer prices in the model change only through tax changes and not through changes in production coefficients and factor price changes. The absence of any change in the choice of technique and factor prices implies that indirect taxes are 100 percent shifted. In this section we indicate some of the consequences of relaxing some of these assumptions. Our focus is on the effect of taxes on prices rather than the full detail of welfare calculations.

In chapter 3 we examined markets and tax shifting without the competitive assumption. It was seen that 100 percent shifting is an intermediate rather than a polar case. (See also Stern, 1985.) Below we show how the general equilibrium effects of tax changes in competitive models, which are more general than our initial simple structure, should be incorporated into the analysis of welfare and revenue changes, and we comment on relationships with analyses using shadow prices. We then discuss the calculation of price responses to taxes in competitive models with more than one factor and where there is substitution among inputs. Next we discuss some possibilities for implementing the competitive models.

General Equilibrium Effects on Welfare and Revenue

In this subsection we show how general equilibrium effects on welfare and revenue may be studied in models that are more complicated than those discussed in which basic prices are unaffected by taxation. If households buy at prices $\mathbf{q}$, sell factors at prices $\mathbf{w}$, and have lump-sum incomes M^h, then their utility, demands, and factor supplies can be written: $V^h(\mathbf{q}, \mathbf{w}, M^h)$, $\mathbf{x}^h(\mathbf{q}, \mathbf{w}, M^h)$, $\mathbf{l}^h(\mathbf{q}, \mathbf{w}, M^h)$. If we write total social welfare as a function W of the V^h, its rate of change with respect to a tax t_i is

$$(11\text{-}64) \qquad \frac{\partial W}{\partial t_i} = -\sum_h \beta^h \sum_j \frac{\partial q_j}{\partial t_i} x_j^h + \sum_h \beta^h \sum_k \frac{\partial w_k}{\partial t_i} l_j^h + \sum_h \beta^h \frac{\partial M^h}{\partial t_i}$$

where t_i is the nominal tax on the ith good (that is, t_i falls on all sales intermediate or final). The change in government revenue is

$$(11\text{-}65) \qquad \frac{\partial R}{\partial t_i} = \frac{\partial}{\partial t_i}(\mathbf{t} \cdot \mathbf{Y}) + \frac{\partial}{\partial t_i}(\hat{\tau} \cdot \mathbf{L})$$

where $\mathbf{Y}$ is the vector of total outputs (intermediate and final), $\hat{\tau}$ is the vector of per unit taxes on factors, and we have ignored other types of taxes. The formal generalization of 11-65 to a more complicated tax structure is in principle straightforward but would raise obvious difficulties of practical implementation. Equations 11-64 and 11-65 would form the basis of marginal tax reform calculations just as they did in our earlier work, where we calculated λ_i as $-(\partial W/\partial t_i) \div (\partial R/\partial t_i)$. Note that only household welfare and government revenue enter the calculations—in the general equilibrium model, profits affect welfare through lump-sum incomes M^h.

It is important to take some care with the definition of the derivatives in equations 11-64 and 11-65. They are general equilibrium derivatives when we consider the equilibrium to be a well-defined function of the tax vector. Then it is easy to check that, if individuals are on their budget constraints, then the government budget constraint

$$(11\text{-}66) \qquad R \equiv \mathbf{t} \cdot \mathbf{Y} + \hat{\tau} \cdot \mathbf{L} = \mathbf{p} \cdot \mathbf{Z} \equiv E$$

will always be satisfied in equilibrium where $\mathbf{Z}$ is the vector of government final demands for goods (we ignore factor services for simplicity) that are purchased at prices $\mathbf{p}$, and thus E is government expenditure. Notice, then, that, if $\mathbf{Z}$ is fixed, revenue can change only with the revaluation of $\mathbf{Z}$ through changes in $\mathbf{p}$—a relatively uninteresting effect that does not reflect real demand over resources. Hence the general equilibrium derivative of revenue is interesting only when government demand for real goods and services is endogenous. Thus we can think, for example, of the government seeking to increase its purchases of a particular commodity so that all the elements of $\mathbf{Z}$ are fixed except one. Then $\partial R/\partial t_i$ and the other partial derivatives will be well defined, but it is clear that their values will in general depend on the particular government demand function that is specified. As we should note, however, it will be true that if λ_i is not equal to λ_j, then an available readjustment of taxes from i to j will leave government demand for real resources $\mathbf{Z}$ unchanged and will raise welfare W.

The first terms in equations 11-64 and 11-65 embody our discussion of effective taxes in the model with one factor and fixed coefficients. We defined the effective tax $\mathbf{t}^e$ as $\partial R/\partial X_i$ where X_i is final demand and showed that

$$(11\text{-}67) \qquad\qquad \mathbf{t}^{e'} = \mathbf{t}'(I - A)^{-1}.$$

Consumer prices were given by the fixed basic price vector plus $\mathbf{t}^{e'}$ (see equations 11-4, 11-5, and 11-6), and so $(\partial q_i/\partial t_i)$ and $(\partial t_j^e/\partial t_i)$ coincide and are equal to $(I - A)^{-1}$. The government demand function is specified in terms of the single scarce factor—all increases in revenue are devoted to purchases of this factor.

The effective tax on good i defined as $\partial R/\partial X_i$, where X_i is final demand, remains an interesting concept in the more general model and would have to be calculated as before, by considering the response of total output and factor supplies to changes in final demand. We would use $\partial R/\partial X_i$ in the estimation of revenue responses to final demand shifts. We are no longer able, however, to use the expression for $\partial t_j^e/\partial t_i$ to switch the analysis from nominal tax space to effective tax space, and we would need to carry out our discussion of reforms from the viewpoint of nominal taxes. The matrix $(\partial q_j/\partial t_i)$ plays a central role and will be discussed further below.

The complication of equations 11-64 and 11-65 contrasts with the simplicities that come from using shadow prices. As we explained in chapter 3, we must specify which variables are considered exogenous (the ω in that chapter) and which endogenous (the s, determined by policy subject to balance in the markets). In this case we consider the taxes $\mathbf{t}$ as exogenous (among the ω) and then specify an appropriate set of prices and scale levels for constant-returns industries as the endogenous variables. We suppose that these variables are specified so that the model is fully determined and the government has no real choice in optimization. We then consider the effect on welfare and net demands of a change in t_i, holding the other exogenous and endogenous variables constant. Thus the analysis of shifts in parameters such as t_i is greatly simplified, although, of course, the simplicity comes from our having already summarized the general equilibrium effects in the shadow prices. Thus it is still of interest to ask about the general equilibrium effects of taxes on prices and allocations, and for the remainder of this section we concentrate on these.

Where there are flexible coefficients, then efficiency losses from the taxation of inputs appear in the first term of equation 11-65, whether or not profits are zero. Firms will substitute away from inputs whose price has risen and thus there may be a loss in government revenue from increasing taxes on inputs. Notice that gains in revenue are possible if firms substitute toward inputs that are already taxed particularly heavily. This is a reminder that the notion of increasing marginal damage from taxation, which we might retain from the discussions of triangles, is particularly treacherous in the general equilibrium context.

There are equations analogous to equations 11-64 and 11-65 for marginal changes in the factor taxes $\hat{\tau}$ or for other parameters of the income tax system. These together with equations 11-64 and 11-65 allow us to examine reforms involving switches between direct and indirect taxes in models that are more general than those considered in the second section of this chapter. As we emphasized there, however, we cannot assume a general superiority of one form of taxation over the other. The appropriate directions for reform would depend quite sensitively on the context, and it must be remembered that inefficiencies arise with the income tax and supply of labor as with indirect taxes and the demand for goods. It is sometimes suggested that the social losses associated with the income tax may be quite substantial for developed countries (see, for example, Hausman, 1983). A judgment of this aspect for developing countries must be suspended because relevant data are not available and the income tax takes a very different form in its coverage of the population.

There are, of course, a number of difficulties in modeling the terms such as $\partial q_j / \partial t_i$, $\partial w_k / \partial t_i$, and $\partial M^h / \partial t_i$ that arise in equations 11-64 and 11-65 in more complicated cases and in implementing the models. Some of these will be discussed in the following subsections.

Flexible Coefficients

We examine here the problem of calculating $\partial q_j / \partial t_i$ and $\partial w_k / \partial t_i$ where we have flexible coefficients in production. To keep things simple and to bring out the main points, we consider a competitive, closed economy with constant returns to scale and no joint production. Thus we may write the cost of production on the jth good as $c_j(\mathbf{q}, \hat{\mathbf{w}})$ where all purchasers of inputs buy at prices $\mathbf{q}$, and $\hat{w}_k$ is the purchasers', or gross-of-tax, price of factor k (the sellers' price w_k, or net-of-tax wage, is $\hat{w}_k - \hat{\tau}_k$). The price received by producers, the seller's price $\mathbf{p}$, differs from $\mathbf{q}$ through the vector of taxes $\mathbf{t}$. Thus we have

(11-68) $$\mathbf{p} + \mathbf{t} = \mathbf{q}$$

where

(11-69) $$\mathbf{p} = \mathbf{c}(\mathbf{q}, \hat{\mathbf{w}})$$

and combining the two preceding equations,

(11-70) $$\mathbf{q} = \mathbf{c}(\mathbf{q}, \hat{\mathbf{w}}) + \mathbf{t}.$$

Transposing and differentiating with respect to the tax t_i we have

(11-71) $$\frac{\partial q_j}{\partial t_i} = \Sigma_k \frac{\partial c_j}{\partial q_k} \frac{\partial q_k}{\partial t_i} + \Sigma_m \frac{\partial c_j}{\partial \hat{w}_m} \frac{\partial \hat{w}_m}{\partial t_i} + \delta_{ij}.$$

In matrix form

(11-72) $$\Delta = \Delta A + WB + I$$

where $(\Delta)_{ij}$ is $\partial q_j / \partial t_i$, $(A)_{kj}$ is $\partial c_j / \partial q_k$, $(B)_{mj}$ is $\partial c_j / \partial \hat{w}_m$, and $(W)_{im} = \partial W_m / \partial t_i$. Note that A is the familiar input-output matrix, because $\partial c_j / \partial q_k$ is simply the input of good k into the jth industry at unit production levels. Similarly, B is the matrix of factor requirements. Thus

(11-73) $$\Delta = (I - A)^{-1} + WB(I - A)^{-1}.$$

The result (equation 11-73) establishes, if we look at the first term, that our assumption of fixed coefficients for intermediate goods extends immediately to flexible coefficients. The effective tax $\mathbf{t}^e$ calculated using the existing A no longer reflects the price difference between the equilibrium with and without taxation (see the third section of this chapter), but the important feature is the rate at which prices change with respect to the tax, and that is given by $(I - A)^{-1}$ both with flexible coefficients and with fixed coefficients for intermediate goods.

We can extend the analysis of flexible coefficients in a straightforward way to the open economy. We distinguish between domestically produced goods and their prices by the superscript d and imported goods by the superscript m; the buyer's price is the producer price plus the tax. Then

(11-74) $$\mathbf{q}^m = \mathbf{p}^* + \mathbf{t}^m$$

and

(11-75) $$\mathbf{q}^d = \mathbf{p}^d + \mathbf{t}^d$$

where $\mathbf{p}^*$ is the (exogenous) world price of the import and $\mathbf{t}^m$ and $\mathbf{t}^d$ are taxes on imports and domestically produced goods, respectively.

(11-76) $$\mathbf{q}^d = \mathbf{c}^d(\mathbf{q}^d, \mathbf{q}^m, \hat{\mathbf{w}}) + \mathbf{t}^d$$

and

(11-77) $$\frac{\partial q_j^d}{\partial t_i^d} = \Sigma_l \frac{\partial c_j^d}{\partial q_l^d} \frac{\partial q_l^d}{\partial t_i^d} + \Sigma_f \frac{\partial c_j^d}{\partial \hat{w}_f} \frac{\partial \hat{w}_f}{\partial t_i^d} + \delta_{ij}$$

(11-78) $$\frac{\partial q_j^d}{\partial t_k^m} = \Sigma_r \frac{\partial c_j^d}{\partial q_r^d} \frac{\partial p_r^d}{\partial t_k^m} + \Sigma_f \frac{\partial c_j^d}{\partial \hat{w}_f} \frac{\partial \hat{w}_f}{\partial t_k^m} + \frac{\partial c_i^d}{\partial q_k^m},$$

where the last two equations are analogous to equation 11-71. We have, corresponding to equation 11-72, for

$$\Delta^d = \frac{\partial q_j^d}{\partial t_i^d}$$

and

$$\Delta^m = \frac{\partial q_j^d}{\partial t_k^m}$$

(11-79) $$\Delta^d = \Delta^d A^d + W^d B + I$$

and

(11-80) $$\Delta^m = \Delta^m A^d + W^m B + A^m$$

where A^d is the domestic input-output matrix $(\partial c_j^d / \partial q_i^d)$ giving the coefficients of domestic goods into domestic production, A^m is the coefficient matrix giving imported inputs into domestic production $(\partial c_j^d / \partial q_k^m)$, W^d is the matrix of factor price responses to the taxation of domestic inputs, and W^m is the corresponding matrix for taxes on imported goods. Finally, we have

(11-81) $$\Delta^d = (I - A^d)^{-1} + W^d B (I - A^d)^{-1}$$

and

(11-82) $$\Delta^m = A^m (I - A^d)^{-1} + W^m B (I - A^d)^{-1}.$$

These two equations generalize equation 11-73 to the open economy and are the marginal versions of equation 11-25 (which used fixed coefficients) for the case of flexible coefficients. Thus if we confine ourselves to marginal changes, we do not have to insist that imported inputs are strict complements in domestic production.

The second term in equation 11-73 (and similarly in equations 11-81 and 11-82) gives us the effect on commodity prices of changes in factor prices resulting from the tax change. In the nonsubstitution theorem, there is only one factor, and if this is the numeraire, the price change is zero. Thus our previous reform analysis applies to flexible coefficients with only one factor, and with more than one factor we have to examine $WB(I - A)^{-1}$. Note, however, that the effect is additive, so that direct examination of $(I - A)^{-1}$ does give us an important part of the effect on prices of a tax change. To this should be added any effect on goods prices through the change in factor prices.

In principle, W or $(\partial \hat{w}_f / \partial t_i)$ cannot be calculated without a full model of the economy. We cannot tell, for example, how the relative prices of land and labor will change without knowing whether the demand changes brought about by the taxes will lead to greater emphasis on land or on labor-intensive commodities. The analytical attractiveness of the nonsubstitution theorem is obviously that it permits the analysis of price without introducing demand. At some point we cannot avoid introducing demand-side considerations. There are, however, some ways of simplifying in certain cases, and we comment briefly on this point in the next subsection.

Some Problems of Implementation

The discussion in the preceding section has indicated ways in which our earlier analysis might be generalized, but more work is required before the generalizations could be implemented. We indicate here three directions that might be pursued in the incorporation of factor price changes. We could use the technique suggested by Hughes (chapter 20), where in certain sectors prices of final goods are determined by world markets and the factors in the corresponding sectors are fixed. Second, we could attempt to implement the Ricardo-Viner model with one mobile factor that is allocated across sectors and sector-specific fixed factors (see Dixit and Newbery, 1985). Third, we could consider two (or possibly more) mobile factors (and no fixed factors) with, say, Cobb-Douglas or CES technology in the individual sectors. The three approaches may perhaps be interpreted as representing the short, medium, and long run, respectively.

Hughes (chapter 20) has shown how his technique could be implemented in practice. For each sector we specify whether the price is determined by cost or is fixed exogenously by the world market. In the former case we have an equation for price and in the latter an equation for the factor reward in the sectors, and this obviously yields (with the corresponding exogenous factor reward and prices) the right number of equations and unknowns, so that we can solve out for prices and factor rewards. The result then is the required input into the welfare analysis. Hughes suggests that the allocation of sectors into exogenous prices and "cost-plus" prices has an important bearing on the result.

The Ricardo-Viner model would require estimates of demand functions for labor (if this is the mobile factor) for each sector. These may be available for some sectors, but a certain amount of inventiveness would be necessary for other sectors. Similarly, with more than one mobile factor we might be forced to use simple ad hoc estimates. If information on factor shares by industry is available, for example, we might simply use it to give point estimates of Cobb-Douglas production functions.

Where increasing returns are thought to be significant, then we should expect to be forced back to partial-equilibrium examples of particular industries. Finally, agriculture both is very important and poses special problems. (See part 4 for a discussion of some of the issues.) We have various possibilities: substitution among outputs; diminishing returns through fixed land; pricing of major inputs such as irrigation; the particular structure of peasant households as producer and consumer units; and so on. The importance of agriculture and the special structure of the problems deserve a substantial direct study.

Conclusions

Our main purpose in this chapter has been to demonstrate the potential shown by some simple but formal methods of analyzing tax reform in the context of the Indian economy in 1979–80. In so doing we have provided a number of extensions and modifications of the methods. Second, although the calculations are illustrative, they do allow a useful commentary on possible tax reforms in India. Third, we have examined a number of theoretical issues that may be of value in future research, particularly those concerning the effects of taxes on prices. In this concluding section we comment briefly on these three aspects of our work. We begin with a summary of worked examples for India, thereby providing the raw material for an assessment of the potential of the methods.

The calculation of effective taxes provides a systematic way of describing the tax system in terms of its consequences for the prices of final goods. Governments may well be unaware of the effects of tax policy, and thus the calculation of effective taxes could have a direct impact on policy, for example if it reveals consequences that are unintended. We can show, for example, that goods which receive substantial subsidies are effectively taxed. Thus in our investigation of indirect taxes we analyzed the consequences of the taxation of intermediate goods. We argued that a useful measure of the impact of this taxation from the point of view of cost of production was the difference between effective taxes and nominal taxes. The inefficiencies arising from input taxation are associated with shifts in production technique, however, and although we are not in a position to address the question empirically, we indicated the theoretical issues that arise.

We also applied the effective tax analysis in our calculations of the extent to which export subsidies might be increased if they were fully to reflect the taxation of inputs in the production of exports. The result depends on the extent to which taxes are already rebated, but the assumption that many such rebates occur leads us to suggest that the subsidies could be increased in some cases.

We examined the balance between state and central taxes in terms of the taxation of inputs and the social marginal costs of funds from the different sources. Our analysis suggests that the major source of the taxation of intermediate goods in India are the union excise taxes, which bear largely on heavy industry and manufacturers. State taxes seem to be more heavily concentrated on certain types of final goods. Furthermore, it appears that the welfare losses from the consumption standpoint of raising extra revenue via union excises are greater than for state sales taxes at lower levels of inequality aversion. The reasons seem, in general terms, to be that the excise taxes cause increases in prices of goods that are more regressive in that the taxes are spread over a wider range of goods through the input-output process; second, they bear more heavily on goods that are in elastic demand. We must be careful here, however, because state sales taxes fall on a number of food items, and the welfare loss for state sales taxes exceeds that for union excises at higher levels of inequality aversion. The relation between union import duties and state sales taxes has a similar "switch."

An examination of the total "effective tax" also permits a comparison of the balance of taxes across goods in terms of the marginal cost of raising revenue. We referred earlier to results from our work (Ahmad and Stern 1983a, 1984, forthcoming), which discusses this issue in greater detail. Two main conclusions emerge for India for 1979–80. First, regardless of the level of inequality aversion, it is possible to identify several directions of welfare-improving marginal reform. Second, these directions do not lead to a movement toward the uniformity of effective taxes. Third, for most levels of inequality aversion, a marginal switch to a uniform poll subsidy financed by commodity taxation would be desirable (if feasible). Thus we cannot regard an optimal poll subsidy as being in operation, as is required for the results in chapters 2 to 4 on the uniformity of commodity taxation.

Furthermore, a consideration of major reform, for instance a uniform VAT, also suggests that "uniformity" is not desirable if there is positive inequality aversion. This is not an argument against the VAT, however, which avoids the distortionary effects of the taxation of inputs. It is possible to have a system of nonuniform VAT so as to equate the cost of raising a unit of revenue across final goods. For administrative reasons, the "appropriate differentiation" might be best achieved with a combination of two or three bands for the VAT, supplemented by specific taxes or subsidies on certain goods.

In discussing the income tax, we showed how the welfare loss could be calculated from different possible reforms of the income tax system sufficient to raise a marginal rupee. Most of the analysis and all of the empirical applications were based on the assumption of no supply response: the analysis can be extended to avoid this assumption, but we argued that the data to implement it were not available. In general the income tax does seem a desirable way (relative to indirect taxes) to raise extra income, provided that we are concerned with inequality, that we are prepared to presuppose no severe adverse incentive effects, that extra collections are not too costly, and that incidence is on the posttax incomes of taxpayers. The underlying reason is that the welfare weights attached to income tax assessees are quite low, given that their incomes are relatively high. The issue is not, however, quite so simple, for in addition to the assumptions already indicated, we must take explicitly into account the effects of changes in disposable income on indirect tax collections.

The question of administrative feasibility and that of collection costs are obviously of importance in a country like India. Thus certain options may not be feasible without major constitutional changes, and issues involving center-state relations are also particularly sensitive. The costs of collection are very relevant and need to be kept in mind when we reach policy conclusions. We illustrated how information on such costs could be incorporated into the analysis. It should be easy for the policymaker to modify estimates of collection costs according to experience and still to conduct an analysis of the balance of taxation across types of goods and taxes along the lines indicated in this chapter.

Our discussion of the supply side and tax shifting was theoretical and built on the discussion in chapter 3. We concentrated on the effect of taxes on prices, but we identified a number of possible directions for further theoretical and empirical research. We suggested that some of our earlier results were fairly robust in the sense that they could accommodate substitution among intermediate goods and furthermore that changes in factor prices could be treated as being additive to the marginal effects already calculated. The calculation of changes in factor prices would involve extensive further work that would include the pattern of demand shifts and calculations of production functions. We indicate some ways in which the investigation might proceed. Additional work should include the analysis of tax shifting and welfare for (partial-equilibrium) noncompetitive industries and explicit modeling of the taxation of inputs and outputs in peasant agriculture. The models we discuss at present are essentially static, but the methods and questions may readily be applied in a dynamic context, and the research should be extended to this direction.

We emphasized that, for complex and distorted economies, a system of shadow prices provided a convenient summary of general equilibrium effects on welfare of tax reform as described in chapter 3. In this way we can examine the question of whether export industries (and which ones) *should be* encouraged using subsidies (rather than considering only whether such subsidies are permissible under international agreements). This issue will be examined in our further work on India and in our study of the Pakistan tax system, now in progress (see Ahmad and Stern, 1986; Ahmad, Coady, and Stern, 1986; and Ahmad and Stern, forthcoming).

We hope these examples of the potential of the methods we have introduced show that they can indeed be of considerable value for the analysis of important questions of current policy, but they clearly raise a number of questions for further research. Among the many possibilities we would indicate: first, a further theoretical and empirical examination of the use of shadow prices in the analysis of reform. Second, the effects and desirability of government expenditure can be examined using analogous methods and may be linked to the expenditure side using the social marginal cost of funds. Third, effective tax calculations and the desirability of expansion of certain industries should be examined at the sectoral level (using the economywide calculations as a framework). Fourth, the effects of taxes on prices could be examined empirically using some of the models indicated in our last section. In any case, questions of the incidence of taxes, as discussed in chapter 3, will be a key issue. Finally, the treatment of agriculture raises a number of substantive issues that require separate analysis. We have tried here to justify our view that such research will prove fruitful.

Notes

1. This would depend on where inputs were purchased. If they were largely from other firms subject only to MANVAT and imports, then it would be reasonably easy to rebate taxes on inputs.

2. Note that a VAT presents the same incentives to cheat at the point of final purchase as a purchase tax, although a rebate on taxed inputs has to be justified, and this prerequisite permits a cross-check.

3. Note that state taxes are levied by individual states, and there may be important differences in rate structures and collections across states. Here we treat total sales tax collections, and the following examples are "as if" illustrations that treat *changes* in sales taxes as uniform across India.

4. See Ahmad and Stern (1983a). This figure does not include the effects of the taxation of capital goods and is subject to revision in subsequent work—see Ahmad and Stern (forthcoming).

5. Exemption, as opposed to zero rating, would mean that there would be no rebates for taxes on inputs, hence "effective taxes" would not be precisely zero, although input taxation is fairly low (see table 11-1).

6. See the technical note to the Sixth Five Year Plan.

12

Some Lessons from Mexico's Tax Reform

Francisco Gil Díaz

TAX REFORM BECAME A POLITICAL ISSUE in Mexico during the political campaign of the administration that took office in December 1970. The tax structure had been portrayed as unjust and tax revenue as inadequate, judged by the comparatively low tax/GDP ratio. These criticisms were not entirely justified.

The corporate income tax/GDP ratio was quite high compared with those of other countries. Other taxes fared reasonably well in an international comparison. The system was and is in some cases unjust but for reasons quite different from the ones used to condemn it. As for insufficiency, the tax ratio rose four points of GDP in six years (1970–76), and it was to rise quite a bit more because of oil revenues, but the increase in public expenditures was simply unattainable. Some important changes in the tax structure appeared to be justified, however, and in 1976 the new administration committed itself to reform.

The reform was carried out from 1978 to 1982. The statements that introduced the executive initiatives to Congress stated that the reforms intended to change the pattern of taxation in order to help enforcement of the law and to distribute the burden of taxation more equitably. It was also intended to make the tax system less distortive or more neutral. The objective was therefore to change the structure of the tax system rather than to raise tax rates or schedules.

This chapter will examine the degree to which these objectives were attained and will note some of the most important problems that remain in the tax structure. The reform was immensely rich in detail. Every existing tax act was completely revamped. It is impossible to do it justice in a short chapter, and I will discuss only the main features. I begin with a section that outlines the economic constraints underlying the tax environment in Mexico. I will then describe and analyze the main features of the reform and will present the effect of the reform on the structure of tax collections and on the incidence of taxation on households before briefly summing up.

The Tax Environment of a Small Open Economy

Whatever the utility of economic theory for tax design, policymaking must face not only demographic, cultural, and institutional realities but also the international dependence and mutual interaction of tax systems. The proximity of other tax areas presents limits and opportunities. The limits apply to tax bases and to tax rates. If Argentina taxes wealth, including vacation homes, then wealthy Argentinians will own vacation homes in nearby Punta del Este, Uruguay. If Mexico applies stiff excises or high import duties, tax collections may diminish, with no effect on consumption but with considerable trade diversion. In the first half of the 1970s, a 30 percent excise tax on mink coats caused tax collections to fall to below one-third of former levels, when the tax had been 10 percent, but well-to-do Mexican buyers continued to purchase them in U.S. border towns.[1] The same consequences followed when the luxury tax on jewels was raised from 10 percent to 30 percent.

Optimal tax theory or just sound economic theory is a policy guide within the strict restraints created by the international movements of goods, factors, and services. We could perhaps consider optimal tax design on a world basis, but only if national governments arranged a coalition against taxpayers, exchanging information and agreeing to end tax havens, would such optimal tax designs be feasible on a local level.

International awareness has made economists recognize that the monetary theory of inflation applies to the world economy but not to local economies with fixed exchange rates. Small economies with depreciating exchange rates on the other hand soon discover that the only freedom they have attained is that of a higher local inflation. Something analogous happens when local tax policy falls significantly out of step with world tax patterns. I do not mean, however, that there is no room to correct distortions—sometimes major ones—or to reduce gross inequities.

To provide a perspective on the openness of the Mexican economy, I will comment on the two basic items of the balance of payments: the capital account and the trade account. First, there is no question that the Mexican economy has been open to international currency and financial transactions. It also shares a large border with the largest capital market in the world.

As a result, financial interest income cannot be taxed. If a tax is applied to interest, it will have to be grossed up to maintain the net-of-tax interest rate. In this case, the tax is borne by credit users, most likely smaller firms and less wealthy individuals without access to international credit markets. The tax will also affect domestic financial intermediaries, making them smaller in size than they would otherwise be.

A second result will be that corporate tax rates cannot exceed international rates. If the tax on corporate profits is above the international standard, investment (foreign and local) will be inhibited unless the excessive part of the tax can be shifted, but in this case the excess tax is borne by consumers and/or labor, not by the owners of capital. The taxation of corporate capital abroad also means that corporate tax rates should not be lower than the prevailing international rates, because the difference would be taxed by the foreign treasury, thus transferring tax collections abroad without a favorable effect on corporate investment.

Third, inheritance and net wealth taxes would be easily avoided. If capital is internationally mobile, inheritance and wealth taxes only strike once and for all real estate owners and middle-income individuals. The truly wealthy, who know well the diverse international investment alternatives, would be unaffected by an inheritance tax.

With respect to foreign trade, the Mexican economy is also quite open, more so than official statistics suggest. The channel that makes it open and competitive is illegal trade. A measure of its influence appears in a study by M. Cavazos (1976) of implicit nominal protection in Mexico (price differences between Mexican and U.S. products). It showed that most Mexican products were below the U.S. CIF price plus the Mexican import duty.

Such market integration restricts the level that consumer taxes can reach and severely constrains the ability of Mexico's tax authorities to raise the tax burden through excises. On the other hand, goods that were subsidized, notably gasoline, diesel, gas, and other oil-derived products, could generate a much higher stream of revenue either by raising the producer prices or by raising the rates of ad valorem taxes on prevailing producer prices.

International labor movements are another limitation. Although some types of labor skills have domestic value but may not be able to find employment abroad, income tax schedules that apply the same rate to different categories of labor must take into account those workers who would be displaced to foreign markets.

It can be seen, therefore, that in many key decisions concerning the optimal design of tax schedules, international parameters must be superimposed on theoretical considerations and on political requirements based on equity or redistributive considerations, the pursuit of which would prove fruitless and, in many cases, counterproductive.

The Major Items of the Tax Reform

In 1978, the first year of the tax reform, individual income taxation was overhauled. Congress also approved a value-added tax to go into effect one year later, so that taxpayers and tax administrators would have an opportunity to know and experiment with the new law before it was applied. At the same time, a different system of revenue sharing with the federal states was approved, also with a one-year delay in its application. In the succeeding years, there were further changes on the personal income tax, a new corporate income tax was introduced, and some profound changes were performed on excise taxes as well. Finally, a new tax code was set up outlining new administrative and compliance procedures and fines.

Reforms on Personal Income Taxation

The base of the individual income tax was broadened, including in it all realized income in cash or in kind. Thus, capital gains, rents, dividends, nonfinancial interest income, labor income, and so forth are now part of the tax base. Financial interest income, gains derived from transactions on shares listed in the stock exchange, imputed income from owner-occupied housing, fringe benefits, and income from authorship rights all remain outside the individual global income tax. It will be seen below why some of these items were omitted from the income tax base. There is some economic or administrative reason for most of them, but the exclusion of fringe benefits and authorship rights reflects solely political considerations.

Authorship rights are exempt from the income tax, although some of the possibilities they offered for tax evasion have been eliminated. This privilege is hotly defended by the press, which has applied considerable pressure whenever the government has tried to eliminate it. Aside from obvious considerations regarding the fairness of totally exempting a group, which incidentally contains some of the most vociferous advocates of confiscatory taxation or soak-the-rich measures, the exemption was considerably abused by many who managed to stretch its scope. To give an example, a controlling shareholder in a firm could take out profits tax free by simulating a contract between his wife and the firm, which made the wife appear to be the recipient of royalties for her alleged authorship of the firm's emblem.

Fringe benefits have been growing in importance in the wage bill because they provide a tax-free vehicle but also because they have become an indexed part of the wage. Their uncontrolled and haphazard growth, without guidelines and restrictions from tax authorities, has produced a situation very difficult to disentangle. In some cases they are very difficult to measure and even harder to apportion to an individual. If the firm provides sporting facilities for its employees, for instance, should they be valued at cost or at comparable market prices? What cost and which prices in the case of either answer? If the valuation problem is solved, how should it be allocated to individual workers? Fringe benefits can go from 10 percent to 60 percent of salary, and the highest percentages usually appear in government firms with strong unions. Therefore, a solution such as lowering the income tax schedule in exchange for making its base all-inclusive would not work using averages. The policymaker faces here a serious problem both for tax equity and for revenue considerations.

THE INCOME TAX SCHEDULE AND PERSONAL DEDUCTIONS. Concern about labor disincentives from stiff marginal tax rates led to a revision of the global income tax schedule, which was modified, reducing substantially marginal tax rates without lowering as much, and sometimes even increasing, average tax rates. Individuals who formerly faced a 57.5 percent marginal tax rate now pay a 40 percent marginal tax on the same incremental real income. Those with a

39.9 percent marginal rate now pay 26.2 percent. Even though the schedule was streamlined, the rate at the top end was increased from 50 percent to 55 percent, with the pretense of improving the distribution of income. These "envy" rates, which apply to very few people and collect little revenue, have been superimposed little by little over the last years, raising the schedule imperceptibly to extremely high levels.

The schedule was fully adjusted for inflation in each of the four years during which the reform was carried out (1979–82). This revision, plus the new deduction explained below, kept tax collections from labor income at a constant fraction of GDP, from 1980, the second year the reform was in effect, until 1983. In 1979, as a result of the new deduction, labor income tax collections actually decreased slightly as a proportion of GDP because of the considerable reduction in tax collections from lower-income laborers. Until 1978, tax from labor income had been increasing every year as a proportion of GDP.

The change for lower-income individuals, people barely above the minimum-wage threshold, was more dramatic. People in this range entered the schedule at an extremely high marginal rate because the Constitution exempts the minimum wage from the income tax, so in order to avoid taxing at 100 percent income slightly above the minimum wage, the worker entered the schedule through a special formula that still resulted in a marginal tax above 50 percent. To solve this problem, itemized deductions for oneself, for the spouse, and for economic dependents were eliminated and were replaced by a single deduction equal to the annual minimum wage. Individual taxable income is now calculated subtracting one annual minimum wage from gross taxable income, whether the individual is single or married. The new deduction may appear strange, for it makes no allowance for family size. Still, it is a fact that the vast majority of taxpayers earning between one and four minimum wages did not use itemized deductions even though they had the right to file a return. The new common deduction has several advantages.

1. It considerably simplifies the administration of the tax. This is no trivial matter for a country with a relatively greater scarcity of administrative resources.

2. It moves up automatically with price and productivity increases. This property is important because of bracket creep in an inflationary environment.

3. It changed the tax burden. It reduced by 30 percent the value of deductions of middle- and higher-income people while increasing as much as 200 percent the amount of deductions for lower-income individuals.

4. It should improve labor effort and should facilitate overtime and seasonal two-shifts for lower-income workers by lowering the marginal tax on their labor income from 55 percent to 3.1 percent.

The only itemized deductions remaining are funeral expenses, medical expenses within the country, and charitable contributions to government-authorized institutions.

TAXATION OF CAPITAL GAINS. Capital gains were added to the income tax base, but because considerable price increases had occurred in the 1970s and more were expected, some sort of correction had to be allowed on their purchase cost. The solution was to insert a table in the law built with the price indexes of fifty years. The table is actually a price index, base 1932, updated every year.

Because capital gains are a nonrecurrent event for most individuals and can therefore be taxed at too high a marginal rate if the total gain is simply added to other taxable income, a simple averaging procedure was introduced to smooth the impact of their accumulation. If the asset is held for less than two years, the whole gain is cumulated to income; if more than two but less than three years elapse between purchase and sale, half of the gain is taken and is cumulated to income. The ratio of the resulting increase in tax with respect to the cumulated gain then is the rate of tax applicable to the whole gain. If more than three but less than four years have elapsed between the purchase and the sale of the asset, one third of the gain is taken and cumulated to income, and so on. When ten years or more have elapsed, gain slicing stops. The economic rationale is that 10 percent is the real permanent stream of income derived from a long-term gain, so that lifetime and other complicated averaging procedures are given a simple solution.

In the case of shares issued by corporations, reinvested profits corrected for inflation are also added to the adjusted purchase cost, whereas distributed profits and corporate losses must be subtracted. These procedures apply to individuals as well as to firms except that gains on stock-listed shares owned by individuals are simply exempt on the grounds that the new rules are difficult for them to understand. The tax exemption for individuals on gains from listed stocks is not new; it has been in effect for several years and has almost no fiscal consequences because, once corrections have been made for inflation and reinvested earnings, the tax base generated by true capital gains turns out on the average to be negative. This exemption, however, creates asymmetry problems and the possibility that there will be some manipulative transactions between corporations and individuals on the shares of the 100 corporations eligible for this treatment. Some of the loopholes have been plugged through rules on the loss deductions that arise from share trading by corporations. As long as the asymmetry persists, however, tax authorities will have to keep outguessing tax schemes.

The changes on the taxation of capital gains were introduced because of equity considerations but also to lubricate the functioning of the capital market. An efficient capital market is of paramount importance for efficient resource allocation. The taxation of nominal gains only led to the locking in of asset transactions. When nominal gains were taxed, firms and individuals preferred to hold onto their assets, showing their portfolios valued at current market prices and failing to indicate on their balance sheets the tax liability contingent upon the sale of the asset. This tactic helped their borrowing potential, because the appropriation of an asset by a bank upon a bankruptcy allowed the bank to enter the asset onto its balance sheet at the declared collateral value, so that it paid tax only on the capital gain obtained above such a value.

To suggest the meaning of these inflationary corrections for revenues, tax collections from asset transactions increased 53 percent in 1979 and 51 percent in 1980, the first two years the new system was applicable. The income tax in those two years increased 31 percent and 41 percent, respectively, whereas nominal income increased 39.1 percent in 1980 and 38.2 percent in 1981.

REINFORCEMENT OF COMPLIANCE. Mexico took cues from tax legislation in other countries, such as the presumption of income based on individual transactions in excess of declared income (which sent the gangster Al Capone to jail in the United States), and several measures of this sort were introduced into Mexican legislation. It now seems, however, that such changes should not have been made in the absence of a network of international taxation treaties. The effect of the new measures on additional compliance has been nil, despite their having been in effect now for more than four years, but they have effectively prevented taxpayers from returning to Mexico part of the wealth they have transferred abroad in anticipation of the 1982 devaluations of the peso. The lack of tax treaties means Mexican authorities have no information or proof of taxable income abroad, while the new law would tax the whole repatriated asset at the personal income tax rate, because the purchase of Mexican currency with the proceeds of, say, a dollar deposit abroad becomes the purchase of an asset that will often be in excess of declared income. Taxpayers in this situation prefer to keep their wealth outside the country.

Reforms of the Taxation of Corporate Profits

Inflationary adjustments are not only convenient but practically necessary when inflation reaches the levels that Mexico has been experiencing lately. Some items, however, are quite difficult to correct when the corporate income tax with its traditional distortions in favor of debt finance has been in operation for many years and has produced a high leverage of firms. The classical distortion toward debt finance is accentuated when even moderate inflation is present. To illustrate the problem, let i and r be the nominal and real interest rates, respectively, and π expected inflation. The relationship between these three rates can be found from the formulas

$$(12\text{-}1) \qquad 1 + i = (1 + r)(1 + \pi)$$
$$i = r(1 + \pi) + \pi.$$

If the intent is only to tax the real interest receipts at rate t, then the after-tax returns will be

$$[1 + (1 - t)r](1 + \pi)$$

and the liability in money terms at the end of the year will be $tr(1 + \pi)$. Equivalently, the tax should be levied on $i - \pi = r(1 + \pi)$.

Such a change in the income tax would involve a considerable redistribution of taxes, creating great losses and gains to corporations. For individuals the solution adopted was simple: only an approximation of $r(1 + \pi)$ is taxed at a flat rate if interest is paid by a financial institution. Individual interest expenditures are not deductible. Corporations are taxed a flat 42 percent of their profits but in addition must pay an 8 percent compulsory profit share to their workers.

Full inflation adjustments for corporations would have involved changes in inventory costing, the redefinition of interest expenditures and income as $r(1 + \pi)$, and revaluation of depreciable assets. Inventory costing was dealt with by allowing LIFO from 1981 into the future. A redefinition of interest, however, would have meant a considerable redistribution of wealth and on average a considerable capital loss to corporations.

Although a redefinition of interest would leave the tax base unaltered in a closed economy, in an open net-debtor economy it means a considerable increase in the tax base. On the other hand, the revaluation of depreciable assets would decrease the tax base of corporations, but there was no information to ascertain the total net effect of a comprehensive correction on the tax base nor on the status of individual corporations. An intermediate solution was devised. An additional deduction from the corporation tax base allowed additional depreciation expenses only insofar as firms have not benefited from indebtedness; this deduction was set as

(12-2) $A \cdot B/E$

where

    A = "Adjusted depreciation" + inflation loss on consumer credit
    B = "Adjusted depreciation" + inflation loss on all financial assets less
        inflation gain on debts
    E = "Adjusted depreciation" + inflation loss on financial assets.

"Adjusted depreciation" is calculated in the following manner: book value depreciation expenditures (dep exp) for each year from 1978 to 1982 are reflated and added:

$$AD = \sum_{t=1}^{5} \left[(\text{dep exp})_t \sum_{i=1}^{t} (1 + \pi_i) - 1 \right]$$

where $t = 1$ for 1982,
       $t = 2$ for 1981, and so on,

and inflation loss on consumer credit (C) is πC, the inflation loss on financial assets (F) is πF, and the inflation gain on debt (D) is πD. It is apparent from this procedure that after twenty years (the longest depreciable assets are buildings at 5 percent per year) all depreciable assets will be fully revalued for depreciation purposes. Such is the case at the present time for all new investments undertaken since the reform was initiated.

This procedure may be interpreted as follows. For a firm that has no debt and no portfolio, $B/E = 1$, and the only additional deduction stems from the "adjusted depreciation" (AD) procedure. If it has some debt but no portfolio, however, AD is multiplied by a factor less than 1 to the extent the firm is in debt, or in other words, to the extent it has benefited from inflation. This latter outcome can be expressed as

$$AD \cdot \frac{AD - \pi D}{AD}.$$

The same logic applies to the correction of opposite sign when the firm has financial assets in its portfolio. Interfirm loans were not included because, on average, they cancel. Finally the inflation loss on consumer credit is added to adjusted depreciation to allow firms some relief on their credit to consumers and to induce through competition, as this deduction becomes more attractive with the passage of time, a reduction on interest charged to consumers.

The deduction discussed above amounts to a partial inflationary correction that allowed firms to deduct their net-of-debt inflationary losses, but the lack of a comprehensive inflationary adjustment creates or accentuates possibilities for tax avoidance. Because individual interest income is taxed only on its real component and nominal interest expenditures are fully deductible at the firm level, interfirm loan swaps are encouraged.

Because a firm can deduct i_ℓ (nominal lending interest rate) from taxable income, the owner of a corporation can make a deposit in a bank conditional on having the amount lent back to his firm, getting a deduction for the full interest payment and obtaining a tax saving of $\frac{1}{2}[\pi + i_\ell(1 + \pi)]$ on its debt. On the negative side, there is a tax payment of only tr_b by the individual, plus the loss due to the bank's margin $i_\ell - i_b$ (where i_b is the nominal borrowing rate of interest). Only full adjustment for inflation would remedy this situation, of course.

DIVIDED INTEGRATION. Another reform in the simultaneous pursuit of equity and efficiency concerns the taxing of dividends. Distributed profits are now taxed, so that the corporate tax and the personal income tax are integrated. With a top marginal rate of 55 percent on individual income and taking 50 percent of corporate profits (through a 42 percent essentially flat corporate tax plus an 8 percent compulsory profit share to workers), there was no other practical way to tax distributed profits. The only caveat is that entities exempt from the income tax that own corporate shares cannot use the integration scheme. For them the corporate income tax paid by the share-issuing corporation is final.

The procedure adopted for integration is to allow the firm the deduction of dividends paid, as if they were any other deductible cost and to require a withholding of 55 percent (the maximum marginal personal income tax rate) creditable by the receiving individual.

Dividend transfers among firms are also deductible and cumulative, thereby allowing interrelated firms the instantaneous offsetting of losses here against profits there. This last possibility was considered particularly important in an inflationary environment.

Another reason for adopting the dividend deduction integration scheme is that in the first stage of the reform a dividend grossing-up method was introduced, but it proved too complex for taxpayers to understand. Partnership profits and taxes are also integrated to the income and to the personal taxes of their members. The net result of integration is that medium- and lower-income individuals are now equitably taxed on their income from profits.

With the reforms mentioned above, and under conditions of price stability, the distortion favoring debt rather than equity financing is eliminated. Even without full correction for inflation, the new rules for dividends and for adjusted depreciation have some interesting implications for the firm's cost of finance (see Solís, 1981).

SOME SPECIAL TAXPAYERS. A common problem in the taxation of corporate profits is that many small taxpayers have little or no administrative ability. The problem posed by these taxpayers is not so much the amount of taxes that go uncollected from them but the fact that their existence has to be accommodated somehow by the authorities, which causes some big taxpayers to find a convenient shelter for their profits.

In Mexico as elsewhere, the procedure has been adopted of taxing small taxpayers on a forfait, or presumptive, basis (where taxable income is assessed by indirect or external indicators such as floor space; see, for example, Goode, 1984, pp. 108–09). The problem with this approach, however, has been that the whole burden of proving that the taxpayer belongs to the small-taxpayer category has rested on the authorities. The taxpayer is not required to keep even the most elementary record of cash inflows and outflows. The result is that an audit starts in a vacuum, with the authorities having to trace nonexistent documents in order to document a tax fraud, a clearly fruitless endeavor. To complicate the matter further, small taxpayers' returns are administered by state authorities, even though a federal tax is involved, on the theory that local authorities have a better idea of their clientele. The theory does not work, because local authorities have very strong incentives (economic and political) to keep taxpayers under their control and stand to benefit practically not at all from making a "minor" taxpayer into a "major" one. The problem was partially tackled by the introduction of reforms that disqualify a taxpayer from remaining minor on the basis of some physical (as opposed to financial) criterion such as the size of the premises. This is an important step but may be insufficient as long as these taxpayers remain in the hands of local authorities.

A qualitatively similar situation, but much more serious because of the amounts involved, arises from the procedure used to tax truckers, agriculture, livestock, forestry and fishing, publishers, and some other groups. In the case of these taxpayers, no distinction is made between big and small ones; all of them are allowed to pay on a per kilo or per truck basis or on some similar basis. They do not have to provide their books to the authorities, and they end up paying a minimal tax on their profits, especially big corporations. Furthermore, the present regime makes it simple to relocate profits by transfer pricing to relocate profits within the country. Thus a corporation may pay high haulage fees to a wholly owned trucking subsidiary, whose tax payments would depend only on the number of trucks operated, not on their profitability. Considerable political resistance has frustrated the efforts by tax authorities to eliminate this situation. The only significant achievement to date in this regard was the elimination of a similar privilege enjoyed by the construction industry.

OTHER TOPICS IN CORPORATE TAXATION. There were many other problems detected in the former legislation on the corporate income tax, and there were some reforms associated with them. I will explain some of the most important.

1. Consolidation of results. Before the reform, large industrial groups were allowed to consolidate results, provided that they met certain requirements of growth, employment, and exports. Consolidation was permitted on the full loss of a subsidiary even with less than 100 percent ownership. The act that permitted this procedure was eliminated, and a new consolidation chapter was written into the law. The new rules demand certain formal accounting and legal conditions but do not require firms to meet economic targets in order to be allowed to consolidate. As a result, any firms that form a group, large or small, and not only the biggest industrial groups in Mexico, will be allowed to consolidate. Furthermore, consolidation can be performed only on a pro rata ownership basis, so that the unjustified subsidy implicit in the former procedure is eliminated.

2. Subsidies. Investment, export, and employment subsidies have never amounted to more than a small fraction of tax collections. Nevertheless, they have attained an important proportion of the investment of some activities. Cement firms, for instance, had their capital goods practically free as a result of the cumulative effects of diverse subsidies. There were also subsidies on the price of energy inputs for firms established in selected seaports to be developed. These subsidiaries were capitalized into the price of land in these areas. Considerable confusion entered the design and administration of subsidies, depending on the influence of particular interest groups, on the interest of the government in developing particular industries or regions, and on the preferences of some bureaucrats.

The major portion of this chaotic structure was eliminated by reforms introduced by the administration that took office in December 1982. New investment incentives were introduced to last only twelve months in order to induce firms to invest during an economically depressed year. Of new investment, 50 percent could be expensed if made outside the congested urban areas; the rest would be depreciated according to the depreciation patterns established by the law (which were revised to approximate as closely as possible economic depreciation).

The few remaining subsidies from the previous scheme were made cumulative to income, and capital was made depreciable only insofar as it had not been subsidized. The new approach is self-administered, and as such it eliminates the considerable administrative expense of the former, which made it accessible mainly to large corporations.

INDIRECT TAXES. The public finance literature has recently begun to favor consumption over income as a tax base. Economic efficiency, horizontal equity, and lifetime fairness are all better achieved if consumption is used as the taxable base. Here again, however, the international context of a developing country comes into play; only partial steps toward consumption as a tax base are feasible as long as developed countries tax income. Take, for instance, the corporate income tax. Developing countries are usually net capital importers, and their corporate income taxes are typically creditable by the treasuries of the countries where the direct investment originates. In such a case, basing the corporate income tax on consumption, allowing for instance the full expensing of investments, would merely transfer tax revenues to foreign treasuries, with no economic advantage to the developing country (see chapter 23 for a discussion of the taxation of foreign investment).

Income taxation of individuals, on the other hand, could be adapted to transform it into the equivalent of a consumption tax. This could be done by allowing individual taxpayers to deduct from their taxable income deposits made into special accounts. The interest on these accounts would not be taxable, and all withdrawals would be fully cumulative to income. If there are inflationary expectations, however, this scheme can work only if the tax schedule is indexed, a step Mexico has not been willing to make. With a nonindexed schedule, individuals will fear ending up with a higher marginal tax rate when withdrawing their deposits, even when their real earned income is no higher than when the saving was first made. With all these complications surrounding the taxation of individual or family consumption, the one area of taxation where progress toward consumption-based taxes is viable in developing countries is perhaps the value-added tax.

VALUE-ADDED TAX. Other economic arguments in addition to those presented above were used to buttress the proposal for a value-added tax in Mexico. Mexico's indirect tax structure had been based on a national turnover tax established at the end of the 1940s and on many federal and state excises.

The federal turnover tax had the well-known defect of encouraging vertical integration and thus favored large firms. Furthermore, it was impossible to know the exact amount of tax to give back to exporters. Agriculture and other primary exporting activities were discriminated against because their exemption from the turnover sales tax made it impossible to calculate the tax built into their costs, and these activities were therefore not entitled to a drawback. Finally, the turnover tax taxed investment, whereas a consumption-based VAT does not.

In addition to the economic arguments that I presented above, which are convincing to economists but insufficient for politicians, VAT was introduced in Mexico to streamline indirect taxation and to reinforce taxpayer compliance. More than 30 federal excise taxes and more than 300 state taxes were eliminated when VAT was introduced. Tax administration was thus considerably simplified (though VAT is collected by the states), helping tax administrators concentrate on one single broad-based tax, with fewer rates and exemptions.

The interlocking effect of VAT was the other practical ingredient of the new system. Under the former multilayered turnover tax, the information provided by an intermediate firm could not be used to check on compliance by the firm that made purchases from it. In contrast, VAT is deductible by the purchaser, so that a whole chain of linkages in intermediate transactions is created, which provides a self-controlling system if final sales reporting is well enforced. Under the old taxes, every sale, intermediate or final, had to be controlled. The fact that VAT is applied to imports is another element that contributes strongly to reduced evasion. If there are tax evaders along the economic chain, taxation at the border means that importers now have cause to believe that they may be caught, and the new system will at least provide a tax collection unavailable under the old system, which did not tax imports.

A peculiarity of the Mexican VAT is the way primary activities are treated (agriculture, forestry, livestock raising, and fishing). As in many other countries, they are exempt. Unlike most other approaches to this exemption, however, Mexico's does achieve a practically zero VAT, making unnecessary the drawback of the tax contained in firms' inputs in the case of firms that process the primary products. This clean zero rate also eliminates any discriminatory tax situation previously endured by these sectors. The new system is quite simple. It zero rates producers of the main inputs specific to these activities. Producers of seeds, farm machinery, fishing boats, and nets, for instance, are treated like exporters: they do not pay the tax and get back any tax they paid on their purchases. The tax on any purchase of inputs not specific to these activities, such as the purchase of a truck by a farmer, can also be claimed by the farmer.

Another characteristic that distinguished the new system from other VAT conventions is the period established for the payment of VAT due to exporters, investing firms, and zero-rated producers. Firms may of course offset the tax they paid on their inputs against other monthly VAT obligation, but any excess of credits over debits must be compensated in cash by the government the month following the firm's tax return.

One of the main problems when introducing VAT was defining its scope, its rates, its exemptions, and as a consequence its expected yields. The fact that it was to replace so many federal and local taxes complicated the calculation of an equal-yield set of rates. A rather dated input-output matrix was used for this purpose as well as evasion-tinged data and census information. Allowing for a few exemptions, the estimated uniform tax was calculated at about 13 percent. There were heated discussions with representatives of the private sector who claimed that the equivalent rate was 10 percent. This rate was finally adopted as a result of the considerable political opposition created by the imminence of the new tax, which was introduced in an inflationary environment.

The revenue effects of VAT on tax evasion were such that indirect taxes maintained the same proportion to GDP the year the VAT was introduced, but corporate income tax collections increased sharply, perhaps reflecting the better compliance generated by the mechanics of VAT.

Nevertheless, political opposition and discontent prevailed after the introduction of VAT. Because continuing inflation was popularly attributed to the new tax, with some distinguished economists as well as the general populace taking this view, VAT was substantially revised with the adoption of a zero rate on all food. As a result, indirect taxes became a slightly lower porportion of GDP. The rate structure was later substantially altered in order to reduce the budget deficit incurred in 1982. The new rates were 6 percent for most food, a 15 percent basic rate, and a 20 percent luxury rate. Those covered by this last category, for the reasons given at the beginning of the paper, are mostly services like fees paid to yacht clubs and such.

LOCAL TAX COORDINATION. Federal tax policy and state taxes are closely related. To prevent excessive multilevel taxation, the federal Constitution and the Value Added Tax Act limit the types of taxes that states and municipalities may impose. There are three distinct periods in federal-state tax relationships. The first ended in 1973 when the federal government raised the nationwide turnover tax from 1.8 percent to 4 percent. The establishment of the new federal rate in 1973 was combined with an offer: those states that eliminated their turnover taxes (at a rate of about 1.2 percent on the average) would share in approximately one-half of the revenues that originated locally. Naturally, no one could refuse this offer, and national tax harmonization was born.

The states also shared in various percentages of the principal federal excises, but in this case tax administration remained with the federal government, whereas the federal turnover tax was administered by the states, thus allowing them something more than just revenue sharing.

The introduction of VAT posed an entirely different situation, because the geographic distribution of value-added tax collections would not be the same as the distribution of the turnover tax. In particular, revenue was going to be even more concentrated in the industrial states. A partial solution to this problem was to make the VAT a local tax, but doing so would have implied setting up interstate borders, an unpalatable approach if a free interstate flow of goods and services is desired.

The solution adopted was imaginative: the share going to the states as a percentage of federal tax revenues was calculated for the three years immediately preceding the new system. The resulting coefficient was slightly above 12 percent, which was upped to 13 percent to make the new system more appetizing to the states. Thus, 13 percent of total federal revenues was to be distributed to the states starting the year that the VAT was introduced. The new coefficient was doubly attractive because until then, because of a lower income elasticity on those taxes in which states participated, the take of the states had been falling when measured as a proportion of federal revenues.

The Federal Participation Fund had been defined, but there was still the problem of how to apportion it to the individual states while at the same time maintaining an incentive for them to administer the new tax efficiently. To this end a formula was devised to calculate the share of each state in period $(t + 1)$ on the basis of the following number. If α_i = share of the state in period $(t - 1)$ times federal taxes geographically identifiable to state i in t, divided by the same concept in $(t - 1)$, the share going to each state will be $\alpha_i / \Sigma \alpha_i$. The formula is intended to deal with various problems simultaneously:

1. It provides stability and respects the initial status quo because the coefficient in $(t + 1)$ depends to a large extent on its value in $(t - 1)$.

2. It provides an incentive to administer VAT, because the main content of the concept "federal taxes transferable to the state" is VAT collected by the state.

3. It reflects the differential growth pattern that may occur in the future among the states, because the other element in "federal taxes geographically identifiable to state i" are the excises collected by the federal government in each state.

In practice the mechanism of the formula turned out to be flawed. A state that believes its percentage rate of increase in the "federal taxes geographically identifiable to it" will be below the national average rate of increase has a strong incentive not to provide the documentation on the VAT collected within its boundaries. Only a few states need to behave in such a manner before the system is disrupted; to succeed, the system needs the simultaneous cooperation of everybody.

The information problems created by the behavior of the states have produced a rigid application of the shares in the years following the introduction of the new coordination procedures. One of the consequences of this state of affairs is that some states have diminished their interest in a good administration of the tax, and the compliance of taxpayers domiciled in those states has been gradually eroding. Also as a consequence, states that for economic and fiscal reasons should be getting a larger tax share have had their relative standing frozen for a few years. The problem may not be solved until a formula for dividing up the FPF is found that does not pit states against each other; the formula must be one that does not generate a pie that must be divided so that somebody's gain is someone else's loss.

Some Broad Results of the Tax Reform

The cumulative effects of the yearly tax changes produce a major reform whose consequences can be seen in some broad tax figures.

Despite yearly adjustments in the personal income tax schedule compensating for inflation, for instance, the distribution of collections per income bracket evolved in the manner described in table 12-1.

Before 1979, the year the tax reform began to take effect, collections were concentrated in the one-to-five minimum-wages bracket. As the tax reform started to seep in, this bracket went from 58 percent of labor income tax collections to only 28 percent, whereas the highest bracket went from a mere 8 percent of the total to 25 percent. The following tables contain aggregated information that shows other structural changes brought about by the recent reform.

The classification of taxes paid by capital and labor does not show how equitable the distribution of the tax burden is. Anyone who takes some care to inspect the composition of income in family cross-section data knows that there is no merit to class classifications, that is, those describing the poor as getting wages, and the rich, rents, interest, and profits. The class distinction does not even hold empirically as a pattern showing that relative capital income rises as income increases. Table 12-2 is shown for another reason. As table 12-1 indicated, before the tax reform the lower income brackets contributed the greater portion of the labor income tax. Table 12-2 shows that, while this was occurring, major corporations, the primary contributors to capital-based collections, until 1978 were contributing a declining share of

Table 12-1. *Tax Collections, by Labor Income Bracket*
(percent)

Bracket[a]	1977	1978	1979	1980	1981
1	0	0	0	0	0
1–5	58	57	40	37	28
5–10	20	19	32	29	26
10–15	14	15	19	18	21
More than 15	8	9	9	16	25
Total	100	100	100	100	100

a. Expressed as a multiple of the national average minimum wage.
Source: Gil Díaz (1984).

Table 12-2. *Income Tax Paid by Capital and Labor*
(percent)

Item	1975	1976	1977	1978	1979	1980	1981
Capital	63.7	60.4	57.6	57.2	64.9	68.5	69.2
Labor	36.3	39.6	42.4	42.8	35.1	31.5	30.8

Source: Gil Díaz (1984).

income tax paid. The trend is reversed in 1979 because of inflationary corrections introduced in the personal income tax, which reduced the tax burden mainly on labor income, and as a result of legislative changes that improved the enforcement of the corporation income tax.

Another way of looking at these results is by considering the distribution of net of taxes disposable national income among capital and labor. In table 12-3 we can observe that capital's share falls from 59.15 percent in 1970 to 49.9 percent in 1981 in row 19, mainly as a result of an increase in taxes, because capital's gross of tax share in the net national product falls from 60 percent in 1970 to only 55.74 percent in 1981 (row 8) (see Gil Díaz, 1982).

Finally, table 12-4 shows how the composition of direct versus indirect taxes has evolved, as a result of a lower ratio of indirect taxes and a higher ratio of income taxes, namely corporate, to GDP.

The Incidence of the Mexican Tax System on Family Income

So that income tax paid in 1977 could be inferred, the information was handled at the individual level, through the application of an iterative tax model.[2] There is no income-expenditure survey for 1980. The analysis for this year was done by simulating the new tax code on the gross income figures obtained with the 1977 data. Expenditure taxes were calculated by applying tax rates to reported family expenditures. Other taxes, such as social security contributions, import taxes, and the inflation tax, were also assigned.

The research undertaken to estimate the incidence of the tax system had the following characteristics: the use of a general equilibrium tax incidence model (see Fernandez, 1980); the recognition of the inflationary tax (see the appendix) as an appropriation of real resources by the government with a concomitant distribution per income bracket; the use of permanent income as the variable to measure tax incidence; and the comparison of two years, one before and one after a major tax reform, to evaluate tax incidence per family income bracket.

It would have been desirable also to assess the incidence of government expenditures per income bracket, but time did not permit this. Reyes Heroles (1978) examines the overall incidence of the Mexican tax system, however,

Table 12-3. Capital-Labor Income after Taxes, 1970–81
(millions of pesos at 1960 prices)

Item	1970	1971	1972	1973	1974	1975	1976	1977	1978	1979	1980	1981
1. GDP	296,530	306,712	329,030	354,057	374,977	390,632	398,572	411,575	441,606	476,905	522,300	561,400
2. Depreciation	20,333	21,673	23,381	24,926	26,707	30,401	33,908	38,687	41,606	45,961	50,347	54,116
3. Indirect taxes	14,731	15,881	18,059	23,041	25,955	29,710	30,411	31,092	32,825	34,788	38,099	40,951
4. Net national product [1 − (2 + 3)]	261,466	269,158	287,590	306,090	322,315	330,521	334,255	341,796	367,175	396,146	433,854	466,333
5. Gross payments to labor minus indirect taxes	104,637	110,908	124,396	130,638	137,370	149,917	163,396	161,640	168,041	175,315	192,003	206,377
6. Share of labor in net national product (5 ÷ 4) (percent)	40.02	41.20	43.25	42.70	42.62	45.36	48.88	47.29	45.77	44.26	44.26	44.26
7. Gross payments to capital minus indirect taxes	156,829	158,249	163,194	175,452	184,944	180,604	170,857	180,156	199,134	220,831	241,851	259,956
8. Share of capital in net national product (7 ÷ 4) (percent)	59.98	58.80	56.75	57.30	57.38	54.64	51.12	52.71	54.23	55.74	55.74	55.74
9. Direct taxes	13,047	13,852	15,834	17,315	19,881	24,376	26,192	30,363	35,650	39,769	59,315	68,744
10. Social security	4,954	5,393	7,396	8,473	9,685	10,653	11,507	11,527	12,029	12,830	14,881	15,903

11. National disposable income [4 − (9 + 10)]	243,465	249,913	264,360	280,302	292,749	295,492	296,554	299,906	319,496	343,547	359,658	381,686
12. Direct taxes paid by labor	4,000	4,491	5,080	5,507	6,184	7,687	9,123	10,364	12,380	11,197	11,914	12,092
13. Social security payments by labor	1,189	1,294	1,578	1,624	1,882	2,071	2,246	2,223	2,309	2,464	2,861	2,991
14. Net payments to labor [5 − (12 + 13)]	99,448	105,123	117,738	123,507	129,304	140,159	152,027	149,053	153,352	161,654	177,228	191,294
15. Net share of labor income in disposable income (14 ÷ 11) (percent)	40.85	42.06	44.54	44.06	44.17	47.43	51.26	49.70	48.00	47.05	49.28	50.12
16. Direct taxes paid by capital	9,047	9,361	10,754	11,818	13,697	16,689	17,069	19,999	23,270	28,572	47,401	56,652
17. Social security payments by firms	3,765	4,099	5,818	6,849	7,803	8,582	9,261	9,304	9,720	10,366	12,020	12,912
18. Net payments to capital [7 − (16 + 17)]	144,017	144,789	146,622	156,795	163,444	155,333	144,527	150,853	166,144	181,893	182,430	190,392
19. Net share of capital income in disposable income (18 ÷ 11) (percent)	59.15	57.93	55.46	55.94	55.83	52.27	48.74	50.30	52.00	52.95	50.72	49.88

Source: Banco de México, National Accounts, 1960–79.

Table 12-4. *Indirect and Direct Taxes as a Percentage of Tax Collections, Excluding Oil Taxes*

Tax	1971	1976	1977	1978	1979	1980	1981
Direct	46.15	46.52	48.49	51.53	50.85	52.42	54.65
Indirect	53.85	53.48	51.51	48.47	49.15	47.58	45.35

Source: Gil Díaz (1984).

and shows the incidence per family income level of government expenditures in 1968. For that year they proved to be progressive, that is, to be a greater proportion of lower incomes, declining as income increases. The main explanation for this pattern lies in government expenditures on primary and secondary education and on health services. Because the structure of government expenditures has changed in the direction of more and expanded social services, this pattern should still hold.

In describing the results it will be useful to comment on the incidence of taxes without considering the inflationary tax and then to add the latter's contribution. Table 12-5 has a subtotal, which shows the percentage of taxes

Table 12-5. *Tax Incidence across Half Deciles in 1977*
(percent)

Half decile	Excise taxes	Other indirect taxes	Direct taxes	Sub-total	Inflation tax	Total
1	6.18	0.82	2.37	9.37	4.21	13.58
2	6.66	0.63	3.29	10.58	4.21	14.79
3	7.13	0.61	3.54	11.28	2.00	13.28
4	7.06	0.51	4.77	12.34	2.00	14.34
5	7.47	0.62	5.26	13.35	2.25	15.60
6	6.81	0.55	6.48	13.84	2.25	16.09
7	7.13	0.64	7.22	14.99	1.39	16.38
8	7.59	0.94	6.71	15.24	1.39	16.63
9	7.39	0.71	7.65	15.75	2.05	17.80
10	7.25	0.84	6.32	14.41	2.05	16.46
11	7.41	0.75	11.77	19.93	1.51	21.44
12	7.52	0.71	10.74	18.97	1.51	20.48
13	6.99	0.78	15.01	22.78	1.73	24.51
14	7.34	0.85	12.55	20.74	1.73	22.47
15	7.07	0.84	15.59	23.50	1.71	25.21
16	7.37	0.86	14.69	22.92	1.71	24.63
17	7.10	0.96	17.31	25.37	2.64	28.01
18	7.88	1.07	13.74	22.69	2.64	25.33
19	7.79	0.95	14.91	23.65	4.29	27.94
20	6.18	2.68	26.22	35.09	4.29	39.38

Sources: Income Expenditure Survey (Mexico City: Secretariat, Department of the Budget, 1977); Gil Díaz (1984); tables 12-A1, 12-A2, 12-A3, 12-A4.

before the inclusion of the inflation tax and in relation to permanent income. It can be seen that in 1977 taxes go from 9.37 percent of income in the first half decile to 35 percent in the top half decile, although the progression is sometimes uneven because the tax falls slightly when between the ninth and the tenth half decile, and again between the eleventh and the twelfth, the thirteenth and fourteenth, the fifteenth and sixteenth, and the seventeenth and eighteenth. The reason can be found in the column of direct taxes. Excises are basically proportional to income, and the concept that includes other indirect taxes is also fairly proportional, except for the last half decile, where it shows some progressivity.

Import taxes, on the other hand, are negligible in amount and prove to be basically proportional except for the last decile. Excise taxes are the combined result of several small taxes, the general 4 percent turnover sales tax and excises on beer, tobacco, liquor, telephone services, soft drinks, and so on. They turn out to be basically proportional, as mentioned above, so that they represent between 6 percent and 7 percent of permanent income.

The overall effect can be described as progressive. The conclusion is unaltered when the inflationary tax is considered. Because of the initial regressivity of the inflation tax, the system becomes proportional down to the fourth half decile and becomes progressive from then on.

In 1980, the year after the reform, the more important changes are in the individual income tax, which was made more encompassing. The individual income tax is progressive except in the top three half deciles, where the incidence decreases somewhat. The corporation income tax and the social security tax more than compensate for this regressivity, so that the total direct taxes shown in table 12-6 are progressive except for very minor deviations. In all cases, however, the individual income tax in the upper strata is higher in 1980 than in 1977 and lower in the lower income levels. The corporation income tax also shows more progressivity in 1980 and represents a higher percentage of income in the upper income levels. The tax on interest income is practically the same in 1980. The total effect is to make direct taxes more progressive, as can be seen in the Direct taxes column of table 12-6 and smoother than was the case in 1977.

The inflation tax reproduces the U-shaped pattern of 1977 except that its initial regressivity combined with higher inflation makes the whole tax system approximately proportional down to the ninth half decile. Other indirect taxes show basically the same pattern, although their load is lighter, because, as I explained above, indirect taxes as a percentage of GDP are smaller after the reform.

Excise taxes, which include VAT, show in 1980 a definite progressive pattern instead of a proportional one. This is a result of the zero rate on food consumption in the value-added tax, food consumption being a declining share of permanent income as income increases.

Abstracting from the inflation tax, the net effect of the tax reform is a more progressive pattern of taxation, with a smooth transition as well from one half

Table 12-6. *Tax Incidence across Half Deciles in 1980*
(percent)

Half decile	Excise taxes	Other indirect taxes	Direct taxes	Sub-total	Inflation tax	Total
1	4.27	0.93	2.33	7.53	6.58	14.11
2	4.33	0.74	3.07	8.14	6.58	14.72
3	4.76	0.69	3.16	8.61	3.14	11.75
4	5.16	0.58	4.17	9.91	3.14	13.05
5	5.70	0.71	4.43	10.84	3.55	14.39
6	4.78	0.63	5.19	10.60	3.55	14.15
7	5.36	0.72	5.85	11.93	2.19	14.12
8	5.73	1.06	4.82	11.61	2.19	13.80
9	5.47	0.79	5.43	11.69	3.25	14.94
10	5.56	0.96	6.83	13.35	3.25	16.60
11	5.63	0.82	9.33	15.78	2.41	18.19
12	5.92	0.84	12.52	19.28	2.41	21.69
13	5.15	0.93	12.24	18.32	2.77	21.09
14	5.90	0.98	15.24	22.12	2.77	24.89
15	5.51	0.98	14.35	20.84	2.73	23.57
16	5.84	1.03	16.14	23.01	2.73	25.74
17	6.07	1.15	17.83	25.06	4.23	29.29
18	6.61	1.31	17.94	25.86	4.23	30.09
19	6.85	1.19	17.37	25.41	6.84	32.25
20	6.18	1.17	29.80	37.15	6.84	43.99

Sources: Income Expenditure Survey; Gil Díaz (1984); tables 12-A1, 12-A2, 12-A3, 12-A4.

decile to another in 1980 in the eleven lower half deciles (except the sixth and eighth) and, including the inflation tax, consistently higher levels from the twelfth half decile on.

Conclusions

It has been said that "an old tax is the best tax." This is a meaningful statement, because when taxes have been in place for several years, people will have adjusted to them as investors, as savers, and as consumers. After several years after-tax rates of return tend to equalize.

If the after-tax rates of return are equal, however, what do we mean when we say that different economic activities are taxed at different tax rates? On purely economic grounds the meaning is clear, because taxation could be arranged so that taxpayers with a smaller relative tax could expand and taxpayers with a higher relative tax would contract. The picture is not so neat when distributional considerations enter, however, because two different groups earning the same rate of return on their investments are going to be treated differently if tax rates are equalized. There is usually no practical way to compensate the losers.

Moreover, the potential loser is frequently an identifiable group with political presence, and the winners are frequently diffused over the economy, so that the political aspects of a tax reform are enormously complicated.

On the other hand, revenue needs, grave distortions on resource allocation, and some glaring inequities in the tax system make it sometimes politically imperative to reform taxes even though there is little room for the fine engineering frequently assumed in the literature. The proposals and changes that will be made will knowingly have a distributional consequence for which it is impossible to compensate. This will always remain a troublesome ethical issue for tax reform, and it appears when the parties affected understandably strive to prevent the proposed changes from taking place.

Obviously, the degree to which the opposition from some groups was successful was directly related to their political power. In some cases, when low taxes were combined with legal loopholes, however, there was room for tacit agreements to make changes that reduced or controlled avenues for tax evasion, even when powerful groups were involved. At this level of generality it should be added that, although a political commitment for tax reform offers many opportunities, it also creates many dangers, because it opens the door for pressure groups that may succeed in bringing about undesirable legislative changes.

Nevertheless, and accepting the possibility that I am a biased judge, I believe that the reform can be said to have attained some of its objectives. These can be summarized as eliminating some inequities, reducing distortions, closing loopholes, adjusting the tax system for inflation, simplifying it, broadening its coverage, and increasing revenue sharing with the states. In some cases progress may not have been totally satisfactory, but it was important. Even then, however, as a national soccer team manager in Mexico used to say, failures or partial failures were extremely educational.

The most difficult part of the reform was obtaining approval for the proposals. This process involved Congress, representatives of many diverse interest and pressure groups, and of course other members of the executive branch. Not least among the factors that contributed to the successful implementation of difficult and delicate structural changes was the unusual combination of political skills and sound economic training in the person of the secretary of the treasury, who was supported by an undersecretary who was a capable negotiator, thoroughly convinced of the importance of his contribution.

I shall now review some accomplishments and pending matters briefly. Substantial progress was made in inflation adjustments, although a full inflationary correction of the income tax is still pending. The reforms performed on excise taxes, which substituted ad valorem taxes for specific excise taxes, created problems. The reform meant to protect excise tax revenue from inflation. In this respect the reform was immensely successful, especially considering the price changes that the Mexican economy had undergone in 1982, 1983, and 1984. The former system would have lagged considerably at least in the first year. On the other hand, however, ad valorem taxes created possibilities for evasion. Firms were taxed at the factory level and could and did set up subsidiaries to buy at low prices from the factory. This problem was tackled by carrying the ad valorem tax until the last stage prior to the sale to the consumer. A considerable simplification of indirect taxation, the effective zero rating of agricultural exports, and the fact that the value-added tax is a consumption-based tax were all changes conducive to a less distortive tax system in terms of resource allocation and were more effective in terms of taxpayers' compliance. In the pursuit of efficiency the reforms on the income tax, which was adjusted for inflation, also rank high, as well as the reforms on personal income deductions and tariff adjustments that contributed to reduce work disincentives without a considerable fall in revenue. There is of course room for improvement in the new tax structure, but it could reasonably be asserted that there were some achievements, to the extent that if taxes are made less disruptive, they make a contribution. Some progress can be cited as well in the direction of reducing some gross inequities and achieving somewhat more progressivity. It must be emphasized, however, that we should not expect too much from taxes except that they should not interfere too much. A given source of revenue can be obtained in a very destructive way or in a least distortive way, so the highest aspiration of a tax system is the modest goal of not interfering too much in resource allocation while exacting a fair contribution from all members of society.

Appendix: Estimates of the Incidence of the Inflationary Tax

The inflationary tax collected by the government can be obtained by multiplying the government's debt by the difference between the real interest rate it would pay on its domestic debt in a noninflationary situation and the real interest rate it currently pays for the stock of the debt.

For banknotes and coins in circulation and noninterest deposits at Banco de México, the difference in real interest rates is simply the inflation rate. For interest deposits and government securities in the current accounts of commercial banks with the Banco de México, it was estimated that the real interest rate paid was 3.5 percent, that is, the average real yield offered by the banking system throughout the 1960s, when there was price stability.

Table 12-A1 shows the methodology used to estimate the inflationary tax at an aggregated level for 1977 and 1980. The inflationary tax obtained by the government on its interest and non-interest-bearing internal debt was distributed among deciles of families ordered by their income level, in proportion to their holdings of bank deposits and money supply. Family holdings of these assets were both direct and indirect. Indirect assets came from imputing the firm's holdings of money and bank deposits to its owners.

The distributions of money supply and bank deposits by deciles of families were estimated as follows. First, data from Cervantes (1982) were used to

Table 12-A1. *An Estimate of the Inflationary Tax Collected by the Federal Government*

Item	1977	1980
1. Bank notes and coins in the hands of individuals and banks, plus noninterest deposits held by Banco de México, individuals, and banks (millions of pesos)[a]	86,130.7	162,660.7
2. Interest deposits and government securities in the bank's current account at Banco de México (millions of pesos)[a]	128,193.9	323,847.0
3. December-to-December growth of the consumer price index (percent)	10.7	29.8
4. Implicit yield on the reserve requirement (2) (percent)	11.3	17.8
5. Inflationary tax rate on (2) = 3.5 − [(4) − (3)]/[1 + (3)] (percent)	11.3	12.7
6. Incidence of the inflationary tax in proportion to the holdings of:		
Money supply, (1) × (3) (millions of pesos)	17,829.1	48,472.8
Deposits with banks, (2) × (4) (millions of pesos)	14,485.9	41,128.6

a. Balance at the beginning of the period.
Source: Banco de México.

obtain an estimate of the distribution of the money supply and bank deposits between families and firms, at an aggregated level, in 1981. The assumptions and results of this estimation appear in table 12-A2. Maintaining the structure of 1981, absolute figures for the distribution of the money supply and bank deposits were obtained for 1977 at an aggregate level.

The proportion (from Cervantes 1982) of direct family holdings of money and bank deposits to family income by decile, were multiplied by the permanent income estimates of Gil Díaz (1984) to obtain family direct holdings of these assets. The income figures by family decile used in this step match with national accounts data. The family holdings of the money supply and bank deposits estimated according to table 12-A2 were larger than the estimate just described. The difference was allocated among the deciles in such a way that the original proportions remained unchanged.

Table 12-A2. *Distribution of Assets between Families and Firms in Mexico, 1981*
(percent)

Item	Families	Firms
Nondemand deposits	90.6	9.4
Money supply[a]	57.5	42.5
Currency	60.0	40.0
Demand	55.4	44.6

a. Average when we use as weights the share of currency and demand deposits in the money supply; these are 46 percent and 54 percent, respectively.
Sources: Rows 1 and 4: Cervantes (1982); row 2: Banco de México; row 3: assumed figures.

Table 12-A3. *Original Data Used to Obtain the Distribution of the Inflationary Tax in 1977*
(percent)

Family decile	Income (millions of pesos)[a]	Money supply (as percentage of income)[b]	Bank deposits (as percentage of income)	Share holdings (as percentage of total)
1	6,227	22.3	1.4	0.005
2	15,091	9.0	1.9	0.251
3	22,993	10.2	3.5	0.016
4	32,364	6.4	2.0	0.000
5	43,746	7.2	6.2	0.148
6	67,728	4.8	5.0	0.507
7	91,088	3.8	8.2	0.883
8	124,330	4.5	6.2	2.422
9	172,773	5.0	13.5	3.205
10	479,748	5.3	13.9	92.563

a. Income is defined as permanent income: see Gil Díaz (1984, p. 72).

b. The percentages shown in this column for the first percentile may appear strange. Those are the numbers supplied by the income-expenditure survey, however, and they are grossly consistent with the income-inelastic estimate for the demand for money in Mexico, in García Bullé (1985).

Source: Cervantes (1982).

Table 12-A4. *Distribution of the Money Supply and Bank Deposits, by Family Deciles, 1977*
(percent)

Family decile	Money supply	Bank deposits
1	1.41	0.07
2	1.48	0.25
3	2.39	0.64
4	2.10	0.52
5	3.26	2.18
6	3.51	2.75
7	3.89	6.10
8	6.70	6.45
9	10.12	18.99
10	65.13	62.05
Total	100.00	100.00

Note: The figures include direct holdings of families and holdings of firms imputed to their owners.

Source: Cervantes (1982).

Finally, the aggregated estimates of the holdings of the money supply and bank deposits by firms were imputed to families, using the distribution of share holdings by family decile, also taken from Cervantes (1982).

The original data used in this step appear in table 12-A3. The final distributions of direct and indirect holdings of money supply and bank deposits are shown in table 12-A4. These distributions were used to assign by decile groups the inflationary tax determined at an aggregate level. The distributions were calculated from balances at the beginning of 1977 and were applied to both 1977 and 1980. The inflation tax collected expressed as a percent of income for these years appears in tables 12-5 and 12-6 in the text.

Because the original incidence study on which the tables in the text are based aggregated the data in twenty half deciles, the inflation tax estimates by decile are broken down on the assumption that the tax of each half decile as a percentage of income is the same. No information was available to do otherwise.

Notes

1. In one form of this particular sort of evasion, smart-looking female employees of some of the large U.S. department stores flew to Mexico City wearing a fur coat. They could be back in Houston or Dallas the same day. The costs involved were a fraction of the tax saved. There is an old Spanish saying: "Lima beans are cooked everywhere." The following news item from Vienna's English newspaper offers another example. "Austrian furriers are almost equally angry at the federal government and at those who buy their minks and sables abroad. According to national guildmaster Karl Szilagyi, furs are smuggled into Austria in the order of 45 million Austrian Schillings every year. Furriers, however, regard the introduction of the luxury tax on furs in 1978 as their main source of complaint. By levying a 30 per cent duty on their products sales have been slow. Szilagyi also criticized the Ministry of Finance for having lost more revenue than it gains through too high a VAT on furs" (*Danube Weekly*, 1984, bus. sec., p. 8).

2. This section presents a revision of Gil Díaz (1984) made on the basis of new information contained in the 1977 Income Expenditure Survey of the Secretaría de Programación y Presupuesto.

PART 4

The Theory of
Agricultural Taxation

THE SIMPLE THEORY set out in chapter 2 and applied in part 3 made assumptions that gave a very simple model of tax incidence—all commodity taxes were on final consumption goods and shifted forward, so that an increase in a particular commodity tax led to an equal increase in the tax-inclusive price facing consumers. In chapter 3 it was argued that, although this model of incidence is legitimate (provided that production takes place under competitive constant returns and only final goods are taxed), it does not apply to more general models. In chapter 11 of part 3 the analysis was extended to include input taxes for an economy satisfying the conditions of the nonsubstitution theorem—that is, conditions that include, in addition to constant returns, no joint products and only one nonproduced factor. Although this may be a reasonable approximation for the manufacturing sector, it is clearly unsatisfactory for agriculture, which uses both land and labor to produce outputs, nor is it possible to fall back on the standard Diamond-Mirrlees tax model described in chapter 3, which requires rents to be completely taxed away. Land taxes and rent taxes are notable by their absence or their minimal level. Furthermore, farmers producing food crops cannot readily be confronted with different prices for their production and consumption.

Part 4 is therefore intended to extend the theory to deal with the agricultural sector. Not only is this a dominant sector in many developing countries, it also exhibits very clearly two of the key features that distinguish tax theory for developing countries from the standard model. The first feature is that there are limitations on the range of tax instruments available. As a result it may be desirable to tax (or to subsidize) inputs. The second is that agricultural taxes have a sector-specific impact on factors, especially labor. The incidence of sector-specific taxes on mobile factors is quite different from that of universal taxes, or taxes on immobile factors, and will depend on the way the factor (labor) markets operate.

The first chapter of part 4 provides an extensive introduction to agricultural taxation and takes up these themes in more detail. It shows the importance of modeling supply responses and discusses the empirical evidence on the magnitude of agricultural supply elasticities. This evidence should be borne in mind in connection with the more theoretical chapters of this part. Chapter 13 also reviews the debate on the desirability of taxing agriculture heavily and the instruments available for agricultural taxation, including land taxes. The chapter concludes with a list of topics that require further research and forewarns the reader of some of the issues that remain to be resolved.

Atkinson's chapter 14 presents a simple model of the agricultural sector in isolation in which to explore the tradeoff between equity and efficiency. The emphasis is on deriving illustrative numerical results from a model that is algebraically easy to manipulate to show how a person's views on tax rates will depend on various features of the model. As such it is useful for illustrating arguments and as an example of the kinds of models that are needed for the agricultural sector. It is to be hoped that this chapter will encourage economists to construct other models as an aid to thinking about these complex issues. Atkinson also illustrates themes that have been discussed elsewhere in the book—the equivalence between apparently different tax structures (discussed in chapters 2, 3, and 7), the importance in this case of a lump-sum tax or subsidy (see chapters 2, 4, and 7), and the special features of the linear expenditure system (see chapter 4). As with the earlier part, the emphasis is on developing a feel for the factors that should influence the tax structure and its progressivity.

Chapter 15 by Heady and Mitra explores the design of optimal taxes in a dual economy in which all individuals are identical. This is a case for which modified single-person Ramsey rules work, and it is therefore possible to see how these are modified by constraints on the set of tax instruments available to the government and by the presence of traditional labor market dualism. Heady and Mitra derive analytical solutions and solve the model numerically so that the sensitivity of the tax rates to various assumptions may be explicitly studied. In particular, the chapter explores the relationships between the tax structure and the level of revenue that the government needs to collect and the consequences of migration in a model in which the social optimum requires utility levels to differ in the two sectors. Chapter 15 considers the impact on the optimum tax structure of large (fivefold) changes in the price of imported oil.

As with the previous chapter, the emphasis is on tax design rather than on tax reform and as such is the appropriate framework within which to ask the more fundamental questions of agricultural taxation. The numerical results obviously depend on the functional forms and parameters chosen, and so it is premature to draw strong conclusions, though a number of results are interesting enough to warrant further investigations in other models. Thus the optimal ad valorem tax rates appear remarkably insensitive to oil price changes; the main problem in adjusting to oil shocks thus seems to be demand management and the adjustment of real wages rather than structural tax reform. Although the tax structure is very sensitive to constraints on the set of feasible instruments, the loss of utility attributable to those constraints is small. Put another way, quite large changes in the tax system made possible by changes in the set of taxes available make very little difference to individual welfare. In large part the reason is that individuals are assumed to be identical.

Chapter 16 by Sah and Stiglitz deals with issues of tax design and tax reform in a fully specified general equilibrium dual-economy model in which urban and rural consumers may confront different prices for agricultural outputs. The institutional arrangement required is a marketing board or government purchasing agency with controls on direct sales from the rural to urban sectors. Whether this arrangement is feasible will depend on the nature of the crop, the type of transport system employed, the geographical separation of town and country, and the extent of control over the transport of the crop. If it is not possible to price discriminate between the sectors, then the government loses a potential tax instrument and will have to worry about the distortionary effects of agricultural taxes on urban consumers as well as on rural consumers. It should also be recognized that, even if it is administratively feasible to price discriminate, the coercive powers given to the marketing board officials over the transport of crops may have unintended and adverse effects.

The model was developed with the Korean economy in mind and thus provides a conceptual framework for the empirical chapters of part 5. It is worth noting that it is feasible to price discriminate in Korea, mainly because urban prices are, if anything, lower than rural prices, and hence transport costs prevent arbitrage. The converse and more typical case would be more difficult to administer. Heady and Mitra explore the consequences of not being able to price discriminate between the sectors, which, they show, can significantly affect the choice of agricultural tax rates.

The chapter by Sah and Stiglitz is in the spirit of the earlier parts of this book in deriving conditions for identifying desirable tax reforms and showing how these also characterize the optimal tax system. It does so within a fully specified dual economy, like that of Heady and Mitra, but includes the distributional issues that were the main concern of Atkinson. It is, however, no longer possible (without substantial extra effort) to derive numerical results. The emphasis is thus on deriving formulas and identifying the parameters needed for the analysis of tax reform. These show precisely how the distributional effects, mediated not only through the direct production and consumption impacts but also through wage changes in the labor market, affect the desirability of raising or lowering specific prices.

One section in the chapter shows how it is possible to make Pareto-improving tax reforms under certain conditions—that is, tax reforms that are revenue neutral but that, by raising one tax and lowering another, make all groups of rural inhabitants better off (although in practice heterogeneity within groups would usually make it impossible to make each individual no worse off). Three conditions need to be satisfied to identify such taxes. First, the impact of the change on the labor market must be negligible (otherwise net sellers and buyers of labor cannot both be made better off). Second, the taxes to be varied must be confined to "production goods," that is, to productive inputs or crops that are not consumed in rural areas (crops such as rubber, fibers, coffee, cocoa, and tea but not sugar, which is also locally consumed). Finally, and equally important, all producers must have equal access to the same constant-returns technology (including land as an input) and must face the same prices. If they do, then they would all choose the same pattern of inputs and outputs per unit of land, and it is in principle simple to check to see if this is the case. If, on the other hand, poorer farmers use fewer hours of tractor service or less fertilizer per hectare than rich farmers, then taxes on tractor services may have additional redistributive effects not captured by these Pareto-improving tax rules.

If, however, the conditions of the argument were to apply, then desirable tax reforms could be derived using relatively little information, of the sort that can be derived from estimates of agricultural production or from profit functions. As Deaton shows in chapter 4, this kind of information can be obtained from a variety of survey and technological sources (such as linear programming models of farm production).

Sah and Stiglitz also ask whether some production goods (for example, tractors) should be taxed while other similar goods (in this case inputs, for example, fertilizer) are subsidized. On the same strong assumption that all farmers have identical production plans and use all inputs in the same proportions, and with the additional strong assumption that the prices of production goods have negligible cross-price effects on the quantities of other inputs and outputs, Sah and Stiglitz show that all production goods in a similar category should be either taxed or subsidized but not both, and the optimal tax rates are then inversely proportional to their own-price elasticities. It remains an open question whether the conditions required for this result ever hold, but the idea suggests a clear program for collecting information. First, define agro-economic zones in which production technologies are reasonably uniform. Then check to see whether there are any systematic differences in inputs or outputs per hectare that correlate with welfare weights. If not, then the conditions of the theorem apply, and it is possible to identify improving reforms. If, in addition, cross-price elasticities are negligible, then optimal taxes can easily be computed; if not, then Sah and Stiglitz provide Ramsey-like expressions for the optimal tax rates on production goods that do not depend on distributional considerations and hence are fairly straightforward to calculate. Unfortunately, these simple rules do not apply to "consumption goods," of which the most important will be cereals, and for these, distributional considerations will obviously be important.

Having calculated the optimal tax rates, the next step is to check whether these computed rates differ between agro-economic zones and, if so, whether the differences are large enough to induce arbitrage. If not, then a desirable set of taxes has been identified.

If, on the other hand, inputs or outputs do differ significantly by farm size (and hence by income level and welfare weight), then there may be market failure or imperfections that it would be socially desirable to remove. If any of these steps fails, then the problem of calculating optimal tax rates becomes more difficult, but we still have the less ambitious task of identifying desirable directions of tax reform—a theme that is taken up in part 5.

13

Agricultural Taxation: The Main Issues

David Newbery

AN OBVIOUS DIFFERENCE between rich countries and poor countries is the proportion of the labor force employed in agriculture. Seventy percent of the labor force is engaged in agriculture in low-income developing countries, compared with 6 percent in industrial market economies (World Bank, 1983, and chapter 7 of this book). Development often consists in transferring labor from relatively low-productivity agriculture to the higher-productivity industrial and service sectors, thereby also ultimately raising the productivity of the remaining agricultural workers. The time has come to inquire into the significance for tax analysis of the prominent position of agriculture and to pursue some of the questions raised in chapter 7.

The first section starts by asking why agriculture raises issues for tax analysis that are not covered in the simple model of chapter 2. The answer is that there are limits on the range of tax instruments available and on their coverage, which will affect their incidence. Below I examine the incidence of taxes on agriculture and the incidence of taxes on nontraded agricultural goods on the urban sector. These issues of incidence then allow us to examine the debate on the appropriate level of agricultural taxation and the related issue of setting the terms of trade between agricultural and nonagricultural goods. The subsequent discussion deals with the constraints limiting the availability of tax instruments and the extent to which they can be circumvented by using alternative feasible taxes, with attention in conclusion to problems that require further research.

The Applicability of the Standard Model

It is useful to take the Diamond and Mirrlees (1971) model of optimal commodity taxation (set forth in chapters 2 and 3) as a starting point. The key features of that model were that all goods can be taxed, so that producers and

I am grateful to Pradeep Mitra and Nicholas Stern for their helpful comments.

consumers can be confronted with different prices, and either production takes place under constant returns to scale, so that there are no profits, or such profits as exist are taxed 100 percent (or the profitable sectors are publicly owned). The main results of the model are that there should be no distortionary taxes on production, so that production is efficient, and that the formulas for the optimal commodity taxes are identical to those that would be obtained if producer prices were fixed. The combination of the two results means that (optimal) commodity taxes can be treated as having very simple incidence: they are shifted forward to fall entirely on the consumer.

Agriculture, particularly in developing countries, does not fit into this model for two reasons. First, agricultural production requires land, which is in inelastic supply and receives profits, or rents. These rents cannot be taxed away completely (and there is some question as to whether they can be taxed at all, as we shall see), nor is it realistic in most countries to suppose that all the land could be publicly owned, so that the rents accrued directly to the government. Second, it is not practical in most countries to tax all transactions between agricultural producers and rural consumers, particularly where, as in subsistence agriculture, the two groups are often the same.

Either characteristic above (diminishing returns or the inability to tax rural transactions) would imply the desirability of taxing production (by, for example, taxing inputs and taxing different outputs at different rates).

In one important case, however, the Diamond-Mirrlees results retain a limited applicability. If there are no rent taxes at all, then the agricultural sector can be included in the consumer sector rather than in the producer sector. Production efficiency in the modern sector (here defined as the set of firms trading at producer prices) would remain desirable, and the tax rules would depend on the derivatives of the net trades of the agricultural sector rather than the usual derivative of consumption (Diamond and Mirrlees, 1971, p. 25). Heady and Mitra make considerable use of this interpretation in chapter 15, though they extend the model in a number of important directions. Sah and Stiglitz show in chapter 16 that the net trade derivatives will depend both on output elasticities and on consumption elasticities. (If there are fixed-rate rent taxes, then government revenue will also be affected by the changes in rent caused by changes in agricultural prices, and the formulas need to be modified, as shown by Stiglitz and Dasgupta, 1971, or Munk, 1980).

A partial-equilibrium geometric picture may help clarify the argument. Consider the net supply from the rural sector of a food crop (such as rice) that is exported and also consumed by urban consumers. Suppose also that the government can set the urban and rural prices independently—which requires it to be able to prevent untaxed transfers of rice between the rural and urban sectors. In figure 13-1, SS is rural net supply, DD is rural consumption demand, q is the urban price, p is the rural price, and P is the export price. Suppose that all urban consumers are identical, that all rural farmers are identical, that there is no migration, and that there are no income transfers between sectors. Using the techniques described in chapter 11 by Ahmad and Stern, we may write the social marginal cost of raising the urban price, q, holding all other prices constant, as

$$(13\text{-}1) \qquad \lambda^m = \frac{-\partial V/\partial q}{\partial R/\partial q} = \frac{\beta^m X^m}{(\partial/\partial q)[(q-P) X^m (q)]}$$

where X^m is urban food demand, or, ignoring all cross-price effects, as

$$(13\text{-}2) \qquad \lambda^m = \frac{\beta^m}{1 - \left(\dfrac{q-P}{q}\right)\epsilon}$$

where ϵ is the urban price elasticity of demand (as a positive number) and β^m is the social marginal utility of urban (manufacturing sector) income.[1] An analogous formula emerges from raising revenue from farmers by depressing their sales price, p. First consider the indirect utility function of a farmer, holding constant (and suppressing) all prices other than the price of rice, p, which he faces as a consumer and producer:

$$V = V(p, m), \quad m = \pi(p).$$

Here m is lump-sum income, which is the profit or rent from the land used to grow rice, and $\pi(p, A)$ is the (restricted) profit function, giving the imputed rent obtained from land of area A when the price of output is p. (Because land area is constant, A is suppressed.) Differentiate with respect to p, holding other prices constant:

$$(13\text{-}3) \qquad \frac{dV}{dp} = \frac{\partial V}{\partial p} + \frac{\partial V}{\partial m}\frac{d\pi}{dp} = \frac{\partial V}{\partial m}(-x + y)$$

where x is consumption, y is production, and $\partial V/\partial m$ is the marginal utility of income.[2] The welfare impact thus depends on net supply, and there is no need to distinguish formally between producers and consumers. Producers will typically have a positive net supply $s = y - x$; consumers will have a negative net supply $s = -x$. (In figure 13-1, the welfare impact of a small change in price, Δq or Δp, is measured by the change in aggregate consumer or producer surplus, $-X\Delta q$ or $S\Delta p$.) The impact on government revenue is

$$(13\text{-}4) \qquad \frac{\partial R}{\partial p} = \frac{\partial}{\partial p}[(P - p)S(p)] = -S\left(1 - \frac{P-p}{p}\frac{\partial \log S}{\partial \log p}\right)$$

and the social cost of raising revenue by lowering the price is

$$(13\text{-}5) \qquad \lambda^a = -\frac{\partial V^a/\partial p}{\partial R/\partial p} = \frac{\beta^a}{1 - \dfrac{P-p}{p}\eta}$$

where β^a is the social marginal utility of rural (agricultural sector) income and η is the elasticity of net supply. (Similar formulas are given by Sah and Stiglitz in chapter 16.) The analogy between the two formulas 13-2 and 13-5 is readily

Figure 13-1. *Net Supply and Demand for a Traded Food Crop*

apparent. The similarity will carry over to the derivation of optimal tax rules, and if all agents within each sector are identical, the optimal taxes will be characterized by the single-person Ramsey rule: (small) taxes should be such that they reduce compensated demands or compensated net trades by an equal proportional amount, when producer prices are held constant. (See chapters 2, 3, 15, and 16.)[3] Ignoring cross-price effects and distributional considerations, the Ramsey rule argues for heavier taxes (lower producer prices) on agricultural goods whose surplus is more inelastic.

To gain some sense of which goods are likely to be more or less elastically supplied, we may consider the net supply of a crop from rural household h:

$$(13\text{-}6) \qquad s^h(p) = y^h(p) - x^h(p, m^h), \quad m^h = \pi^h(p)$$

where m^h is lump-sum income, which, for a farm that neither sells nor hires labor, is just the rent, π^h. Then

$$(13\text{-}7) \qquad \frac{\partial s^h}{\partial p} = \frac{\partial y^h}{\partial p} - \left(\frac{\partial x^h}{\partial p} + \frac{\partial x^h}{\partial m} \frac{\partial \pi^h}{\partial p} \right)$$

$$= \frac{\partial y^h}{\partial p} - \frac{\partial x^h}{\partial p} \bigg|_{\bar{u}} - (y^h - x^h) \frac{\partial x^h}{\partial m}.$$

If we aggregate across all farmers (but ignore impacts mediated by the labor market), the aggregate supply response will be

$$(13\text{-}8) \qquad \frac{\partial S}{\partial p} = \frac{\partial Y}{\partial p} - \sum_h \left(\frac{\partial x^h}{\partial p} \bigg|_{\bar{u}} + s^h \frac{\partial x^h}{\partial m} \right)$$

and the elasticity of marketed surplus, η, will be

(13-9) $$\eta = \frac{Y}{S}\eta^a + \frac{X}{S}\frac{\Sigma\, x^h \epsilon^{h^*}}{\Sigma\, x^h} - \frac{\Sigma\, b^h s^h}{\Sigma\, s^h}$$

where η^a is the elasticity of food *output*, ϵ^* is the *compensated* price elasticity of food demand (as a positive number), and b is the marginal propensity to spend on food out of income. The compensated elasticities ϵ^{h^*} are unlikely to be as large as 0.2, and the marginal propensity to spend on food, weighted by shares in net supply, might be 0.5 or less. If $S/Y = 0.5$, then the elasticity of marketed surplus would exceed the output elasticity if the output elasticity were greater than 0.3–0.4. The evidence presented below suggests that output elasticities may be this low in poorer developing countries (though they might be higher for the more diverse agriculture often found in higher-income countries). Even if different crops have similar output elasticities, it will not be clear on efficiency grounds whether it is better to tax food or nonfood crops (whose supply elasticity will be the same as the output elasticity) more heavily. On the other hand, crops for which S/Y and b are small will typically have high supply elasticities. Cassava and inferior food grains such as sorghum and millet may fit this description very well.

These tax rules depend sensitively on the assumption that the urban and rural prices can be set independently. Different prices for the same good in two different places will provide a motive for arbitrage, however, unless transport costs make this uneconomical. Thus it is relatively easy for governments to set the urban selling price of food grains *below* the transport-inclusive supply price from the rural sector, because it may be too costly for rural consumers to transport the goods back to their villages rather than buy locally. (There will be no incentive for arbitrage if the urban subsidy relative to the rural purchase price is less than twice the transport cost.) Thus the Korean government can apparently subsidize urban rice relative to the producer price without inducing arbitrage, as discussed in chapters 17 and 18. If, however, the government wishes to lower the rural price relative to the (transport-exclusive) urban price, then farmers have an incentive to ship and sell their produce, bypassing the formal market channels. Governments may attempt to prevent this behavior by requiring farmers to obtain permits for grain movements and operating roadblocks to police such movements (as was the case in Kenya and India; see Brown, 1978, p. 91), but their ability to enforce this requirement will depend on the geography of the country, the extent of the transportation system, and the compliance of the populace. In many countries it is unrealistic to price food products separately in urban and rural areas, though agriculture may still be taxed by imposing export taxes (as on rice in Thailand). Figure 13-2 shows the consequences of the government's inability to price discriminate within the country. Any tax on farmers implies a subsidy to urban consumers, and the relevant net supply facing the government is rural net supply less urban demand. Urban and rural consumers must now be aggregated, because it is no longer possible to treat them separately, and it is no longer possible to apply the single-person Ramsey rule; even if all consumers have identical preferences, their net supplies of goods will differ, not only in amount, but also, for agricultural goods, in sign.

This distinction between cases in which urban and rural prices can be separately set, and those in which they cannot should not be overdrawn, however: the simplicity of the single-person Ramsey rule disappears when income distribution is taken into account in any case, and the inability to price discriminate will not greatly add to the resulting complexity.

Even when the government is free to vary the prices facing the agricultural sector, the optimal tax rules need careful interpretation. Because the agricultural sector is being treated as a consuming sector, there is a presumption *against* efficient pricing (from the standpoint of production as a whole). In general, production inputs into agriculture should be taxed or subsidized, and there is no presumption that agricultural producers should face world prices. Because production and consumption cannot be separately taxed, taxes must inevitably trade off efficiency against equity. Although an intellectually respectable case may be made for the elimination of distortions (tax induced and otherwise) in the modern industrial and urban sector, and also for international trade, this case does not apply to agriculture, at least as it exists in developing countries.

Tax Incidence in Agriculture

Consumption taxes levied on the output of a constant-returns modern sector can be analyzed as though they had been shifted forward to fall entirely on consumers, as discussed in chapters 2 and 3. As I remarked above, this statement is not true for agricultural taxes, and it is instructive to take the simplest case of a tax on a traded agricultural good [measured by $(P - p)$ in figures 13-1 and 13-2 and possibly implemented by an export tax]. This tax will reduce the income of farmers and will lead to a fall in the returns to land and labor. Different rural residents will be differently affected, depending on whether they are net buyers or sellers of land and/or labor services, and these distributional impacts may be of first-order importance. Consider the impact of an increased export tax on rice. The apparent gainers in the rural area will be landless laborers who are consumers of rice; we must, however, ask what happens to their incomes. If rural wages fall substantially (because the alternative crops into which farmers substitute are much less labor intensive than rice), then landless laborers may be made significantly worse off overall. These labor market repercussions are discussed in chapter 16 by Sah and Stiglitz and are quantified for Korea in chapters 17 and 18.

If the rural wage falls, then it may be attractive for workers to migrate to the urban sector, and this migration will either tend to reduce the urban wage or increase urban unemployment, as discussed in chapters 7 and 10. Migration modifies the analysis of agricultural taxation in a number of ways that are

Figure 13-2. *Export Taxes on a Traded Food Crop*

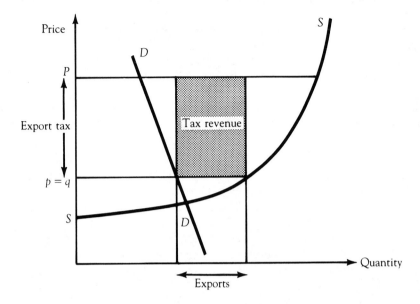

explored further in chapters 15 and 16. It affects not only the incidence of taxes on wages in both sectors and on utility levels but also the return to land and the aggregate net trade elasticities. If workers are free to choose the sector in which they locate, then sector-specific taxes will affect their decision, and this effect will need to be taken into account. Interestingly, if the cost of producing utility is different in the two sectors, then there are social welfare grounds for supposing generally that horizontal equity (to be interpreted here as equal utility levels for identical individuals differing only in their location) is not desirable. Free mobility, which tends to equalize utilities across sectors, will be socially costly. Heady and Mitra show in chapter 15 that the inability of the government to prevent migration will affect the choice of sector-specific taxes. In Heady and Mitra's model, it is more expensive to create utility in the urban sector (higher transport costs, housing costs, pollution, and so forth). Arnott and Gersovitz (1982) analyze a model in which it is more expensive to create utility in the country (higher costs of electricity, water, health care, and so forth). The optimal solution is to give urban residents higher utility ("urban bias") but to restrict migration, as it is socially efficient to produce more utility in towns but desirable to prevent an excessive reallocation of workers from agriculture to urban production. If migration cannot be controlled, they argue, then it may even be desirable to create urban unemployment to discourage migration providing that, in the resulting equilibrium, urban residents consequently enjoy higher welfare than rural residents.

The way in which urban and rural labor markets equilibrate and interact is obviously crucial for determining the incidence of agricultural (and urban) taxes and hence on their distributional impact. If, in addition, the labor markets are fragmented so that the marginal products of labor are not equated in each sector, there is an additional presumption of inefficiency that may be reduced by corrective sector-specific taxes. Sector-specific commodity taxes may act as a partial substitute for corrective labor taxes, as discussed by Heady and Mitra in chapter 15. In one of their models, rural workers lose their claim on rent when they migrate, so that they compare the urban wage with the rural average (not marginal) product of labor. Although there are doubts as to the empirical importance of such "traditional labor market dualism" (Bertrand and Squire, 1980, and chapter 7 in this book), it is useful to see how far it modifies the problem of tax design. Sah and Stiglitz in chapter 16 concentrate their attention on the empirically more soundly based "modern sector dualism" and argue that sectoral differences in marginal products are not necessarily inefficient once training costs, labor efficiency, and other factors have been taken into account.

Tax Incidence in the Urban Sector with Nontraded Food Crops

If all food crops were tradable goods, and if their border price (export or import price as appropriate) were independent of domestic supply or demand (the small-country assumption), then their prices would be fixed and would not respond to changes in taxes on nonagricultural commodities. Many food crops are too bulky (per unit value) to be either exportable or importable (that is, the domestic market-clearing price lies between the high import price and the low export price). Changes in the prices of other goods (and changes in wages or incomes) will, by changing demand for these nontraded goods, typically also change their prices. These price changes will in turn have welfare impacts and revenue effects that may be potentially important. Just how important will depend on the details of the case, but to gain some sense of the magnitudes, it seems useful to examine a very simple model in which the single food crop (subscripted f) is nontraded, whereas all other goods are traded or produced under constant returns. As usual, define producer and consumer prices as $\mathbf{p}$, $\mathbf{q}$, with $\mathbf{q} - \mathbf{p} = \mathbf{t}$, let consumption and production of household h be $\mathbf{x}^h$, $\mathbf{y}^h$, and examine the effect of changing the consumer price of a nonfood commodity i ($\neq f$). Suppose for simplicity (and for realism) that there is no tax on the nontraded food, so that

$$(13\text{-}10) \qquad \frac{\partial q_f}{\partial q_i} = \frac{\partial p_f}{\partial q_i} \equiv \Delta$$

say, and the total welfare impact of changing q_i on urban and rural households is (ignoring all cross-price effects except those through food)

(13-11) $$\frac{\partial W}{\partial q_i} = -\sum_h \beta^h [x_i^h + (x_f^h - y_f^h)\Delta].$$

Total government revenue from taxes on consumption and export taxes on agricultural production (where world prices are $\mathbf{P}$) is (j, $k \neq f$)

(13-12) $$R = \sum_j t_j X_j + \sum_k (P_k - p_k) Y_k$$

so

(13-13) $$\frac{\partial R}{\partial q_i} = X_i + \sum_j t_j \frac{\partial X_j}{\partial q_i} + \sum_j t_j \sum_h \left(\frac{\partial x_j^h}{\partial q_f} + y_f^h \frac{\partial x_j^h}{\partial m}\right)\Delta + \sum_k (P_k - p_k) \frac{\partial Y_k}{\partial p_f}\Delta.$$

The first two terms are the normal effects that arise if all other prices remain constant, and the additional effects are those induced by the price changes Δ and the supply responses $\partial Y_k / \partial p_f$. The price changes can be found by differentiating the market-clearing condition for food:

(13-14) $$\sum_h x_f^h [\mathbf{q}, \pi(p_f)] = \sum_h y_f^h (p_f)$$

(13-15) $$\frac{\partial X_f}{\partial q_i} = \Delta\left[\frac{\partial Y_f}{\partial p_f} - \sum_h \left(\frac{\partial x_f^h}{\partial q_f} + y_f^h \frac{\partial x_f^h}{\partial m}\right)\right]$$

or

(13-16) $$q_f \frac{\partial X_f}{\partial q_i} = \Delta\left[\eta + \bar{\epsilon}^* + \sum_h \left(\frac{x_f^h - y_f^h}{X_f}\right) b_f^h\right] X_f$$

where, as in equation 13-9, η is the output elasticity of the nontraded food, $\bar{\epsilon}^*$ is a (consumption) weighted-average compensated own-price elasticity of food consumption (as a positive number), and b_f^h is the propensity to spend on the food:

$$\bar{\epsilon}^* = -\sum_h x_f^h \frac{\partial \log x_f^h}{\partial \log q_f}\bigg|_{\bar{u}} /X_f; \qquad b_f^h = q_f \frac{\partial x_f^h}{\partial m}.$$

One might expect b_f^h to fall with increasing income and hence to be negatively correlated with x_f and y_f. Because on average $x_f = y_f$, the last term in equation 13-16 is likely to be small (and of uncertain sign). It seems reasonable to ignore it, so that

(13-17) $$\Delta = \frac{q_f \partial X_f / \partial q_i}{X_f (\eta + \bar{\epsilon}^*)}; \qquad \frac{\partial \log q_f}{\partial \log q_i} = \frac{\partial \log X_f / \partial \log q_i}{\eta + \bar{\epsilon}^*}.$$

Given a set of demand and supply elasticities, it would now be easy to modify the standard calculations of the marginal cost of raising revenue by varying prices q_i to take into account the induced price effects. Our object here, however, is to gain a sense of the likely importance of these effects, and it is therefore necessary to make further assumptions. We shall argue that the extra effect on the revenue term is negligible but that it may be moderately important for the welfare impact.

Suppose, following Deaton in chapter 4, household behavior is described by the linear expenditure system:

$$(13\text{-}18) \qquad\qquad x_i^h = \gamma_i + b_i(m^h - q'\gamma)/q_i$$

so that aggregate demand is

$$(13\text{-}19) \quad X_i = \Gamma_i + b_i(M - q'\Gamma)/q_i, \qquad (M = \Sigma m^h, \ \Gamma_i = \Sigma \gamma_i^h).$$

Then

$$(13\text{-}20) \qquad\qquad \frac{\partial \log X_i}{\partial \log q_i} \equiv \epsilon_{ii} = -1 + (1 - b_i)\Gamma_i/X_i$$

and

$$(13\text{-}21) \qquad \frac{\Delta}{X_i} = \frac{-b_f \Gamma_i}{X_i X_f(\eta + \bar{\epsilon}^*)} = \frac{-b_f}{X_f(\eta + \bar{\epsilon}^*)}\left(\frac{1 + \epsilon_{ii}}{1 - b_i}\right).$$

The induced price effects add the following extra terms to the revenue impact:

$$(13\text{-}22) \qquad \Delta\left[\sum_j \frac{t_j b_j}{q_j}(Y_f - \Gamma_f) + \sum_k \left(\frac{p_k - p_k}{p_k}\right)\frac{p_f \partial Y_k}{y_k \partial p_f} \frac{p_k Y_k}{p_f Y_f} \cdot X_f\right]$$

$$(13\text{-}23) \qquad = \Delta X_f\left[\bar{\tau}\left(1 - \frac{\Gamma_f}{X_f}\right) + p_a \eta_{af}\frac{p_a Y_a}{p_f Y_f}\right]$$

where $\bar{\tau} = \Sigma \ t_j b_j/q_j$ is the average indirect tax rate on marginal expenditures, p_a is an average export tax rate on nonfood, η_{af} is the cross-price supply elasticity of nonfood to the price of food (presumably negative), and $p_a Y_a$ is the value of nonfood. From equation 13-20

$$(13\text{-}24) \qquad 1 - \frac{\Gamma_f}{X_f} = \frac{-(\epsilon_{ff} + b_f)}{1 - b_f} = \frac{\epsilon^*}{1 - b_f}, \ \bar{\epsilon}^* = \frac{-\partial \log X_f}{\partial \log q_f}\bigg|_{\bar{u}}.$$

The bracketed expression in equation 13-23 is roughly the difference between two tax-weighted elasticities and is likely to be small. Thus if $b_f = 0.3$, $\epsilon^* = 0.1$, $\eta_{af} = -0.3$, $\bar{\tau} = 0.15$, $p_a = 0.1$, and $p_a Y_a/p_f Y_f = 0.5$, the part in brackets would be 0.006. The whole expression would be, if $\eta = 0.3$, -0.005 $X_i(1 + \epsilon_{ii})/(1 - b_i)$, or, for a typical good i with a small budget share b_i, about $-0.003X_i$, which is negligible.

The extra effect on the welfare impact can be measured by

$$(13\text{-}25) \qquad -\frac{1}{\beta X_i}\frac{\partial W}{\partial q_i} = \frac{X_{\bar{i}}}{X_i} - \frac{X_{\bar{f}} - Y_{\bar{f}}}{X_f}\frac{b_f}{\eta + \bar{\epsilon}^*}\left(\frac{1 + \epsilon_{ii}}{1 - b_i}\right)$$

where $\overline{\beta}$ is the average social weight, and $X_i^=$ is the welfare-weighted demand for good i:

$$X_i^= = \sum_h \beta^h x_i^h / \overline{\beta}.$$

$X_i^=/X_i$ is then the distributional characteristic of good i (Feldstein, 1972, and chapter 3). The second term in expression 13-25 could be quite large, for $X_f^=/X_f$ is likely to be substantially above unity, and $Y_f^=/Y_f$ is likely to be substantially below unity (because output is likely to be concentrated on farms of above-average income levels and hence below-average social weights). The whole of the last term might be as large as one-quarter.

Thus the main impact of the induced price changes is to *lower* the social cost of raising revenue, because taxes will reduce money purchasing power, which will reduce the price of nontraded food and will therefore have beneficial distributional effects. Furthermore, the extra term in expression 13-25 will vary between goods and will be largest for price-inelastic goods, thus appearing to strengthen the case for concentrating revenue collection of these goods. It certainly seems worthwhile to explore alternatives to the linear expenditure system before accepting this second conclusion; as Deaton shows in chapter 4, the LES prejudges some tax reform questions rather seriously.

The Debate on Agricultural Taxation and the Terms of Trade

Many developing countries tax agriculture by lowering the prices of agricultural outputs, and protect manufactured goods by tariffs. Developed countries, notably the European Community and Japan, often subsidize agriculture by raising prices above world market levels. Clearly these policies generate inefficiencies, and as the distortions are often large, there is a widespread belief that these inefficiencies are very costly—a view that is documented in Schultz (1978), *Distortions of Agricultural Incentives*. If land or agricultural output cannot be effectively taxed, however, then agricultural taxation will inevitably be inefficient, as we have seen, and even if it is well designed, it will reflect a compromise between equity and efficiency. This characteristic is evident in the view that justifies turning the terms of trade against agriculture for the following four (related) reasons:

1. Aggregate agricultural supply is relatively inelastic, which fact argues for relatively heavy taxes.
2. Investment in industry provides a higher rate of growth than investment in agriculture, and hence it is desirable to transfer the surplus from agriculture to industry.
3. Because the chief beneficiaries of higher agricultural prices are the larger farmers, a case may be made on grounds of rural equity for lower agricultural prices.
4. Lower food prices would benefit low-income urban and rural consumers.

The first two points are efficiency arguments (static and dynamic), whereas the last two are equity arguments, all suggesting the desirability of possibly quite heavy agricultural taxation. Before accepting the arguments, however, it is important to scrutinize the evidence on which these claims rest. Proponents of lower agricultural taxes (or for more favorable terms of trade) argue as follows (see, for example, Schultz, 1978, and especially Brown, 1978). First, individual crop production elasticities can be quite high, and even aggregate production elasticities may be quite high in the medium to long run, once complementary investments in irrigation, seed improvement, agricultural extension, and rural infrastructure, especially transport, have been made. If the output elasticity is reasonably high, equation 13-9 shows that the *supply* elasticity will be higher than the output elasticity, further strengthening the case. Second, these complementary investments have a high social rate of return, arguably higher than that of many industrial projects, so the case for transferring the surplus out of agriculture is weakened. Third, the distributional impact of lower agricultural prices is not necessarily beneficial, because of the possible impact on rural wages. Fourth, if rural real wages fall, urban real wages may also fall, in which case the fall in urban money wages would be even greater than the fall in food prices. Finally, rural standards of living are on average systematically lower than urban standards of living in almost all developing countries (though Korea *may* be an exception; see chapter 18), and hence on equity grounds the case for agricultural taxation (and the consequential simultaneous taxation of marginal urban workers) is weak.

The efficiency arguments are somewhat easier to quantify, though most of the available evidence relates to individual crop supply responses or acreage responses. (For a recent survey, see Askari and Cummings, 1976.) Thus Timmer, Falcon, and Pearson (1983, p. 108) cite evidence that the supply elasticity of cereals has a median value between zero and one-third, with higher values for more developed agriculture. Looking across countries, Timmer and Falcon (cited in Schultz, 1978) found a close correlation between rice prices and yields (which are a better proxy for an aggregate supply response) among Asian countries ranging from 4–5 tonnes/hectare in Japan and Korea to 1.7–2 tonnes/hectare for Indonesia, Thailand, the Philippines, and Burma. The ratio of rice to fertilizer prices varied from 0.1 to 0.4 for low-yielding countries to 1–1.4 for the high-yielding countries, suggesting high estimates of elasticity. The yield differences cannot be explained by soils or climate, though there are clearly large and systematic differences in rural infrastructure across countries. For tax purposes, what is wanted is the supply elasticity holding constant publicly financed rural investment, and so these high elasticities do not clinch the argument. Recently, Binswanger and Duncan (1985) have attempted to estimate the *aggregate* supply response from cross-country and time-series data, separately distinguishing the effects of investment in infrastructure and research. They find rather low own-price elasticities of between 0.1 and 0.3. At the same time they checked earlier cross-country estimates that found much higher elasticities and showed that, when the price data were carefully corrected, similar low elasticities emerged.

These aggregate elasticities can immediately be used to throw light on a question raised by Sah and Stiglitz in chapter 16: would it be possible by raising agricultural prices to make everyone better off? Atkinson's chapter 14 asks the equivalent question: would government revenue and rural welfare both rise with an increase in agricultural prices? Sah and Stiglitz show that they will if the agricultural terms of trade (the ratio of agricultural to nonagricultural prices, p/P in figure 13-1 above) are more adverse than $\eta/(1 + \eta)$, where η is the aggregate supply elasticity (Sah and Stiglitz, equation 16-8). Putting the higher value of 0.33 gives the critical value for the domestic terms of trade as one-quarter the world terms of trade, which suggests that in few, if any, countries can costless gains be found from raising *all* agricultural prices, though as Sah and Stiglitz note, the conditions for Pareto improvements when the *relative* prices of agricultural inputs and outputs are changed are very much less demanding.

If the static case for the efficiency of quite high agricultural tax rates seems plausible, the dynamic case [argument (ii) above] does not. There is good evidence that the social returns to agricultural investment are high (Binswanger and Duncan, 1985; Lipton, 1977; Schultz, 1978). Thus although it may be efficient to tax agriculture, it is also efficient to invest in agriculture, and there is no presumption that the net transfer out of agriculture (tax revenues less public investment) should be positive (though for poor agrarian economies with no mineral resources there is in fact little other than agriculture to tax.)

The equity issues are thus crucial to any assessment of whether agricultural taxes are too high or too low in particular developing countries, and the logical way to investigate this question is to apply the methods of tax reform analysis. Where any proposed tax or price change is concerned, we need to assess its impact on the prices of goods facing producers and consumers and to consider the prices of factors. These price changes give the welfare impacts on the households in the economy (in the rural and urban areas). They in turn induce supply-and-demand responses that affect government revenue and, given some system of weighting household welfare changes, allow one to calculate the marginal social cost of increasing government revenue by a change in the policy. Comparing this source of government revenue with others, we can then judge whether agricultural taxes are too high or too low (that is, whether output prices are too low or too high). Where the analysis of agricultural price reform differs is that any policy change (the price of some input or output or an export tax) typically affects a wide range of other prices. Thus a decrease in the rice price (an increase in the rice export tax or a decrease in the rice import tariff) will typically cause a fall in rural labor demand, in the rural wage rate, and in land rents. These changes will affect the costs of producing other goods, and if these goods are nontraded, so that their prices are determined by domestic market clearing, then their prices will typically change. Changes in the rural wage rate may lead to changes in urban wages and prices and possibly in the level of unemployment. Chapters 17 and 18 show in detail how to follow this chain of impacts and hence how to evaluate particular policy changes.

Instruments for Agricultural Taxation

Tax reform analysis is well suited to the analysis of small changes in existing taxes or government regulated prices. The argument set forth above—that some of the major conflicts between equity and efficiency derived from the limited range of tax instruments available for agricultural taxation—suggests that it is important to examine these supposed limitations carefully. It may be far better to introduce new methods of taxing agriculture rather than make small adjustments to the present unsatisfactory set of instruments. The next section therefore briefly examines the instruments potentially available and discusses their feasibility.

Land Taxes and Water Charges

Agricultural land, which is in inelastic supply, is an obvious candidate for taxation. It is often distributed in a highly unequal way, with the largest landowners owning a disproportionate fraction of the total. Bird (1974, p. 79) cites evidence that, in Latin America as a whole, 1 percent of the agricultural population controlled less than 2 percent of the farm units but more than 50 percent of the land, accounting for close to one-third of output and receiving more than one-sixth of total continental GNP (Sternberg, 1970).

Such extreme inequality in the distribution of land ownership arises for a variety of reasons. Asset accumulation requires a surplus of income over subsistence, and hence the distribution of wealth will normally be more skewed than the distribution of income. The uncertainties of agricultural production reinforce the process of concentration: small landowners are more likely to suffer below-subsistence production and to be forced to sell their land. Political power often coincides with land ownership and reinforces this process, whereas the absence of taxes, land reform, or revolution allows the process to continue. Hence land taxes also appear very desirable from an equity point of view, though it should be borne in mind that incomes are lower in the agricultural sector than in the rest of the economy. If, however, the choice is to replace other taxes on agriculture with a land tax, then equity and efficiency arguments are likely to favor land taxes. Despite all these obvious attractions, land taxes have declined in at least some countries from a dominant position to their present negligible level. Some of the reasons for this decline were mentioned in chapter 7, and we cited two extensive monographs, by Wald (1959) and Bird (1974), that have been devoted to the analysis of land taxes and a discussion of their potential and actual role in developing countries. Bird's book in particular bears close study and makes an extensive discussion here redundant. Instead, it seems useful to summarize Bird's main conclusions. Bird argues convincingly for a simple proportional tax on presumptive income (that is, normal rent), perhaps with an exemption for small land holdings (though this may be undesirable if it encourages evasion through the registration of land ownership with a wide variety of relatives). Progressive land taxes, or land taxes that depend on the owner's income and wealth, introduce considerable complexity, frequently provoke effective political opposition, and can be evaded by subdivision. The evidence strongly suggests that complex land taxes are impractical. Still, are simple land taxes practical? On administrative grounds, the evidence suggests that they are. The tax requires knowledge of only four facts: the area of the property, its location, its classification, and the name of the person to whom to send the tax bill (presumably the owner). This information can be collected at relatively low cost. Thus Chile managed to complete an aerial survey based land tax assessment in three years, by 1965 (Bird, 1974, pp. 102–5) and recent developments in satellite imaging (using Landsat) ought to simplify the major problem of assessment considerably—calculating the potential fertility of land in different areas. Such information is useful for other purposes, and the lesson from experience is that the fiscal cadastre should be much less detailed and accurate than the traditional legal cadastre used to establish ownership rights. (The term "cadastre" refers to an official record of location, size, ownership, and possibly value of each tract of land in a specified area.) Ownership identification will be greatly facilitated if the land can be seized should no owner come forward.

Once the fiscal cadastre is complete, the next requirement is a clear statement of the tax law, which specifies who is responsible for paying the tax, the method of assessment of tax liability, and the penalties for failure or delay in payment, which, to be effective, must allow the tax authorities to enforce a lien against the property as a final resort (see Bird, 1974, chap. 11; and United Nations, 1968). Finally, of course, tax officials are required to collect the tax. The problem of inflationary erosion of tax yield can be met by indexing the tax base to a price index.[4] The problem of fluctuating income can be met by linking last year's tax liability to the value of agricultural output throughout the country or region.

The three main determinants of presumptive income or rent will be the fertility of the land, the availability of reliable water, and its accessibility to the main market. The first two pieces of information can be obtained by inspection or Landsat imaging, the last by local inquiry into transport costs. This information will be of obvious value in deciding on transport improvements.

Land taxes are easy to analyze no matter which model is chosen, for standard profit-maximizing arguments show that, although they reduce the direct incomes of landowners, they have no direct effect on the wages of agricultural workers or the incomes of tenants. If the supply price of labor to the modern sector is determined by the latter, then the land tax will not affect it. If the supply price depends on the average productivity of small farmers, and if they lose their rights to the implicit land rent upon migration, as in the Heady-Mitra model of chapter 15, then land taxes will lower the supply price, unless smallholders, who supply the migrants, are exempt from the tax. If rents are determined by non-profit-maximizing criteria (for example, by legal fiat or local convention), then we need to know whether the land tax is in part shifted to rent and, if so, whether the rent remains below the official level (as would seem likely with administered rents). If so, then again the impact is on the distribution of income rather than on input choices, but a wider range of agents will be affected).

The obvious empirical question to ask is how desirable a crude land tax would be from an equity viewpoint (because its efficiency is not in doubt). Its desirability could readily be tested with the techniques described in chapter 20, using a detailed socioeconomic survey containing information on incomes, expenditures, and gross agricultural production from owned land (that is, excluding rented land). As a rough approximation, if rent is assumed to be a reasonably stable fraction of gross output, the effect of a tax on rent can be captured by reducing income and household expenditure by a predetermined fraction of the value of gross output from owned land. If data on the fraction of land irrigated are available, it would be interesting to explore the consequences of taxing output from such land at a higher rate (to capture some of the effects of a water charge or to allow for the share of rent in gross output on irrigated land to differ from that on rain-fed land).

If the idea of taxing land is accepted as logical, then an even more powerful case may be made for charging for publicly supplied irrigation water and, indeed, for levying user charges quite generally for agricultural inputs, either directly, where their value is apparent and collection costs can be kept low, or indirectly through the land tax assessment (much as sewerage charges are frequently collected via local rates in the United Kingdom). There are several compelling reasons for levying such user charges. First, if farmers face the correct prices for inputs, they will choose efficient input levels.[5] It is often argued that farmers have little control over irrigation decisions, especially for large, integrated systems, but this argument misses the point. If farmers are not charged, they will lobby for increased water and will strongly resist reductions, whereas if they are charged, their lobbying activities will not impede efficient reallocations. Second, if they are not charged, the landowner will receive a windfall gain in increased land values, and given the arguments advanced above, this windfall is likely to worsen the distribution of income. If farmers are charged, they will typically still enjoy part of this windfall gain and hence will welcome the introduction of irrigation, but the effect will be less inegalitarian. Finally, if water is not charged, the economic viability of the irrigation scheme will be greatly reduced, on the assumption that private benefits have a lower shadow value than revenue received by the government. Furthermore, if the government or water authority collects water charges, and if these are related to water delivered, then they have a more explicit incentive to manage the water distribution system efficiently.

Two further practical points can be made. First, the water may well be effectively charged in one way or another, for if the government fails to levy charges, corrupt local water engineers may levy charges. (For a well-documented case, see Wade, 1979.) Second, if water is not charged, improvements in water allocation that might dramatically raise productivity will be resisted, because they upset the pattern of bribes, because they make some groups of farmers worse off, or because they would create de facto water rights that would restrict the water authority's freedom of action. Thus there is some evidence that, at present in the Indus basin, irrigation water may be randomly allocated to prevent the establishment of water rights, despite the obvious inefficiencies that such allocation generates.

Taxes on Output

Taxes may be levied on gross output or on the marketed surplus. For cash crops, the distinction is not important, but for food crops it is crucial, at least in developing countries. It is also clear that for these crops it may be administratively very difficult to levy taxes on gross output, though tithes were quite common in earlier periods. The distinction between gross and net output taxes can best be seen by looking at a farmer who grows a food crop and a nonfood crop, both of which are exported. Let y be output of the food crop, c farm consumption, x output of the export crop, and m purchases from the nonagricultural sector. World prices are all unity, and we compare uniform taxes on the two agricultural goods, so that the prices facing the farmer are $(1 - t)$. (The variables x, y, c, and m will all depend on t). If the tax is on marketed surplus, the budget constraint of the farmer is

$$(13\text{-}26) \qquad (y - c)(1 - t) + x(1 - t) = m$$

or

$$(13\text{-}27) \qquad y - c + x = \frac{m}{1 - t}.$$

If the tax is on gross output, the budget constraint is

$$(13\text{-}28) \qquad (y + x)(1 - t) = m + c.$$

From equation 13-27 we see that a tax on marketed surplus is equivalent to a tax on purchases from the nonagricultural sector, which is the form that agricultural taxation frequently takes. Equations 13-26 and 13-27 show that a uniform tax on marketed surplus does not change relative producer prices but does change relative consumption prices. Equation 13-28 shows that a tax on gross output leaves both relative producer and relative consumer prices unchanged. If, however, the tax on gross output is combined with a tax on purchases (m), then each consumption commodity can be taxed at a different rate, which in general will be preferable.

A tax on gross output is therefore superior to a tax on marketed surplus, because it provides more independent tax instruments. On the other hand, it is administratively costly and, in one special case, unnecessary. The special case is when the optimal tax on food is zero (that is, the same as the tax on agricultural labor, which is taken as the untaxed numeraire in the above analysis). This is a very common feature of the indirect tax structures of developed countries and is usually defended as the best method of making taxes progressive. This argument is not completely persuasive, as food is a very heterogeneous commodity group. It is furthermore unlikely that the optimum commodity tax is zero for all its members, but it is worth testing the hypothesis that the additional benefit of being able to tax food is small and is hence not worth the administrative difficulty.

Taxes on Purchased Inputs

The main purchased inputs are labor, fertilizers, services of tractors or draft animals, water, chemicals, and seed. It would be as difficult—and hence infeasible—to tax labor as to tax rural incomes. Taxing seed either is the same as taxing gross output or is equivalent to deciding how best to price seed sold from plant breeding stations. We have already dealt with water, so there remain the inputs supplied from the modern sector. The problem in deciding on the appropriate taxes then consists in balancing the various conflicting factors. First, if all inputs except land and all outputs were subject to the same tax, the effect would be equivalent to a rent tax, as the following expression shows. Y is output, A is land, $\mathbf{M}$ is the vector of purchased inputs, including labor, and the production function gives

$$(13\text{-}29) \qquad Y = f(A, \mathbf{M}).$$

If rent is $R/$acre, then total rent is the residual

$$(13\text{-}30) \qquad RA = pY - \mathbf{w} \cdot \mathbf{M}$$

where p and $\mathbf{w}$ are efficiency prices. Still,

$$(13\text{-}31) \qquad R(1 - t)A = p(1 - t)Y - (1 - t)\mathbf{w} \cdot \mathbf{M}$$

so if output prices fall to $p(1 - t)$ and all purchased input prices are subsidized to $(1 - t)\mathbf{w}$, production efficiency is preserved and the effect is equivalent to a rent tax.

For this situation to have the desired effect, all inputs would have to be subsidized, and the rate of subsidy would have to be specific to the sector in which they are employed. Because labor is an important input that is hard to tax or subsidize, any input subsidy would in practice have to be restricted to modern sector inputs such as fertilizers and tractor services. Such a subsidy, together with an output tax, will not be the same as a rent tax and will tend to distort the choice between subsidized and unsubsidized inputs (that is, between labor and bullock plowing, on the one hand, and fertilizers and tractor services, on the other). If the same inputs are used to produce a wide range of crops that are taxed at very different rates (for example, if food crops are untaxed and export crops are heavily taxed), and if, plausibly, inputs cannot be subsidized at different rates when used for different crops, then additional distortions will be introduced by uniform subsidies. On the other hand, taxing outputs without subsidizing inputs, even if only partially and at some compromise rate, will tend to reduce outputs. It may even be desirable to tax inputs where it is not possible to tax output, though again the distortions will depend on the substitutability between inputs, the ratio of input costs to the value of gross output, and the extent to which different crops have different input requirements.

Finally, taxes on inputs or outputs will affect the demand for labor and hence will affect the rural market-clearing wage, which will affect the distribution of income, the supply price of labor to the modern sector, and therefore either the urban wage or the level of unemployment (or both).

Directions for Future Research

The models analyzed in the next two parts (and in the rest of the book) are static models with no uncertainty. As such they are most useful for the analysis of long-run changes in the tax structure on goods whose prices are reasonably stable (though, as Heady and Mitra show in chapter 15, optimal ad valorem tax rates may be relatively insensitive to large changes in relative prices). Agriculture prices are typically volatile, supplies vary, and opportunities for insurance are few in developing countries, so the assumption of certainty should at least be questioned. We may identify two important issues requiring further research. First, the choice of policy instrument has important consequences for risk sharing in the economy, as we see in the Korean case discussed in chapter 18. The government sets the price of rice, which is produced domestically and is marginally imported. The world price is very volatile, but the domestic price is not, so that the implicit tax/subsidy structure is volatile. Government revenue absorbs the larger part of the risk, and the form that price stabilization takes is quite costly, as it involves substantial public storage, some of which might be avoidable. The alternative of setting the import tariff and domestic subsidy rates and letting the domestic price move with international prices would shift the risk from the government to consumers and producers but may significantly lower the operating costs of the Grain Management Fund. The tools for the analysis of this policy choice have been developed in Newbery and Stiglitz (1981) and could usefully be applied to questions of this type.

The second, more difficult issue concerns tax and price policy for food grains, particularly those for which the country is consistently neither an exporter nor an importer. (For countries that consistently either export or import, the main problem is insuring against international price fluctuations, for which futures markets and the Compensating Financial Facility of the International Monetary Fund offer appropriate insurance). Where the food grain is essentially nontraded, its domestic market-clearing price is likely to be quite volatile in the face of supply variations. (Even when it is marginally traded, the price may fluctuate markedly between the FOB and CIF price, and the gap between these two prices may be both large and uninsurable on futures markets.) As Mellor (1978) argues, supply fluctuations for nontraded food crops have very significant distributional impacts. If the market is allowed to operate competitively, the major impact of supply fluctuations will be borne by the poor, because they allocate a much larger share of their budget to food than do the rich. If, on the other hand, food is rationed to prevent the adverse effect on the real incomes of the poor, then the market-clearing price fluctuations will be much increased, as the aggregate demand elasticity will be lowered. The reason can be seen from the Slutsky equation

$$(13\text{-}32) \qquad \frac{-\partial \log x}{\partial \log q} = \frac{-\partial \log x}{\partial \log q}\bigg|_{\bar{u}} + \omega \frac{\partial \log x}{\partial \log m}.$$

The compensated elasticity is likely to be very small for food grains, whereas the budget share, ω, will be substantially larger for the poor than for the rich, tending to make the price elasticity proportional to the budget share and hence fairly large for the poor. If the poor are compensated by food rations, then their demand elasticity will be closer to the (small) compensated elasticity, and the aggregate price elasticity of demand will be reduced. Although this situation will tend to provide better income insurance to food producers, anyone not covered by the ration system (typically poor rural net purchasers of food) will be greatly disadvantaged. Thus the short-run distributional consequences of any food policy (price interventions, rationing, compulsory procurement, storage, and so on) will, in the presence of supply variability, typically be significant, and it may be very misleading to ignore uncertainty.

Conclusions

Limitations on the availability and coverage of tax instruments in agriculture mean that their incidence will depend on the details of production and demand, notably whether the good is internationally traded or not. The positive theory of agricultural tax analysis is therefore more complicated than the simple model of chapter 2 and requires the construction of suitable models that capture the main features of the problem under study. This chapter has briefly described some of the interesting problems. The remaining chapters of this part of the book and the next provide some examples of the kinds of models that are available and of the results of using them for tax design and analysis.

Notes

1. Note that in the present case where the shadow price of the agricultural good is equal to its world price, P, and where we ignore cross-price effects, it is not necessary to draw distinctions between the response of revenue at shadow and producer prices. In more complex cases the distinction will be important, and the methods of chapter 3 will be required.

2. dV/dp is the total impact on the household but holding other prices constant. $\partial V/\partial p$ measures the impact on the household as consumer, holding lump-sum income constant.

3. Heady and Mitra give a more careful statement of the Ramsey rule in chapter 15 in terms of a small, equiproportionate intensification of taxes at the optimum.

4. If this computation is felt to be too crude, then the tax base can be defined by a formula that gives rent as the difference between normal output and assumed input, each of which can be separately indexed, the first to the price of relevant agricultural commodities and the second to an index of inputs. The stability of share rent payments suggests that the gross value of output is probably a satisfactory index. The alternative is to specify rents in kinds.

5. The correct prices are those that would induce the farmer to choose the (constrained) efficient input levels and are the solution to the standard optimal pricing or tax rules discussed in chapters 2 and 3 and in Atkinson and Stiglitz (1980, chap. 15).

14

The Theory of Tax Design for Developing Countries

Anthony Atkinson

How much revenue should the government seek to collect through income taxation? How should the tax burden be distributed? What should be the balance between direct and indirect taxation? These classic questions of public finance have received renewed attention in recent years in the research on optimum taxation and tax reform. The result has been a substantial literature (for a bibliography until 1980, see Atkinson and Stiglitz, 1980, and chapter 2 of this book), much of it concerned to provide answers that are more useful to the policymaker than those found in earlier writing on public finance. The recent work on normative tax theory takes into account the impact of taxation on individual decisions and the tradeoff between raising revenue, or redistributing its burden, and the efficiency losses. It recognizes the need for explicit treatment of government objectives, on the one hand, and the constraints on government activities, on the other. It treats models of the economy that are sufficiently rich to allow for differences between people in incomes or expenditure patterns.

At the same time, the achievements of modern tax theory should not be overstated. Perhaps most important from the standpoint of application to developing countries, the models tend to be constructed in such a way that taxation is introduced into an otherwise first-best world. The literature on optimum taxation has typically taken as its starting point the standard theorems of welfare economics. The second theorem of welfare economics tells us that, under certain conditions, any desired Pareto-efficient allocation can be attained as a competitive equilibrium by the use of lump-sum taxes and transfers to redistribute endowments. (A lump-sum tax is one that does not depend in any way on the actions of the taxpayer.) If such lump-sum taxes and transfers can be made, then the first-best can be attained. In order to levy the requisite lump-sum taxes, however, the government needs information about the characteristics of individuals: for example, about their earnings potential, or consumption tastes, or nonmarketed production. This information will not in general be available to the government, and individuals may have no incentive to provide it (indeed they may have good reason to conceal information).

The optimum tax literature has therefore been largely concerned with the implications of using non-lump-sum taxes, such as those on income or on expenditures. (The specification of the precise instruments at the disposal of the government is an important element in the treatment of the problem.) The resort to such non-lump-sum taxes is seen as a regrettable necessity, the problem of tax design being to minimize the efficiency losses from raising revenue or redistributing income. How can income be redistributed from the rich to the poor while minimizing the distortion to work/leisure choices or to the choice of consumption patterns? As such, the standard optimum tax analysis has a rather negative approach; taxation is not typically seen as making a positive contribution to improving efficiency. This aspect clearly needs to be incorporated. Taxation may help offset distortions elsewhere in the economy, or the revenue raised may finance more rapid development.

The analysis of optimum taxation has taken as its starting point the standard competitive equilibrium model, but it should be emphasized that many of the results relate to special cases of this model, as we shall see in this chapter. There is a striking contrast in this regard with the theorems of first-best welfare economics, which are couched in quite general terms, with only limited assumptions about the form of consumer preferences and technology. The theorems are therefore of considerable power. Once we leave the territory of the first best, by introducing elements of distortion or non-lump-sum taxes or both, however, then such general results are much more difficult to obtain. Most of the findings relate to more specific models or to special functional forms or are based on numerical calculations. The optimum income tax, for example, is considered in a model in which there are two goods, consumption and leisure. Even here few general results can be derived from the conditions for optimality (see Mirrlees, 1971, and chapter 2), and recourse is made to particular functional forms for the utility function, such as the Cobb-Douglas, and to numerical calculations for specified values of the parameters.

This lesser generality may appear disappointing, but it reflects the more complex structure of the problem. It is necessary to reconsider the level of generality appropriate for the analysis. It may be that—in the absence of general theorems—more insight can be obtained from specific examples than from the partial characterization of the conditions for optimality in a more general model. If so, we should not claim too much for the analysis, particularly when we take into account the difficulties of empirical implementation. Optimum tax theory cannot, at its present stage of development, demonstrate that a shift to a uniform value-added tax would be desirable, or that 50 percent of the revenue should be raised from income taxation. The concern is not with obtaining concrete answers but with the structure of arguments leading to such answers. The goal is to illuminate the relationship between specified government objectives, assumptions about how the economy operates, and policy recommendations. What kind of arguments could be made for the shift to a uniform value-added tax? How are they related to particular objectives or to particular views about economic behavior?

This chapter begins with a simple example, designed to illustrate the equity-efficiency tradeoff at the heart of much of the analysis. The first section describes a simplified version of the economy that is carried throughout the chapter to illustrate the application of the optimum tax theory: an economy consisting entirely of peasant households, producing food, which they sell to purchase imported manufactured goods. I consider the choices open to the government in this simple model, where it is concerned to balance the effect on revenue, used to finance future growth, against that on current welfare. After setting forth the general framework for the discussion of direct and indirect taxes in the context of the peasant household economy, I review a number of the results on optimum taxation, as applied to the model being considered here. In a final section I discuss some ways of extending the analysis.

A Simple Example of a Peasant Economy

It is often easier to understand results if we can solve explicitly for the revenue, tax rates, levels of social welfare, and so on. The purpose of the simple example presented in this section is to permit such explicit solutions. (A model of this kind was used in Atkinson, 1973, and in Atkinson and Stiglitz, 1980, lecture 13. The results have been extended by Deaton, 1983.)

The economy is assumed to consist entirely of peasant households, which produce food under fixed technological conditions and with no uncertainty about the level of output or about any other variables. The food output of an individual household is denoted by Q. The household sells a quantity $(Q - X)$ of its food output to purchase another good, "manufactures," which are imported at a fixed price (and are taken as the numeraire). The quantity of manufactures consumed, M, is, in the absence of government intervention:

$$(14\text{-}1) \qquad\qquad M = p(Q - X)$$

where p is the price of food. The household determines the amount marketed to maximize the utility function $U(M, X)$.

The essence of the problem is that the peasant households differ. For the purpose of the present highly simplified example, we assume that households have different amounts of land, N, and that household size, A, increases with the amount of land:

$$(14\text{-}2) \qquad\qquad A = N^{\delta}$$

where $0 < \delta < 1$. That is, we are assuming that households with more land are larger in size but that the size increases less than proportionately. If, furthermore, we assume that output is a constant-returns Cobb-Douglas function of land and labor, and labor is assumed to be proportional to household size, then, using equation 14-2:

$$(14\text{-}3) \qquad\qquad Q = cA^{\rho}N^{1-\rho}$$

(14-3a) $= cN^{\delta\rho+1-\rho}$

(14-3b) $= cA^{\rho+(1-\rho)/\delta}$

so that observed output per unit of land falls with N but observed output per person rises with A. In this and the next section, we take A as the index of the difference between households (this is simply a matter of exposition) and assume that the distribution of A is given by the cumulative distribution function, $F(A)$, with a range from one to infinity. For convenience, we normalize such that

(14-4) $$\int_1^\infty dF(A) = 1$$

so that all quantities are expressed as averages per household.

The final simplifying assumptions concern the form of the utility function. We suppose that for the individual member of the household, per capita food consumption enters the utility function (consumption being shared equally), but manufactured goods have the characteristic of a public good. Moreover, individual utilities are assumed to take the special form:

$$X/A + \log(M + b)$$

where b (≥ 1) is a parameter. If we sum across all household members, the household utility function becomes:

(14-5) $$U(M, X) = X + A\log(M + b).$$

This is a very special form, but it has the virtue of leading to particularly simple results.

The supply of marketed food by an individual household may be obtained by maximizing equation 14-5 subject to equation 14-1. This procedure yields the solution:

(14-6) $$Q - X = A - b/p$$

where $p \geq b/A$, and equals zero otherwise. The supply of a given household is therefore zero if the price is below b/A; supply is an increasing function of price above this point. Across households, the supply is an increasing function of A. Because A has a lower bound of one, we can see that if $p \geq b$, then all households enter the market, but that, if $p < b$, some consume only food. In general, there is a cutoff level of A, defined by

(14-7) $$\underline{A} = \max(b/p, 1).$$

The total supply of marketable food is thus:

(14-8) $$\int_{\underline{A}}^\infty (A - b/p)\,dF.$$

Below we shall consider only the case where all households are in the market (the reader can readily derive the results where this condition is not satisfied).

We may then write the total supply of marketable food as $\bar{A} - b/p$, where $\bar{A}$ is the mean value of A. It follows that the elasticity of total supply, η, is given by

(14-9)
$$\frac{1}{\eta} = \frac{\bar{A}p}{b} - 1$$

so that with, for example, $\bar{A} = 3/2$ (the mean 50 percent higher than the lowest value) and $b/p = 0.3$, the elasticity is 0.25.

The Taxation of Marketed Surplus

We suppose first that the government can tax neither output nor land but only the marketed surplus, at a proportional rate. As a result, the price received by peasant households becomes $p(1 - \tau)$ and the budget constraint

(14-1a)
$$M = p(1 - \tau)(Q - X).$$

The supply of marketed output is now:

(14-6a)
$$Q - X = A - b/[p(1 - \tau)]$$

where

$$p \geq \frac{b}{A(1 - \tau)}$$

and equals zero otherwise. The cutoff level of output, at which a household enters the market, is therefore an increasing function of the tax rate:

(14-7a)
$$\underline{A} = \max\left[\frac{b}{p(1 - \tau)}, 1\right].$$

In other words, all households remain in the market only if the tax rate is limited to the range $\tau < 1 - b/p$, and we assume that this is the case. The revenue from the tax, measured in terms of food, is:

(14-10)
$$R = \int_1^\infty \tau\left[A - \frac{b}{p(1 - \tau)}\right] dF = \tau\bar{A} - \frac{b\tau}{p(1 - \tau)}.$$

The derivative with respect to the tax rate is:

(14-11)
$$\frac{\partial R}{\partial \tau} = \bar{A} - \frac{b}{p(1 - \tau)^2}.$$

It is positive at $\tau = 0$, and the turning point is reached where

(14-12)
$$\tau = 1 - \sqrt{\frac{b}{\bar{A}p}}.$$

In figure 14-1, we show the revenue from the tax, taking one particular set of values ($\bar{A} = 3/2$ and $b/p = 0.3$). The revenue reaches a maximum and then declines; at a tax rate of 70 percent, the smallest households would begin to leave the market.

Figure 14-1. *Revenue from a Tax on Market Sales*

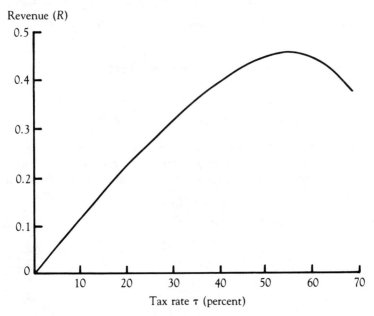

Note: Calculated for $\bar{A} = (3/2)$ and $(b/p) = 0.3$.

The Equity-Efficiency Tradeoff in Our Simple Model

The hump-shaped curve plotted in figure 14-1 captures in a simple way the restrictions on what the government can achieve as a result of supply-side responses. The possibility that revenue may reach a maximum has been popularized among U.S. congressmen by Arthur B. Laffer but has been well known for many years: for example, Jules Dupuit noted in 1844, "If a tax is gradually increased from zero up to the point where it becomes prohibitive, its yield is at first nil, then increases by small steps until it reaches a maximum, after which it gradually declines until it becomes zero again" (quoted in Arrow and Scitovsky, 1969, p. 278).

How should the government choose the tax rate? If its sole concern is with extracting the maximum revenue, then it will seek the top of the hump. Such an objective may be appropriate if the aim is to grow as rapidly as possible, a goal corresponding to the maximization of the investible surplus in the literature on the choice of techniques (for example, Marglin, 1976; Sen, 1960). In the present case, the revenue-maximizing choice of tax rate is given by equation 14-12. With the particular numbers used in figure 14-1, the optimum tax rate is 55.3 percent. The revenue-maximizing tax rate can in fact be seen to be related to the parameter η, which is the elasticity of total supply *in the absence of taxation*. Using equation 14-9, we can write

$$(14\text{-}12a) \qquad \frac{1}{1-\tau} = \sqrt{1+1/\eta}.$$

Treating η as an indicator of the degree of supply response, we can see that the tax rate falls with η—as would be intuitively expected.

It is, however, possible that the government attaches weight to the current levels of welfare of the peasant households. In the present case more is involved than simply a tradeoff between future and present consumption, because we must consider the *intratemporal* distribution as well as the *intertemporal* distribution. Suppose that the government has an additive social welfare function, formed by summing the current household utility, U, over all households:

$$(14\text{-}13) \qquad W = \int_1^\infty U dF.$$

If we use equations 14-5, 14-1a, and 14-6a, the total level of household utility may be seen to be:

$$(14\text{-}14) \qquad U = Q - A + \frac{b}{p(1-\tau)} + A\log[p(1-\tau)A]$$

(because all households are assumed to be in the market). Alternatively, writing utility as a function of the tax rate:

$$(14\text{-}15) \qquad U(\tau) = U(0) + \frac{b\tau}{p(1-\tau)} + \bar{A}\log(1-\tau).$$

The change in total welfare, treated as a function of τ, is:

$$(14\text{-}16) \qquad \Delta W \equiv W(\tau) - W(0) = \frac{b\tau}{p(1-\tau)} + \bar{A}\log(1-\tau).$$

The derivative with respect to τ is:

$$(14\text{-}17) \qquad \frac{\partial \Delta W}{\partial \tau} = \frac{b}{p(1-\tau)^2} - \frac{\bar{A}}{1-\tau}.$$

Because $b/[p(1-\tau)] < 1 < \bar{A}$ (otherwise some households would have left the market), this term is negative. We may also note that at $\tau = 0$, the derivative is equal to $(-\partial R/\partial \tau)$—see equation 14-11—so that, with an infinitesimal tax, the marginal loss of welfare (measured in this way) is equal to the marginal gain in revenue. A comparison of equations 14-17 and 14-11, however, shows that, for $\tau > 0$, the marginal loss of welfare is greater.

The choice of the tax rate will therefore depend on the tradeoff between current welfare, represented by W, and revenue, R. In order to capture this tradeoff, we assume that the government maximizes

$$(14\text{-}18) \qquad \Omega = \Delta W + \lambda R$$

where $\lambda \geq 0$. The parameter λ measures the relative weight attached to revenue, and in a dynamic treatment of the problem it may be expected to change over time (this point is discussed later). From equations 14-11 and 14-17, we can see that:

$$(14\text{-}19) \qquad \frac{\partial \Omega}{\partial \tau} = \bar{A} \left(\lambda - \frac{1}{1-\tau} \right) - \frac{b}{p(1-\tau)^2} (\lambda - 1)$$

and the relevant turning point is given by (for $\lambda \neq 1$):

$$(14\text{-}20) \qquad \frac{1}{1-\tau} = \frac{1}{2} \frac{(1 + 1/\eta)}{(\lambda - 1)} \left[\sqrt{1 + \frac{4\lambda(\lambda - 1)}{1 + 1/\eta}} - 1 \right].$$

Again it should be noted that η is the supply elasticity in the absence of taxation. We can now plot the optimum choice of tax rate as a function of the relative weight, λ, given to the two elements in the objective function—see the lower curve in figure 14-2 (where we take $\eta = 0.25$, as in figure 14-1). We have already seen that, where $\lambda = 1$, the turning point is at $\tau = 0$, because at that point the marginal loss of current welfare is equal to the marginal gain in

Figure 14-2. *Optimum Tax Rate as a Function of Relative Weight (λ) Attached to Revenue*

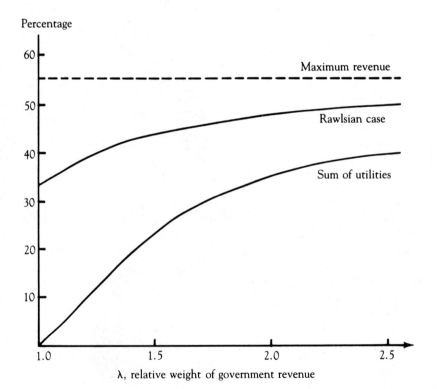

Percentage

Maximum revenue

Rawlsian case

Sum of utilities

λ, relative weight of government revenue

revenue. For $\lambda > 1$, more weight is given to revenue, and there is a positive tax rate. In the limit, as $\lambda \to \infty$, the tax rate rises toward the revenue-maximizing level, given by equation 14-12a.

Alternative Government Objectives

The valuation of current welfare has so far been based on the sum of household welfares. Alternative specifications of the government's objectives may be introduced. For this purpose let us define (following Deaton, 1983):

$$(14\text{-}13a) \qquad\qquad W^* = \int_1^\infty J(A)U dF$$

where $J(A)$ are a set of weights depending on A (but not on the tax parameters) and are normalized such that

$$(14\text{-}13b) \qquad\qquad \int_1^\infty J(A)dF = 1.$$

The change in total welfare is then:

$$(14\text{-}16a) \qquad\qquad \Delta W^* = \frac{b\tau}{p(1-\tau)} + A^* \log(1-\tau)$$

where we have replaced the "average" person's level of $\bar{A}$ by a "representative" level, A^*, defined by

$$(14\text{-}21) \qquad\qquad A^* = \int_1^\infty J(A)A dF.$$

The derivative with respect to τ is now:

$$(14\text{-}17a) \qquad\qquad \frac{\partial \Delta W^*}{\partial \tau} = \frac{b}{p(1-\tau)^2} - \frac{A^*}{(1-\tau)}.$$

We can see that where $\lambda = 1$, the optimum tax rate is now (where the right side is greater than unity):

$$(14\text{-}22) \qquad\qquad \frac{1}{1-\tau} = 1/a^*$$

where $a^* = A^*/\bar{A}$. Otherwise the formula for the turning point is:

$$(14\text{-}20a)\ \frac{1}{1-\tau} = \tfrac{1}{2}\frac{(1+1/\eta)}{\lambda - 1}\left[\sqrt{a^{*2} + \frac{4\lambda(\lambda - 1)}{1 + 1/\eta}} - a^*\right] \qquad \text{for} \quad \lambda \neq 1.$$

Two examples may be helpful. First, the government may be concerned with the welfare of only those households with the smallest holdings (a "Rawlsian," 1973, objective). Then $a^* = 1/\bar{A}$. With the numerical values used earlier, the optimum tax with weights such that $\lambda = 1$ is given by $\tau =$

1/3, and the tax rate is higher for all (finite) values of λ than in the sum-of-utilities case. Second, the weights $J(A)$ may be proportional to the rank $[1 - F(A)]$ in the distribution (that is, going from 1 at the bottom to 0 at the top). It may then be calculated (Deaton, 1983) that a^* is one minus the Gini coefficient for the distribution of A, so that with a Gini coefficient of 0.2, the value of a^* is 0.8, and with $\lambda = 1$, the optimum tax rate is 20 percent. In both cases, the greater the "inequality" of land holdings, the higher the tax.

Alternative Taxes on Agriculture

The tax on the marketed surplus of food drives a wedge between the price received in the market and the rate of transformation between goods in production. This distorting effect would be avoided if the government were able to relate the tax to variables not subject to decision by the household. In the present model this statement would apply to a tax based on land ownership. This type of taxation has long been advocated as desirable on both efficiency and equity grounds, and we now briefly consider its implications.

Suppose that a household of size A pays $T(A)$ in terms of food. The budget constraint becomes

$$(14\text{-}1b) \qquad\qquad M = p[Q - X - T(A)]$$

and the supply of marketed output (where $p \geq b/A$)

$$(14\text{-}6b) \qquad\qquad Q - X = A + T(A) - b/p.$$

The level of utility is

$$(14\text{-}14b) \qquad U(T) = Q - A - T(A) + b/p + A\log(pA)$$
$$= U(0) - T(A).$$

It follows that, with the additive social welfare function 14-13,

$$(14\text{-}23) \qquad\qquad \Delta W = -\int_1^\infty T(A)dF.$$

The loss of welfare is exactly equal to the revenue; this equality holds for finite revenue and not just infinitesimally at a zero tax rate. There is, in this case, no additional cost associated with taxation.

What may therefore prevent such a tax from being employed? First, the tax cannot be levied at a rate that drives the household into destitution; it would then be uncollectible. There is therefore an upper limit to $T(A)$ for each value of A. A second restriction that may prevent the government from levying the desired lump-sum tax is that the tax cannot rise so sharply with A that it makes a household with more land actually worse off than a smaller one. This restriction may arise from considerations of horizontal equity (that taxation should not reverse the ranking of households), or it may arise because households would then have an incentive to "destroy" their endowments (see Dasgupta and Hammond, 1980, for discussion of this aspect). This restriction was not necessary with the tax on marketed surplus, because $U(\tau)$ is an increasing function of A for all $\tau < 1$.

The force of these restrictions may be seen if we suppose that the government has distributional objectives that lead it to attach a weight $J(A)$ to household utilities where J declines with A. The optimum would then involve taxing all households above some level of A, say $\hat{A}$, up to the maximum permitted by the first restriction. Such taxation would, however, violate the second constraint, because those at $\hat{A}$ would be worse off than those just below.

Considerations such as the ones just described, together with the costs of obtaining and processing information, may mean that only simple forms of lump-sum taxes may be employed. The simplest is the uniform poll tax per household, although even this may raise administrative difficulties, such as identifying who has paid. In the next section, we suppose that this is the only lump-sum tax at the disposal of the government.

Direct and Indirect Taxation in the Peasant Economy

In this section and the next, we consider the choice of tax policy by a government that can impose a linear direct tax, with a single marginal rate of tax over the whole range, and indirect taxes at different rates on different goods. This treatment is selective in that it does not allow for nonlinear taxes, nor does it take into account the fact that taxes may be partial in their coverage. Nonetheless, it allows us to consider some of the central issues. What factors determine whether an income tax should be employed? In what circumstances is there a case for taxing one class of goods more heavily than another?

The model employed is more general than that which we just considered in that we assume the household to have a utility function $U(M_1, M_2, X)$ defined over two manufactured goods, M_1 and M_2, and food, X, where this function is assumed to be quasi-concave, continuously differentiable, and strictly increasing. The budget constraint is:

$$(14\text{-}24) \qquad q_1 M_1 + q_2 M_2 = p(Q - X)$$

where q_1, q_2 are the prices to the consumer, including taxes, of the two manufactured goods. Again producer prices are taken as fixed, and food is now untaxed. The differences between households are now described in terms of food production, Q, which has a cumulative distribution function $G(Q)$, normalized to have the same properties as $F(A)$.

The government is assumed to be able to levy ad valorem taxes at rates τ_1 and τ_2 on the two manufactured goods, and a uniform poll tax, T, per household. The prices of all goods are normalized at unity before tax, so that the household budget constraint becomes:

$$(14\text{-}25) \qquad (1 + \tau_1)M_1 + (1 + \tau_2)M_2 = Q - X - T.$$

The government revenue is then

$$(14\text{-}26) \qquad R = \int_1^\infty (\tau_1 M_1 + \tau_2 M_2 + T)dG(Q).$$

It may be noted that this formulation does not include the tax considered in the first two sections—that on the market sale of food. It is clear, however, that the effect of such a tax can be achieved by increasing $(1 + \tau_1)$, $(1 + \tau_2)$, and T proportionately. If we were to tax food sales at rate τ, the budget constraint would become

$$(1 + \tau_1)M_1 + (1 + \tau_2)M_2 = (1 - \tau)(Q - X) - T$$

or

$$(14\text{-}27) \qquad \frac{1 + \tau_1}{1 - \tau}M_1 + \frac{1 + \tau_2}{1 - \tau}M_2 = Q - X - \frac{T}{1 - \tau}.$$

(Equivalence from the point of view of government revenue can also be demonstrated.) In this context, a linear direct tax on income is achieved by an equal proportionate tax on the two manufactured goods plus a lump-sum grant. The latter is equal to the value of the personal exemption in the income tax, and it should be noted that we are assuming that there is a negative income tax (incomes below the exemption are subsidized at the same rate as they are taxed above the exemption).

The result given above illustrates the kind of equivalence result that is often used in the theoretical public finance literature (and see the appendix to chapter 3). It also illustrates the kind of difficulties that may arise in trying to identify, for instance, "direct" and "indirect" taxes. A proportionate tax on cash income, $(Q - X)$, is equivalent, with an appropriate adjustment to T, to equal proportionate taxes on the consumption of M_1 and M_2. Our analysis therefore allows us to clarify the precise meaning of "direct" versus "indirect" taxation (Atkinson, 1977). Where there is no saving, a proportionate tax on income is the same as a uniform sales tax. What is at stake when we consider the choice between direct and indirect taxation, in this context, is (1) the level of the uniform poll tax, T, which is clearly a component of the direct tax system, and (2) the extent to which we tax the manufactured goods at different rates. We pay particular attention to these issues.

The government's objective function is taken to be represented by:

$$(14\text{-}28) \qquad H \equiv \int_1^\infty \phi[U(Q)]dG(Q) + \lambda R.$$

where ϕ is an increasing and concave function of the household utility, U. This expression may be interpreted as the maximization of current welfare subject to a revenue constraint, with λ being the Lagrange multiplier associated with the constraint. This is the form in which the optimum tax problem has usually been stated since Ramsey's original article: "The problem I propose to tackle is this: a given revenue is to be raised by proportionate taxes on some or all uses of income, the taxes on different uses being possibly at different rates; how should these rates be adjusted in order that the decrement of utility may be a minimum?" (Ramsey, 1927, p. 47). Alternatively, the government may attach a weight to revenue as such, as in the discussion in the third section of this chapter.

Optimal Taxation

We now describe some of the results in the optimal tax literature stemming from Ramsey (1927), as applied to the peasant economy.

In Ramsey's formulation, the government could vary τ_1 and τ_2, but there was no poll tax, T. As we shall see, this is an important restriction. Let us in fact start with the effect of variations in T, where this can take either sign. For the individual household, the derivative of U with respect to T is $-\alpha$, where α is the marginal utility of income. The effect on revenue is

$$(14\text{-}29) \qquad 1 - \tau_1 \frac{\partial M_1}{\partial I} - \tau_2 \frac{\partial M_2}{\partial I}$$

where $\partial M_i / \partial I$ denotes the income derivative ($i = 1, 2$). The revenue gain from a one dollar tax is thus less than one dollar if taxed goods are normal goods ($\partial M_i / \partial I > 0$). Suppose now that we consider the effect taken over all households, where we assume throughout that all households are in the market (which imposes restrictions on the range of variation in tax rates). The derivative is

$$(14\text{-}30) \quad \frac{\partial H}{\partial T} = \int_1^\infty \lambda \left[-\frac{\phi'\alpha}{\lambda} + \left(1 - \tau_1 \frac{\partial M_1}{\partial I} - \tau_2 \frac{\partial M_2}{\partial I}\right) \right] dG \equiv -\int_1^\infty \lambda \beta(Q) dG.$$

The expression $\beta(Q)$, corresponding to the square brackets in the middle, may be interpreted as the social value, in units of revenue, of one dollar transferred to a household with output Q, the social valuation taking account of the net loss of revenue (Atkinson and Stiglitz, 1976; Diamond, 1975). It is assumed that $\beta(Q)$ is a nonincreasing function of Q. There is no reason why this should be the case in general, because the income effect via taxed goods (see expression 14-29) may rise with Q, but it is a not unreasonable first assumption.

Suppose now that we consider a rise in the tax τ_i on M_i. The effect on household utility is $-\alpha M_i$, and that on revenue

$$(14\text{-}31) \qquad M_i + \tau_1 \frac{\partial M_1}{\partial \tau_i} + \tau_2 \frac{\partial M_2}{\partial \tau_i}.$$

From the Slutsky equation,

$$(14\text{-}32) \qquad \frac{\partial M_j}{\partial \tau_i} = S_{ji} - M_i \frac{\partial M_j}{\partial I}$$

where S_{ji} denotes the substitution term. It follows that we can write

(14-33) $\quad \dfrac{\partial H}{\partial \tau_1} = \displaystyle\int_1^\infty \lambda \left[-\dfrac{\phi' \alpha M_1}{\lambda} + \left(M_1 - \tau_1 M_1 \dfrac{\partial M_1}{\partial I} - \tau_2 M_2 \dfrac{\partial M_2}{\partial I} \right) \right.$

$$\left. + (\tau_1 S_{11} + \tau_2 S_{21}) \right] dG$$

(14-34a) $\qquad = \lambda \displaystyle\int_1^\infty (-\beta M_1 + \tau_1 S_{11} + \tau_2 S_{21}) \, dG.$

Symmetrically,

(14-34b) $\quad \dfrac{\partial H}{\partial \tau_2} = \lambda \displaystyle\int_1^\infty (-\beta M_2 + \tau_1 S_{12} + \tau_2 S_{22}) \, dG.$

The effect of the tax on a commodity differs from that of the uniform poll tax in two respects (compare equations 14-34a or 14-34b with 14-30). First, the burden is proportional to M_i (first term in the integral); second, the substitution terms now enter the expression, reflecting the distortion that is introduced.

Where the taxes (T, τ_1, and τ_2) may be freely varied, the first-order conditions for a social optimum are that $\partial H/\partial T$, $\partial H/\partial \tau_1$, and $\partial H/\partial \tau_2$ be zero. It does not follow that these conditions will uniquely define the optimum; there may be several candidates, and a comparison may have to be made between them. (Given the mechanical approach often adopted by economists to maximization problems, the need for understanding the structure of the problem should be emphasized. One cannot just crank the handle.) At the same time, the first-order conditions provide insight.

To begin with, let us consider the conditions under which the uniform poll tax is sufficient for the government's purpose. We would expect this to be only the case in which the government is not concerned about distribution, but how can we make this precise? The answer lies in the "social valuation of income," $\beta(Q)$. Suppose that this quantity was constant at $\bar{\beta}$, independent of Q. Then from equation 14-30, the choice of T implies that $\bar{\beta} = 0$. From equations 14-34a and 14-34b we can see that the derivatives $\partial H/\partial \tau_1$ and $\partial H/\partial \tau_2$ are zero when evaluated at $\tau_1 = \tau_2 = 0$. We have therefore the conclusion that indirect taxes are employed in this context only where the government is concerned about distribution, in that β varies with Q. This may at first appear surprising, but as Adam Smith noted, "in countries where the ease, comfort and security of the inferior ranks of people are little attended to, capitation taxes are very common" (1892, p. 690).

The presence of constraints on the use of particular taxes may therefore be of considerable importance. (We may note that Ramsey implicitly assumed that a poll tax was impossible; if it had been possible, then his problem would have disappeared, there being no distributional reasons for taxation.) Suppose that we consider the case where β decreases with Q, so that the social valuation of income is less for households with larger levels of output. Let us now define the aggregate substitution effect and elasticity:

(14-35) $$\bar{S}_{ij} \equiv \int_1^\infty S_{ij} \, dG \quad \text{and} \quad \bar{\epsilon}_{ij} \equiv \frac{\bar{S}_{ij}(1 + \tau_j)}{\bar{M}_i}$$

where

(14-36) $$\bar{M}_i \equiv \int_1^\infty M_i \, dG.$$

We also define the "distributional characteristic" (Feldstein, 1972) of good i:

(14-37) $$d_i \equiv \int_1^\infty \beta \frac{M_i}{\bar{M}_i} \, dG.$$

Because the marginal effect on household utility of a rise in τ_i is proportional to M_i, this provides an indication of the distributional desirability of reducing the tax on good i: if M_i rises sharply with Q, then it gives relatively more weight to the lower values of β (the good is consumed proportionately more by the "less deserving").

The first-order conditions for the choice of τ_1 and τ_2 may be rewritten, from equations 14-34a and 14-34b:

(14-38) $$d_1 = \frac{\tau_1}{1 + \tau_1} \bar{\epsilon}_{11} + \frac{\tau_2}{1 + \tau_2} \bar{\epsilon}_{12}$$

$$d_2 = \frac{\tau_1}{1 + \tau_1} \bar{\epsilon}_{21} + \frac{\tau_2}{1 + \tau_2} \bar{\epsilon}_{22}$$

(where we have used the symmetry of the substitution terms $S_{ji} = S_{ij}$). These equations may be solved to yield:

(14-39) $$\frac{\tau_1}{1 + \tau_1} = \frac{d_1 \bar{\epsilon}_{22} - d_2 \bar{\epsilon}_{12}}{\bar{\epsilon}_{11} \bar{\epsilon}_{22} - \bar{\epsilon}_{21} \bar{\epsilon}_{12}}$$

$$\frac{\tau_2}{1 + \tau_2} = \frac{d_2 \bar{\epsilon}_{11} - d_1 \bar{\epsilon}_{21}}{\bar{\epsilon}_{11} \bar{\epsilon}_{22} - \bar{\epsilon}_{21} \bar{\epsilon}_{12}}.$$

We assume that the denominator is positive (ensured in the individual case by the properties of the Slutsky matrix but not guaranteed in the aggregate). We also assume that the goods are both normal and aggregate Hicksian substitutes ($\bar{\epsilon}_{ij} > 0$ where $i \neq j$), which does not seem unreasonable for broad commodity groups.

The role of the distributional characteristic now becomes apparent. Suppose that the government is able to set the poll tax optimally or that it is constrained in its use of the poll tax but would like to increase it. This implies that (from equation 14-30):

(14-40) $$\bar{\beta} \equiv \int_1^\infty \beta(Q) \, dG \leq 0.$$

This, combined with the assumption that M_i is increasing (goods are normal), means that d_i is negative. It follows from equation 14-39 that both goods should be taxed positively where the government sets the poll tax optimally or would like to increase it but is constrained not to do so. Moreover, the relative rates of tax depend on the substitution elasticities and on the distributional characteristics of the good. In the latter case, the good that is more responsive to income will have the larger value, in absolute terms, of d_i. From equation 14-39 we see that such a "luxury" will be taxed more heavily. This finding quite accords with intuition, in that distributional considerations are represented by this term.

The effect of the substitution terms may be seen in the situation where $d_1 = d_2$, for example, when the government is concerned only about revenue ($\lambda \to \infty$), so that β depends on Q only via the income effects and when these are constant (constant marginal propensities to consume). Suppose further that the government would like to use the poll tax but cannot. Then in the formula for τ_1 and τ_2, we have $d_1 = d_2 = \bar{\beta} < 0$, and (from equation 14-39) the optimum tax structure depends solely on the substitution elasticities. At the level of the individual household

$$(14\text{-}41) \qquad (1 + \tau_1)S_{i1} + (1 + \tau_2)S_{i2} + S_{i3} = 0$$

for $i = 1, 2, 3$, where 3 denotes food (X). Aggregating for $i = 1$ and 2, and dividing by $\bar{M}_i$, it follows that

$$(14\text{-}42) \qquad \bar{\epsilon}_{12} = -\bar{\epsilon}_{11} - \bar{\epsilon}_{13}$$

$$\bar{\epsilon}_{21} = -\bar{\epsilon}_{22} - \bar{\epsilon}_{23}.$$

Hence from equation 14-39,

$$(14\text{-}43) \qquad \frac{\tau_1}{1 + \tau_1} = \frac{\tau_2}{1 + \tau_2} \left[\frac{-(\bar{\epsilon}_{11} + \bar{\epsilon}_{22}) - \bar{\epsilon}_{13}}{-(\bar{\epsilon}_{11} + \bar{\epsilon}_{22}) - \bar{\epsilon}_{23}} \right].$$

The tax rate will thus be higher on the manufactured good with the smaller cross-elasticity of (compensated) demand with the price of food (this is in effect the result of Corlett and Hague, 1953).

Such use of the first-order conditions helps us understand the key elements in the solution. At the same time, it does not permit an explicit solution for the policy parameters. The aggregate elasticities, $\bar{\epsilon}_{ij}$, and the distributional characteristics, d_i, are in general functions of the tax rates. As a result, although it is tempting to try to obtain comparative static results, we cannot do so using this form. For this reason, the optimum tax literature has commonly made particular assumptions about the functional form.

To illustrate the results obtainable with a particular specification for $U(M_1, M_2, X)$, we take the Stone-Geary (linear expenditure system) form:

$$(14\text{-}44) \qquad \log U = \gamma_1 \log(M_1 + b_1) + \gamma_2 \log(M_2 + b_2)$$
$$+ (1 - \gamma_1 - \gamma_2)\log(X + x),$$

where γ_1, γ_2, and γ_3 are positive parameters, and b_1, b_2, and x are parameters that may take either sign. This form has been widely used in empirical studies of consumer demand (see, for example, Lluch, Powell, and Williams, 1977) and is discussed by Deaton in chapter 4. The resulting demand functions are:

(14-45)
$$(1 + \tau_1)M_1 = \gamma_1 Z - (1 + \tau_1)b_1$$

$$(1 + \tau_2)M_2 = \gamma_2 Z - (1 + \tau_2)b_2$$

$$X = (1 - \gamma_1 - \gamma_2)Z - x$$

where

(14-46)
$$Z = (Q + x) - T + (1 + \tau_1)b_1 + (1 + \tau_2)b_2$$

and Z is equal to (U/α).

Suppose further that in the social welfare function $\phi = \log(U)$. Therefore

(14-47)
$$\phi'\alpha = \alpha/U = 1/Z.$$

Hence (from equation 14-30)

(14-48)
$$\beta = \frac{1}{\lambda}Z^{-1} - \left(1 - \frac{\tau_1}{1 + \tau_1}\gamma_1 - \frac{\tau_2}{1 + \tau_2}\gamma_2\right) \equiv \frac{1}{\lambda}Z^{-1} - \beta_0$$

using the properties of the demand system 14-45. It may further be calculated that:

(14-49)
$$S_{11} = \frac{\gamma_1(\gamma_1 - 1)}{(1 + \tau_1)^2}Z; \qquad S_{12} = \frac{\gamma_1\gamma_2 Z}{(1 + \tau_1)(1 + \tau_2)}$$

with symmetric expressions for S_{21} and S_{22}. Substituting in equation 14-39 and using equation 14-45, we may derive (after rearrangement):

(14-50)
$$\frac{\tau_1/(1 + \tau_1)}{\tau_2/(1 + \tau_2)} = \frac{\dfrac{1}{\lambda} - \beta_0\bar{Z} - \bar{\beta}\left[\dfrac{1 - \gamma_2}{\gamma_1}b_1(1 + \tau_1) + b_2(1 + \tau_2)\right]}{\dfrac{1}{\lambda} - \beta_0\bar{Z} - \bar{\beta}\left[b_1(1 + \tau_1) + \dfrac{1 - \gamma_1}{\gamma_2}b_2(1 + \tau_2)\right]}$$

where $\bar{Z}$ and $\bar{\beta}$ denote the mean values.

We can draw a number of conclusions. First, if $b_1 = b_2 = 0$, then uniform taxation is desirable. In this case, the goods have unitary income elasticities; there is an argument for differential taxation only if the income elasticities differ. Second, if $\bar{\beta} = 0$, then uniform taxation is again desirable (even where $b_1, b_2 \neq 0$). $\bar{\beta} = 0$, however, is the first-order condition for the choice of T (from equation 14-30). As a result, if the government is free to levy a uniform tax or subsidy, then it would not want, with the linear expenditure system and this social welfare function, to have differential sales taxation. In other words, if the government levies an optimum linear income tax (T plus equal proportionate sales taxation), then there is no welfare gain from the use of indirect taxation. (See also the discussion by Deaton in chapter 4.)

With the specific Stone-Geary functional form, we do not obtain an explicit solution for τ_1 and τ_2. The tax rates enter β_0, $\bar{Z}$, and $\bar{\beta}$, so that equation 14-50 does not provide a direct numerical answer. For this reason, a number of authors have made numerical calculations of the optimum tax rates (see, for example, Stern, 1976). The interest in these calculations depends on the validity of the parameters used, and there can be little doubt that at present we lack adequate evidence. At the same time, calculations provide some feel for the likely numerical magnitudes and, perhaps more important, indicate the directions in which the assembly of data and statistical analysis needs to be improved.

Extensions of the Analysis

In the previous section, we have tried to give some flavor of the results obtained in the recent optimum taxation literature. The analysis evidently needs to be deepened. In this section, attention is drawn briefly to some of the areas that seem particularly relevant to developing economies.

The Household and the Agricultural Sector

The model has been cast in terms of a peasant economy, but even within this type of agriculture a number of aspects need to be considered. We have not taken into account the household structure and the relation between the decisions of different members. This has been explored by Sen (1966) and others, who have shown that labor inputs and other decisions may depend on the rules according to which income is shared within the household and the degree of sympathy of household members for each other. The imposition of taxation may affect the distribution *within* households as well as *between* households: for example, the relative position of men and women. The role of land ownership has not been treated explicitly (although it is one of the elements assumed to lie behind the distribution of Q).

In addition to labor and land, there are purchased inputs, and these may be affected by government policy. The decision to plant new, higher-yielding varieties, for example, may be affected by the tax on market sales. It is also the case that the government may have other instruments at its disposal. The government may be able to vary the price of inputs such as fertilizer; it may be able to supply capital inputs such as irrigation or transport facilities. The question of tax design has to be considered in relation to the pricing of inputs and supply of infrastructure. The literature on optimum taxation itself indicates that "partial" optimization (considering only one subgroup of instruments) may yield misleading conclusions for policy, and it is a valid objection to optimum tax analysis that it ignores other controls that the government has at its disposal. Some of those questions are explored by Sah and Stiglitz in chapter 16.

Finally, we need to consider the implications of other forms of agricultural organization. The model of a peasant economy was chosen here as approximating most closely the treatment of the household in the tax design literature; the presence of landlords and landless laborers raises other issues. How is the response to taxation affected by the renting of land? What are the differences between fixed rent contracts and sharecropping? How is the outcome influenced by money lending and debt? Here the analysis needs to draw on recent studies of the microeconomics of different market systems (for example, Newbery and Stiglitz, 1979). Quite a lot of the theory carries over to these alternative systems, but at the very least some distributional effects must be taken into account.

The Industrial Sector

The industrial sector needs to be brought into the analysis, and we must also examine the way in which it is affected by taxation. As a minimum, we need a dual-economy model, which allows for intersectoral relations and for the effects of taxation on producer prices. Chapters 15 and 16, by Heady and Mitra and Sah and Stiglitz, provide examples.

Of particular interest is the question of migration between the sectors. People may leave the peasant sector seeking employment in the industrial sector, according to some process such as that described by Todaro (1969) and Fields in chapter 10. This is relevant to the analysis of taxation, in that geographical migration may imply that the person then enters the taxable net. It may, for instance, be possible to levy a standard income tax on the workers in the modern industrial sector but not on those in the traditional sector. This may act as a counterweight to wage subsidies (such as low-cost housing) in the industrial sector. Here, again, the study of the public finance questions needs to be based on a model of the economy more closely attuned to the issues discussed in a development context.

Dynamics of Optimization

The discussion thus far invites consideration of the dynamics of optimization. Discussions of such questions as choice of technique or rate of investment have typically been embedded in a dynamic model, where the economy grows over time, with the advanced industrial sector playing an increasingly important role.

In the present context, the implications of such a dynamic approach may be seen in terms of the weight λ attached to revenue in the objective function (as noted in the third section of this chapter). If revenue is used for investment, then H in equation 14-28 corresponds to the Hamiltonian in a dynamic optimization (the choice of notation was deliberate), with λ corresponding to the multiplier associated with the differential equation for capital. In the typical planning model of a dual economy (for example, Newbery, 1972, and

Stern, 1972), the value of this multiplier falls as the economy develops. The implications for the design of taxation policy can then be deduced, and some of them have been discussed in chapter 5.

The dynamic approach may be taken further, in that we may view the design of taxation as a dynamic process, with the government seeking to adjust taxes in a welfare-improving direction but being limited in the speed with which changes can be made (for example, taxes can be increased by only a specified percentage in any one year). We would then have a set of differential equations governing the adjustment of taxes—in which case we would of course be taking the perspective of tax "reform" (see, for example, Fogelman, Guesnerie, and Quinzii, 1978) rather than tax optimization. This development represents an interesting problem for further research, incorporating an important real world limitation on what governments can do. In this and other respects, a great deal remains to be done.

15

Optimal Taxation and Shadow Pricing in a Developing Economy

Christopher Heady and Pradeep Mitra

THE MAIN PURPOSE of this chapter is to explore the design of optimal taxes in a simple model of a developing country. It is thus similar in spirit to the approach adopted by Atkinson in chapter 14 and by Sah and Stiglitz in chapter 16. Recent interest in optimal commodity taxation largely dates from the work of Diamond and Mirrlees (1971), but their model makes strong assumptions about the structure of the economy and the instruments available to the government. In particular, they initially assume that all transactions between producers and consumers can be taxed and that changes in private production need not change the distribution of goods in the economy, so that the organization of production and the distribution of the goods that are produced can be separately addressed; the Diamond-Mirrlees result is discussed in chapter 2. In most developing countries, a large fraction of the population is typically employed in agriculture and consumes goods produced on family-owned farms. It is often hard to tax agricultural output but relatively easy to tax trade between the agricultural and nonagricultural sectors. Diamond and Mirrlees (1971, p. 25) showed that they could accommodate this problem in their model by including subsistence agriculture in the consumer sector rather than in the producer sector, in which case the tax rules would depend on the derivatives of net trades rather than consumption. The production efficiency results would apply only to the restricted definition of the producer sector, not to subsistence agriculture. This chapter extends the analysis of Diamond and Mirrlees by considering its application to an economy with internal migration in which other tax restrictions may be present. It also provides numerical results to illustrate the tax rates implied by the theory and their sensitivity to the features that we introduce.

The main case for examining simple optimal tax models such as those of the

The authors thank Christopher Harris and Hector Sierra for exceptionally able research assistance. Useful comments from James Mirrlees and David Newbery on an earlier draft are gratefully acknowledged. The World Bank does not accept responsibility for the views expressed herein, which are those of the authors and should not be attributed to the World Bank or to its affiliated organizations. The findings, interpretations, and conclusions are the results of research supported by the Bank; they do not necessarily reflect official policy of the Bank.

present chapter is not to derive quantitative results for the tax rates on specific goods but rather to explore the factors that will influence these tax rates and hence to identify the important determinants of tax design that will need to be examined carefully in any particular case. The case for exploring optimal taxes in addition to simple tax reform has been made in chapter 3 but can usefully be restated. Small changes in taxes give fairly predictable changes in welfare, and hence it is possible to be reasonably confident about modest improvements. Large changes in taxes, associated with attempts to redesign the tax system in accordance with the imperatives of optimal taxation, have less predictable consequences but offer potentially larger improvements. The results reported here allow us to understand the sensitivity of optimal taxes to differences in the underlying economic model. They therefore indicate the sort of information that is required before a major tax change can be formulated.

The model analyzed in this chapter has several special features. First, it distinguishes between the rural and urban, or modern, sectors. Modern sector production satisfies all the assumptions of the Diamond-Mirrlees producer sector, which allow it to be treated as though it were in the public sector. The only transactions that can be taxed in the rural sector are net trades with the modern sector. The present model thus shows similarities to Atkinson's model but also important differences—it explicitly considers the role of land ownership and the ability of the government to control the price of the agricultural input, fertilizer. It also treats the industrial sector explicitly and models rural-urban labor migration under two different assumptions about the working of the rural land market. As in Atkinson's chapter 14, the emphasis is on calculating numerical solutions for the tax rates and showing how taxes will respond to the government's revenue needs. In contrast to Atkinson, the model that we analyze assumes all agents to be identical, and it thus ignores distributional issues in order to concentrate on various specific features. The tax rules explained below would be modified in the usual way if distributional considerations were introduced. It would obviously be desirable to extend the numerical model to include distributional considerations, but the data are not available.

The model also has close affinities with that studied by Sah and Stiglitz in chapter 16 and shares some of its analytical results (and indeed shares results with the reinterpreted model of Diamond and Mirrlees, 1971, p. 25). It differs in deriving numerical estimates for the tax rates and exploring their quantitative robustness, whereas Sah and Stiglitz show how empirical estimates of critical elasticities may be used to inform the choice of tax policy. The specific advantage of these numerical estimates is that we can explore the significance of the various constraints implied by dualism as well as examining such interesting questions as the sensitivity of the tax rates to changes in the trading environment (specifically, to large changes in the import price of oil).

The questions addressed in this chapter are the following:

1. What can be said about the optimal structure of commodity taxation in

each sector, and how is this structure affected by restrictions on the government's tax powers and the possibility of migration?

2. How do tax rates on different commodities change as the revenue requirements of the government increase? How do they respond to changes in the world price of oil?

3. Is it desirable to influence migration by changing the balance of urban and rural taxation?

4. To what extent is it desirable to tax or subsidize agricultural inputs (fertilizer)? (If the government could tax agricultural output, factor payments, and consumption separately, input taxes would be undesirable.)

5. Should the government intervene in either sector's transactions with the rest of the world by using tariffs or other trade policies?

6. How should accounting or shadow prices for use in social cost-benefit analysis differ, if at all, from market prices?

The first four questions are clearly important issues in tax policy, and the fifth is a question of trade policy, whereas the sixth is concerned with cost-benefit analysis of government projects. As has been remarked in chapters 1, 3, and 6, however, there is a very close connection between tax policy, trade policy, and social cost-benefit analysis, and this connection will again be apparent in the present chapter.

The Structure of the Model

The economy is divided into a rural sector and an urban sector. The rural sector produces food, using land, labor, and fertilizer. The urban sector produces three goods: clothing, services, and fertilizer. It uses three factors, which are assumed to be fully mobile within the urban sector: capital, labor, and energy. All markets are competitive, and food, clothing, fertilizer, and energy are internationally traded at fixed world prices. With the exception of energy, which must be imported, the direction of trade is determined endogenously in the model. The model is static (a dynamic version is discussed in Heady and Mitra, 1984), and everyone is assumed to be identical and to have identical tastes except that some people live and work in the rural sector and the rest live and work in the urban area.

Assumptions Concerning Migration

Individuals can choose whether to migrate from one sector to the other, and this requires us to specify the rural outmigrant's rights to income from land. We consider two polar alternatives. Model 1 assumes that migrants from the rural sector give up their rights to land, whereas migrants into the rural sector acquire rights to land. Thus, land is divided equally among all rural residents. Model 2 assumes that the ownership of land and the income accruing from it are divided equally among the entire population. Because it is not obvious whether rural-to-urban migrants can maintain their rights to land income (by renting or selling the land), it is interesting to examine the sensitivity of optimal policy to these alternatives. In addition, people dislike living in urban areas, so that their utility is reduced by a given proportion. Thus, if a particular consumption and leisure choice would result in a utility level u_m in the rural sector, it would only produce θu_m (where $\theta < 1$) in the urban sector. Equilibrium occurs when the utility of rural residents, u_a, is equal to the effective utility of urban residents, θu_m (where u_i is the same function of consumption and leisure in each sector).

Finally all capital stock is owned by the government, although as usual nothing would be altered if it were privately owned but were subject to a 100 percent profits tax. We shall analyze the significance of this assumption shortly.

Restrictions on the Government's Ability to Tax

The main instruments of government policy are taxes. It is assumed that all urban consumer goods and labor supply can be taxed. Given the institutional structure of agriculture, however, it may be virtually impossible to tax some rural activities. The rural consumption of food, for example, cannot be taxed, because it is produced within the household. Similarly, land and labor cannot be taxed, because they are supplied and used in the family farm. Thus, as in Atkinson's model (chapter 14), the only taxes on agriculture are those levied on its sales to and purchases from the rest of the economy.

Another natural restriction is that, because of the ease of arbitrage, the consumer price of clothing should be the same in both sectors. This is not a real tax restriction, however, as only *relative* prices in each sector matter. Thus the urban consumer prices can be scaled up or down to satisfy the arbitrage condition without altering utility or production. The restriction does, however, assume significance if any other good must also have the same price in both sectors, and we will consider the case in which arbitrage also forces the urban and rural consumer prices of food into equality. Note that services are unlikely to be subject to arbitrage and so can be taxed at different rates in the two sectors.

Subject to these restrictions, the government chooses taxes to maximize social welfare and to balance its budget. For simplicity, government expenditures (as opposed to transfer payments) are assumed to have no effect on current welfare (administration, defense, investment, and so forth). The social welfare function has the form

$$(15\text{-}1) \qquad W = \frac{1}{1 - \epsilon} [L_a u_a^{1-\epsilon} + L_m (\theta u_m)^{1-\epsilon}] \qquad \epsilon \neq 1,$$

(15-2) $= L_a \log u_a + L_m \log(\theta u_m)$ $\epsilon = 1,$

where L_a is the number of people in the rural or agricultural sector, L_m is the number in the urban or manufacturing sector, u_i is the same function of consumption and leisure in each sector, and ϵ is the Atkinson's degree of inequality aversion, or the rate at which the social marginal utility of consumption falls with increasing consumption. When migration equalizes utility, so that $u_a = \theta u_m$, then social welfare is just

(15-3) $$W = \frac{1}{1-\epsilon} L u_a^{1-\epsilon}$$

where $L = L_a + L_m$ is total population.

Analytical Results

The model is similar to those used in other work on optimal taxation (including restricted taxation) and public production (Diamond and Mirrlees, 1971 and 1976; Heady and Mitra, 1982; Munk, 1980; Stiglitz and Dasgupta, 1971). This section extends their results to take into account the special features of the present model. The main differences are that we allow migration and must make assumptions about rights to land rent. The fact that some goods are allowed to have different prices in different sectors introduces no new point of principle, because they can be regarded as different goods that can be transformed into each other by the government.

Migration means that the government must take into account the effect of its policies on intersectoral labor mobility. Because migration equalizes utility, however, any policy that increases the utility of urban residents will promote rural-urban migration, and vice versa. Consequently, if the government wishes to encourage rural-urban migration, the tax policies will be the same as they would be if it put a higher weight on urban utility and lower weight on rural utility.

We are interested in the structure of taxation in each sector, and it is useful to start with a situation in which there are no tax restrictions other than the unavailability of lump-sum taxes and subsidies. Because in our model everyone is identical, the standard one-consumer Ramsey rule for efficient taxation applies to both urban and rural consumer taxation. Thus a small equiproportionate intensification of optimal consumer taxation, with constant producer prices, would produce equal proportionate reductions in compensated demands for all urban consumer goods. A similar statement would apply to rural consumer goods, but the proportionate reduction in agricultural output would be zero, as the tax would fall entirely on the inelastically supplied land. If it is not possible to tax agriculture directly, this option is not available. We can follow Diamond and Mirrlees (1971), however, by regarding a farm as a consumer that purchases clothing, services, and fertilizer and sells food. Thus the net trades of the agricultural sector can be treated as if they were consumer demands and supplies. In this case the Ramsey rule must be modified to state that efficient agricultural taxation requires an equiproportionate increase in taxation (where taxes are defined as the difference between agricultural prices and urban producer prices, and the urban producer of food is taken to be its world price), with constant urban producer prices, to produce equal proportionate reductions in compensated *net trade* for all goods, just as in the urban sector it should produce equal proportionate reductions in compensated *consumption*. Evidently tax rates will differ in the two sectors, and it will be desirable to tax (or subsidize) the net trade in fertilizer. These Ramsey rules do not apply without further modification to model 2 (in which migrants keep their land rights) because agricultural taxation also affects urban income. If in addition to the restrictions on agricultural taxation, it is assumed that food must have the same price in each sector, the tax rules given above must be modified so that within each sector, the proportionate reductions for food and clothing can be different from those for other goods.

The next set of questions concerns the balance of the tax burden between the sectors, which in turn involves balancing the social costs and benefits of migration. A marginal rural-to-urban migrant has no direct effect on social welfare because the extra urban utility gained exactly balances the rural utility lost. In model 2, everyone owns an equal amount of land, and the indirect net benefit of the move is the cost of the rural consumption bundle the migrant gives up less the cost of the urban consumption bundle to which he (or she) lays claim. Because this must be zero at an optimum, the cost of a consumption bundle in the two sectors must be equal. This equality can be shown to imply an equal tax burden on rural and urban consumers, and hence the tax system should neither encourage nor discourage migration. The result is similar to a production efficiency result in that it forbids government intervention in all allocative processes despite the existence of distortionary consumer taxation.

The situation is different in model 1, where rural-to-urban migrants lose their land rights. Migration then creates an externality in the form of an increase in land income for those left behind in the rural sector. The corresponding policy implication is that the tax burden on rural consumers should exceed that on urban consumers by the net social value of the ensuing change in land incomes.

We shall now turn to trade policy and public production. Consider first the urban sector of the economy. The government can vary urban consumer prices independently of producer prices, even when food and clothing prices must be the same in both sectors, because these restrict the number of consumer price instruments but do not link consumer prices to urban producer prices. Consequently the Diamond-Mirrlees result holds, and production efficiency is desirable in the manufacturing sector. The implication is that there should be no tariffs or other interventions on manufacturing trade with the rest of the world and also that the government should use producer prices as accounting or shadow prices.

The government cannot vary rural consumer prices independently of rural producer prices, however, and so the Diamond-Mirrlees results do not apply. As we argued above, it becomes desirable to tax (or subsidize) intermediate inputs (fertilizer). Agricultural production will be inefficient (relative to world prices, that is, to comparative advantage). In addition, shadow prices for rural goods need not equal their market prices, because government use of rural resources (for example, land) will affect all rural prices and incomes. These will affect government revenue, the social value of which must be added to the simple output forgone. It is still possible, however, to say something about shadow prices of rural goods, as all production activities, including agriculture, experience constant returns to scale, and so all activities used at an optimum have zero profits at producer prices. Despite the presence of production inefficiency, those activities will have zero profits at shadow prices as well (Diamond and Mirrlees, 1976). Indeed, this argument leads to the Little and Mirrlees (1974) rule for shadow pricing a small country's tradables at their world prices.

Numerical Results

This section reports the results of solving models 1 and 2 with specific functional forms (regarding the algorithm used, see Drud, 1985). Consumer behavior is described by a linear expenditure system that gives rise to additive separability (see chapter 4, by Deaton). Production functions are the nested constant elasticity of substitution forms. (In the rural sector, land and fertilizer are combined to form a subaggregate, which is then combined with labor to produce output. The manufacturing industries are treated similarly, but capital and energy rather than land and fertilizer form the subaggregate.) The parameter values were chosen to approximate the Turkish economy (for which a larger computable model and associated data base exist in Lewis and Urata, 1983). The calculated tax rates appear in the following tables and are defined as

$$(15\text{-}4) \qquad \text{Tax rate} = \left(\frac{\text{Consumer price}}{\text{Producer price}} - 1 \right) \times 100 \text{ percent.}$$

Thus, for goods purchased by consumers, a positive tax represents a transfer to the government, whereas a negative tax represents a transfer from the government. The reverse is true for goods such as labor and agricultural output, which are supplied by consumers, however: a consumer price higher than the producer price represents a transfer to the consumer from the government.

As we remarked above, consumer welfare depends only on relative prices, and hence it makes no difference if we scale consumer prices up or down relative to urban producer prices, giving rise to nominally different tax rates. A zero tax on urban labor and positive urban sales taxes, for example, is equiva-

Table 15-1. *Optimal Taxes When the Rural Population Owns Land*
(percent)

Item	Base case[a] (1)	Base case[a] (2)	DFT[b] (3)	DFT[b] (4)	Base case[c] (5)	Base case[c] (6)	Base case[c] (7)	No tax restrictions[d] (8)	No tax restrictions[d] (9)
Price of energy[e]	1	5	1	5	1	1	1	1	5
Urban									
Food	−43.8	−43.6	−55.5	−54.2	−27.2	−30.5	−42.1	−51.2	−50.6
Clothing	−56.3	−54.4	−48.3	−47.0	−53.5	−54.0	−56.1	−44.1	−43.3
Services	−48.1	−45.5	−46.0	−44.0	−41.7	−42.9	−47.4	−41.6	−40.9
Rural									
Food (− is tax)	−43.8	−43.6	−25.3	−22.9	−27.2	−30.5	−42.1	} −44.1[f]	−43.3[f]
Clothing	−56.3	−54.4	−48.3	−47.0	−53.5	−54.0	−56.1		
Services	−61.3	−59.4	−46.4	−42.4	−58.6	−59.2	−61.1		
Fertilizer	−47.2	−46.5	−26.7	−24.0	−33.1	−35.9	−45.7		
Rural[g]									
Clothing	−22.2	−19.1	−30.8	−27.9	−36.1	−33.9	−24.1	0	0
Services	−31.2	−28.1	−28.3	−25.3	−43.1	−41.4	−32.9	0	0
Fertilizer	−6.0	−5.2	−1.9	−1.4	−8.2	−7.8	−6.2	0	0
u_a (note h)	99.0	94.2	99.2	94.4	109.6	107.9	100.3	100	94.9
θu_m	99.0	94.2	99.2	94.4	89.1	93.4	98.0	100	94.9
L_a/L	50	49	52	51	50	50	50	59	57

Note: In all columns except column 6, θ = 0.972.

a. Effect of energy price change. Base case: rural and urban prices of food and clothing are the same; there are no taxes on land or labor.
b. Energy price change. DFT = Differential food taxation feasible: different rates in each sector, same clothing tax in each sector.
c. No migration. Labor allocation constrained to that of column 1.
d. Energy price changes.
e. Other parameters: in column 5, ε = 0. In column 6, θ = 1. In column 7, ε = 6.
f. Tax on rural consumption, not on food production.
g. Taxes or subsidies relative to food. In this model, rural workers are concerned only about the prices of purchased goods relative to that of food.
h. Utility as a percentage of that achievable with no tax restrictions (column 8). Utility is proportional to income less subsistence requirements.

lent to a negative tax on labor (which drives the after-tax wage below the before-tax wage and yields positive government revenue) and lower rates of sales taxes. This apparent indeterminacy has been avoided by setting labor taxes at zero in both sectors in model 1.

The initial calculations were designed to explore the sensitivity of the tax rates to tax restrictions, model choice, labor mobility, and the price of energy, with government revenues held constant. The effect of varying the revenue requirement is studied in the next section. As the model is set up, the government receives all the profits of the public sector (either by ownership or profits taxes). In the early experiments, government expenditure was set at zero, so that these profits had to be handed back as subsidies. Obviously the assumption involved is implausible, for normally these profits would be reinvested, repatriated, or consumed, and the government would require revenue for administration, public goods, and development expenditures. Fortunately, the next section shows that tax rates vary in a steady way as the revenue requirement increases, and so the tables below, which report the results of transferring revenue to consumers, are still a good guide to the way the distortions (subsidies rather than taxes) vary with the specification of the model.

Table 15-1 reports the results for model 1. In the base case the government cannot tax agricultural production but only net sales and is constrained to tax food and clothing equally in each sector. This can be achieved by an export tax on food grains of 77.9 percent (for column 1), which lowers the domestic price to 56.2 percent of its world price, equivalent to domestic taxes of $56.2 - 100 = -43.8$ percent. Similarly, clothing is subsidized at the same rate in both sectors (whereas services are differentially priced). Fertilizer is subsidized at 6 percent relative to food in the rural sector, as is best seen from the lower part of table 15-1, which gives rural tax rates relative to agricultural output, food. The reason for the subsidies is that the government is redistributing its profits, and the interest of table 15-1 is that it permits us to compare tax rates along the rows, and as *relative* magnitudes within columns, rather than considering merely their absolute level.

The effect of not being able to price food differently in each sector can be seen by comparing columns 1 and 3. If food can be differentially priced, then its rural price rises relative to the urban price, improving the welfare of rural workers, who sell food for higher prices. Consequently the other rural subsidies decline, and fertilizer is only subsidized 1.9 percent relative to food. Urban workers receive more of their subsidies from food and less via other goods, because it is no longer necessary to worry about an adverse food supply response as the urban food price is lowered. Agricultural output rises (rural labor increases from 50 percent to 52 percent of the labor force), but real income increases by only 0.2 of 1 percent. Though the constraints have powerful effects on the tax structure, they have little effect on welfare.

The effect of not being able to tax trades between rural producers and rural consumers can be seen by comparing column 8 with columns 1 and 3. The most dramatic effect occurs in agriculture when inelastically supplied land is now the sole taxed (actually subsidized) good, and resources can be transferred in a nondistortionary way, resulting in larger agricultural output. By comparing columns 3 and 8 we see that the urban subsidies are lower, with no tax restrictions, but their real income rises by 0.8 of 1 percent as agricultural output increases in response to eliminating rural distortions.

The significance of migration can be examined if we look at columns 5, 6, and 7 of table 15-1, which report the optimal tax rates with all the tax restrictions in place but with no migration. The distribution of the labor force between urban and rural areas has been fixed at the optimal level of column 1. Two sets of results are reported because the absence of migration means that the urban-rural utility differential is no longer fixed, and so the government will take distributional considerations into account when setting taxes. Column 5 gives the results for $\epsilon = 0$, where the government is not concerned about inequality. Column 7 gives the results for $\epsilon = 6$, where the government is greatly concerned to reduce inequality (see below for a discussion of the results of column 6).

A comparison of columns 5 and 1 shows that, if migration is not able to equalize rural and urban welfare, then rural subsidies are all increased (in terms of the price of food); rural workers are made better off than urban workers and are absolutely 10 percent better off. Urban subsidies are reduced, so that urban workers are 10 percent worse off. The reason is that, in model 1, rural outmigration creates an externality (higher remaining rural income), which tends to cause too little migration. The government attempts to correct this deficiency by subsidizing urban consumers relative to rural consumers. When migration cannot occur, and the government is indifferent to inequality, resources are shifted back to agriculture and the urban subsidy is removed. In model 2, discussed below, this issue does not arise.

The resulting inequality, shown in column 5, is not what a government interested in equality would desire. Thus, column 7, in which the government worries about inequality, shows a pattern of subsidies much closer to that of column 1, which produced the same value of L_a/L when equality was achieved by migration.

The final set of experiments explored the impact on the structure of optimal commodity taxes (subsidies) of a fivefold increase in the real price of oil. Columns 2, 4, and 9 report the taxes corresponding to the cases considered in columns 1, 3, and 8. Services (such as transport and electricity) are the most energy-intensive goods, and the effect of an increase in the oil price is to reduce government profits and hence the level of subsidies. Labor also moves out of agriculture to import substitute in clothing in order to pay for the increased cost of oil imports, and this shift further reduces the subsidies available. As might be expected, the subsidy rates on the most energy-intensive good (services) fall the most, though the changes are all small compared with the welfare cost (of 5.8 percent of real income). Thus the *pattern* of ad valorem taxes appears to be relatively insensitive to large changes in the price of oil. (The absolute level of taxes on energy-intensive goods would therefore change appreciably, as we would expect the price to change.)

It is also interesting to see whether tax restrictions affect the government's ability to deal with the oil price increases. A comparison of columns 3 and 4 shows the effect when it is possible to price food differentially, whereas a comparison of columns 8 and 9 shows the effect when there are no tax restrictions at all. All the effects are very similar to those in the base case, and there appears to be little connection between the extent of tax restrictions and the ability of the government to deal with energy price changes, at least over the range of restrictions analyzed here.

The Effect of Land Ownership

Table 15-2 presents the results for model 2 in which everyone owns land (and rural outmigrants retain their land rent). If the government were able, it would wish to subsidize the land rent of urban workers, which is an inelastic good. If this were not possible, the government would achieve the same effect by rescaling all other urban prices, *including* the price of labor. It is then no longer possible to treat urban labor as an untaxed good, and hence its tax rate is reported in table 15-2. The consequences of this choice of numeraire can be seen by comparing the upper and lower parts of table 15-2. In the lower part, urban labor and rural food are the (relatively) untaxed goods, but it is now necessary to subsidize urban land income to achieve the same effective tax system.

The first point that stands out in table 15-2 is that it is always desirable to tax urban labor and services at the same rate, because they are sector specific. Food and clothing tax rates are influenced by the need to tax agriculture inefficiently. If food prices can be set differently in each sector, then column 3 shows that the urban sector should face uniform taxes, or, equivalently, only inelastically supplied land rent is subsidized. The same is also true when there are no tax restrictions. By comparison with model 1, there is now no argument for favored treatment of the urban sector to encourage migration, and the fraction of agricultural workers consequently drops dramatically, raising real income levels. The market failure or externality implied by the inability to transfer land rights in model 1 has resulted in a loss of output and a considerable distortion in the allocation of labor.

Agriculture is subsidized more in model 2 than in model 1, again because there is no need to relatively favor the urban sector. When migration is impossible, columns 5–7 show that the agricultural sector is worse off than the urban sector, whereas the opposite was true in model 1. As the government's inequality aversion increases (column 7), so the disparity narrows and the tax structure approaches the base case with migration. When $\theta = 1$ (column 6), there are no nonpecuniary disadvantages to living in the urban area, and

Table 15-2. Optimal Taxes When the Entire Population Owns Land
(percent)

Item	Base case[a] (1)	Base case[a] (2)	DFT[b] (3)	DFT[b] (4)	Base case[c] (5)	Base case[c] (6)	Base case[c] (7)	No tax restrictions (8)	No tax restrictions (9)
Price of energy[d]	1	5	1	5	1	1	1	1	5
Urban									
Food	−67.8	−66.2	−74.6	−73.1	−78.4	−79.0	−69.7	−72.1	−70.8
Clothing	−79.0	−77.7			−79.0		−79.0		
Services	−76.7	−75.3			−78.8		−77.0		
Labor (− is tax)	−76.7	−75.3			−78.8		−77.0		
Rural									
Food (− is tax)	−67.8	−66.2	−74.6	−73.1	−78.4	−79.0	−69.7	−72.1[e]	−70.8[e]
Clothing	−79.0	−77.7	−86.0	−84.8	−79.0		−79.0		
Services	−82.3	−80.9	−85.3	−84.0	−79.4		−82.2		
Fertilizer	−71.1	−69.4	−75.9	−74.4	−78.6		−72.4		

418

Urban[f]									
Land (+ is subsidy)	329.0	305.7	293.7	271.7	372.0	376.2	334.8	258.4	242.5
Food	38.1	36.8	0	0	1.9	0	31.8	0	0
Clothing	−9.9	−9.7	0	0	−1.0	0	−8.7	0	0
Services	0	0	0	0	0	0	0	0	0
Fertilizer	0	0	0	0	0	0	0	0	0
Rural[g]									
Clothing	−34.8	−34.0	−44.9	−43.6	−2.7	0	−30.8	0	0
Services	−44.9	−43.6	−42.1	−40.7	−4.7	0	−41.1	0	0
Fertilizer	−10.2	−9.6	−5.2	−4.9	−0.8	0	−9.0	0	0
u_a (note h)	100.6	95.7	100.9	96.0	76.5	74.8	97.2	102.3	97.2
θu_m	100.6	95.7	100.9	96.0	110.2	113.8	102.1	102.3	97.2
L_a/L	24.7	25.8	26.9	27.7	24.7	24.7	24.7	40.1	39.4

Note: In all columns except column 6, $\theta = 0.972$.

a. Base case: rural and urban prices of food and clothing are the same; there are no taxes on land or labor.

b. DFT = differential food taxation feasible: different rates in each sector, same clothing tax in each sector.

c. No migration. Labor allocation constrained to that of column 1.

d. Other parameters: in column 5, $\epsilon = 0$. In column 6, $\theta = 1$. In column 7, $\epsilon = 6$.

e. Tax on rural consumption, not on food production.

f. Taxes and subsidies when urban labor is untaxed.

g. Subsidies relative to food. For these rates to be implemented, urban food, not urban labor, would need to be the numeraire, with consequent changes in the structure of urban tax rates.

h. Utility as a percentage of that achievable with no tax restrictions (column 8). Utility is proportional to income less subsistence requirements.

419

Table 15-3. *Optimal Taxes When the Rural Population Owns Land: Base Case with Varying Revenue Requirements*
(percent)

Item	Government expenditure[a]							
	0	5	10	20	30	36.6	50	60
Net tax requirement[b]	−36.6	−31.6	−26.6	−16.6	−6.6	0	13.4	23.4
Urban and rural[c]								
Food	−43.8	−43.2	−42.5	−40.6	−38.0	−36.2	−31.1	−31.7
Clothing	−56.3	−52.8	−48.6	−37.8	−22.3	−8.9	40.4	136.9
Services								
Urban	−48.1	−45.0	−43.4	−33.2	−22.6	−14.9	5.7	20.7
Rural	−61.3	−57.6	−53.1	−40.8	−21.8	−4.5	57.3	96.9
Fertilizer	−47.2	−45.9	−44.4	−41.1	−37.0	−34.3	−27.7	−28.4
Rural taxes in relation to food								
Clothing	−22.2	−16.8	−10.7	4.6	25.4	42.9	103.7	247.1
Services	−31.2	−25.3	−18.5	−0.3	26.1	49.7	128.3	188.5
Fertilizer	−6.0	−4.7	−3.4	−0.8	1.6	3.0	4.9	4.9
u_a	99.0	95.4	91.9	83.9	75.1	69.3	54.7	40.7
L_a/L	50.3	49.3	48.4	46.3	44.2	42.7	39.3	37.0

Note: The table depicts the base case shown in table 15-1.

a. Government expenditure = modern sector profits *less* transfer to consumers, as a percentage of GDP.

b. Net tax = 36.6 − government expenditure as a percentage of GDP.

c. Urban and rural labor untaxed.

efficiency requires that the government intervene solely in the sector with fewer tax restrictions (that is, in the urban sector) and only on the inelastic land rent. All other tax rates are thus uniform.

The remaining columns present the effect of a fivefold rise in the price of oil on the tax rates, with similar (small) results to model 1.

The Effect of Increasing Revenue Requirements on the Tax Structure

What happens in model 1 as the government revenue requirement increases? The question is important, not only because countries differ in their tax share, but also because it is hard to calibrate simple models such as this for a realistic revenue requirement. The model was originally constructed to be capable of generating investment from modern sector profits, and in the case of the static version it was natural to assume that this surplus should be redistributed rather than ignored—hence the unrealistic problem of finding the least distortionary way of redistributing, rather than collecting, revenue. It is thus important to check that the lessons of this early version continue to apply when positive transfers to the government are required.

The share of profits in GDP is 36.6 percent, and this is assumed to be available to the government for expenditure or redistribution. When government expenditure is equal to profit income, there is no net transfer to consumers as a whole, though table 15-3 shows that there are still substantial tax interventions, mainly intended to encourage migration.

The lower part of the table shows the effective tax rates in the rural sector relative to food, from which it can be seen that the input, fertilizer, is very lightly taxed or subsidized relative to the output, food. Agriculture is essentially untaxed at a level of government expenditure of 20 percent, which involves transferring a surplus of 16.6 percent of GDP largely to the urban sector. Rural clothing and services are fairly equally taxed, as are urban clothing and services. The urban tax structure is fairly uniform when subsidies are distributed but becomes less uniform as tax requirements rise, probably as a result of the changes in demand elasticities as relative prices change substantially (and to that extent as a result of the functional forms chosen).

The results of table 15-3 are presented graphically in figure 15-1, which shows that tax rates change smoothly and monotonically with the revenue requirement and that tax rates rise rapidly as net revenue required becomes positive. As expected, goods that are relatively heavily subsidized initially (clothing, rural services) are relatively heavily taxed at high revenue requirements, showing that these goods are the most efficient available for the distortionary activity of either distributing or collecting revenue. To that extent, the lessons of tables 15-1 and 15-2 should continue to hold for different revenue requirements.

Figure 15-1. *The Sensitivity of the Tax Structure to the Revenue Requirement*

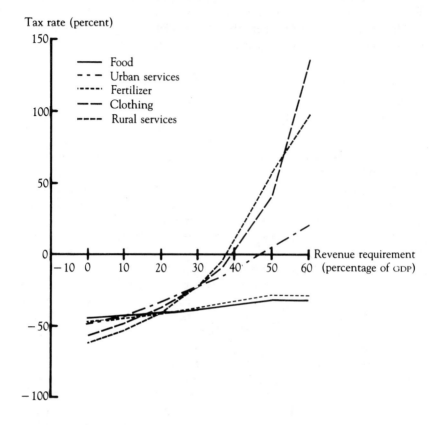

Source: Table 15-3.

Shadow Pricing

Earlier in this chapter we argued that the Diamond-Mirrlees efficiency result applied to the urban sector and hence that the government should treat urban producer prices or world prices as shadow prices for goods used or produced in the urban sector (including food). It also showed, however, that shadow prices would not necessarily equal producer prices in the rural sector because of the tax restriction. The shadow prices of interest are those of rural land and labor, whose producer prices are equal to their marginal products at market prices, and are hence affected by the distortionary tax on food. The same need for normalization applies to shadow prices as for taxes, and the figures reported in table 15-4 take (rural) food prices as numeraire. If, as would be the case in the Little-Mirrlees method of cost-benefit analysis, uncommitted foreign exchange is taken as numeraire, then all these accounting ratios would need to be multiplied by the ratio of the domestic price of food to its export price, which, for the base case of column 1, would be 0.562 in model 1 (= 1 − 0.438) and 0.322 in model 2. The ratios for fertilizer are simply another way of representing the taxes on it reported in tables 15-1 and 15-2, because shadow prices equal urban producer prices (and world prices) for urban goods. We therefore concentrate on the accounting ratios for labor and land.

Looking first at the ratios of the shadow price to the producer price of labor in model 1, we see that it is always greater than unity except for columns 8 and 9, where there are no tax restrictions. The government thus is restraining its demand for rural labor because it wants to reduce the market price for rural labor. Part of the reason may be to reduce the demand for fertilizer, which is subsidized, but the main consideration is that the lower wage will discourage work and will thus reduce rural demand for goods that the government subsidizes. The significance of this explanation of shadow pricing in terms of revenue effects is demonstrated by the fact that the ratio is highest in column 5, the case that involved the largest subsidies to rural consumption.

This result does not appear to carry over to model 2, where the ratios are nearer unity and are usually below it. The reason for this difference lies in the different pattern of land ownership. In model 1, the fall in the market wage raised the rent on land so that the rural population did not suffer a fall in real income, only a change in the work incentive. In contrast, a significant part of any rent increase in model 2 will go to urban residents, so that the rural population will suffer a real income loss and, as a result, will work longer hours. This tendency will offset, and could even outweigh, the reduction in hours that results from the wage reduction, and diminishes—usually reverses—the government's desire to reduce rural wages.

Turning to the ratios for land, we see that its ratio is always on the other side of unity from labor's. The reason is that labor and land are the most significant agricultural inputs. Therefore, the market wage for rural labor depends very strongly on the land/labor ratio. Any reason to restrict government use of labor is thus also a reason to encourage government use of land: they both lower the land/labor ratio in agriculture.

Table 15-4 corresponds to the case in which the government is subsidizing consumers out of profit income. If, as will generally be the case, the government needs to raise net tax revenue, the signs of the differences between shadow prices and producer prices will be reversed, and the government will wish to encourage work in model 1, not discourage it.

Conclusions

This chapter started with a series of questions, and it is therefore appropriate to finish with a summary of the answers obtained.

1. Optimal consumer taxation in the manufacturing sector must be such that a small equiproportionate intensification of it, at constant shadow prices,

Table 15-4. *Ratios of Shadow Prices to Rural Producer Prices*

Item	Base case^a (1)	Base case (2)	DFT^b (3)	DFT (4)	Base case^c (5)	Base case^c (6)	Base case^c (7)	No tax restrictions (8)	No tax restrictions (9)
Price of energy^d	1	5	1	5	1	1	1	1	5
Model 1									
Labor	1.07	1.06	1.07	1.06	1.12	1.11	1.07	1.00	1.00
Land	0.91	0.93	0.91	0.93	0.85	0.86	0.91	1.00	1.00
Fertilizer^e	1.06	1.05	1.02	1.01	1.09	1.08	1.07	1.00	1.00
Model 2									
Labor	0.96	0.97	1.00	1.01	1.00	1.00	0.97	1.00	1.00
Land	1.04	1.03	0.99	0.99	1.00	1.00	1.03	1.00	1.00
Fertilizer	1.11	1.11	1.05	1.05	1.01	1.00	1.10	1.00	1.00

Note: In all columns except (6), $\theta = 0.972$. Rural producer prices are measured in food units.

a. Base case: rural and urban prices of food and clothing are the same; there are no taxes on land or labor.

b. DFT = differential food taxation feasible: different rates in each sector, same clothing tax in each sector.

c. No migration. Labor allocation constrained to that of column 1.

d. Other parameters: in column 5, $\epsilon = 0$; in column 6, $\theta = 0$; in column 7, $\epsilon = 6$.

e. Market price less shadow price = fertilizer tax (negative, hence a subsidy).

424

would produce equal proportionate reductions in compensated demand for all urban consumer goods. This rule needs modification for goods that must be uniformly taxed in both sectors. If land ownership is confined to the agricultural sector, optimal agriculture taxation must be such that a small equiproportionate intensification in it, at constant shadow prices, would produce equal proportionate reductions in compensated marketed surplus for all goods. This rule also needs modification for goods in cases where sector-specific pricing is not feasible. It does not apply if urban residents own land.

2. Tax (and subsidy) rates change smoothly and monotonically in response to increasing revenue needs, and relative consumer prices do not change dramatically. Oil price increases have remarkably little effect on ad valorem tax rates in these models.

3. The government should not interfere with rural-to-urban migration unless migration gives rise to externalities. The implication is that the tax burden per capita should be equal for rural and urban consumers. When the migration confers an externality on people left in rural areas, the rural tax burden should exceed the urban tax burden by the social value of the externality. It turns out to be quite important to specify migrants' rights to land.

4. It is desirable to tax or subsidize inputs into agriculture.

5. The government should not intervene in the urban sector's transactions with the rest of the world. If food must be uniformly priced in both sectors, however, this can most easily be achieved by a trade (export) tax.

6. The government should use urban producer (that is, world) prices as shadow prices for goods that are produced or used in the urban sector. Rural shadow prices, however, will generally be different from market (producer) prices.

In general, we found that the tax structure was quite robust to some changes (energy prices and revenue requirements) and very sensitive to others (tax restrictions and land rights). Welfare was less sensitive than the tax structure, so the cost of an inappropriate tax structure may not be very large. Labor allocation (in this very neoclassical open economy) was surprisingly sensitive.

We think that this kind of modeling exercise can be useful in obtaining a feel for issues in tax design and that it could usefully be extended.

16

The Taxation and Pricing of Agricultural and Industrial Goods in Developing Economies

Raaj Kumar Sah and Joseph Stiglitz

IN MOST DEVELOPING COUNTRIES governments play an active role in setting the food prices received by farmers and the food prices paid by city dwellers. They do so through a variety of mechanisms, such as agricultural marketing boards, which often have a monopoly on the purchase of certain goods from farmers and their sale to consumers; through price regulation authorities, which control the prices at which private traders can sell; by explicit food subsidies, sometimes accompanied by rationing; and by export and import taxes and subsidies. Their aims in attempting to alter the prices that would emerge in the absence of government intervention are several. In this chapter, we focus on the following objectives:

- To increase the income of peasants, who are often among the poorest in the economy

- To subsidize the poorer city dwellers. In most developing countries, direct income subsidies are not feasible, and food subsidies may be an effective way of helping the poor

- To generate revenue for financing investments and public expenditure, to attain some level of self-sufficiency in specific goods, and to avoid excessive dependence on the international market[1]

- To counteract the effects of rigidities in the economy, such as price and wage rigidities in domestic markets and the country's lack of access to a free international trade and borrowing environment.[2]

In some cases, the policies adopted seem at variance with the stated objectives. Though the government may claim that food subsidies are meant to help the urban poor, it may subsidize not the grain consumed by the poor (millet, for example) but rather that consumed by those relatively better off (such as rice). In other cases, the government may fail to achieve its objectives because of corruption and incompetence. Though the intended objective of a marketing board may be to help producers and consumers, in some cases it may actually harm both groups by running excessively costly operations.

Sometimes the stated objectives appear inconsistent or confused. The government attempts to subsidize everyone, to increase the prices received by farmers, and to lower the prices paid by city dwellers, without articulating who is paying for the subsidies and indeed without a clear view of the full incidence of the complicated set of taxes and subsidies that are levied. This confusion is further compounded when many different agencies set the prices of different goods. Often these agencies act independently of one another, under contradictory assumptions about society's objectives and about the constraints facing the economy.[3]

Different agricultural pricing policies have markedly different effects on the welfare of farmers versus city dwellers, on government revenue, on investment, and on the distribution of income within each sector. Similarly, in economies where different commodities are produced or consumed in different regions, or by different ethnic groups, different agricultural policies have different impacts on the welfare of these regions and groups. A study of these effects requires a general equilibrium analysis in which the dependence of demands and supplies on pricing policy is modeled and in which the overall constraints facing the economy (such as those of the balance of trade and government revenue) are also taken explicitly into account.[4] Here we develop such a model, which can be used not only to identify circumstances in which changes in the pricing policy can make each of the groups in the society better off but also to characterize the qualitative aspects of the optimal pricing policy.

This chapter is a part of a research program we have undertaken that examines the reform and the design of taxation and pricing policies in developing countries, using models that reflect not only the institutional features of developing economies but also the limitations on the policy instruments available to the governments of developing countries.[5] Our research makes use of two important strands of economic literature: modern development economics and the recent advances in public economics. We follow much of the modern development economics literature in modeling a developing country as a dual economy in which the forms of economic organization in the agricultural (rural) and industrial (urban) sectors may differ markedly. The specific features of developing countries that we take into account include (1) the presence of widespread urban unemployment, which may be caused by (2) urban wages set above market-clearing levels, inducing (3) migration from the rural sector to the urban sector. Thus, although a central concern of the standard tax theory, which has been developed in the context of economies with full employment, is the effect of tax policies on individuals' labor supply, a more relevant concern in the context of developing countries may be the effect of public policies on unemployment and migration.

The development experience of the past quarter century has also made it abundantly clear that there is no single "model" of a developing country. Although in some countries sharecropping may predominate, in others family farmers may be more typical. Although landless peasants may constitute a large fraction of the agricultural population in some countries, they may not in others. One of the objectives of our research program has been to ascertain which features of the economy are critical in determining the consequences of changes in prices and taxes. We have succeeded in developing formulas that hold for a variety of institutional arrangements. The values of the parameters within these formulas may differ, of course, from one institutional setting to another.

In analyzing the consequences of alternative institutional features, it is also important to understand the economic forces that may have given rise to them, particularly in the case of high urban wages. Governments may be well aware that the urban unemployment is induced by high urban wages; it may be of little use to tell them once again that their first order of business should be the reduction of urban wages and to predicate all other taxation and pricing policies on the assumption that wages will be cut. It may be no more realistic to assume that, although direct wage cuts are not feasible, indirect wage cuts through increased prices are. Moreover, wage reductions (direct or indirect) may not always be desirable if they lead to a significant decrease in productivity through, for instance, their effects on workers' health, incentives, and turnover (see Stiglitz, 1982a, 1982d, and Yellen, 1984 and references therein).

The correspondence between the problems of pricing and of taxation has long been recognized (see Atkinson and Stiglitz, 1980). Pricing decisions, like tax decisions, have many indirect effects on the economy; the first question, then, in assessing the impact of any pricing or tax decision is to determine its *incidence*—that is, how it affects each of the variables of interest (the welfare of workers in the rural and urban sectors and the investable surplus, for example). To do so, we construct a two-sector general equilibrium model of the economy. This is like Harberger's (1962) model for analyzing the consequences of a tax on corporate capital, but unlike his model, each of our two sectors contains many different income groups; also, our assumptions—for example, those concerning wage flexibility, factor mobility, and price determination—are different from those of Harberger.

Having described the effects of policy changes, we then develop a framework for evaluating them. This entails first ascertaining circumstances in which there exist Pareto-improving policies, or policies that make all individuals better off. Those taxation (pricing) policies for which there does not exist any possible change (given the limitations on government's policy instruments and given the structure of the economy) that can make someone better off without making someone else worse off are called *Pareto-efficient* tax *structures* (see Stiglitz, 1982e). In choosing among Pareto-efficient tax structures, we follow the approach of modern public finance theory in which the effects on different groups are evaluated by means of a Bergson-Samuelson social welfare function. We develop formulas that can easily be used to show, for example, how views concerning the desirability of any price reform (that is, a small change in policy) as well as the nature of the optimal policy (that is, the policy that maximizes the social welfare function) depend on attitudes toward inequality.

The main differences between a meaningful approach toward the problems of pricing and taxation in developing countries and the approach that has typically been followed in the standard tax literature concern the salient features of the economy (some of which we have indicated above) and the limitations on the instruments available to the government. The governments of most developing countries employ an extremely limited set of instruments, and as we shall see below, these constraints have important consequences for the analysis of pricing and taxation policies.[6]

An important example of the constraints on policy instruments in the context of developing countries is as follows. If the government can set different prices in the two sectors for the goods traded between the sectors, then a change in the prices in one sector has no direct effect on individuals in another sector. If, on the other hand, the government cannot do so for some goods (because, for instance, it is too expensive or difficult to monitor the movement of these goods between the two sectors), or does not wish to do so, then changes in the prices of these goods have simultaneous direct effects on the individuals in both sectors. This situation alters the nature of desirable price reforms as well as the characteristics of optimal prices (see Sah and Stiglitz, 1984a and 1985a for the corresponding analysis). We assume in this chapter that the government can set different sets of taxes (prices) in the two sectors and that the individuals within the same sector (tax regime) face the same set of prices. The latter assumption (which underlies much of public economics) may not be satisfied in the presence of certain types of market imperfections; their consequences are discussed later.

A practical problem in the implementation of desirable pricing policies in developing countries is that reliable estimates of many of the critical parameters of the economy are not easily available.[7] One would, therefore, like to know what kinds of statements one can make on the basis of qualitative information. Similarly, there is no reason why there should be unanimity, or even consensus, about what social weights to attach to different groups. Thus, one would like to be able to ascertain how differences in welfare judgments would affect one's views concerning the desirability of different policies.[8] We have, therefore, derived a number of qualitative results (for example, identifying situations when some commodity might be taxed and another commodity might be subsidized) that make use only of qualitative information, concerning both the parameters representing the structure of the economy and the welfare weights.

In fact, given the well-known obstacles to reaching a consensus on the social weights to be associated with different groups of individuals, it is important to analyze the properties of Pareto-efficient tax structures; these properties are desirable regardless of one's views concerning the social welfare function. We have devoted considerable attention to such analyses and report here several rules for price and tax reforms that lead to Pareto improvements. Our rules of reform have the additional virtue that they can be implemented with very little information.

We base our analysis on models of the economy that are quite general (of course, these are not the most general models one can construct).[9] Our model of migration and unemployment, for instance, can be specialized to common hypotheses such as no migration, free migration with no unemployment, and the Harris-Todaro hypothesis, in which the expected utility of the marginal migrant is the same in the two sectors; it can also be specialized to other specifications, such as the one in which an individual's utility in one sector is some fixed fraction of that in the other sector (see chapter 15, by Heady and Mitra in this volume). Our model for the determination of agricultural wages and earnings is consistent with a wide variety of competitive as well as noncompetitive rural labor markets. Furthermore, in our general model, we do not impose any restriction on the number of goods in the economy or on the nature of intrasectoral and intersectoral inequality.

Also, we do not assume any functional forms to represent individuals' responses. Not surprisingly, strong special assumptions are typically employed both in econometric estimations of behavioral parameters and in simulation exercises on taxation and pricing policies. The results of such simulations must be interpreted with care because, as is well known, certain types of parameterizations seriously prejudge the optimal tax structure one obtains. (For a dramatic example of the consequences of the LES assumption, together with uniform lump-sum taxes, on optimal commodity taxes, see Atkinson and Stiglitz, 1980.)

We believe that one of the main uses of the kind of formal analysis we present here is to contribute to a more informed policy debate, to identify, for example, those instances in which there is an important equity-efficiency tradeoff from those in which there is not or to help see the full ramifications of any policy decision, ramifications that become apparent only within a general equilibrium model in which careful attention is paid to the institutional structure of the economy. Our research thus provides the conceptual background that is a necessary prelude to empirical attempts to investigate the consequences of taxation and pricing policies.

Outline of the Chapter

This chapter is divided into ten sections. Though it would clearly be possible to begin our analysis by presenting the most general model and then specializing to obtain more specific results, a better understanding of what is at issue is obtained by beginning our analysis with a simple model, in which there is a single commodity produced in each sector. Our concern in these sections is to identify the central tradeoffs in the analysis of pricing and taxation. We then analyze the disaggregated structure of taxes first within the agricultural sector and later within the industrial sector.

Our objective in this chapter is not to present the general formulations that we have analyzed elsewhere but rather to provide an exposition that brings out as clearly as possible some of the central issues, including the role of alternative institutional structures. We therefore use a simple model to examine the consequences of migration and unemployment on pricing policy. We subsequently discuss several other variations of our model, including alternative agricultural institutions and international trade environment. Furthermore, because there are differences (concerning the salient features of the economy, the feasibility of various policy instruments, and the emphasis of analysis) between our models and those examined in the standard tax literature, we devote one section to an explanation of some of those that are critical. We articulate some of our misgivings with the general approach of this chapter, as well as that of modern public economics, and present concluding remarks at the end of the chapter.

The Basic Model

Consider an economy in which there are two commodities and two sectors: food and related products, produced in the agricultural sector (sector a) and a generalized industrial good, which can be used either for consumption or for investment, produced in the manufacturing or industrial sector (sector m). Both goods are freely traded; the international price of the agricultural good in terms of the industrial good is denoted by P.

Agricultural Sector

The agricultural sector consists of homogeneous peasants who decide how much labor to supply, given the prices at which they can sell their surplus. We denote this price (in terms of the industrial good) by p. Clearly, the level of utility that peasants can attain is a function of this price, and the utility level of a representative peasant can be written as $V^a(p)$.[10] Some of the agricultural output is consumed within the agricultural sector and the surplus quantity, s per peasant, is sold to the industrial sector or abroad. This quantity is a function of the price that the peasants receive. We denote the price elasticity of the surplus by $\eta_{sp} = (\partial \log s)/(\partial \log p)$. Economic theory puts no constraints on the sign of η_{sp} (there may be a backward-bending supply schedule of the surplus), but it is empirically reasonable to assume that an increase in the price increases the marketed surplus. That is, $\eta_{sp} > 0$. Our formulas can be reinterpreted for the case in which $\eta_{sp} < 0$.

We assume that the government has very few policy instruments to control peasants' behavior; it cannot directly control their output or their consumption. This, we believe, is the correct representation in most developing countries, because much of the farming in these economies is done on numerous small plots, and the ability of the government to monitor and control the actions of peasants seems sufficiently limited that only indirect incentives are administratively feasible. We also assume that complex pricing schemes are infeasible. Nonlinear pricing schemes, for example, in which the unit price paid to a peasant depends on the amount the peasant sells, typically lead to underground (unaccounted) transactions. Accordingly, we restrict ourselves to schemes that pay a common price to all peasants, regardless of the quantities they transact.[11]

Industrial Sector

We assume that there are many policy instruments in the industrial sector, in contrast to the agricultural sector. In many developing countries, the government not only is the largest industrial producer and employer but also taxes private producers' profits and can sometimes control their prices and quantities. Here we make the polar assumption that the government has sufficient instruments so that the distinction between direct and indirect control can be virtually ignored.[12]

For simplicity, we ignore at present the intrasectoral income distribution and assume that the number of hours for which an industrial worker works is fixed. The government takes the wage, w, it pays workers as given, but it can control the price, q, at which its marketing board sells food in the industrial sector. (The case in which the government can alter w is discussed later.) Thus, we write the welfare of an industrial worker as $V^m(q, w)$. An industrial worker takes his income w and the price q as given and decides how much food to consume. This quantity is represented as $x^m(q, w)$. The price elasticity of the urban consumption of food is $\epsilon^m = -\partial \log x^m / \partial \log q$, which is a positive number, because consumption goods are assumed to be normal.

Investment

Government revenue available for investment is denoted by R. This equals the difference between the value of industrial output and the industrial wage payment, plus the net profit of the marketing board:

$$(16\text{-}1) \quad R = N^m(z - w) + (P - p)N^a s(p) + (q - P)N^m x^m(q, w)$$

where N^a is the number of peasants, N^m is the number of industrial workers, and z is the output per industrial worker.

A Simple Analysis of Agricultural and Industrial Pricing

Price Reforms for Pareto Improvements

There are three groups in the present model: the peasants, the industrial workers, and the government, which represents future generations through its control of investment. For each value of p and q, we can calculate the feasible

Figure 16-1. *The Utility Possibilities Schedule*

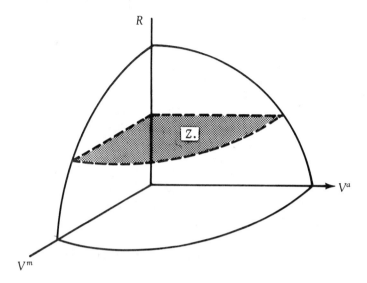

combinations of V^a, V^m, and R (see figure 16-1). We first show that certain price changes can make all groups in a society better off.

The utility possibilities schedule gives the maximum value of revenue for investment consistent with any level of utility of peasants and industrial workers. If the existing prices are at inefficient points such as Z, then a change in prices can make every group in the society better off.

In the above-described model, an increase in the rural food price makes the peasants better off, but it does not affect the industrial workers. Also, investment increases with an increase in p if $dR/dp > 0$. This happens, we see from equation 16-1, if

(16-2) $$p < P/(1 + 1/\eta_{sp}) = \bar{p}.$$

Thus, if the price of food in the agricultural sector is less than $\bar{p}$, then an increase is unequivocally desirable, because it will increase the government revenue and will also improve the welfare of peasants without affecting the welfare of industrial workers.

Similarly, raising the urban food price makes urban workers worse off and does not affect the peasants. It lowers government revenue if $dR/dq < 0$, or, from equation 16-1,

(16-3) $$q > P/(1 - 1/\epsilon^m) = \bar{q}$$

and $\epsilon^m > 1$. Thus, if $\epsilon^m > 1$, and if the urban food price is above $\bar{q}$, then a price reduction is unequivocally desirable for the society. Though at the aggregate level of analysis in this section, it seems plausible to assume that the demand elasticity of "food" is less than unity (in which case, Pareto improvement in urban prices is not possible), it is clear that there are particular agricultural commodities for which the demand elasticity may be greater than unity; thus, as the price of rice increases, urban workers may switch to lower-quality grains that face lower taxes; urban workers will be worse off, and the public revenue will decrease. See below for a disaggregated analysis.

These rules of price reform have several virtues. First, they identify a lower limit for the rural food price and an upper limit for the urban food price. Second, the questions of reform in the rural and the urban prices can be addressed independently of one another.[13] Third, the use of these rules requires very little information. Apart from the world price, only the demand and supply elasticities are needed. The rules do not require social weights, which are needed to implement optimal prices, as we shall see later. Moreover, the elasticities that are needed to use these rules of reforms (as well as other rules of reform that we derive later) are those associated with the current equilibrium, which can be calculated from the local properties of the demand and supply functions. These rules should be contrasted with the optimal pricing rules, to be discussed below, in which the elasticities are to be evaluated at the social optimum, for which purpose one needs to know the global properties of the demand and supply functions.

In addition, these rules hold in models much more general than the one considered above. The only conditions required are that

$$(16\text{-}4) \qquad \frac{\partial V^a}{\partial p} > 0 \quad \text{and} \quad \frac{\partial V^m}{\partial q} < 0,$$

respectively. Interpret, for instance, V^a and V^m as representing the aggregate welfare of the entire group of peasants and industrial workers, respectively. Then expression 16-4 implies that the aggregate welfare of peasants increases if the price of their output is increased and that the welfare of industrial workers decreases if the food price they face is increased. As long as these conditions are satisfied, the above-described rules of price reform continue to hold.

The rule for reform in the urban food price, for instance, holds regardless of the distribution of income among industrial workers. Similarly, the rule for reform in the rural food price may hold no matter how agricultural land is distributed among peasants, provided peasants are not net buyers of food.[14] Moreover, as we shall see later, these rules of reform can be extended in a straightforward manner when prices and wages affect individuals' productivity and when there is migration between the two sectors.

The main point we wish to establish in this section, however, is not that the specific rules of price reform proposed above are valid in every circumstance (of course, they are not if the economy is very different) but that one can often determine a set of rules to identify those price reforms that improve the welfare of all groups in the society.

Other Price Reforms

The approach discussed above weeds out inefficient pricing policies, but it does not distinguish between numerous pricing policies that are efficient. A choice among these policies necessarily entails tradeoffs between the interests of peasants, industrial workers, and future generations. In this section, we show how to analyze these tradeoffs. First, we express the aggregate social welfare as

(16-5) $H = N^a W(V^a) + N^m W(V^m) + \lambda R$

in which λ is the social value of marginal investment, $W(V)$ is social welfare defined over an individual's utility level, and H is the value of social welfare as a function of the welfare of peasants and industrial workers, and the level of revenue.[15] Conceptually, this approach allows us to draw social indifference curves, that is, those combinations of V^a, V^m, and R among which the society is indifferent (see figure 16-1).

Differentiation of equation 16-5 with respect to p and q, and a rearrangement of the resulting expressions, yields

(16-6) $\dfrac{dH}{dp} \gtreqless 0,$ if $p \lesseqgtr P\mu^a$

(16-7) $\dfrac{dH}{dq} \gtreqless 0,$ if $q \lesseqgtr P\mu^m$

where

(16-8) $\mu^a = 1/\left[1 + \left(1 - \dfrac{\beta^a}{\lambda}\right)\dfrac{1}{\eta_{sp}}\right]$

(16-9) $\mu^m = 1/\left[1 - \left(1 - \dfrac{\beta^m}{\lambda}\right)\dfrac{1}{\epsilon^m}\right].$

$\beta^i = \gamma^i \, \partial W/\partial V^i$ is the social weight or the social marginal utility of extra income to a worker in sector i, and γ^i is the (positive) private marginal utility of income to a worker in sector i.[16]

Expression 16-6 implies that the social welfare is increased by increasing (decreasing) the rural food price if the current price is lower (higher) than $P\mu^a$. A similar rule for changing the urban food price is given by expression 16-7. These rules are sharper than those we obtained earlier—not surprisingly, because rules 16-6 and 16-7 require more information. Specifically, they need the social weights (at the current equilibrium) associated with the rural and the urban incomes relative to the social weight associated with investment. On the other hand, like the previous rules, they require information about supply and demand elasticities only at the current equilibrium.

Optimal Prices

The optimal prices are those at which the possibilities of reform have been fully exhausted. Using expressions 16-6 and 16-7, thus, the optimum is represented by

$$(16\text{-}10) \qquad\qquad p = P\mu^a$$

$$(16\text{-}11) \qquad\qquad q = P\mu^m.$$

Diagrammatically, the optimum represents that point on the utility possibilities surface (see figure 16-1) that is tangent to the social indifference curve.

We have thus obtained optimal pricing formulas, of a remarkably simple form, in terms of the welfare weights and the price elasticities. The optimal price in the agricultural sector depends only on the social weight on the income of peasants (relative to investment) and on the price elasticity of agricultural surplus. Similarly, the optimal price in the industrial sector depends only on the social weight on the income of industrial workers and the price elasticity of their demand for agricultural goods.

The above results have some natural interpretations. In the early stages of development, the social value of investment might be thought to exceed the weights on private incomes, that is, $\lambda > \beta^i$. Under such circumstances, peasants should receive less than the international price of food, and city dwellers should pay more than the international price of food. That is, both sectors should be taxed.[17] Also, a higher elasticity of agricultural surplus corresponds to a higher price paid to peasants, because the marginal increase in the revenue from a price increase is higher, and a higher demand elasticity of food in the industrial sector corresponds to a lower price charged to city dwellers, because the marginal increase in the revenue from a price increase is lower. Furthermore, the smaller the social weight on peasants' income, the lower the price in the agricultural sector; the smaller the social weight on city dwellers' income, the higher the price paid by them.

Implicit Tax Rates

The optimal pricing formulas derived above can also be stated in terms of commodity taxes. Let $\tau = (P - p)/p$. Then τ is the tax rate on the output of peasants; it can also be interpreted as the rate of subsidy on their consumption. Denote the food output and the consumption of a peasant with y and x^a, respectively. Then the marketed surplus per peasant is

$$(16\text{-}12) \qquad\qquad s = y - x^a.$$

Furthermore, define $\eta^a = \partial \log y / \partial \log p$, and $\epsilon^a = -\partial \log x^a / \partial \log p$ as the price elasticities of food output and consumption of a peasant. Then the surplus elasticity can be expressed as $\eta_{sp} = (1 + \alpha)\eta^a + \alpha\epsilon^a$, where $\alpha = x^a/s$ is the ratio of peasants' consumption to their marketed surplus. With these definitions, the optimal tax rate is obtained from equation 16-10 as

$$(16\text{-}13) \qquad \tau = \left(1 - \frac{\beta^a}{\lambda}\right) \frac{1}{(1 + \alpha)\eta^a + \alpha\epsilon^a} = \left(1 - \frac{\beta^a}{\lambda}\right) \frac{1}{\eta_{sp}}.$$

The above expression for the tax rate has some similarities with those in the traditional tax literature, but there are also some differences. According to equation 16-13, the magnitude of the tax rate is inversely proportional to the price elasticities of output and consumption. This dependence is similar to the one suggested in some of the earliest writings on taxation, for example, those by Ramsey and Pigou. There is a basic difference, however, between the present policy problem and the standard taxation problem in which production and consumption decisions are made separately by corporations and consumers. In the latter case, the relative roles played by output and consumption elasticities depend very much on the government's taxation of profits; the output elasticity does not appear in the tax formula, for example, if the profits are entirely taxed away (see Atkinson and Stiglitz, 1980, p. 467, and Stiglitz and Dasgupta, 1971).

In the present problem, it is nearly impossible for the government to distinguish between producers and consumers within the agricultural sector, because peasants are simultaneously producers as well as consumers. The key elasticity is therefore that of marketed surplus. Even though this elasticity can be restated in terms of output and consumption elasticities, as in equation 16-13, it is the combined effect that matters. This statement should not be surprising. In the formulations of standard general equilibrium models, what matters is the individual's net trade; for farmers, this is just their marketed surplus.

Many Income Groups in Agricultural and Industrial Sectors

The formulas derived earlier can be used even when the distribution of income in the agricultural sector is explicitly taken into account. We need only to reinterpret β^a as the "average" social weight corresponding to the agricultural sector. To see this point, consider an agricultural sector in which there is a continuum of land ownership ranging from large landlords to landless workers. Denote an individual by the superscript h, whose land holding is A^h, whose marketed surplus is s^h (which can be negative) and whose net labor supply (labor hours supplied minus labor hours used on his farm) is L^h. $A^h = 0$ for landless workers. The rural wage per hour, w^a, is determined in the rural labor market, and so it depends on the price of agricultural goods, p. We define $\eta_{wp} = \partial \log w^a / \partial \log p$ as the elasticity of rural wage with respect to p. Furthermore, let $\bar{s}$ denote the average marketed surplus, that is, $\bar{s} = \Sigma_h s^h / N^a$. Expression 16-5 is now modified to be: $H = \Sigma_h W(V^{ah}) + \Sigma_h W(V^{mh}) + \lambda R$, where V^{ih} is the utility of person h within sector i.

Then it is easily verified that equation 16-10 still characterizes the optimal pricing rule, with the modification that now

$$(16\text{-}14) \qquad \beta^a = \Sigma_h \beta^{ah} \left(s^h + \frac{w^a L^h}{p} \eta_{wp}\right) / N^a \bar{s}$$

where β^{ih} is the social weight on the income of individual h in sector i. It is obvious from equation 16-14 that β^a is a weighted average social weight on rural incomes, because $\Sigma_h L^h = 0$ from the rural market-clearing condition, and the sum of the terms multiplying β^{ah} is unity.

An important property of the average social weight derived above is that it takes into account the general equilibrium effects of prices on incomes.[18] Also, our pricing formula, equation 16-10 in combination with equation 16-14, is largely independent of the precise nature of the labor market (for example, on whether or not the labor market is competitive). The relevant parameter is the elasticity of rural wage with respect to price, which would take specific values, depending on the features of the rural labor market.

The same approach applies to the industrial sector. With wage (income) differences among city dwellers, equation 16-11 is the optimal pricing formula, with a modification that

(16-15) $$\beta^m = \sum_h \beta^{mh} x^{mh} / \sum_h x^{mh}$$

where x^{mh} is the food consumption of the city dweller h. Once again, it is obvious from equation 16-15 that β^m is a weighted average of the social weights on the incomes of city dwellers.[19]

It is perhaps important to explain here the difference between applying the rules for optimal prices on the basis of the assumption of homogeneous individuals within a sector versus the rules in which the intrasectoral heterogeneity of individuals is explicit. In both cases the required information on sectoral price elasticities is the same, because the government's budget, equation 16-1, is the same. The application of rules based on heterogeneous individuals requires additional information on the quantities (of goods and net labor supply) and the social weights corresponding to different groups of individuals. If the society cares about the intrasectoral distribution of welfare then, clearly, the government should use the coefficients β^a and β^m from equations 16-14 and 16-15 in its calculations.

The Structure of Prices in the Agricultural Sector

A major issue facing many developing countries is whether fertilizer and cash crops should be subsidized to increase production or should be taxed as a way of raising revenues to finance government services and investment. Sometimes it is argued that cash crops are grown more by the wealthier peasants, and such crops provide a particularly desirable basis for taxation by a government concerned with redistribution.

On the face of it, government policies in this area often seem contradictory. Although the government provides a subsidy on fertilizer, allegedly to encourage production, it taxes the output, which discourages production. Would it not be better to eliminate the subsidy and reduce the tax—in short, to reduce the extent of government intervention in this market? The model in the preceding section can be extended to give us insights into these issues.

A General Formulation

The range of goods produced in the agricultural sector can be divided into several distinct categories. They include those goods that are consumed by peasants and are also sold to outsiders, like food grains; those that are produced solely for sale, like rubber, fiber, and other cash crops; and those that are inputs to agricultural production itself, like manure. Similarly, the agricultural sector buys some goods from outside for consumption, like textiles and radios, and other goods for use as inputs in production, like fertilizers, pesticides, and tractors (tractors, though, are used occasionally to provide transportation services).

All of these goods can be incorporated within our earlier model by interpreting s^h as a vector, of which an element s_i^h represents the *net* supply of the ith good from the household h to the rest of the economy. If the peasant is a net seller of this good, s_i^h is positive, and it is negative if the peasant is a net buyer of this good. The per capita surplus of good i is denoted by $\bar{s}_i = \Sigma_h s_i^h / N^a$. For those goods that are produced and utilized solely within the agricultural sector, $\bar{s}_i$ is zero. We assume that the government can influence the prices of only those goods that cross the border between the two sectors and that there are no taxes on trades within the agricultural sector.[20] Naturally, $\mathbf{p}$, $\mathbf{P}$, and $\mathbf{q}$ are now vectors, and z now denotes the value of the entire vector of industrial output, measured at international prices, if we take one of the industrial goods as the numeraire. The effects of a change in the price of good i on an individual's utility and on the government revenue are respectively given by

$$(16\text{-}16) \qquad \frac{dV^{ah}}{dp_i} = \beta^{ah}\left(s_i^h + \frac{dw^a}{dp_i} L^h\right)$$

$$(16\text{-}17) \qquad \frac{dR}{dp_i} = N^a(\mathbf{P} - \mathbf{p}) \cdot \frac{d\bar{s}}{dp_i} - N^a\bar{s}_i$$

where $d\bar{s}/dp_i$ includes the induced effect due to a change in the rural wage. That is, $d\bar{s}/dp_i = \partial\bar{s}/\partial p_i + (\partial\bar{s}/\partial w^a)(dw^a/dp_i)$, where d and ∂ denote derivatives including and excluding induced wage effects; both exclude the effects of changes in other prices. We can immediately calculate the effect of a change in prices on the social welfare. Expressions 16-5, 16-16, and 16-17 yield

$$(16\text{-}18) \qquad \frac{\partial H}{\partial p_i} \gtreqless 0$$

if

$$(16\text{-}19) \qquad (\mathbf{P} - \mathbf{p}) \cdot \frac{d\bar{s}}{dp_i} \gtreqless \left(1 - \frac{\beta_i^a}{\lambda}\right)s_i$$

where

$$(16\text{-}20) \qquad \beta_i^a = \Sigma_h \beta^{ah} \left(s_i^h + \frac{w^a L^h}{p_i} \eta_{wi} \right) / N^a \bar{s}_i$$

and $\eta_{wi} = \partial \log w^a / \partial \log p_i$ is the elasticity of rural wage with respect to the price of good i. We thus obtain a straightforward modification of our earlier analysis. Note that the above expressions take into account the fact that different commodities will have different distributional effects, depending on the marketed surplus of the commodity for the rich versus the poor. They also emphasize that we need to take into account not only the direct effects (for example, large surplus suppliers are hurt more by a reduction in the prices they receive) but also indirect effects due to price-induced changes in wages, η_{wi}, which would be different for changes in the prices of different goods. A tax on a crop that is largely a cash crop may have deleterious distributional effects if it depresses the labor demand and agricultural wage significantly, because small landholders and the landless, who are net suppliers of labor, may well be hurt more than the large landholders. The above expressions differ from our earlier analysis in a second way: when other taxes are in place, a change in the tax on one commodity may change demands for other commodities, increasing or decreasing tax revenues. These effects are incorporated in the left-hand side of expression 16-19.

As before, the optimal prices are characterized by expression 16-19, in which the inequality is replaced by an equality. This yields a multiperson Ramsey-like optimal rule, with a difference that induced general equilibrium effects on wages and earnings are now taken into account. This rule has the standard interpretation of how the proportional reduction in the quantity of a good should be related to its distributional characteristics (see Atkinson and Stiglitz, 1980, pp. 386–90).

The implementation of this optimum, however, requires more information than might be available. It requires estimates of the values of all the elasticities and of social weights at an equilibrium that may be far removed from the current situation. The use of expressions 16-18 and 16-19 for reform analysis may also be inhibited, because we seldom have good estimates of all the own and cross-elasticities or of the general equilibrium responses of agricultural wages to changes in prices of particular goods. We show now that it is possible to reform prices of certain goods based on much more limited information.

Pareto-Improving Price Reforms That Require Very Little Information

Pareto-improving price reforms can be made for "production goods" (that is, for those agricultural inputs and outputs that are not used for consumption, such as fertilizers, machine inputs, cash crops, and so on) solely on the basis of the elasticities of inputs and outputs (on unit land) with respect to the prices of production goods. In certain circumstances, we do not need any information concerning consumption responses, the distribution of land, or the social weights.

For the analysis in the remaining part of this section, we assume that there are constant returns to scale in agricultural production when all inputs, including land, are taken into account, and that all farmers have access to the same production technology. The latter assumption is not required if farmers with different production technologies are in different regions and can be subjected to different sets of taxes (some aspects of pricing policy, when this assumption is not satisfied, are discussed below). We should point out here that the above assumptions not only are made in most of the empirical work on farmers' responses (on which an implementation of price policy must ultimately be based) but also underlie typical simulation exercises on tax policy (see, for example, chapter 15, by Heady and Mitra in this volume). Though these assumptions are unlikely to be satisfied by every single farmer, the relevant empirical question is whether one can identify systematic differences between the observed technologies and those with the above assumptions. If the differences are not significant in a statistical sense, then one can use our reform rules with extreme parsimony in information; otherwise, one would need to use expressions 16-18 and 16-19.

Denote the net output vector of the hth household by $\mathbf{y}^h$, such that the outputs are represented as positive quantities and the inputs are represented as negative quantities, and $\mathbf{y}^h = A^h \mathbf{y}$ where $\mathbf{y}$ is the net output vector per unit of land. If the consumption vector of the household h is denoted by $\mathbf{x}^{ah}$, then $\mathbf{s}^h = A^h \mathbf{y} - \mathbf{x}^{ah}$ denotes the surplus vector of household h. Now consider a change in the prices of those goods that are employed in the rural production (as inputs and outputs) but are not consumed. If the good is a production good, then $s_i^h = A^h y_i$. Also, because the prices of production goods affect the consumption quantities only through changes in full income, it follows that $\partial x_j^{ah}/\partial p_i = A^h y_i \, \partial x_j^{ah}/\partial M^h$, where M^h denotes the full income of the household h, and $\partial M^h/\partial p_i = A^h y_i$ is the change in full income due to a change in p_i. Now assume that the induced wage effect is negligible (this assumption is relaxed below). Then 16-17 can be written as

$$(16\text{-}21) \qquad \frac{dR}{dp_i} = (c_i - 1 - B)N^a A y_i$$

where $A = \Sigma_h A^h/N^a$ is the per capita land, $\tau_j = (P_j - p_j)/p_j$ denotes the rate of tax or subsidy, $\eta_{ij} = \partial \log y_i/\partial \log p_j$ represents the price elasticities of the production goods per unit of land, $c_i = \Sigma_j \tau_j \eta_{ij}$ is the proportional change (due to taxation) in the quantity of the ith production good per unit of land, and $B = (\mathbf{P} - \mathbf{p}) \cdot [\Sigma_h A^h(\partial \mathbf{x}^{ah}/\partial M^h)]/N^a A$. In deriving equation 16-21, we have also used the standard symmetry property of inputs and outputs that $\partial y_j/\partial p_i = \partial y_i/\partial p_j$. Expression 16-21 provides the basis for the following rules of price reform.

Calculate c_i for all of the production goods. If $c_i > c_k$, and i and k are both outputs (inputs), then increase (decrease) the price of the ith good by a small amount, say Δp_i, and decrease (increase) the price of the kth good by ($y_i/y_k)\Delta p_i$. On the other hand, if the ith good is an output (input) and the kth good is an input (output), then increase (decrease) the price of the ith good and increase (decrease) the price of the kth good in the same proportion as above. This procedure should be continued until all values of c_i are as close to one another as possible.

The above rules of reform have the property that they increase the government revenue while leaving unchanged the utility level of every individual. The reforms therefore lead to strict Pareto improvements. This can be verified as follows. If Δp_i is the change (positive or negative) in the price of the ith good, then $-(y_i/y_k)\Delta p_i$ is the change in the price of the kth good. From equation 16-16, then, V^{ah} remains unchanged, because $s_i^h = A^h y_i$ for production goods. From equation 16-21, on the other hand,

$$(16\text{-}22) \qquad\qquad \Delta R = (c_i - c_k)N^a A y_i \Delta p_i.$$

Recalling that y_i is positive for an output and negative for an input, it follows from equation 16-22 that our rules of reform increase investment. It is also clear from equation 16-22 that a necessary condition for the optimality of taxes is that values of c_i should be equal for all production goods.

These reform rules are highly parsimonious in their use of information, as should be obvious. The information required consists solely of the current taxes on inputs and outputs, current quantities of inputs and outputs on unit land, and the response of these quantities to the changes in the prices of production goods. Also, the above-described reform analysis applies to those cases in which different groups of producers (in different regions, for example) face different sets of prices.

In fact, these reform rules can be applied even when the induced wage effects are significant. If the production goods have the same (but not necessarily constant) elasticity with respect to the wage, for instance, then not only do our rules of reform hold, but also one does not need to know anything whatsoever concerning the labor supply behavior of households to be able to use them.[21] Though we do not expect the restriction on elasticities noted above to hold in every circumstance, once again the relevant empirical question is: how different are the actual wage effects from those predicted by the technology with the above restrictions? If the difference is not significant in a statistical sense, then our reform rules continue to hold.

Should Some Cash Crops or Production Goods Be Taxed and Others Subsidized?

To gain insight into this question, recall that a necessary condition for the optimality of taxes is that

$$(16\text{-}23) \qquad\qquad c_i = \Sigma_j \tau_j \eta_{ij}$$

should be the same for all production goods. That is, the proportionate change due to taxation in the quantities of production goods per unit of land should be equal for all such goods.

Now assume for a moment that changes in the prices of production goods have negligible cross-price effects on the quantities of inputs and outputs (that is, $\eta_{ij} = 0$ if $i \neq j$) then, from equation 16-23, $\tau_i \eta_{ii}$ is the same for all i. Next, from the standard properties of production functions, $\eta_{ii} > 0$ for an output and $\eta_{ii} < 0$ for an input. Also, from our definition of τ_i, a positive (negative) τ_i implies a tax (subsidy) on an output and a subsidy (tax) on an input. It follows, then, that either all of the production goods (inputs as well as outputs) should be taxed or they should all be subsidized. Also, the taxes (or subsidies) on these goods should be inversely proportional to their own-price elasticities.

These results are important not because we believe that the cross-price effects are negligible or that the induced wage effects are always of the type considered above. They are important because we have isolated the reasons why the sign of taxes might differ among different production goods. Specifically, we often find that a fertilizer is being subsidized, whereas a pesticide is being taxed, or vice versa—or that cotton is being subsidized, whereas another cash crop is being taxed. If it is true that farmers use inputs in the same relative proportions, then our analysis suggests that the justification for such taxation must lie in the presence of large cross-price effects or in the presence of specific induced wage effects. If it is found from empirical analysis that input patterns are similar, that there are no large cross-price effects or wage responses, then the existing tax structure is not optimal, and it can be improved upon, regardless of what the social weights might be.

This analysis casts some doubts on the oft-given advice that, on the grounds of equity, some agricultural inputs (like machinery) should be taxed, because they are used primarily by rich farmers, whereas other inputs (like fertilizer) should be subsidized, because they are used by poor as well as rich farmers. The above analysis suggests that all inputs should be used by rich and poor alike and that such policies, when aimed at cash crops and production inputs, cannot be justified on the ground of equity alone; the primary justification for them should reflect the importance of cross-price effects and specific kinds of induced effects of prices on the rural wage.

Given the importance of the results obtained above, it is probably useful to evaluate a central assumption, that of constant returns to scale in production, which underlies these results. As we noted earlier, much of the existing theory of taxation assumes constant returns to scale; our results can thus be viewed as simply indicating one of the important logical implications of this assumption. By the same token, simulation-based models of taxation that begin with a specification of a constant-returns-to-scale production function must necessarily yield results that conform with our analysis. Moreover, a number of empirical studies (see Singh, Squire, and Strauss, 1986, for a review) of farm-household models have found that the hypothesis of constant returns to scale cannot be rejected in most circumstances.

Yet one might feel a certain unease concerning constant returns, in particular because (under the standard microeconomic model of a farm) it predicts identical factor ratios across farmers with different sizes of landholding, whereas casual observation sometimes suggests differences in factor ratios (for example, smaller farmers use more bullocks, whereas larger farmers use more tractors). When such differences are systematically observed (in a reliable statistical sense), then one needs to understand the sources of these differences (whether it is, for instance, deviations from homotheticity, deviations from uniform prices due to credit constraints, or differences in information about best practices), and what the appropriate policy response should be (to attempt to correct price distortions, if that is the reason for differences in input ratios; to provide better information, if lack of information is the source of differences in input ratios). Depending on the source of differences in factor ratios, and depending on the available policy responses to counteract them (if it is desirable to counteract them), then, the model for tax analysis would have to be modified. A full analysis of such modified models is beyond the scope of the present chapter. It is in any case by no means obvious that the results (presented earlier in this section) concerning tax policy would be significantly modified under such extensions; the reason is that constant factor ratios are a *sufficient* but not a *necessary* condition for our results. See "Caveats and Misgivings" for a more complete discussion of the limitations of the model presented here as well as those found elsewhere in the literature.

The Structure of Prices in the Industrial Sector

Urban food subsidies not only are widespread in developing countries but are often also a source of large public deficits. Attempts to cut food subsidies have precipitated riots in more than one country. Modern public finance theory does not give us a clear qualitative picture. As Atkinson and Stiglitz (1972) noted, for instance, and as Deaton illustrates in chapter 4, in the demand systems that are typically estimated in practice, the commodities with a low income elasticity are often also the commodities with low price elasticity. If one ignored distributional consequences, these would be the commodities to tax, but if one focused on distributional considerations, then these would be the commodities to subsidize. Thus, whether a particular consumption commodity should be taxed or subsidized may depend relatively sensitively on the social weights as well as on other critical features of the economy, such as what other instruments for redistribution are available to the government (see Atkinson and Stiglitz, 1980).

Four features of the economy, we would argue, are central in analyzing the structure of urban prices and taxes in developing economies. These are the presence of urban unemployment, intersectoral migration, wage-productivity effects, and the urban wage determination mechanisms. In the presence of significant unemployment, the effect of taxation on the hours of labor that an individual might hypothetically be willing to supply—a basic feature of the standard tax analysis in developed countries—does not seem to us to be of central importance in the context of the industrial sector in developing countries.

Moreover, the migration between the agricultural and the industrial sector is closely related to the nature of urban unemployment, as has been emphasized in the recent development economics literature, and its implications on tax analysis can be significant. If the agricultural wage is fixed, for instance, then an urban food subsidy would make living in the urban sector more attractive, so that there would be a higher flow of migration from the agricultural to the industrial sector. This effect in turn might mean that there would be an increase in the urban unemployment rate, little or no increase in the welfare of the poor (in terms of their expected utility), and a possible reduction in the funds available for investment.

It has also been argued sometimes that urban food subsidies may be desirable in developing economies, because they may improve the health of workers and, hence, the efficiency of the industrial labor force. This argument is, in fact, a part of a class of hypotheses that postulate a relationship between industrial wages, industrial productivity, and the level of unemployment in the economy. According to these hypotheses, the output per worker of an industrial firm (net of hiring and training costs) depends on the wages paid, because wages affect workers' efficiency, quality, and turnover. Employers (public or private) therefore take these effects into account when setting the wage that, in turn, affects the level of unemployment.

The reason why we believe that the mechanism of industrial wage determination is a key issue in the analysis of taxes in developing countries is that, if the government can control industrial wages, then under certain circumstances (but not always), commodity taxation may be unnecessary in the industrial sector. If, on the other hand, wages are determined endogenously, then one needs to specify the precise mechanism through which industrial wages are determined (such as competitive wage setting by private firms), because a change in the tax policy would result in induced effects on the industrial wages (similar to those discussed earlier in the context of the agricultural sector), and these effects need to be incorporated in the design of tax policy.

Elsewhere (in Sah and Stiglitz, 1984a, 1985a, 1985b), we have developed a framework that provides a unified treatment of unemployment, migration, wage-productivity effects, and the determination of wages and earnings in the two sectors. Using this framework, we have analyzed the consequences of taxation and pricing as well as the determination of shadow prices and wages for cost-benefit analysis. Moreover, this framework can be specialized to many different hypotheses concerning, for instance, migration, wage-productivity effects, and the determination of wages. Limitations of space do not permit us to describe such an analysis here. We therefore present below a highly simplified model that emphasizes wage-productivity effects, whereas the consequences of migration and unemployment are briefly discussed in the next section.

If the wage-productivity hypothesis holds—that is, the hypothesis that the wage rate affects a worker's productivity—then efficiency may entail paying high wages in the industrial sector. Also, real wages may be relatively insensitive, for instance, to the unemployment rate. Wage-productivity effects have typically been studied within models in which prices are fixed. A natural extension, in the present context, is that the productivity of a worker is a function of his (or her) wage as well as the relative prices he (she) faces.

For simplicity, consider the case of homogeneous industrial workers (its extension to the case of heterogeneous workers is discussed later). The wage-productivity effects are represented in a reduced form as

$$(16\text{-}24) \qquad\qquad z \equiv z(\mathbf{q}, w).$$

This representation is consistent with a hypothesis that the productivity depends on the level of worker's utility. It is also consistent with a hypothesis that the productivity may be more closely related to the consumption of certain goods, such as health care and food, than to the consumption of other goods. The standard assumption in the literature is that higher wages lead to higher productivity, that is, $\partial z/\partial w > 0$. The effects of prices on productivity, which have not received attention in the past, are likely to be ambiguous in general. In the special case in which a worker's productivity depends only on his utility level, however, that is,

$$(16\text{-}25) \qquad\qquad z \equiv z[V^m(\mathbf{q}, w)]$$

and $\partial z/\partial V^m > 0$, it is easy to see that higher prices reduce productivity.

Taking expression 16-24 into account, and assuming that the urban wages are fixed and there is no migration, we maximize the aggregate social welfare with respect to prices. The corresponding optimal price structure is given by the solution to

$$(16\text{-}26) \qquad \Sigma_j \, \tau_j \, \epsilon_{ij}^{mu} = \left[1 - \frac{\beta^m}{\lambda} - (\mathbf{q} - \mathbf{P}) \cdot \frac{\partial \mathbf{x}^m}{\partial w} \right] + b_i$$

where $\tau_j = (q_j - P_j)/q_j$ is the tax rate on good j, $\epsilon_{ij}^{mu} = -\partial \log x_i^{mu}/\partial \log q_j$ represents various compensated elasticities, and $b_i = (1/x_i^m)/(\partial z/\partial q_i)$.

As is well known, the left side of equation 16-26 represents the (tax-induced) proportional reduction in the compensated consumption of good i. The standard result that this reduction should be equal for all goods, however, does not hold here, because of the wage-productivity effects, which are captured in the last term, b_i, of equation 16-26. This term can be interpreted by noting that $b_i = -\epsilon_{zi} z/q_i x_i^m$, where $\epsilon_{zi} = -\partial \log z/\partial \log q_i$. Therefore b_i is a larger negative number for a good if an increase in the price of this good decreases the productivity to a larger extent (that is, ϵ_{zi} is larger), and if the worker's expenditure, $q_i x_i^m$, on this good is smaller. Obviously, from equation 16-26, the proportional reduction corresponding to such goods should be smaller.

Moreover, a basic prescription of standard tax theory, that there should be no commodity taxation if the government can set the wages, also does not hold in the present context. To see this point, we first obtain the expression for optimal wage, taking prices as fixed. The optimal wage is characterized by $1 - \beta^m/\lambda - (q - P)\partial x^m/\partial w = b_w$, where $b_w = \partial z/\partial w$. Next, if both the prices and the wage are set optimally, then by substituting the last expression into equation 16-26 we obtain

$$(16\text{-}27) \qquad\qquad \Sigma_j \, \tau_j \, \epsilon_{ij}^{mu} = b_w + b_i.$$

Now, in the absence of wage-productivity effects, the right side of equation 16-26 is zero. Hence $\tau_j = 0$, and

$$(16\text{-}28) \qquad\qquad q_i = P_i.$$

That is, there should be no commodity taxes in the industrial sector. This, however, is not the optimal policy if the wage-productivity effects are significant.

A special case in which the standard results are restored, even though the wage-productivity effects are present, is when a worker's productivity depends on the level of his utility. In this case, $b_i = -\beta^m \partial z/\partial V^m$, which is the same for all goods, and therefore, from equation 16-26, the proportional reduction should be equalized across goods. Also, the right side of equation 16-27 is zero (because $b_w = -b_i$), which implies that commodity taxation in the urban sector is unnecessary if the government sets the wages.

In fact, the above results concerning the desirability or undesirability of urban commodity taxation may hold even if the government does not entirely control industrial wages. Consider a situation, for instance, in which wages are determined through bargaining between the government and a trade union that does not suffer from money illusion. That is, the union knows that an increase in the price of food represents a worsening of workers' welfare in the same way that a reduction in their wage does. Now, if the wage-productivity effects are of the type represented in expression 16-25, then it is better to have no urban commodity taxation, as in equation 16-28, whereas the wages should be the instrument of bargaining. The substitution of a lump-sum (or wage) tax subsidy for an equal utility distortionary tax subsidy, in this case, generates increased revenues for the government. On the other hand, if the wage-productivity effects are more general, as in expression 16-24, then it is desirable to have urban commodity taxation.[22]

The above-described model is easily generalized to incorporate heterogeneity of individuals in the industrial sector. The main implication of this extension is that, in general, various goods will differ not only in their productivity effects (b_i) but also in their distributional effects. Goods such as food may have larger distributional effects (because the welfare of the poor is more sensitive to the food prices) as well as larger productivity effects (because of the effect of food consumption on workers' health, for example), and if this is the case, then the (tax-induced) proportional reduction in food consumption should be smaller than in other goods. Furthermore, it can be verified that this extension does not alter our earlier results concerning the desirability or undesirability of urban commodity taxes or subsidies.

Migration and Unemployment

Recent research has drawn attention to the importance of labor mobility across sectors. In particular, it has been noted that migration from the agricultural to the industrial sector might increase industrial unemployment indirectly, because only some of the migrants can find industrial employment. This possibility has important consequences for tax policy, as the following extension of the basic model illustrates.

Consider three population groups: peasants, industrial workers, and unemployed workers. For brevity, we abstract from the heterogeneity of individuals within each of these groups and also assume that there is a single agricultural good and a single industrial good. One would expect that, for peasants who are net sellers of food, a lower rural food price will decrease the attractiveness of living in the agricultural sector, compared with living in the industrial sector. The same effect would arise if the urban food price is lower. On the other hand, additional migration to the industrial sector will tend to increase the level of unemployment in this sector, which in turn will discourage further migration.

We therefore need to calculate the consequences of the induced migration due to price changes. First, we need to redefine the elasticity of the agricultural surplus to account for the fact that the size of the rural population itself is sensitive to prices; this also affects the government revenue from taxation. Second, an outward migration from the agricultural sector reduces the population pressure on agricultural land, which in turn increases the welfare of those living in this sector. Third, migration has direct welfare effects as well, because workers move from one group to another that, in general, has a different level of utility.

In a general model of migration that we have proposed elsewhere, the rural population is represented as: $N^a = N^a(p, q, w, N^m)$, and the number of unemployed is given by: $N^u = N - N^a - N^m$. If V^u denotes the utility of an unemployed worker, then equation 16-5 is replaced by $H = N^a W(V^a) + N^m W(V^m) + N^u W(V^u) + \lambda R$. The optimal rural food price is characterized by

$$(16\text{-}29) \qquad p = \frac{P + \phi}{1 + \left(1 - \frac{\beta^a}{\lambda}\right)\frac{1}{\bar{\eta}_{sp}}}$$

where $\bar{\eta}_{sp} = \partial \log(N^a s)/\partial \log p$ is the redefined price elasticity of agricultural surplus (taking into account the effect of price on rural population), and ϕ represents the welfare effects of price-induced migration.[23] If there is no migration, then $\bar{\eta}_{sp} = \eta_{sp}$, and $\phi = 0$. Not surprisingly, equation 16-29 is the same equation as 16-10 in this special case. When there is migration, $\bar{\eta}_{sp}$ exceeds η_{sp}, and ϕ is positive, under plausible circumstances.

Now compare the above expression for the optimal price, equation 16-29, to the special case equation 16-10 when there is no migration. The effect of migration, then, is to increase the numerator and decrease the denominator in equation 16-29 if investment is more valuable than consumption. Heuristically, the implication is that migration increases the price that should be paid to peasants for their surplus. This notion makes sense, because by paying a higher price to peasants, the government can reduce the pressure of migration to cities and can hence reduce the resulting urban unemployment that otherwise lowers society's welfare. This insight appears to be particularly relevant in the context of some cities (for example, Bangkok, Cairo, and Mexico City) in which the inmigration from the rural sector has led to serious social degradation.

Another special case of the above formulation is the Harris-Todaro hypothesis (discussed by Fields in chapter 10), in which migration continues to the point where the expected utility of the marginal migrant (taking into account the probability of being unemployed) is equal in the two sectors and the marginal productivity of a worker in the rural sector is fixed. Then our pricing formula becomes

$$(16\text{-}30) \qquad p = \frac{P}{1 + \left(1 - \dfrac{N\gamma^a}{N^a\lambda}\right)\dfrac{1}{\bar{\eta}_{sp}}}$$

where recall that γ^a is the marginal utility of income to a rural worker.[24]

This expression has an interesting implication. In the early stages of development, when the relative social weight on investment, λ/γ^a, is expected to be quite large and when the fraction of the population in the agricultural sector is expected to be large, the price paid to peasants should be less than the international price. As the economy develops, however, the price paid to peasants should increase, and it could quite possibly even exceed the international price.[25]

Further Extensions

The major components of our models of developing economies involve (1) the organization of the agricultural sector, (2) the organization of the industrial sector, (3) the mechanism of migration and unemployment, and (4) the international trade environment. In our basic model, the agricultural sector consisted of homogeneous owner-peasants, the industrial sector had homogeneous workers receiving a rigid wage, and there was no induced migration. This basic model was extended to include such features as the heterogeneity of individuals within the two sectors, migration and unemployment, and endogenous determination of industrial and agricultural wages. These features are clearly important in many developing countries. In this section, we illustrate ways of extending the model further to incorporate additional features that might be important in certain economies.

Sharecropping in Agriculture

In some economies, sharecropping is important. In such cases, all we need to do is to interpret s^h as the net surplus of an individual after the landlord's share has been paid or after the share has been received from the tenant. Furthermore, if the share contract is endogenously determined (see Stiglitz 1974b), then the individual's surplus elasticity will be based in part on the elasticities of equilibrium shares with respect to price. Clearly, the values of price elasticities might differ between economies with sharecropping and with peasant holdings even if the underlying utility functions and production functions were identical.

Composition of Households

This aspect, though ignored in much of the standard tax literature, is important, because we know that households have heterogeneous demographic characteristics, particularly when we contrast rural and urban households or rich and poor households in the agricultural sector as well as in the industrial. This affects the social weights, β^{ih}, which depend not only on the income of the households and on the social aversion to inequality but also on the demographic composition of the households. Moreover, the households' response to prices would implicitly depend on their demographic characteristics. (See Sah, 1983b, regarding a methodology for analyzing intrahousehold allocations.)

International Trade Environment

So far we have assumed that all goods can be exported or imported. Some goods, however, have such high transportation costs that neither alternative is attractive, whereas in other cases, even though it may be economically attractive to export a good, the country may face quantity restrictions and quotas from potential importers. In yet other cases, the government may restrict imports of certain goods because of self-sufficiency considerations. In addition, there may be constraints on international borrowings, restricting the level of trade a country can sustain. These and other similiar situations entail additional constraints within which pricing policies need to be determined.

Suppose that the government wishes to achieve a certain degree of self-sufficiency in food (a self-sufficiency objective for other goods can be treated similarly). One way to express this objective is as a constraint that the quantity of food imported cannot exceed a certain prespecified fraction of the domestic production. Obviously, such a constraint influences pricing decisions only when it is binding. Once it is binding, however, the government's flexibility in setting prices decreases. In the simple model described in our second section, for instance, the two prices (p and q) can no longer be varied independently of one another.

Self-sufficiency objectives may also result in higher food prices for both the peasants and the city dwellers, because the government, with self-sufficiency in mind, may use price policy to increase the surplus from peasants and also to curtail urban food consumption. In this case, then, peasants would be relatively better off, and city dwellers relatively worse off, compared with a situation in which there were no self-sufficiency objectives.

Goods such as infrastructure and inputs into human capital formation are nontraded. Also, a large number of ordinary consumption and industrial goods produced in developing countries have virtually no international markets, in part because of quality considerations, even though these goods are traded domestically. For the purpose of tax policy, these goods must also be viewed as nontraded goods. If, in addition, it happens that a developing country faces export constraints on goods that it sells abroad, then the actual traded quantities would be nearly insensitive (at the margin) to the pricing policies. In determining prices and taxes, therefore, such an economy should be treated like a closed economy.

The difference in the treatment of a traded versus a nontraded good is simple. The shadow price for a traded good is its international price, whereas the shadow price of a nontraded good is determined, in our model, endogenously (and simultaneously with the determination of optimal prices) on the basis of its social marginal value. Specifically, those elements of the vector $\mathbf{P}$ that correspond to nontraded goods are replaced by the vector $\mathbf{P}^*/\lambda$, where elements of the vector $\mathbf{P}^*$ are the Lagrange multipliers to the market-clearing conditions of various nontraded goods. Now recall that we had defined taxes for traded goods as the difference between the international price and the price faced by consumers and producers. Taxes for nontraded goods can be defined correspondingly with respect to their shadow prices. This redefinition, however, does not change the expressions for the optimal tax rates that we have derived earlier. Our discussion of the qualitative properties of optimal taxation thus applies to the traded goods as well as to the nontraded goods.

Rigidities in the Economy

An important rigidity on which we have focused is the one in the labor market. The urban wage influences the output through labor productivity and other effects, and the migration decisions are based on expected utility, which includes a probability of remaining unemployed. The equilibrium market wage (that is, the wage that private or public employers would choose to pay) is therefore such that there is unemployment. An important consequence of this approach is that the market wage would change if the tax policy changes, and

that the government would not, in general, be able to eliminate unemployment through taxes and subsidies.

This point has been missed in some of the earlier literature, which has
assumed that some government policies capable of eliminating unemployment
always exist. This supposition, in turn, has sometimes led to a belief that,
because the government can eliminate unemployment, it would do so. Consequently, unemployment must necessarily be a short-run phenomenon that can
be ignored in a long-run policy analysis. These views are clearly misleading if
the endogeneity of wages is taken into account.

Our analysis has also abstracted from the possibility that the adjustments in
the economy, particularly in the labor market, might be lagged. In such a case,
there are possible intertemporal consequences of taxation policies (for example, wage subsidies today may lead to higher wages and higher unemployment
in the future), and a myopic taxation policy (based on this period's consequences alone) might differ from the one in which the dynamics of adjustment
is taken into account.

Tax Analysis for Developing versus Developed Economies

Often policy analysts show a temptation to borrow results from the standard
tax literature and to prescribe them in the context of developing countries
without examining the premises on which these results are based. Such an
approach overlooks what we consider to be two fundamental differences
between developing countries and developed economies: one concerns the tax
instruments that the government can or cannot use, and the other concerns
the salient features of the economy. A related issue, discussed in the next
section, is the possible unwillingness of the government to use certain policy
instruments even if it is economically feasible to do so.

The constraints on the government's ability to employ particular instruments of taxation are, in turn, related to the information available and to the
administrative costs associated with different tax instruments. In developing
country agriculture, for example, it is virtually impossible to tax labor transactions. This inability to tax can be viewed as an information problem: though
the concept of labor transaction is a perfectly well-defined economic concept,
a tax system must be based only on those variables that are quantitatively
ascertainable (at a reasonable cost) by an outside party. Our assumption that
the labor transactions cannot be taxed in the agricultural sector of a developing
country with heterogeneous individuals, we therefore believe, is more realistic
than the one made in the standard tax model (Diamond and Mirrlees, 1971,
for example) that the government can tax all trades that an individual
undertakes.

Moreover, in many versions of the standard tax model, all profits are taxed
away. Its counterpart in the agricultural sector requires the government to

impose a 100 percent tax on land rent. For obvious reasons (such as the government's inability to distinguish between the returns from land and those from other inputs), such a tax is almost certainly infeasible. The issue of land taxation, in fact, provides a good example of the constraints on tax instruments. This tax has been recommended by conventional economic theory since David Ricardo, but it faces the following problem. If the land tax is based on land area, irrespective of the quality, then it is viewed as unfair. On the other hand, it is inherently difficult to base a land tax on land quality: a direct measurement of land quality requires, once again, disentangling the effect of land quality from that of other inputs, whereas the absence of good land markets makes it difficult to obtain an indirect measure of land quality. It is perhaps not surprising that negligible use is made of the land tax in most developing countries and that its use has steadily declined over time. The reason is possibly that the coercion required to administer such a tax is less feasible today than it was earlier.

These differences have important consequences for tax policy. Oft-quoted results (Diamond and Mirrlees, 1971) that the producer prices should be the same as the shadow prices and that there should be no tax on international trade, for instance, need to be interpreted with considerable caution. The former result not only requires the government to be able to impose taxes on all trades, as well as 100 percent tax on profits but also is based on the standard definition of firms that purchase all of their inputs and sell all of their output. Firms by definition do not consume, and their transactions can be monitored. Under this definition, the farms of our model are not firms, because farmers are both producers and consumers (at least for certain goods, like food grains), and it is virtually impossible to implement different producers' and consumers' prices, because the transactions (of food, for example) within a household and across households cannot easily be monitored.

Also, by this definition, those establishments are not firms where an owner-manager's effort has an effect on the outcomes, and that effort cannot be monitored. Such establishments are in this formal sense just like the farms in our model (see Stiglitz, 1974b), in which a direct tax on labor (effort) cannot be imposed. It is impossible to separate out that fraction of an owner-manager's income which is due to his efforts from the fraction that represents pure profits. Thus the standard results may be almost as inapplicable to developed economies as they are to developing countries.

Caveats and Misgivings

We indicated above several important directions in which our model could be extended, to reflect better the variety of institutions and economic environments found in developing countries. The analysis presented in this chapter (as well as in other chapters on taxation in this volume), however, has several limitations that cannot so easily be remedied. Though we are currently engaged in research on these problems, it is only fair to warn the reader and to present some of our thoughts on their consequences.

The first limitation has to do with market imperfections. Though our model incorporates several types of rigidities, it has abstracted from those market imperfections that may cause different individuals (within the same sector and region) to face different *effective* prices for goods, even though the market prices they face are the same. To assess the consequences of such imperfections on pricing policy, one first needs to ascertain their sources. Among the examples are differential credit constraints faced by different individuals due, for instance, to the problems of imperfect information (note, however, that the effects of credit constraints may be considerably ameliorated by rental markets in capital goods) and to the incomplete access of particular ethnic groups to specific markets. Unfortunately, the available empirical work does not adequately characterize the importance of such imperfections or the precise nature of the underlying mechanisms. If these imperfections are important in a given economy, then one must take them into account in the analysis of taxation and pricing policies.

Market imperfections may either decrease or increase the ability of the government to tax. Improvements in the capital markets in developed countries have enabled smart investors to engage in tax arbitrage and have thus impaired governments' ability to impose capital taxation to the point where there is a widespread belief that capital taxation is not feasible. At the other extreme, in general, it is difficult for governments to tax transactions that do not pass through formal markets. Such transactions are undoubtedly of greater importance in developing countries than in developed countries. Moreover, tax policy affects the extent to which transactions occur in formal versus informal markets: tax-induced shifts in the "choice" of markets have both efficiency and equity effects that have not yet been studied.

Individuals not only make decisions about the extent to which they participate in formal (taxed) versus informal markets; they also decide on the extent to which they participate in tax avoidance activities. Such activities range widely, from those that are legal loopholes to those that involve outright corruption (including bribery of tax officials). Again, the tax structure may have a marked effect on the extent to which individuals participate in these activities, with consequences not only for equity and efficiency but also for the political process itself.

The second limitation has to do with differential knowledge and learning. It has been argued that many farmers may be uninformed about the best available practices, and diffusion of new technologies may be quite slow. It has also been argued that pricing policies can be used to help overcome peasants' resistance to the adoption of new techniques or to "protect them" while they learn the new technology. (The analogy with the infant industry argument should be obvious.) If this argument is correct, then it suggests that the equity-efficiency tradeoff in taxation analysis has another dimension: subsidizing tractors may indeed provide greater benefit (in the short run) to faster learners (those who adopt the new technology more quickly), but subsidizing bullocks may simply serve to perpetuate inefficient technologies. On the other hand, it is plausible that extension services provide a better (more economical) instrument of policy to spread technological information than incentives through pricing and taxation policies.

The third limitation has to do with the political economy of pricing and taxation. Here we have provided a technical answer to the question "what 'advice' would you give if the government were to ask you what the Pareto-improving reforms are and what the structure of optimal prices is (for any social welfare function), given a set of policy instruments?" We have not asked how the government would arrive at the particular social welfare function it uses or whether it will use (or misuse) the economist's advice to pursue its own political objectives; nor have we asked whether the constraint on the set of available instruments is caused by economic (technical) or "political" factors.

Concerning the last question, it is apparent that some of the constraints on the available instruments may have primarily economic reasons. As we argued earlier, for instance, progressive land taxes may be precluded in developing countries because of the government's lack of information concerning the quality of land at different locations and the prohibitive costs of acquiring such information. A similar argument may preclude the use of progressive income taxation in some (but not all) cases if the quality of information concerning individuals' income is low. On the other hand, a uniform lump-sum subsidy (directly or indirectly through tradable food rations) or land reforms may be feasible on technical and economic grounds, in which case, the government's unwillingness to use them would reflect a "political" choice.

The issues noted above may have fundamental consequences for the study of taxation and pricing. Assume, for a moment, that redistribution (from the rich to the poor) is indeed a key government objective. A basic question we then need to ask is: how much redistribution is *possible*, given the set of instruments? Note that this is a positive question (in contrast to the normative question "how much redistribution is *desirable?*") and that it can be examined quantitatively by devising appropriate measures of the redistribution achieved. Suppose it turns out that very little improvement in the welfare of the poor can be achieved, say, through taxation and pricing of goods (which happen to be the only instruments the government can employ or wishes to employ); then the discourse on tax policy is modified in at least two ways. First, the redistributive objective of government loses much of its practical relevance because given the set of instruments, very little redistribution can be achieved regardless of what the government desires. By the same token, it becomes clear that, if the government indeed wants redistribution, then it must enlarge the set of instruments.

Sah (1983a) has examined the maximum extent to which the welfare of the poorest can be improved (when the only instruments are taxation and pricing of goods) and has shown that the achievable redistribution can indeed be quite small. There are at least four reasons for this result. First, if there are significant substitution possibilities, then there is a limit to how much revenue can be collected by taxing luxuries; this, in turn, restricts the extent to which necessities can be subsidized. Second, the (marginal) deadweight losses associated with commodity taxation are often large, and therefore, even if a (marginal) change in taxes imposes a large burden on the rich, it may not be of any help to the poor. Third, if the poor consume even small amounts of luxuries and if the rich consume some amounts of necessities, then an excessively high tax on luxuries can be quite damaging to the poor, and large subsidies on necessities would, to some extent, benefit the rich. Fourth, the extent to which differential commodity taxation can achieve redistribution also depends on how finely one can differentiate among commodities. Differences in the consumption of particular types of grains across income groups may be larger than the differences in the total consumption of grains, but informational requirements and enforcement costs are likely to increase rather rapidly with the degree of differentiation. This analysis clearly suggests that there might be hitherto unrecognized limitations on the redistributive capabilities of commodity taxation and pricing.

Now, assume that redistribution from the rich to the poor is not the objective of taxation. Instead, taxation is used by the more powerful groups in the society for their own advantage. It is obvious that the analytical apparatus developed in this chapter can be applied with these objectives as well. If the city dwellers control the political system and they maximize their own welfare, for example, then the prices they will set will correspond to the rules we developed earlier, where the social weights on the income of peasants are set at zero.

Empirical studies have not so far provided much guidance on which one of these two polar assumptions concerning the government's objective is more realistic or what particular combination of these two cases is most plausible. Casual observation suggests that the latter objective (in which tax policies are employed by some groups against others) might be playing an important role. Some of the most important historical conflicts have been associated with one group of individuals attempting to use discriminatory policies against other groups. Among the landmarks are: the conflicts associated with corn laws in England, the discord between the North and the South in the United States leading to the Civil War, and the conflicts between the advocates of peasants and the proponents of industrial workers in the precollectivization U.S.S.R.

It is quite plausible, then, that the domination of one group by another is an important factor determining pricing policies in present-day developing countries. Whether an analysis such as the present one would serve to improve the equity and efficiency in an economy, or whether it will be used by some groups to enhance their ability to discriminate against others, is a question of concern to us.

Conclusions

Developing countries display an enormous variety of institutional arange-ments, and these arrangements critically influence the impact of taxation and pricing policies and hence the design of these policies. Clearly, then, no single model, no single prescription, is applicable to all countries. We have therefore constructed a general framework that can be adapted to the special circum-stances facing individual countries. For the agricultural sector, for example, we have considered family farms (which can hire in or hire out labor), landless workers, and sharecropping. Plantations are important in some countries, and our framework can easily be adapted to take that importance into account. Our framework also incorporates the effects that pricing and taxation have on the distribution of agricultural earnings and on land congestion and the conse-quences that these effects have in turn on the welfare of those in the agricul-tural sector.

At the same time, we have shown that one cannot simply transfer the policy conclusions reached for developed economies—no matter how sophisticated the reasoning—to developing countries. Developing economies face fun-damental restrictions on their ability to levy certain taxes (which in part are due to the administrative costs and informational constraints, which can be severe in many developing countries), and also the salient features of these economies are different. Our framework is sensitive to the restrictions on the feasibility of various tax instruments, and we show how these restrictions cause many of our results to differ from those in the standard tax literature.

Concerning the salient features of the developing countries, we have emphasized the dependence of taxation and pricing policies on the nature of wage-productivity effects, on the nature of migration and unemployment, and on the nature of wages (and earnings) determination mechanisms in the agricultural and the industrial sectors. The government may not always be able to eliminate industrial unemployment, even if it wishes to do so, because of the endogeneity of industrial wages. Moreover, it may not even wish to do so if it considers the corresponding costs (due to the wage-productivity effects, for example) to be too high. A change in taxes and prices would then affect unemployment, which in turn has output effects as well as welfare effects. This concern of ours with unemployment differs markedly from the central concern of standard tax theory, which assumes full employment and focuses on the deleterious effect of reductions in labor supply.

Finally, in most developing countries there is only limited information on the parameters of the economy (such as various elasticities and social weights). We have therefore derived rules for price reform that can be applied on the basis of qualitative (and local) information. Moreover, agreements on the relative magnitudes of social weights corresponding to different groups of individuals are often difficult to achieve. We have therefore proposed rules that lead to Pareto improvements, reforms that increase not only the welfare of each individual in the economy but also the investable surplus.

Notes

1. A long tradition that cuts across ideological boundaries views the agricultural sector as the desirable source of public revenue. In the Marxist tradition, this approach was advocated by many leaders of the October Revolution in what came to be known as the "Soviet industrialization debate" and the "scissors problem." Sah and Stiglitz (1984a, 1985a) analyze this problem both in the context of the Soviet debate and in the context of present-day developing countries. In the classical laissez-faire tradition, similarly, the agricultural sector has been viewed as an ideal source of public revenue, at least since David Ricardo claimed that the land tax is the best form of taxation. We discuss the issue of land taxes later. Economists are often reluctant to deal with so-called noneconomic objectives such as self-sufficiency. The fact of the matter is that, in many countries (for example, India and Korea), self-sufficiency is an unambiguously stated national policy. We show how these objectives may be incorporated into a policy analysis while noting the associated economic costs.

2. The objectives include the stabilization of prices faced by consumers and producers (see Newbery and Stiglitz, 1981) and to redistribute income away from middlemen toward consumers and producers or from one region to another.

3. The above remarks apply outside developing countries as well. Not only are farm price interventions widespread in developed economies, but so is the confusion associated with them. Some of the most bitter controversies among the members of the European Economic Community have arisen in the past, for example, because of their disagreements on farm price policies.

4. These issues have not received much attention in the literature. See, however, Dixit (1969, 1971), and Dixit and Stern (1974). Some researchers have analyzed agricultural pricing with approaches based on consumer and producer surplus; for example, Tolley, Thomas, and Wong (1982). Sah (1982b) notes the limitations of such approaches and provides an empirical framework to implement an approach such as the one developed in this chapter.

5. For a more detailed discussion of the issues treated, see Sah (1978, 1982b, 1983a), Stiglitz (1982c), and Sah and Stiglitz (1984a, 1985a, 1985b).

6. The fact that limitations on the instruments available to the government may have significant effects on tax policy has long been recognized. Stiglitz and Dasgupta (1971), for instance, showed that the Diamond-Mirrlees (1971) result on the desirability of productive efficiency and its corollary, the undesirability of taxes on intermediate goods and imports and exports, depended critically on the assumption that the government could impose 100 percent taxes on profits and could levy taxes on all commodities and labor, assumptions that are even less persuasive in the context of developing countries than in the context of developed countries. Similarly, Atkinson and Stiglitz (1980) show that the structure of optimal commodity taxes depends critically on whether income taxation is feasible or not.

7. The problem may be almost as severe in developed countries. Calculation of optimal tax rates requires knowledge of all cross-elasticities, both in consumption and in production. It appears virtually impossible to obtain reliable estimates of these; most estimating procedures impose considerable structure on the demand and supply systems, which implicitly constrain the values of some of the cross-elasticities.

8. It is important to note here, however, that different social welfare functions, although giving rise to different sets of optimal taxes, may not always lead to significant differences in the total amount of taxes that an individual pays or in the resulting levels of welfare of different individuals. A simulation of optimal commodity taxes for India, for example, based on heterogeneous individuals in the two sectors, showed that the amounts of taxes paid by different individuals were quite insensitive to the society's inequality aversion (see Sah, 1978). This result is consistent with the argument we

present later that commodity pricing and taxation may be rather inadequate instruments for a significant redistribution from the rich to the poor.

9. In particular, we do not examine all of the potentially important features of the economy, and it is conceivable that some features to which we have given insufficient attention may prove to be important in subsequent research. It should be noted, however, that we have analyzed a much wider variety of considerations than those reported here. We do not discuss here the consequences of capital allocation and mobility between the two sectors, for instance, and of private savings, which, in the long run, may indeed be important. These aspects can easily be incorporated within our general framework. See Sah and Stiglitz (1984b), an earlier version of this chapter, for a discussion of some of these aspects.

10. We are at present abstracting from migration and capital flows. With migration, the utility of a peasant is also a function of the number of persons in the agricultural sector. If there are capital flows, then the utility is also a function of the interest rates at which peasants can borrow and lend.

11. It should be obvious that nonlinear tax-subsidy-pricing schemes, if administratively feasible and not too expensive, are better (in a Pareto sense) than the standard (linear) pricing. The reason is simply that a nonlinear scheme provides "more" instruments to the government than the standard pricing, and the government cannot do worse by having more instruments. Also, restricted nonlinear schemes, such as those entailed by (nontradable) quotas and rations, are desirable additions to standard pricing because, once again, one cannot do worse by having more instruments. Still, these schemes are not necessarily desirable alternatives to standard pricing. See Sah (1982a) for an analysis. Also note that some simple schemes, such as the provision of fixed tradable rations below market prices, are often feasible. Such schemes may provide a way of implementing a uniform lump-sum subsidy.

12. This assumption is not completely satisfactory. Though the government can, for instance, tax profits, it can seldom impose a 100 percent profits tax. There are numerous discussions of the problems that developing countries have in controlling multinationals. In fact, questions may even be raised whether the government controls nationalized industries. Our assumption that the government can control the industrial sector is partly to simplify the analysis, partly to dramatize the difference between the urban and rural sectors. As we note later, the analysis can be modified for those cases in which the government's control on the industrial sector is limited and indirect.

13. This independence is partly because the economy is open to external trade. In a closed economy, a Pareto-improving price reform typically involves simultaneous changes in both the rural price and the urban price, because corresponding to a value of p there is a value of q that clears the market for the agricultural good.

14. In an agricultural sector in which individuals buy and sell labor services, an additional requirement for the above-mentioned rule of price reform to hold is that the rural wage should not be significantly sensitive to the rural food price. A disaggregate analysis of the agricultural sector with heterogeneous individuals is presented later in this chapter.

15. W is increasing and concave in V. H is the Hamiltonian representing the current value of the time-discounted social welfare. The results presented in this chapter hold at every point in time. The same formulation can also be employed to trace the path of optimal prices and other variables over time; this, however, is beyond the scope of the present chapter. For a discussion of the alternative uses of the investable surplus, see the earlier version (Sah and Stiglitz, 1984b) of this chapter.

16. To obtain these expressions we have used Roy's formula: $\partial V^a/\partial p = \gamma^a s$, and $\partial V^m/\partial q = -\gamma^m x^m$. Also, we assume that μ^a and μ^m are positive. From equation 16-8, μ^a is positive if $\eta_{sp} > \beta^a/\lambda - 1$. We expect this condition to be met in developing countries at early stages of development, because the social weight on investment is likely to be higher than that on the rural income. From equation 16-9, $\mu^m > 0$ if $\epsilon^m > 1$

$- \beta^m/\lambda$. This condition may not always be met, especially if the urban demand elasticity of food (with respect to price) is very small and if the government does not care about the industrial workers. If $\mu^m < 0$, then the urban price should be increased. Note, however, that the present model abstracts from effects such as that of consumption and wages on workers' productivity, which we discuss later. Increasing the urban price beyond some level would not be desirable when these effects are taken into account even if the government does not care about the welfare of industrial workers.

17. The observed pattern in many developing countries in which the urban food price is often lower than the international price thus seems inconsistent with equalitarian social welfare. Note, however, that our results need to be qualified by concerns such as intrasectoral inequality, and wage-productivity effects. See below.

18. The social weights proposed in the earlier literature have often abstracted from these general equilibrium effects, as in Feldstein (1972), Diamond (1975), and Atkinson and Stiglitz (1976). The difference arises because these papers assume that the government can impose wage taxes, so the wages received by individuals need not depend on commodity taxes.

19. The wage elasticity term does not appear in equation 16-15, whereas it does in equation 16-14. The reason is simply that at present we are assuming industrial wages to be fixed. In more general models, such as those that we discuss later, wage elasticity terms would appear in the expressions analogous to equation 16-15. Also, though we are considering here a single type of labor, its generalization to a multitude of skill types is straightforward.

20. In practice, there are some ambiguities in the precise geographical definition of such a border, because agricultural activities are sometimes undertaken on the fringe areas of cities that fall under cities' tax jurisdiction. Also, our assumption that trades within the agricultural sector cannot be taxed somewhat overstates the constraints on the government. What is crucial for our purpose is whether a transaction can be monitored, so that a tax can be imposed. If a farmer can sell directly to another farmer, then a tax can probably not be collected. The developing country governments can (and frequently do) attempt to impose taxes and marketing controls on transactions within the agricultural sector. One of the implications of such interventions is to encourage individuals to avoid making use of formal markets, so that the taxes can be avoided. This implication is discussed later.

21. This happens if the profit function (on unit land) is separable between prices of the production goods and other prices. Denote the unit profit function as $G = G[G^1(\mathbf{p}^1, w^a), G^2(\mathbf{p}^2)] = \mathbf{p}\mathbf{y} - w^a L_d$, where $\mathbf{p}^2$ is the vector of production goods' prices and L_d is the labor applied to unit land. Then, for the production good i, $\partial y_i/\partial w^a = -\partial L_d/\partial p_i = g_1 y_i$, where $g_1 = [(\partial G^2/\partial G^1 \partial G^2)(\partial G^1/\partial w^a)]/(\partial G/\partial G^2)$. Therefore, the elasticity $\partial \log y_i/\partial \log w^a = g_1 w^a$ is the same for all i. For details on the underlying production technologies, see Lau (1978). Next, the labor market–clearing condition is $\Sigma_h L^h(\mathbf{p}, w^a) = 0$, which, upon differentiation, gives $dw^a/dp_i = -(\Sigma_h \partial L^h/\partial p_i)/(\Sigma_h \partial L^h/\partial w^a)$. Next, $L^h = L_s^h - A^h L_d$ where L_s^h is the labor supply of the household h. Because the prices of production goods affect the labor supply only through full income, $\partial L^h/\partial p_i = A^h y_i \partial L_s^h/\partial M^h - A^h \partial L_d/\partial p_i$. Now, recall from above that $-\partial L_d/\partial p_i = g_1 y_i$. It follows that $dw^a/dp_i = g y_i$, where $g = -\Sigma_h A^h (g_1 + \partial L_s^h/\partial M^h)/\Sigma_h \partial L^h/\partial w^a$. Using these equations, the earlier reform analysis can be reproduced, with a difference that now $B = (\mathbf{P} - \mathbf{p})\{\Sigma_h s[A^h(\partial \mathbf{x}^{ah}/\partial M^h) - g(\partial s^h/\partial w^a)]\}/N^a A$. One special case, of course, is when there are no induced wage effects. For this case, simply substitute $g = 0$.

22. An alternative institutional setting is the one in which private firms set wages to maximize their profits, taking into account wage-productivity effects. The resulting wage, in general, would differ from the one that the government would set (to maximize H) and thus, in certain cases, commodity taxes may be used for a partial "correction" of private decisions.

23. Here we are ignoring the consumption of unemployed workers and are assuming that the industrial wage is fixed in terms of industrial goods. Also, the level of industrial employment is fixed because it is derived from an equalization of the industrial wage and the marginal product of labor. These assumptions are being made solely to simplify the exposition. $\phi = [W(V^a) - W(V^u) - \beta^a pY_A A]m_p/\lambda s\bar{\eta}_{sp}$, where A is the agricultural land per peasant, $Y_A = \partial Y/\partial A$ is the marginal output (per peasant) of land, and $m_p = \partial\log N^a/\partial\log p$ is the elasticity of rural population with respect to the rural price. We assume $V^m > V^a > V^u$, that is, the industrial workers are better off than peasants, who in turn are better off than those who are unemployed. We also assume that agricultural land is not too scarce (that is, Y_A is small) and that ($\eta_{sA} = \partial\log s/\partial\log A$), which is the elasticity of agricultural surplus per peasant with respect to the land per peasant, is smaller than one. Next, note in the expression for ϕ that the expression in square brackets represents the net welfare gain if one unemployed worker migrates to the agricultural sector. Specifically, $W(V^a) - W(V^u)$ is the direct welfare gain, and $\beta^a pY_A A$ is the welfare loss due to the congestion effect of migration on others in the agricultural sector. This net gain is positive, as we see from the above assumptions. Furthermore, $\bar{\eta}_{sp} = \eta_{sp} + (1 - \eta_{sA})m_p$. We assume that the agricultural population increases if the price of agricultural surplus is higher, that is, $m_p > 0$. (This assumption is automatically satisfied under the Harris-Todaro migration hypothesis, which we discuss below.) Thus, $\phi > 0$, and $\bar{\eta}_{sp} > \eta_{sp}$.

24. For simplicity, we assume here that the social welfare function is utilitarian, that is, $\beta^a = \gamma^a$. The main implication of the Harris-Todaro hypothesis then is that $H = NV^a + \lambda R$ rather than equation 16-5. The corresponding results thus hold, regardless of the migration mechanism, in all those circumstances in which the government is concerned with the rural welfare alone. Other migration hypotheses can be similarly obtained as special cases of our formulation. If it is posited that there is free migration and no unemployment, for instance, but the utility of a worker in one sector is a fraction of the utility in another sector (see chapter 15 by Heady and Mitra), then we have a special case of our formulation in which N^u is set at zero and the expression $N^a = N^a(p, q, w, N^m)$ is implicitly defined by $V^a(p, N^a) = eV^m(p, w, N^m)$, where e is a parameter. A further special case is $e = 1$, which implies the standard neoclassical assumptions that there is no unemployment and that free migration equalizes workers' utilities across sectors.

25. Pricing in the industrial sector in the presence of endogenous migration can be analyzed similarly. Also note that the rules of price reform derived earlier apply with some modifications in the present case as well. The rule for reform in the rural food price, equation 16-2, for example, applies in the present case if η_{sp} is replaced by $\bar{\eta}_{sp}$.

PART 5

Empirical Studies of Agricultural Taxation

THREE EMPIRICAL CASE STUDIES of agricultural price reform in the Republic of Korea make up this part. Korea is unusual in having high-quality statistics for both the agricultural sector and the nonagricultural sector and thus shows how far the techniques presented in this book can be pushed under good conditions. Most developing countries lack Korea's statistical coverage, though many nonetheless have micro surveys, farm management studies, consumer budget surveys, and the like. An additional advantage of Korea is that many of the data are readily accessible because good summaries are published.

Korea is unusual in other respects, notably in its rapid industrial growth to the extent that policy toward the agricultural sector is more similar to that in developed countries than to that in developing countries. Thus the main aims are to raise rural standards of living, to protect farm incomes, and to aim for self-sufficiency rather than to tax agriculture and transfer the surplus for industrial investment. Korean grain prices are higher than world prices, whereas in most developing countries they are below world prices. Moreover, the policy appears to have been fairly successful in equalizing urban and rural real incomes and in achieving near self-sufficiency, though subsidy payments have become high (about 1 percent of GDP). Thus the main policy question is whether to reduce the grain subsidy, rather than, as in other developing countries, whether to increase or reduce agricultural taxes (to lower or to raise agricultural prices).

Conceptually, however, the questions are essentially the same, and so is the strategy for answering them. The aim of this part of the book is to illustrate this strategy, not to draw general conclusions about agricultural pricing from an admittedly atypical case. It would of course be desirable to apply these techniques to a country such as India or Pakistan, where the issues of rural poverty and agricultural taxation take on a very different complexion, but time and space preclude that option. Fortunately Braverman and his colleagues are vigorously applying their techniques to a growing list of countries and are extending their methodology to cover a broader range of questions, so it may be possible to offer more firmly based general conclusions in the near future.

463

The three chapters that follow are closely complementary, but they also build on the theoretical models of part 4. In particular, in chapter 16 Sah and Stiglitz construct a model motivated in part by the Korean experience, and chapter 13 discusses how far Korea is a special case for agricultural policy analysis. The core chapter in this part is chapter 17 by Braverman, Hammer, and Ahn, which describes a model for the simulation of the effects of agricultural price policy and the results of applying it to Korea. The model is calibrated and used to derive the consequences, given changes in policy, the costs and benefits of which are then evaluated. The following chapter, by Newbery, shows how an analytical version of the model can be used to derive improving directions of policy change. There is no difficulty in principle in extending the computable model to address those questions, and work on Cyprus by Braverman, Hammer, and Gron (1985) does just that. The main value of Newbery's chapter is to demonstrate that it is not necessary to construct a computer-based model in order to probe issues of price reform quantitatively.

One advantage of the approach is that it is flexible. Particular repercussions can be added sequentially without the need to reprogram the entire model. It is then possible to see whether, on the basis of the evidence available, the extra repercussion is important enough to warrant inclusion. Once the modeler is satisfied that all the major interactions have been included, then there are obvious advantages in moving to a computer-based model, which is far better suited to the large number of repetitive calculations needed to explore robustness and to generate confidence intervals for the policy impacts.

Chapters 17 and 18 both deal with conventional microeconomic questions of changing the urban and rural price of rice and barley, notionally holding constant the government budget. Macro effects are thereby ignored, and the focus is on medium-run issues of equity and efficiency rather than on short-run issues of stabilization and dynamic adjustment. Both chapters also ignore the possible impact of agricultural price policies on the urban money wage, though they acknowledge that the supply price of migrant labor from the rural sector may respond to these policies, and may ultimately affect the urban wage, in ways discussed more fully by Sah and Stiglitz in chapter 16. In the interests of brevity, however, these questions were sidestepped by holding the urban money wage constant. Chapter 19 by van Wijnbergen differs in focusing entirely on the possible macroeconomic impacts of a large fall in the domestic rice price. Van Wijnbergen has constructed and estimated a dynamic macroeconometric model of the Korean economy in which urban workers bargain over the real wage, so that the urban money wage responds (with a lag) to changes in the cost of living and is thus sensitive to the price of a major consumption item such as rice. Changes in the money wage induce changes in export competitiveness and hence have impacts on the balance of trade, the exchange rate, and the rate of inflation. Changes in the rice price affect the intersectoral distribution of income and hence affect the level of savings, the level of demand, and the balance of payments. This chapter stresses that large agricultural tax reforms may have significant macro effects if they are not countered by offsetting macro policy. Put another way, elsewhere in the book it is often assumed that revenue-neutral tax changes will have no macro consequences, but this assumption may be incorrect if the tax changes have large income redistributional effects between sectors with very different propensities to save and invest. Agriculture and nonagriculture apparently exhibit this property in Korea. This finding further strengthens the case for being cautious in predicting the consequences of large policy changes, though of course if the economy is in fundamental and substantial disequilibrium, there is little alternative to such reforms.

All three chapters demonstrate the importance of the way the labor market works for the analysis of tax incidence, at both the micro and the macro levels. Chapters 17 and 18 concentrate on the rural labor market and compare two polar cases—one in which the rural money wage is insensitive to the cereal price (that is, a perfectly elastic supply of rural labor to cereal production) and one in which the labor supply to cereal production is perfectly inelastic, and the wage adjusts to equilibrate demand to this supply. Chapter 18 shows that the alternative labor market specifications make a large difference to the social cost of raising revenue by changing agricultural prices, though in the Korean case they had little effect on the ranking of alternative policies. This result is similar to the finding in chapter 13 that allowing for changes in the prices of nontaxed, nontraded goods may affect the social cost of raising revenue but may not have much effect on the relative attractiveness of alternative policies. It is clearly desirable to explore this issue further, however, particularly for the labor market, which has such direct distributional implications.

Chapters 17 and 18 both illustrate very clearly the way in which empirical estimation raises important methodological issues. Urban workers appear to work longer hours than rural workers, though the disutility of effort when someone is farming may be much greater than that when a person is sitting in a comfortable office. The two groups face different prices. How, then, are their utility levels to be compared? What is the value of rural leisure, some of which may be seasonally enforced—or, indeed, of peace and quiet, or of the absence of bright lights and urban services? Any attempt to address income-distributional issues must take some position on these questions. Another empirically important feature of agriculture intrudes at various points—that of the volatility of the market-clearing price, caused by fluctuations in production within the economy or fluctuations in world market prices. If, as in Korea, the government stabilizes the domestic price, then the immediate problem is one of valuing surpluses that are stockpiled. When goods remain tradable, as in Korea, this problem can be sidestepped by valuing stocks at world prices, though one must be careful to specify whether these are to be current import or export prices or present discounted expected future import or export prices. The second point that is quantitatively very important is that the implicit tax and subsidy rates become very unstable (being the difference between the fixed agricultural price and the unstable world price). One solution is to work with the "normal" tax rates implied by the "normal," or trend value, of the world price. To do so requires a careful study of the relevant world commodity market (though futures markets may be able to answer the question "what world price did the government anticipate when it announced the domestic price?"). Agricultural uncertainty has other implications as well, as mentioned in chapter 13. To take one example relevant to chapters 17 and 18, uncertainty may affect crop choices and may explain why farmers do not specialize. To ignore the effect of uncertainty may be to bias the econometric estimates of the production function, though we must acknowledge that it would be a challenging task, requiring careful theoretical and econometric specification and rich data sets, to model the effects of risk adequately.

In sum, the following three chapters show some of the variety of agricultural policy analysis that appears useful and possible as well as suggesting a rich field of research topics for further work.

17

Multimarket Analysis
of Agricultural Pricing Policies
in Korea

Avishay Braverman, Jeffrey Hammer,
and Choong Yong Ahn

THE PURPOSE OF THIS CHAPTER is to present a methodology developed for the World Bank's economic analyses of agricultural pricing policies and to illustrate its application to Korea. This methodology has evolved considerably since this chapter was first written in 1984. Our current emphasis is on models that are easily accessible to operational economists. They are implemented on personal computers and require less mathematical sophistication than the model described here. For a detailed discussion of the Korean problem and model, see Braverman, Ahn, and Hammer (1983). Similar methodology has been applied (under different institutional constraints) to Senegal, Sierra Leone, Cyprus, and Malawi by Braverman, Hammer, and Levinsohn (1983); Braverman and Hammer (1986); Braverman, Hammer, and Jorgensen (1983, 1984); and Singh, Squire, and Kirchner (1984). Applications to other countries are discussed below. For discussion of past rice price policies in Korea, see Hasan and Rao (1979), and Moon (1975). In this introduction, we briefly discuss the motivation for our study and the gap in policy analysis of agricultural pricing that it is intended to fill. We then present the Korean problem and the basic model and policy scenarios. We subsequently discuss the main results and conclude by summarizing the lessons we have drawn about the role of modeling and tax analysis in the policy dialogue between the Bank and officials in developing countries.

Any Bank economist who discusses or advocates agricultural price reforms with officials of developing countries is expected to address the consequences

The research for this chapter was done under World Bank Research Project no. 672-61. We thank Jim Levinsohn, Karen Messer, and Ann Case for excellent research assistance. Many other persons in the World Bank, in the International Monetary Fund, in Korea, and in U.S. academia—too numerous to mention all by name—contributed. In particular, we thank Joseph Stiglitz, Raaj Sah, Angus Deaton, Avinash Dixit, and Lyn Squire. Special thanks are due to Alex Meeraus, Tony Brooke, and Arne Drud, whose modeling system, GAMS, we have used for the numerical solutions of the model and who provided us with most valuable assistance. We alone are responsible for any remaining errors and for all views expressed. Our opinions do not necessarily reflect the official views of the World Bank.

of the suggested price changes for (1) the public budget, (2) foreign exchange, (3) real income distribution (often rural versus urban), and (4) production and consumption of key agricultural commodities. These are the issues on which the immediate political economy debate will center.

Domestic agricultural prices often differ from world prices. It is neither helpful nor particularly effective, however, simply to propose that domestic agricultural prices be equated with world prices without trying to assess the consequences of such changes and to evaluate their merit both on utilitarian grounds and in terms of the other variables mentioned above. Frequently, trade liberalization is the best policy to recommend, but even then a policy-maker needs to know the likely consequences of the decisions taken (particularly in a distorted economy).

Bank economists mainly use two standard techniques in their quantitative assessment of agricultural pricing policies. The first involves measuring the domestic resource cost and the effective protection rate for various crops. (Scandizzo and Bruce, 1980, use this method in the context of agricultural pricing.) These measures are modified ratios of domestic prices to international prices and do not address the income distribution and public revenue issues, nor can they address the quantitative impact of taxes and subsidies on production and consumption. The second technique calculates the single-market or partial-equilibrium consumers' and producers' surplus but typically does not address the interaction among markets, that is, the substitution effects in consumption and production, and does not devote sufficient attention to income distribution beyond the classification of agents into consumers and producers (for an excellent demonstration of this methodology with application to the Republic of Korea, see Tolley, Thomas, and Wong, 1982, and also Anderson, 1981). It also ignores the impact on and feedback from the rural labor market. Because agricultural price reforms often include simultaneous changes in several prices, the interaction among the different commodities is critical, and there is no guarantee that the effects of policies are additive across commodities.

In order to address these concerns and to bring them into operational work at the Bank, we devised a major work program. This chapter represents the first stage. The second stage was designed to make the multimarket method more accessible to operational economists. Such models have already been installed on personal computers with user-friendly software for the cases of Argentina, Brazil, Cyprus, Hungary and Indonesia. For discussion and comparison of the two multimarket approaches with an application to Cyprus, see Braverman, Hammer, and Gron (1987). For the cases of Brazil and Hungary, see Braverman, Hammer, and Brandão (1987) and Braverman, Hammer, and Morduch (forthcoming), respectively. Because this book focuses mainly on analysis of directions of change in taxes (subsidies), the present chapter illustrates the alternative approach, which handles large policy changes in a natural way, whereas the next chapter, by David Newbery, utilizes our model in analyzing directions of change.

The approach presented here can be viewed as extending the single-market surplus method to include income distribution and some general equilibrium considerations. This extension comes at the cost of further complexity but stops far short of a full computable general equilibrium analysis. A similar approach that models only the agricultural sector and is applied to Taiwan is set forth in Lau and others (1981). Instead, we devised a "small" two-sector (rural and urban) multimarket model that endogenously generates incomes (rents and wages) in the rural sector but takes the money incomes of urban residents as exogenously given. This approach may be viewed as a synthesis of the work on agricultural household models (such as Ahn, Singh, and Squire, 1981, for Korea; Barnum and Squire, 1979; and Yotopoulos and Lau, 1974) and the new public economics literature (for example, Atkinson and Stiglitz, 1980). It uses simple models of farm-household behavior as its basic building blocks. These models allow a microeconomic investigation of both producer and consumer response to exogenous price changes within an integrated consumer-cum-producer framework. Variations in rural incomes are due to different sizes of holdings and to different labor endowments. Through aggregation over households, aggregate supply and demand functions, including those of labor, are generated and can be used to evaluate the impact of price changes at the market level. In the Korean case, we derive the marketed surplus functions, that is, the net domestic supplies of rice and barley to the urban sector, and evaluate the impact of these price changes on the welfare of the individual household.

Four more points should be made clear:

1. The analysis is at the short to medium run, where technology is given.
2. Demand and supply functions are derived econometrically, using duality theory.
3. Because large, computable general equilibrium models are expensive to construct and solve, and are too complex to be intuitively understandable, we have chosen to restrict the size of the model. We attempt to model only key commodities whose production, consumption, and prices have major effects on public finance and on income distribution.
4. The analysis examines alternative policies through simulation exercises, which provide a detailed set of results for discussion. Although it is possible to impose an objective function (that is, a social welfare function) and to find "the optimal" policy, we often find the single optimal solution not very useful for policy dialogue. Most practical economists and public officials are suspicious of recommendations from social welfare maximization exercises and prefer to discuss the scenarios emerging from alternative price reforms.

The Korean Problem

Though the Republic of Korea is rapidly becoming a modern industrial country, World Bank data suggest that the agricultural sector is still a significant part of the economy, generating approximately 16 percent of GNP and employing 30 percent of the labor force. The price of rice for both farmers and urban consumers has always been a major policy issue. In the past, the government of Korea tried to fulfill three objectives with its rice price policy: to achieve self-sufficiency in rice production; to maintain rural incomes at parity with urban incomes; and to keep prices low in the cities in order to restrain urban workers' demands for wage increases.

Objectives 2 and 3 hold for barley too. Korea is already self-sufficient in barley. In addition to these three objectives, the government of Korea aimed at stabilizing urban consumer prices, especially that of rice, during the calendar year and across years. We shall not deal in this chapter with the price stabilization issue. Tolley, Thomas, and Wong (1982) discuss this aspect of Korean price policy, and some of the issues are discussed further in chapter 18, by Newbery.

In order to fulfill these three objectives, the government lowered the urban prices of rice and barley below the rural price and as a result generated large deficits. The GMF (through which the rice and barley price policies are executed) ran a deficit of about 0.7 percent of GNP in the late 1970s.[1] The prices for urban consumers of both rice and barley are still substantially higher than the world price, however, and so part of the cost of the farm support policy is borne directly by urban consumers. For the base year 1979, the rural price of rice was approximately 65 percent above the world prices, and the urban price was approximately 50 percent above. For barley, the rural price was more than two and one-half times the world price, whereas the urban price was about 30 percent above.

In addition, fertilizers are produced domestically at guaranteed prices significantly higher than international prices. There are two main reasons: (1) Korea produces urea from naphtha rather than from natural gas, the cheaper source, and (2) the Korean government entered into disadvantageous joint ventures with foreign companies. By the Joint Venture Decree, these companies are guaranteed both a rate of return on their capital and a volume of government purchases (all domestic demand is handled through government channels). These guarantees, the last of which is to expire in 1986, imply high price support for the fertilizer industry. To compensate farmers partially for the inefficient production of fertilizers, the government sells farmers fertilizers through the FF at subsidized prices, that is, at prices lower than factory prices. The FF deficit was approximately 0.2 percent of GNP in 1979. The subsidized prices, though, are still above international prices—in 1979 they were about 20 percent higher than international prices—and are therefore really a tax on farmers and a transfer to the fertilizer industry.

After the 1980s' "new awareness" of large government deficits, the government decided to reduce both GMF and FF deficits. Because there are alternative ways to do so, and because the three commodities in question (rice, barley, and fertilizer) are linked through production and consumption to each other, the task of comparing the quantitative impact of these alternative policies on the conflicting targets can be carried out using the basic methodology outlined above. In tailoring the general methodology to the Korean problem, however, we had to respond to the particular institutional details of the country, of which the most important is the existence of two distinct types of rice, HYV and TV. Although TV is much preferred by consumers, the government provides price support only for HYV in its drive for self-sufficiency. It is obviously important to allow for the effects of substitution between the two products in evaluating the impact of government price intervention in the HYV market.

The Model

In this section, we shall briefly describe the basic structure of the model and shall then discuss a number of modeling issues: the assumption of constant returns to scale and the possibility of complete specialization, the choice of functional form for the demand system, and the use of real disposable income rather than full income in welfare comparisons.

The basic structure of the model is straightforward. The model explicitly considers the supply and demand for three consumer goods: high-yield rice, which is marketed and subsidized by the government; barley, which is also subsidized and passes through government channels; and traditional rice, which is traded on private markets. It also considers the supply and demand of two factors of production: chemical fertilizer, which is government controlled, and labor. The basic outcomes of the model are determined by supply and consumption responses to the price changes engendered by the policy experiments.

Agricultural Production

The production structure for all commodities is assumed to be given by the translog restricted profit function (Lau, 1976). This is a flexible functional form in the sense that it can accommodate a large variety of substitution possibilities and factor demand elasticities. Inputs to production are classified as fixed or variable. Rents accruing to the fixed factor (land) are considered part of family income. The variable inputs to production are fertilizer, labor, and other inputs. Because the farm is assumed to be competitive in factor markets, the family endowment of labor does not affect the use and allocation of labor in production. If family labor is insufficient to meet demand at current factor prices, the farm will hire workers from outside, and if family labor is excessive, the family is assumed to hire members out. Therefore, profits on the farm depend on the prices of the variable factors and on the quantities of the fixed factor. Using duality theory, the profit function yields the supply of the product, the demand for the factors of production, and, directly, the net return to the farm from land ownership. These are all functions of the commodity and input prices. The production function exhibits constant returns to scale.

Although land is fixed to the sector, it is not fixed between uses. In particular, paddy land can be used in production of either the high-yield or the traditional variety of rice. The equilibrium condition for land allocation is that the marginal revenue product of land in each use is equated. In the absence of information about the production functions of the two types of rice, they are assumed to differ only by a shift parameter. The above-described equilibrium condition, essentially identical production functions, and constant returns to scale imply a linear production possibility frontier between the two crops. The producer price ratio will be fixed in this case, and equilibrium in the full model will require the rural traditional rice price (left endogenous) to be proportional to the rural price of high-yield rice. Perfect substitutability between goods on the production side may imply specialization for a typical farmer but not for the market as a whole (unless they are perfect substitutes in demand or the indifference curves hit the axis). Even an allowance for slightly more intensive use of fertilizer and labor in HYV production (the likely case) will not significantly alter the shape of the production possibility frontier. (On this point see Johnson, 1971.)

Because barley is grown in a completely different season from rice, though usually on the same land, no explicit substitution is considered between these commodities. Indeed, the usual alternative to barley production is to let the land lie fallow, and there is no need to incorporate the opportunity cost of barley into family income that is not already handled by labor time and factor costs.[2]

Rural Incomes and Commodity Demands

Incomes in the rural areas derive from three sources. The first is profit from barley and rice production, as described above. The second is wage income, and the third is income from nonagricultural pursuits. The rural sector was divided into four groups, corresponding to the presentation of the large majority of the data from Korean sources. The division into classes was solely on the basis of the amount of land owned, taken from the Farm Household Economy Survey. The classes are: (1) those owning less than 0.5 hectares (33.6 percent of the rural sector); (2) those owning between 0.5 and 1.0 hectares (34.3 percent); (3) those owning between 1.0 and 1.5 hectares (18.2 percent); and (4) those owning more than 1.5 hectares (13.9 percent). Wages for farm workers are assumed to be equal across the classes.

Two versions of the model were originally used in this exercise, corresponding to the definitions of income. The first and the most straightforward version uses disposable income, which is broken into three components: profits from the rice and barley production, wage income, and income from other sources. In the simulation exercise, only profits and labor income will be affected by policy intervention, the other component being held fixed.

The second version uses the concept of "full" income associated with Gary Becker (1965). In this case, the value of leisure time is incorporated into the model, and "income" includes the value of the family's total time endowment. If we assume that people choose the number of hours that they work, the opportunity cost of an hour of leisure is the amount earned by an hour of working, that is, the wage. Full income, then, includes the entire time available to potential workers (for example, twenty-four hours a day) evaluated at the wage rate plus profits and other nonlabor income. This approach enables us to derive "demand" functions for leisure and hence supply functions for labor. If the impact of price support policies on agricultural labor supply and wages is ignored, the appraisal of the welfare consequences of the policy options may be severely biased. Inclusion of a complete demand system that accommodates labor supply decisions can shed considerable light on both the distributional effects of pricing policies and the effects on production.

The valuation of leisure is the main problem in comparing urban and rural incomes and welfare. Most observers agree that urban workers spend more time on the job than do their rural counterparts. If so, the value of the latter's leisure should be included in the welfare comparison. Unfortunately, it is not easy to do so, as time is not a single homogeneous quantity. Agricultural labor demand is very seasonal, and the scarcity wage rate varies over the year in an unobserved fashion, making the valuation of this "leisure" time problematic. We avoid the issue by giving the results in terms of real disposable income derived from the implicit hours worked in the model. We discuss this recommendation—that real disposable income be used—below.

The demand system to be used in the model is the AIDS of Deaton and Muellbauer (1980*b*), which is a flexible functional form in which goods are assumed separable from leisure, that is, the marginal rate of substitution between any pair of goods is independent of the amount of leisure, or equivalently, the allocation of goods from total expenditure is independent of leisure once expenditure has been given. The choice of this functional form and the separability assumption are discussed below.

Urban Incomes and Demand

The urban sector is divided into four income groups roughly equal in size that are assumed to differ only in their wage rates. In 1979, the classes chosen were: (1) disposable incomes less than 150,000 won/month (21.4 percent); (2) incomes between 150,000 won and 210,000 won (24.3 percent); (3) incomes between 210,000 won and 300,000 won (24.3 percent); and (4) incomes over 300,000 won (30 percent). Because the wage structure and nominal urban incomes are assumed to be fixed in the model, the specific cause of such differences is not of crucial importance.

Urban real incomes are assumed to depend on the prices of consumer goods. Several price indexes were examined for suitability in calculating changes in real income. The one reported is the Stone index, specific to income group, which closely approximates compensating variations implicit in the AIDS framework. In the absence of independent information on demand structure in the urban sector, AIDS parameters were chosen such that price elasticities at each sector's average income are the same.

Market-Clearing Conditions

The controlled high-yield rice market equilibrates in the following way: the government sets the price to farmers, who decide how much to produce and consume and hence how much surplus to sell to the government marketing agents. The government sets the urban price of rice, and the discrepancy between urban demand and marketed surplus supply is met by imports, which are also completely controlled by the government.[3] Although much of the rice imported by the government is actually of the traditional type and is not the high-yield variety, it is included in the market of the latter because it is of lower quality then the domestic traditional type.

The *traditional rice* market is assumed to be in a private, closed-economy equilibrium, with the marketed surplus equaling urban demand (the surplus being net of animal feed and waste).

The *barley* market, like high-yield rice, is assumed to be completely in government hands. The purchase price of the government is the rural producer and consumer price; the release price is the urban consumption price. Supply is entirely domestic, as imports have never been significant. Market clearing is brought about by inventory accumulation or reduction if any discrepancy arises between the marketed surplus (a function of rural prices) and urban demand. In recent years this discrepancy has been substantial, resulting in large increases in inventories.

Fertilizer production is exogenous to the current model, as the agreements between the government and foreign producers are assumed to be binding. Prices that farmers face are a matter of policy and influence the demand for fertilizer in rice and barley production. The residual farm demand for fertilizer in other uses is assumed to be a function of the price also. Any discrepancies between total demand and contractual supply are met by exports to world markets (total production has always run ahead of demand) and changes in inventory.

Four versions of the model can be run, each making different assumptions about the *rural labor market*. A major advantage of detailed modeling of the rural sector is the ability to incorporate factor market conditions for the analysis of output and income determination. The precise institutional assumption regarding labor market equilibrium is likely to have a substantial effect on the response of incomes to policy changes, particularly the effect of food prices on rural incomes.

The four alternative assumptions are: the rural (money) wage rate is fixed; the rural wage is endogenous, but the rural population and labor supply are fixed; the rural wage and labor supply are endogenous, but the rural population is fixed; and all three variables are endogenous.

The first assumption implies the smallest impact of pricing policy on rural incomes: only the profitability of crops will be affected by policy changes. Family endowments of labor will retain their original value, and labor supplied will remain constant. Changes in the demand for agricultural labor will be balanced by compensatory changes in demand for off-farm labor, which is assumed to be elastically demanded, with negligible changes in the wage rate.

Fixing the labor supply and off-farm employment but allowing the wage to vary to clear the market will have the strongest impact on rural income and welfare. A reduction of the purchase price of rice will lead to a fall in the demand for labor. With supply fixed, this situation translates immediately into lower wages.

Only the results of the above two versions have been computed, because they represent the possible extreme assumptions about the behavior of the labor market. The remaining two versions may be considered in future work.

By allowing the supply of labor to vary in accordance with the estimated utility function, we compromise between the two previous cases. With a properly estimated demand system, it should be the case closest to reality in the short run, defined as the time horizon within which no migration can take place.

The last assumption allows migration to affect the size of the rural population. The equilibrating factor in this version is the level of utility in the rural and urban sector. One characterization of migration equilibrium is modeled by equating the average utility of the rural dwellers (a function of rural wages and prices) with that of the urban dwellers (a function of urban wages and prices). This version of the model is likely to have effects similar to those of the fixed-wage case on income and prices, because the option to migrate will add extra responsiveness to the labor supply function. For a discussion of current migration issues in Korea, see Yusuf and others (1983).

Deficits

Finally, the deficits in the funds devoted to the government price policies are calculated in a straightforward manner. For the Grain Management Fund, the deficit is equal to the differential between purchase and sale prices times the marketed surplus, plus handling and storage costs, and minus the implicit tariff revenue from importing cheap rice and selling it at higher urban prices. Barley is not assumed to be traded except in the version that simulates completely free trade. The excess of supply over demand is assumed to increase inventories at a cost to the government but with no implicit economic return. This assumption sidesteps the intertemporal issues involved with inventory carryover and interest payments. For the Fertilizer Fund, the deficit is the differential of purchase and sales prices times the volume of sales to domestic consumers plus the cost of acquiring new inventories less the revenue from sales abroad.

Methodological Issues

1. Constant returns to scale and complete specialization. The first thing the analyst should check is the number of exogenously fixed prices and the number

of fixed factors to the economy. It is well known from trade theory (originally stated by Paul Samuelson) that, if the number of exogenously fixed prices is larger than the number of fixed factors, then under constant returns to scale, complete specialization will result. In the Korean case (recall that barley is completely separable from rice because it is grown in a different season), this issue did not arise, and we have assumed constant returns to scale. In our studies of Senegal, Sierra Leone, and Cyprus, however, the number of fixed prices exceeded the number of fixed factors, and to allow curvature of the production possibility frontier, we imposed decreasing returns to scale. This assumption can be justified on an "as if" basis as capturing either the diversification of the farmer's "crop portfolio" under uncertainty or crop-specific fixed factors—that is, land of different qualities is suitable for different crops.

2. Choice of functional form for demand. AIDS (see chapter 4, by Deaton) permits a greater variety of price elasticities, to be determined by estimation or by a priori information, than most other common demand systems, but its most important feature in the Korean case is the flexibility it allows income elasticities. Barley is generally considered to be an inferior good. Consumer expenditure surveys suggest that the consumption of high-yield-variety rice tends to increase with income at low levels of income but reaches a peak and thereafter decreases with income. This inverse U-shaped Engel curve is often encountered when foodstuffs are finely disaggregated. The demand system chosen can accommodate that pattern rather than forcing the income elasticities to be positive everywhere.

The implications of positive versus negative income elasticities are substantial in the Korean context, because they will have very different consequences concerning the elasticity of marketed surplus and hence of the cost of government programs as farm prices are manipulated. The linear expenditure system would not be appropriate for the present study; it does not allow inferior goods. It also imposes strong restrictions on the relationship between income and price elasticities.

AIDS assumes separability between goods and leisure and hence allows labor supply to be either perfectly elastic or perfectly inelastic. This feature gives us upper and lower bounds on labor market responses. In principle, any conventional labor supply function can be combined with AIDS (see, for example, Deaton, 1984). Because we do not recommend the use of full income as a welfare measure for developing countries, this separability assumption seems appropriate.

3. Concavity of the expenditure (cost) function. AIDS, like other flexible function forms, cannot guarantee global concavity. Because many of the policies analyzed imply significant price changes from the existing equilibrium, we had to check numerically for concavity in the calibration process. In fact, in the first construction of the model, concavity was violated. During the calibration of the model, this problem was corrected by changing parameters in such a way that the relevant elasticities were altered as little as possible.[4]

4. Real versus full income as welfare measures. The welfare comparison is

conducted using real disposable income. We recommend in general the application of this measure rather than full income for the following reasons. A real income measure using full income must include the price of leisure in the price index, and income distribution comparisons are contingent upon the choice of labor time endowment, T. It can be shown that alternative choices of T can produce alternative welfare rankings at one's will. (See Deaton, 1984, on this point.) In addition, the full income calculations implicitly assume that there is no involuntary unemployment and would therefore often lead to an overstatement of rural welfare that may be improperly used in the rural-urban debate. The issue is important enough to merit further careful study, however.

Policy Scenarios

The set of policies to be analyzed was determined by discussions with Bank regional economists and Korean officials. All situations that are analyzed lead to smaller deficits. The standard of comparison is one in which deficits are eliminated completely—the Korean target for 1986—but this target is to be approached gradually. We analyze both single and multiple price changes. (They are listed in the table in the next section.) The scenarios entailing multiple price changes include closed-economy laissez-faire and free trade.

The model is calibrated for 1979 data. The responses analyzed are presented in the form of percentage changes from the base run. These include:

1. Changes in the deficits of the rice, barley, and fertilizer funds.
2. Total production, consumption, and marketed surplus of rice and barley as well as the self-sufficiency ratio of production divided by consumption.[5]
3. Changes in rural incomes, both on average and divided into the four classes.
4. Changes in the rural and urban consumer price index. Combined with the changes in incomes, the price index can be used to calculate real incomes and can reflect the true cost of proposed policy changes for the different rural and urban income groups.
5. Changes in an aggregate welfare measure that is a "weighted national income" in which different income groups are given different weights. We use the Atkinson measure (see Atkinson, 1970), and calculate results for several degrees of the inequality aversion parameter, ϵ. (See note g of table 17-1 for the formal definition of this measure.)

The higher the value of the parameter ϵ, the more the poor are valued relative to the more affluent. As ϵ becomes very large, only the very poor are counted in the evaluation of social welfare (this being Rawls's criterion of justice [see Rawls, 1971]).

Two points should be raised here regarding the calculation of real disposable incomes and their aggregation into a welfare measure. The first is that the real incomes reported here are compensated variations rather than equivalent variations. Though the equivalent variation is the correct measure to rank alternative price changes (for example, Morey, 1984), the compensated variation measure allows us to answer the following question: how much money would the government have to pay the losers to make them as well off as before? Because actual compensation to accompany price changes is a policy option, we have used this measure.

The second issue is the disposition of the money saved through GMF deficit reduction. We assume that these savings are distributed to the public on a uniform per capita basis, and we incorporate them into the Atkinson social welfare measures. This assumption implies a very progressive tax rebate scheme. There are other possible ways to redistribute the tax, though none affects the results very much. A reduction of taxes in proportion to those paid would benefit the urban sector most and the relatively affluent within the sector especially. As a result, an inequality-averse Atkinson measure would be a bit lower, because groups with little weight in the welfare function would get most of the government revenue. A second possibility is to give the extra resources to the poor, either by reducing taxes borne by the poor or by redirecting government expenditure. This approach would raise the measure, the more so for large values of ϵ. Finally, the government revenue may be used to compensate the people who are adversely affected by a deficit-reducing policy. For the rural price reduction, the deficit gain is returned to the rural sector, particularly to larger farmers, with ambiguous effects on the social welfare measure (relative to per capita revenue distribution), but it may reduce rural opposition to the policy, though full compensation is not possible from the increase in government revenue because of rural price reductions.

The deficit might alternatively be financed by simply increasing the money supply or by borrowing. Indeed, the government used a combination of these devices to finance the deficit until summer 1983. The distributional consequences of these changes in macroeconomic policy are difficult to identify, and we have ignored them, though there is clearly a need to assess the distributional implications of a reduction in deficits associated with such monetary changes. The recent change in government financing of GMF and FF, however—shifting them to the general budget—makes our model description more accurate.

Results

In this section we shall briefly describe the results that are generated by the model. For a more detailed discussion of the results, see Braverman, Ahn, and Hammer (1983). We shall mainly focus on issues that are of methodological interest. The results corresponding to the shortest-run version, which assumes perfectly inelastic labor supply, are presented in tables 17-1 and 17-2. These results illustrate the conflict among the various goals of government policy.

Rice Policy

The rice market best illustrates the conflict. In 1982, Korean officials were debating whether to decrease the rural purchase price of HYV rice by 10 percent or to increase the price of HYV rice by 10 percent.

For a 10 percent reduction in the rural prices of high-yield rice (see row 1 in table 17-1):

The combined GMF and FF deficit will decline by 32 percent.

National income will increase by 0.13 percent (the case with $\epsilon = 0$).[6]

Average rural incomes will decline by 5.5 percent.

The proportion of rice consumption met by local production will fall from 93 percent to 88 percent.

For a 10 percent increase in the urban price of high-yield rice (row 3 in table 17-1):

The combined GMF and FF deficits will decline by 20 percent.

National income will decline by 0.44 percent.

Average urban incomes will decline by 0.65 percent.

The proportion of rice consumption met by local production will increase from 93 percent to 94 percent.

We find:

1. In general, the deficit is more sensitive to changes in rural prices than in urban prices.
2. If the government is constrained to the use of rice prices, the goals of self-sufficiency and rural income conflict directly with national income and the cost of living. The orders of magnitude are provided above and appear in greater detail in the tables.
3. Specification of the weights given to different income groups is critical in ranking the evaluated two policies on welfare grounds. In particular, a Rawlsian criterion ($\epsilon = \infty$) that puts the emphasis on the poorest group will favor a decrease in rural prices, because the poorest are concentrated in the urban area. It will produce the same ranking as the efficiency principle ($\epsilon = 0$). Intermediate inequality aversion weights of $\epsilon = 1$ and $\epsilon = 2$, however, will favor the rural sector because, on average, the rural sector is poorer than the urban.

Each of the goals mentioned above is of genuine value for Korean society. The difficulty, and the need to evaluate tradeoffs, arises from the fact that all of these goals cannot be satisfied by changes in agricultural prices alone. Too many different effects are expected from the application of these limited tools. Instead, priority should be given to expanding the number of policy instruments.

Table 17-1. *Single Price Changes, Rural Wages Endogenous, Fully Estimated System*

Price change	Deficit change due to government domestic expenditure[a] (A)	Deficit change due to tariff revenues[b] (B)	Total deficit (A + B)	Self-sufficiency ratio of rice (base year = 0.93)[c]	National real disposable income[d]	Rice supply Total	Rice supply HYV	Rice supply Traditional	Rice demand	Barley supply	Barley demand
High-yield-variety rice											
Rural price decreases 10%	-22.2	-9.8	-32.0	0.88	0.13	-5.90	-11.41	3.18	0.43	4.64	-4.88
Rural price decreases to urban level	-36.6	-21.8	-58.4	0.81	0.32	-13.29	-25.45	7.2	1.00	9.96	-10.26
Urban price increases 10%	-20.6	-1.0	-21.6	0.94	-0.44	-0.07	-0.68	0.95	-1.10	0	1.29
Urban price increases to rural level (26.8%)	-35.0	-14.1	-49.1	0.96	-1.11	-0.18	-1.70	2.38	2.86	0	3.19
Barley											
Rural price decreases	-17.5	4.7	-12.8	0.96	0.012	1.64	3.46	1.46	-1.38	-35.5	4.84
Rural price decreases to urban level (54.1%)	-26.3	9.1	-17.2	0.98	0.02	3.14	6.65	-2.80	-2.64	-79.87	17.06
Urban price increases 20%	-0.9	-0.3	-1.2	0.93	0.005	0	-1.09	0.152	0.16	0	-2.05
Urban price increases to rural level (118%)	-3.9	-1.1	-5.0	0.93	0.02	0	-4.65	0.65	0.67	0	-9.64
Fertilizer											
Raised 20%	-6.35	-0.7	-7.05	0.93	0.018	-0.70	-1.04	-1.86	-0.16	-3.92	-0.21
Raised to purchase price	-15.75	-2.0	-17.75	0.92	0.029	-1.91	-2.73	-0.54	-0.44	-7.95	-0.47
Lowered to world price	6.82	0.7	7.52	0.94	-0.028	0.67	0.94	-0.181	0.12	2.81	0.20

480

Price change	Rural real disposable income, by class[e]				Urban real disposable income, by class[f]				Change in social welfare[g]				
	1	2	3	4	1	2	3	4	$\epsilon=0$	$\epsilon=.5$	$\epsilon=1$	$\epsilon=2$	$\epsilon=\infty$
High-yield-variety rice													
Rural price decreases 10%	-3.54	-5.01	-5.78	-6.94	0.62	0.62	0.62	0.62	0.13	-0.16	-0.34	-0.63	1.37
Rural price decreases to urban level	-7.24	-10.25	-12.35	-14.62	1.48	1.48	1.48	1.48	0.32	-0.23	-0.40	-0.83	1.95
Urban price increases 10%	0	0	0	0	-0.91	-0.73	-0.63	-0.55	-0.44	-0.37	-0.31	-0.19	-0.60
Urban price increases to rural level (26.8%)	0	0	0	0	-2.28	-2.10	-1.59	-1.08	-1.11	-0.95	-0.79	-0.52	-1.40
Barley													
Rural price decreases	-2.82	-2.01	-1.51	-1.02	0	0	0	0	0.012	-0.20	-0.28	-0.42	0.40
Rural price decreases to urban level (54.1%)	-4.32	-3.18	-2.22	-1.30	0	0	0	0	0.02	-0.33	-0.42	-0.72	0.70
Urban price increases 20%	0	0	0	0	-0.02	-0.02	-0.02	-0.01	-0.005	-0.007	-0.008	-0.011	-0.088
Urban price increases to rural level (118%)	0	0	0	0	-0.10	-0.08	-0.07	-0.06	-0.02	-0.03	-0.04	-0.05	-0.04
Fertilizer													
Raised 20%	-0.48	-0.49	-0.49	-0.51	0	0	0	0	0.018	0.008	-0.002	-0.017	0.195
Raised to purchase price	-1.28	-1.31	-1.33	-1.39	0	0	0	0	0.029	-0.001	-0.030	-0.075	0.488
Lowered to world price	0.459	0.467	0.475	0.494	0	0	0	0	-0.028	-0.020	-0.012	0	0.209

(Notes to table are on the following page.)

481

Notes to table 17-1

Notes: All entries are percentage changes from base-period levels except for the self-sufficiency ratio.

Disposable income per capita, rural (won)		Disposable income per capita, urban (won)	
class 1:	429,550	class 1:	319,938
class 2:	474,752	class 2:	459,455
class 3:	544,442	class 3:	619,502
class 4:	743,553	class 4:	1,016,774

Base values (hundreds of millions of won)

Deficit change due to government domestic expenditure	3,625
Deficit change due to tariff	380
Total deficit	3,245

Base value: national real disposable income per capita (won)   617,500

Rice supply (tons)

Total	4,809,642
HYV	2,869,855
Traditional	1,939,787
Rice demand (tons)	5,161,000
Barley supply (tons)	1,562,000
Barley demand (tons)	497,000

a. Includes the change in government costs due to the price differential multiplied by quantity processed plus the handling cost. Change is relative to the total deficit.

b. Includes the change in the government deficit due to changes in tariff revenues; for example, if the rural price of rice is decreased, there will be a reduction in the marketed supply of rice, and in order to equilibrate the market at these prices, rice imports will increase. The increase in imports that are sold to urban consumers at a price higher than the purchase price of imports, the international price, increases government revenues and hence reduces the government deficit. Change is relative to the total deficit.

c. (Total consumption − imports) ÷ total consumption. Expressed in levels.

d. Real disposable income = (nominal full income − value of leisure) ÷ P where P is the price index from the demand system.

e. Income classes by size of landholding.
   1: less than 0.5 hectare
   2: 0.5 to 1.0 hectare
   3: 1.0 to 1.5 hectare
   4: more than 1.5 hectare

f. Income classes by wage income.
   1: lowest 21.4 percent
   2: next 24.3 percent
   3: next 24.3 percent
   4: highest 30 percent

g. Social welfare is measured by the Atkinson index

$$W = \bar{Y}\left[\sum_i \left(\frac{Y_i}{\bar{Y}}\right)^{1-\epsilon} N_i\right]\left(\frac{1}{1-\epsilon}\right)$$

where $\bar{Y}$ is mean real income, N_i is fraction of population in class i, and Y_i is real income of class i. (Atkinson's index of inequality is then $1 - W/\bar{Y}$.) Changes in social welfare are then expressed as percentage changes in W. For $\epsilon = 0$, the measure is average private real income; for $\epsilon > 0$, an "inequality equivalent" real income, with increasing ϵ representing increasing inequality aversion. Government expenditure reductions are assumed to be redistributed on a uniform per capita basis.

Source: Braverman, Ahn, and Hammer (1983).

Single-Market versus Multimarket Analysis

The results of this study were contrasted with the findings of a single-market analysis of the same problem by Case and Squire (1984): there were substantial differences. The reason is that substitution possibilities are of central importance to the results reported here. For producers, the ability to substitute traditional rice for high-yield-variety rice leads to considerably higher supply elasticities for the subsidized commodity than would emerge from an analysis of the aggregate commodity "rice." This result has profound effects on the calculation of deficit reductions due to price changes. It also helps to identify indirect effects of policies, such as the reduced cost of traditional rice in urban areas when the rural high-yield price declines.

On the demand side, the spillover effects of related markets are substantial. When rural rice prices are reduced, for example, barley sales to the government increase, partially offsetting the savings in the deficits. Such multimarket effects have substantive policy implications, such as the need to coordinate price changes in related commodities, and require a general approach to modeling the rural sector.

Robustness

In our case, the robustness issues relate mainly to the choice of model for the labor market and the choice of functional forms for demand and supply.

As expected, a major change in modeling of the rural labor market implies significant quantitative changes in the results. We modeled the two bounds on labor market response in the short to medium run: perfectly inelastic supply and perfectly elastic supply at a fixed nominal wage. In particular, the two versions of the model have different distributional implications. In the fixed-wage case, the rural sector does not uniformly suffer from a reduction in the farm subsidy. Landless workers and the very small farmers (together making up about 30 percent of the rural population) actually benefit from rural price reductions. The landless get no benefit from the subsidy either directly (because they own no land) or indirectly (through increased demand for their services and, therefore, increased income from their services). The higher prices for basic grains merely increase their cost of living. Indeed, they seem to be the biggest gainers from a cut in the subsidy. Small farmers, who are also net purchasers of grain, also benefit from a price fall though less than the landless, because they purchase a smaller percentage of their consumption of grains. In the fixed-wage case, there is a conflict of interests between the small and large farmers.

In the flexible-wage case, the differences between residents in the rural area disappear. One consequence of a grain price reduction in this case is a lessened demand for labor, which translates into a lower wage that affects all workers in farming, not just the landowners. A flexible wage brings about a unification of interests. Through the labor market mechanism, the costs of the lower support

Table 17-2. Multimarket Interventions, Rural Wage Endogenous, Fully Estimated System

Policy intervention	Deficit change due to government domestic expenditure (A)	Deficit change due to tariff revenues (B)	Total deficit (A + B)	Self-sufficiency ratio of rice (base year = 0.93)	National real income	Rice supply			Rice demand	Barley supply	Barley demand
						Total	HYV	Traditional			
Rural											
Rice and barley prices to urban level; fertilizer price rises to government purchase price	-74.7	-4.1	-78.8	0.903	0.18	-5.79	-9.48	0.458	-2.44	-76.88	8.04
As above, with world fertilizer price	-62.55	-1.0	-63.55	0.924	0.03	-3.10	-5.42	0.814	-2.11	-73.92	13.15
Rural barley price falls to urban level; urban high-yield rice price rises to farm-gate level	-70.19	6.6	-63.59	0.864	0.40	0.864	2.41	-1.76	-4.34	-78.29	16.6
Urban prices both rise to farm-gate levels	-52.94	5.3	-47.64	0.929	1.47	-1.97	-3.93	1.34	-1.44	-7.91	-8.80
Urban barley price rises to farm-gate level; rural high-yield rice prices fall to urban level	-43.87	-13.1	-56.97	0.849	-0.03	-8.81	16.33	3.93	0.801	-2.97	-14.3
Closed-economy laissez-faire equilibrium	—	—	-1.00	1.00	-1.5	2.83	3.88	1.06	-4.25	-28.22	-0.94
Free trade equilibrium	—	—	-1.00	0.731	2.48	-23.5	-39.9	4.26	-0.69	-83.15	-12.94

Table 17-2 (continued)

Price change	Rural real disposable income, by class				Urban real disposable income, by class				Change in social welfare				
	1	2	3	4	1	2	3	4	$\epsilon = 0$	$\epsilon = .5$	$\epsilon = 1$	$\epsilon = 2$	$\epsilon = \infty$
Rural													
Rice and barley prices to urban level; fertilizer price rises to government purchase price	-10.61	-10.65	-10.77	-11.22	0.73	0.73	0.73	0.73	0.18	-0.40	-0.66	-0.98	0.80
As above, with world fertilizer price	-9.40	-9.42	-9.50	-9.76	0.73	0.73	0.73	0.73	0.03	-0.32	-0.59	-0.89	0.75
Rural barley price falls to urban level; urban high-yield rice price rises to farm-gate level	-5.98	-4.3	-3.47	-2.71	-1.18	-1.18	-1.18	-1.18	-0.40	-0.85	-0.82	-1.00	-0.28
Urban prices both rise to farm-gate levels	-1.28	-1.31	-1.33	-1.39	-2.40	-2.40	-2.40	-2.40	-1.47	-1.35	-1.24	-1.04	-1.10
Urban barley price rises to farm-gate level; rural high-yield rice prices fall to urban level	-5.3	-7.2	-8.2	-9.46	-0.51	-0.51	-0.51	-0.51	-0.03	-0.26	-0.40	-0.58	-0.78
Closed-economy laissez-faire equilibrium	-1.15	0.135	0.8	1.52	-4.63	-3.89	-3.63	-3.50	-1.5	-1.3	-1.01	-0.57	-1.15
Free trade equilibrium	-18.7	-20.6	-24.8	-28.7	8.25	7.47	6.70	6.20	2.48	0.88	-0.77	-3.82	6.74

Note: See notes to table 17-1.

price are shared by the whole sector. The truth presumably lies between these two bounds that are provided to the policymaker.

On the *supply* side, we used Lau's (1976) restricted translog profit function. Statistical tests rejected the hypothesis that the production structure is Cobb-Douglas. In the simulation model, however, it made little difference to the results whether we used the Cobb-Douglas or the estimated profit function. Because it is easier to estimate the parameter of the Cobb-Douglas function, we have used this form. The parameters are then the average shares of output spent on each input, and survey data are not needed; data at the regional, or even national, level are adequate, though in our case we used the information from farm household surveys.

On the *demand* side, we use AIDS. Clearly, other flexible functional forms can be used, but we were not interested in comparing different flexible forms. For cross-elasticities, we used our best estimate from an econometric exercise. Experimentation with a structure, allowing similar own-price elasticities to these estimates but with zero cross-elasticities, did not alter the results substantially. The assumption of unitary price elasticities together with zero cross-elasticities, however, something an analyst might be tempted to make in the absence of data, made a substantial difference.

Given the limitations of data and the obvious dependency of results on the model specification, we must rely on judgment regarding plausible model structures. A close interaction between the modeler and the "clients" is a prerequisite. Furthermore, because the model is not a full general equilibrium model, it is important to state which interactions and linkages could not be included. In the present model, we have ignored the impact of the change in agricultural subsidies on government revenues generated from taxation of other commodities and on nominal urban wages.

Conclusions

Two important directions for future research in this area are the following: better theoretical and empirical understanding of the operation of rural labor markets and alternative closure rules with the industrial sector that can extract insights from a fully general equilibrium framework. We are investigating these issues for the various countries that we have already analyzed, utilizing our current easy-to-use approach.

We have accumulated experience in applying this methodology to support policy dialogue between the Bank and the officials in several developing countries. All our studies evolve from requested policy desires to cut government budget deficits that provide the major impetus for reducing subsidies. Our aim is to provide a quantitative structure for a more informed political debate. This seems also to be the desire of the policymakers. Without an assessment of the short-run impact of changes in taxes and subsidies, the credibility of any Bank advice may be questioned. Numbers can also be used out of context, of course, and abuse of models by political advocates is frequent. In our judgment, however, the advantages of our approach in providing a consistent framework and quantitative structure for discussion greatly outweigh this drawback.

Appendix

Table 17-A1. *Demand Structure Used in the Model*

Elasticity of demand	Rural price[a]			Urban price[a]			Income	
	Barley	High-yield rice	Tradi-tional rice	Barley	High-yield rice	Tradi-tional rice	Rural	Urban
Barley	−0.51	0.03	0.02	−0.15	0.49	0.44	0.33	−0.20
High-yield rice	0.01	−0.46	0.06	0.01	−0.45	0.12	0.78	0.62
Traditional rice	0.01	0.07	−0.50	0.01	0.15	−0.53	1.0	1.0

a. Demand structure is presented for the class in each sector whose income is closest to its sector's average.
Source: Braverman, Ahn, and Hammer (1983).

Table 17-A2. *Production Structure Used in the Model*

Grain	Share of output paid to variable factors	
	Labor	Fertilizer
Barley	0.33	0.06
High-yield rice	0.20	0.03
Traditional rice	0.20	0.03

Source: Braverman, Ahn, and Hammer (1983).

Notes

1. The GMF deficit has been financed by direct loans from the Bank of Korea, and hence it was *institutionally* tied directly to increases in the money supply and to inflationary pressures. In principle, it could have been financed from the general budget, whereas other items of public expenditure could have been financed by direct borrowing from the Bank of Korea. Given that this type of financing was taking place, however, the deficits of the GMF (and similarly those of the FF) were more connected to money creation than to other components of government expenditures in the political debate over the size of the deficit. Recently, however, the government is planning to finance the GMF from the general budget.

2. There is a form of intertemporal substitution between barley and rice via the depletion of nutrients in the soil from barley production. This, however, is too subtle for present concerns.

3. The implication is that the price wedge generated by this policy is not circumvented by arbitrage or by black market operations. This assumption can be justified on the basis of the relatively strict adherence to the law in Korean society. Although the assumption is not plausible in many places in the world, the chance that the marketing laws are respected in Korea is high.

4. We shall not discuss the calibration issues here. For a detailed discussion of this topic, see Braverman, Ahn, and Hammer (1983) and Braverman, Hammer, and Jorgensen (1985).

5. Readers must be aware that it may be very misleading to refer only to a self-sufficiency *ratio*, that is, a large increase in urban consumer prices may decrease consumption substantially so as to achieve a 100 percent self-sufficiency rate. The public notion of an increase in self-sufficiency, however, is usually associated with increased production under given real prices.

6. National income is defined here as total private real disposable income plus the reduction in total government deficit.

18

Identifying Desirable Directions of Agricultural Price Reform in Korea

David Newbery

THE FOREGOING CHAPTER described a model of the Korean agricultural sector designed to predict the impact of agricultural price policies on outputs, consumption levels, government revenue, foreign exchange, and real incomes of urban and rural consumers. It also estimated the change in social welfare of these policies using various sets of social weights β^h. The approach adopted by Braverman and others has various advantages and limitations that were discussed in the introduction to part 5. The main disadvantage in the present context is that the approach does not identify desirable directions of price reform but instead provides a wealth of detail about the predicted consequences of prespecified reforms.

The aim of this chapter is to show how to develop a method of marginal tax reform analysis that can be applied to the study of agricultural price reforms and hence to identify desirable directions for price reform to take. The marginal method has the advantage of lending itself to an analytical approach. The approach of analytical modeling, in contrast to computer modeling, has several other advantages, of which the most important is its great flexibility. The welfare and revenue impacts of particular price changes depend on which other prices change, how large these induced price responses are, and the size of the consequent quantity responses. Changing the price of rice will typically change the rural wage rate and the prices of various nontraded agricultural goods such as vegetables. It is reasonably straightforward to extend the simple model to include more of these repercussions, whereas in a computer-based model, substantial reprogramming would be required to handle each additional market impact.

The analytical and computer-based approaches should therefore be seen as complementary. Initial explorations are most effectively done with an analytical model, and order-of-magnitude estimates can quickly be derived to

I thank Jeffrey Hammer and Avi Braverman for their help in preparing the chapter, though they are not to be held responsible for the use to which I have put their model and estimates. Nicholas Stern provided helpful comments.

determine the importance of a particular set of repercussions. Once the form of the model has been chosen, it may be worth constructing a computer-based model, which is better suited to performing a large number of repetitive calculations that explore the sensitivity and robustness of the results. Such a model is also better suited to calculating the wide range of impacts about which policymakers may need to know—changes in levels of supply, imports, exports, consumption, and so on. It can also give some sense of why a particular policy is less costly than some other policy: does it have a small diffuse impact, an adverse impact on the rich, or an impact of some other sort?

The chapter, then, extends the analysis of marginal tax reform exhibited in chapter 11 to the agricultural sector. It derives quantitative estimates of the marginal social cost of raising government revenue in Korea by changing the prices of key agricultural commodities. Because I did not have access to primary data and am not familiar with Korea, it should also be seen as a desk study, a preliminary to more intensive analysis of the problem and dialogue with the country's economists and policymakers. Consequently, the figures are to be treated with great caution, and the conclusions even more so, as they have not been subjected to the necessary next step of critical scrutiny and modification. In the meantime, the exercise is best viewed as an example of what can be done using limited information and indicates the kinds of questions that analysts will need to answer when undertaking an exercise of this sort. It builds heavily on the interpretation of the Korean agricultural sector provided in the previous chapter and complements that exercise. In particular, it is not able to answer some of the questions addressed there, such as the effects of large price changes, and additional work would be required to adapt the present approach to identify other useful consequences, such as the impact on supplies, foreign exchange, self-sufficiency, and so forth. In principle, though, these other (marginal) impacts could also be derived if they were needed.

The chapter is organized in the following way. The next section briefly summarizes the main lessons that can be drawn from this kind of exercise. I then describe the Korean agricultural sector, list the policy options to be explored, and begin the policy analysis by setting forth the equations for the welfare and revenue impacts of the price changes to be studied. I present the marginal social cost of rural price interventions and urban price interventions. Finally I derive and discuss the social weights and consider the social cost of raising revenue by the various policy choices on various assumptions. The following section examines their sensitivity to other parameter variations, and the final section presents conclusions.

Summary of Lessons Learned

It might be useful briefly to summarize the main lessons to be drawn from this exploratory exercise. First, it appears to be reasonably straightforward to gain some sense of the determinants of desirable policy reform from the available data (though it must be admitted that Korea is particularly well endowed with the right data). It is possible to use the available econometrically estimated price elasticities and to "invent" not unreasonable price elasticities for the remaining commodities that at least allow us to explore the sensitivity of the conclusions. In many cases, the cross-price terms, which are so difficult to estimate, appear to have relatively little effect on the ranking of policies. Second, agricultural price policy typically takes the form of setting prices to farmers and consumers, whereas the import price fluctuates significantly from year to year. The effective tax or subsidy rate is the difference between these two and is thus both variable and hard to predict. Because the desirability of price reform depends on the size of the tax or subsidy, it will depend on our view of the likely future world price, which is uncertain (though futures markets provide both a prediction and the option of hedging that prediction). The implication is that agricultural price reform requires a careful study of world market prospects for tradable goods and raises wider questions about the best methods of intervening in volatile markets.

Third, the exercise demonstrated the importance of identifying the structure and costs of operating the marketing system, including transport, handling, and storage costs. Fourth, it was possible to extend the analysis to include other interactions and linkages in the demand and supply of noncereals. These affect both the distributional impact of reform and the impact on revenues and hence it is useful to assess the importance of ignoring these interactions. Finally, we confirmed the importance of specifying labor market behavior and valuing leisure, both of which Braverman and others regarded as important for the results.

It would also be possible to examine the importance of identifying the way the government procurement of rice works. In the present model the government is assumed to purchase all the rice offered at the announced price. If producers are subject to quotas, however, and have to sell excess rice on the free market, the welfare impacts of price changes might be quite different. Although it would not be difficult to extend the model to explore this alternative, it has not been possible to do so in the time available.

A Brief Description of the Korean Problem

We follow Braverman and others closely, and a more complete description of the Korean problem appears in the preceding chapter. The year chosen for the policy analysis is therefore 1979, although this is in some ways a rather unsatisfactory year, as the won was devalued substantially shortly afterward, at the end of a long period during which it was pegged to the U.S. dollar. The government sets the purchase price of barley and high-yield variety of rice and sells both to urban consumers at a (substantial) loss. Traditional rice, in contrast to HYV, is freely marketed and accounts for 30–50 percent of production. Fertilizer is sold to farmers at a substantial loss as a result of the government's purchases involving unfavorable long-term contracts from domestic producers. Urban barley and rice prices are typically below rural prices but above import parity prices. At 1979 prices, barley was in (marginal) export surplus and rice is (marginally) imported. The government controls imports (and exports) and sets the urban price to stabilize prices through the crop year. The result is that the government bears most of the cost of storage. Traditional rice is presumably sold and consumed in the first half of the crop year, whereas HYV rice is sold in the second half of the year.

The problem facing the government is that it incurs substantial losses in subsidizing grain and fertilizer producers, and the policy issues that need to be examined are whether to lower rural rice and barley prices, whether to raise or lower urban grain prices, and whether to raise or lower fertilizer prices. We can formulate this as a problem in tax reform by asking what impact on welfare and the government budget changes in the following policy instruments would have: the rural prices of barley and HYV rice, the price of fertilizer to farmers, and the urban prices of barley and HYV rice. The impact on consumers and producers will depend on the amounts of these and related agricultural goods that they consume and/or produce, whereas the impact on government revenue will depend on the tax and subsidy rates on these and other goods. Production and consumption data are needed for the first, whereas data on taxes and prices are needed for the second, as well as information about price elasticities of demand and supply. The first step is to identify the relationship between the policy instruments, the prices facing the various agents, and the implied subsidies and taxes.

The Price Structure of Grain Marketing

The first step is to identify the prices, taxes, and subsidies for rice and barley. This apparently simple calculation turns out to be quite complex, and because similar problems are likely to arise in other countries, it seems useful to describe the steps in the calculation rather carefully. Table 18-1 gives the structure of pricing for the various grains and shows the relationship between the urban and rural price and the various taxes and subsidies. For rice, which is imported, the government collects tariff revenue on the imports but pays subsidies to the rural producers. If barley were to be exported, the government would have to pay an export subsidy of t_i as well as a production subsidy s_i. Fertilizer is exported and is therefore similar except that there are no urban consumers, and it is purchased, not sold, by farmers.

If the government is committed to setting prices, then it seems logical to regard the prices as expected at the start of the crop year (the previous June for rice and December/January for barley). In order to calculate the implied taxes and subsidies, it is necessary to forecast the import or export price, whichever is appropriate. Because Korea has typically imported barley in the past and, similarly, has imported rice, we shall assume that the relevant figures for

Table 18-1. *Presumed Price Structure for Korean Grain in 1979*
(1979 won/kilogram)

Item	Notation[a]	Barley January	Barley July	HYV rice January	HYV rice July	TV rice January	TV rice July
Import price							
Actual		(68)		(139)		—	
Central forecast	P_i	90	90	242	242	—	
High forecast		(106)		(329)		—	
Handling cost (wholesale)	$\{H_i$	5	5	5	5	—	
Storage costs		17	0	0	45	—	
Tariff on central forecast	t_i	20	37	157	112	—	
Wholesale price							
Free market	q_i	—	—	(328)	—	385	437
Government price	q_i	132	132	404	404	—	—
Subsidy	s_i	218	143	−14	126	—	—
Storage costs	$\{c_i$	93	0	0	140	—	92
Handling		15	15	15	15	15	15
Farm gate							
Average	p_i	—	—	332	—	370	—
Support price		(242)[b]	260	(375)	—	—	—
Free market		—	—	(313)	—	—	—
Average tax rates on central forecasts	$\dfrac{(s_i + t_i)}{p_i}$	—	0.83		0.63	0	0

— Not applicable.

Note: Braces indicate items that were not used in the calculations but are plausible alternatives. Exchange rate: 484 won to the U.S. dollar.

  a. Relationships: $q_i = P_i + H_i + t_i = p_i + c_i - s_i$, where the notation is defined in the first column.

  b. For June 1978 (that is, the start of the crop year for January harvest).

Sources: Braverman, Ahn, and Hammer (1983); Korea (1980).

cereals are the import prices. The first problem is to calculate the exchange rate to use for the calculation. The exchange rate, after being pegged from 1974 to the end of 1979 at 484 won per U.S. dollar, moved sharply to an average of 586 won/dollar in the first quarter of 1980. If this rate is assumed to be in equilibrium, then the 1979 equilibrium rate can roughly be calculated assuming purchasing power parity and deducting for domestic inflation. This procedure gives an average rate for 1979 of 520 won/dollar, but if we take as our reference price level January 1979 (that is, just after the rice harvest) then the official rate of 484 appears roughly correct and will be the rate used in the forecasts.

    The next problem is that world grain prices fluctuate substantially from year to year. Thus the Thai export price in 1979 U.S. dollars averaged $471/tonne over the ten years 1970–79, with a coefficient of variation (cv) of 38 percent.

The actual 1979 price was $334, the lowest in real terms for the decade (and indeed for at least three decades, though it was close to the troughs of 1971 and 1977). The reported import price in 1979 was $287 (Braverman, Ahn, and Hammer, 1983, p. 88, hereafter cited as BAH), which is substantially below the export price from the United States and Australia for 1979, though not for Australian rice in 1978, which may be the relevant price for delivery in 1979. A government worried about the potential costs of having to import rice if the price suddenly rose, and announcing the support price for rice in 1978 before planting the 1979 crop, might reasonably have planned on a rice import price (allowing for freight costs of $30/tonne) of between $500 (the trend price) and $680 (average plus one standard deviation) or 242–239 won/kilogram.

Barley was imported every year from 1972 to 1977 except for 1976, according to BAH, p. 94, and in 1978 and 1979 (according to the FAO *Trade Yearbook*). Its reported import price in 1979 was $141/tonne (FAO), which historically may again be on the low side. If we take the ten-year average U.S. maize price of $156 (real) as a rough proxy and add transport of $30, we obtain $186, compared with an actual maize price FOB in 1979 of $115.5, CIF of $145.5, in line with the actual barley price. Again, a risk-averse government might take the ten-year average plus one standard deviation (of $33).

Handling charges from farm gate to wholesale (with no storage) appear to be about 15 won/kilogram (BAH, p. 129: = wholesale less farm-gate price of traditional rice) and are arbitrarily put at one-third this level for handling from CIF to wholesale.

Next we must face the problem that grains are produced over a short period and are stored for gradual release over the year. The government stabilizes the price over the year, which means that TV rice (which is freely marketed) appears to have a comparative advantage at and soon after harvest time, whereas HYV and barley appear relatively cheaper to consumers later in the year. One way of treating this difficulty is to divide the year into two subperiods: November to May and June to October. In period 2, rice supply costs are higher because of storage costs, but barley supply costs are lower because it is harvested in period 2. One of the obvious policy options to consider is reducing the extent of price stabilization so that the relative consumer costs of rice and barley more nearly approximate their relative supply prices. Storage costs are taken as 1 percent per month plus interest costs of 2 percent (real) per month, or 3 percent per month altogether. The government carries significant stocks from year to year, and the effective period in storage is therefore about one year.

With these issues resolved, the next step—finding the farm-gate and wholesale prices of various crops—should be simple. This is done in appendix 18-1 and the results are reported in table 18-1. What emerges strongly from this exercise is that it may be quite difficult to identify the effective tax and subsidy rates with any precision, particularly where marketing agencies in their operation parallel the free market and where prices fluctuate substantially. The tariff rate (expressed as a proportion of the wholesale price) for rice may be 39 percent on the central forecast if we use the government release price as the base or 25 percent if we use the January free market price, or 64 percent if we use the actual import cost and the controlled price, or 56 percent if we use the actual import cost and the free price, or effectively zero, if we take a pessimistic high forecast price and the free market rice price. Similarly, the subsidy to producers depends very much on the price they effectively receive and on the date when the rice is sold. If the support price is treated as a quota based on acreage, then it will act as a land tax (subsidy), and the free market price is the relevant price for allocative decisions. If, as seems to be the case, the government allocates its purchases in proportion to production of HYV, then the support price will act as a subsidy, raising the average price above its equilibrium level.

Fertilizer Pricing

Fertilizers are purchased at (high) contract prices in predetermined amounts from domestic producers and are sold at a subsidized price to farmers; the surplus is exported. The relevant opportunity cost is thus the export price, which, as with grains, fluctuates significantly from year to year (its CV over the ten previous years was 50 percent). For reasons that are unclear, the relative prices of nitrogen and phosphate that farmers confront differ from those on the export market and from relative production costs (BAH, p. 113). One costless policy reform would be to correct these relative prices (assuming that they are in fact wrong and not just wrongly reported). We ignore this possibility and average the various fertilizer types to give an average fertilizer, and the presumed price structure is as shown in table 18-2.

Pricing of Other Goods

Apart from labor, which will be considered below, we shall distinguish two other kinds of goods that are potentially important to a tax reform analysis. The first category includes goods that are either priced on world markets or produced at constant cost in the nonagricultural sector and are also taxed. These will generate revenue whose amount will change as supplies and demands change in response to changes of other prices in the economy. The second category includes nontraded goods produced in the rural sector, which we shall assume are untaxed and whose prices will change as wages change. These will be considered later—here we attempt to estimate the tax on the remaining goods, which are assumed to be both taxed and traded. The IMF's *Government Financial Statistics* gives the indirect tax rates shown in table 18-3.

Modeling Supply and Demand

Braverman and others assume that barley and rice are noncompetitive for land, as they are grown in different seasons. Supply responses thus depend on

Table 18-2. *Fertilizer Prices in Korea in 1979*
(1979 won per kilogram gross weight)

Item	Notation[a]	Urea	DAP	Weighted average
Weights	—	0.44	0.56	1.0
Export prices				
Actual		92	106	100
Central forecast	P_0	110[b]	123[c]	117
Handling cost	c_0	15	15	15
(Actual subsidy)[d]		(−15)	(23)	(6)
Subsidy on central forecast	s_0	3	40	23
Price to farmer	p_0	122	98	109
Average subsidy				
On central forecast (fraction)	s_0/p_0	—	—	0.21
(Actual)[d]		—	—	(0.06)

— Not applicable.
a. Relationships: $p_0 = P_0 + c_0 - s_0$ in the notation of the first column.
b. $SD = 54$.
c. $SD = 64$.
d. Parentheses mean that figures are based on the actual export price.
Sources: Braverman, Ahn, and Hammer (1983), pp. 113, 115, 132; World Bank (1980a).

Table 18-3. *Indirect Tax Rates in Korea in 1979*

Item	Percentage or share
Indirect taxes as percentage of GDP	8.0
Trade taxes as percentage of imports	9.2
Indirect taxes as percentage of private consumption	13.0
Average share of expenditure on remaining goods	
1979 urban	0.855
1979 rural	0.327
1979 total	0.719
Indirect taxes as percentage of remaining goods	
(taken as 0.7)	18.1
Taxes as percentage of selling price	15.3

Sources: International Monetary Fund, *Government Finance Statistics, International Finance Statistics;* table 18-A2 (remaining goods share = ω_5).

increased inputs of labor, fertilizers, and so on and may, as estimated, adequately capture possible substitution between these and other crops. They further assume that HYV and TV rice are perfect substitutes in production and thus yield equal profit per acre. The higher yield of HYV is compensated by higher risk and a lower farm-gate price than TV rice. We shall follow these assumptions (that HYV and TV rice are perfect substitutes and that rice and barley are noncompetitive) and note that they have strong implications for the effects of price interventions. Specifically, raising the producer price of barley has no direct effects on the supply of rice and vice versa. The producer price of HYV rice determines that of TV rice and also the consumer price of TV rice. Given the consumer price of HYV rice, the demand for TV rice then determines the equilibrium supply of TV rice. TV rice is treated as nontradable, though this appears to be a policy decision—at present imported rice is apparently stored until its quality has declined to that of local HYV rice.

The response of wages to food price changes will be important in determining the desirability of policy changes, and a wide range of alternatives might be defended under various assumptions about the time frame of the analysis. We follow Braverman and others rather than van Wijnbergen (in chapter 19) in assuming that the urban money wage does not change. The rural wage may respond in various ways to be explored below but is assumed not to affect (or to be affected by) the urban (real) wage.

Policy Options

Minor reforms would preserve the structure of price setting but would change the prices of grain facing producers and consumers (and the price of fertilizer to farmers). More drastic reforms would involve a partial or complete abandonment of seasonal price stabilization, a reduction in government grain stocks, and perhaps a complete dismantling of the present structure of price intervention, possibly to be replaced by alternative policy instruments such as tariffs, subsidies, acreage subsidies, or other rural income support measures. This chapter, like the preceding one, considers only the analysis of minor reforms, maintaining the present seasonal price stabilization, but the other reforms may be substantially better. The calculations of Newbery and Stiglitz (1981) suggest that the optimal degree of price stabilization is likely to be well below that practiced in Korea, and it should be possible to make producers and consumers on average better off at no revenue cost by simply reducing the size of average stocks and hence reducing storage costs. Moreover, allowing rural and urban grain prices to reflect seasonal availabilities will lower the relative price of barley to rice in July (the barley harvest) and will raise it in December, encouraging (some) substitutions in consumption and a further reduction in average storage costs (as argued by Tolley, Thomas, and Wong, 1982). Moving to trade-related grain prices (that is, fixing tariff rates and subsidies rather than fixing domestic producer and consumer prices) will again encourage substitutions in production and consumption and will reduce storage requirements and costs, at the cost of greater price instability. This cost is likely to be small except for the poorer consumers and for producers (to judge from similar calculations in Newbery and Stiglitz, 1981). The latter could be ensured by offering them contract delivery prices (that is, forward markets).

Policy Analysis

We are now in a position formally to specify the problem, which is to calculate the social cost of increasing government revenue by one unit by changing one of the policy instruments in the appropriate direction. Goods are numbered 0, 1, 2, 3, 4, 5 for fertilizer, barley, HYV rice, TV rice, nontraded rural produced goods, and other goods. The convention is that producer prices are **p**, and consumer prices are **q**. The policy instruments are the price of fertilizer (p_0), the rural producer prices of barley (p_1) and HYV rice (p_2), and the urban consumer prices of barley (q_1) and HYV rice (q_2). One of the purposes of this chapter is to determine the sensitivity of the answer to alternative specifications of the rural labor market and of the market for rural goods. As in the preceding chapter, the simplest assumption is that rural money wages and hence the price of rural goods (which are assumed to depend only on the wage rate) are insensitive to the policy instruments (perhaps because there are rural employment opportunities producing tradable goods for which there is elastic demand). The alternative assumption is that labor is inelastically supplied, but its demand is sensitive to the wage, so changes in the prices of grain will lead to changes in demand for labor and hence in the wage rate and the prices of nontraded goods. The more general case is the second, and the first can be obtained by suppressing the wage sensitivity term.

Welfare Impacts

In this subsection we calculate the impact of the policy reforms on urban and rural household welfare and then aggregate these impacts using social weights β^h to evaluate the change in social welfare. Changes in the price of a good have a direct impact measured by the levels of production and consumption but also affect the profit from production of the good, possibly the wage rate, and the prices of other goods. These effects can be seen most clearly for an agricultural household that faces a vector of prices $\mathbf{q}^a$ for its consumption goods, **p** for producer goods, and w for the rural wage rate. Its indirect utility function is:

$$V^h(\mathbf{q}^a, m^h), \qquad m^h = \Pi^h(\mathbf{p}, w) + wl^h.$$

Here m^h is lump-sum income, equal to farm profits (rent) Π^h, and the value of its labor endowment l^h, which is assumed to be inelastically supplied. From the properties of the profit function and indirect utility function

$$\frac{\partial \Pi^h}{\partial p_i} = y_i^h; \qquad \frac{\partial V^h}{\partial q_j} = -x_j^h \frac{\partial V^h}{\partial m^h}$$

where y_i^h is the output of good i (negative for an input such as fertilizer or farm labor) and x_j^h is the consumption of good j. (The second derivative holds lump-sum income constant.) The vector of consumer prices is $\mathbf{q}^a = (p_1, p_2, p_3, p_4, q_5)$, which reflects the assumption that, for barley, rice, and rural goods, the consumer and producer prices are the same. The urban consumer price vector

$\mathbf{q}^u = (q_1, q_2, q_3, q_4, q_5)$, with $q_4 = p_4$, as rural goods are not taxed. The producer price vector facing farmers is $(p_0, p_1, p_2, p_3, p_4)$, where p_0, p_1, and p_2 are set by the government. A change in any one of these may affect some of the consumer prices, and possibly the rural wage, which will in turn affect the price of rural goods, p_4. Changes in the price of HYV rice, p_2, will affect the rural price of TV rice, p_3 (and also the urban price, q_3), but not the price of barley.

Social welfare will be written as the sum of agricultural and urban welfare:

(18-1) $$W = W^a + W^u$$

where

(18-2) $$W^a = \sum_h V^h[\mathbf{q}^a, \, \Pi^h(\mathbf{p}, w) + wl^h].$$

The effect on rural household h of a change in price p_i $(i = 0, 1, 2)$ is then given by

(18-3) $$\frac{\partial V^h}{\partial p_i} = \beta^h \left\{ y_i^h - x_i^h + (y_3^h - x_3^h) \frac{\partial p_3}{\partial p_i} \right.$$
$$\left. + y_i^h \left[\frac{p_4(y_4 - x_4^h)}{p_i y_i^h} \frac{\partial \log p_4}{\partial \log p_i} + \frac{w(l^h - l^a)}{p_i y_i^h} \epsilon_{wi} \right] \right\} \quad i = 0, 1, 2$$

where β^h is the social marginal utility of income to household h, l^a is the labor used on the farm, and so $(l^h - l^a)$ is net sales of labor, y_3^h is production of TV rice, y_4 is noncereal farm production, and ϵ_{wi} is $\partial \log w / \partial \log p_i$, the elasticity of wages with respect to p_i.

The first term in equation 18-3 is the net supply of good i (possibly negative) and measures the direct impact. The second term is the effect of the induced change in the price of TV rice, zero except for $i = 2$, and, because $p_3 = kp_2$ where $k = 1.114$, $\partial p_3 / \partial p_2 = k$. The third term is the effect of the induced change in the price of rural goods, p_4, and the final term is the effect of the induced change in the rural wage rate. In all cases the effect depends on the size of the net sales of goods or labor. If the government sets the farm-gate price of both barley and HYV rice, as we shall assume, then urban consumer prices q_1 and q_2 will have no effect on rural producers, so[1]

(18-4) $$\frac{\partial W^a}{\partial q_i} = 0, \quad i = 1, 2.$$

The effect of urban grain prices on urban consumers is readily found:

(18-5) $$\frac{\partial W^u}{\partial q_i} = -\sum_h \beta^h x_i^h, \quad i = 1, 2.$$

Note that an increase in the price of HYV rice (q_2) has no effect on the urban price of TV rice (q_3), which is determined by the (fixed) producer price of HYV rice. The effect on urban consumers of changing rural producer prices is given by

(18-6) $\qquad \dfrac{\partial W^u}{\partial p_i} = -\sum_h \beta^h \left(x_3^h \dfrac{\partial q_3}{\partial p_i} + x_4^h \dfrac{\partial q_4}{\partial p_i} \right) \qquad i = 0, 1, 2.$

Only changes in p_2 will affect q_3, and because $q_3 = kp_2 + c_3$ (c_3 is the handling cost), $\partial q_3 / \partial p_2 = k$.

Revenue Impacts and Calculation of Supply Responses

The next step in the calculation of the social marginal cost of raising government revenue by changing the various policy instruments is to calculate their effect on government revenue. The part of government revenue that varies with the policy instruments will be denoted R. The assumption is that neither TV rice nor rural goods (that is, goods 3 and 4) are taxed, so that

$$(18\text{-}7) \qquad R = Y_0(P_0 + c_0 - p_0)$$

$$+ \sum_{i=1}^{2} [(Y_i - X_i^a)(P_i - p_i - c_i) + X_i^u(q_i - p_i)]$$

$$+ (q_5 - P_5)(X_5^u + X_5^a).$$

(Capital letters for prices denote world prices, and c_i is the handling cost.) This equation can be written in terms of taxes and subsidies as

$$(18\text{-}8) \qquad R = s_0 Y_0 + \sum_{i=1}^{2} [(X_i^a - Y_i)(s_i + t_i) + t_i X_i^u] + t_5 X_5.$$

The effect of price changes on revenue will depend, among other things, on supply responses. These can be calculated from the profit functions $\Pi^h(\mathbf{p}, w)$. With detailed microeconomic data it might be possible to estimate profit functions for the various crops and hence to estimate the various supply responses as discussed by Deaton in chapter 4. In the previous chapter, Braverman and others report that they found little difference in their results when they replaced the estimated translog profit function by a Cobb-Douglas function, which has the great merit of requiring only data on average input shares. Because it considerably simplifies the formulas we shall follow them and assume a Cobb-Douglas production structure for each crop. The aggregate profit function is assumed to be

$$\Pi = \sum_{i=1}^{3} \Pi^i = \sum_{i=1}^{3} A_i K_i p_i^{1 + \eta_i} p_0^{-\alpha_{i0}} w^{-\nu_i}$$

where K_i is land allocated to crop i (determined by total demand). The supply responses can then be derived from the profit function in terms of the share parameters α_{i0}, η_i, and ν_i in the following way. Outputs (and inputs) can be recovered from the profit function by differentiation

$$(18\text{-}9) \qquad Y_i = \dfrac{\partial \Pi}{\partial p_i} = \dfrac{(1 + \eta_i)\Pi^i}{p_i} = (1 + \eta_i)A_i K_i p_i^{\eta_i} p_0^{-\alpha_{i0}} w^{-\nu_i}$$

and so the response of output Y_i to, for example, the price of fertilizer, p_0, is given by

$$(18\text{-}10) \qquad \frac{\partial Y_i}{\partial p_0} = \frac{\partial^2 \Pi}{\partial p_i \partial p_0} = \frac{-\alpha_{i0} Y_i}{p_0} \qquad i \neq 0$$

$$\frac{\partial Y_0}{\partial p_0} = \frac{-\sum_j (1 + \alpha_{j0}) Y_0^j}{p_0} = \frac{-(1 + \bar{\alpha}_0) Y_0}{p_0} \qquad i = 0$$

where α_{i0} is the share of fertilizer expenditure in net profit in crop i, $-Y_0^j$ is the input of fertilizer into crop j, and $\bar{\alpha}_0$ is a weighted-average fertilizer share. The same approach can be used to find the impact of prices on the wage rate and the price of rural goods.

Rural Wage Determination

Rural labor supply is assumed to be inelastic, but it can be freely allocated to agricultural production or to the production of rural handicrafts (that is, to rural nonagricultural employment). Nontraded rural producer goods (indicated by subscript 4) thus consist of rural handicrafts (indicated by subscript z) and other agricultural crops, such as vegetables. Because there is little information available about nonagricultural production, we shall assume that it is produced under constant returns by labor alone and is not taxed. By a suitable choice of units, the output of handicrafts can thus be measured by its labor input, or conversely, and its unit (producer and consumer) price will be the wage rate, w. The demand for agricultural labor (L^a) can be found by differentiating the profit function, Π. Thus if total labor supply is $\bar{L}$:

$$(18\text{-}11) \qquad \bar{L} = L^a + L_z = -\Pi_w + X_z$$

and the price of rural handicrafts is $q_z = p_z = w$.

We wish to know the effect on wages of changes in the rural policy instruments—the prices of barley and the two kinds of rice. Because rice prices move together, it is convenient to let p_r denote the producer price of (undifferentiated) rice. Differentiate equation 18-11 with respect to p_i, $i = 1$, r (for rice)

$$(18\text{-}12) \qquad 0 = -\Pi_{wi} - \Pi_{ww} \frac{\partial w}{\partial p_i} + \frac{\partial X_z^a}{\partial p_i} + \frac{\partial X_z}{\partial q_z} \frac{\partial w}{\partial p_i} + \sum_h \frac{\partial x_z^h}{\partial m^h} \frac{\partial m^h}{\partial p_i}$$

where m^h is money income ($= \Pi^h + wl^h$). From equation 18-9

$$\Pi_{ww} = \frac{\sum_i \nu_i(\nu_i + 1)\Pi^i}{w^2} = \frac{\sum_i (1 + \nu_i)L_i}{w}$$

$$-\Pi_{wi} = \frac{\nu_i(1 + \eta_i)\Pi^i}{w p_i} = \frac{\nu_i Y_i}{w} \frac{(1 + \eta_i)L_i}{p_i}$$

where η_i is the supply elasticity and ν_i is the ratio of labor costs to profit for crop i. Also

$$\frac{\partial m^h}{\partial p_i} = \frac{\partial \Pi^h}{\partial p_i} + \frac{\partial m^h}{\partial w}\frac{\partial w}{\partial p_i} = y_i^h + (l^h - l^a)\frac{\partial w}{\partial p_i}.$$

Multiply equation 18-12 by p_i and substitute these expressions, remembering that $X_z = L_z$, and rearrange to obtain

$$(18\text{-}13) \qquad \frac{p_i}{w}\frac{\partial w}{\partial p_i} = \frac{(1 + \eta_i)L_i + \epsilon_{zi}^a(X_z^a/X_z)L_z + \sum_h \mu b_z^h p_i y_i^h/w}{\sum_i (1 + \nu_i)L_i - L_z\epsilon_{zz} - \sum \mu b_z^h l_z^h}.$$

Here μb_z^h is the marginal income share spent on rural handicrafts (the product of the marginal expenditure share, b_z^h, and the marginal propensity to spend out of income, μ) and $l_z^h (= l^h - l^a)$ is nonagricultural employment for household h. It is convenient to replace $p_i y_i^h/w$ with $a^h(1 + \eta_i)l_i/\nu_i$, where $a^h = y_i^h/Y_i$ is the fraction of total land owned by household h. If in addition the marginal shares b_z^h are constant across rural households, then

$$(18\text{-}14) \qquad \frac{p_i}{w}\frac{\partial w}{\partial p} = \frac{(1 + \eta_i)(1 + \mu b_z/\nu_i)L_i + \epsilon_{zi}^a(X_z^a/X_z)L_z}{\sum (1 + \nu_i)L_i + (-\epsilon_{zz} - \mu b_z)L_z}.$$

Tables 18-6 and 18-A1 give estimates for these parameters, and if in addition we assume that $\mu b_z = 0.22$, $\epsilon_{zz} = -0.07$, $\epsilon_{z1} = -0.02$, and $\epsilon_{z2} = -0.13$, then

$$\epsilon_{w1} \equiv \frac{p_1}{w}\frac{\partial w}{\partial p_1} = 0.09 \qquad \epsilon_{wr} \equiv \frac{p_r}{w}\frac{\partial w}{\partial p_r} \equiv 0.32.$$

These figures would be substantially lower if rural handicrafts were tradable (which would increase the price elasticity, ϵ_{zz}, substantially).

The effect of fertilizer prices on wages can similarly be calculated, and the denominator will be as in equation 18-14, but the numerator will be

$$-\left(\sum \alpha_{i0}L_i/\bar{L} + \frac{-b_4 p_0 Y_0}{wL^a}\cdot L^a/\bar{L}\right).$$

Here $-p_0 Y_0/wL^a$ is the ratio of expenditure on fertilizer to wage costs in agriculture, which is 0.09, imputing the going rural wage to agricultural labor. The average value of α_0 across all agriculture is 0.04, though the figure is possibly much higher in cereal production. Because labor per hectare is fairly constant across crops, the average of 0.04 is a reasonable estimate, in which case the response of wages to the price of fertilizer

$$\frac{p_0}{w}\frac{\partial w}{\partial p_0} = -0.01$$

can safely be ignored.

The impact of policies on the prices of other crops (assumed to be non-traded) and on rural handicrafts can now be roughly calculated. Other crops are assumed to be competitive with barley but not rice, so a rise in the price of barley is assumed to raise the supply price of other crops by an equal proportional amount (in the absence of any information on the structure of costs for these other crops). This is clearly a rather strong assumption that requires scrutiny. Rice prices affect other crops only via the wage effect. Rural handicrafts are assumed to be produced by labor alone, so their price changes in line with wage changes. They account for 65 percent of rural consumption of x_4 but probably a lower fraction of urban consumption. It is therefore assumed that "other crops" and rural handicrafts account for equal shares of the aggregate good, x_4, so the resulting impacts are

$$\frac{\partial \log p_4}{\partial \log p_1} = 0.5 \times 1.0 + 0.5 \, \epsilon_{w1} = 0.54$$

$$\frac{\partial \log p_4}{\partial \log p_r} = (0.5 \times 0.4 + 0.5) \, \epsilon_{w2} = 0.22.$$

On these assumptions, then, the price of rural goods is quite sensitive to changes in the rural prices of barley and rice. If wages are not responsive to grain prices, then these figures will be (slightly) lower.

The Marginal Social Cost of Rural Price Interventions

We are now in a position to calculate the marginal cost of raising revenue by suitably varying the policy instruments. The easiest case to consider is the effect of varying the price of fertilizer, p_0. Remember that Y_0 is negative, differentiate equation 18-7, and use equation 18-10 to find the revenue impact

$$(18\text{-}15) \quad -\frac{1}{Y_0}\frac{\partial R}{\partial P_0} = 1 + \frac{s_0}{p_0}\left(1 + \bar{\alpha}_0\right) + \sum_{1}^{2}\left(\frac{s_i + t_i}{p_i}\right)\alpha_{i0}\frac{p_i Y_i}{(-p_0 Y_0)}$$

$$- \sum_{i=1}^{5}\left(\frac{s_i + t_i}{p_i}\right)\sum_{h}\mu b_i^h y_0^h / Y_0.$$

In the last term μb_i^h is the marginal share of expenditure on good i out of income by household h, and this term captures the effect of changes in farm incomes induced by fertilizer price changes. The effect via wage changes has been ignored as insignificant. If $\alpha_{i0} = \bar{\alpha}_0$, constant across crops, and if we assume that marginal expenditure shares $b_i^h = b_i$, constant across households (that is, linear Engel curves), then

$$(18\text{-}16) \quad -\frac{1}{Y_0}\frac{\partial R}{\partial p_0} = 1 + \frac{s_0}{p_0}\left(1 + \bar{\alpha}_0\right) + \sum_{1}^{5}\left(\frac{s_i + t_i}{p_i}\right)\left(\frac{p_i Y_i}{\Pi} - \mu b_i\right).$$

The welfare effect is given by equation 18-3, and we note that p_0 does not affect the prices of any other goods or wages.

$$-\frac{1}{Y_0}\frac{\partial w}{\partial p_0} = -\Sigma \beta^h y_0^h / Y_0.$$

The social cost of raising government revenue by increasing the price of fertilizer to farmers is then

$$(18\text{-}17) \quad \lambda_0 = -\frac{\partial W/\partial p_0}{\partial R/\partial p_0} = \frac{\Sigma \beta^h y_0^h / Y_0}{1 + \frac{s_0}{p_0}(1 + \bar{\alpha}_0) + \Sigma\left(\frac{s_i + t_i}{p_i}\right)\left(\frac{p_i Y_i}{\Pi} - \mu b_i\right)}.$$

Food Price Interventions

Changes in the producer price of barley, p_1, from equation 18-7, have the following impacts:

$$(18\text{-}18) \quad \frac{1}{Y_1}\frac{\partial R}{\partial p_i} = -\left\{1 + \frac{s_0}{p_0}(1 + \eta_1)\left(\frac{-p_0 Y_{01}}{p_1 Y_1}\right) + \left(\frac{s_1 + t_1}{p_1}\right)\eta_1\right.$$

$$+ \Sigma_i \left(\frac{s_i + t_i}{p_i}\right)\left[-v_i\frac{p_i Y_i}{p_1 Y_1}\epsilon_{w1} + \mu b_i^a\left(1 + \frac{wL^z}{p_1 Y_1}\epsilon_{w1}\right)\right]\right\}$$

$$+ \frac{X_1^a}{Y_1}\left\{1 + \Sigma_i\left(\frac{s_i + t_i}{p_i}\right)\left[\left(\frac{\omega_i}{\omega_1}\right)^a\epsilon_{i1} + \frac{X_1}{X_1^r}\frac{\omega_i}{\omega_1}\epsilon_{i4}\frac{\partial \log q_4}{\partial \log p_1}\right]\right\},$$

again assuming that b^h is constant across (rural) households. Here η_1 is the supply elasticity of barley, calculated from equation 18-9 in a way similar to equation 18-10, whereas v_i is the wage share. The main problem with equation 18-18 is that the expenditure share of barley, ω_1, is extremely small, and hence the ratio ω_i/ω_1 is large. The other problem is the standard one that it is extremely difficult to estimate the cross-pricing elasticities ϵ_{ij}. It helps in obtaining a quantitative sense of the importance of both these uncertainties to assume that the aggregation is possible over consumers, so that each sector behaves as a single consumer. In that case the price elasticity terms can be rewritten as follows

$$\frac{\omega_i}{\omega_j}\epsilon_{ij} = \epsilon_{ji}^* - \omega_i\epsilon_i = \epsilon_{ji} + \omega_i(e_j - e_i)$$

where ϵ_{ji}^* is the compensated elasticity, e_i is the expenditure elasticity of good i, and $\omega_i e_i = b_i$ the marginal expenditure share. The large multiple ω_i/ω_1 now disappears, though we are left with another elasticity, equally hard to estimate, namely, ϵ_{1i}. This approach does not work equally well for the term in ϵ_{i4}. The welfare impact is given by equation 18-3:

$$(18\text{-}19) \quad \frac{1}{Y_1}\frac{\partial W}{\partial p_1} = \Sigma_h \beta^h\frac{y_1^h}{Y_1}\left[1 - \frac{x_1^h}{y_1^h} + \frac{p_4(y_4^h - x_4^h)}{p_1 y_1^h}\frac{\partial \log p_4}{\partial \log p_1} + \frac{wl^z}{p_1 y_1^h}\epsilon_{w1}\right]$$

$$- \frac{\Sigma \beta^h q_4 x_4^{uh}}{p_1 Y_1}\frac{\partial \log p_4}{\partial \log p_1}.$$

If we assume that urban consumption of rural goods is equal to net rural sales (consistent with their nontradability), then $\Sigma p_4 x_4^{uh} = \Sigma p_4 (y_4^{ah} - x_4^{ah}) + wL_r^z$, and the only effect of changes in the price of rural handicrafts will be the differential distributional effect.

Changes in the producer price of HYV rice, p_2, have the following impacts on revenue:

$$(18\text{-}20) \quad \frac{1}{Y_2} \frac{\partial R}{\partial p_2} = -\left\{ 1 + \frac{s_0}{p_0}(1 + \eta_2)\left(\frac{-p_0 Y_{0r}}{p_2 Y_2}\right) + \left(\frac{s_2 + t_2}{p_2}\right)\frac{Y_2}{Y_r} \eta_r \right.$$

$$+ \Sigma_i \left(\frac{s_i + t_i}{p_i}\right)\left[-v_i \frac{p_i Y_i}{p_2 Y_2} \epsilon_{w2} + \mu b_i^a\left(1 + \frac{wL_r^z}{p_2 Y_2}\epsilon_{w2}\right)\right]\Big\}$$

$$+ \frac{X_2^a}{Y_2}\left[1 + \sum_i^5 \left(\frac{s_i + t_i}{p_i}\right)\frac{\omega_i}{\omega_2}\left(\epsilon_{ir} + \epsilon_{i4} \frac{\partial \log q_4}{\partial \log p_2}\right)\right]$$

$$+ \frac{kX_3^u}{Y_2}\left[\sum_i \left(\frac{t_i}{q_i}\right)\frac{\omega_i}{\omega_3^u}\left(\epsilon_{i3}^u + \epsilon_{i4}^u \frac{\partial \log q_4}{\partial \log p_2}\right)\right].$$

Here the subscript r refers to total rice, and ϵ_{ir} can be found from the equation $\epsilon_{ir}^* = \Sigma \omega_j \epsilon_{ij}^* / \Sigma \omega_j, j = 2, 3$. The main difference between equations 18-20 and 18-18 lies in the effect on the urban consumer price of rice, q_3. The impact on welfare is found from equation 18-3 as for barley:

$$(18\text{-}21) \quad \frac{1}{Y_2}\frac{\partial W}{\partial p_2} = \frac{Y_r}{Y_2}\left\{\sum_h \beta^h \frac{y_r^h}{Y_r}\left[1 - \frac{x_r^h}{y_r^h} + \frac{p_4(y_4 - x_4)}{p_r y_r^h} \cdot \frac{\partial \log p_4}{\partial \log p_2} + \frac{wL_r^z}{p_r y_r}e_{w2}\right]\right.$$

$$- \frac{kX_3^u}{Y_2}\sum_h \beta^h \frac{x_3^h}{X_3^u}\left(1 + \frac{\omega_4}{\omega_3}\frac{\partial \log q_4}{\partial \log p_2}\right)\Big\}.$$

The Marginal Social Costs of Urban Price Interventions

Urban prices do not affect rural producers, which fact greatly simplifies the analysis.[2] Thus the revenue inputs are given by

$$\frac{\partial R}{\partial q_j} = X_j^u\left[1 + \sum_{i=1}^5 \left(\frac{t_i}{q_i}\right)\left(\frac{\omega_i}{\omega_j}\right)e_{ij}^u\right] \quad j = 1, 2.$$

The marginal social costs of raising revenue by increasing the urban food prices are then

$$(18\text{-}22) \quad \lambda_j^u = -\frac{\partial W/\partial q_j}{\partial R/\partial q_j} = \frac{\sum_h \beta^h x_j^h / X_j^u}{1 + \sum_{i=1}^5 \left(\frac{t_i}{q_i}\right)(\epsilon_{ji}^* - \omega_i e_i)} \quad j = 1, 2.$$

The Calculation of Social Weights

For illustrative purposes we assume that the social weight is based on real per capita consumption. Three difficulties arise in comparing real consumption levels in the urban and rural sectors: there are substantial differences in hours worked (or recorded), there may be differences in savings rates, and there may possibly also be differences in prices. Rural hours worked seem to be one-half urban hours, which reflects the seasonality of agriculture and possibly the underrecording of other productive activity. Savings rates are 25 percent in the rural sector but about 22 percent in the urban sector (Korea, *Statistical Yearbook*, 1980, pp. 97, 418, 423), and hence the difference in savings rates is apparently not as large as might be expected.[3] Even for urban daily laborers, reported consumption is 83 percent of income. Cereal prices may be somewhat lower in urban areas because of subsidies, but, as table 18-1 shows, the subsidies largely offset transport costs, and for other agricultural goods the converse is probably true. Thus the main difference between the two sectors superficially appears to lie in the number of hours worked. It is likely that a rural hour of work is more demanding or unpleasant than an urban hour, and so the difference in disutility may not be as great as the difference in hours observed.

Our solution is to consider two alternative assumptions. The first is to value possibly enforced rural leisure at one-half the rural wage rate (of 411 won/hour), if we assume that a worker has 2,200 hours available per annum (urban workers average fifty-nine hours per week). This leisure is calculated as the residual after deduction of recorded agricultural hours worked and estimated nonagricultural hours worked (assumed at the going wage rate) and is shown in table 18-4. The alternative assumption is to ignore the differential rural leisure, which reverses the relative position of the average urban and rural consumers, as can be seen by comparing tables 18-4 and 18-5. The fact that migration is from rural to urban areas suggests that the second alternative may be more plausible, though it still seems true that the poorest urban group is poorer than the poorest rural group.

Three different sets of social weights were calculated, representing a range of views about the desirability of redistributing income. The social weight of household h, enjoying consumption c^h, is given by

$$\beta^h = \left(\frac{c^h}{\bar{c}}\right)^{-\epsilon}$$

where $\bar{c}$ is the consumption of the poorest rural group, or 371,000 won per year. (By coincidence this amount is almost exactly equal to the average urban consumption.) The parameter ϵ measures the degree of inequality aversion (Atkinson, 1970), and values of $\epsilon = 1$, 2, and zero are taken. When $\epsilon = 0$, $\beta^h = 1$ for all h, and the government is assumed to be uninterested in improving the distribution of income. It can be interpreted as identifying the pure efficiency effects of the policy reform. The various social weights are shown in tables 18-4 and 18-5.

Table 18-4. *Rural Expenditure and "Real" Income, 1979*

Item	Average, all groups	Groups[a]				
		1	2	3	4	5
Fraction of farms		0.31	0.367	0.267		0.056
Fraction of land a^h		0.11	0.304	0.410		0.174
Expenditure[b]	1,662	1,286	1,489	1,777	2,095	2,681
Expenditure per capita[b]	320	292	299	316	353	433
Income per capita[b]	(428)	(345)	(384)	(438)	(513)	(653)
Value of leisure[b]	525	346	536	592	535	733
Total real consumption[b]	2,187	1,632	2,025	2,369	2,630	3,414
Consumption per capita[b]	421	371	407	421	443	552
Social weight[c] with inequality aversion ϵ						
$\epsilon = 1 \ \beta^h$	0.88	1	0.91	0.88	0.84	0.67
$\epsilon = 2 \ \beta^h$	0.84	1	0.83	0.78	0.70	0.45
Social weight[c] ignoring leisure with $\epsilon = 2 \ \beta^h$	1.438	1.614	1.540	1.378	1.105	0.734

Note: Parentheses indicate figures not directly used in the calculations that show savings rates.

a. Size categories of farms: 1: less than 0.5 cheongbo (hectare). 2: 0.5–1.0 cheongbo (hectare). 3: 1.0–1.5 cheongbo (hectare). 4: 1.5–2.0 cheongbo (hectare). 5: more than 2.0 cheongbo (hectare). Groups 3 and 4 are aggregated for the first two rows.

b. Thousands of won per year.

c. Numeraire is 317,000 won per year—consumption of group 1.

Source: Korea (1980).

Table 18-5. *Urban Expenditure, 1979*

Item	Average	Groups[a]			
		1	2	3	4
Fraction		0.315	0.275	0.265	0.145
Family size	4.65	4.27	4.55	4.85	5.2
Expenditure per capita[b]	372	248	327	412	604
Social weight[c] with inequality aversion ϵ, $\epsilon = 1 \ \beta^h$	1.00	1.50	1.13	0.90	0.61
Weighted by fraction	1.11	0.473	0.311	0.239	0.088
$\epsilon = 2 \ \beta^h$	1.00	2.24	1.29	0.81	0.38
Weighted by fraction	1.33	0.705	0.354	0.215	0.055
Expenditure share on cereals	0.149	0.191	0.171	0.141	0.114

a. Groups are defined by family income: (1) less than 130,000 won/month; (2) 130,000–190,000 won/month; (3) 190,000–300,000 won/month; (4) more than 300,000 won/month.

b. Thousands of won per year.

c. Numeraire as in table 18-4.

Source: Korea (1980), p. 432.

Quantifying the Social Cost of Raising Revenue

Table 18-6 collects some of the values assumed for the parameters that appear in the formulas for the revenue and welfare impacts. The tax rates are taken from tables 18-1–3, and most of the other data come from the *Korea Statistical Yearbook* for 1980, supplemented by data from BAH and from chapter 17 (especially the supply elasticities and the division between HYV and TV rice). The underlying farm data are presented in appendix 18-3, tables 18-A4 and 18-A5, whereas the expenditure shares and elasticities are given in appendix 18-2, tables 18-A2 and 18-A3. The implied values for the impacts and the social cost of raising government revenue are presented in table 18-7. The social costs (the values of λ_i) take the full consumption per capita of the poorest rural groups as numeraire, and these values can be compared with the social benefit of giving a uniform lump-sum transfer to everyone, shown in the

Table 18-6. *Assumed Parameter Values*

Item	Description	Central estimate	Variant (actual)
Taxes and subsidy rates			
s_0/p_0	Rural fertilizer subsidy	0.21	0.06
$(s_1 + t_1)/p_1$	Rural barley	0.83	0.93
$(s_2 + t_2)/p_2$	Rural HYV rice	0.63	0.91
t_1/q_1	Urban barley	0.22	0.38
t_2/q_2	Urban HYV rice	0.33	0.59
t_5/q_5	Both other goods	0.15	—
		Parameter values	
Labor market data			
Hours per year per household[a]	$L_1, L_r, L_a, L_z, \bar{L}$	138, 598, 917, 1,693, 3,346	
Shares $L_i/\bar{L}$	$i = 1, r, a, z$	0.04, 0.18, 0.27, 0.51	
Wage shares	v_1, v_r, v_a	0.9, 0.4, 0.9	
Wage rate		411 won per hour	
Other rural data			
Crop supply elasticities	η_1, η_r, η_a	1.2, 0.5, 1.2	
$\bar{\alpha}_0$	Average fertilizer share	0.04	
μ	Marginal propensity to consume	0.75	
$p_i Y_i / \Pi$	Output/farm profit, $i = 1, 2, 3, a$	0.14, 0.64, 0.39, 0.5	
k	Ratio of productivity of HYV rice to TV rice	1.114	
ϵ_{ir}^r	Cross-elasticities with rice, $I = 1, 2, 5$	0.072, −0.294, −0.024	
Shares			
$X_1^q/Y_1, X_1/X_1^q, q_4 X_4^u/p_1 Y_1$		0.25, 1.47, 1.00	
$Y_2/Y_r, X_2^q/Y_2, X_3^u/Y_2$		0.62, 0.19, 0.28	

a. 1 = barley, r = all rices, a = other crops, z = nonfarm labor, $\bar{L}$ = total hours. Other parameters are defined in the text and in equations.

Source: Korea (1980), and text.

last line of table 18-7. (These social benefits take account of the tax that is paid on the extra expenditure, as can be seen most clearly in the final two columns, which ignore distributional considerations.) If the social cost of instrument i, λ_i, is lower than this social benefit, then it would be desirable to finance an increased lump-sum transfer by raising more revenue from policy i. (An alternative way of presenting the results would be to take the social value of the lump-sum transfer as the numeraire.)

Eight alternative estimates are shown and give some idea of the sensitivity of the results to the social weights, the operation of the rural labor market, and the valuation of rural leisure. In one case the rural wage is assumed not to respond to any of the policy instruments, whereas in the other case it responds strongly, as calculated above. The extent to which the price of rural goods $p_4(= q_4)$ responds also depends on the size of the wage response.

In all the eight cases considered in table 18-7, the most desirable way of increasing government revenue appears to be to reduce the support price of barley, p_1, which has the lowest value of λ. The ranking of the next two most attractive policies depends on whether the rural wage is sensitive to agricultural price changes or not. If the wage does respond, then it is better to raise the price of fertilizer (p_0) rather than lower the support price of HYV rice (p_2). If the money wage rate remains unchanged, then it is better to lower the rural rice price rather than raise the fertilizer price. It is always better to change agricultural prices rather than urban consumer prices, and in the urban sector, it is better to raise the price of barley than rice. It is always better to reduce rural subsidies and use the money to finance lump-sum transfers, but it is even better to reduce lump-sum transfers in order to lower urban rice prices.

Several lessons emerge from table 18-7. First, though the numerical values of λ are quite sensitive to all three assumptions (regarding the social weights, the responsiveness of the rural wage, and the valuation of rural leisure) the ranking of policies is fairly insensitive, as the only policy whose rank changes is reducing the fertilizer subsidy. In part, this robustness is illusory, for if a wide range of alternative policies also under consideration were relatively insensitive to these assumptions, then the relative attractiveness of these agricultural price policies might depend quite sensitively on these assumptions. The ranking of the policies does not change with the social weights over the range considered (inequality aversion from zero to two), which means that the ranking of the desirability of policy interventions would be the same if it were judged solely on efficiency grounds. At least over the range considered, there is no obvious conflict between equity and efficiency. At very high levels of inequality aversion, this situation would change, for the poorest group is in the urban sector, and although the data are not available, it seems likely that barley would have the highest distributional characteristic. Lowering the urban barley price might then be the most desirable reform (the highest λ), and lowering the producer price of rice (which lowers the urban price of TV rice) might be the least-cost way of raising revenue (and, indeed, would have a negative cost).

Table 18-7. Magnitude of Policy Impacts

Item	ε = 1 RL		ε = 2 RL		ε = 2 No RL		ε = 0	
	No WR Alt. 1	WR Alt. 2	No WR Alt. 3	WR Alt. 4	No WR Alt. 5	WR Alt. 6	No WR Alt. 7	WR Alt. 8
Revenue impact, $[(1/Y_i)(\partial R/\partial p_i)]$								
Fertilizer, p_0	1.635	1.635	1.635	1.635	1.635	1.635	1.635	1.635
Barley support, p_1	−2.454	−2.343	−2.454	−2.343	−2.454	−2.343	−2.454	−2.343
Rice support, p_2	−1.147	−1.066	−1.147	−1.066	−1.147	−1.066	−1.147	−1.066
Urban barley, q_1	0.963	0.963	0.963	0.963	0.963	0.963	0.963	0.963
Urban rice, q_2	0.751	0.751	0.751	0.751	0.751	0.751	0.751	0.751
Welfare impact, $[(1/Y_i)(\partial W/\partial p_i)]$								
Fertilizer, p_0	−0.863	−0.863	−0.755	−0.755	−1.297	−1.297	−1.0	−1.0
Barley support, p_1	0.307	0.746	0.076	0.472	0.747	1.351	0.75	1.24
Rice support, p_2	0.484	0.894	0.257	0.567	0.788	1.388	0.39	0.78
Urban barley, q_1	−1.155	−1.155	−1.400	−1.400	−1.400	−1.400	−1.0	−1.0
Urban rice, q_2	−1.256	−1.256	−1.554	−1.554	−1.554	−1.554	−1.0	−1.0
Social cost of revenue, λ_i								
Fertilizer, p_0	0.53	0.53	0.46	0.46	0.79	0.79	0.61	0.61
Barley support, p_1	0.13	0.32	0.03	0.20	0.30	0.58	0.31	0.53
Rice support, p_2	0.42	0.84	0.22	0.53	0.69	1.29	0.34	0.53
Urban barley, q_1	1.20	1.20	1.45	1.45	1.45	1.45	1.04	1.04
Urban rice, q_2	1.60	1.60	2.07	2.07	2.07	2.07	1.33	1.33
Social value of uniform lump-sum benefit, β	1.22	1.22	1.38	1.38	1.58	1.58	1.16	1.16

Notes: WR = wage response. RL = rural leisure valued. Alt. = alternative.

510

Second, the rural policies are remarkably cheap ways of raising revenue, for the double reason that the distortions are large and the standards of living of the rural poor appear higher than those of the urban poor. Only if rural leisure is not valued and the wage responds to agricultural price changes is the social cost of raising revenue from the rural sector ever greater than 1.0 in table 18-7. Even in this case it is still below the value of uniform lump-sum subsidies to everyone or the cost of a uniform lump-sum tax. Conversely, raising taxes further on urban rice is a very costly way of raising revenue, or equivalently, it is very desirable to lower these taxes.

Sensitivity of the Results to Other Parameters

It is instructive to examine the size of the indirect contributions to the revenue and welfare impacts, as these are typically overlooked in simple partial analysis and are also quite difficult to quantify.

In the case of fertilizer, the major indirect effect on revenue is by reducing the supply of heavily subsidized crops. If rice were not subsidized, the revenue impact would fall by 0.34, with barley accounting for 0.11.

In the case of rural barley, the major indirect revenue effect is the one most difficult to estimate, the effect on q_4 and hence on the demands for other goods. If q_4 did not respond, then the revenue impact would be -1.955 rather than -1.642, or 20 percent larger, whereas the welfare impact would be raised to 0.645 ($\epsilon = 1$) or 0.556 ($\epsilon = 2$), giving values of λ of 0.33 and 0.28, respectively (compared with 0.22 and 0.10). Although this effect is substantial, it does not alter any policy ranking and is comparable in magnitude to the effect of allowing the labor market to operate. The main reason why the effect via p_4 is so large lies in the term $\omega_i e_{i4}/\omega_1$, in equation 18-18, which, in the rural sector for $i = 4$, is -15.9. Such is the power of the assumption of additivity used to derive the cross-price elasticity terms. Ignoring all cross-price effects gives a revenue impact of -1.852 rather than -1.642, and values for λ of 0.35 ($\epsilon = 1$) or 0.30, close to the values obtained from ignoring the labor market repercussions.

For rural rice, the consequence of ignoring all cross-price effects is hardly to change either the revenue or the welfare impacts, by comparison with the case of zero wage response, and in that sense the estimates appear quite robust, depending only on own-price effects. If the urban price of TV rice is unaffected by the support price of HYV rice, then the social cost of lowering the support price rises from 0.45 to 0.93, which although not altering the ranking, is a considerable increase, comparable to the effect of allowing for the responsiveness of the rural wage.

For urban barley, the results are insensitive to the cross-price effects.

In the case of urban rice, ignoring the cross-price effects lowers the social cost by 8 percent, or from 1.60 to 1.47 ($\epsilon = 1$).

Table 18-6 gives the actual tax and subsidy rates for 1979, compared with the central estimates used in the calculations of table 18-7. If these are used, then the revenue impacts change (but not the welfare impacts). With zero inequality aversion (that is, if we ignore distributional considerations), the ranking of policies p_1 and p_2 is reversed when the wage response is ignored, and that of p_0 and p_2 is reversed where the wage is assumed to respond. At an inequality aversion of 2, valuing rural leisure, there is no change in the ranking ignoring the wage response, but again policies p_0 and p_2 switch when wages respond. If rural leisure is not valued, then the rankings are unaffected.

Thus the ranking of some policies does depend on the assumptions made about the expected import and export prices, though it remains true that it appears desirable to lower urban and rural cereals prices.

Conclusions

The main policy conclusion appears to be that reducing the rural subsidies to barley and rice is a way of raising revenue at relatively low social cost, as is increasing the domestic price of fertilizer. Social welfare would increase if these rural subsidies were replaced by uniform lump-sum subsidies to the whole population. Conversely, reducing the taxes on urban rice appears desirable, even if the revenue lost had to be replaced by uniform lump-sum taxes. A revenue-neutral change that lowered urban cereal taxes and rural cereal subsidies would be even more desirable. This set of conclusions is fairly robust to alternative assumptions, although the ranking of the desirability of reducing rural barley and rice prices, or of raising the fertilizer price, does depend on the way the labor market responds. It is perhaps more surprising that the policy rankings do not change with the range of social weights considered, or equivalently, that there is no obvious conflict between equity and efficiency. The reason is that the most distortive subsidies most benefit the rural producers who are relatively quite well off, and the most distortive taxes fall most heavily on the urban poor.

In many cases the cross-price terms, which are so difficult to estimate, have relatively little effect on the ranking of policies, which implies that the main determinants of the desirability of various policies are, in increasing order of uncertainty, the quantitative impacts, the tax and subsidy rates, and the own-price elasticities of supply and demand. In the Korean case the uncertainties on the tax and subsidy rates are quite remarkably large, compared with the other components, and the ranking of policy intervention depends on one's judgment about the relevant world prices of grains and fertilizers.

The other main lessons that may be drawn have already been summarized in the first part of this chapter and need not be repeated here, although we should note that this marginal approach is very flexible in allowing for additional or alternative responses to the policy changes. Although a systematic exploration of the results' sensitivity to the data and behavioral assumptions would be easier if the equations were put in a computer, the results reported here were all derived using no more than a pocket calculator. It would, however, be desirable to explore the sensitivity more systematically than has been attempted here. More systematic analysis would rapidly identify those parameters critical for the policy advice. The next stage would obviously be to attempt to refine the estimates of the key parameters and to clarify important structural assumptions by discussions with knowledgeable Korean economists. It would be useful to know exactly what quantitative impact the rice support system has on farmers and to clarify the various prices and handling costs between farmers and urban consumers. The rural labor market and the rest of rural economy would merit further investigation, as would the setting of the urban real wage and the links between the wages rates in the two sectors. The main conclusion is that, in Korea, the main food grain is a traded good, but the domestic price is well above its world price. Because standards of living in urban and rural areas are not very different, and because, if anything, the urban poor may be worse off than the rural poor, eliminating some of these distortions improves efficiency without compromising redistributive objectives.

Appendix 18-1:
Calculating the Tax Rates on Cereals

It is not straightforward to deduce the relevant prices from the available evidence. Thus the average farm-gate price of HYV is given as 332 won/kilogram (average November 1978–January 1979, BAH, p. 129), whereas the government purchase price is given as 375 won/kilogram. It is noted that farmers are not necessarily able to sell all their HYV rice to the government, and it is not clear what costs are incurred delivering to the government store, though it is unlikely to be as high as 10 won/kilogram. If the government purchased 30 percent of the total HYV at 375 won, then the effective price of freely marketed HYV would be 313 won, compared with the free market farm-gate price of TV rice during this period of 370 won—an 18 percent differential that seems reasonable, given the different productivities of the two crops discussed above.

The wholesale price for HYV averaged 408 won/kilogram over 1979, whereas the government release price is variously stated to be 400 won/kilogram (BAH, pp. 102, 129), 323 won/kilogram (BAH, p. 108), or 331.3 won/kilogram (p. 88). A correction for storage cost and interest must be made to obtain the appropriate real price at the start of 1979, and the approach adopted in table 18-1 is to take the observed farm-gate price of TV rice and add handling to obtain the January TV price of 385 won/kilogram. (The observed price was 386 won, which is close—BAH, p. 129.) To this is added eight months' storage to yield the "July" price of 477 won. The July price of HYV rice is then set at 404 won to reflect the observed differential, and this is taken as the stabilized, or release, price of government rice. The storage costs of on average twelve months then give the subsidy on HYV as 126 won/kilogram. This is not very different from the recorded deficit of 100 won/kilogram (BAH, p. 108), which, however, probably does not include the correct real rate of interest on storage. The free market wholesale price of HYV might be 328 won/kilogram in January, maintaining a reasonably constant differential against TV rice.

Faced with these wholesale prices, consumers would presumably buy free market HYV rice in the first period and government HYV rice in the second period. If the price of free market HYV has been underestimated (and the average wholesale HYV price from November—January is 338 won/kilogram), then TV rice may be preferentially consumed in the earlier rather than the later period, otherwise, as the differential remains constant, it will be consumed through the crop year.

Barley prices are similarly difficult to identify, and barley appears to be stored by the government for more than twelve months. July barley is presumed to have a farm-gate price of 288 won/kilogram (BAH, p. 108) or a real price of 260 won/kilogram in January 1979 prices.

Whereas flows of rice are reasonably well accounted for, and losses amount to between 5–10 percent of production (consistent with the assumed storage costs), flows of barley are most unclear, as "losses and other uses" account for between 22–42 percent of total consumption. Presumably a significant fraction of this is "other uses," though feed grains are separately accounted for. No doubt brewing is one of these other uses. It is unclear what prices are paid for these uses.

Appendix 18-2:
Calculating the Demand Elasticities

The previous chapter gives the demand and income elasticities for goods 1–3 (cereals) for both urban and rural sectors, evaluated for the class in each sector whose income is closest to the sector average. This procedure should give estimates reasonably close to the aggregate sector elasticities. The budget shares ω_i are available from the *Statistical Yearbook*. It remains to complete the matrix of elasticities, and the simplest (and effectively the only) method available is to suppose that cereals (goods 1–3), nontraded rural goods (x_4), and other goods (x_5) are additively separable. In that case the demand price elasticities are (from Deaton and Muellbauer, 1980a, p. 138):

$$(18\text{-}A1) \qquad \epsilon_{ii} = \phi e_i - e_i \omega_i (1 + \phi e_i) \qquad i = c, 4, 5$$

$$\epsilon_{ij} = -e_i \omega_j (1 + \phi e_j) \qquad i \neq j$$

where subscript c refers to cereals, the appropriate subaggregate of goods 1–3, and e_i is expenditure elasticity. The parameter ϕ is found in the following way. The own-price and income expenditure of cereals are calculated from

$$(18\text{-}A2) \qquad \epsilon_{cc} = \sum_{i=1}^{3} \sum_{j=1}^{3} \omega_i e_{ij} \Big/ \sum_{i=1}^{3} \omega_i$$

$$(18\text{-}A3) \qquad\qquad e_c = \sum_{i=1}^{3} \omega_i e_i \Big/ \sum_{i=1}^{3} \omega_i.$$

Then

$$(18\text{-}A4) \qquad\qquad \phi = \frac{\epsilon_{cc} + e_c \omega_c}{e_c(1 - \omega_c e_c)}.$$

The remaining demand elasticities can be calculated as follows. Weak separability between goods in group c (cereals) and the other two subaggregates implies that the elements of the substitution matrix s_{ij} satisfy

$$(18\text{-}A5) \qquad\qquad s_{ij} = \epsilon_{cj}^* \frac{x_i e_i}{p_j e_c} \qquad i \in c$$

(Deaton and Muellbauer, 1980a, pp. 128–29) and hence the compensated elasticities ϵ_{ij}^* are

$$(18\text{-}A6) \qquad\qquad \epsilon_{ij}^* = \frac{s_{ij}p_j}{x_i} = \epsilon_{cj}^* \frac{e_i}{e_c} = -\omega_j e_i e_j \phi$$

from equation 18-A1. The uncompensated elasticities can then be found from $\epsilon_{ij} = \epsilon_{ij}^* - e_i \omega_j$, and the remainder of the table completed, as shown in tables 18-A1 and 18-A2.

Table 18-A1. *Rural Demand Elasticities*

i	ω_i	e_i	b_i	ϵ_{ij} 1	2	3	4	5
1	0.020	0.33	0.0066	−0.51	0.03	0.02	−0.09	−0.07
2	0.167	0.78	0.1303	0.01	−0.46	0.06	−0.21	−0.16
3	0.073	1.00	0.033	0.01	0.07	−0.50	−0.27	−0.21
4	0.453	1.11	0.5020	−0.02	−0.13	−0.02	−0.70	−0.23
5	0.327	1.00	0.3281	−0.02	−0.12	−0.02	−0.27	−0.57

Source: Table 17-A1 and text.

Table 18-A2. *Urban Demand Elasticities*

i	ω_i	e_i	b_i	ϵ_{ij} 1	2	3	4	5
1	0.002	−0.20	−0.0	−0.15	0.49	0.44	0.00	0.11
2	0.085	0.62	0.0527	0.01	−0.45	0.12	−0.01	−0.33
3	0.034	1.0	0.034	0.01	0.15	−0.53	−0.01	−0.53
4	0.024	1.11	0.026	0.00	−0.07	−0.02	−0.44	−0.59
5	0.855	1.04	0.888	0.00	−0.07	−0.02	−0.02	−0.93

Source: Table 17-A1 and text.

Variations in the Substitutability of Rice

It is hard to attach much plausibility to econometric estimates of the cross-elasticities of demand for HYV and TV rice, and we would obviously wish to explore the sensitivity of the results to the substitutability of one kind of rice for the other. It is therefore useful to develop some sense of what might be "reasonable" values for the elasticity of substitution between the two kinds of rice. If both kinds of rice can be aggregated into a composite "rice," whose cost is given by the cost function

$$p_r = C(p_2, p_3),$$

then one natural measure of the elasticity of substitution is given by

$$\sigma_{23} = \frac{C_{23}C}{C_2 C_3} = \frac{x_2 \epsilon_{23}^* C}{p_3 x_2 x_3} = \frac{\epsilon_{23}^*}{\omega_3}\omega_c.$$

From the data given in tables 18-A1 and 18-A2, the two elasticities can be calculated for the two sectors, rural and urban:

$$\sigma_{23}^r = 0.52 \qquad \sigma_{32}^r = 0.28$$

$$\sigma_{23}^u = 0.49 \qquad \sigma_{32}^u = 0.33.$$

In principle, for a single consumer, these figures should be equal, though it is not clear whether symmetry of the substitution matrix was imposed in estimation. The figures look low, and it might be interesting to examine the consequences of increasing the elasticity dramatically, to 2, for example. If we require that the own-price elasticity of "rice" is unchanged, then

$$\epsilon_{rr} = \sum_i \sum_j \omega_i \epsilon_{ij}/\omega_c \qquad i, j = 2, 3$$

should be unchanged, as should ϵ_{rr}^*. In the rural sector $\epsilon_{rr} = -0.40$, $\epsilon_{rr}^* = -0.24$. If $\sigma_{23} = \sigma_{32} = 2.0$, $\epsilon_{23}^* = 0.33$, and $e_{32}^* = 1.67$, and if both ϵ_{22}^* and ϵ_{33}^* are to be increased by the same proportion, their new values will be -0.74 and -1.05. The uncompensated elasticities for both sectors are given in table 18-A3.

Propensities to Consume

Where tax changes affect the cost of consumption, the assumption is that total expenditure is held constant, rather than, for example, changing savings. The impact of these tax changes requires only information about expenditure shares and elasticities. Where policies affect income (as they will in the rural sector), then it is plausible that the effect on expenditure will depend on the marginal propensity to consume out of income. A quick estimate from the available time-series and cross-section data (based on five observations in each case) gives the rural cross-section MPC and APC as 0.61 and 0.79, and from time series, the MPC is 0.87, and APC = 0.73. An average of the two marginal propensities gives 0.75, which will be the figure used for μ.

Table 18-A3. *Alternative Elasticities* ϵ_{ij}

	Rural		Urban	
i	$j=2$	$j=3$	$j=2$	$j=3$
2	−0.87	0.30	−1.06	0.55
3	1.50	−1.08	1.34	−1.29

Appendix 18-3: Data Used in Calculations

Table 18-A4. Farm Data

Item	All or average	Less than 0.5	0.5–1.0	1.0–1.5	1.5–2	2 or more
Households						
Number (thousands)	2,080	644	764	556		117
Fraction	1.000	0.310	0.367	0.267		0.056
Holdings						
Total (thousands of hectares)	1,845	205	561	757		322
Fraction	1.000	0.111	0.304	0.410		0.174
Average size	0.887	0.32	0.73	1.36		2.75
Labor						
Number of family members	5.2	4.4	4.97	5.63	5.94	6.19
Number of workers	2.58	2.12	2.48	2.79	2.79	2.39
Annual hours farming						
Total	1,654	774	1,422	2,012	2,405	3,102
Male family	806	362	713	1,028	1,164	1,296
Female family	582	383	550	686	743	731
Hired	224	75	154	225	381	806
Income (thousands of won)						
Gross agricultural receipts $\Sigma p_i y_i$	2,027	809	1,656	2,419	3,223	4,546
Expenditure	496	228	400	556	794	1,160
Value of own labor ωl^a	582	287	521	734	832	944
Profit (imputed rent) Π	949	293	735	1,129	1,597	2,442
Net agricultural income	1,531	580	1,256	1,863	2,429	3,386
Nonagricultural income (ωl^z)	696	937	650	604	620	656
Farm income	2,227	1,517	1,906	2,467	3,049	4,042
Agricultural/total income (%)	69	38	66	76	80	84
Gross crop receipts						
Rice	920	348	770	1,165	1,638	2,761
Barley	127	77	134	158	174	175
Other crops	445	199	404	614	760	915
Total crops	1,491	624	1,308	1,937	2,572	3,851
Expenditure						
Fertilizer	56	22	48	71	101	156
Wages	85	33	63	90	158	340
Expenditure/income	0.75	0.85	0.78	0.72	0.69	0.66
Gross agricultural income less food		90	717	1,278	1,829	3,013
Agricultural expense		228	400	556	794	1,160
Modern sector purchases, $q_5 x_5$	544	425	477	579	687	937
Other nonfood, $p_z x_z$	489	327	421	539	665	906
Barley, x_1/y_1	0.25	0.38	0.26	0.22	0.22	0.18
$p_4 x_4$	753	556	667	815	972	1,259
$p_4 y_4$	888	384	752	1,096	1,411	1,610
$p_4(y_4 - x_4)$	135	−172	85	281	439	351
x_r/y_r	0.33	0.79	0.40	0.30	0.24	0.16

Notes: A cheongbo is approximately 1 hectare (0.991). Modern sector purchases are fuel, clothes, education, medicine, and other items. $p_4 x_4$ = food minus cereals plus other nonfoods. $p_4 y_4$ = gross agricultural receipts minus cereals. Numbers may not sum to total because of rounding.

Source: Korea, *Statistical Yearbook*, 1980, sect. 4.

Table 18-A5. Consumption of Grains, Food, and Nonfood
(thousands of won)

| Item | All or average | Share | Size range[a] | | | | | | | | | |
			Less than 0.5	Share	0.5–1.0	Share	1.0–1.5	Share	1.5–2	Share	2 or more	Share
Barley	34	0.02	30	0.02	35	0.02	34	0.02	38	0.02	32	0.01
Rice	331	0.20	275	0.21	310	0.21	349	0.20	398	0.19	453	0.17
Food	669	0.38	534	0.42	591	0.40	659	0.37	743	0.35	838	0.31
Nonfood	1,033	0.62	752	0.58	898	0.60	1,118	0.63	1,352	0.65	1,843	0.69
Total	1,662	1.00	1,286	1.00	1,489	1.00	1,777	1.00	2,095	1.00	2,681	1.00

a. Hectares or cheongbo.
Source: Korea, Statistical Yearbook, 1980.

Notes

1. This statement is not strictly true, as changes in q_i will affect the demand for rural goods and, as they are nontraded, their price and the rural wage rate. This effect will be examined in the discussion of the rural labor market.

2. This statement is not strictly true, as induced changes in the demand for non-traded goods will affect wages and nontraded-goods prices. This effect is ignored in the present calculations but would be worth modeling and quantifying. The main effect will be redistributive and hence probably relatively small, given the similarity in urban and rural real income levels.

3. Van Wijnbergen, in chapter 19, however, reports substantial differences in marginal propensities to save out of rural or urban incomes when these propensities are estimated from aggregate time-series data. The figures reported above are estimated from cross-section data and hence are consistent with the other elasticity parameters.

19

Short-Run Macroeconomic Effects of Agricultural Pricing Policies

Sweder van Wijnbergen

THE DISCUSSION OF AGRICULTURAL PRICING POLICIES is usually confined to a partial-equilibrium, microeconomic analysis of static efficiency losses. In many developing countries, however, agriculture makes up a substantial part of GNP. Agricultural products, especially food grains, are often "wage goods," with a high share in wage earners' consumption basket. As a consequence, large changes in food grain prices have significant effects on the distribution of income between farmers, urban workers, and the government and hence on wage levels, profits, aggregate savings, and external balance. It may therefore be necessary to coordinate macroeconomic policy to minimize any potential adverse effects arising from a major agricultural price or tax reform.

The macroeconomic effects may be beneficial or adverse, depending on whether the reform lowers or raises urban food costs. In the Republic of Korea, the subject of this chapter, a reform that adjusted cereal prices toward import parity prices would lead to a substantial cut in urban food costs and, accordingly, to macroeconomic benefits together with microeconomic efficiency gains. In most developing countries, however, food prices are kept below world price levels, so that a switch to border pricing will involve transitional macroeconomic costs if no offsetting measures are implemented.

Korea, although one of the most advanced of the developing countries in terms of industrial development, still has a large agricultural sector: about 30 percent of its population lives in agricultural areas, and a similar proportion of its labor force derives its income from agriculture, contributing roughly 20 percent of total GNP. The disastrous harvest in 1980 (a 25 percent shortfall due to bad weather) and the ensuing food price increases were among the major factors explaining the unprecedented decline in GNP and the increase in inflation that took place in 1980, as documented in van Wijnbergen (1981).

In this chapter I will focus on two crucial links between the agricultural sector and the rest of the economy that are relevant from a short-run macroeconomic point of view. The first moves from food prices via real wage resistance or explicit CPI indexation to real wage pressure on manufacturing, with the concomitant problems for export competitiveness. The second derives from well-documented differences in savings propensities between rural and urban areas. Agricultural price changes imply major income transfers between these two groups, so the existence of differential savings propensities implies that income transfers between them will affect aggregate savings and therefore the current account of the balance of payments.

I first analyze the link between food costs and export competitiveness via real wage indexation using a simple analytical model and then discuss the empirical relevance of both channels by incorporating them in an econometric macro model of the Korean economy in order to simulate the macroeffects of agricultural price reform. I briefly describe the relevant characteristics of the model used; a more extensive description of a version without an agricultural sector can be found in van Wijnbergen (1982); the extension of that model with an agricultural sector is described in detail in van Wijnbergen (1981). Later in this chapter I use this model to simulate the macroeconomic effects of a price reform leading to a gradual decline of agricultural prices to world levels.

Relative Food Prices and Export Competitiveness

An increase in the real price of food will lead to a lower real wage in terms of food, all other things being equal. If workers try to maintain their real consumption wage, via explicit indexing arrangements, implicit agreements, or social pressure, they will put upward pressure on the real wage in terms of other, nonfood items. The real wage pressure will in turn lead to a loss of competitiveness unless the real wage increase is offset by higher productivity. In what follows, the preceding argument is formalized with a simple model that is then used to derive estimates of the amount of investment that would be required to maintain external competitiveness in the nonagricultural sector, given real wage pressure caused by higher food prices. The structure is kept very simple so that we can obtain analytical solutions.

Assume that workers consume domestically produced food and an imported consumer good with local currency price q_c. The price of food is q_a (the agricultural good), and w is the nominal wage. Wage indexation on the consumer price index implies:

$$(19\text{-}1a) \qquad\qquad \hat{w} = \alpha\, \hat{q}_a + (1 - \alpha)\hat{q}_c$$

or

$$(19\text{-}1b) \qquad\qquad \hat{w} - \hat{q}_c = \alpha(\hat{q}_a - \hat{q}_c)$$

where carets denote proportional rates of change and α is the food share in the consumption "basket" underlying the CPI.

Assume furthermore that only one other good (apart from agricultural commodities) is produced in this economy, with output level Y_m. This good (manufacturing) is produced for export only, so that its domestic price p_m does not show up in the CPI. World demand for Y_m depends on world real income, $\bar{Y}^w$, and its relative price with respect to world traded goods:

(19-2)
$$Y_m^D = f\left(\frac{p_m}{q_c}, \bar{Y}^w\right)$$

with price elasticity of demand η (defined positive). Empirical estimates suggest that the long-run value of η may be as high as 6.

Domestic producers are assumed to set their output price to maximize profits subject to production possibilities and the downward-sloping demand curve 19-2. Production possibilities are represented by the production function

(19-3)
$$Y_m = K^{\psi_k} g(L, Y_I)^{1-\psi_k}$$

where K is capital stock and ψ_K is the competitive capital share in gross output. The function g is homogeneous of degree one and a function of labor use, L, and the volume of intermediate imports, Y_I, whose domestic price is p_I. Profit maximization ($\max p_m Y_m - wL - p_I Y_I$) then leads to an output price response equation:

(19-4a)
$$\hat{p}_m = \frac{\psi_K \eta}{1 + \psi_K(\eta - 1)} \hat{q}_c + \frac{(1 - \psi_K)\gamma}{1 + \psi_K(\eta - 1)} \hat{w} + \frac{(1 - \psi_K)(1 - \gamma)}{1 + \psi_K(\eta - 1)} \hat{p}_I$$
$$- \frac{\psi_K(1 - \psi_K)}{1 + \psi_K(\eta - 1)} \hat{K}$$

or

(19-4b)
$$\hat{p}_m - \hat{q}_c = \frac{(1 - \psi_K)\gamma}{1 + \psi_K(\eta - 1)} (\hat{w} - \hat{q}_c) + \frac{(1 - \psi_K)(1 - \gamma)}{1 + \psi_K(\eta - 1)} (\hat{p}_I - \hat{q}_c)$$
$$- \frac{\psi_K(1 - \psi_K)}{1 + \psi_K(\eta - 1)} \hat{K}$$

where γ is the wage share in variable costs. Inserting the wage indexation formula 19-1b in equation 19-4b and setting the change in foreign relative prices equal to zero ($\hat{p}_I - \hat{q}_c = 0$) yields a relation between changes in external competitiveness (p_m/q_c), relative food prices (q_a/q_c), and the capital stock in manufacturing:

(19-5)
$$\hat{p}_m - \hat{q}_c = \frac{(1 - \psi_K)\gamma\alpha}{1 + \psi_K(\eta - 1)} (\hat{q}_a - \hat{q}_c) - \frac{\psi_K(1 - \psi_K)}{1 + \psi_K(\eta - 1)} \hat{K}.$$

Now it is easy to follow the effects of an increase in the real price of food. If $\hat{q}_a - \hat{q}_c > 0$, nominal wages will be pushed up to maintain purchasing power in terms of the CPI. This rise will increase the real wage in terms of nonagricultural goods and so will put pressure on producers in the export sector. Equation 19-5 shows that part of it will be passed on, leading to a loss of competitiveness, unless K is increased sufficiently to offset the higher wage costs. Equation 19-5 also allows us to calculate how much investment is needed to do that. The increase in K needed to maintain external competitiveness in the face of real wage pressure caused by higher food prices can be obtained from equation 19-5 by setting $\hat{p}_m - \hat{q}_c = 0$; then

$$(19\text{-}6) \qquad \hat{K}\bigg|_{\hat{p}_m = \hat{q}_c} = \frac{\gamma\alpha}{\psi_K}(\hat{q}_a - \hat{q}_c).$$

Thanks to the stark simplification introduced in the model, we gain some sense of the numbers using readily available "basic" parameters. Consider the following exercise. In Korea the capital share in nonagricultural value added was 0.42 in the midseventies, and the value-added gross output ratio is about 2/3 in manufacturing, so $\psi_K = 0.28$. Some manipulation will allow us to derive the wage share in variable costs, γ, from these numbers. The wage share in value added is $1 - 0.42 = 0.58$, and so the wage share in gross output, ψ_L, is $0.58 \times 2/3 = 0.39$.

Therefore the wage share in variable costs is

$$(19\text{-}7) \qquad \gamma = \psi_L/(1 - \psi_K) = 0.54.$$

Finally, the share of cereals in the CPI (based on 1979 consumer surveys), α, is 0.15.

Putting all this together gives us the required increase in the nonagricultural capital stock after an increase in relative food prices:

$$(19\text{-}8) \qquad \hat{K} = \frac{0.54 \times 0.15}{0.28}(\hat{q}_a - \hat{q}_c)$$

or an increase in the real price of food of 10 percent will lead to an increase in labor costs in nonagricultural sectors of the economy comparable with the fall in labor productivity caused by a 3 percent decrease in the capital stock.

If we take 1976 as a "normal" year as far as the ratio of investment to GNP is concerned (25 percent), and regard 2 as a reasonable estimate of the ratio of nonagricultural capital to GNP, we get a "normal" gross investment—capital ratio of 12.5 percent. Accordingly the increase in nonagricultural capital needed to maintain export competitiveness in the face of real wage pressure caused by a 10 percent increase in real food prices amounts to 25 percent of one year's investment.

To put this situation in perspective, we should realize that moving the urban price of rice to import parity in Korea would involve a 30 percent cut in the consumer price of rice (based on the "normal" border price of rice—see table 18-1). Rice and barley make up 15 percent of consumer expenditure, though it is likely that other nontraded foodstuffs would fall in price as the market price of rural inputs falls in response to the reduction in cereal prices. Altogether the move to import parity pricing might be equivalent to a 10 percent increase in the nonagricultural capital stock, or to 75 percent of one year's investment.

Model Description

The next two sections report the results of a simulated agricultural price reform within the context of a quarterly macroeconometric model of the Korean economy. A version of that model without an agricultural sector is described extensively in van Wijnbergen (1982), so we will only give a summary description here, followed by a list of the changes made to incorporate an agricultural sector in that model. (A full list of the equations is given in appendix A-2 in van Wijnbergen [1981].)

The real part of the model is in the mainstream of open-economy macroeconomics. Output is demand determined in the short run (one quarter) but with aggregate supply responding via a system of wage-price dynamics. The financial component distinguishes between the formal financial market where bank lending rates are artificially low and credit rationed, and informal "curb" markets where lending rates are determined by demand and supply.

Export demand depends on Korean export prices in terms of foreign competitors' prices and real income in the main trading partners (the United States and Japan). Aggregate private consumption depends on the real curb market interest rate and disposable income. Government consumption and investment are considered policy instruments. Tax payments are endogenous and linked to nominal GNP and nominal imports. Investment depends mainly on financial market conditions, as no empirically significant accelerator effects could be found. Current investment depends on the real curb market rate and the *change* in the real volume of credit extended by the banking sector to the private sector. Capital goods imports are linked to investment; imports of intermediate goods depend on the real price of oil (in terms of Korean output prices), on real wages, on aggregate output, and on the real cost of credit needed to finance imports.

Nominal wages are driven by unemployment and the consumer price index according to a standard expectations-augmented Phillips curve. Unemployment follows a variant of Okun's law, where the difference between actual and potential real GNP drives unemployment rates. Domestic (nonfood) prices are explained by wages, local currency cost of intermediate imports, and credit conditions, following the theory outlined in van Wijnbergen (1983). Export prices depend in similar fashion on competitors' prices, wage and local currency intermediate import costs, direct export subsidies, and the cost of credit to exporters. The financial side of the model is fairly elaborate, and I will not attempt to summarize it here. The structure is similar to Tobin's (1975) portfolio model, with explicit incorporation of the unorganized money markets or curb markets and a detailed model of the financial intermediary system. Econometric estimates of all these relations are presented in van Wijnbergen (1982).

The following extensions are made to incorporate agriculture in the model. Agricultural exports are ignored (the amounts involved are trivial and involve fish to Japan)—agricultural output is heavily dominated by rice and barley, all of which is consumed domestically. The domestic price indexes (consumer and wholesale, that is, CPI and WPI) that play a role in the model are broken up into agricultural and nonagricultural components. The pricing equations for the WPI and the CPI are reestimated using the nonagricultural components. Aggregate indexes can then be derived by combining the two components. Agricultural prices can be treated either as policy variables, in which case food imports become endogenous, or as endogenous in the case where food imports are the policy variable. Agricultural producer and consumer prices differ more than is justified by transport and distribution costs, because the Grain Management Fund buys up a substantial part of the rice output and sells it at a loss, as described in chapter 17. This feature is explicitly incorporated in our model. The GMF deficit is added to the government deficit.

To break down changes in aggregate consumer expenditure in food and nonfood components, we used the linear expenditure system budget allocation model. The parameters are derived from actual budget shares and Taylor's (1979) "stylized values" for the substitution indicator (taken as 0.5) and income elasticity of food (taken as 0.5). The most important parameters are base-year budget shares, however, and these correspond to actual values. In line with the short-run nature of the model, we keep agricultural supply exogenous.

Finally, we also incorporated the second link between the agricultural sector and the rest of the economy mentioned before, the one that hinges on differential savings propensities between farmers and nonfarmers. For that purpose we estimated a consumption function that explicitly incorporated different savings propensities:

$$(19\text{-}9) \quad \frac{C}{P} = \underset{(3.04)}{2.15} - \underset{(2.79)}{2.94} \log[(1+r)/(1+\pi)] + \underset{(1.71)}{0.12} \frac{Y^{ag}}{P}$$

$$+ \underset{(7.20)}{0.50} \frac{Y^{nonag}}{P} + \underset{(5.94)}{0.42} \frac{C_{-1}}{P_{-1}} \qquad R^2 = 0.99$$

where C is private consumption, P is the CPI, r is the nominal curb market interest rate, π is the rate of inflation ($\dot{P}/P$), Y^{ag} is agricultural income, Y^{nonag} is nonagricultural income, and C_{-1} is one-quarter lagged consumption. The figures in parentheses are t statistics. With these modifications in place, we are ready to look at the macroeconomic effects of agricultural price reform. In the econometric model we assume that all food prices (not just cereal prices) are reduced to import parity.

Simulating an Agricultural Price Reform

In the first run presented, we assume a gradual reduction of consumer prices and producer prices to world levels, to be achieved within four quarters, that is, at the end of 1981 (the simulation run starts at the end of 1980). This implies a somewhat smaller reduction in nominal terms than an instantaneous reform would imply, because world prices are assumed to increase by 9 percent over 1981, in line with world inflation. It works out to a cumulative cut of somewhat more than 25 percent in consumer prices and nearly 50 percent for producer prices.

The results are summarized in table 19-1 and should be compared with those obtained in the "control" run (table 19-2), where all exogenous and policy variables have the same value except for agricultural prices, which are frozen at their end of 1980 level.

The most dramatic outcome has to do with inflation (WPI), which drops to 10 percent, a twelve-percentage-point reduction from the 22 percent predicted under the control-run scenario. Eight percentage points are due to direct effects (the WPI weight of food is 0.17, so a 50 percent reduction in food prices will by sheer mechanical accounting knock off eight percentage points of the WPI rate), an additional four-percentage-point reduction is obtained via reduced wage pressure, and so on. Given nominal money targets, the real money stock therefore comes out 12 percent higher than under the control run, with the predictable positive impact on investment: investment ends up 3 percent

Table 19-1. *Agricultural Prices Gradually Reduced to World Prices over 1981*

Item	Q_1	Q_2	Q_3	Q_4	1981
Government					
Revenues (+)[a]	2,046.8	2,281.1	2,148.3	2,317.4	8,793.6
Expenditures (−)[a]	2,852.3	2,503.8	2,290.0	2,588.0	10,234.1
Saving (budget surplus)[a]	− 805.5	− 222.7	− 141.7	− 270.6	− 1,440.5
Saving as a percentage					
of GNP	− 10.8	− 2.4	− 1.6	− 1.8	− 2.5
Private sector					
Private saving (+)[a]	754.3	1,685.3	1,769.0	1,368.1	5,576.8
Private investment (−)[a]	1,086.9	1,696.8	1,892.8	2,414.6	7,091.1
Investment as a					
percentage of GNP	14.6	18.5	20.8	16.2	17.5
Current account surplus[b]					
Billions of won	− 1,138.1	− 234.1	− 265.5	− 1,317.1	− 2,954.8
Billions of U.S. dollars	− 1.7	− 0.34	− 0.38	− 1.8	− 4.2
As a percentage of GNP	− 15.3	− 2.6	− 2.9	− 8.8	− 7.2
GNP current prices[a]	7,424.8	9,159.4	9,109.3	14,890.9	40,584.9
GNP constant prices					
seasonally adjusted[c]	36.4	37.2	37.9	39.2	150.7

a. Billions of won.

b. The sum of the budget surplus and the excess of private saving over private investment is equal to the current account surplus.

c. Index numbers, base year 1975 = 100.

Source: Computer simulations.

Table 19-2. *Agricultural Prices Frozen at 1980 Levels*

Item	Q_1	Q_2	Q_3	Q_4	1981
Government					
Revenues (+)[a]	2,046.8	2,311.6	2,167.3	2,322.4	8,848.1
Expenditures (−)[a]	2,852.3	2,503.8	2,290.0	2,588.0	10,234.1
Saving (budget surplus)[a]	− 805.5	− 192.2	− 122.7	− 265.6	− 1,386.0
Saving as a percentage of GNP	− 10.7	− 2.0	− 1.3	− 1.8	− 3.3
Private sector					
Private saving (+)[a]	690.8	1,616.9	1,742.2	2,044.6	6,094.5
Private investment (−)[a]	1,105.2	1,643.2	1,758.3	2,284.8	6,791.5
Investment as a percentage of GNP	14.6	17.4	18.5	15.2	16.3
Current account surplus[b]					
Billions of won	− 1,219.9	− 218.5	− 138.8	− 505.8	− 2,083.0
Billions of U.S. dollars	− 1.8	− 0.32	− 0.20	− 0.71	− 3.03
As a percentage of GNP	− 16.2	− 2.3	− 1.5	− 3.4	− 5.0
GNP current prices[a]	7,552.7	9,426.5	9,508.6	15,062.4	41,550.2
GNP constant prices seasonally adjusted[c]	36.4	36.9	37.2	35.5	146.0

a. Billions of won.

b. The sum of the budget surplus and the excess of private saving over private investment is equal to the current account surplus.

c. Index numbers, base year 1975 = 100.

Source: Computer simulations.

higher than in 1980 in real terms rather than the real fall of more than 8 percent obtained under the control-run scenario.

Private saving, rather than matching the increase in investment, actually goes down because of the transfer from high savers to low savers implied by the reduction of food prices. The net effect is of course a deterioration in the current account, to a substantial extent in fact: the deficit increases from US$3 billion under the control-run scenario to US$4.2 billion. The increased investment and consumer expenditure do stimulate aggregate demand, which, in view of the considerable slack in the Korean economy at that time, leads to further growth: more than three percentage points are added to the 7.1 real growth rate of the control-run scenario to arrive at a 10.3 percent annual growth rate for real GNP.

The lower food prices did slow down wage claims, but a two-quarter delay between wages and export prices and a further one-quarter delay between export prices and the volume of real exports precludes any significant effect on competitiveness and real export growth within the short horizon considered (the model was run for four quarters to simulate 1981 values, whereas food prices were lowered gradually during that period). To explore the link between relative food prices, real wage pressure, and export competitiveness, we also ran the model for an additional five years under the assumption that food prices would gradually decline to world levels over the first two years instead of one and would follow international inflation from there on. The cumulative effect on export growth compared with a base run where the high real price of food was maintained throughout the five-year time horizon showed quite a strong effect on competitiveness and real export growth: lowering food prices to world levels would have added 4 percent per year to real export growth over the five-year horizon (that is, the final-year volume of exports was slightly above 20 percent higher in the low-food-price case than in the constant-real-food-price run). This is a clear indication that the high real price of food threatens Korea's competitiveness in export markets via the induced pressure on real product wages.

Conclusions

In this chapter we demonstrated that agricultural pricing policies do indeed have major macroeconomic consequences. Changes in food prices have a major impact on inflation for several quarters after they take place; their impact spreads via wage indexation mechanisms and gradual markup pricing rules. Large changes in food prices imply major income transfers, which clearly have income-distributional consequences. Because of the differences in savings behavior between the groups involved (farmers and urban food consumers), we should expect important short-run effects on total savings and thereby on the current account of the balance of payments—and, depending on the state of the business cycle, on economic activity. Finally, high food prices lower the real wage in terms of food and so will lead to upward pressure on the real wage in terms of other goods via wage indexation on the CPI. High agricultural prices accordingly lead to real wage pressure on nonagricultural sectors; in the Korean context we demonstrated a clear link, via this mechanism, between food prices and export competitiveness.

All of these findings emerged using analytical and empirical models that focused explicitly on the *short-run* spillover from the agricultural sector on the rest of the economy. Accordingly, little attention was paid to supply responses of agriculture; it was assumed to be exogenous over the time horizon considered. This assumption seems realistic for a one-year forecasting exercise but is of course unsatisfactory if longer-run responses are of interest.

The proper conclusion is of course not that agricultural prices should always be "low." I want to note only that, if changes in agricultural pricing policies are considered, for whatever reason, major macroeconomic side effects should be expected and incorporated in transition planning. In the case of Korea, the subject of our empirical work, it seems clear that important macroeconomic benefits on top of possible microeconomic efficiency gains can be expected if agricultural prices are gradually lowered to world market levels. Most developing countries will face a more difficult problem, however, when they shift to border prices for agricultural commodities, because the shift nearly always implies large *increases* in food prices. The message of this chapter is that such pricing reforms need to be complemented by carefully designed macroeconomic policy to minimize adverse effects arising from major price or tax reforms. Neglect of this point has often resulted in so much turmoil that the reforms have had to be abandoned (Egypt in 1976, Tunisia in 1983).

PART 6

Taxation and Pricing
in Other Sectors

A NUMBER OF SECTORAL ISSUES—energy pricing, the pricing of publicly supplied services, education subsidies, and the taxation of foreign private investment—are considered in this part. As with parts 4 and 5, which dealt with the
agricultural sector, the aim is to show how the special features of the sector, or
its characteristic problems, affect the analysis of policy reforms. Thus the
energy sector is special because energy is an important input as well as a final
consumption good. Typically, commercial energy prices either are set by
government agencies or are readily influenced through the tax system. Different fuels are often close substitutes, and although on distributional grounds it
might be desirable to tax them at very different rates, this substitutability
imposes important constraints on what is feasible and desirable. In chapter 20,
Hughes develops a method for determining the incidence of fuel price changes
that takes into account two important facts: that fuel is an input into almost
every economic activity and that the output prices of many of these activities
are set on world markets. To assume that final-goods prices will increase in line
with calculated cost increases is therefore inappropriate, and alternative
assumptions are required.

The distributional impact of the resulting price changes of goods and factors
resulting from changes in specific fuel tax changes is then calculated. These
calculations show that kerosene taxes are highly regressive, diesel taxes are
roughly neutral, and gasoline taxes are very progressive. Kerosene is a close
substitute for diesel (and is frequently added as an adulterant to transport diesel
fuel), whereas diesel and gasoline are substitutes for light vehicles. It is
therefore potentially very misleading to aggregate all petroleum products or all
energy into one commodity when analyzing potential tax reforms; the characteristics of the individual fuels are sufficiently different to merit careful disaggregation.

Chapter 21, by Katz, provides the theoretical underpinnings for the analysis
of the pricing and supply of publicly supplied goods and services such as health
and education. Typically these goods and services are supplied below cost and
represent claims on the expenditure side of the budget. The subsidies can,

however, be viewed as negative taxes, and we can ask whether it is desirable to raise the tax (that is, reduce the rate of subsidy). The two distinguishing features of the goods on which Katz concentrates are that they are frequently allocated by nonmarket methods and that quality, as well as price, is often a choice variable. Katz discusses the important practical question of when the government should increase the price in order to increase either supply or quality without increasing the cost to the budget. The chapter therefore aims to identify criteria that will apply in various circumstances.

The following chapter, by Armitage and Sabot, provides a particular example of this general problem. State-provided secondary education in Kenya is heavily subsidized and accounts for a large fraction of public expenditure. It is not universal, and it competes with a very lightly subsidized private sector. An increase in fees, with quality and public expenditure held constant, would permit more children to receive high-quality secondary education, and in the Kenyan case, this reform appears desirable on both equity and efficiency grounds.

It would obviously be desirable to study social services to see whether the framework developed by Katz can be applied with similarly clear-cut results. In many countries the cost of these subsidies is increasing rapidly, and they obviously compete with other productive uses of government revenue, so that the problem is of considerable importance.

The last chapter, by Gersovitz, asks how a developing country can best structure its corporate tax (and subsidy) system to maximize the domestic benefits from foreign private investment. He shows how the answer depends sensitively on the tax system of the home country of the foreign company, as well as on the creditworthiness of the host country. In a period that has seen a rapid increase in the public indebtedness of many developing countries, and an evident reluctance of banks to make loans, the role of direct foreign investment is likely to be still more important than it has been in the past, and the study of its proper tax treatment is of comparable significance.

20

The Incidence of Fuel Taxes: A Comparative Study of Three Countries

Gordon Hughes

THE ANALYSIS OF THE INCIDENCE OF TAXES imposed on goods and services used as intermediate inputs into the production of other goods or services necessarily involves an attempt to estimate the indirect effect of such taxes on the prices of other goods and services. This analysis is particularly important in the case of fuels, both because fuel taxes/subsidies are a major item in the government budgets of most developing countries and because energy prices affect the prices or profitability of a wide range of goods and services. To allow for this indirect effect of taxes, it is conventional to assume that changes in costs are passed on completely as price changes and then to use data from an input-output table to estimate the composition of average costs. I shall refer to this approach as the "cost-plus pricing rule." Provided that a suitable input-output table—or similar source of data concerning the average cost structure of sectors—is available, this approach is relatively straightforward to implement.

There are, however, two major objections to the cost-plus pricing rule:

1. It is strictly valid only for marginal changes in the relative prices of inputs, whereas specific taxes designed to collect significant amounts of revenue will almost always involve quite large changes in the relative prices of some inputs.
2. For many sectors in developing countries, prices may be determined not by costs of production but by the price of competing traded goods—for example, by the landed price of competing imports or by the world market price for exported goods.

Estimating the impact of nonmarginal price changes on the cost of production requires detailed information on the cost function for each sector, which is

I am grateful to Esra Bennathan, David Newbery, and Nicholas Stern for their comments and to the national statistical offices of Indonesia, Thailand, and Tunisia, which gave me access to the data used in this study. The paper reports on research that I carried out as a consultant to the World Bank in connection with research project RPO 672-83, funded by the World Bank, on the pricing and taxing of transport fuels in developing countries.

certainly not available for any developing country at a reasonable level of sectoral disaggregation. It might be possible to make use of cost functions estimated for developed countries, but the work involved could be justified only if a simpler analysis suggested that there might be scope for significant cost savings by substitution between inputs in production. Reliance upon input-output data has the merit of *overestimating* the indirect effect of tax changes, so that it is possible to identify the sectors for which more extensive analysis of the cost function might be justified. For these reasons the conventional approach is modified in this study by allowing a greater variety of pricing rules. The most important of these is the traded-goods pricing rule, which assumes that the domestic price is determined by the appropriate border price of competing traded goods.

Once the impact of tax changes upon the prices of goods and services supplied by various sectors has been estimated, the analysis of tax incidence proceeds by examining their effect upon households. Here, as in other studies reported in this book, it is important to use data on individual households from a household budget survey because substantial within-groups variation in expenditure patterns means that the use either of average expenditures for groups of households or of simple systems of demand equations will fail to capture the diversity of the impact of tax changes affecting specific items on different households. Because of the difficulty of obtaining plausible parameter values for household expenditure functions, the analysis of the welfare effects of tax changes relies upon current expenditure patterns, which is strictly valid only for marginal tax changes. The approach followed will therefore overestimate the impact of larger tax changes on households, so that it is again possible to identify the categories of household expenditure that might warrant further investigation.

The analysis in this chapter concentrates on extending the descriptive investigation of tax incidence by examining the impact of taxes on the distribution of real income for large samples of households. I have not attempted to calculate welfare measures indicating whether particular taxes should be increased or decreased. These require much fuller information than was necessary for the work reported here on the structure of the existing tax system and on the elasticities of aggregate demand in order to estimate the overall revenue changes associated with particular tax reforms. Nonetheless, it is necessary to compare tax reforms that have approximately the same revenue impact, so in this chapter I have calculated the net yield of tax reforms by focusing entirely on the changes in revenue from indirect taxes. Furthermore, I have assumed that the total quantities of different goods and services purchased remain constant despite the tax changes. Neither assumption is appropriate for anything other than very small tax reforms, but the complexity of attempts to trace changes in income and hence in revenue from direct taxes and also to estimate the changes in aggregate production or consumption resulting from policy-induced changes in relative prices is a serious barrier to the adoption of more satisfactory assumptions.

This chapter applies the above-described approach to the analysis of the incidence of fuel taxes in three countries—Indonesia, Thailand, and Tunisia. The basic model is outlined in the next section, which also discusses the data required to implement the analysis. The third and fourth sections examine the results of the comparison of a number of alternative tax reforms in each country, focusing on their effects on prices and on the distribution of income, respectively.

Analytical Method and Data Requirements

The model that has been used to estimate the impact of fuel taxes on consumer prices in the three countries is simple in its basic conception but becomes rather difficult to implement because of the need to distinguish between taxes imposed at different points of the production/distribution chain and because of the need to allow for those prices that are influenced by various forms of government intervention. Full details of the model for Thailand are given in Hughes (1986), but for present purposes it is sufficient to concentrate on the basic framework. Suppose that the producer price vector is denoted by $\mathbf{p}$, the vector of factor prices $\mathbf{w}$, and the vector of fuel prices—which we treat as being fixed by the government—is $\mathbf{v}$.[1] The unit cost function for the output of sector i is $c_i(\mathbf{p}, \mathbf{w}, \mathbf{v})$. Under competitive conditions with constant returns to scale, the cost-plus pricing rule implies:

$$(20\text{-}1) \qquad \Delta p_i = \Sigma_j \frac{\partial c_i(\mathbf{p}, \mathbf{w}, \mathbf{v})}{\partial p_j} \Delta p_j + \Sigma_k \frac{\partial c_i(\mathbf{p}, \mathbf{w}, \mathbf{v})}{\partial w_k} \Delta w_k$$

$$+ \Sigma_f \frac{\partial c_i(\mathbf{p}, \mathbf{w}, \mathbf{v})}{\partial v_f} \Delta v_f + \Delta t_i$$

$$(20\text{-}2) \qquad = \Sigma_j a_{ij} \Delta p_j + \Sigma_k b_{ik} \Delta w_k + \Sigma_f g_{if} \Delta v_f + \Delta t_i$$

where the a_{ij}, b_{ik}, and g_{if} coefficients are the unit input requirements obtained from an input-output table and t_i is production taxes on i.[2] This pricing equation is assumed to apply for all nontraded goods and services and also for goods that might be traded if it were not for the protection provided by tariffs or import restrictions.

The other pricing rules may all be regarded as special cases of a general pricing equation linking the producer price of good i to some price p_i^* that may be exogenously determined. The general equation is

$$(20\text{-}3) \qquad \Delta p_i = \Delta p_i^* + \Sigma \alpha_{ij} \Delta p_j \qquad \beta_{ik} \Delta w_k + \Sigma \gamma_{if} \Delta v_f + \Delta t_i.$$

There are two simple applications of this general pricing equation.

1. For traded goods we put

$$(20\text{-}4) \qquad \Delta p_i^* = \Delta P_i$$

where P_i is the port-gate price of imports or exports of good i, which allows for the impact of import duties and export taxes. This pricing rule should be applied to items that are exported or imported directly as well as to those whose prices are directly linked to movements in the prices of traded goods—that is, paddy whose farm-gate price is linked by distribution and processing margins to the traded price of rice in Thailand. In the latter case the α_{ij} and other coefficients would reflect the processing, transport, and distribution costs involved in converting paddy at the farm-gate price into milled rice that competes with imported rice or might be exported rather than being sold for domestic consumption.

2. In many countries the government fixes the prices of certain items—providing, if necessary, subsidies to producers to compensate for the losses caused by price controls. In this case, we have

$$(20\text{-}5) \qquad\qquad \Delta p_i^* = \Delta \overline{p}_i$$

where $\Delta \overline{p}_i$ is now a policy choice.

For each sector or item included in the analysis, it is necessary to decide upon an appropriate pricing rule of the form outlined above. For small changes, the coefficients in these equations may be treated as constants, and hence each equation may be regarded as a local linear approximation of a more elaborate pricing model. In general, cost-minimizing behavior or profit-maximizing behavior will ensure that the relevant functions are concave, so that linearization tends to overestimate the impact of exogenous price changes. The set of pricing equations may be expressed as a general matrix equation and may be solved to give the change in the producer price vector, $\Delta \mathbf{p}$, in terms of the changes in the exogenous price vectors $\Delta \mathbf{P}$, $\Delta \mathbf{v}$, and so on. Thus, with the aid of an input-output table and subsidiary data, it is possible to estimate the impact of changes in fuel prices on other producer prices. The extent of the differences between these estimates and those yielded by the strict cost-plus pricing model will depend upon the importance of traded goods and of government price controls in fixing prices. For a small open economy with substantial government intervention, such as that of Tunisia, the differences between the two models are substantial, whereas for a country like Brazil or India (see chapter 11) they would be relatively minor.

In order to examine the incidence of the price changes on households we need to add a further set of equations that express changes in consumer prices q_i in terms of changes in the various producer and other prices. These equations may, if appropriate data are available, distinguish between complementary and competitive imports for each sector in computing the effect of tax changes on the average prices paid by consumers. Furthermore, though this has not proved feasible in the studies reported here, it may be possible to differentiate between the price changes faced by different categories of households—for example, between urban and rural households.

The changes in consumer prices associated with various tax reforms will affect the distribution of real income between households. If the consumption vector of household h is $\mathbf{x}^h$, then total household expenditure is $e^h = \mathbf{q} \cdot \mathbf{x}^h$. For small changes in consumer prices, the welfare change for the household due to the price changes is

$$(20\text{-}6) \qquad\qquad \Delta u^h = -\beta^h \sum_i x_i^h \, \Delta q_i$$

where β^h is the marginal utility of income for household h at its initial income and set of prices. This formula also measures the change in social welfare if β^h is interpreted as the income distributional weight assigned to the household. In cash terms, the proportional change in real income (denoted by $\Delta e^h / e^h$) is found by dividing both sides of equation 20-6 by $\beta^h e^h$ to give

$$(20\text{-}7) \qquad\qquad \frac{\Delta e^h}{e^h} = \frac{\Delta u^h}{\beta^h e^h} = -\sum_i w_i^h \frac{\Delta q_i}{q_i}$$

where w_i^h is the budget share of good i for household h at initial prices and income.

The pricing rules imply that, in the sectors for which cost-plus pricing is not operative, there must be some changes in factor incomes if the changes in unit costs of production and in producer prices differ. If we assume that there are certain immobile factors of production in each sector and that all pure profits and rents can be attributed to these factors, then the change in pure profits per unit of output, $\Delta \pi_i$, will be:

$$(20\text{-}8) \qquad\qquad \Delta \pi_i = \Delta p_i - \Delta c_i.$$

Provided that suitable information on the sources of income received by households is available, it is possible to estimate the impact of the tax-induced price changes on the income account of households. This will usually involve making some rather strong assumptions because of the nature of the data. For two of the countries studied—Indonesia and Tunisia—data on sources of income were not available in the household budget surveys used, but some illustrative calculations were carried out for Thailand and are reported in Hughes (1986). These were based on the assumption that profits and earnings from self-employment, π_i, are the residual after the cost of material inputs, hired labor, and taxes have been met. Equation 20-8 was then used to estimate the proportional change in such income for each sector. The Thai socioeconomic survey provides information on entrepreneurial income and rents from a range of activities. These data were combined with the estimates of $(\Delta \pi_i / \pi_i)$ by matching activities and sectors as far as was possible in order to estimate the income changes that might be experienced by the households. In this case the net change in each household's income was, of course, the sum of the changes in the expenditure and income accounts. The latter could be extended to take account of changes in wage rates if these are expected to accompany the tax changes.

In this chapter, I will concentrate on the "expenditure transfers" experienced by households as measured by $\Delta e^h / e^h$ in equation 20-7, because these have been calculated in a similar manner for each of the three studies. Again, these estimates will tend to overestimate the effect of the large tax changes, because no allowance is made for substitution in consumption away from items whose relative price has risen. The results may therefore be regarded as indicating the short-run incidence of the taxes or as providing a "worst-case" analysis.

The primary data sources used for the studies were:[3]

- Indonesia: input-output data for 1975 and a household budget survey for 1981;
- Thailand, 1975: input-output data for 1975 and a household budget survey for 1975–76;
- Thailand, 1982: input-output data for 1982 and a household budget survey for 1981;
- Tunisia: input-output data for 1977 and a household budget survey for 1979–80.

For Indonesia and for Thailand, 1975 and 1982, the sectors in the original input-output tables were aggregated to yield tables for each country on almost identical 73-sector bases, whereas for Tunisia the original sectoral breakdown was largely retained by working with a 111-sector table. The two studies of Thailand using data for 1975–76 and 1981–82 enable us to examine the robustness of conclusions concerning the impact of fuel taxes in the face of changes in production and consumption brought about by substantial changes in relative fuel prices and rapid income growth.

To contrast the general pricing model adopted in this work and the cost-plus model, table 20-1 shows that, after investigation, it has been assumed that more than one-third of the sectors in each country do not follow the cost-plus pricing rule and that these sectors account for between 25 percent and 41 percent of domestic output. On the demand side a higher proportion of intermediate demand than of final demand is fulfilled by non-cost-plus sectors—as we would expect because of the greater role of services in final demand—but the share of cost-plus sectors in final demand is still no more than 75 percent in Thailand. The major difference between Thailand and Indonesia lies in the effects of government price intervention in Indonesia for two important foodstuffs, milled rice and wheat flour. Tunisia is a much smaller and more open economy than the other two, though its size is partly offset by its higher income per capita and by its generally more developed industrial sector. As a result, the traded-goods pricing rule applies to a large number of sectors that represent more than 35 percent of total demand. The figures in the table show clearly that there is considerable scope for differences between the analysis of tax incidence based on cost-plus pricing and the general model adopted in this study. Furthermore, the impact of tax changes will differ across the four studies because of the cross-country variations in the importance of cost-plus pricing. Note, however, that the difference between the two Thai studies is quite small.

Table 20-1. *Input-Output Sectors, by Pricing Rule*

		Pricing rule		
Item	Cost plus	Traded	Government controlled	Market nontraded
Indonesia				
Number of sectors	45	21	3	4
Percentage of domestic output	58.6	22.0	14.8	4.6
Percentage of intermediate demand	55.2	23.2	19.3	2.3
Percentage of final demand	58.3	25.6	11.0	5.1
Thailand, 1975				
Number of sectors	44	26	0	3
Percentage of domestic output	71.0	25.1	0	3.9
Percentage of intermediate demand	56.3	42.8	0	1.0
Percentage of final demand	73.0	21.9	0	5.1
Thailand, 1982				
Number of sectors	44	26	0	3
Percentage of domestic output	73.0	23.6	0	2.5
Percentage of intermediate demand	62.3	37.0	0	0.7
Percentage of final demand	75.1	21.6	0	3.3
Tunisia				
Number of sectors	56	42	5	8
Percentage of domestic output	62.0	26.2	3.1	8.7
Percentage of intermediate demand	50.2	37.9	3.4	8.5
Percentage of final demand	57.1	33.5	2.7	6.7

For the principal focus of the study, I have assumed that in each country taxes need to be increased in order to collect net revenue—after allowing for the higher cost of government purchases—amounting to 1 percent of total final demand on the assumption that aggregate consumption of all products remains unchanged.[4] In addition to taxes on petroleum products, a number of nonfuel taxes have been examined in order ro provide the basis for investigating revenue-neutral tax reforms—that is, by raising some taxes and lowering others. The discussion will concentrate upon five alternative methods of collecting the additional revenue:

1. A sales tax on all petroleum products
2. A sales tax on motor gasoline and aviation fuel
3. A sales tax on petroleum products other than motor gasoline and aviation fuel
4. An import sales tax on the landed price (including existing customs duties) of all imported goods other than food items whose domestic price is controlled or subsidized by the government—for example, wheat in Tunisia and rice and flour in Indonesia (these items are excluded on the grounds that the tax would simply lead to a transfer from one government account to another)
5. An industrial sales tax, which was assumed to be a cascading sales tax on the output of all domestic enterprises plus imported items for the follow-

ing industries: beverages, nonfood manufacturing, electricity, and gas, water, and petroleum products.

The last two taxes were chosen as being typical of general taxes used in many developing countries.

In addition to these five general tax reforms, I have examined the impact of excise taxes on specific fuels in order to identify the possible impact of policies designed to alter the domestic relative prices of different petroleum products by taxing or subsidizing particular fuels. To normalize these taxes in terms of their potential revenue/cost, I have calculated the tax rates required to collect net revenue—defined as above—equal to 0.25 of 1 percent of final demand and have used these in the four studies. Unfortunately, for at least one fuel in each case, this procedure implies a very large change in its price relative to other fuels, so that the assumption of unchanged demand is hardly plausible. It would have been possible to have set a lower net revenue target—say, 0.1 percent of total final demand—but the effects of the resulting taxes are so small as to be well within the margins of error in the data. Hence the figures are reported in order to indicate the direction and relative magnitudes of the impact of specific fuel taxes, but they should not be interpreted as forecasts of the actual impact of the larger tax changes, because they will certainly overestimate their impact over any period other than the very short run.

The impact of the price changes on households was calculated by reclassifying the several hundred budget items identified in each household budget survey so that they matched the sectors distinguished in the pricing analysis. The surveys recorded separately items purchased in the market, items received as pay in kind, and items consumed out of the household's production. The estimates of the expenditure transfers are based only on items purchased in the market for consumption. Price changes for goods that are received as pay in kind or are consumed out of domestic production will have an effect on the cost of a given consumption basket that is exactly offset by the corresponding change in imputed income. The expenditure transfers associated with each tax reform were calculated for all of the households for which complete data on expenditure patterns were available, so the analysis of the incidence of the taxes in section 4 is based on large samples. The number of households for each country was: (1) Indonesia, 15,213, (2) Thailand, 1976, 11,300, (3) Thailand, 1981, 11,897, (4) Tunisia, 5,957.

The Impact of Fuel Taxes on Prices

In order to judge the magnitudes of the fuel taxes required to raise the fixed amount of revenue in the three countries, it is useful to note the structure of petroleum product prices in each country. These are shown for the relevant year in table 20-2; the indexes in the table refer to indexes of the relative prices of petroleum products in each country with regular gasoline equal to 100. To

Table 20-2. *Petroleum Product Prices*

| Product | Domestic purchaser prices | | | | | | | | Border prices, Thailand CIF, 1982 | |
| | Indonesia, 1981 | | Thailand, 1975 | | Thailand, 1982 | | Tunisia, 1981 | | | |
	Price	Index	Price	Index	Price	Index	Price	Index	Price	Index
Premium gasoline	1.33	146	0.81	106	2.21	118	2.08	113	1.04	107
Regular gasoline	0.91	100	0.77	100	1.88	100	1.94	100	0.97	100
Kerosene	0.23	25	0.54	70	1.01	54	0.47	26	1.11	115
Motor diesel oil	0.32	35	0.43	56	1.22	65	0.71	39	1.07	111
Industrial diesel oil	0.32	35	0.51	67	0.77	41	0.52	28	1.05	109
Heavy fuel oil	0.27	30	0.32	42	0.72	38	0.22	12	n.a.	n.a.
Crude oil[a]	32.00	—	11.51	—	34.00	—	32.00	—	34.00	—

— Not applicable.

n.a. Not available.

Note: Prices shown are midyear prices in U.S. dollars per U.S. gallon at official exchange rates.

a. Saudi Arabian light, U.S. dollars per barrel.

Sources: Domestic prices from U.S. Department of Energy, *International Energy Annual,* and local sources. Border prices computed from *Petroleum Economist* (prices posted in Singapore plus freight and other charges to Bangkok). The crude oil is the Saudi official selling price.

complete the comparison, CIF prices for five petroleum products delivered to Bangkok (based on prices posted in Singapore) are also shown in order to illustrate the structure of border prices for petroleum products. The crude oil price allows us to compare prices in 1976 and the early 1980s. To simplify the comparison, we may assume that the border price of all petroleum products other than heavy fuel oil are approximately equal.

For Thailand in 1982, gasoline was quite heavily taxed, whereas kerosene was slightly subsidized and industrial diesel oil was more heavily subsidized. In the case of both of these last two products, the subsidies represented a major change in policy since 1976, as the dollar price of crude oil had increased by nearly 200 percent, whereas the domestic prices in dollars of regular gasoline, kerosene, and industrial diesel oil had increased by 144 percent, 87 percent, and 51 percent, respectively.

Indonesian domestic prices for petroleum products in 1981 were all low in absolute terms, but, as in Tunisia, the implicit subsidies were concentrated on kerosene—with prices equal to one-quarter that of regular gasoline in both countries—as well as diesel oil and heavy fuel oil. The large differences between domestic relative prices and border relative prices in all three countries indicate how far governments have intervened in setting petroleum product prices. We may also infer that it may be very difficult politically to bring relative domestic prices into line with relative border prices—as would be desirable on standard efficiency arguments—especially for kerosene and diesel oil.

In all three countries, domestic prices for petroleum products are controlled directly by the government. The ex-refinery prices paid to the refiners are usually set according to cost-plus criteria, as domestic transport and distribution costs are also. The governments then levy taxes on or provide subsidies for different products in order to make up the difference between the controlled purchaser prices and ex-refinery prices plus distribution margins. Any decision to raise or lower the purchaser prices of fuels may thus be regarded as equivalent to a change in fuel taxes/subsidies in terms of the effects on both government revenue and fuel prices facing energy consumers. The two nonfuel general taxes—sales taxes on imports and industrial goods—are widely used in developing countries. Both Indonesia and Tunisia levy sales taxes on imports and industrial output, though in Tunisia the tax on domestic industrial production operates like a value-added tax rather than like a cascading sales tax. In Thailand import duties and a business tax generate almost one-half of central government revenue; these are very similar in effect to the import and industrial sales taxes examined here.

The effects of taxes designed to raise net revenue equal to 1 percent of total final demand in the case of the general taxes and 0.25 percent of total final demand for the specific fuel excises on purchase prices appear in table 20-3. The tax rates are calculated on the assumption of a zero price elasticity of demand, as I stressed above, so they will only yield equal net revenue over the short term. The differences in the price increases reflect variations in income per capita and economic structure. A higher proportion of GDP goes for fuels and imported goods in Tunisia, for example, than in Indonesia. The price increases for petroleum products also reflect the very different initial levels of petroleum product prices and the effect that these have had on patterns of consumption. The high price of gasoline in Tunisia relative to motor diesel oil,

Table 20-3. *Percentage Increases in Purchase Prices Associated with Taxes to Raise Fixed Net Revenue*

Tax reform	Indonesia	Thailand 1975	Thailand 1982	Tunisia
General taxes[a]				
All petroleum products	43.3	20.0	14.3	29.4
Gasoline	103.9	52.0	37.7	81.6
Other petroleum products	73.3	32.2	22.7	46.3
Import sales tax	9.7	8.7	8.8	5.4
Industrial sales tax	3.8	2.3	1.5	2.4
Fuel excises[b]				
Gasoline	26.0	13.0	9.4	20.4
Kerosene	46.7	174.5	75.8	167.2
Diesel oil	33.9	14.0	9.2	20.3
Fuel oil	115.2	22.8	22.6	71.7

a. To raise 1 percent of total final demand.
b. To raise 0.25 percent of total final demand.

for example, has encouraged both the use of small fuel-efficient cars and the purchase of diesel-engined cars/pickups rather than ones with gasoline engines. Adjustments of this kind mean that the tax bases for the excises on each fuel are determined in each country by complex sets of institutional, geographical, and other factors, so that there is no simple correlation between fuel prices and the tax rates required to raise a given fraction of final demand as tax revenue. Comparing the price changes implied by the tax changes for the two Thai studies, we observe the effects of both the rise in domestic fuel prices relative to other prices between 1975 and 1982 and the growth of income reflected in a higher share of expenditure on industrial goods.

The principal results of the general pricing model with respect to the impact of these tax reforms on price levels in the three countries appear in table 20-4. A preliminary point to note is that the figures in the first five rows are naturally scaled by the requirement that the tax reforms collect net revenue equivalent to 1 percent of total final demand. We would expect the change in the consumer price indexes to fall in the 1.5–2.0 percent range if all the additional revenue were to come from private consumption, because this constitutes between 47 percent and 60 percent of final demand in these countries. Figures significantly below 1 percent indicate that the pricing system has the effect of shifting the tax burden backward onto factor incomes either directly by affecting the profitability of various activities or indirectly by increasing the relative cost of investment.

The general ranking of the tax reforms in terms of their impact on both producer and consumer prices is very similar for Indonesia, Thailand in 1975, and Tunisia. The largest rises in consumer prices are associated with the tax on petroleum products other than gasoline and the import sales tax, whereas the smallest rises are associated with the tax on gasoline and the industrial sales

Table 20-4. *Percentage Changes in Price Indexes under Alternative Tax Reforms*

	Producer prices				Consumer prices			
		Thailand				Thailand		
Tax	Indo-nesia	1975	1982	Tunisia	Indo-nesia	1975	1982	Tunisia
General taxes								
All petroleum products	1.46	1.23	1.35	0.99	0.85	0.86	1.19	0.81
Gasoline	1.55	1.13	1.26	0.96	0.76	0.68	1.21	0.65
Other petroleum products	1.38	1.29	1.39	1.00	0.92	0.98	1.17	0.90
Import sales tax	2.43	1.38	1.35	1.39	1.36	0.89	1.02	1.60
Industrial sales tax	0.96	0.98	0.78	0.61	0.83	0.81	0.66	0.50
Fuel excises								
Gasoline	0.39	0.28	0.32	0.24	0.19	0.17	0.30	0.16
Kerosene	0.26	0.69	0.59	0.15	0.38	1.08	1.15	1.37
Diesel oil	0.31	0.26	0.26	0.23	0.12	0.19	0.24	0.10
Fuel oil	0.54	0.37	0.42	0.38	0.17	0.16	0.16	0.11

tax. With the exception of the import sales taxes for Indonesia and Tunisia, the increases in the consumer price indexes are substantially lower than they would be with a value-added tax that fell only on private consumption and yielded the same amount of revenue. As a result, a major portion of the tax burden falls upon factor incomes rather than on consumption. If we compare the three countries—still excluding Thailand in 1982—the magnitudes of the changes in consumer price indexes associated with the three general petroleum taxes are very similar. As we would expect, there are significant differences in impact between the import and industrial sales taxes across the three countries because of the differences in economic structure that I noted above.

The differences between the effects of the fuel taxes on consumer price indexes in Thailand for 1975 and 1982 are striking. In part, they may be accounted for by the rise in direct private consumption of petroleum products as a share of total consumption from 9.3 percent to 10.4 percent over the same period, combined with a decline in the share of kerosene and a rise in the shares of gasoline and liquefied petroleum gas in private consumption. It also seems, however, that the growth in indirect private consumption—that is, via the increased share of relatively energy-intensive industrial goods—must account for a substantial proportion of the differences between the two years. The income elasticity of private consumption of petroleum products is substantially larger than unity, so that the change from 1975 to 1982 illustrates the effects of income growth on fuel consumption that were not outweighed by the much slower response of consumption to the rise in the real prices of petroleum products.

Among the specific fuel excises, kerosene stands out as producing much the largest increases in consumer price indexes in each country, but there are considerable differences between the four studies that are associated with differences in the patterns of kerosene consumption. In Indonesia, kerosene constituted approximately 19 percent of total expenditure on petroleum products, whereas in Thailand and Tunisia the shares fell in the 3–4.5 percent range. These differences in the importance of kerosene in total fuel consumption account for the large differences in the price rises associated with taxes to raise revenue equivalent to 0.25 percent of total final demand. Furthermore, in Indonesia nearly 30 percent of total kerosene consumption is outside the household sector, whereas this proportion is less than 5 percent in the other two countries. Kerosene is used primarily for domestic cooking and lighting, though if it is cheap enough it may be substituted for diesel oil in small generators, may be used in motor vehicles, and may have certain industrial applications. The crucial difference between Indonesia and the other two countries is the very underdeveloped state of its distribution networks for electricity and liquefied petroleum gas, which, combined with a relatively low price for kerosene, has made kerosene dominant in domestic use and has caused it to be substituted for other fuels in many industries. As a consequence, a given percentage tax on kerosene will collect more revenue in Indonesia than in the other countries, but its impact will also be felt much more widely.

In the Thai studies, the price of kerosene has a significant impact upon the consumer price indexes because of its indirect effect upon the price of firewood/charcoal, which I discuss below. In consequence, the effects of a kerosene tax are larger and more widespread than an examination of the figures for kerosene consumption alone might suggest. It would have been desirable to have included the same effects in the Indonesian model, but unfortunately the input-output table aggregates firewood and charcoal with logging and other forest products whose prices are determined by export opportunities. Hence the Indonesian model understates the full impact of a tax on kerosene.

Considerations of space mean that it is not possible to present tables showing the effects of the various tax reforms on the relative prices for different sectors, but it is worth identifying the sectors whose prices are most significantly affected by the fuel taxes. I will concentrate on producer price changes of more than 2 percent as a result of the tax on all petroleum products. The main sectors affected in all countries are predictable: electricity; road, air, and water transport; cement and similar nonmetallic mineral products; and fertilizers and other petrochemicals as long as they are not treated as traded goods. Two sets of changes in particular countries are also worth noting.

First, in Thailand, fuel tax reforms have the effect of increasing the price of charcoal and firewood quite substantially. This effect results from the assumption that the price of these items is determined by a market-clearing condition combined with substitution of kerosene for them (and vice versa) as fuels for rural cooking and heating. Thus an exogenous increase in the retail price of kerosene is assumed to induce a sympathetic increase in the price of charcoal and firewood.

Second, in Indonesia the prices received by farmers in the sugarcane, coconut, and logging sectors are *reduced* significantly by the general fuel tax. The commodities produced by these sectors are exportable, so that their prices are determined by trade possibilities, but exportation involves quite heavy costs of energy-intensive processing or transport. Because processing and transport are treated as cost-plus activities, any increase in their costs is simply passed backward in the form of a reduction in the price paid to the raw material producers. Thus, the fuel taxes fall in these sectors primarily upon the income of factors employed in these sectors.

These two examples illustrate the importance of distinguishing between cost-plus pricing and a framework in which many prices are determined by exogenous factors. Thus there are considerable differences in the changes in overall price indexes predicted by the two approaches. For the three reforms involving fuel taxes, the cost-plus pricing model indicates substantially larger increases in both producer and consumer prices than does the general model used here, whereas for the import sales tax the difference is reversed, with the general model yielding a much higher estimate of the pricing impact of the tax. As a rule, the contrast between the two models is more substantial for the change in the producer price index than for the change in the consumer price index. The reason is that nontraded items, for which cost-plus pricing applies in both cases, have a considerably greater weight in consumption than in output.

Expenditure Transfers and the Distribution of Real Income

Before we examine the magnitude of the expenditure transfers associated with the tax reforms, it is worth comparing the patterns of direct household expenditure on petroleum products in the three countries. The average percentages of total household expenditure spent on various petroleum products by urban and rural households are shown in table 20-5 together with their standard deviations. The figures show large differences between expenditure patterns both in different countries and for urban and rural households. Kerosene is much the most important fuel for households in Indonesia, where petroleum products also comprise a substantially larger fraction of household expenditure than in the other two countries. In contrast, kerosene is the most important fuel only for rural households in Thailand and Tunisia because liquefied petroleum gas is used for cooking by many urban households. In Tunisia the high relative price of gasoline has also led to significant expenditure on diesel oil, which is used essentially as a substitute for gasoline. The standard deviations of the expenditure shares show that there is a wide diversity of expenditure patterns. The associated coefficients of variation are lowest for expenditure on all petroleum products, which finding indicates that

Table 20-5. *Share of Household Expenditure Allocated to Petroleum Products*
(percent)

Expenditure	Average shares				Standard deviations			
	Indo-nesia	Thailand		Tunisia	Indo-nesia	Thailand		Tunisia
		1976	1981			1976	1981	
Urban households								
Gasoline	0.71	1.26	1.66	0.34	2.56	3.53	4.00	1.09
Kerosene	3.49	0.11	0.06	0.54	2.69	0.49	0.37	0.84
Diesel oil	0.0	0.0	0.0	0.36	0.0	0.0	0.0	1.12
Liquefied petroleum gas	0.14	0.56	0.52	1.00	0.52	1.34	1.28	1.28
All petroleum products	4.34	1.94	2.24	2.29	3.56	4.13	4.44	2.52
Rural households								
Gasoline	0.19	0.46	0.77	0.10	1.72	2.42	2.59	0.58
Kerosene	3.05	1.08	0.80	1.23	2.53	1.13	1.17	1.19
Diesel oil	0.0	0.0	0.0	0.14	0.0	0.0	0.0	0.63
Liquefied petroleum gas	0.04	0.10	0.13	0.47	0.38	0.58	0.65	1.23
All petroleum products	3.28	1.64	1.71	1.94	3.15	2.80	2.94	1.90

Table 20-6. *Median Expenditure Transfers*
(percent of original expenditure)

Expenditure transfer	All petroleum products	Gasoline	Other petroleum products	Import sales tax	Industrial sales tax	Excise taxes[a]		
						Kerosene	Diesel oil	Fuel oil
Indonesia								
Urban	2.02	0.48	2.85	1.48	0.87	1.37	0.18	0.18
Rural	1.10	0.16	1.84	1.36	0.61	1.17	0.03	0.01
All	1.26	0.20	2.06	1.39	0.67	1.21	0.06	0.03
Thailand, 1975								
Urban	1.02	0.59	1.17	0.69	0.86	1.18	0.17	0.24
Rural	0.70	0.30	0.88	0.65	0.68	1.95	0.13	0.09
All	0.74	0.33	0.92	0.66	0.72	1.82	0.14	0.10
Thailand, 1982								
Urban	0.64	0.30	0.67	0.65	0.46	0.25	0.07	0.16
Rural	0.43	0.21	0.49	0.62	0.39	0.66	0.05	0.08
All	0.46	0.22	0.51	0.63	0.40	0.59	0.05	0.08
Tunisia								
Urban	0.55	0.03	0.86	1.64	0.56	0.28	0.03	0.21
Rural	0.51	0.02	0.81	1.65	0.48	1.55	0.03	0.03
All	0.52	0.02	0.84	1.64	0.53	0.85	0.03	0.12

a. To collect one-quarter of the revenue of the first five columns. To calculate comparable figures for the gasoline excise tax, divide column 2 by four.

households with high expenditure shares for one fuel have relatively low expenditure shares for other fuels. Note also that the standard deviations of the shares of expenditure on all petroleum products are lowest in Tunisia, the country with the highest income per capita of the three.

The medians of the expenditure transfers for each household—that is, $\Delta e^h/e^h$ expressed as a percentage of original expenditure—for the five tax reforms and three of the excise taxes are shown in table 20-6. Again, the specifications of the tax reforms provide a natural scaling that helps in interpreting their expenditure transfers, as a strictly proportional tax on private consumption alone would raise the same amount of revenue with rates of 1.90 percent in Indonesia, 1.67 percent in Thailand (1975), 1.89 percent in Thailand (1982), and 2.10 percent in Tunisia. To compare the effects of the specific fuel excises, we must divide the figures for the general tax on gasoline by 4 to give estimates equivalent to those for kerosene and the other fuels.

The figures in the table highlight the differences between the countries in the incidence of the fuel taxes, which reflect the large differences in fuel prices and use between countries. If we concentrate on the impact of taxes on specific fuels, the major point to note is that in all three countries there is no great variation in the impact of taxes raising similar revenue that are imposed on gasoline, diesel oil, and fuel oil, whereas kerosene stands out as having a much more substantial impact on households, especially on those in rural areas. This finding is not surprising in view of the large differences between the impacts of the kerosene tax and the other fuel taxes on the consumer price indexes. The differences between the impact of the taxes on kerosene and, say, diesel oil, are, however, much smaller when we compare the changes in the consumer price indexes (which reflect average expenditure patterns) than for the median expenditure transfers. The implication of this observation is that taxes on kerosene affect households in the lower tail of the income distribution particularly severely. In part, this is an automatic consequence of the greater impact of kerosene taxes on rural households than on urban households, because the average expenditure per person of the former group is substantially lower than for the latter group, but even within sectors the distributional impact may be unfavorable.

Turning to the effects of the five general tax reforms, we see that the median expenditure transfers are lowest for the tax on gasoline and highest for the tax on other petroleum products in Indonesia, Thailand (1975), and Tunisia. Between 1975 and 1982, patterns of fuel consumption in Thailand clearly changed significantly; the median expenditure transfers associated with all of the general and specific fuel taxes declined by large fractions of their 1975 values—the drop was particularly marked for kerosene and diesel oil—despite the increase in the impact of the taxes on the consumer price index. Such a change is consistent with a response to increased fuel prices that was much more rapid among low-income households than among high-income households.

The complexity of the factors that determine median and average expenditure transfers is illustrated by the significant difference between Thailand and Indonesia in the incidence of the import sales tax. By most criteria—including the figures in table 20-1—Thailand would be judged to be a significantly more open economy than Indonesia, yet the median expenditure transfers associated with an import sales tax in Indonesia are more than twice as large as the equivalent transfers for Thailand, which are very similar in both years. The implication, of course, is that in Thailand the burden of this tax must fall disproportionately on factor incomes—especially in export sectors.

Overall, the general taxes seem to favor rural households relative to urban households—even for the tax on other petroleum products—though the difference between the two sectors is marginal in Tunisia. It is, however, inadvisable to draw from this evidence firm conclusions concerning the distributional impact of the taxes; as we have seen, there is large variation within (as well as between) income groups and sectors. As a preliminary to discussion of the distributional implications of the taxes, table 20-7 shows the distributional characteristics, calculated in the manner described in part 1, for a number of commodities in the four household budget surveys. Kerosene stands out as having distributional characteristics that are very similar to those for the primary cereal in each country and is therefore very close to the top of the ranking of commodities by their distributional characteristics in all cases.

Table 20-7. *Distributional Characteristics for Petroleum Products*

Product	Distributional characteristic				Rank of distributional characteristic			
	Indo-nesia	Thailand		Tunisia	Indo-nesia	Thailand		Tunisia
		1976	1981			1976	1981	
Petroleum products								
Gasoline	0.236	0.379	0.406	0.253	48	52	49	68
Kerosene	0.754	1.035	1.136	0.871	9	2	1	1
Diesel oil	—	—	—	0.276	—	—	—	65
Liquefied petroleum gas	0.245	0.395	0.397	0.461	47	51	51	37
Other items								
Primary cereal (rice/wheat)	0.724	1.048	1.082	0.765	10	1	2	5
Fats and oils	0.685	0.747	0.765	0.549	14	15	15	25
Tobacco products	0.635	0.736	0.715	0.572	18	17	22	20
Clothing	0.522	0.717	0.737	0.468	23	21	21	35
Electrical goods	0.172	0.496	0.545	0.396	51	41	38	53
Electricity	0.359	0.454	0.457	0.465	45	49	44	36
Number of items	n.a.				52	55	57	73
Median characteristic value	0.501	0.673	0.625	0.461	—	—	—	—

— Not applicable.

Notes: The distributional characteristic for item k is defined as $(1/H) \Sigma_h \beta^h (x_k^h/\bar{x}_k)$ where β^h is scaled so that $\bar{\beta} = 1$. The values of the distributional characteristics are based on β^h calculated using the isoelastic social welfare function $W = \Sigma_h [1/(1 - \epsilon)] e_h^{1-\epsilon}$ with an inequality aversion parameter of $\epsilon = 1$, which corresponds to the social welfare function $W = \Sigma_h \log \epsilon_h$. Rankings for distributional characteristics with $\epsilon = 1$ and $\epsilon = 2$ are almost identical.

Gasoline, on the other hand, is close to the bottom of the ranking, as also is liquefied petroleum gas except in Tunisia—where it is widely used by poor urban households for cooking. Because indirect consumption of kerosene and gasoline is a small fraction of total consumption, it may be assumed that the distributional impact of specific excises on these fuels will reflect their distributional characteristics. For general taxes on all petroleum products and for specific excises on diesel and fuel oil, it is not obvious where the distributional impacts will lie, relative to the polar cases of kerosene and gasoline.

As a first step in the analysis of the distributional implications of the alternative tax reforms, table 20-8 gives the average expenditure transfer for all households and an index of progressivity that I will discuss below. The average expenditure transfers in the table were calculated by averaging the expenditure transfers for each household without weights and are not the same as the expenditure-weighted averages, which are equal to the total tax cost for each reform divided by total expenditure. As we might expect, the fuel taxes have a heavily skewed impact, with the means of the distributions exceeding the medians by substantial amounts. The skew is particularly marked for the

Table 20-8. *Indexes of Expenditure Transfer Progressivity*
(percent of original expenditure)

Tax reform	Mean expenditure transfer				Progressivity indexes			
	Indo-nesia	Thailand		Tunisia	Indo-nesia	Thailand		Tunisia
		1975	1982			1975	1982	
General taxes								
All petroleum								
products	1.59	0.89	0.58	0.69	0.092	0.221	0.140	0.053
Gasoline	0.55	0.68	0.56	0.23	0.367	0.500	0.301	0.163
Other petroleum								
products	2.47	1.02	0.59	0.97	−0.139	0.049	0.056	−0.016
Import sales tax	1.38	0.73	0.71	1.65	0.038	0.161	0.132	−0.066
Industrial sales								
tax	0.76	0.78	0.44	0.56	0.248	0.133	0.108	0.054
Fuel excises								
Gasoline	0.14	0.17	0.14	0.06	0.092	0.125	0.075	0.041
Kerosene	1.50	2.36	0.83	1.42	−0.175	−0.605	−0.187	−0.538
Diesel oil	0.06	0.15	0.08	0.09	0.032	0.013	0.014	0.040
Fuel oil	0.10	0.13	0.11	0.18	0.061	0.053	0.037	0.020

Notes: The progressivity index for a particular reform was calculated by regressing the expenditure transfer for each household on total original household expenditure and household size and then multiplying the coefficient for total expenditure by the average value of total expenditure in the sample. It is regarded as a percentage of original expenditure.

gasoline tax, which implies that this tax affects small numbers of households rather heavily though its impact on most households is small. The differences between the means and medians for the import and industrial sales taxes are slight, indicating that the distributions of their expenditure transfers are much more symmetrical than those of the fuel taxes.

Skewness of the distribution of expenditure transfers across households is not per se a disadvantage, because, for example, both highly progressive and highly regressive taxes may display substantial degrees of positive skewness. One problem is that a tax that is roughly proportional across households overall but displays considerable skewness may generate considerable opposition because a small number of households gain or lose disproportionately by comparison with apparently similar households. I will discuss the issue of the horizontal equity/inequity of any tax reform below. First we must examine how far the incidence of the taxes is progressive or regressive. This question may be analyzed in a number of ways, and the main conclusions are independent of the measure of progressivity adopted. In table 20-8, I have adopted a relative approach: (1) the expenditure transfer expressed as a percentage of original expenditure was regressed upon total household expenditure and household size and (2) the regression coefficient for household expenditure was multiplied by average household expenditure to give the index of progressivity. Formally this index is calculated by estimating the coefficients μ_0, μ_1, and μ_2 in equation 20-9:

(20-9)
$$\frac{\Delta e^h}{e^h} = \mu_0 + \mu_1 e^h + \mu_2 N$$

where N is total household size. We then define IP, the index of tax progressivity:

(20-10)
$$IP = \mu_i \bar{e}$$

where $\bar{e}$ is the average value of e^h. This index may be regarded as the predicted difference between the proportional expenditure transfers for households of a fixed family size with expenditures equal to 0.5 and 1.5 times average household expenditure respectively. The index is expressed as a percentage of original household expenditure; negative values mean that the incidence of the tax is regressive.

The values of the progressivity indexes in the table should be interpreted with caution. Perhaps the most important conclusion to be drawn from the regressions estimated in order to compute the indexes is that the R^2 values are exceedingly low (less than 0.15), even by comparison with other cross-section studies. The regression coefficient μ_1 had substantial t values (greater than 9) because of the very large sample sizes, but the relationships between the expenditure transfers and total household expenditure are very noisy. Bearing this warning in mind, we see that the tax on gasoline is consistently the most progressive of those examined, whereas the excise tax on kerosene is consistently regressive. For both Thai studies, the tax on all petroleum products is significantly progressive; the tax on other petroleum products is neutral. The regressive effect of the taxation of kerosene means that the tax on other petroleum products in Indonesia is strongly regressive and the tax on all petroleum products is neutral. Diesel oil is more important in Tunisia than in the other two countries, and its progressive impact largely outweighs the regressive impact of the tax on kerosene.

Although indexes of progressivity indicate the nature of the correlations between the expenditure transfers and total expenditure, they do not show how important these correlations may be in affecting overall inequality and social welfare. For this purpose I have calculated two measures of the welfare impact of the tax reforms. The first is based upon Atkinson's index of inequality in Atkinson (1970)—see Hughes and Islam (1981). This is associated with the social welfare function for parameter ϵ:

(20-11)
$$W(\epsilon) = \sum_h \frac{1}{1 - \epsilon} e_h^{1 - \epsilon}$$

and the inequality index is defined by

(20-12)
$$I(\epsilon) = 1 - \left[\left(\frac{1}{H} \sum_h e_h^{1 - \epsilon} \right)^{\frac{1}{1 - \epsilon}} \Big/ \bar{e} \right].$$

After a little manipulation, the impact of a tax reform on social welfare can be expressed as

$$(20\text{-}13) \qquad \Delta W(\epsilon) = (1 - \epsilon) W(\epsilon) \left(\frac{\Delta \bar{e}}{\bar{e}} - \frac{\Delta I(\epsilon)}{1 - I(\epsilon)} \right).$$

The formulas for $\epsilon = 1$ differ slightly because $W(1) = \Sigma_h \log e_h$, but for all values of ϵ the change in social welfare depends upon the proportional change in average household expenditure, that is, the amount of tax collected from households, and the proportional change in $1 - I(\epsilon)$, since an increase in $I(\epsilon)$ denotes an increase in inequality. If we focus specifically on the impact of the tax reforms on vertical inequality, table 20-9 gives $-\Delta I(\epsilon)/[1 - I(\epsilon)]$ as a percentage for $\epsilon = 1$.

The second measure of the impact of the tax reforms on social welfare is an extension of the concept of the distributional characteristic of a commodity to the effect of a tax reform on real income or expenditure. The distributional characteristic for a reform is defined as

$$(20\text{-}14) \qquad DC = \Sigma \, \beta_h \Delta e_h / \Sigma \, \Delta e_h$$

which is simply a weighted average of the social welfare weights, β_h, using the

Table 20-9. *The Impact of Tax Reforms on Social Welfare*

Tax	Index of welfare change[a]				Distributional characteristic for the reforms			
		Thailand				Thailand		
	Indo-nesia	1975	1982	Tunisia	Indo-nesia	1975	1982	Tunisia
General taxes								
All petroleum products	0.14	0.13	0.12	0.08	0.551	0.627	0.572	0.523
Gasoline	0.58	0.29	0.26	0.22	0.293	0.497	0.469	0.315
Other petroleum products	−0.26	0.02	0.04	0.00	0.662	0.705	0.643	0.581
Import sales tax	0.06	0.11	0.11	−0.08	0.571	0.638	0.601	0.608
Industrial sales tax	0.17	0.11	0.08	0.08	0.482	0.643	0.598	0.525
Fuel excises								
Gasoline	0.15	0.07	0.07	0.06	0.293	0.497	0.469	0.315
Kerosene	−0.30	−0.48	−0.20	−0.66	0.747	0.876	0.881	1.005
Diesel oil	0.05	0.01	0.01	0.05	0.331	0.688	0.601	0.388
Fuel oil	0.09	0.04	0.03	0.03	0.313	0.584	0.538	0.503
Uniform lump-sum transfer	2.79	1.24	1.53	2.19	—	—	—	—

— Not applicable.

Notes: The index of welfare change and the distributional characteristic for the impact of the reform are defined in the text. The values in the table are based on an inequality aversion parameter of $\epsilon = 1$.

a. $-100 \, \Delta I/(1 - I)$.

expenditure changes as weights in calculating the average. To ensure compara-
bility between the distributional characteristics for the tax reforms and those
for goods reported on table 20-7 and also between the two measures of the
impact of the reforms, the distributional characteristics in table 20-9 are based
upon β_h values calculated using $\epsilon = 1$. The table also shows the effect on
inequality of a uniform lump-sum subsidy to all households distributing the
same amount of revenue as is raised by the general taxes—that is, amounting in
total to 1 percent of total final demand. The distributional characteristic for
such a transfer is by definition equal to 1.0, because β_h is scaled so that its
average value is equal to 1.0.

For Indonesia and Thailand, the household expenditure figures used in
computing the inequality indexes $I(\epsilon)$ were deflated by price indexes reflecting
variations in prices, for example between urban and rural areas and across
regions of the countries. These price variations are small in Tunisia and were
therefore ignored. The inequality indexes were calculated using expenditure
per member of the household so that they allow for variations in household
size, but the values of the indexes remain measures of the inequality of the
distribution across households. The results in the table show that, among the
general taxes, the tax on gasoline has the most substantial impact in reducing
inequality, though by comparison with the size of the taxes—raising revenue
in excess of 1.5 percent of household expenditure in all countries—this effect
is small in Thailand and Tunisia. The tax on other petroleum products worsens
inequality in Indonesia and is neutral in its impact in the other two countries.
If we combine these two, the tax on all petroleum products leads to a small
improvement in the extent of inequality and has an impact that is very similar
to that of the industrial sales tax. The comparable figures for the uniform
lump-sum transfer, however, show that all of these general taxes are poor
methods of attempting to correct inequalities in the distribution of income.

The fuel excises raise only a quarter of the revenue of the general taxes, but
the tax on kerosene has a larger absolute effect on inequality than all of the
reforms except the uniform lump-sum transfer. This finding confirms the
regressive impact of taxing kerosene, whereas taxes on the other specific fuels
are either neutral or beneficial in terms of their effect on inequality. Although
a tax on kerosene worsens inequality in all four studies, this effect can be
largely or entirely offset by redistributing the revenue via a uniform lump-sum
transfer. Thus, if it was thought necessary to raise the price of kerosene on
efficiency grounds, it would be possible to mitigate the impact of this reform on
overall inequality at a very small net cost in terms of government revenue.
Such a package of tax changes would be neutral only overall, and many
households would still experience substantial changes in their real incomes.

The distributional characteristics in table 20-9 confirm the conclusions
drawn from the analysis of the inequality measure of the welfare change. The
distributional characteristics for the full impact of taxing gasoline are somewhat larger than those calculated for gasoline consumption alone, which

implies that the indirect effects of a gasoline tax are less progressive than the direct effects. In Thailand the distributional characteristics of the kerosene excise are substantially lower than for kerosene consumption, so that the indirect effects of this tax offset its direct impact. On the other hand, in Tunisia the indirect effects reinforce its regressive impact on household consumption. The distributional characteristics for the excises on fuel oil and diesel oil fall close to or below the median distributional characteristics in table 20-7 in Thailand and Tunisia, whereas in Indonesia all fuels other than kerosene seem to fall near the bottom of the ranking of distributional characteristics.

Although the effect of the general fuel taxes on aggregate inequality may be small, they do generate substantial horizontal inequity because of their differential impact on households with similar levels of expenditure per capita. Economists disagree as to whether the horizontal effects of a tax reform should be taken into account when assessing its merits. In political terms, however, large differences between the expenditure transfers experienced by apparently similar households may undermine support for a reform and may provide the leverage sought by pressure groups that wish to subvert the objectives of the reform. Hence policymakers must be concerned about the horizontal inequity associated with alternative tax proposals. There are a variety of ways of measuring the effects of a tax reform on horizontal equity. One approach, discussed in King (1983b), is to compute indexes of horizontal inequality similar to the Atkinson indexes of vertical inequality. These measure, in effect, the extent to which the ranking of households in the overall distribution has been shuffled by the tax reform. King shows that the indexes of vertical and horizontal inequality can be combined to give an overall index reflecting the net effect of a reform, whose value for a rank-preserving reform will simply be equal to the Atkinson index. I have computed this overall inequality index for each of the reforms, using various values of the horizontal and vertical inequality aversion parameters. Only if the sensitivity to horizontal inequality is very low does the gasoline tax lead to a net improvement in inequality, whereas for all of the other tax changes, the horizontal inequity outweighs any improvement in vertical inequality.

Another, more concrete method of measuring horizontal inequity relies on examining the residuals of a regression equation with the expenditure transfer as the dependent variable and total household expenditure as the independent variable. Suppose that we estimate the simple linear equation

$$(20\text{-}15) \qquad\qquad \frac{\Delta e^h}{e^h} = \mu_0 + \mu_1 e^h$$

and calculate the residuals

$$(20\text{-}16) \qquad\qquad d_h = \frac{\Delta e^h}{e^h} - \frac{\Delta \hat{e}^h}{e^h}$$

where the caret denotes the predicted value from equation 20-15. Then we can

Table 20-10. *Indexes of Horizontal Inequity Due to the Tax Reforms*
(percent of original expenditure)

| | | Thailand | | |
Tax	Indonesia	1975	1982	Tunisia
General taxes				
All petroleum products	2.63	1.04	0.89	1.02
Gasoline	0.71	1.10	1.26	0.37
Other petroleum products	4.03	1.18	0.87	1.37
Import sales tax	1.27	0.78	0.89	0.99
Industrial sales tax	1.10	0.94	0.59	0.62
Fuel excises				
Gasoline	0.18	0.27	0.31	0.09
Kerosene	2.50	4.64	1.84	3.46
Diesel oil	0.33	0.20	0.16	0.21
Fuel oil	0.49	0.17	0.17	0.38

Notes: The index of horizontal inequity given in this table is defined in the text. Average values of the expenditure transfer appear in table 20-8.

analyze the distribution of d^h across households. In table 20-10, the index of horizontal inequity is computed as the difference between the tenth and the ninetieth percentiles of this distribution. In other words, we have shifted equation 20-15 vertically upward so that 10 percent of households lie above the line, and similarly we have shifted it downward so that 10 percent of households lie beneath it; see figure 20-1. The index is then equal to the vertical distance between these two lines and is measured as a percentage of original household expenditure.

The figures in the table confirm that the horizontal inequity associated with the tax on kerosene and—to a lesser extent—on other petroleum products is high when compared with the horizontal effects of the sales taxes on imports and industrial products. For specific fuels, the tax on gasoline generates relatively little horizontal inequity, as also does the diesel oil excise, but the excise tax on kerosene leads to large degrees of horizontal inequity. If we compare countries, it is interesting to note that the index of horizontal inequity for the gasoline tax is relatively high in Thailand, but the indexes for the taxes on all petroleum products and other petroleum products are relatively low. Thus, in Thailand there seems to be little advantage to concentrating fuel taxes on gasoline, whereas in Indonesia and Tunisia the differences between the indexes for a gasoline tax and general taxes on petroleum products favor concentration on gasoline.

Conclusions

In this chapter I have outlined an approach that makes possible the analysis of the incidence of any indirect taxes imposed upon intermediate goods as well

Figure 20-1. *Illustrative Plot for Calculation of the Index of Horizontal Inequity: Thailand, 1982, Tax on All Petroleum Products*

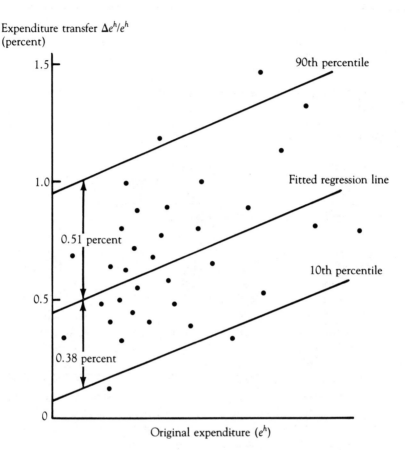

Source: Table 20-10.

as final goods. Because of the difficulties involved in collecting the requisite information on tax rates and price elasticities, I have not tried to calculate welfare measures indicating whether particular taxes should be increased or decreased. Instead the discussion of the incidence of the taxes has, in effect, extended the descriptive approach adopted in standard tax analysis by examining the impact of the taxes on the distribution of real income for large samples of households. This procedure can be implemented with relatively limited resources and can easily be updated as better information becomes available. At the same time, it can be made the starting point for a more thorough welfare analysis, or it can be used to answer specific questions concerning the impact of proposed reforms on particular groups of the population.

The adoption of a pricing model that is more general than the conventional cost-plus pricing rule has a substantial effect on the results of the analysis, because it leads to a lower overall increase in both producer and consumer price indexes and to a rather different pattern of relative price changes. Furthermore, the divergence from cost-plus pricing means that the incidence of the taxes is shifted backward onto factor incomes to a significant extent. The analysis of the incidence of the tax reforms on net real incomes in Thailand shows that the changes in factor incomes can have a significant effect on conclusions about the impact of certain tax changes on the distribution. The inclusion of changes in factor incomes in the analysis did not alter any of the main conclusions about the impact of the five general taxes examined in this chapter. On the other hand, the income changes associated with an export sales tax were large but very erratic in their distribution across households, so that the index of horizontal inequity for the tax was greatly increased.

Focusing specifically on the fuel taxes, we have seen that their effect on the price indexes is small and that, for example, a reduction in taxes on imports offset by an equivalent increase in fuel taxes would tend to lower consumer price indexes. There is therefore no reason to object to fuel taxes on the grounds that they are inflationary. The major objection to fuel taxes on distributional grounds arises from the adverse impact of a tax on kerosene in each of the three countries, though this is most serious in Indonesia, whereas the taxation of liquefied petroleum gas in Tunisia has similar but less severe effects. Unfortunately, there are very powerful efficiency arguments for not discriminating between kerosene and diesel oil in setting taxes and, in the longer run, a large discrepancy between taxes on gasoline and diesel oil leads to substitution away from the former in transport. Hence, apart from distributional considerations, there are good a priori reasons for preferring a tax system that imposes similar tax rates on all petroleum products. A uniform tax on all petroleum products would not worsen the overall vertical inequality of the distribution of real income, but it would lead to substantial horizontal inequity because of its differential impact on households with similar total expenditure levels. The ideal solution would be to find a tax/subsidy that could be used to offset the effects of kerosene taxation on poorer (especially rural) households, but the very high values of the distributional characteristic for kerosene reported in table 20-7 mean that a suitable commodity or group of commodities is unlikely to be identified for this purpose. Even in Indonesia, for which kerosene ranks only ninth in the list of distributional characteristics, the correlation coefficients between household expenditure on kerosene and on other products with high distributional characteristics are typically below 0.3. Thus, any combination of commodity subsidies designed to offset the overall distributional impact of taxing kerosene would generate substantial horizontal effects—that is, there would be a redistribution of real income between households at similar initial levels of income per person.

One interesting implication of the comparison between the effects of the fuel taxes in the three countries is that relative price distortions of the kind that have persisted in Indonesia and Tunisia for some time, due to differential taxes, can become so deeply embedded in economic behavior that they are exceedingly difficult or painful to correct. In both countries, the dependence of rural households on kerosene for cooking and other fuel requirements is such that attempts to adjust relative prices are seen as being regressive—and also as having a detrimental impact on the environment as they affect woodcutting for charcoal and firewood—whereas similar price changes have been easier in Thailand, where domestic relative prices are much closer to border relative prices. This conclusion offers little reassurance to policymakers who wish to correct long-standing price distortions, but it should strengthen the resistance of those who wish to prevent the introduction of similar price distortions as devices to mitigate the inflationary and other effects of exogenous increases in energy prices.

Overall, the analysis of fuel taxes may be interpreted in two ways.

1. It can be argued that there is no real basis for using fuel taxes as a method of achieving other social or economic objectives, so that they should be set to achieve efficiency in the use of different sources of energy and in the major energy-consuming sectors, such as transport.

2. These taxes have a very limited impact on the economy as a whole. They may thus be seen as a desirable method of raising government revenue, with an industrial sales tax being an almost equally attractive alternative.

The choice between these two interpretations depends on the weight given to government revenue relative to the efficiency losses associated with higher fuel prices and taxes. That remains a matter for future research.

Notes

1. The establishment of a consistent basis for valuing inputs and outputs can present major problems in implementing the model in different countries. It will be assumed that items are valued at producer prices—that is, on exit from the factory—or at farm-gate prices, which include taxes paid by producers. In this spirit the vector of factor prices, w, includes direct taxes such as payroll taxes, social security taxes, and profits taxes, which affect the cost of employing factors of production. Production subsidies, of course, are treated as negative taxes. Unfortunately, this approach, though relatively simple to implement for most developing countries, does pose problems of implementation for countries (Tunisia in this study) with differential rates of VAT or similar taxes on production.

2. This rule poses obvious problems in relation to major agricultural commodities when land is a binding constraint on production, because changes in total output may lead to changes in land rents and hence in the unit cost functions.

3. Further details on data sources and methods are available from the author. For Indonesia, the real price of gasoline (but not of other fuels) rose between 1975 and 1981, so an adjustment was built into the tax calculations to allow for this increase. In the case of the other countries, differences between the dates of the two primary data sources caused no difficulties.

4. For each country it has been assumed that 25 percent of gross fixed domestic capital formation is financed by the government, so that the increase in government expenditure caused by the price changes is the sum of the extra cost of government consumption plus one-quarter of the extra cost of gross investment, if we assume that the volume and composition of government consumption and gross investment are not altered by the relative price changes.

21

Pricing Publicly Supplied Goods and Services

Michael Katz

MANY GOODS AND SERVICES are supplied by governments, typically at prices below the costs of production. Most countries, for example, have public education systems in which education services are sold at heavily subsidized prices (often equal to zero). Similarly, many countries have publicly operated health services, public housing authorities, and government-run programs to provide drinking water.

The prices, quality, and availability of these publicly provided goods and services can have major impacts on the welfare of the population. Government provision of goods and services is likely to be particularly important in a developing nation, where the government may be the sole source of supply for many households. The majority of households may be totally dependent on the government for provision of health and education services, for example. The government may be a crucial supplier of food or may determine the supply of food indirectly through price controls.

As a supplier of a good or service, the government must choose the price at which to sell the output, the aggregate level of production, and the quality of the output. In providing schooling, for example, the government must choose the user fee, the total number of students to whom to offer education, and such dimensions of quality as the number of pupils per teacher, the educational attainment of the teachers, per pupil expenditures on textbooks, and the number of miles that students must travel to reach the school.

The government authority makes these choices subject to a budget constraint. The government, in its role as a producer, typically cannot sustain losses greater than some given level. If the government sets price at a low level and quality at a high level, it may be unable to afford to meet all of the demand that is generated. In order to satisfy its budget constraint, the authority must make tradeoffs between the good's price, its quality, and its total supply (the good may be rationed). These tradeoffs are likely to be very important in developing countries, where public budget constraints are tight.

The present chapter examines the welfare effects of making these tradeoffs for a publicly supplied good or service for which the aggregate subsidy is fixed. A completely general analysis of the problem would consider the simultaneous

560

determination of the entire tax system, treating the level of aggregate subsidy for the publicly provided good as one of the parameters of the system. The more limited case of a fixed aggregate subsidy examined here is of practical importance, however, for a number of reasons.

First, although there are clearly interactions between the pricing of publicly produced goods and the design of the overall commodity and income tax system, it may not be politically feasible to change the price of the publicly provided good and the overall tax system simultaneously. The analysis of a fixed aggregate subsidy is also relevant in cases where the government decentralizes its decisionmaking by granting the government health authority, say, a fixed budget with which to meet its goals. Finally, the possibility of rationing and the choice of product quality are the two features that set government supply decisions apart from usual questions of taxation, and it is useful to focus on these novel aspects of the problem by ignoring the more standard issues that arise when the government designs the remainder of the tax system.

A simple general equilibrium model with one publicly supplied good and one privately produced good, presented below, provides the framework for the analysis. I use this model to examine the efficiency and distributional consequences of marginally increasing the price of the publicly provided good in order to finance an increase in total output (the aggregate subsidy is held constant) when the good is subject to rationing. For simplicity, the level of product quality is held fixed. Conditions under which an increase in the user fee will raise consumer welfare are demonstrated, and these conditions are related to observable demand data. The key condition that determines whether a household is better off as a result of the price increase is whether the additional benefits from the increase in the household's ration allotment exceed the increase in the price that the household must pay for units of the good that would have been allotted to the household anyway.

I proceed to analyze the government's choice of product or service quality. Here the model is used to examine the efficiency and distributional consequences of marginally increasing the price of the good so as to finance an increase in quality (again, the aggregate subsidy is held constant). It is shown that some or all of the consumers of the publicly provided good may benefit from an increase in its price; the increase in the quality of the output supplied may more than compensate consumers of the good for the associated price rise. Moreover, such a price increase may redistribute income toward the poor. The minimal amount of data on the basis of which one could reasonably make predictions about welfare effects would be changes in household consumption levels that result from simultaneous price and quality changes. It is shown that, although the use of the change in consumption as a proxy for the change in welfare is not valid in all cases, the test is valid for several important cases, which I discuss.

I subsequently consider a method for increasing consumer welfare that requires essentially no a priori demand information. Households are presented with a menu of options, with one of the options being to have the original price, quality, and rationing level. Faced with this menu, each household chooses its most preferred combination of price, quality, and rationing. In effect, a household is allowed to purchase higher quality or shorter queues if it chooses to do so. Because the household's choice set is enlarged, the household cannot be made worse off by this policy. It is shown that quantity-dependent pricing may be used in a similar fashion to make Pareto-optimal policy improvements.

I briefly discuss the relationship between the fixed and variable subsidy cases. When the aggregate subsidy can be varied, there are additional tradeoffs between the subsidy to this good and the tax rates on other goods and income. The chapter closes with a brief summary.

A Model

Consider a two-good economy. Good 1 is the publicly produced good. Good 2 is the privately produced good and is taken as the numeraire, with a price equal to one. All agents are assumed to have zero initial endowments of good 1. A household's initial endowment of good 2 is positive and is denoted by n, which may be regarded as household income. Generalization to the case of an arbitrary number of goods would be straightforward.

Production of X units of good 1 with quality z requires $C(X, z)$ units of good 2 as input, where z is a measure of some attribute of the good such that all households value the good more highly if it has a higher level of z. Good 1 is sold at price p by the government, which is the sole producer of the good. As a producer, the government faces the following budget constraint:

$$(21\text{-}1) \qquad\qquad pX - C(X, z) + A \geq 0$$

where X is the aggregate amount of good 1 supplied and A is the fixed amount of aggregate subsidy for good 1. A is assumed to be exogenously generated (for example, it represents foreign aid) so that we can make the simplifying assumption that there are no other taxes or subsidies present in the economy.

The quantity that the government can supply will depend on both the price and the quality of the publicly supplied good. Let $S(p; z)$ denote the maximal quantity that the government can afford to produce when the quality level is z and the user price is p. This quantity is determined by the requirement that $S(p; z)$ must satisfy the social budget constraint, expression 21-1:

$$(21\text{-}2) \qquad\qquad pS(p, z) - C[S(p; z), z] + A = 0.$$

Holding quality fixed and varying the price, we can solve equation 21-2 for the maximal feasible quantity and can graph the supply curve for a good of given quality, as is illustrated in figure 21-1 for two quality levels. Clearly, a higher price makes it feasible to supply a greater quantity; the supply curve is upward sloping.

Figure 21-1. *Supply and Aggregate Demand for a Publicly Produced Good with Given Quality* z

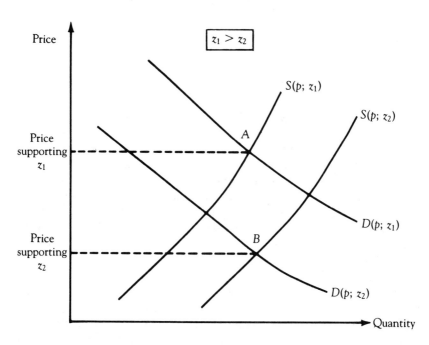

Now consider the demand side of the market. Faced with the price and quality of the publicly supplied good (which are set by the government), a household chooses its consumption levels to maximize its utility subject to any government-imposed rationing constraints and to its household budget constraint. Thus, in the absence of rationing, the household chooses its consumption levels of goods 1 and 2 (denoted by x and y, respectively) to

$$(21\text{-}3) \qquad \underset{x,\ y}{\text{Maximize}} \quad u(x, y, z) \qquad \text{subject to} \quad px + y \leq n.$$

At the household's maximum, it will spend all of its income on the two goods, and $px + y = n$. Thus, we can rewrite the household's problem as

$$(21\text{-}4) \qquad \underset{x}{\text{Maximize}} \quad u(x, n - px, z).$$

Differentiating expression 21-4 with respect to x, the household's first-order condition for utility maximization is

$$(21\text{-}5) \qquad \qquad u_x - pu_y = 0.$$

Let $x(p; z, n)$ denote the unrationed demand for the publicly provided good by a single household.

Summing demand over all of the households in the economy, let $D(p; z)$ denote the aggregate quantity of good 1 demanded when the price is p and the quality level is z. By holding quality fixed and varying the price, we can trace the aggregate demand curve for the publicly produced good with a given quality. Two such curves are illustrated in figure 21-1.

Price and Rationing Changes

Although the government could change the price, quality, and rationing scheme for the publicly provided good simultaneously, the exposition is simplified by considering pairwise changes. In this section, the possibility of rationing is considered, with the quality level held fixed. In the following section, it is assumed that the government changes the price and quality level to satisfy the social budget constraint, without resorting to rationing.

When the price of the publicly provided good is p, and the quality level is z, $D(p, z)$ units of the good will be demanded. The government may be unable to afford to meet all of the demand generated at that price. In response the government may ration the publicly provided good in order to satisfy the social budget constraint.

We can also apply the analysis of rationing to the case of price controls, where production and sales of the good are undertaken by private profit-maximizing firms. When production decisions are made by private firms that take the price ceiling into account, production will be insufficient, and rationing will be necessary if the government sets a price that is below the market-clearing level.

As long as there is excess demand at the current price, consumers will be willing to purchase the additional output even when the price is increased to finance the additional production. Thus, when the price is below p^e in figure 21-2, consumption is rationed, and a price increase leads to movement along the supply curve. (Here the supply curve has been drawn under the assumption of constant marginal costs.) When the price is above p^e, there is no rationing, and a price increase leads to movement along the demand curve (with equation 21-1 a strict inequality); total consumption falls, and clearly consumers are worse off. The analysis of this section focuses on the case in which the initial price is below the market-clearing level, so that a price increase leads to a movement along the supply curve and an increase in total consumption. In this case, the increased consumption benefits may outweigh the loss in consumer surplus due to the higher price. To determine whether a household gains or loses from a price increase, we must consider both supply and demand conditions.

The Price-Quantity Tradeoff

Consider the supply side of the market first. Suppose that the government raises the price of the publicly provided good, and for expositional conveni-

Figure 21-2. *Rationing of a Publicly Provided Good*

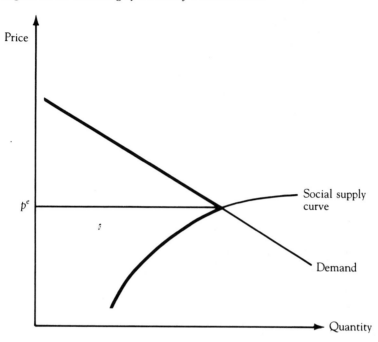

ence assume that the level of quality is fixed. If we totally differentiate the social budget constraint, equation 21-2, and rearrange terms, we obtain

$$(21\text{-}6) \qquad \frac{dS}{dp} = \frac{-S}{p - C_S}.$$

Note that here and throughout this section, z is suppressed in the notation, because quality is fixed. From equation 21-6, it is clear that rationing can be optimal only in those cases where $(p - C_S)$ is negative; if the price is greater than marginal cost, then increasing output (relaxing the rationing constraint) will raise "social profits," making it possible to increase the amount of good 1 supplied while lowering the price.

The Rationing Scheme

The welfare effects of raising the price and aggregate consumption of the publicly provided good (when $p < C_S$) depend on the way in which the additional output is distributed to households. The ration allotments must depend only on household characteristics that the government can observe. Suppose that the government cannot observe n directly but that it is able to observe some other characteristic, b, which may be some imperfect but observable measure of n. Alternatively, b may be some feature of the household that is not a proxy for income; for example, b may be the number of children.

For simplicity, assume that characteristic b has no direct effect on household utility or social welfare.

The rationing scheme is parameterized so that $x^r(b; S)$ denotes the rationing ceiling faced by a household with characteristic b when total output of the publicly supplied good is S. That is, the household is allowed to purchase and consume up to x^r units of the publicly produced good.

If a household's ration ceiling is greater than the quantity that the household would wish to purchase in the absence of rationing, then clearly the ceiling will have no effect. When a household is subject to a ration ceiling that is lower than the level that the household would like to consume, then the actual consumption level will be at the ceiling. Thus, the household's consumption level, $x^*\{p; x^r(b; S), n\}$, will be equal to its unrationed demand, $x(p; n)$, or its ration allotment, $x^r(b; S)$.

The government does not ration good 2. As before, the household spends all of its income on the two goods, and thus the household consumes $n - px^*[p; x^r(b; S), n]$ units of good 2.

The rationing scheme must satisfy the constraint that rationed consumption (summed over all households) is less than or equal to production,

$$(21\text{-}7) \qquad\qquad \sum_h x^{*h}[p; n, x^r(b; X)] \leq S$$

where the h superscript is the index denoting the household. It always is socially desirable to have all output that is produced consumed, and expression 21-7 will hold with equality under any efficient outcome.

For all consumers for whom the ceiling is binding, consumption is equal to $x^r(b; S)$, which is less than $x(p; n)$. The first-order condition for unrationed utility maximization, equation 21-5, implies that the ratio of marginal utilities is equal to the price ratio; $u_x/u_y = p$. Hence when rationing drives the consumption of x down and thus raises the consumption of y, $u_x/u_y > p$. For small price changes, this inequality will continue to hold. The household would like to trade consumption of the privately produced good for consumption of the publicly produced good at the prevailing prices. Thus, such a household will increase its consumption by the full amount of the increase in its ration ceiling; the change in consumption due to an increase in price and total output is $\partial x^r/\partial S$. For a household for which the ceiling is not binding, consumption is equal to the unrationed level, $x(p; n)$, and $u_x - pu_y = 0$. The only effect of a price and rationing shift comes through the price effect. The change in household consumption is $x_p \cdot dp/dS < 0$.

How is a household affected by an increase in price that is used to finance an increase in the aggregate quantity of the publicly produced good? The essential property of the rationing scheme is the relationship between the increase in consumption and the increase in payments. It is useful to think of the policy change in terms of an increase in the level of total output, S, and to treat the concomitant changes in the price and household ration levels as consequences. Suppose that the rationing constraint is binding. The change in household welfare from a unit change in total output is

(21-8) $(u_x - pu_y)\partial x^r/\partial S - x^r(dp/dS).$

The first term represents the increase in the household's utility from being allowed to shift some consumption from the privately produced good to the publicly produced good. The second term represents the loss in utility due to the increase in the price of the publicly produced good. In general, either effect may dominate.

How does the sign of expression 21-8 vary across income groups? One factor is the extent to which consumption by a given income group is distorted by the rationing scheme. Suppose that $u_{xy} \geq 0$, and the ration allotment is the same for all households. Then as income rises, $(n - px^r)$ rises, u_x rises, and the marginal utility of income u_y falls (given $u_{yy} < 0$). The other variables in expression 21-8 are constant across income groups. Hence the rich will favor an increase in the price and total output more than will low-income households. That is, there will be a critical income level such that all richer households benefit from the policy shift, whereas all poorer households are made worse off. The intuitive reasoning is the following. When the publicly provided good is a normal one and all households are forced to have the same level of consumption, high-income households find their consumption more distorted than do low-income households. High-income households have the most to gain from a marginal relaxation of the rationing ceiling. At the same time, all income groups bear equal shares of the additional costs of production.[1]

Admissions-Test Rationing

There is an important special case of the rationing scheme described above. In many significant markets, rationing takes the form of a nonprice admission decision. Aptitude tests or school records, for example, are used as the basis of admission decisions to college or secondary school. The decision as to whether to permit hospitalization or to transfer to a more sophisticated facility may depend on a measure of the severity of the illness.[2] In some cases, whether or not a given household is allowed to purchase the rationed good may essentially be decided randomly, for example in the case of queues for subsidized housing. In all of these examples, each household faces either a ceiling of zero or no ceiling, depending on whether its value of the test statistic is above or below some standard or, in the case of a random allocation, on whether the household was lucky.

Formally, this type of scheme can be modeled by interpreting b as the test statistic and letting $\hat{b}$ denote the cutoff value. Then, this type of rationing scheme has the form

(21-9) $x^r(b; S) = \begin{cases} 0 \text{ for all } b < \hat{b} \\ \infty \text{ for all } b \geq \hat{b}. \end{cases}$

The cutoff value $\hat{b}$ is set high enough to ensure that the quantity demanded by households meeting the standards is just equal to the quantity supplied (that is, $\hat{b}$ is set to satisfy expression 21-7 with equality).

Raising the price and the total amount supplied will make it possible for the government to lower the cutoff value; $d\hat{b}/dp < 0$. If a household met the standard prior to the price increase, then the reduction in $\hat{b}$ is of no value to that household. Therefore, such a household is made worse off by the shift because the household must pay more for the service that it would have been allowed to purchase anyway. A household that fails to meet the admissions standard before or after the price increase is obviously unaffected by the policy change. The only households that can gain from the price increase are those that failed to meet the standard at the original level but meet it at the new level. These households cannot be worse off, because they could continue to buy none of good 1. They may be strictly better off; purchasing the good at the new price will typically yield positive consumer surplus.

Consider the average effects across income classes. Households with the same level of income may have different values of b. We must consider the expected effects of a price and output shift on a household with income n, taking the expectation over the possible values of b. Let $f^n(b)$ denote the probability that a household has a test score of b, given that it has income n. The change in the expected utility of a household with income n from a (unit) marginal change in price is:

$$(21\text{-}10) \quad [u(x, n - px) - u(0, n)]f^n(\hat{b})(-d\hat{b}/dp) - xu_y \int_{\hat{b}}^{\infty} f^n(b)db.$$

The first term represents the additional utility that the household derives from being allowed to purchase the publicly supplied good multiplied by the household's chance of being at the admissions margin times the change in the cutoff level. In the second term, x is the quantity purchased by a household that is not subject to the zero consumption ceiling. The term $\int_{\hat{b}}^{\infty} f^n(b)db$ is the probability that a household with income n will be above the cutoff level. Thus, the second term represents the welfare effects of the price rise, because a household above the cutoff level will have to pay xdp more for the output that it was purchasing prior to the shift.

As before, the burden of the price increase (given by the second term) is distributed according to preshift consumption levels. The benefits are given by the increase in the chance that the household is allowed to purchase the publicly supplied good. Households at the admissions margin benefit from a price increase that is used to finance expansion of supply, whereas households already meeting the standard bear the costs but receive no benefits from expansion.

An income group is most likely to benefit from the price and output increases if its members were unlikely to have been allowed to purchase the service before the changes but had values of b near the cutoff level. If b is highly correlated with income, for example, then households currently allowed to purchase the good will tend to have higher incomes than those households that are at the margin of being allowed to purchase. Hence in this sense, a price *increase* and accompanying reduction in the cutoff level will be a *progressive* policy move. Armitage and Sabot (chapter 22) suggest that this relationship holds for the case of admission to secondary school in Kenya.

Data Requirements

For the theory to be of use, the planner must be able to estimate the values of the key parameters in the model. In order to calculate the set of feasible price and total output pairs, the government needs to know its cost function and the overall level of subsidy available. To know which rationing schemes are feasible, the planner must also have information about the quantities demanded by households at the proposed price. Observation of present consumption levels may provide reasonable estimates of these quantities.

The estimation of the parameters needed to make welfare calculations is likely to pose much greater difficulty. Given sufficient data, the planner could estimate a complete system of household demand equations and the underlying utility functions (subject to certain integrability conditions). These utility functions then could be used to calculate indifference curves or actual changes in utility levels.

Typically, however, the government will not have sufficient data or resources to estimate a complete system of household demands. Recognizing these constraints, the analysis in this section focuses on the extent to which the government can make inferences about the sign of household welfare changes solely on the basis of a simple and intuitively appealing test: taking the change in the household's consumption level that is due to the shift in the price and rationing scheme as a proxy for changes in household welfare.

When households are subject to a rationing scheme of the first type considered above [where a household with characteristic b faces a ceiling of $x^{\tau}(b; S)$], changes in household consumption levels yield relatively little information about changes in welfare. Clearly, if a household's consumption falls when the price rises and the rationing scheme is altered, then household welfare falls. If a household's consumption rises at the same time that the price is raised, however, we cannot in general tell whether household welfare has risen or fallen. If for simplicity we assume away income effects, household welfare is given by the area under the demand curve and above the price line, as shown in figure 21-3. As drawn, household consumption will be equal to the rationing ceiling before and after the policy shift. The level of utility will increase only if the increase in consumer surplus due to the extra consumption (area $abde$) is greater than the loss in surplus due to the price increase (area $cdfg$). The level of consumption will increase in response to a relaxation of the rationing constraint as long as the price is less than marginal utility. As illustrated in figure 21-3, even though consumption rises, area $abde$ is less than $cdfg$, and household utility declines. Some inferences are possible, however. From the diagram, we can see that households with near-zero consumption levels under the old ceiling are very likely to gain from any policy that raises their consumption under the new ceiling.

Figure 21-3. *Rationing: Changes in Consumer Surplus*

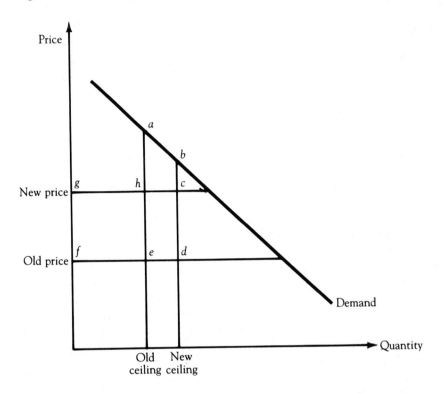

For the case of an admissions-type rationing scheme as given in equation 21-9, the change in a household's level of consumption is a much more powerful measure of the change in welfare. The inferences that can be drawn from consumption data are straightforward and immediate. Suppose that the household faces a ration ceiling of zero under the old price and has a positive consumption level under the new, higher price. Prior to the price increase, consumer surplus is zero. Under the new price and relaxed rationing constraint, surplus is positive. In terms of figure 21-3, area *abde* will be larger than area *cdfg* because area *efgh* is equal to zero. Thus, if a price rise allows the government to expand its output, those households that choose to purchase the service and were previously excluded from receiving the service definitely benefit from the price increase. The households that were admitted under the old ceiling are of course made worse off by the price increase; consumption will fall for a non-Giffen good.

Optimal Pricing

Thus far we have examined the effects of a policy shift on the welfare of a single household. This approach is helpful for understanding the distributional consequences of a policy change and can reveal Pareto-optimal changes. The government may, however, wish to choose among prices where in moving from one price to another there are gainers and losers.

The planner must have some sort of social welfare function in order to compare the losses suffered by some households with the gains enjoyed by others when choosing its pricing policy. To understand the form of the government's social welfare function, we must answer the question "why is the government intervening in the market at all rather than relying on private supply?" Possible motives for government intervention (subsidization) in the market for the publicly produced good include (1) income redistribution goals (see, for an example, Wilson and Katz, 1983); (2) economies of scale in production (so that there is a conflict between marginal cost pricing and covering average costs); (3) the failure of a profit-maximizing monopolist to provide the optimal level of quality (see Spence, 1975); (4) externalities in the consumption of the subsidized good; (5) government paternalism (so-called merit goods); and (6) the presence of capital market imperfections (so that consumers cannot borrow against future income or there are incomplete markets for the risk associated with investment in education).[3]

Under motives 1, 2, and 3, the government does not care about consumption levels per se; it is concerned with the resulting utility levels. We can express the social welfare as a function of household utility levels, which are in turn functions of household consumption levels:

(21-11) $W = G[u^1(x^1, y^1, z), \ldots, u^h(x^h, y^h, z), \ldots, u^H(x^H, y^H, z)].$

H is the number of households in the economy (I have included the quality notation here because this welfare function will be used in the next section as well). A useful and tractable special case of W is one in which

(21-12) $$G(u^1, \ldots, u^h, \ldots, u^H) = \sum_h u^h.$$

Objectives 4, 5, and 6 are all similar to one another in that, from the government's perspective, households will choose to consume too little of x relative to y. The following function captures this type of relationship between social welfare and individual utility:

(21-13) $$W = \sum_h [u^h(x^h, y^h, z) + E(x^h)]$$

where dE/dx^h is greater than zero. The values u and E are normalized so that $E(0) = 0$. The term $E(x^h)$ is the level of external (or perhaps we should say "paternal") benefits that arise when a household consumes x units of the publicly provided good. The term $E(x^h)$ is the amount by which the government values household h's consumption of the publicly supplied good more than the household itself does.

When the social welfare function is of the form given in equation 21-13, the change in welfare is given by the household utility effects and external effects aggregated over all households. Suppose that the rationing scheme is such that

$x^r(b; S)$ is differentiable with respect to S (that is, small changes in the overall supply lead to small changes in any given household's ration ceiling). The change in social welfare from a marginal increase in the level of total output and the accompanying price increase is

$$(21\text{-}14) \quad \sum_h [(u_x^h - pu_y^h)(dx^{rh}/dS) - x^h u_y^h(dp/dS)] + \sum_h E'(dx^{rh}/dS)$$

$$= \sum_h (u_x^h + E')(dx^{rh}/dS) - \sum_h u_y^h [p(dx^{rh}/dS) + x^h(dp/dS)].$$

Under the admissions cutoff type of rationing scheme, a small change in S may lead to a jump in $x^r(b; S)$ for a household that is on the admissions margin. For this type of rationing, the change in welfare is given by

$$(21\text{-}15) \qquad \sum_{h \in M} [u^h(x^h, n^h - px^h) - u^h(0, n^h) + E(x^h)$$
$$- E(0)] - \sum_{h \in M} x^h u_y^h$$

where M is the set of households at the admissions margin. The first sum in equation 21-14 or expression 21-15 represents the private and public (external) increases in gross consumption benefits. The additional revenues raised are equal to the additional costs of production; $Sdp + pdS = C_x dS$. Thus the second sum in each of formulas 21-14 and 21-15 represents the social cost to consumers of additional output (the cost weighted by the social marginal utility of income of those consumers who bear the additional cost). For a given level of production costs, the socially weighted costs will be lower when u_y and x are negatively correlated than when they are positively correlated.

More generally, the essential features of any rationing scheme are whether marginal output is distributed in a socially efficient way and whether the marginal revenues are raised in a socially efficient way. The marginal social benefits of the additional output depend on the covariance of u_x and dx^r/dS across households. When those consumers receiving the additional output are the ones for which the social marginal utility of consumption is high, the price and output increases will be more likely to raise welfare. The social costs depend largely on the relationship between u_y and x^r. When those consumers with low social marginal utilities of income are the ones who pay the largest share of the increased costs (that is, the ones who consume large amounts of the publicly provided good prior to the price increase), the socially weighted costs will be low. Thus, the price increase will be more likely to be socially beneficial when u_y and x^r are negatively correlated. Finally, note that a price and output increase is more likely to lead to a welfare increase when there are strong externalities so that the increase in consumption has a high marginal social value.

What about consumption data and aggregate welfare changes? Given the difficulty in evaluating individual welfare changes, it is not surprising that we can say little in general about the overall welfare changes. To see why, continue the assumption of no income effects and, furthermore, assume that all households are identical, so that it is valid to consider a representative

Figure 21-4. *Small Price Rise with External Benefits*

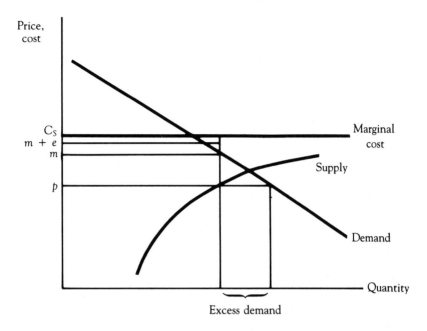

Excess demand

household. Clearly, this case is the one for which we have the greatest chance of being able to make correct inferences. As illustrated in figure 21-4, however, even in this case an increase in consumption does not indicate an increase in aggregate welfare when price is set below marginal cost (recall from equation 21-6 that rationing is never optimal when price equals or exceeds marginal cost). For households with a binding rationing constraint, the gain in utility from a marginal unit of good is m, which is greater than p. There is excess demand, and an increase in the price leads to an increase in the total amount of the good consumed as output moves along the social supply curve generated by the budget constraint. The increase in social benefits is the sum of the increases in the household and external benefits, $(m + e)$, where e is the level of external benefits measured in monetary units. For sufficiently weak externalities, $(m + e)$ is less than C_S even though m is greater than p. Thus, the increase in social benefits is less than the increase in social costs. A small price rise may lead to inefficiently high consumption.

Price and Quality Changes

In this section, it is assumed that the government does not ration the publicly provided good. Instead, the planner adjusts the price and quality levels to satisfy the social budget constraint while meeting all of the demand that is generated.

The Government's Price-Quality Tradeoff

Suppose that the government raises the price of the publicly provided good in order to finance a change in the quality level, z. Again, we must consider both the supply and the demand for the good in order to find the set of price and quality levels that are feasible. In the absence of rationing, the quantity supplied must be equal to the quantity demanded in equilibrium, or

$$(21\text{-}16) \qquad\qquad S(p; z) = D(p; z).$$

This condition yields the set of feasible price and quality combinations. If p and z satisfy equation 21-16, then the government can afford to meet the demand for the good at this price and quality. Points A and B in figure 21-1 are two such price/quality pairs. The feasible pairs can be found algebraically by substituting equation 21-16 into the social budget constraint, equation 21-2, to obtain

$$(21\text{-}17) \qquad\qquad pD(p; z) - C[D(p; z), z] + A = 0.$$

For any particular price of the publicly provided good, equation 21-17 can be solved to find the maximal quality level for which the government can afford to meet demand at that price. The only way for the government to provide still higher quality without rationing or violating the social budget constraint is to adjust the price of the good.

Consider increasing the user fee charged for the publicly provided good by dp. Totally differentiating equation 21-17 and rearranging terms, we obtain

$$(21\text{-}18) \qquad dz/dp = -[(p - C_x)D_p + D]/[(p - C_x)D_z + C_z]$$
$$= -\pi_p(p, z)/\pi_z(p, z)$$

where $\pi(p, z) = pD(p; z) - C[D(p; z), z]$ is the public producer's profit as a function of price and quality. Thus, the denominator is the change in the producer's profits due to the quality change. Because quality is set at a level as high as is feasible, given the price and the social budget constraint, it must be the case that $\pi_z < 0$; otherwise the planner could afford to raise z while holding p constant. The numerator is minus one times the change in the producer's profits due to the price change. If p is greater than the monopoly price (for the given quality level), then profits will fall as price rises because of the cutback in the quantity demanded. In this case, dz/dp will be negative; the decrease in profits makes the government less able to afford providing the publicly supplied good at its current quality level. Therefore, any price increase above the monopoly level would be unambiguously bad—the price would rise, and the quality would fall.

When price is initially below the monopoly level, an increase in the user fee will lead to an increase in profits, which can be used to finance additional quality. In this case, there is a tradeoff between price and quality. Figure 21-5 illustrates the resulting upward slope in the government's "production possibility frontier" for price and quality (that is, the set of all price and quality pairs

Figure 21-5. *Change in Household Welfare, p' Preferred to p''*

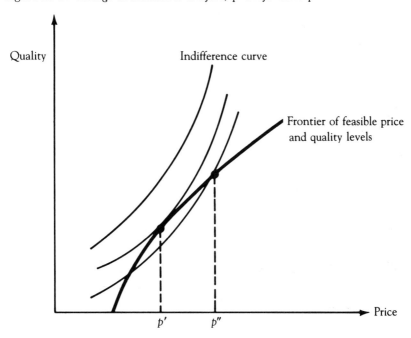

such that the government can meet demand while satisfying the social budget constraint).

The Household's Price-Quality Indifference Curve

Is a household better off or worse off when the government raises price and quality along its price-quality frontier? To answer this question, we must compare the rate at which the household is willing to make tradeoffs between price and quality with the rate at which the government can make these tradeoffs.

The maximized value of the household's utility when it faces price p and quality z is found by substituting the quantities demanded into the utility function:

$$(21\text{-}19) \qquad u[x(p; z, n), n - px(p; z, n), z].$$

Differentiating this expression with respect to price and quality, the change in the household's welfare from a price-quality shift is given by

$$(21\text{-}20) \qquad du = -xu_y dp + u_z dz.$$

The first term represents the loss in the household's utility due to the price increase. We can regard u_y as the marginal utility of income, and xdp is the extra amount of income that the consumer has to spend to pay for x units of the publicly provided good. The second term in equation 21-20 represents the gain from the increase in product quality.

For any given price and quality pair, we can calculate all of the other combinations of price and quality that yield the same level of utility. These combinations trace the household's indifference curves for p and z. Starting from the original p and z, we look for changes in price and quality, dp and dz, such that du is equal to zero. Solving equation 21-20 for dz in terms of dp, we obtain the slope of the indifference curve: $dz/dp = xu_y/u_z$. The household's indifference map is illustrated in figure 21-5. The indifference curves are upward sloping to reflect the fact that the consumer prefers low price and high quality.

The Change in Household Welfare

From figure 21-5 we see that the sign of the change in utility when the government moves from p' to p'' is determined by whether the indifference curve is flatter or steeper than the government's production possibility frontier. Thus, we must compare $-\pi_p/\pi_z$ with xu_y/u_z. In general, welfare may rise or fall; a household may *gain or lose* when the price and quality are increased. The steeper the frontier (that is, the larger $-\pi_p/\pi_z$), the more likely it is that the household's utility will increase as a result of the price rise.

Planners are often interested in the distributional effects of a policy move and the way in which the change in household welfare varies across income groups. One case is of particular interest, both because of its simple functional form and because it is a dividing line. Suppose that utility can be written as $u[\rho(z)x, n - px]$. In effect, each unit of the publicly provided good is equivalent to $\rho(z)$ quality-adjusted units. This form of utility is known as "pure repackaging" because it includes the case of goods where $\rho(z)$ is the amount of service provided by one unit, or "box," of the good. According to this interpretation, x boxes yield $\rho(z)x$ units of service, and changes in z can be thought of as changes in the box size, or "repackaging." As will be seen in the next section, utility functions of this form go well beyond the case of true repackaging, and such a utility function is implied by the common functional form of a demand curve that is linear in the logarithms of price and quality.

In the so-called pure repackaging case, $p/\rho(z)$ can be regarded as the quality-adjusted (or hedonic) price of good 1, because each unit of the good provides $\rho(z)$ quality-adjusted units of service at a cost to the household of p. A household's utility will rise if and only if the hedonic price falls. All households will agree on whether this hedonic price is increased by a given price and quality shift, and the *sign* of the welfare effects will not vary across income classes, because we have assumed that $\rho(z)$ is the same for all consumers.

To verify this intuition, note that differentiation of $u\{\rho(z)x, n - px\}$ with respect to quality yields $du/dz = u_1\rho_z x$. If we substitute the first-order condition for utility maximization, equation 21-5, into this expression, $du/dz = (pu_2/\rho)\rho_z x$.[4] Further substitution into equation 21-20 yields

$$(21-21) \qquad du = -xu_2\,dp + (pu_2/\rho)\rho_z x\,dz$$
$$= pu_2 x(\rho_z dz/\rho - dp/p)$$

the sign of which is independent of x and is thus independent of income, n. According to equation 21-21, household utility rises if and only if p falls proportionately faster than $\rho(z)$ rises (that is, if and only if the hedonic price, $p/\rho(z)$, falls).

More generally, the way in which welfare effects vary across income groups depends on the way in which the burden of the price increase and the benefits of the quality increase are distributed across income classes. From equation 21-20, we can see that the burden of the price increase, $xu_y\,dp$, rises proportionately with consumption. If x is a normal good, a household's consumption rises with income, and richer households bear a larger burden of the price increase (in terms of increased expenditures). How do the benefits of the increased quality vary with the level of consumptions and thus with income?

In the pure repackaging case, the value of the additional quality rises proportionately with x. Thus, the burden of the price increase and the benefits of the quality increase rise at the same rate, and the signs of the household utility changes are the same for all income classes. For more general utility functions, the valuation of the additional quality may rise proportionately more or less than the level of consumption. The net benefits of the price and quality changes may therefore rise or fall with household income. If the benefits derived from a marginal quality increase rise less than proportionately with the quantity consumed, we obtain the surprising result that the poor may benefit from a price increase while the rich are harmed. One example in which the poor would benefit from a price and quality increase would be if utility took the form

$$u(x, y, z) = \begin{cases} x + y^{1/2} + z & \text{if } x > 0, \\ y^{1/2} & \text{if } x = 0 \end{cases}$$

Data Requirements

In order to calculate the set of feasible price and quality pairs, the government needs to know its cost function, the overall level of subsidy available, and the aggregate demand for the publicly produced good. Obtaining these data should pose *comparatively* little difficulty. The estimation of individual price-quality indifference curves is much more problematical. Again, given sufficient data, the planner could estimate a complete sytem of household demand equations and the underlying utility functions or indifference curves. Such estimation, however, is likely to be impractical. Hence the analysis of this section examines the extent to which the government can make inferences about the sign of household welfare changes by taking the change in the household's consumption level due to the price-quality shift as a proxy for changes in household welfare. As with rationing, there is one case in which this test is clearly valid. If a price and quality shift induces a household to raise its consumption of the publicly produced good from zero units to some positive number of units, then the price-quality shift raises that household's welfare.

Unfortunately, when initial consumption levels are positive, this test is not, in general, valid. The fact that a household raises its consumption of the publicly provided good in response to simultaneous changes in the good's price and quality does not imply that the household is better off as a result of the changes. Fortunately, however, using observable demand data solely for the publicly provided good, we can determine whether the test is valid for any particular application.

To see the difficulty with applying the test in general, suppose that the household utility function is separable in the consumption of the two goods:

$$(21\text{-}22) \qquad u(x, y, z) = \phi(x, z) + \theta(y).$$

If we solve for the comparative statics of the consumer's utility maximization problem, equation 21-19, a household increases its consumption in response to the price and quality shifts if and only if

$$(21\text{-}23) \qquad (px u_{yy} - u_y)dp + u_{xz} dz > 0.$$

Dividing equation 21-20 by x, we see that household utility increases if and only if

$$(21\text{-}24) \qquad -u_y dp + (1/x)u_z dz > 0.$$

The difference between expressions 21-23 and 21-24 is

$$(21\text{-}25) \qquad px u_{yy} dp + [u_{xz} - (1/x)u_z]dz.$$

The first term represents the income effect of a price change on the demand for x. The term in brackets is equal to the difference between the value of the extra quality in the marginal unit and the value of the extra quality averaged across all units.

Ignoring the income effect for the moment, we see that a household's willingness to pay for a marginal unit of the publicly provided good (the household demand curve) is given by $u_x = \phi_x$. Thus, $u_{xz}(x, y, z)$ is the amount by which a quality increase raises the value of the xth unit of the publicly provided good and shifts the demand curve upward. In the absence of income effects, the utility derived from consumption of the publicly provided good is equal to the area under the household's demand curve. As figure 21-6(a) illustrates, utility will rise only if the upward shift in the demand curve due to the quality increase is on average greater than the price rise. Although utility changes depend on the relationship between the price rise and the *average* shift in the demand curve $\{(1/x)u_z(x, y, z)dz\}$, the change in the level of consumption depends on the relationship between the price increase and the shift in the

Figure 21-6. Quality Increase: (a) Utility Change Depends on Price Rise and Demand Shift, and (b) Consumption Rises If New Price Is Less Than p_2

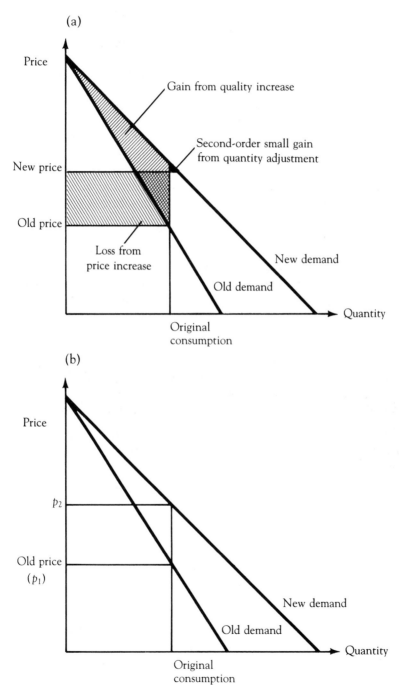

demand curve at the *margin* $[u_{xz}(x, y, z)dz]$. Thus, in figure 21-6(b), consumption will rise as long as the price rise is less than $p_2 - p_1$. When the shift in the demand curve at the margin exceeds the average shift, consumption of the publicly supplied good may rise while utility falls. When the marginal shift is less than the average shift in the demand curve, however, a price-quality shift may raise a household's utility even though it induces the household to consume less of the publicly supplied good.

If the publicly produced good is a normal good, then $u_{yy} \leq 0$. Hence, if the term in brackets in expression 21-25 is negative, then whenever expression 21-23 is satisfied, so too is expression 21-24. This term will be negative when u_{xz} is negative, and the value of the extra quality is lower at the margin than on average. In this case, any shift in price and quality that induces a household to increase its consumption of the publicly provided good also raises that household's utility. Thus, if policymakers believe that a quality increase raises a consumer's willingness to pay for the good by more for initial units of consumption than for later units, then a price and quality increase that raises the household's consumption level also raises its welfare. The government has available a one-sided test in this case.

A more practical way to identify cases for which the test is valid is to look at the form of the demand function for the publicly produced good.[5] Consider the earlier pure repackaging case. By the analysis of the previous subsection, a household's utility will rise if and only if the hedonic price, $p/\rho(z)$, falls when p and z are changed. The quantity change test is therefore valid in the pure repackaging if the change in quantity is indicative of the change in the hedonic price. If we assume that the publicly produced good is not a Giffen good, a fall in the hedonic price will raise the quality-adjusted consumption level, $x\rho(z)$. When z increases, however, a rise in $x\rho(z)$ may be accompanied by a fall in x. Thus, the use of the change in consumption, x, as a proxy for a change in welfare is valid in one direction only. Let us summarize this finding:

If the household utility can be expressed in the form $u[x\rho(z), y]$, then a price and quality increase that raises household consumption of the publicly produced good raises household utility.

As stated earlier, the pure repackaging case does not apply solely to the size of the box. A necessary and sufficient condition for the pure repackaging function to hold is that household expenditures on the publicly produced good, $px(p, z, n)$, can be expressed in the form $F[g(p, z), n]$ (proposition 3 of Willig, 1978). In this case, we can express utility as a pure repackaging function, and $p\rho(z) = g(p, z)$. The functional form for household expenditures on the good is restricted so that all of the interaction effects between income and the price and quality of the publicly produced good come through the $g(p, z)$ term.[6]

To determine whether or not the pure repackaging form is valid, the planner must examine the functional forms of demand for, and expenditures on, the publicly produced good. It turns out that an important functional form often fitted to demand data falls into this category. Suppose that demand is linear with the familiar log-log form

$$(21\text{-}26) \qquad \log x = \alpha + \beta \log p + \gamma \log z + \delta \log n$$

where α, β, γ, and δ are coefficients of the demand function. This specification is equivalent to

$$(21\text{-}27) \qquad x = \xi p^{\beta} z^{\gamma} n^{\delta}$$

where $\xi = \exp(\alpha)$. If we multiply by the price to obtain expenditures,

$$(21\text{-}28) \qquad px = p^{\beta+1} z^{\gamma} \xi n^{\delta}.$$

This equation is of the form $px(p, z, n) = F[g(p, z), n]$, with $F[g, n] = g\xi n^{\delta}$ and $g(p, z) = p^{\beta+1} z^{\gamma}$. Therefore, when demand is of the log-log form, any increase in p and q that raises household consumption also raises household utility.

There is another important class of utility functions for which the direction of utility changes can be inferred from the direction of consumption changes. Suppose that the household utility function can be written in the form $u[x, y + xf(z)]$. To see intuitively how such a functional form might arise, suppose that the publicly produced good is medical care. Then z may be the distance that the consumer has to travel to reach the health facility, x the number of trips made to the facility, and y household purchases of transportation services. An improvement in the quality of health care in the form of closer facilities will reduce the amount of travel that is necessary and may be equivalent to giving the consumer $xf_z(z)dz$ units of transportation service. Alternatively, y may be privately produced health care and z some measure of the quality of the publicly provided health care such that an increase in z allows the household to attain a given level of health and utility while reducing purchases of private health care.

Given this form of utility function (discussed by Willig, 1978), household demand for the publicly produced good can be expressed in the form

$$(21\text{-}29) \qquad x[p - f(z), n].$$

Here $[p - f(z)]$ can be regarded as the hedonic price of the publicly produced good. For a non-Giffen good, household consumption and utility will rise if and only if $[p - f(z)]$ falls:

If household utility is of the form $u[x, y + f(z)]$, then a price and quality shift raises household utility if and only if it raises household consumption of the publicly produced good.

Note that this test is stronger than the earlier one because here a fall in the quantity purchased indicates that household utility has decreased.

Several specifications of demand that are commonly used imply that the underlying utility function is of this form. Suppose, for example, that the investigator finds the linear demand specification appropriate:

(21-30) $$x = \alpha + \beta p + \gamma z + \delta n.$$

If we define $f(z) = -\gamma z/\beta$, equation 21-30 can be written in the form $x\{p - f(z), n\} = \alpha + \beta\{p - f(z)\} + \delta n$. Hence a demand function of the form given by equation 21-30 falls within the class of demand functions given by equation 21-29. Therefore, when the household's quantity demanded is a linear function of price, quality, and income, the use of the change in consumption as an indicator of the change in welfare is appropriate.

Finally, suppose that the researcher fits a log-linear function to the data. Then

$$\log x = \alpha + \beta p + \gamma z + \delta n$$

which is equivalent to

(21-31) $$x = \exp(\alpha + \beta p + \gamma z + \delta n).$$

In this case, demand can be written in the form of equation 21-29 by taking $f(z) = \gamma z/\beta$ and $x[p - f(z), n] = \exp\{\alpha + \beta[p - f(z)] + \delta n\}$. Hence, when the logarithm of the household's quantity demanded is a linear function of price, quality, and income, the use of the change in consumption as an indicator of the change in welfare is appropriate.[7]

In summary, the analysis of this subsection shows that, although the signs of the changes in utility and consumption may in general differ, there are several important cases for which the two signs will agree. The change in consumption can often serve as a proxy for the change in welfare in cases of practical interest.

Socially Optimal Pricing

When the social welfare function is of the additive form given in equation 21-13, the change in welfare is given by the household utility effects and external effects aggregated over all households:

(21-32) $$\sum_h u_z^h dz - \sum_h x^h u_y^h dp + \sum_h E'(x_p^h dp + x_z^h dz).$$

The first two sums in equation 21-32 are the effects of price and quality shifts on household utility, as before. The final sum is the change in the level of external benefits that results from the change in consumption of the publicly supplied good. This term may be positive or negative.

Other things being equal, the price and quality changes are most likely to increase social welfare when households with high levels of consumption (x^h) are ones for which the marginal utility of income (u_y^h) is low, so that the social burden of the cost increase is low. If poor households value additional quality highly but have low levels of consumption *prior* to the price-quality shift, then an increase in price and quality is likely to be socially desirable when the government has a progressive welfare function. A price increase and concomitant quality rise are also more likely to be socially beneficial when the external effects (E') are strong and the changes lead to increased consumption levels.

Unfortunately, the data requirements are much more severe when determining whether a feasible price and quality shift raises social, rather than household, welfare. The difficulty arises because it is necessary to calculate the magnitude of the household utility changes, not just their sign. For certain special cases, we may be able to say something on the basis of changes in individual consumption levels. In the case of strong redistributional motive, if the conditions described in the preceding subsection are satisfied, then a price and quality shift that raises the consumption levels of the poorest households is likely to increase social welfare. If the external effects are strong, the third term in equation 21-32 may dominate. The government can tell the sign of this term by observing the change in x^h for each household.

Menus of Options for Consumers

Thus far, the analysis has focused on the provision of a good or service with a single price and either a single quality level or a single rationing scheme. The government may, however, be able to provide the good or service at several different prices, with varying levels of quality or strictness of the rationing constraint. By offering a menu of consumption options in such cases, the government can implement a Pareto-improving policy that requires no data about consumer preferences.

First, consider that the government offers several different quality levels. Different quality levels of health care could be made available, for example, with higher levels of care having higher user fees. Essentially such a scheme would allow households to purchase quality. In the analysis of a single quality offering, raising the price to finance additional quality could lead to lower welfare for some or all households. The welfare losses occurred when a household lost more from the price increase than it gained from the quality increase. Such losses cannot arise when the government offers a high-quality, high-price option while retaining the original low-quality, low-price service—a household can always remain with its original service. Thus even in the absence of any demand information, the planner can be sure that no household has reduced utility as a result of the policy.

This type of plan will be feasible as long as the costs of administration are not too great, and there are not overly severe cost diseconomies associated with offering multiple options. In order to be able to retain the original option, the government must set the price of the new options so that they cover their incremental costs (minus any subsidy that the households would have received buying the original option). Thus, when these technical considerations are satisfied, Pareto improvements in welfare can be made by allowing households to purchase quality at cost.

The same value of offering options to households arises in the case of rationing as well. Suppose, for example, that the government constructs housing that it then rents at subsidized prices and that there is a shortage of housing. The extent of rationing can be measured by the length of time that the consumer must wait to obtain housing. If the government were to charge higher rents, it could finance a more rapid construction program. Some consumers might prefer to wait rather than pay higher rents. The government could operate two programs. One would hold the length of waiting and rents at their present levels. The other would involve a shorter queue but higher rents. Again, each household would be free to choose the program in which it participated. Because participation in the high-price, short-queue program would be optional, only those consumers who preferred it to the original program would participate. As long as the households participating in the new program are receiving subsidies (relative to marginal costs) that are no larger than those that they would have received had they participated in the original plan, the government will be able to continue to offer the old option. Thus, consumers who do not switch to the new option will be unaffected, and the new option will be a Pareto improvement.

One way to generate subsidy-free options is to allow private provision of the good. (In chapter 22, Armitage and Sabot discuss privately supplied education.) Given the analysis of this section, we obtain the following powerful policy conclusion about the desirability of competition from the private sector:

> Social welfare is raised if unsubsidized private suppliers are allowed to compete with the government to serve households to which the government offers prices that are less than or equal to the government's marginal costs of supply.

Care must be taken in applying this conclusion. In the presence of adverse selection or externalities, calculation of the government's marginal cost of supply may be difficult. Consider first the problem of adverse selection. Suppose that the government offers health care services such that, on average, price is below marginal cost but some individual services are priced above cost. If private competition is allowed, profit-maximizing providers are likely to seek the patronage of those patients who need services that the government sells at prices greater than cost. The government health authority may find itself left with only those patients who seek heavily subsidized services. Faced with a limited budget, the health authority may be forced to raise prices, to lower quality, or to institute more stringent rationing for its remaining patients, making those households worse off.

More generally, across-the-board private sector competition will limit the government's ability to engage in cross-subsidization, which may lower social welfare. When the government practices cross-subsidization, the conclusion that private sector competition is desirable holds only for the *subset* of services that are provided by the government at less than marginal cost.

Similar issues may arise when some households confer positive externalities on others through their consumption of the publicly provided service. Consider education, for example. Good students may confer positive externalities on their classmates. If the government charges students of all ability levels the same price, then, in effect, high-ability students may be cross-subsidizing low-ability students. Private schools might attempt to pull away high-ability students, leaving the public schools with only those of low ability. As a result, low-ability students could be made worse off by private sector competition. To ensure that private sector competition is desirable, it must be the case that high-ability students are being charged less than true social marginal cost by public schools, where the nominal marginal cost is adjusted downward by the value of the positive externality. If this condition holds, then the government resources saved when high-ability students are no longer served can be used to compensate—even to reward—the remaining, low-ability students for their loss.

The menu of options need not consist solely of different quality levels offered at different prices. Quantity-dependent pricing, whereby the price paid per unit of the good varies with the amount that the household purchases (for example, quantity discounts), can also be used to create new options. Consumers would face a menu of price/quantity offerings. The use of such quantity-dependent pricing deserves more serious consideration and greater application than it has seen to date. This conclusion follows from the following important fact:

> For any rationing scheme of the form discussed in "The Rationing Scheme," above, there is a feasible quantity-dependent pricing scheme that Pareto dominates it.

(Spence, 1977, discusses this point further.)

To see this fact, suppose that $x^r(b; S)$ units are available to the household at some price, p_0, below marginal cost, C_S. This scheme represents an extreme form of quantity-dependent pricing. As illustrated in figure 21-7(a), the price per unit is p_0 for the first $x^r(b; S)$ units and infinite for all units thereafter. Suppose that this rationing scheme is replaced with the following price schedule. If the household buys $x^r(b; S)$ units or less, then it pays p_0 per unit as before. Additional units may be purchased at a price equal to marginal cost. The government can afford to offer these extra units, because they are sold at cost. A household with a low level of demand, such as D_1 in figure 21-7(b), will be indifferent between the two pricing schemes. A household with a high level of demand, such as D_2 in figure 21-7(b), will strictly prefer the nonrationed scheme. Thus, this second pricing scheme is a Pareto improvement on the original rationing scheme and should be no more difficult to administer.

The Presence of Other Taxes and Subsidies

The analysis above assumes that there are no other taxes or subsidies present in the economy. Clearly this condition will not be satisfied in actual cases. Thus, it is useful to consider the effects that the presence of other taxes would

Figure 21-7. *Quantity-Dependent Pricing: (a) Infinite Price above* $x^r(b; S)$
and (b) Units above $x^r(b; S)$ *Sold at Marginal Cost*

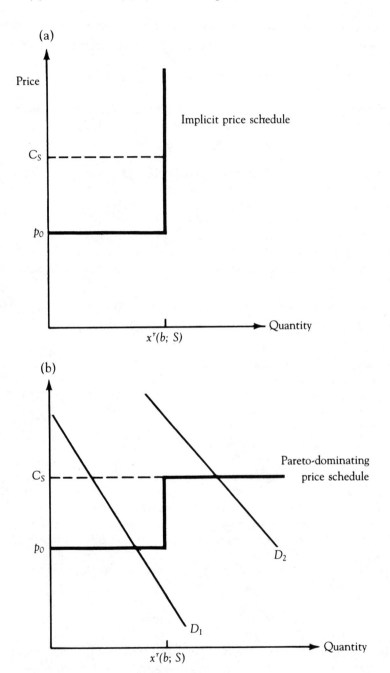

have on the results derived above. Essentially, there are three types of interaction between the price of the publicly provided good and the overall tax system.

First, if the other tax rates can be adjusted, there is no need to hold the aggregate subsidy, A, at a fixed level. With a fixed aggregate subsidy, the additional revenues necessary to finance an increase in the quality or total quantity of the publicly supplied good have to be raised by increasing the price of the good. When the aggregate subsidy is variable, some or all of the additional funds can be raised through changes in other tax rates. Instead of a fixed level of subsidy, the budget constraint would contain a shadow price for public funds, reflecting the social costs of raising additional revenues through optimal (feasible) tax changes. This shadow price could be greater or less than the shadow price of funds used in the analysis above, which reflected the social costs of raising additional revenues through an increase in the price of the publicly produced good for a given level of contribution by other taxes, A. The relationship between the two shadow prices depends on whether the fixed level of aggregate subsidy considered above is greater or less than the socially optimal level of aggregate subsidy.

Second, the presence of a tax system will affect the benefits of changes in the consumption of, and expenditures on, the publicly supplied good. The presence of redistributive taxes may reduce the need to use the price of the publicly produced good as a means of income redistribution. Furthermore, by distorting relative prices and, hence, consumption decisions, other taxes will alter the marginal benefits associated with an increase in the consumption of the publicly produced good.

Finally, changes in the price, quality, and quantity of the publicly provided good will affect the revenues raised by other taxes. If there are commodity taxes on goods other than the government-supplied one, for example, an increase in expenditures for the publicly produced good will reduce expenditures on other goods and will lower the revenues collected from fixed taxes on these goods. Similarly, a quality change may induce shifts in consumption patterns that alter the revenues collected by other taxes.

Conclusions

The principal findings of this chapter have been several.

1. When there is a social budget constraint, a price increase may allow the government to increase the quality or the quantity of a publicly provided good or service in a way that raises the aggregate welfare of the consumers of the good.

2. A price increase may raise the welfare of low-income households, particularly if prior to the price change these households consumed little of the good or service. Consequently, even when the government has strong redistribu-

tional objectives that favor low-income households, it may be socially desirable to raise the prices of publicly supplied goods and services.

3. Simple tests based on the demand for the publicly provided good may often be used to determine whether a household's welfare is raised or lowered by a policy shift. For quality increases, the planner can look at the sign of the change in the quantity purchased. For increased rationing ceilings, all households with zero initial consumption and positive consumption after the price increase are better off.

4. Wherever feasible, the government should offer a menu of options, allowing consumers to purchase additional quality or quantity at marginal cost. Such a policy will lead to a Pareto improvement in household welfare.

5. Private, profit-maximizing firms may be a useful source of these options. Unsubsidized private firms should be allowed to compete with the government for sales to those households to whom the government offers prices below social marginal cost (provided that there are no externalities between consumers and no problems of adverse selection). Under these conditions, even if the private firms charge prices above their marginal cost, their presence cannot lower welfare.

Notes

1. In his work on voting for the government provision of goods and services, Usher (1977a) obtained a similar result.

2. Of course, in some of these cases, the assumption that b is independent of the social or private value of the household's consumption may not be valid. Society may, for example, more highly value the education of those who have demonstrated an aptitude for learning. It is straightforward to extend the current analysis to such cases.

3. We could of course argue that government-provided loans or insurance are more appropriate solutions to the type of problem identified in point 6.

4. These conditions are derived as follows. The household chooses x to maximize $u[\rho(z)x, n - px]$. The first-order condition is $u_1\rho - pu_2 = 0$, or $u_1 = pu_2/\rho$.

5. Willig (1978) has considered a more general problem using demand data for the publicly produced good only. With more than two goods, this data requirement is a weaker one than knowledge of all demands. I base this subsection largely on Willig's analysis. In a series of papers, Birdsall has investigated the difficulties with, and the methodology for, estimating the welfare effects of price changes in developing nations. See, for example, Birdsall (1982).

6. When there are more than two goods in the economy, the prices of other goods may affect household expenditures on the publicly produced good. Interaction between these prices and z must also come through $g(p, z)$ in this case.

7. As the reader may have noticed, the two forms considered here are special cases of the fact that, given any function of quality, $g(z)$, and any invertible transformation of the quantity variable, $h(x)$, if $h(x) = \alpha + \beta p + g(z) + \delta n$, then $x = h^{-1}\{\alpha + \beta[p + g(z)/\beta] + \delta n\}$, which is the requisite form.

22

Efficiency and Equity Implications of Subsidies to Secondary Education in Kenya

Jane Armitage and Richard Sabot

PRACTITIONERS OF THE NEW ECONOMICS of public finance use a rule of thumb when searching for candidates for taxation: goods and services that have low price elasticities of demand and high income elasticities of demand are likely to prove to be particularly appropriate choices. These characteristics imply that the reduction of demand (and of potential revenues) and the consequent distortion of consumption patterns resulting from the imposition of a tax will be relatively small and that the share of revenue accruing from those in the upper portions of the income distribution will be relatively large. The same rule of thumb applies when an existing program of subsidies is scrutinized to identify candidates for reduction. In this chapter we exploit this symmetry, using a Kenyan example to show how such an assessment might be conducted in the education sector.

That education expenditures should be subjected to critical scrutiny is obvious: public spending on education as a proportion of GDP and as a proportion of public expenditure is high in all regions of the world. In 1970, on average, developing countries spent 4 percent of GDP and 15 percent of total public expenditure on education (Zymelman, 1982). Moreover, enrollment ratios that remain low by comparison with those of industrialized countries, combined with rapid population growth and high private rates of return to investment in education, mean that demand for education (and hence pressure to increase subsidies) is high and growing.

As a consequence of the recession of the early 1980s, and as much for structural reasons, budgetary constraints on educational expenditure in developing countries are tighter than they were in the 1950s and 1960s, when many subsidy programs were put into place or were greatly expanded. Governments' share of output grew substantially over the last twenty years; today public expenditure is no longer growing as a percentage of GDP. Likewise the

We are grateful to P. Diamond, J. Seade, and the editors of this volume for detailed comments on an earlier draft of the present chapter.

proportion of the budget spent on human resources increased in the 1960s and 1970s. Today expenditures on education and health face increasing competition from other claims (Bowman and Sabot, 1982).

There is a further reason for scrutinizing education expenditures: after twenty to thirty years of economic development, the original justification for the subsidies may not apply with equal force or may not have proven sound. The belief that the distribution of school places (and thence the rate of intergenerational mobility) should not be determined by the ability to pay school fees provided one justification for these subsidies. Capital market imperfections generally prevent the poor from borrowing to finance education expenditure.

There is also the belief that various externalities generated by the educational process drive a substantial wedge between private and social returns and that, in the absence of subsidies, investment in education would be less than socially optimal. These externalities include the compression of the earnings structure and consequent reduction of the inequality of pay resulting from an increase in the supply of human capital relative to other factors of production.[1] If, as it has been argued, education has a negative effect on fertility and on child mortality and a positive effect on political awareness and participation, then these external benefits also support subsidization (see Bowen and Sabot, 1983; Cochrane, 1979).

The need to set standards of quality in the face of inadequate information is a third reason for government regulation and possibly also subsidization of schooling. In an environment in which many parents of school children are themselves uneducated and are thus unable to reach informed judgments about the relative costs and benefits of relatively high-quality schooling, there is concern that quality will be less than socially optimal.

The public finance rule of thumb and the arguments advanced to justify educational subsidies suggest that an assessment of a program of education subsidies should address the following questions:

- Would a reduction of subsidies have a large negative impact on enrollments, or is the price elasticity of demand sufficiently low for that not to be the case?
- Would a reduction of subsidies have an adverse effect on the distribution of schooling, or contrary to intentions, have the relatively well-to-do benefited disproportionately from the subsidization of education?
- Would a reduction of per pupil subsidies result in a deterioration of school quality, or would private funds simply substitute for public funds, leaving per pupil expenditures on education inputs unchanged?

We attempt to answer these questions with regard to government subsidies of secondary education in Kenya. In so doing we will find it important to distinguish between the consequences of the two means of reducing per capita subsidies of secondary education: first, by raising fees in government schools, and second, by leaving the growth of secondary enrollments to relatively unsubsidized private schools.

The next section presents background information on the Kenyan secondary system and program of education subsidies. The model of a dual school system suggested by the stylized facts can be used to make a prima facie case for raising user fees in government secondary schools. We then discuss the various econometric methods employed in the subsequent empirical analysis, our sources of data, and a possible problem with sample selection bias. Wage functions and educational attainment functions are used to improve measures of key relationships, to test competing hypotheses regarding the interpretation of those relationships, to estimate, using simulation techniques, the extent to which user fees can be raised, and to assess the efficacy of leaving further secondary expansion to private schools.

The Dual Secondary System in Kenya

Between 1963, the year of independence, and 1980, enrollments in the highly subsidized government secondary system expanded rapidly at 12 percent per year. Demand grew even faster than supply. The excess demand was satisfied by the establishment of large numbers of harambee, church, and private schools, which receive only small subsidies from the government.[2] Since 1963, private school enrollments, including assisted harambee school enrollments, have been growing at the rate of 21 percent. Secondary school enrollment in nongovernment schools first exceeded that in government-supported schools in 1975. In 1981, 40 percent of enrollment was in government schools, about 20 percent in assisted harambee schools and unaided harambee schools, respectively, and the remainder in church or private schools. The state secondary system is clearly the system of preference. With few exceptions, harambee schools are filled with primary school leavers who did not qualify (on the basis of meritocratic criteria) for a government secondary education. Tables 22-1–22-3, and the tables in the text below, which present characteristics of government and harambee schools for 1980, explain

Table 22-1. *Costs per Pupil, Government and Harambee Schools, 1980*
(shillings per year)

School	Private direct	Public direct	Total direct	Wages forgone[a]
Government	1,557	2,071	3,628	6,960
Harambee	2,460	227	2,687	6,960

a. Primary wages forgone, annual average over first four years, predicted with wage functions presented in table 22-8.

Source: Annual Census of Primary and Secondary Education (1979), the Appropriations Account, 1980–81.

Table 22-2. *Distribution of Highest Secondary Form Achieved, 1980*
(percent)

School	Form 1	Form 2	Form 3	Form 4	Form 5	Form 6
Government	2.6	9.7	2.6	64.1	0.2	20.7
Harambee	9.1	40.9	8.4	40.2	0.0	1.3

Note: Rows sum to 100.
Source: Kenya Survey of Wage Employment and Education, 1980.

Table 22-3. *Distribution of O-Level Examination Scores, 1980*
(percent)

School	Division				Failed	Did not sit
	1	2	3	4		
Government	19.4	27.5	32.7	16.5	2.9	1.2
Harambee	3.2	6.3	33.3	42.9	12.7	1.6

Note: Rows sum to 100.
Source: Kenya Survey of Wage Employment and Education, 1980.

why. Table 22-1 indicates that, because subsidies are much larger in the government system than in the harambee system (2,071 shillings per student per annum as compared with 227 shillings), the cost borne by parents is much smaller in the government system (1,557 shillings per student per annum as compared with 2,460 shillings for harambee schools).[3] Moreover, government schools appear to be of higher quality. Total expenditures are roughly 1,000 shillings per pupil per annum higher in government than in harambee schools; this difference translates into better-educated teachers, smaller classes, more textbooks, and better physical facilities.[4]

The difference in inputs is reflected in differences in outputs from the two systems. Table 22-2 indicates that only 15 percent of the students in government schools drop out prior to reaching form 4; for harambee schools, the figure is 58 percent. Similarly, 21 percent of government school pupils attend upper secondary (forms 5 and 6)—the gateway to a university education—whereas the equivalent proportion for harambee schools is only 1 percent. Table 22-3 indicates that government school leavers perform markedly better than their harambee school counterparts on the standardized exam taken at the conclusion of form 4. Forty-seven percent of government school leavers scored in the top two divisions, as compared with 10 percent of harambee school leavers. Fully 56 percent of harambee leavers either placed in the lowest division or failed, as compared with 19 percent of government school leavers.

The difference between government school and harambee school leavers in performance on exams is consistent with our other evidence of a difference in school quality. It could also partly result, however, from differences in student quality, given the meritocratic selection criterion for entrance to government schools. Although we do not have evidence on ability levels for the entire sample, a subsample of form 4 leavers was given Raven's Progressive Matrices, a test of reasoning ability that is widely used in developing countries. The results, shown below, indicate that the difference in ability scores between harambee and government school leavers is small; indeed, it proved to be statistically insignificant.[5]

Item	Government	Harambee
Mean ability	30.52	28.32
SD	4.85	7.90

Nevertheless, government school students are likely to be better qualified on entrance than harambee school students because of differences between the two groups in the quality of primary schooling and in academic skills acquired at home.

The difference between government and harambee school leavers in levels of skills measured by the exams is, in turn, reflected in a large difference between the two groups in the earnings they command in the labor market. As we see from the table below, although the predicted mean wages of workers (with ten years' experience) from both types of secondary school are substantially higher for 1980 than the predicted wages of primary school leavers, those from government secondary schools earn 23 percent more in shillings per year than those from harambee schools.[6]

Leaver group	Wage
Primary school	9,273
Harambee form 4	12,518
Government form 4	16,897

In the parlance of cost-benefit analysis, these stylized facts suggest that the private costs of investing in a secondary education are lower and the private returns are higher for those who gain access to a government secondary school than for those who must attend a harambee school. The resulting difference in net private returns explains parents' strong preference for sending their children to government schools. If we abstract, for now, from individual constraints on financing secondary education when the market for secondary education is segmented, the implication is that per pupil subsidies to government schools can be reduced (with user fees increased) without affecting the demand for places in government schools or the level of expenditure per pupil and hence school quality. A simple economic model of the demand for schooling predicts that, in a dual school system, there will be excess demand for places in the relatively small, highly subsidized segment of the system. The elasticity of demand in that segment will therefore be zero and will remain zero until fees are raised sufficiently to equate the private net rates of return in the two segments.[7] If the highly subsidized segment is also higher in quality, hence in gross returns, the fees charged in that segment will actually have to be higher than the fees in the other segments before net rates of return are equalized.

Raising user fees in Kenyan government secondary schools would ease budgetary constraints on education, which have tightened in the 1980s.[8] Moreover, public resources for secondary education will also be limited by the higher government priorities attached to primary and higher education. The Kenyan government is committed to free and universal primary education.[9] Whether the Kenyan government takes advantage of the revenue-generating potential of user fees in government schools, however, also depends on the consequences of a rise in those fees for the distribution of secondary school places and for the aggregate size of the secondary system. An important consideration is whether a substantial increase in user fees would force children of relatively low-income families either to transfer their children to the private school system or to terminate their education.

The predicted probability of a child's attending a government secondary school rises monotonically and steeply with the educational level of the child's parents, an indicator of socioeconomic status (probability is predicted at mean age for those born outsde Nairobi).

	Probability
Both parents with no education	.16
One parent with no education, one with primary	.23
Both primary or one with secondary or more, one with none	.33
One with primary, one with secondary or more, or both with secondary or more	.51

The probability rises from .16 for the children of uneducated parents to .51 for children of parents with at least some secondary education. Those with the greatest ability to bear the cost of their education are the most likely to receive large subsidies. The explanation may lie with differences among socioeconomic groups in the quality of primary schooling, in the quantity and quality of training provided within the home, or in the ability to "purchase" places in government schools. Whatever the cause, it appears that in Kenya the incidence of subsidies of secondary education, a private "good" that substantially raises the lifetime income of the recipient, strongly favors those households that stand relatively high with respect to the distribution of income. A rise in user fees is likely, therefore, to reduce the inequality of income (consumption) among households.

A zero aggregate price elasticity of demand (given the rationing of places) implies that a rise in user fees will not result in any underutilization of government schools. If some students withdraw from the government system, others from the harambee system will take their places in the preferred system. The nature of the change in aggregate secondary enrollments as user fees are increased, however, depends on the numbers who leave the government system and on whether they switch to the harambee system or leave the secondary system entirely.[10] These magnitudes will depend on the composition of the government system. If, at one extreme, the government system is entirely composed of the children of the group with the highest education (income), then a rise in fees is unlikely to induce withdrawals. As we see from the table below, in Kenya, despite their low probability of attendance, children of parents with no formal education still compose 38 percent of the government secondary system, because such a high proportion of parents had little or no formal education. Another 25 percent of places are filled by children who have one parent with primary education. This statistic suggests that, unless the rise in school fees is discriminatory, that is, imposed only on those "able to pay," it may induce substantial withdrawals from the government system and perhaps entirely from the secondary system.

| | Percentage of children in | |
	Government system	Harambee system
Both parents with no education	38.2	49.0
One parent with no education, one with primary	24.6	27.1
Both primary or one with secondary or more, one with none	27.1	20.0
One with primary, one with secondary or more, or both with secondary or more	10.1	3.9

Methods and Data

Our concern is with the apparent dualism in the market for secondary education between the high-quality, high-subsidy government system and the low-quality, low-subsidy harambee system. Therefore, we depart from the conventional procedure and disaggregate the benefits and costs of secondary schooling by type of school and calculate separate rates of return to government schooling and to harambee schooling.

In the conventional measurement of the rate of return to (say) secondary education, the benefit stream is measured by means of an earnings function (see Mincer, 1974), of which the following, estimated first for a sample of primary school leavers and then for a sample of secondary school leavers, is an example:

$$(22\text{-}1) \quad \log W = a + bL + cL^2 + \sum_j d_j X_j + u$$

where

$\log W$ = log of earnings of the individual

L = the number of years of employment experience of the individual

X = a vector of other characteristics of the individual

u = a disturbance term

These cross-section earnings functions are used to simulate two time series, $\hat{W}_p$ and $\hat{W}_s$, representing the predicted wages, over their expected working lives, of primary and secondary school leavers, respectively. The difference between the educational groups in predicted lifetime earnings is interpreted as a proxy for the cognitive skills or other marketable traits acquired in secondary education and is used as the estimate of the gross benefits of secondary education. When we calculate the internal *private* rate of return that equates the present value of these benefits to zero, we net out only the opportunity costs (wages forgone) of attending secondary school and the private direct costs.[11] When calculating the *social* rate of return, we must also take into account the public direct costs (subsidies).[12]

On the benefits side, disaggregation involves estimating earnings functions that will yield $\hat{W}_{sg}$ and $\hat{W}_{sh}$, representing the predicted wages, over their expected working lives, of government and harambee secondary school leavers, respectively. We do this with the following modification of equation 22-1:

$$(22\text{-}2) \quad \log W = a + bL + cL^2 + \sum_j d_j X_j + \Sigma_i e_i S_i + u$$

where S_i = dummy variables signifying type of school.[13] Excess demand for government schooling is sufficient to establish that the price elasticity of demand is zero. The comparison of the private rate of return to investment in government schooling, r_g^p, with the private rate of return to harambee schooling, r_h^p, provides the basis for assessing the extent to which user fees can be raised (subsidies lowered) without inducing a reduction in enrollments. Given that $r_g^p > r_h^p$, and there are no financial constraints, this procedure involves raising direct costs in our calculation of private rates of return until $r_g^p = r_h^p$.

Does the practice of reducing per pupil subsidies of secondary education by leaving further expansion to the low-cost, low-quality private sector result in the sacrifice of allocative efficiency? Because both the total costs and the total benefits of government schooling appear to exceed those of harambee schooling, our stylized facts did not permit even a preliminary answer to this question, which involves the comparison of social rates of return, r_g^s and r_h^s. The answer depends on whether the difference between the two systems in costs or the difference in benefits has the greater effect on the relationship of r_g^s and r_h^s. If $r_g^s \leq r_h^s$, then reducing per pupil subsidies in this way would not reduce the aggregate economic productivity of the school system. If $r_g^s > r_h^s$, then allowing the harambee system, as currently constituted, to increase its share of enrollments would result in expected output forgone.

The deficiencies of cost-benefit analysis as a guide to the allocation of resources between secondary schools and other types of investments such as health clinics or railroads are well known (see chapter 10, by Fields), and various more or less ad hoc adjustments have been devised to correct them (see Knight and Sabot, 1983b; Psacharopoulos and Hinchliffe, 1973). Our more limited aim of comparing social rates of return to two components of the secondary system as a means of assessing the efficiency consequences of reducing per pupil subsidies is less subject to some of the biases that have been a source of concern. The precise nature of the relationship between wages and the marginal product of labor in the public sector, for example, may have a large influence on the aggregate social rate of return to secondary education but only a small impact on the relative rates of return to government and harambee schooling.[14] Wage-experience profiles derived from cross-section data are only crude approximations of earnings over the life cycle.[15] Again, the aggregate rate of return to secondary education is likely to be more subject to bias from this source than is the relative rate of return to government and harambee schools.[16]

We do, however, empirically examine the following four issues that could have an important bearing on relative private or social rates of return, and where appropriate we devise methods—described in detail below—of adjusting our estimates:

- We use more refined measures of human capital—scores on the O-level exams taken in form 4—to assess whether the lifetime earnings of government school leavers are higher than those of harambee school leavers because of the former group's higher level of skills. The difference could instead be due to credentialism, that is, to discrimination by employers on the basis of the worker's "old school tie."

- We have measures of time devoted to job search on leaving school (unemployment) that allow us to assess whether government and harambee school leavers differ in this regard and whether relative rates of return are sensitive to the observed differences.

- We assess whether relative rates of return must be adjusted for the difference noted above between government and harambee schools in wastage rates. The answer depends on whether the returns to schooling, as well as the costs, are a linear or nonlinear function of years of schooling.

- We assess the extent to which the difference between government and harambee school leavers in skill levels and earnings is due to the government system's greater tendency to select children from more educated backgrounds rather than to differences in the quality of schooling. To this end we estimate an education production function to isolate the effect of family background, independent of type of school, on performance on the exam at the end of schooling. We then simulate the difference between government and harambee school leavers in performance and in earnings if the two groups did not differ in family background.

Apart from opportunity costs (derived from the earnings function estimated for primary school leavers using data from our survey, described below), we do not have individual data on costs. In our rate-of-return calculations, all government school leavers are assumed to have paid the average current costs of government schools; similarly, all harambee school leavers are assumed to have paid the average current costs of harambee schools. Official government statistics provided our sources for the private and public cost data. Our estimates of private direct costs—tuition and board, uniforms, caution fees, activity fees, medical fees, books and equipment, and contributions to the building fund—are obtained from the *Annual Census of Primary and Secondary*

Schools (1979).[17] Our estimates of public costs are obtained from *The Appropriation Accounts, 1980–81.*[18]

The *Kenya Survey of Wage Employment and Education, 1980* is our source for
the opportunity costs and returns to government and harambee secondary
education. The survey was designed and administered in 1980 by a team that
included one of the authors. The sample, containing nearly 2,000 employees,
was randomly selected on an establishment basis, using a two-stage procedure,
from among the wage-labor force of Nairobi.

For our purposes the survey has two strengths—accuracy and richness—
though it also has a weakness. Data on wages collected from an establishment-
based survey are likely to be more accurate than similar data derived from a
household survey because the inquiry does not rely solely on the recollection of
the employee; confirmatory information can be (and was) obtained from the
employer. The richness of the data is a product of the specially designed
questionnaire. Respondents were asked detailed questions about their educational and employment histories, their family background, and other things.
One advantage is that it is possible to identify the type of secondary school
attended and hence to compare the rates of return that are central to our
analysis. The experience variable in our earnings functions is the actual
number of years in wage employment rather than the usual crude proxy based
on age and years of education. The variable indicating performance on O-level
exams permits the test of competing hypotheses regarding the cause of the
difference between harambee and government school leavers in earnings
streams (essential for the measurement of the gap between the two types of
school in gross *social* returns). It also permits us to estimate an education
production function and to correct, if only crudely, for the bias in the measure
of the gap that arises from the selectivity of the government system.

The weakness of an establishment-based survey such as the *Kenya Survey* for
cost-benefit analysis is that the sample does not include those educated workers
who are *not* in urban wage employment.[19] Our estimate of the relative rate of
return to government and harambee schools may therefore be subject to
sample selection bias. In particular it seems likely that a higher proportion of
harambee school leavers than of government school leavers are not in urban
wage employment and that those harambee school leavers who were unsuccessful in obtaining such employment are from the poorest-quality schools. If
those schools have below-average costs as well as below-average returns, then
our comparison need not be biased. If, however, the returns alone are below
average, the implication would be that we are overestimating the returns to
harambee schools relative to the returns to government schools.

Private and Social Rates of Return to Government
and Harambee Schools and Some Adjustments

Table 22-4 presents estimates of the various earnings functions used in the
analysis. In both equation 22-1, estimated for primary leavers, and equation

Table 22-4. *Earnings Functions*

Independent variable	Leavers			
	Standard 7 or 8	*Form 4 or more*	*Form 4 or more*	*Form 4 or more*
Equation	(22-1)	(22-2)	(22-3)	(22-4)
Years of employment experience (L)	0.045	0.099	0.099	0.099
	(4.8)	(9.7)	(10.0)	(9.5)
(L^2)	−0.0005	−0.0016	−0.0019	−0.0019
	(1.6)	(4.3)	(4.6)	(4.2)
Harambee secondary school (S_2)[a]	—	−0.21	−0.024	—
		(2.9)	(0.3)	
Private secondary school (S_3)[a]	—	−0.20	−0.016	—
		(3.2)	(0.2)	
Government technical school (S_4)[a]	—	−0.15	−0.20	—
		(1.6)	(1.8)	
Post–form 4 schooling (E_5)[b]	—	0.64	0.30	0.42
		(10.9)	(4.4)	(6.5)
First division (D_1)[c]	—	—	1.00	—
			(8.5)	
Second division (D_2)[c]	—	—	0.70	—
			(7.6)	
Third division (D_3)[c]	—	—	0.47	—
			(5.5)	
Fourth division (D_4)[c]	—	—	0.27	—
			(3.1)	
Upper division (D_1 or D_2)[d]	—	—	—	0.41
				(7.7)
Constant	6.25	6.58	6.08	6.40
$\bar{R}^2$	0.19	0.40	0.45	0.45
Number	458	508	456	456

— Not applicable.

Notes: The dependent variable is the log of monthly wages (log$W$). The figure in parentheses beneath a coefficient is its t statistic.

a. Government school S_1 is the base.

b. Lower secondary leavers is the base.

c. Failed or did not sit O-level exams is the base.

d. Lower divisions (third, fourth, or fail) are the base.

22-2, estimated for leavers at form 4 or later, the coefficient on the experience variable is positive and highly significant and the coefficient on the quadratic term is negative and highly significant. Differences between the two equations in constant terms and coefficients on the experience variables indicate that, as usual, the earnings profile of secondary school leavers lies above and rises more steeply than that of primary school leavers.

Figure 22-1. Costs and Benefits of Government and Harambee Secondary Schooling

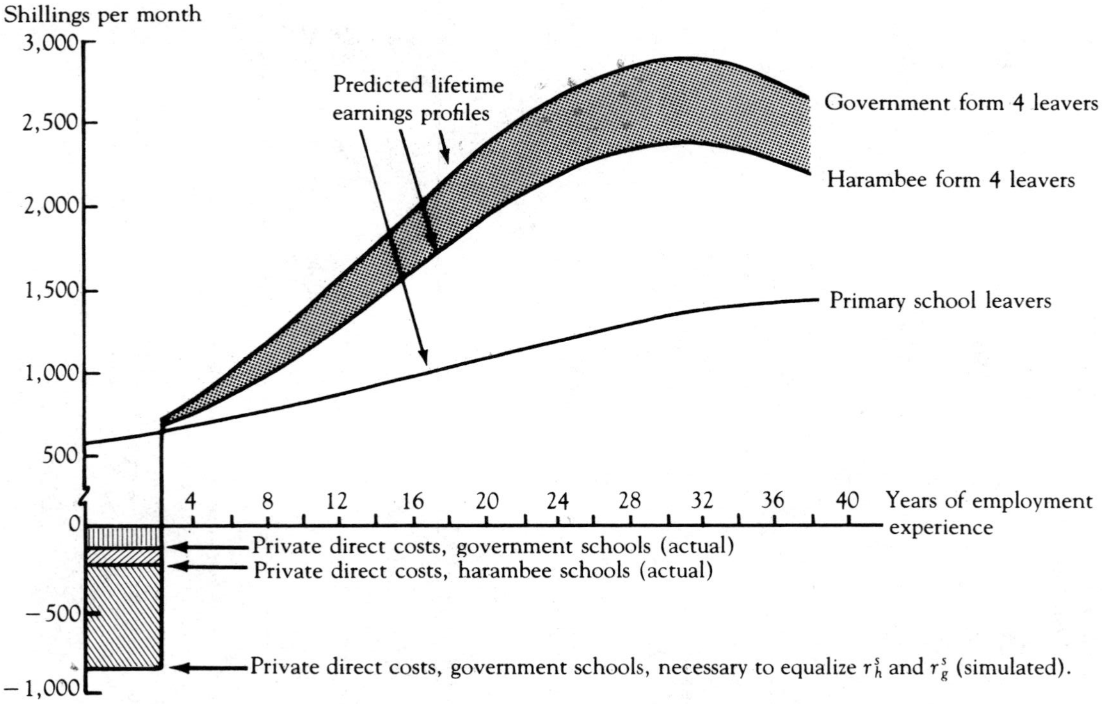

Shillings per month

3,000

2,500

2,000

1,500

1,000

500

0

−500

−1,000

Government form 4 leavers

Harambee form 4 leavers

Primary school leavers

Predicted lifetime earnings profiles

4 8 12 16 20 24 28 32 36 40 Years of employment experience

Private direct costs, government schools (actual)

Private direct costs, harambee schools (actual)

Private direct costs, government schools, necessary to equalize r_h^s and r_g^s (simulated).

Source: Armitage and Sabot (1983).

600

The coefficient on the harambee dummy variable in equation 22-2 is negative, large, and significant: the implication is that, if we standardize for employment experience, the earnings of harambee school leavers are considerably lower (more than 21 percent) than those of government school leavers. This estimate of the standardized differential in earnings may be biased, because in equation 22-2 the returns to experience are constrained to be the same for government and harambee school leavers. An F test on an unconstrained version of the equation (not shown), however, did not allow us to reject the null hypothesis that the returns to experience are the same for both groups. The F statistic was below the critical value, at the 5 percent level of significance.

Figure 22-1, a rendering of the lifetime earnings streams of primary school leavers, government school form 4 leavers, and harambee school form 4 leavers derived from equations 22-1 and 22-2, summarizes these findings. The lower shaded areas represent the opportunity cost of secondary schooling; the upper shaded area represents the higher gross private returns to government secondary schooling than to harambee secondary schooling.[20]

Table 22-5 presents our estimates of private and social rates of return to government and harambee schooling based on the data underlying the

Table 22-5. *Private and Social Returns to Secondary (Form 4) Education*
(percent)

Item	Government schools	Harambee schools
Base calculation		
Private return	14.5	9.5
Social return	13.0	9.5
Adjusting for credentialism		
Private return	14.5	9.5
Social return	13.0	9.5
Adjusting for wastage		
Private return	14.5	7.5
Social return	13.0	7.5
Adjusting for search time		
Private return	21.0	11.5
Social return	17.0	11.5
Adjusting for selectivity of government schools[a]		
Base private	15.5	11.0
Base social	13.5	11.0
Adjusted private	15.0	—
Adjusted social	13.0	—

— Not applicable.

a. The base private and social returns are recalculated because a slightly different specification of the earnings function underlying our estimate of returns is used to make the adjustment.

above-mentioned estimates of returns and opportunity costs and on the estimates of private and government expenditures presented in table 22-1. Confirming what the stylized facts strongly suggested, the private returns to government schooling are higher—50 percent higher—than the private returns to harambee schooling. The implication is that user fees in government schools would have to be raised substantially to equalize private returns in the two systems. Our simulations indicate that, to accomplish such an equalization, private direct costs in government schools would have to be raised from 1,557 shillings per year to 10,000 shillings per year (see figure 22-1).[21] The difference between what the government could charge, given perfect capital markets, and what it actually charges over four years is therefore in excess of 33,000 shillings. This sum is double the mean annual earnings of all workers in our sample, considered by some observers to be the urban elite; it is 3.5 times the mean annual earnings of the manual workers in our sample.

If, as we have assumed, the elasticity of demand for government schooling remains zero until private returns in the two segments of the system are equalized, the revenue potential of raising user fees is then simply the difference between current user fees and the maximum potential fee multiplied by aggregate enrollment in government lower secondary schools. This amount is 75,600,000 pounds, a sum that represents more than 300 percent of government recurrent expenditures on lower secondary education.[22] Capital market imperfections imply that it is not feasible to levy the maximum potential user fee without a decline in demand for government schooling. Nevertheless, the potential revenue associated with an increase in school fees is likely to be substantial.[23]

The private and social returns to harambee secondary schools are essentially the same. Adding the negligible government subsidies onto private costs of harambee schools increases total costs by only 9.2 percent. This increase does not measurably reduce the rate of return. There is, however, a gap between the private and social returns to government schools because per pupil subsidies in that system are far from negligible. Adding government subsidies onto private costs increases total costs by 133 percent. The result is that the social rate of return to government schools is some 13 percent, which is less than the private rate of return of 14.5 percent.

The gap between government and harambee schools in the social rate of return is less than the gap in private returns. Nevertheless, social returns to investment in government schools remain substantially higher than the social returns to investment in private schools. This difference suggests that, from the perspective of costs and benefits to the economy as a whole, not just to the individual or household, the government system is the more cost-effective system—output per shilling of input is higher in government schools than in harambee schools.[24]

The measured difference between the two systems in economic efficiency could be due to a difference in the quality of management. Alternatively, it could reflect increasing returns in the education production function. Recall that total per pupil expenditures are substantially lower in harambee schools than in government schools. The returns to the extra 1,000 shillings per pupil per year spent in government schools may have substantially exceeded average returns. Educationalists generally presume that the learning curve, relating inputs on the horizontal axis and skills acquired on the vertical axis, has a logistic form, increasing rapidly at first, then more slowly. Kenyan secondary schools may be on the steeply sloped portion of an aggregate version of such a curve where a small increase in inputs yields a disproportionately large increase in outputs (Armitage and Sabot, 1983).

One implication of this efficiency differential for the assessment of government subsidies of secondary education is that a policy of reducing per pupil subsidies by allowing the relatively unsubsidized harambee system to provide a disproportionate share of new secondary places would entail allocative inefficiency. Such a policy would result in potential output forgone. Because of the higher total costs of the government system, however, the efficiency differential between the two systems is less than the 20 + percent differential between government school leavers and harambee school leavers in economic productivity estimated by our wage function. If, as hypothesized, the education production function is characterized by increasing returns, it may take only a small increase in the quality of harambee schools to reduce the difference between the two systems in gross social returns. Narrowing the gap between the two systems in total expenditure per pupil may therefore narrow the gap in social rates of return.

Just how robust are these assessments of the economic costs and benefits of reducing per pupil subsidies of secondary education in Kenya? The following adjustments of our estimates of relative private and social rates of return to government and harambee schooling provide a basis for judgment.

Adjusting for Credentialism

To what extent does credentialism account for the higher earnings of government than of harambee school leavers? To what extent is the difference in earnings due to the greater skill of government leavers as indicated by their superior performance (see table 22-3) on the nationwide form 4 exam? To answer these questions, we add to the wage function for form 4 or more (equation 22-2 above and in table 22-4) a set of dummy variables (D_j) signifying the division achieved on the O-level exams. The estimated equation 22-3 is presented in table 22-4.

Exam scores clearly have a powerful influence on earnings. The coefficients on the dummy variables increase monotonically and in large increments; all four are highly significant. The equation predicts that, if we standardize for other characteristics, a form 4 leaver who was placed in the first division will earn in excess of 100 percent more than a form 4 leaver who failed or did not sit the exam. Most striking is that adding exam scores to the explanatory variables entirely eliminates the influence of type of school on earnings. If we compare equations 22-2 and 22-3, the coefficient on the harambee dummy (S_2) declines from -0.21 to -0.024 and is no longer statistically significant.

All of the difference in earnings between government school and harambee school leavers appears to reflect differences in skills; none appears due to credentialism.[25] Therefore, no adjustment needs to be made to our estimate of the rate of return to harambee schools; the rates of return in rows 3 and 4 of table 22-5 are the same as the base calculations.

Adjusting for Wastage

As documented in table 22-2, the dropout rate from harambee schools (59 percent) is greater than the rate of dropouts from government lower secondary schools (15 percent). Whether our estimates of rates of return have to be adjusted for differential wastage depends on whether gross returns to schooling are a linear function or an increasing function of the number of years of schooling. If the returns function is linear, then no adjustment need be made; if the cost function is linear, the rate of return per year of harambee school will be the same, irrespective of the number of years completed, as will the relative rates of return of government schools and harambee schools.[26] If, however, returns per year of harambee schooling are lower for form 2 than for form 4 leavers, our base estimates of rates of return to harambee schooling are biased upward. To assess this issue of linearity, we calculate the rate of return to two years of harambee schooling. This involves estimating a wage function for form 2 harambee school dropouts and predicting the lifetime stream of net benefits, taking into account only two years of forgone primary wages and direct costs. The result of these calculations is a rate of return (private and social) of 6.5 percent, considerably less than the rate of return to four years of harambee schooling (9.5 percent).

To arrive at an adjusted aggregate rate of return to harambee schools, we weight the rates of return to forms 2 and 4 by the proportions of students who left harambee school at those levels. Rows 5 and 6 of table 22-5 indicate that the adjusted rate of return is 7.5 percent, thereby widening the gap between government and harambee schools in private and social rates of return.[27]

Adjusting for Search Time

No wages are earned during the time spent searching for a job on completion of schooling.[28] We did not take into account this period of search when we predicted the lifetime earnings of school leavers and calculated the base rates of return. Because there are large differences between harambee and government school leavers in search time, relative rates of return may be biased by this omission. Thirty-five percent of government school form 4 leavers found a wage job immediately, compared with 19 percent of harambee school leavers. The average time taken to find a wage job for government school leavers was

9.5 months, as compared with 18 months for harambee school leavers and 32 months for primary school leavers.

Rows 7 and 8 of table 22-5 show the results of taking into account search time.[29] Because primary school leavers take a longer time to find a job than secondary school leavers, the rates of return to both government and harambee schools are higher than in the base calculation. The returns to government schools rise more, however. Therefore, as in rows 5 and 6, the gap between government and harambee schools in both private and social rates of return is widened by the adjustment.

Adjusting for Selectivity of Government Schools

Although we have confirmed that the difference between government and harambee school leavers in wages results from differences in cognitive skills, the question remains: how much of this difference in cognitive skills is due to the higher quality of government schools, and how much is due to the higher achievement at the start of secondary schooling of government school entrants and to their higher ability and socioeconomic background? If, to take an extreme case, all of the difference in skills is due to the selectivity of the government system, then there would be no gap between the two systems in either gross private or gross social returns. Because of differences in costs, net private returns would still be higher in the government system, but net social returns would actually be higher in the harambee system.

We attempt to answer this question with regard to socioeconomic background; because we do not have measures of cognitive skill levels at the beginning of secondary school, we cannot answer it with regard to this dimension of selectivity. Recall, however, that we were able to show for a subsample of form 4 leavers that there is no significant difference in ability between government and harambee school leavers. Family background may, however, be partly serving as a proxy for differences in achievement at the start of secondary school. Table 22-6 presents probit estimates of the following simple educational production function for form 4 leavers, together with predicted probabilities for different family background groups and for government and harambee students:

$$(22-5) \qquad \text{Prob}(H = 1) = \Phi(\mathbf{X'B})$$

where H is a dichotomous variable that takes the value 1 where the individual obtained a high score (division 1 or 2) on the O-level exam. The vector of exogenous variables, X_i, includes P_j, the family background dummies; S_j, the type of school dummies; and, to capture the cohort effect, A_j, the age of the worker. Φ is the cumulative-unit normal-distribution function.

The three coefficients on the family background variables are significantly positive. They indicate that the probability of attaining a high grade increases monotonically as the educational level of the parents of students increases.

Table 22-6. *Probit Educational Production Functions*

Independent variable	Coef-ficient	Probability of attaining high grade[a]		
		P	Government leaver	Harambee leaver
One parent with no education, one with primary (P_2)	0.337 (2.1)	P_1 P_2 P_3 P_4 Average[b]	.34 .47 .55 .71 .47	.06 .11 .15 .27 .10
Both parents with primary, or one with secondary or more; one with none (P_3)	0.539 (3.5)			
One parent with primary, one with secondary or more, or both with secondary or more (P_4)	0.979 (4.3)			
Harambee secondary school (S_2)	-1.159 (4.9)			
Private secondary school (S_3)	-0.903 (4.9)			
Government technical school (S_4)	0.153 (0.5)			
Age (A)	0.010 (0.5)			
Constant	-0.699			
χ^2	78.2			
Number	496			

Note: Figures in parentheses are t statistics.

a. The probability that $Y = 1$ is the area under the standard normal curve between $-\infty$ and $\mathbf{X'B}$. Probabilities are predicted for individuals with mean age.

b. Averaged over all family background groups, with weights equal to mean family background for sample.

Nevertheless, the coefficient on the harambee dummy (S_2) is of larger absolute size and more highly significant than the coefficients on any of the family background variables. The predicted probabilities more clearly illustrate these findings. In both the government and the harambee systems, there is considerable variation in performance on O-level exams by family background. The impact of type of school on the probability of attaining a high grade on the O-levels, however, appears to be larger still: it is nearly five times higher for government school leavers (0.47) than for harambee school leavers (0.11). For reasons noted above, the composition by family background of the two secondary systems is not very different (see the text table above). The effect of family background on performance in school is therefore unlikely to have a large effect on the difference between government school leavers and harambee school leavers in predicted cognitive skill levels and thus in predicted wages and returns to secondary schooling. The results of simulating the returns to government and harambee schooling in the absence of government school selectivity by family background, presented in rows 5 and 6 of table 22-5, confirm this point.[30] The gap in both private and social returns narrows only marginally.

In sum, although our adjustments are not comprehensive, neither do they give conflicting signals. Two of our four adjustments—for credentialism and for the selectivity of government schools—have little impact on the relative rates of return of government and harambee schools. The other two adjustments—for differences in length of job search and in wastage rates—widen the gap between government and harambee schools in both private and social rates of return. The widening of the gap in private returns implies that our simulations with the base-rate calculations underestimated the increase in user fees necessary to equalize private returns to investment in the two systems. It appears that 8,000 shillings per annum would not be sufficient. The widening of the gap in social returns implies that allowing the harambee system to increase its share of enrollments entails somewhat higher efficiency costs than we had supposed.

Access to Government Schools and Family Background

Our assessment of the consequences for the distribution of schooling of reducing per pupil subsidies is based on estimates of a simple educational attainment function. Using binomial probit, we obtain maximum likelihood estimates of the parameters in the following reduced-form equation:

$$(22\text{-}6) \qquad \text{Prob}(G = 1) = \Phi(X'B)$$

where G is a dichotomous variable that takes the value 1 where an individual attended a government secondary school (and thus benefited from government subsidies) and 0 where the individual did not; X is a vector of exogenous variables. The exogenous variables include a set of four dummy variables signifying the education level of the parents of the individual. In another specification of the education attainment function, estimated only for individuals whose fathers were farmers, a variable signifying the size of the farm is also included among the exogenous variables. $\Phi(X'B)$ is the cumulative-unit normal-distribution function.[31]

Table 22-7 presents estimates of our probit educational attainment function and predicted probabilities of attending a government secondary school for various family background groups. In equation 22-7, estimated for the entire sample, the coefficients on the parents' education variables are positive and increase monotonically; all are significant. As we noted above, the predicted probabilities of reaping the very large private benefits from the subsidies of government education rise sharply with the educational level of the parents.

Table 22-7. *Probit Educational Attainment Functions*

Independent variable	Coefficient		Probability of going to a government secondary school[a]	
	(1)	*(2)*		
Equation	(22-7)	(22-8)		
One parent with no education, one with primary (P_2)	0.261 (2.9)	0.181 (1.2)	From (22-7) P_1 P_2 P_3 P_4	.16 .23 .33 .51
Both parents with primary, or one with secondary or more; one with none (P_3)	0.581 (6.1)	0.597 (3.4)	From (22-8)[b] 1.5 acres 3.5 acres 7 acres 15 acres 25 acres	.17 .19 .19 .21 .24
One parent with primary; one with secondary or more, or both with secondary or more (P_4)	1.042 (6.1)	0.743 (1.3)		
Born in Nairobi (N)	0.176 (3.8)	— —		
Age (A)	−0.043 (8.1)	−0.041 (4.6)		
Acreage of farm (A_c)	—	0.010 (2.5)		
Constant	0.355	0.319		
χ^2	193.2	48.0		
Number	1,650	539		

Note: Figures in parentheses are *t* statistics.

a. The probability that $Y = 1$ is the area under the standard normal curve between $-\infty$ and **X′B**. Probabilities are predicted for individuals born outside Nairobi, at the mean age.

b. Probabilities are predicted for individuals with uneducated parents, at the mean age.

Access to the government secondary system is meritocratic; selection is based largely on performance on the examination at the end of primary school. The education production function we estimated (table 22-6) therefore suggests one explanation for the relationship between parents' education and access to government secondary schools. It indicated that the education level of parents matters to performance in both high-quality (government) and low-quality (harambee) schools.[32] Though we have no direct evidence, there is a strong presumption that, standardizing for school quality, the educational level of parents is also positively related to performance in primary schools.[33] Moreover, children of more educated parents are likely to attend primary schools of above-average quality because of the concentration of both educated parents and high-quality primary schools in urban areas.

Our second educational attainment function (equation 22-8 in table 22-7) indicates that family wealth has an influence on the probability of attending a government secondary school independent of parents' education. The equation is estimated only for those workers whose fathers were farmers and includes a measure, A_c, of the size in acres of the family farm among the independent variables. Although coefficients of the parents' education variables continue to be positive and increase monotonically, they are reduced in both magnitude and significance relative to equation 22-7. The coefficient on the size-of-farm variable is positive and significant. For students with uneducated farmers as parents, the predicted probability is some 40 percent higher for those from farms of 25 acres than for those from farms of 1.5 acres. This relationship may indicate a nonmeritocratic component in the influence of family background on access to government secondary schooling.

The equations represented by table 22-7 measure the relationship between the socioeconomic status of the parents of the workers in our sample and the educational attainment of the workers. To confirm that the effect of family background is not merely a historical phenomenon, we also estimated by probit the relationship between the educational attainment of the workers and the probability that their children would attend a government secondary school. The results (not shown) for the younger two generations are qualitatively the same as those for the older two generations: the richer the family, the greater the likelihood that it will benefit from government subsidies of secondary education.[34] This outcome is especially perverse, because in Kenya, as in many developing countries, the government generates much of its revenue from regressive import and excise duties rather than from progressive income taxes.[35]

Conclusions

The private rate of return to investment in secondary education is markedly higher for children who attend government secondary schools than for children who attend harambee schools. The reason is partly the lower private costs of government schooling and partly the higher gross returns. The latter phenomenon is the result of the higher level of cognitive skills of government school graduates.[36] Moreover, a positive relationship between family income and the probability of reaping the subsidies to government schools contributes to the difference in private rates of return. These findings provide the basis for efficiency and equity arguments for reducing per pupil subsidies in government schools by selectively increasing user fees.

Our simulations indicate that it would take an increase in user fees in excess of 8,000 shillings per student per annum to equalize private rates of return in the two systems. The revenue potential of user fees in government schools is therefore substantial—more than 300 percent of government per student recurrent expenditures on secondary education. In part, the revenue potential is so large because in the relevant range the price elasticity of demand for government schooling appears to be so small. It must be emphasized, however, that, in practice, the revenue potential will be less than the amount indicated because of the inability of some families to borrow in formal credit markets to finance schooling. Nevertheless, a substantial proportion of students in government schools are from families with the means to pay the cost of their children's education who would be willing to do so in the absence of a highly subsidized alternative. The willingness of relatively low-income families paying high fees to send children to low-quality harambee schools that yield low private returns provides the evidence for the latter assertion.

Government schools are unlikely to be underutilized as a consequence of even substantial increases in user fees, nor would a reduction of per pupil subsidies result in a deterioration of school quality, as private funds would simply substitute for public funds, leaving per pupil expenditures unchanged. There is some danger of inefficient changes in the composition of the student body of government schools and of a reduction in the size of the secondary system as a whole as a consequence of increases in user fees. There is some reason to believe that those students from uneducated (poor) backgrounds forced to withdraw from the school system by the rise in fees will be the most able. The reason is that students who gain access to government secondary schools without having the advantages of educated parents are likely to be unusually bright. If the increases in fees are uniform, relatively bright but poor students may terminate their education and may be replaced by less able students from higher-income families who would otherwise have gone to harambee schools.

To avoid this eventuality, increases in user fees could be discriminatory. In effect, a needs-based scholarship program could ensure that admissions decisions would continue to reflect solely meritocratic criteria. Such a program is bound to suffer from one of the two following problems: if the criteria for awarding scholarships are too loose, the scholarship program will cost too much; if the criteria are too tight, then the government secondary system may lose students who would qualify on meritocratic grounds. Though the difficulties of assessing ability to pay should not be underestimated, this system is likely to distribute government subsidies more equitably than the current system. At present, the least needy have the highest probability of obtaining a subsidy. The gap between what the government could charge and what it does charge is equal in value to income from two years of work at the mean urban wage. One alternative to raising school fees and providing scholarships to the needy would be to raise fees and then to provide all students with loans to finance the private costs of a government secondary school education. This approach would have the advantage of avoiding the application of means tests. The disadvantage lies in the administration of a program for repayment. In Kenya the "pay-as-you-earn" tax system could be used for this purpose.

Reducing per student subsidies by allowing low-subsidy harambee schools to satisfy an increasing proportion of the growing demand for secondary schooling has been a de facto policy of the Kenyan government for more than a decade. Our results suggest that, for reasons of allocative efficiency, the case for this approach is actually not as strong as the case for raising user fees in government schools. The difference between the two systems in social rates of return indicates that harambee schools are less efficient than government schools, that is, they raise worker productivity less per shilling of total expenditure. Government regulation of quality in harambee schools together with small subsidies (relative to those given to government schools) for quality-improving purposes, however, may substantially curtail the efficiency costs of this means of reducing per student subsidies in the entire secondary system.[37] Such would be the case if the difference in efficiency between the two systems was explained by the higher total expenditure per pupil in government than in harambee schools and by the finding that Kenyan secondary schools lie on a portion of the education production function that is characterized by increasing returns.

Notes

1. The wider gaps observed in the structure of earnings in low-income countries than in high-income countries could be attributed to the relative scarcity of educated labor in the former. For evidence of substantial compression of the educational structure of wages and reduction in the inequality of pay in East Africa as a consequence of the expansion of secondary education, see Knight and Sabot (1983a).

2. Harambee is a Swahili word meaning "let's pull together": harambee schools are those built and financed by the local community.

3. The exchange rate in 1980 was 7.57 shillings to the U.S. dollar. The mean annual earnings of the manual workers in our sample was about 9,500 shillings. Per capita income was about $420 in 1981. Throughout, our analysis compares government with harambee schools to the exclusion of other private schools. The reason is the heterogeneity of the "other" category. Some few of these private schools are very good and very costly; most are of very poor quality and low in cost. Thus this category would have had to be further disaggregated, and some key data were not available for the component parts. The omission does not pose a serious problem, as it appears that harambee schools are representative in key respects of the larger group of low-cost private schools.

4. We do not suggest that harambee schools are attempting to offer a qualitatively different type of education, for example more practical or vocational training rather than an academic education. Their curriculum is oriented toward preparation for the same lower exams at the end of secondary school that are taken by government school students.

5. For detailed discussion of the nature of the ability tests and the influence of ability on accumulation of cognitive skills and on earnings, see Boissiere, Knight, and Sabot (1985).

6. Predictions are made with wage functions presented in table 22-2. They do not allow for any compression of the educational structure of wages that might result from educational expansion.

7. In this model, whether an individual demands secondary schooling depends solely on whether the expected present value of net benefits is positive and on whether the individual chooses between segments of the secondary system solely on the basis of the relative magnitude of present values.

8. Government guidelines call for holding expenditures for education to 30 percent or less of the recurrent nondefense budget. For 1981–83, the share was estimated to be nearly 35 percent.

9. The estimated net enrollment ratio in primary schools in 1981 is still only 0.83. Hence, in addition to keeping pace with population growth (3.8 percent per annum),

the primary system must expand sufficiently to enroll the 17 percent of school-age children who are not yet in school.

10. Although the returns to government schooling are high if people are capital constrained, a rise in user fees may force them to withdraw from the government system. A reduction of government school fees to a level below that of harambee school fees will mean students' withdrawal from the secondary school system entirely. When fees in government schools are raised above those in harambee schools, people facing liquidity constraints may be forced to switch into the harambee system even though the private returns are lower.

11. If the net benefits of secondary education are B_t per year, extending over a period of n years, the internal rate of return (r) to investment by an individual in four years of secondary education (during which B_t is negative) is calculated by solving the following equation for r:

$$\sum_{t=1}^{n} \frac{B_t}{(1+r)^t} = 0.$$

12. Such estimates of social returns of course do not take into account the externalities mentioned above that are generated by the secondary system, which would tend to increase the social returns.

13. We also estimate a version of equation 22-2 in which S_i interacts with the other dependent variables, but we conclude, using F tests, that this is not a superior specification.

14. The assumption here is that, although there will be a large difference between primary and secondary school leavers with respect to their proportions in the white-collar intensive public sector, the difference between government and harambee secondary school leavers in this regard will be relatively small.

15. There are likely to be differences in profiles between cohorts of school leavers because of the changes in the education-occupation matrix associated with rapid educational expansion. See Knight and Sabot (1981).

16. Recall that both the government and the harambee secondary systems have been growing very rapidly.

17. The survey is administered by the Central Bureau of Statistics in collaboration with the Ministries of Basic and Higher Education. The figure for average private expenditure per student for harambee schools is a weighted average of the expenditures in assisted harambee schools and unaided harambee schools, where the weights are the proportion of total harambee enrollments in the two types of schools. Similarly, the figure for private expenditure per pupil for government schools is a weighted average of the expenditures in the various types of government schools where the weights are the proportions in the different types of government schools.

18. The government expenditure figures are aggregates; to obtain per pupil expenditures, it is necessary to use the appropriate enrollments. Although public expenditures on harambee schools are confined to assisted harambee schools, the appropriate enrollment figure for our purposes is total harambee enrollments. Because our other costs and our returns data refer to 1979, it is necessary to deflate government expenditures. To do so we use 12 percent, the official government estimate of the rate of inflation for 1980.

19. The large majority of rate-of-return studies share this weakness of focusing exclusively on urban wage employment. See Psacharopoulos and Hinchliffe (1973).

20. We assume that the wages of primary school leavers are an accurate measure of opportunity costs of secondary school leavers. If entrance to secondary schools is meritocratic, this measure of opportunity costs will be too low. Moreover, to the extent that government secondary entrants are of higher quality than harambee entrants, the opportunity costs of the former will be still higher.

21. The 6,372-shilling difference between the total cost of schooling (3,368 shillings per annum) and the fee that could be charged, given perfect capital markets, would be a tax on educational expenditure.

22. See Bertrand and Griffin (1983). This estimate ignores the general equilibrium effects of a rise in user fees: if people spend more of their income on education, they may spend less on other goods that the governmnent taxes, which will have a negative impact on public revenues, or less on goods that are subsidized, which will have a positive impact on public revenues.

23. High-cost, high-quality private schools enroll only a small proportion of secondary students. Some expansion could drain revenue from the government system.

24. The actual cost of one shilling in public money is greater than the nominal cost because of the administrative and efficiency costs of collecting public money via the tax system. Taking this factor into account would lower the social return to government schools. Harambee schools, however, are often built and supported with voluntary labor and other inputs that are not "costed," in which case one shilling of private money may also be an underestimate of resources used.

25. The fact that government and harambee school leavers with the same exam scores are predicted to earn the same wages reinforces our assumption that the only characteristic that differentiates government and harambee leavers is their exam results.

26. Strictly speaking, linearity of wages in education does not imply constancy in rate of return over education of different lengths, because the length of the working life decreases as years of education increase. This qualification is unlikely to be quantitatively important.

27. Because so few pupils drop out of government school, there is no need to adjust these returns.

28. School leavers may have obtained income from other sources during this period. The survey does not yield estimates of such income.

29. The following procedure was adopted: when we predict the lifetime wage profile for primary school leavers we impose zero wages for the first two years, a third of a year's wage for the third year, and wages in the Tth year equivalent to $(T - 2.7)$ years of experience. When we predict the wage profile for government secondary school leavers, the wages for the first four years after primary school are zero as before. In the fifth year, 0.2 of a year's wages are imposed, and in the Tth year wages equivalent to $(T - 4.8)$ years of experience. For harambee school leavers zero wages are imposed for the first five years after primary school, in the sixth year half of a year's wages, and in the Tth year wages equivalent to $(T - 5.5)$ years of experience.

30. The simulation was conducted as follows: wage function 22-3 in table 22-4 was reestimated (see equation 22-4), and we substituted for the disaggregated set of dummies the more aggregate exam score variable used in the probit education production function. We then substitute the O-level scores for the graduates of the two types of school that were predicted when family background is set at the sample mean into the wage function to predict, in turn, the respective earnings streams for the graduates from the two types of school. The simulation removes the part of the higher cognitive achievement and earnings of government school leavers due to their more educated family background.

31. Note that in this model the coefficients do not represent the marginal change in the probability associated with each independent variable as they do in a simple linear probability model. For heuristic reasons, therefore, in our results, predicted probabilities for various representative groups are presented.

32. This relationship is not unique to Kenya. For reviews of studies that have documented such a relationship in other contexts, see Alexander and Simmons (1975) and Bridge, Judd, and Moock (1979).

33. Virtually all primary education is provided by the government; there is no equivalent to harambee schools at the primary level in Kenya.

34. Kenya is not unique in this regard. For evidence of a similar outcome in the United States, see Hansen and Weisbrod (1969), and in Colombia see Jallade (1974).

35. See Fields (1975a) for evidence that the overall incidence of taxes in Kenya is regressive.

36. There is some expectation that the scarcity rents earned by the highest achievers in secondary schools may be reduced over time. See Knight and Sabot (1983a).

37. Such as buying textbooks, hiring better-trained teachers, and reducing teacher/student ratios.

23

The Effects of Domestic Taxes on Foreign Private Investment

Mark Gersovitz

FOREIGN INVESTORS weigh the effects on their total after-tax profits of allocating the capital available to them among different countries. The tax policies of countries that receive capital (the hosts) are therefore an important influence on this allocation. Such a host affects its own benefits from foreign investments by taxing the profits that these investments generate. In this chapter I will discuss issues relevant to the taxation of the income from foreign direct investments, arising when a nonfinancial corporation invests in production facilities in a host. In the case of financial investments, the situation is often far simpler, and many of the issues raised in some sections below obviously do not arise.

In the case of an individual developing country, the opportunity cost for foreign investors is the marginal return they earn in investments outside this nation. In determining a country's optimal taxation of foreign investment, a useful distinction is between situations in which the host can affect this opportunity cost and those in which it cannot. This chapter begins with the theory of tax policy when the host can affect the opportunity cost of foreign investors. Few developing countries, if any, are likely to be in this situation, however, and the main focus is on a fixed opportunity cost.

In the simplest case, a fixed opportunity cost implies that a host should neither tax nor subsidize foreign investment. Various important exceptions to this rule exist, however, and are developed in subsequent sections. The issues discussed include tax policies abroad, especially the distinction between deductions and credits for taxes paid to developing countries; the option of consolidating tax paid abroad rather than reporting on a host-by-host basis; deferral of taxes owed to the investor's home country; transfer pricing by the investor; separate accounting versus formula apportionment; and constraints imposed by investors' fears of expropriation. A final section raises some issues in the implementation of tax policies and investment incentives. Caves (1982, chap. 8), Corden (1974, chap. 12), and Shoup (1974) are excellent earlier

I thank Richard J. Arnott, Mervyn King, Russ Krelove, and David Newbery for helpful discussions of this topic. Roger H. Gordon and John D. Wilson very kindly allowed me access to their unpublished work on formula apportionment, which I mention in my text.

surveys that this chapter seeks to complement. Kopits (1976) and Kyrouz (1975) provide some evidence on the international variation in corporate tax rates, on tax bases, and on other aspects of taxation of international investment by both host and home countries.

The Large Host

Trade theorists have done considerable work on international factor mobility when the return required by foreign investors depends positively on the quantity of foreign capital they provide. In this case, the host can act as a monopsonist, choosing the quantity-return combination it most prefers via a tax on foreign capital (Corden, 1974). I describe this classical case for the taxation of foreign capital to show that it is not relevant to the developing countries.

It is not always stated why the return paid to foreign investors depends on the quantity of capital they provide. Instead, an upward-sloping supply curve of foreign capital is often posited as an assumption. When a reason is given, however, it is usually that transferring capital from abroad makes it scarcer there, raises its marginal product, and therefore increases the opportunity cost of foreign investors.[1]

If, in addition, the host has monopoly power in trade, optimal policy is to choose a tariff and a capital tax jointly (Batra, 1973, chap. 13). In Gehrels's (1971) analysis, a host country that also imports the capital-intensive good improves the terms on which it obtains foreign capital together with its terms of trade when it raises its trade duty. Similarly, for such a country, the optimal restriction of foreign capital is made greater by the fact that the host's terms of trade are simultaneously improved. Although it is true that the average developing country is both capital poor and an importer of capital-intensive goods, no developing country is large enough to affect its terms of trade and the terms on which it imports capital.

Because the typical developing country is hardly large enough to affect the stock of capital abroad appreciably, the monopsonist justification for taxation of foreign capital seems largely irrelevant to the type of host under discussion in this paper. In the following sections, I will consider only cases where the opportunity cost of investors is fixed and will instead examine reasons other than the classical one for taxing foreign capital.

No Taxation of Foreign Capital

If the opportunity cost of investors is fixed, it is often argued, the host should not tax foreign capital. Such a conclusion depends, however, on a very particular set of assumptions. The two most important for practical purposes are (1) that foreign taxes on capital are zero and (2) that the returns that

Figure 23-1. *A Case in Which Foreign Capital Should Not Be Taxed*

Marginal product of capital

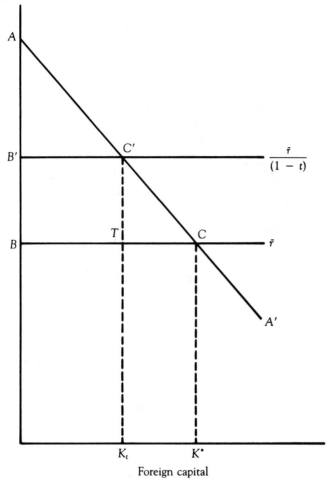

Foreign capital

foreign investors receive can be specified in advance by a binding agreement. Corden (1974) lists a number of additional assumptions.

Under these assumptions, any tax on foreign capital will be borne entirely by the host, and in addition, there will be a deadweight loss consequent on the diminished use of foreign capital. This case is useful as a benchmark for the models of subsequent sections. Figure 23-1 makes this argument for an industry with no domestically owned capital. Domestic labor is available in a fixed amount, L, and cooperates with foreign capital, K_f, to produce a single good sold at a fixed price. The fixed return to capital abroad is $\bar{r}$. The curve AA' is the marginal product of capital curve.

A tax (t) on profits raises the return gross of taxes required by investors to $\bar{r}/(1 - t)$, capital is reduced from K^* to K_t, and national income falls from ABC to $AB'C'$ plus the revenue $B'BTC'$, for a net loss of $C'TC$. If revenue must be raised, a tax on labor income, ABC, should be used, because labor is supplied in a fixed quantity. Even if the quantity of labor fell in response to a tax, say, because there is a labor-leisure tradeoff, a labor-income tax would still be preferred to a capital tax even though there would be some deadweight loss. Although labor may not be supplied perfectly inelastically, the assumption of a fixed supply price of capital means that capital is supplied infinitely elastically.

Even under these assumptions, an exception to the rule that profits should not be taxed arises if the government provides services for which it cannot otherwise charge. In this case, it will in general be appropriate to tax foreign capital to ensure that firms' decisions reflect the costs of these services. The user charge, however, should fall exclusively on profits only if the government-provided services are used in fixed proportion to capital.

Foreign Tax Rules and Developing Country Taxation of Foreign Firms under Separate Accounting

How other countries tax potential multinational investors in a developing country critically affects the way in which the developing country should treat these firms. In this section, I will be discussing variants of the so-called separate accounting system currently employed by most OECD home countries and by most developing country hosts. For tax purposes, every multinational firm has a country of residence, its home country. This home country may tax the worldwide profits of the firm, after taking into account taxes paid abroad, or, it may tax only profits arising from the firm's activities in the home country. Regardless of this choice by the home country, the essence of separate accounting is that the developing country host responds only to activities by the firms that are defined as taking place in the host.

How multinational firms choose their country of residence in response to tax codes is an important topic, of potential interest especially to OECD policymakers. The actions of an individual developing country, however, will probably have little effect on any firm's choice between different potential OECD homes, and developing countries are unlikely to be potential candidates for the status of home country. I have, however, encountered no theoretical treatment of the endogenous choice of home country, and for this and the preceding reasons I will treat the residence of the investor as exogenous.

The most frequently discussed alternative to a separate-accounting-with-residence system of taxation is formula apportionment, which I examine in more detail below. Under this option, host countries tax the proportion of world profits that is attributed to the firm's activities in the host on the basis of various indexes. In contrast to separate accounting, a change in the firm's profitability abroad, all other things equal, can affect its tax obligation to the host.

The firm acts to maximize its world profits (π_W) net of all taxes paid to the home and host countries. Initially, I assume that the firm's only choice relevant to this goal is the allocation of its fixed capital stock ($\bar{K}$) between production in the developing country host (K_f) and at home ($\bar{K} - K_f$). Each unit of capital invested at home earns a fixed before-tax return of $\bar{r}$ and an after-tax return of $(1 - \theta)\bar{r}$ where θ is the home country's corporate income tax rate.

One important factor influencing the optimal tax treatment of foreign firms is whether the home country treats taxes levied abroad as a deduction from income earned abroad or as a credit against the tax it assesses on this income.[2] The deduction provision means that the home country taxes income earned abroad net of taxes paid abroad. Under the credit option, tax on income earned abroad is calculated without reference to taxes paid abroad, and then taxes paid abroad are subtracted from these taxes due, up to the whole amount of taxes calculated in the first step. An analysis of these two situations leads to the following rules for profits taxation by the developing country:

1. If the home country treats foreign taxes as a deduction, the host should not tax the foreign firm.
2. If the home country treats foreign taxes as a credit against taxes on foreign income, the host should tax foreign firms at rate θ, the foreign corporate income tax rate.

A sketch of a proof for these rules is as follows. In the case of a tax deduction, the foreign firm will see its foreign operations (K_f) as contributing π_f to its world profits over and above what they would be if it invested only at home at rate $(1 - \theta)\bar{r}$:

$$(23\text{-}1) \qquad \pi_f = (1 - \theta)(1 - t)[pF(K_f, L) - wL] - (1 - \theta)\bar{r} K_f$$

where L is the amount of domestic labor employed at wage w, t is the corporate income tax rate in the host, and $(1 - t)[pF - wL]$ is income subject to home taxes. The price of output is p, and output is produced using the production function $F()$. Taking the derivative of π_f with respect to K_f yields:

$$(23\text{-}2) \qquad (1 - \theta)(1 - t)pF_K - (1 - \theta)\bar{r} = 0$$

so that the foreign firm sets $(1 - t)pF_K$ equal to $\bar{r}$. Any increase in t will decrease K_f, raising pF_K above the before-tax rate abroad. The incidence of the tax will be borne entirely by the host.

On the other hand, if the home country allows a credit for taxes paid abroad up to the amount due on that income when no foreign taxes are levied, then

$$(23\text{-}3) \qquad \pi_f = [1 - \theta - t + \min(t, \theta)][pF(K_f, L) - wL]$$
$$- (1 - \theta)\bar{r} K_f.$$

Table 23-1. *Illustrative Projects*

Item	Home project	Host project, no subsidy	Host project, with subsidy
1. Output	10	8	8
2. Host subsidy	—	—	2
3. Host tax on (1) + (2)	—	4	5
4. Tax credit = min$(t, \theta)[(1) + (2)]$	—	4	5
5. Home tax = $\theta[(1) + (2)]$	5	4	5
6. Net income to firm = (1) + (2) − (3) + (4) − (5)	5	4	5
7. Net income to host if project done = (3) − (2)	—	4	3
8. Host project done after comparison to home project	—	no	yes

— Not applicable.

The firm's first-order condition is

$$(23\text{-}4) \qquad [1 - \theta - t + \min(t, \theta)] \, pF_K - (1 - \theta)\bar{r} = 0.$$

As long as $t \leq \theta$, t has no effect on the firm's decision on K_f because $\min(t, \theta)$ = t. Above θ, increases in t lead to a fall in K_f as in 23-2, and so $(t > \theta)$ should not be adopted. To tax at less than θ, however, only transfers tax revenue from the host to the home country. Note also that with $t = \theta$, $pF_K = \bar{r}$ as in the tax deduction model with $t = 0$; the country does, however, gain revenue.

Still, the host can do better than rule 2 by driving the marginal value product of capital, pF_K, below $\bar{r}$ by subsidizing foreign capital if this is allowed by the home country. In this case, it turns out that the country's opportunity cost of capital is $(1 - \theta)\bar{r}$ rather than $\bar{r}$. Consider the projects described in table 23-1. All are assumed to use an equal amount of capital, and the home country tax rate is $\theta = 0.5$.

Because the home project pays 5, the host project will not be undertaken without a subsidy, and the host receives no income. With a subsidy, however, the firm can be provided with its opportunity cost income of 5, and the host can at least realize a tax income of 3 over the subsidy. In fact, the host will find it worthwhile to subsidize any project that provides output of more than five units. The general rule is

3. If the home country treats foreign taxes as a credit, the host should tax the profits of foreign investors at rate θ and subsidize them at rate $s = \theta/(1 - \theta)$. The marginal value product of capital will then be $(1 - \theta)\bar{r}$, the after-tax return to capital abroad.

In this case,

$$(23\text{-}5) \qquad \pi_f = [1 - \theta - t + \min(t, \theta)](1 + s)[pF(K_f, L) - wL]$$
$$- (1 - \theta)\bar{r} K_f.$$

The intuitive reasoning behind rule 3 is that, by both taxing and subsidizing profits, the host need not be constrained to share in the distortion that the home country has imposed. Instead the host can profitably undertake any projects that give a return equal to the opportunity cost of capital to the firm, $(1 - \theta)\bar{r}$. On the other hand, from a viewpoint of global efficiency, hosts should be forbidden to use such subsidy schemes, because they result in different marginal products of capital in the home and host countries.

This strategy presupposes that the home country is willing to allow a tax credit based on the gross tax rather than on the tax net of subsidies. In fact, several OECD countries have had programs allowing developing country hosts to forgo a profits tax while allowing their firms to take a tax credit for the amount that would have been paid (Lent, 1967). This provision can correspond exactly to the tax-subsidy scheme described above. For the example of table 23-1, it would mean a host tax of 5 with a remission of 2 and a home country tax credit of 5. Because rule 3 applies to the marginal product, it can be restated as "tax at rate θ but then remit this tax entirely to the investor," who nonetheless receives a full home country credit. Programs that allow tax credits for remitted taxes are, however, not widespread and many OECD governments may consider only the tax paid net of the subsidy as eligible for a tax credit.

If such a tax-subsidy scheme were disallowed by the home country, various suboptimal strategies would be available to the host. It might be possible to subsidize the output of the firm rather than its profits. In this case,

$$(23\text{-}6) \qquad \pi_f = [1 - \theta - t + \min(t, \theta)](1 + s)[pF(K_f, L) - wL]$$
$$- (1 - \theta)\bar{r}K_f.$$

The subsidy then applies equally to all other factors the firm hires, in this case labor. There is consequently a distortion of decisionmaking relative to equation 23-5, a distortion that increases with the elasticity of supply of these other factors. For this reason, if the host is restricted to an output subsidy, the optimal one will attract less capital than the optimal profits subsidy.

A third, even less direct policy is to protect the firm with a tariff.[3] In this case the definition of investor profit is the same as equation 23-6, with $s = \tau$, the tariff rate. Relative to a subsidy that is equivalent from the firm's viewpoint, a tariff discourages domestic consumption, resulting in a deadweight loss to consumers. Thus tariff protection is inferior to a production subsidy, which is in turn inferior to a profits subsidy. The optimal tariff will always be less than the optimal production subsidy. Nonetheless, if a production subsidy is ruled out by the tax codes of home countries, whereas tariffs are clearly not, some protection is justified.[4] This result contrasts sharply with the conclusions of trade and investment models that ignore host corporate taxes and tax credits. In these models, tariff-induced inflows of capital make the country worse off.[5]

A number of secondary considerations may affect developing country taxation of foreign investors. Some of these factors suggest a tax below the foreign rate even in the presence of foreign tax credits, whereas others argue for a rate above this one. These factors include most-favored-nation (or equal treatment) rules, effects on domestic savings, foreign tax deferral, transfer pricing, foreign tax consolidation, and taxation of rents.

It may not be possible to tax investors from different countries differently. The motivation for such a policy of differentiation comes from the fact that home countries themselves differ in the tax policies each has adopted, for instance with regard to allowing credits or deductions on taxes paid abroad (Kopits, 1976). If the host were constrained to treat investors equally, regardless of their home countries, and some investors from each type of country were present in equilibrium, then it would be optimal to tax at a rate between the highest and lowest that would be optimal if discrimination by origin were possible. The most-favored-nation principle is not, however, well established in the area of foreign taxation, so this constraint may not be important in practice (Mutén, 1983).

Another form of discrimination in taxation is between foreign investors and domestic investors in the host country. The preceding models ignore domestic capital. If domestic saving behavior depends on the after-tax return on capital, this response will influence the optimal taxation of foreign investors if all capital must be taxed in the same way. In general, the optimal tax may be above or below the rates indicated by the preceding models. It may be possible to tax foreign investors differentially, however, say, via a withholding tax, in which case these considerations are not relevant.[6]

Most home countries tax profits earned abroad only when these earnings are repatriated (Mutén, 1983). To the extent that foreign investors value this option of tax deferral, host countries that tax foreign investors' profits as they accrue rather than at the time of repatriation will reduce the incentive to invest. This statement is true even when taxation at the home country tax rate would post no disincentive because there is a foreign tax credit. For neutrality to prevail, taxation by the host not only cannot exceed the home tax rate but also must be imposed at the same time.[7]

The discussion has so far assumed that taxes above rate θ can be imposed, although I have argued that it is suboptimal to do so. The foreign investor may, however, be able to use transfer pricing to prevent a country from successfully collecting revenues. A firm may, for instance, import an input from its production facilities abroad, and the host country may not be able to control the price that is used in intrafirm transfers of the input and therefore the income that is paid abroad. If there is no host country tariff on the input, then the investor can set the transfer price sufficiently high to ensure that it pays no more tax than the home country assesses. If there is a foreign tax credit, it may be especially difficult to prevent this practice by controlling the transfer price, because the firm need only set this price sufficiently high to absorb the difference between the host and home tax rates. Tariffs on the input will undermine the investor's ability to avoid paying taxes, because a high transfer price will subject the investor to high tariff charges.[8] On the other hand, research and development expenditures, head office expenses, and interest rate charges can be allocated between the home and host components of the multinational firm and can be particularly good channels for transferring profits abroad. In fact, home country rules that require the allocation of these expenses in proportion to the gross income attributed to operations in different jurisdictions can generate incentives similar to the formula apportionment rules discussed below (see Adler, 1979).

An exception to the undesirability (and the impossibility) of taxing above the home country rate can occur when the firm invests in more than one host. In this case, whether the firm is able to and chooses to consolidate its worldwide income in reporting to the home country tax authorities is crucial. The alternative method of reporting is on a host-by-host basis. Prior to 1976, firms resident in the United States had this choice; since that time only the former method has been allowed (Adler, 1979).

As Jenkins and Wright (1975) note, consolidation permits excess tax credits generated in one host to be used as an offset against home country taxes due on income from hosts with tax rates below the home country's rate. On the other hand, unconsolidated reporting has the advantage that a loss in one host (A) can be deducted from taxable income generated in the home country itself even if profits are made in a second host (B). These profits in B, taxed by B without regard to the losses in A, may already be protected from home country taxation by tax credits generated by B taxation. Consolidation with the losses from A would then generate unusable excess tax credits only as the consolidated income falls relative to income from B without affecting taxes paid to B or generating the tax deduction against home country income allowed under unconsolidated reporting.

Jenkins and Wright (1975, pp. 2–3) report that consolidation is generally practiced by manufacturing firms. Petroleum companies, however, have found it beneficial to adopt unconsolidated reporting when high exploration and other initial costs generate losses at the beginning of operations. Subsequent dispersion of those companies' investments into high tax countries has tended to move them to adopt consolidated reporting. Such a conversion may be legally irreversible for any parent corporation.

If the firm consolidates, and if other hosts tax below the home country rate, then the firm will be short of tax credits for the income generated in these hosts. In this case, other developing countries can tax above the home country rate (to the point where the shortage of tax credits is exhausted) without affecting the firm's investment decisions. Such low-tax developing country hosts may exist, as mentioned above, if tax policy cannot discriminate among investors by home country and if these developing countries get a relatively large amount of their investments from home countries with low tax rates or without foreign tax credit provisions in their tax codes.

So far, I have assumed that no rents are generated by a firm's investment activities. Either there are many firms in any particular industry in the host, or in the case of very small hosts, the competition comes from world trade, which is likely to be relatively competitive. If there are rents, however, it may be possible to tax them away without affecting the firm's incentives to invest. Particular instances are mineral investments when the deposits are richer than the marginal deposits being mined. In this case, the country will want to ensure that it appropriates these rents through either royalties or a corporate income tax that taxes away these rents without preventing investments in mining capacity. One such tax would be a 100 percent tax on cash flow that allows all investment costs as well as labor costs to be deducted in the year incurred with a loss carry-forward provision (that includes a payment of a return on losses carried forward). The host tax on rents is likely to exceed the home tax due on this income. To the extent that a tax on rents can qualify as an income tax under the home country tax code, and the firm can use these credits to shelter income earned elsewhere, the return required by the firm on its investment in extraction can be driven below even $(1 - \theta)\bar{r}$ because the firm receives an implicit return in the form of tax credits. This type of tax has been suggested by Garnaut and Clunies-Ross (1974). As Jenkins (1974) notes, however, it presupposes that the host can stop transfer pricing that diminishes the rents subject to taxation if the firm cannot use the tax credits. Furthermore, the firm must be given an incentive to produce efficiently, because under these rules it has little reason to minimize costs. Although I raise these issues, a comprehensive discussion of taxation of resource rents, including mechanisms for auctioning resource concessions, is beyond the scope of this chapter.

The Formula Apportionment Alternative

An alternative to separate accounting in defining the tax base is the formula apportionment system. Many U.S. states have adopted this type of system in assessing their corporate tax; see McClure (1974). Under this system, the tax authority claims the right to tax a share of the worldwide profits of any company doing business in its jurisdiction. The share subject to taxation may depend on the firm's capital, wage bill E, or sales S located in the jurisdiction relative to the worldwide values of these variables. For instance, in the so-called three-factor formula with equal weights, the firm's tax liability in the jth jurisdiction, T_j, would be

$$(23\text{-}7) \qquad\qquad T_j = \frac{t_j}{3} \left(\frac{K_j}{K_W} + \frac{E_j}{E_W} + \frac{S_j}{S_W} \right) \pi_W$$

where the variables subscripted by W refer to the worldwide values of capital, wage bill, sales, and profits, respectively, and t_j is the jth authority's tax rate. Such a three-factor tax is really a hybrid, because it depends not just on the value of profits or even of capital.

One advantage of formula apportionment is its elimination of opportunities to avoid tax payment through transfer pricing. On the other hand, tax authorities in any jurisdiction will find it difficult to verify the world components of the formula. These administrative considerations, however, are not the only ones relevant to the choice between separate accounting and formula apportionment. As Gordon and Wilson (1983) show, the two systems may raise different amounts of revenue, given the level of deadweight loss. In this section, I follow their analysis. A minor change is that I allow the firm to invest at the fixed opportunity cost of capital in the home country as well as to borrow at it. Unless otherwise indicated, one small host considers its own benefits (in terms of revenue) and costs (in terms of deadweight loss) from adopting either a formula apportionment or a separate accounting system. In either case, the (single, large) home country taxes foreign source income and allows a foreign tax credit as in the preceding section.

As Gordon and Wilson show, the three-factor model is extremely difficult to analyze. Important aspects of formula apportionment can, however, be indicated by a model in which capital is the only factor in the apportionment formula. The host defines the tax base to be

$$(23\text{-}8) \qquad \pi_W = pF(K_f, L) - wL + \bar{r}(K_W - K_f).$$

Total taxes paid by the investor to the host are

$$(23\text{-}9) \qquad T_a = t_a \frac{K_f}{K_W} \pi_W$$

where t_a is the host's rate on the apportioned profits. The investor maximizes income from investments in the host and home countries net of taxes and factor payments:

$$(23\text{-}10) \qquad \pi_f = \pi_W - T_a - \theta\bar{r}(K_W - K_f) - (1 - \theta)\bar{r} K_W.$$

The next-to-last term accounts for home country taxes on the assumption that

$$(23\text{-}11) \qquad T_a \geq \theta[pF(K_f, L) - wL]$$

so that the firm has excess tax credits. (If the firm is short of tax credits, the method by which T_a is raised would be of no interest.) The last term represents the cost of capital.

The firm maximizes equation 23-10 with respect to K_f, K_W, and L to yield:

$$(23\text{-}12a) \qquad \frac{\partial \pi_f}{\partial L} = \left(1 - \frac{t_a K_f}{K_W}\right)(pF_L - w) = 0$$

so that there is no distortion in labor use and

$$(23\text{-}12b) \qquad \frac{\partial \pi_f}{\partial K_f} = pF_K - (1 - \theta)\bar{r} - t_K(pF_K - \bar{r}) - t_a \frac{\pi_W}{K_W} = 0$$

where $t_K \equiv t_a K_f / K_W$, the capital-weighted average formula apportionment tax rate. Finally,

(23-12c)
$$\frac{\partial \pi_f}{\partial K_W} = -t_K \frac{\pi_W}{K_W^2} + t_K \frac{\bar{r}}{K_W} = 0$$

which, with 23-8, 23-12a, and 23-12b, implies $t_K = 0$, $K_W = \infty$, and π_W/K_W = $\bar{r}$. Substituting for π_W/K_W into 23-12b and rearranging yields

(23-12d)
$$pF_K = (1 - \theta + t_a)\bar{r}$$

whereas from 23-9 total tax revenue is

(23-13)
$$T_a = t_a K_f \bar{r}.$$

Compare this equation to the case of separate accounting with a host tax of t_s > θ on profits earned in the host, as defined in 23-3, so that

(23-14)
$$pF_K = \frac{1 - \theta}{1 - t_s} \bar{r}$$

and revenue, T_s, is

(23-15)
$$T_s = t_s \frac{1 - \theta}{1 - t_s} K_f \bar{r}.$$

Now consider imposing taxes t_a and t_s such that pF_K and therefore K_f and the distortion are all the same. If we use the equality of the right sides of equations 23-12d and 23-14, it can be proved that $T_a = T_s$, so that it does not make any difference whether the host adopts a separate accounting or an apportionment scheme from the perspective of deadweight loss. This result generalizes to any number of small hosts as long as the firm invests in the large home country (as indicated by the $\bar{r}(K_W - K_f)$ term in equation 23-8.

By contrast, if the only investment opportunities are in small countries, the model can be modified to:

(23-8')
$$\pi_W = pF(K_f, L) - wL + \tilde{p}\tilde{F}(\tilde{K}_f, \tilde{L}) - \tilde{w}\tilde{L}$$

and

(23-9')
$$\pi_f = \pi_W - T_a - \tilde{T}_a - (1 - \theta)\bar{r}K_W,$$

where $K_W = K_f + \tilde{K}_f$ and the tilde denotes the second host. In this case, it can be shown that $T_s \gtrless T_a$ as $t_a \gtrless t_K$, where $t_K \equiv (t_a K_f + \tilde{t}_a \tilde{K}_f)/K_W$.

For an equal distortion, revenue under apportionment using a single capital factor differs from revenue under separate accounting when there is no large investment available. To put it another way, for a given amount of revenue, the deadweight loss experienced by the host under separate accounting is less than under apportionment when its tax rate on apportioned profits exceeds the world tax rate on apportioned profits calculated using capital share weights (t_K). In a multihost world, this result on revenue for a given deadweight loss holds for the jth host if $t_{aj} > t_K$ where $t_K \equiv \Sigma(K_j t_j)/K_W$. Conversely, if in the developing country $t_{aj} < t_K$, it gains more revenue under apportionment. As Gordon and Wilson argue, this property tends to make the system unstable, as the authorities for which $t_a > t_K$ have an incentive to switch to separate accounting to raise their revenue, given deadweight loss, and thereby lower t_K, causing more defections as other authorities find that their t_a exceeds the new, lower t_K. This aspect of apportionment must, however, be weighed with the administrative properties of these systems mentioned at the beginning of this section when the tax base is defined. Other formulas for apportionment must be investigated to understand how these results generalize.

Country Risk

We have seen a somewhat surprising result: optimal policy for a developing country is to subsidize foreign investors. If this policy were feasible and implemented, capital would be more abundant in the developing countries in the sense that there would be a lower marginal product than in the capital-exporting countries, although its ownership would be concentrated in the developed countries. These unrealistic conclusions suggest that influences constraining the international movement of capital have been neglected.[9] Factors are likely to operate to prevent the international distribution of capital implied by the subsidy rule, and they may undermine the validity of these subsidy schemes.

One very important factor that has been omitted so far is often called "country risk" by market participants. This term denotes their fear that sovereign governments will renege on contracts with foreign investors, will expropriate direct investments, or will repudiate international loans, and in general will prevent investors from realizing returns on their investments that justify the initial decision to invest. Concerns by foreign direct investors on this score seem well founded. For a large sample of developing countries, Williams (1975) estimates that about 20 percent of the value of foreign investments carried into or made from 1956 to 1972 was expropriated without compensation during this period.

Table 23-2 reproduces data country by country from the Williams study. It shows that there has been a great variation in investors' experience in different developing countries. Some countries have expropriated most or all foreign investments; others have expropriated more selectively. There has also been great variation in the compensation paid.

Outright, uncompensated expropriation is of course not the only type of action hosts can take that adversely affects foreign investors. Other threats to foreign investors include changes in: taxes, tariffs on inputs, rules for remitting profits, indigenization of ownership, and domestic content laws. It is difficult to model the motivations of hosts, and several complementary paradigms are necessary. On the one hand, investors may suffer losses consequent on revolutions or other large-scale upheavals. In these cases, there is probably little any individual investor can do to affect the risks faced, and in Eaton and Gersovitz (1983) these risks were therefore termed exogenous.

Table 23-2. The Coefficient of Nationalization

Country	Foreign investment stock, end 1972 (millions of dollars) (S)	Assets nationalized (millions of dollars) (A)	$\dfrac{A}{A+S}$ (percent)	Compensation paid (millions of dollars) (C)	C/A (percent)	$\dfrac{A-C}{A+S}$ (percent)
Algeria	250	1,746	87.5	202	11.6	77.4
Argentina	2,540	224	8.1	224	100.0	0
Bangladesh	110	810	88.0	10	1.2	87.0
Bolivia	87	83.1	48.9	81.6	98.2	0.9
Brazil	6,000	239	3.8	239	100.0	0
Burma	9	49.9	84.6	17.2	34.5	55.4
Chile	152	908	85.7	471	52.0	41.1
Congo, People's Rep.	110	3.5	3.1	3.0	85.7	0.4
Cuba	0	1,250	100.0	50	4.0	96.0
Ecuador	510	7.4	1.4	7.4	100.0	0
Egypt	40	518	92.8	279	53.9	42.8
Ghana	300	6	2.0	5	83.3	0.3
Guatemala	218	50	18.7	50	100.0	0
Guinea	110	108	49.5	69	63.9	17.9
Guyana	141	53.5	27.5	53.5	100.0	0
Haiti	42	0.5	1.2	0.5	100.0	0
India	1,211	33	2.7	33	100.0	0
Indonesia	566	1,510	72.7	730	48.3	37.6
Iraq	10	414	97.6	214	51.7	47.2
Jamaica	1,122	16.5	1.4	16.5	100.0	0
Kampuchea, Dem.	80	5	5.9	5	100.0	0
Lebanon	183	7.3	3.8	7.3	100.0	0
Libya	700	127	15.4	15	11.8	13.5
Mexico	2,826	171	2.4	171	100.0	0
Morocco	210	9	4.1	9	100.0	0
Nigeria	1,250	5	0.4	5	100.0	0
Pakistan	250	5	2.0	5	100.0	0
Peru	559	197	26.1	37	18.8	21.2
Sierra Leone	89	6.1	6.4	6.1	100.0	0
Somalia	9	15.4	63.1	7.7	50.0	31.6
Sri Lanka	110	14.5	11.6	14.5	100.0	0
Sudan	15	30	66.7	22.5	75.0	16.7
Syria	0	70	100.0	32	45.7	54.3
Tanzania	50	58	53.7	37	63.8	19.4
Trinidad	781	10	1.3	10	100.0	0
Tunisia	190	46	19.5	28	60.9	7.6
Uganda	20	70	77.8	21	30.0	54.4
Yemen (PDR)	38	15.6	29.1	7.8	50.0	14.6
Zaire	540	850	19.1	620	72.9	5.2
Zambia	500	354	41.5	354	100.0	0
Total	21,928	10,096	—	4,171	41.3	—

— Not applicable.

Notes: Figures to nearest $0.1 million where data are available; totals to nearest $1 million.

Source: Williams (1975).

In other situations, however, country risk may be the outcome of rational choice by a host that weighs the costs and benefits of taking hostile actions against foreign investors. Although the benefits are the obvious gains from not having to share the project's proceeds, the costs are less clear. If hosts are influenced by costs, however, the nature and extent of the sanctions that investors can use to prevent hostile acts critically determine their willingness to invest abroad. These sanctions are likely to be quite indirect because international property law hardly exists, and so international enforcement of contracts is severely circumscribed. They include loss of access to capital from abroad in the future, to trade in goods and services, to skilled manpower and technology, or to inputs, especially where manufacturing firms produce differentiated products. These and other aspects of the strategic interactions between hosts and investors are discussed in Eaton and Gersovitz (1981, 1983, and 1984) and in Gersovitz (1983). The important feature of these models is that country risk is endogenous.

A capital-importing government may wish to make a binding promise to foreign investors to forgo hostile actions with the goal of attracting investments. Binding promises are not generally feasible, however, because there is no international forum to enforce this type of contract. Once the investments have occurred, the strategy of allowing a return to investors may be time inconsistent (Kydland and Prescott, 1977). It may be optimal for a government to renege on its promise. Rational investors anticipating this situation will invest less than otherwise or possibly not at all, depending on the availability and force of penalties just described.

The wide variation in circumstances makes it impossible to present a general model of these phenomena. In particular, whether the foreigner is a direct investor or a financial lender may make a difference in the sanctions available (Eaton and Gersovitz, 1983). Thus if one form of investment is limited by country risk, it may still be possible to obtain additional funds in another form if additional sanctions are available.

One useful illustration of the interaction between the considerations of the last section and country risk can be developed using the model of Eaton and Gersovitz (1984). This is basically a static one-period model with the following sequence of behavior: first foreigners invest, then hosts decide on expropriation, next production takes place, and finally investors receive their returns, which depend on the host's previous decision on expropriation. Despite its static nature, the model illustrates some important considerations; Eaton and Gersovitz (1981 and 1983) present some explicitly dynamic models.

Assume that output can be produced with a constant-returns-to-scale production function using capital K_f, skilled manpower H, and unskilled labor L. The first two factors are entirely provided by the firm; the last is domestically supplied. Skilled manpower earns a constant return of v. If I continue the discussion of the models used in examining tax rules 1, 2, and 3, above, and include H in equation 23-5, the implication is

$$(23\text{-}5') \qquad \pi_f = [1 - \theta - t + \min(t, \theta)](1 + s)[pF(K_f, H, L) \\ - vH - wL] - (1 - \theta)\bar{\tau} K_f.$$

Firms choose H so that

$$(23\text{-}16) \qquad\qquad\qquad pF_H = v.$$

Furthermore, if investors are perfect competitors, the host can choose s so that for any level of K_f, $\pi_f = 0$. The relationship implied by equations 23-5' and 23-16 between host income from labor and taxes net of subsidies, Y, and K_f, given an s such that $\pi_f = 0$, is illustrated in figure 23-2 by the curve II. This locus is in effect the relation examined in the last section, and as stated in rule 3, Y reaches a maximum at K_f^* when $s = \theta/(1 - \theta)$.

So far, the model has neglected country risk. Eaton and Gersovitz (1984) assume that, if the investor is expropriated, H is withdrawn and cannot be replaced, whereas K_f is left behind in the possession of the host. All returns from the now-impaired project accrue to the host, so that host income after expropriation, Y^E, is

Figure 23-2. *Equilibrium of Investor and Host with Country Risk*

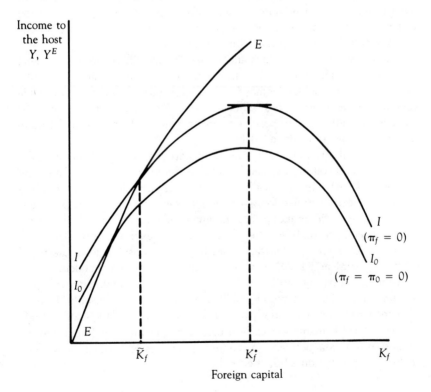

(23-17) $$Y^E = F(K_f, 0, L).$$

Host income is increasing in K_f. This relation is illustrated in figure 23-2 by the EE curve.

For any given K_f, the rational host chooses expropriation if Y, as determined by equations 23-5' and 23-16 is less than Y^E. Rational investors recognize this decision rule and never invest beyond $\tilde{K}_f$ in figure 23-2, the point where $Y = Y^E$. Depending on technology, the EE curve may cut the II curve to the left of K_f^*, and investment is constrained to $\tilde{K}_f$, or the intersection may be to the right of K_f^*, with K_f^* and $s = \theta/(1 - \theta)$ chosen because these levels maximize host welfare.

For purposes of this chapter, the important observation is that for $\tilde{K}_f < K_f$, $s < \theta/(1 - \theta)$. In fact, $\tilde{K}_f$ may be such that a negative subsidy, $s < 0$, is required to make $\pi_f = 0$ for $K = \tilde{K}_f$:

4. Country risk may not only make a positive subsidy undesirable but may also require total taxes on foreign profit at a rate above θ.

The case of a negative subsidy arises if the threat of expropriation makes it impossible to attract enough investment to drive the marginal product of capital below $\bar{r}$, let alone down to $(1 - \theta)\bar{r}$. The country should at least ensure that it pays no more for capital than $\bar{r}$, the opportunity cost of capital abroad, and it can do so by taxing foreign investors' profits. Otherwise, investors would earn rents that they do not require to invest but that provoke the host to expropriate.

Indeed, to forgo this tax and allow $\pi_f > 0$ is to attract even less capital because the gains to the host from expropriation will be increased. This result can be seen as follows: Assume $\pi_f = \pi_0 > 0$. Define $I_0 I_0$ as the locus of points in figure 23-2 such that $\pi_f = \pi_0$. For any given K_f, this locus must lie below the II curve and therefore intersects the EE curve to the left of $\tilde{K}_f$. These points are made in more detail in Eaton and Gersovitz (1984) in a model without home country tax credits.

In the preceding discussion it is known with certainty whether or not the host will expropriate. Rational investors therefore invest only to the point where the host would choose expropriation, and acts of expropriation would never occur. In models with uncertainty, however, rational investors may invest when the probability of expropriation is positive. They do so in the expectation that, if expropriation does not occur, they will earn enough profits to compensate for the risk of expropriation. As in Eaton and Gersovitz (1984, sec. 6), for instance, the host may have some endowment of skilled manpower H, say $\bar{H}$, that is a random variable only realized after the investment is made. For high values of $\bar{H}$, the host expropriates, as it can then operate the foreign capital relatively successfully.

In this model, risk-neutral competitive investors invest until expected profits, including the loss from expropriation, are driven to zero. There is therefore no need to impose a tax to achieve zero (expected) profits as in the certainty model. The probability of expropriation fills this role of the tax. Even in the absence of foreign tax credits, however, it may still be optimal for the host to tax or subsidize investors. First, in a model with an exogenous, positive probability of expropriation, investment should be subsidized to offset the tax implicit in expropriation. Second, in situations with an endogenous probability of expropriation, each investor may view the probability of expropriation as given with respect to the size of its own particular investment, although it recognizes that this probability depends on aggregate foreign investment. In this case, an externality leads to suboptimal investment even given the constraints imposed by country risk, something that can be corrected by government action. Finally, an increase in the subsidy not only makes it more attractive to invest, given the probability of expropriation, but also increases this probability by making it more attractive to seize the capital and forgo the need to pay a subsidy. With a foreign tax credit, it may be desirable to tax *and* subsidize investors rather than to do only one or the other.[10] It is unfortunately not easy to quantify the model in ways that provide guidance in specific situations.

Attracting Foreign Investment: Tax Holidays

Many countries have various programs that seek to attract foreign investments; see Shah and Toye (1979). The provisions of these programs are frequently different from the annual profits subsidy at a constant rate that I discussed above. One popular device is a tax holiday: either new firms or the profits from new investments are exempt from taxes for a number of years, after which taxes are paid at the same rate as other firms. Tax holidays have a number of shortcomings from the host's point of view and are probably not desirable relative to an annual subsidy at a constant rate.

First, such schemes may be less likely to be treated by home countries as a tax that can be used by the firm as a credit, with a subsidy added. Tax holidays may therefore result in a loss of tax revenue without a compensating increase in investment, because the investor finds the tax liability to the home country rising in an offsetting manner.

Second, firms may dissolve after the tax holiday ends, selling their capital to new firms if these are eligible for a tax holiday based on the purchase of used plant and equipment. Thus, the total subsidy may be larger than expected as the same equipment is passed on from one firm to another. Bond (1981) provides some evidence on this phenomenon in Puerto Rico. He further suggests that, if firms cannot resell their equipment, they may choose to invest in equipment that depreciates more rapidly than is optimal. In this way, they are able to exit soon after the tax holiday expires. Usher (1977b, p. 136) argues that tax holidays will bias investors against projects with long gestation periods, creating a further inefficiency.

Usher (1977*b*, p. 133) also notes that firms may transfer price between the project eligible for a holiday and other activities. By shifting profits from these activities, it can avoid taxes on them. This problem also applies to the subsidization at a constant annual rate of profits from individual projects. Once again, the extent of the subsidy may be much larger than is apparent initially, underlining a general problem in discriminating between old and new projects.

Conclusions

The taxation of foreign capital is no simple matter. Optimal policy depends on

1. Whether host countries are large in the sense of affecting the opportunity cost of investors
2. Whether home countries allow tax credits or tax deductions for taxes paid to hosts
3. Whether the investor reports to the home country on a consolidated or an unconsolidated basis
4. Whether home countries calculate taxes paid to hosts as gross or net of profits or production subsidies paid by hosts
5. The size of inefficiencies caused by production subsidies or tariffs that are used when profits subsidies are not allowed by home country tax codes
6. The scope for tax avoidance through transfer pricing
7. The extent to which firms value the opportunities for tax deferral by retaining earnings in the host
8. Whether foreign and domestic firms must be taxed at the same rate, and, if so, the elasticity of domestic savings
9. Whether the investor has the potential to earn rents
10. The importance of country risk.

These factors probably differ by industry and by home country of the investors. Thus the rules adopted should optimally vary in these ways as well. This statement, however, implies a complicated tax code that will be difficult to administer and leaves latitude for discretion and ultimately corruption. Furthermore, any discrimination among investors that depends on their country of origin violates most-favored-nation principles. Finally I note some important topics for future research: the determinants of the choice of home country by the investor, the value to the investor of deferral, the role of international differences in depreciation rules and in inflation, and the role of country risk.

Notes

1. Feldstein and Hartman (1979) analyze tax credit and deduction rules under exactly this assumption. They also assume, however, that the host takes as given the home country tax policy. This combination of assumptions seems somewhat inconsistent in that the host is large relative to the total capital stock but not relative to the home country tax authority.

2. Hamada (1966) discusses ways in which international tax agreements can emerge from strategic behavior by host and home countries.

3. Batra and Ramachandran (1980) discuss a model of trade and investment in the presence of tax credits and tariffs, but they do not discuss optimal tax/tariff policy. See also Khandker (1981) for correction of their model.

4. With a tariff at rate τ, the firm maximizes (23-6) with $s = \tau$. Let the international price be P and the domestic price be $p = (1 + \tau)P$, so that demand is $X(p)$, a function of the tariff-inclusive price. Then the host's goal is to choose t and τ to maximize social welfare, W, given by

$$W = \int_p^{X^{-1}(0)} X(x)dx + \tau P[X(p) - F(K_f, L) + wL$$
$$+ t[pF(K_f, L) - wL].$$

The first term is consumer's surplus, the second is the tariff revenue, the third is labor income, and the fourth is income from the corporate income tax. Maximize with respect to τ and t, holding L constant, and eliminate $\partial K/\partial\tau$ and $\partial w/\partial\tau$ by differentiating the first-order conditions of profit maximization from (23-6) with respect to τ and t (also using homogeneity) to give $t = \theta$ and

$$\tau^* = \frac{t}{\epsilon\xi/d + (1 - t)}$$

where $\epsilon = -X'p/X$ is the elasticity of demand, $\xi = -d\log F_K/d\log F = -FF_{KK}/F_K^2$ is an output elasticity, and $d = F/X$ is the ratio of domestic production to consumption. If there is a constant elasticity of substitution σ between K_f and L, and if α is the share of profits, then $\xi = (1 - \alpha)/\alpha\sigma$. Because $\partial\tau/\partial(d\sigma) \geq 0$ and $d \leq 1$, take high values of d and $\sigma = 1$ to obtain an upper bound $\tau^* \leq t/[(1 - \alpha)\epsilon + (1 - t)]$. If $\alpha = 0.4$, $\theta = t = 0.5$, and $\epsilon = 1.0$, then $\tau^* \leq 0.25$. Thus, the optimal second-best tariff that substitutes for the first-best profits subsidy, $s = \theta/(1 - \theta) = 1.0$, is likely to be relatively low.

5. See Brecher and Diaz Alejandro (1977), Brecher and Findlay (1983), and Yabuuchi (1982).

6. Horst (1980 and 1982) and Dutton (1982) discuss some aspects of the simultaneous taxation of foreign and domestic capital. Horst sees the issue, however, primarily from the perspective of world welfare maximization.

7. Horst (1977) discusses deferral provisions from the viewpoint of the home country. In this model the firm is assumed to defer a fixed proportion of its profits in the host country and maximizes world profits without regard to whether they are deferred or not. For the firm's perspective, see Adler (1979), Hartman (1977), Kopits (1972), and Mutti (1981). I am not aware of any work that endogenously determines the proportion of profits a firm would wish to defer and the extent to which this proportion is affected by host tax policy. The analogy to the retained earnings/dividend question (Feldstein and Green, 1983), one that has not been resolved, is apparent. It is therefore difficult to suggest what the disincentives from taxing on an accrual basis will be.

8. Horst (1971), Bond (1982), and Eden (1983) discuss transfer pricing in greater detail.

9. See Reddaway (1968, p. 219), Harberger (1978 and 1980), and Feldstein and Horioka (1980) for some evidence on the extent of international capital mobility and cross-country rates of return.

10. In this note, I sketch the results to which I alluded in the text on the assumption, made for reasons of space, that the reader is fully familiar with section 6 of Eaton and Gersovitz (1984). In the notation of this chapter, the modifications to the Eaton-Gersovitz model needed to prove these assertions are as follows: Let $H(x)$ be the host's endowment of H, with $H' > 0$ and x a uniform random variable distributed between 0 and 1. Ignore the possibility that $H(1)$ is so high as to lead to the export of H by an expropriating host. The host's income in case of expropriation, $Y^E(x)$, is

$$Y^E(x) \equiv G[K_f, \bar{H}(x), L] \equiv F[K_f, \bar{H}(x), L].$$

Income if expropriation does not occur, $Y^N(x)$, when there is a foreign tax at rate θ, a foreign tax credit and a domestic tax $t = \theta$, and a subsidy at rate s is

$$Y^N(x) = F(K_F, H, L) - (1 + s)F_K K_f - v(H - \bar{H}) + t(1 + s)F_K K_f$$

with H chosen so that $F_H = v$. The curve EE of Eaton and Gersovitz is given by $Y^E(x) = Y^N(x)$, which determines a value of x, x^*, for a given K_f such that $x > x^*$ implies expropriation. The curve II is given by

$$(1 + s) x^* F_K = \bar{r}.$$

Simultaneous solution of the curves EE and II determines x^* and K_f in equilibrium. The host's expected income is

$$EY = \int_0^{x^*} Y^N(x)dx + \int_{x^*}^1 Y^E(x) \, dx.$$

By totally differentiating the EE and II curves and using the property that the absolute value of the slope of the curve II must exceed that of the curve EE in equilibrium, it can be shown that $dEY/ds \gtreqless 0$.

PART 7

Findings
and Implications

THE LAST TWO CHAPTERS suggest directions for further research and assemble some conclusions from the theoretical developments and applied analyses in the earlier chapters.

First, we have seen that the theory can now be applied productively to many substantial practical problems of public policy. Second, it provides an approach that can be followed in a systematic way to organize the analysis of many issues that have not been covered in detail in this book. Third, by focusing attention in a direct and coherent manner on the identification of the consequences of policy changes, we define the topic of debate and thereby show how the desirability of proposed reforms may be questioned. Fourth, we have seen that the approach generates interesting, fruitful, and important directions for further research. The first chapter by Diamond describes some major programs of research, and the second, by the editors, underlines the main conclusions.

24

Optimal Tax Theory
and Development Policy:
Directions for Future Research

Peter Diamond

THIS CHAPTER CONSIDERS the directions that research on optimal tax theory might take to make the theory more useful for development policy questions. I first contrast the optimal tax approach with first-best analyses as they are normally taught in graduate economics programs. A background of the differences between these two approaches will facilitate the argument for the appropriateness of the optimal tax approach as a basis for both policy and continued research. Second, I discuss the problem of policy recommendation in general and the necessity of using some framework resembling that of optimal tax theory. Only after considering these two preliminary issues do I turn to the actual assumptions made in the development of the theory to date and suggest the directions of further research that I regard as most fruitful to pursue.

First- and Second-Best Analyses

First-best welfare theory as normally taught in graduate schools around the world is centered on the fundamental theorem of welfare economics. The theorem has two parts. The first is that, under suitable conditions, every competitive equilibrium is a Pareto optimum, and the second is that, under a somewhat different set of suitable conditions, every Pareto optimum can be achieved as a competitive equilibrium, provided that the income distribution is corrected before equilibrium is sought. That is, the theory assumes that lump-sum taxes are available. Lump-sum taxes can vary from person to person and are unaffected by any individual actions. This theorem plays a major role in organizing much of economics for both research and teaching purposes as well as affecting policy recommendations. I do not suggest that anyone regards the theorem as directly applicable, making it an appropriate basis for the simple derivation of policy conclusions in all settings (or even in one setting).

Rather, the conditions under which the theorems become true are used as a guide for the many ways in which actual economies deviate from desired allocations and simultaneously as a guide to the potential for policy intervention to improve social welfare. Thus, in industrial organization courses, the focus is on noncompetitive behavior, holding constant the other assumptions of the theory. In urban economics, much attention is focused on externalities associated with pollution and congestion, again holding the rest of the assumptions constant. Traditional public finance theory, for example, has analyzed public goods, again preserving all other assumptions.

Optimal tax theory also involves primarily a single deviation from the fundamental welfare theorem. The central rejected assumption is that it is feasible to make income distribution right, using nondistorting taxes. It is necessary to distinguish between poll taxes and the lump-sum taxes required for the fundamental welfare theorem, which are potentially different from person to person and do not vary with the behavior of the person. It is feasible to have a poll tax that is the same for all persons and does not vary with the behavior of the person, provided that the tax is a social dividend. If the poll tax is positive, some people are likely to be unable to pay. It is useful to reflect that, if all of the other conditions of the fundamental welfare theorem hold and income distribution is the only problem, then the first small move away from nonintervention has a zero impact on efficiency, by the usual envelope conditions, and a nontrivial impact on income distribution if there are differences among people that can be used as a basis for redistribution. Thus if income distribution is a problem, as it is in every country in the world, then we must consider the design of policy interventions to improve income distribution. That is, under these circumstances, efficiency concerns are never sufficient to imply an absence of all interventions to improve income distribution.

The optimal design of these interventions will involve a balancing at the margin between the further costs in efficiency loss from distorting interventions and the further gains from continuing to pursue redistribution. Naturally, this balancing includes intertemporal redistributions, which are a central focus of development. Although balancing between efficiency and redistribution occurs at the margin, in some circumstances we can find interventions that improve both efficiency and income distribution. I have phrased the problem in this way rather than in terms of the need of the government to get resources because, if we were unconcerned about income distribution, we could finance all government expenditures from poll taxes, which are equal for everyone in the economy. I do not distinguish between the need to get resources and the need to obtain tax revenues, because, in general equilibrium, they are equivalent. If the government obtains the resources it needs and sets taxes so that all markets clear, then Walras's law tells us that the government's budget constraint is satisfied whenever all other agents satisfy their budget constraints.

The opening premise of optimal tax theory is that lump-sum taxes are unavailable and that we must analyze optimal policy in an economy where the set of available policy tools is limited. This assumption is far more realistic than the first-best assumption that income distribution is not a problem. Although the first step in optimal tax theory is to consider a model with this single altered assumption, we can proceed to analyze additional simultaneous deviations from the assumptions of the fundamental welfare theorem. Such analyses represent an agenda for reworking much of economics that has been pursued over the last fifteen years.

Ideally the choice of policy tools would be analyzed as a reflection of deeper technological and administrative factors. Optimal tax theory has taken the simpler route of selecting a class of taxes to be treated as available for use at no cost (or available at a cost independent of tax rates), also assuming that all other policies are unavailable (that is, are infinitely costly to use). This simplification is an enormous help in the analysis and may do little damage to the policy conclusions if the set of feasible policies is well chosen, although the problem of choosing well is a difficult one.

Second-best theory, exemplified by Lipsey and Lancaster (1956–57), makes the important point that, in the absence of satisfaction of all of the conditions of the fundamental welfare theorem, the optimal choice of a single control variable in the hands of the government was generally not to use that policy tool the same way it would be used if all of the other conditions of the fundamental welfare theorem were satisfied. Optimal tax theory is an attempt to go beyond the negative result of rejecting first-best analysis, to explore a general class of positive results, and thus to develop the theory of optimal intervention. The terms "first best" and "second best" are unattractive. They are perhaps also misleading, as they suggest that somebody is choosing a second best when the first best might be available. I will deviate only partially from conventional usage and will refer to "optimal plans," meaning optimal plans constrained by both the production technology, which is viewed as a constraint in standard first-best theory, and any limitations on feasible policies that represent administrative technologies. These limitations are as real a restriction on actual policies as production technologies. Increasingly, economic analyses are recognizing the presence of additional constraints on the allocation of resources. Examples include the difficulties associated with individual decisionmaking, with coordinated decisionmaking within a firm, and with coordinating potential trading partners throughout the economy.

Optimal tax theory has developed two types of results. One result is an exploration of the circumstances when aggregate efficiency is desirable over some aggregation of production sectors in the economy. The minimal aggregation for which efficiency is desirable is over all of the sectors that the government itself controls. The conditions for the desirability of this aggregate efficiency are merely that the government be operating under a single budget constraint and the usual conditions for equilibrium in the economy. If, in addition, parts of the economy have constant returns to scale and are subject to taxes on all inputs and outputs, then it is desirable to have aggregate efficiency over the sum of government-controlled projects and private constant-returns projects that are controlled by price-taking profit-maximizing firms. This result follows from the fact that private profit-maximizing price takers can be induced to behave in the same way as public production planners who are following an optimal plan. The fact that a private firm cannot be induced to choose an inefficient production plan is irrelevant when efficiency is desired. For a small country (that is, one facing fixed prices in international trade), international trade opportunities are constant-returns projects. When applicable, this efficiency result is very handy for planning purposes because it implies that the planner needs only look to market prices in equilibrium when designing small projects, provided that the tax authorities have acted optimally. That is, overall optimization by the government can be decentralized, with tax planners choosing optimal taxes according to appropriate first-order conditions while project planners use shadow prices, many of which are simply market prices.

The second type of result of optimal tax theory is the calculation of first-order conditions for the optimal control of policy tools for taxation and government expenditure. These first-order conditions represent a balancing of the alternative equity and efficiency considerations for the economy. The purpose of this chapter is not to explore first-order conditions in detail but rather to talk about their use. For such an exploration, see chapter 2.

Policy Recommendations

Having considered some of the differences between first-best and second-best analyses, I turn now to the problem of policy recommendations. A policy adviser uses some model, implicit or explicit, consistent or not consistent, in making policy recommendations. A policy adviser often also needs detailed data about an economy. Sometimes we can make do with much less information about the economy. It should be recognized, however, that some information about the economy is always needed to check the applicability of a model even when calibration is not important. Let us begin by considering a first-best situation. If the fundamental welfare theorems apply, then the problem for the adviser is simplified by the use of the well-developed analyses of resource allocation in first-best economies. The implications of knowing that first-best theory applies are that marginal-cost prices should be used, that production efficiency is desirable, that everyone in the economy should have the same social marginal utility of consumption, and that public goods and lumpy investments can be evaluated using the traditional adding-up and consumer surplus frameworks. Before we leap to these policy recommendations, however, it is necessary in fact to confirm that all of the conditions of the fundamental welfare theorem are applicable. My experience in underdeveloped countries is somewhat limited, but I feel safe in assuming that there exists no country where all of the conditions apply. Thus I conclude that a good policy adviser is always doing second-best analysis, recognizing the complications that are relevant and important.

If we cannot apply first-best policies, the natural next step is to see when second best can reasonably be approximated by a simple policy (with limited data requirements), such as aggregate efficiency or uniform taxes or tariffs. As I indicated above, there are certainly interesting, relevant cases in which this simpler form of advice is possible, provided that we believe that other policy tools are simultaneously being used appropriately. These other policy tools do not have the easy way out of looking to market prices because, at a minimum, someone must worry about income distribution, and that person must balance efficiency against equity. This tradeoff requires knowledge about demand patterns by income brackets and elasticities and cross-elasticities of demand. Unless some policymakers are addressing income distribution questions appropriately, the efficiency case for uniformity crumbles before the need for income redistribution, as discussed above (see also chapters 2, 3, 4, and 11). Moreover, efficiency alone frequently calls for nonuniform taxes or prices. This point is made clear in the analyses of one-consumer economies by Ramsey (1927), Meade (1955b), and Boiteux (1971).

We should recognize that the appeal of simple policies is not just in their ease of applicability but also in the important role they may play in the political process. I take the role of optimal tax theory to be the design of the policies we would like to see implemented under certain circumstances. Political constraints are a necessary part of the description of the circumstances. We also, however, need to know the importance of particular political limitations (rather than administrative costs), because no one seems to have a theory of the political process that is well developed enough for us to accept any particular limitations with confidence. Because policies are frequently adopted that were considered politically impossible shortly before, it is important to know what policies we would like to see adopted before bowing, when necessary, to political limitations. The choice of a policy framework will also frequently affect the political process. The development of a satisfactory theory of political economy that reflects economic allocation problems, administrative limitations, and the real workings of the political process is a tall order well beyond the current state of analysis. I will therefore continue in this chapter with the optimal tax tradition of selecting the policy that the political adviser would prefer while recognizing that this perspective is incomplete because it omits the feedback from current allocation decisions onto the future of the political process.

The problem facing a policy adviser in most circumstances will have important implications for both income distribution and efficiency. We cannot legitimately duck the necessity of facing that tradeoff by appealing to other policies. That is, lump-sum taxes are clearly not available. Aggregate efficiency theorems give some cases in which optimally set taxes reduce some production decisions to simply finding the efficient allocation. In many cases, and probably in most, aggregate efficiency theorems are not applicable (for example, because of the incompleteness of the tax structure). Striking the optimal balance between equity and efficiency is thus the central problem. To fall back on simple policies that are not justified by an appropriate second-best model of the economy is to be derelict about the correct role of a policy adviser. Thus we need to examine existing policies for their consistency and the appropriateness of the implicit equity-efficiency tradeoff. We need a list of plausibly feasible policy tools not currently in use. We need a usable model of the workings of the economy, perhaps described in terms of deviations from the fundamental welfare theorem conditions. We also need a way, or a set of alternative ways, for evaluating income redistributions. Furthermore, we need some data or estimates for the critical parameters in this tradeoff.

Optimal Tax Theory

Having completed these preliminaries, I turn now to a qualitative description of the current state of optimal tax theory, which will lead us, in turn, into a discussion of desirable directions for theoretical development. The current theory in its well-developed form is a variation on the Arrow-Debreu model. Thus it is basically static, having the same intertemporal interpretation as the Arrow-Debreu model (see chapter 5), which provides a highly limited, and inaccurate, picture of intertemporal problems in actual economies. That is, the Arrow-Debreu model distinguishes commodities by physical characteristics and by date, place, and state of nature for delivery. Given this complete list of commodities, all trades for all time are coordinated before any economic activity takes place. In this sense, the resource allocation process is completely static. In actual economies, the problem of coordinating plans and trades uses both resources and time. The fact that the resource allocation process takes place only over time is central for understanding the workings of the credit market. Furthermore, some of the recent work on the micro foundations of macroeconomics is based on the presumption that the difficulties of coordinating economic activities are central for the behavior of aggregate unemployment over time (see, for example, Diamond, 1984). Following Arrow-Debreu, the optimal tax model in its well-developed form assumes competitive equilibrium and the possibility of using all available excise taxes and tariffs.

The theory has been built upon the implicit supposition that it is appropriate to develop a theory of the allocation process under the assumption that the relevant economic parameters are known by the planner. Ideally we would integrate the problems coming from estimation of demand and supply elasticities (see Deaton, chapter 4) into the design of optimal tax and spending plans. The combined problems of extracting information and of determining the optimal allocation of resources with limited information seem to me just too hard a problem to permit rapid development, and I thus conclude that it is satisfactory to proceed with a theory that assumes knowledge of parameters while we are simultaneously attempting to better our knowledge of those parameters. It would of course be wrong to have all researchers following the same strategy and good to have some of them tackling the simultaneous estimation and optimization problem.

To look at the strict assumptions of the theory is to point to the directions that it needs to take in order to be developed for use. Some of these directions have been explored. Others are relatively straightforward, although they often lead, unfortunately, to complicated analyses that require careful application rather than simple, easy-to-use rules. The basic theory has been extended to include producer and consumer externalities as well as pure public goods. I will consider in turn four areas for further development: limitations on available taxes, the presence of noncompetitive behavior, the presence of and opportunities in nonequilibrium resource allocation, and the fact that the economy is open-ended in time and is not equivalent to a static model.

It is clear from administrative considerations that taxing every single commodity at a (possibly) different rate is not a good idea. A resource-saving device is to lump large categories of commodities and to subject them to uniform ad valorem taxes. This procedure raises two questions, one regarding the criteria for grouping and the other regarding the design of tax and expenditure policies in the presence of tax tools limited in this way. The latter theory has been developed and is straightforward (see, for example, Diamond, 1973). The former question is analytically much more difficult and has received little attention (see chapter 3). Administrative reality is also evident in the conclusion that many taxes are hard to collect at the retail level and are easier to collect at the wholesale level, at least in the case of large wholesalers. In the case where there are no large wholesalers, many taxes are easy to collect only at the manufacturing level. I take it as given that many tariffs are relatively easy to collect in most countries, at least if the incentives for smuggling are not made too great. The basic approach of the theory can easily accommodate these limitations on taxes available for use. The first-order conditions obviously change, and the scope of applicability of aggregate efficiency also changes, but the basic approach of the theory is unaffected by these limitations. (See, for example, chapters 3, 15, and 16.) The basic approach is to choose the appropriate point in the production and distribution chain for the levying of taxes, to describe transactions in terms of whether or not they cross the tax line, and then to develop the theory as usual. There is obviously room for many useful examples to be worked out (see, for example, Stern, 1983a).

It may be useful briefly to consider tourism, one example that has appeared in the literature. Tourists can be modeled as individuals having special (presumably low) weight in a social welfare function and special preferences representing their access to untaxed foreign work and consumption. Alternatively, and more in line with the discussion above, we can view tourism as another production possibility set. In contrast to the situation with conventional international trade opportunities, it is difficult to create tax barriers around this production possibility set that are independent of domestic economic activity. Then we have a constraint on feasible taxation possibilities.

For many goods, the constraint is that tourists are subject to the same taxes as domestic consumers (although exceptions are widespread and can be introduced, especially for services, which are not subject to resale). In this way we create a framework for modifying taxes in the presence of tourism and for evaluating expenditures that encourage tourism (see, for example, Diamond, 1969). Another extension that can be modeled similarly is the combination of mobility (rural-urban, for example) and geographically varying taxes. The modeling problems seem straightforward, so there may be considerable room for analysis of the interaction of this important phenomenon with tax and expenditure theories.

Large firms, and thus noncompetitive behavior, are widespread in modern economies. Even with small firms, the presence of limited information and shopping costs, rather than the familiar Walrasian auctioneer, introduces, at a minimum, monopolistic competition rather than perfect competition and in some circumstances, even larger deviations from competitive pricing. Again, it seems to me both feasible and highly relevant for optimal tax theory to incorporate firm behavior that is different from competitive behavior. To carry out such a development, it is natural to proceed in two steps, first developing tax theory in partial-equilibrium models and then embedding such models in a general equilibrium framework. Except where the details of several noncompetitive industries interact strongly (which should be part of a good partial-equilibrium model), I do not expect the move to general equilibrium to introduce important new elements that have not already appeared in the move from partial to general equilibrium with the competitive model. For a survey of general equilibrium monopolistic competition models, see Hart (1985). The replacement of the assumption of competition and price-taking behavior by a richer description of the behavior of firms requires the use of additional empirical knowledge about the workings of the economy in order to be applicable. It also requires a careful treatment of profit income. This, however, is a common tradeoff in policy. The more detailed the model, the greater the potential for accuracy but also the greater the need for data to make the more detailed model accurate.

The third item on my list is nonequilibrium. We can usefully distinguish three ways in which equilibrium can differ from that of traditional market theory. First, the government may choose policies that imply that the economy is out of equilibrium. The minimum wage is the most familiar of these. Many governments follow policies of price minima and maxima different from market-clearing values, which generate nonequilibrium as part of policy. In some circumstances with limited policy tools, some attainable nonequilibria are more desirable than any of the attainable equilibria. The simplest example offsets a lemons problem. Wilson (1980), for example, has analyzed a model in which the quality of individual used cars is known to potential suppliers but is not distinguishable by potential buyers. The average quality of the used car sold increases with the price of used cars, because individuals with good used cars are willing to sell only at higher prices. There may be multiple equilibria in this market, because the quantity demanded can increase with price over a range of prices as a consequence of the increase of average quality with price. Among these equilibria, the one with the highest price Pareto dominates (in expected utility terms) the equilibria with lower prices. Moving to a price above the highest equilibrium price will require allocating demanders among the greater number of suppliers. If the latter are not too averse to the risk of not making a sale, a small move in this direction can be Pareto improving (in expected utility terms). The circumstances under which disequilibrium is desirable have received very little attention even though such policies are in widespread use. This question needs exploration. Perhaps it would be fruitful to pursue Weitzman's (1977) pioneering efforts.

The second possibility, still within the framework of conventional micro-economics, is that the private economy may achieve allocations that are not classical market equilibria. In the development setting, the most familiar of the hypotheses resulting in such an allocation is the efficiency wage hypothesis, in which firms prefer to pay a higher wage than necessary to attract labor because of the greater efficiency of more highly paid labor (see, for example, Mirrlees, 1975). Because most economic relations are ongoing and are not spot transactions of the kind modeled by a Walrasian auctioneer, it is not surprising that there are many situations in which, in response to the difficulty of complex contracts, economic agents choose contracting relations that are not classical market equilibria. Because the study of ongoing relations under contract (rather than allocation by classical markets) is still very much in its infancy, I fear it will be a while before optimal tax theory can be satisfactorily developed in the world of contracts, although it should be straightforward to incorporate taxes in the simplest contracting equilibria. For a survey of contract equilibria, see Hart (1983).

The third class of nonequilibria are those that we associate with macroeconomics. It is clearly true that the economy may move a considerable distance away from its desirable, normal full employment equilibrium (or micro disequilibrium), perhaps in response to a shock. The need to design a good micro policy does not obviate the need for good macro policy. Ideally, micro and macro would be integrated in that one would have a model of the economy that could incorporate both the familiar efficiency and equity problems of micro economics and the phenomena that lead modern economies often to exhibit large deviations from what seem to be a more desirable, feasible allocation. In the absence of such an integrative theory, we must continue our schizophrenic policy advice of trying to do micro policy well, trying to do macro policy well, and hoping that the one effort does not obstruct the other. Unfortunately, it is necessary to worry about macro impact effects from large changes in micro policies. Apart from concern about such impacts, it seems best to consider medium-to-long-run elasticities as appropriate for optimal tax considerations because of the problem of dynamic inconsistency inherent in any attempt to take advantage of short-run elasticities "just this once." That is, differences in short- and long-run elasticities create a dynamic inconsistency problem for tax setting. It will always seem worthwhile to change taxes once new production facilities have been set in place, but such moves inhibit investment in long-lived facilities. Thus the government needs consistently to avoid taking short-run advantage of these opportunities because it is impossible for the government to commit itself not to take such advantage in the future.

The last item on my list is that the economy is open-ended in time. Trade occurs period by period, with some intertemporal trade possibilities. Similarly, tax setting is repeated period by period. This open-endedness is most obviously relevant when we think of the problem of credit, that is, the difficulty of converting possible future incomes into current usable resources. There is a major long-run need to develop a theory that is truly dynamic in this way, one that pays attention not merely to the short-run resource allocation problem but also, and more important, to the full problem of resource allocation in the present and in the future, recognizing the complicated reallocation process that takes place as the economy evolves. Tax policy affects portfolio choice and so the structure of credit availability. Anticipated future tax policies affect anticipated revenues and so again credit availability. The large spread in intertemporal marginal rates of substitution and transformation in the economy makes this an important micro problem as well as one of consequence for aggregate demand.

In conclusion, I have identified two highly feasible short-run research topics (alternative choices of the set of feasible taxes and alternative descriptions of firm behavior) and two topics that require more fundamental basic research into modeling before applications become feasible (the role of nonequilibria and the role of the open-endedness of time and of the resource allocation process). As I indicated at the outset, this research agenda seems to me essential for the development of good policies. The appropriate justification of any policy needs to be based on a satisfactory view of the full resource allocation process. The better the view of the process, the more likely the policy advice is to be correct. Although it is sometimes appropriate to make shortcuts in our policy design by using the powerful theorems that are available with some descriptions of the economy, that approach must rely first on an analysis of the applicability of such conclusions, an analysis that is often subtle and difficult. In the general case there is really no alternative to knowing, estimating, or guessing the critical parameters in the inevitable tradeoff between equity and efficiency. Optimal tax theory provides a usable, consistent framework for evaluating this tradeoff. Further research will make the theory even more helpful for a wider class of problems.

25

Conclusions

David Newbery and Nicholas Stern

OUR PURPOSE THROUGHOUT THIS BOOK has been the examination of the potentialities of a particular approach to the analysis of tax reform in developing countries. This approach may be summarized as a formal treatment of the consequences of tax changes for different members of the population and for government revenue plus a judgment of whether those consequences, taken together, are beneficial. The contributions to the volume have included theoretical studies that attempt to analyze and derive principles, rules, and methods that can be used in the preparation and evaluation of possible reforms and also applied studies in which the theory is put to use and assessed. Our emphasis, however, has been on empirical implementation. Thus we have asked how the theory can be cast in a form that can guide the study of practical problems, what data are required, and how appropriate use can be made of the existing data. As one of the participants in the July 1984 workshop observed, "we are getting formal about policy proposals."

The structure of the book has reflected our intentions. Thus, in the first part we set forth the theory, examined the principles and data requirements that arise, and related the theory to earlier ideas in public finance and to other aspects of the economics of policy. In the second part we examined the taxation possibilities and economic structure in developing countries to show the context and difficulties of tax reform. The third part reported on the development and application of the methods in the analysis of possible tax reform in India and on the practical experience of designing, implementing, and evaluating a major tax reform in Mexico. The fourth part developed models that are appropriate for tax analysis in developing countries. The main feature of these models that distinguishes them from the standard tax model is that many taxes apply to only a fraction of the population or to one sector. The incidence of taxes that are partial or sector specific is typically quite different from that of taxes which are economywide. The fifth part of our book paid special attention to agriculture, which poses particular problems for tax analysis and is a major sector in many developing countries. The sixth part investigated tax and pricing policies in other areas.

In the next section we shall identify what we see as the main contributions of the methods described in this book and in the third we shall discuss problems and omissions. The fourth section will indicate some fruitful areas for further research and applications.

Contributions

The theories and methods can help our understanding and analysis of tax reform in many ways. First, they suggest a set of questions that we can ask regarding any system or proposed change. Second, they provide a set of rules or principles that can guide tax design or reform. Third, they indicate how the analysis of taxation can be integrated with other aspects of public policy, in particular cost-benefit analysis, and with industrial and commercial policies. Fourth, and this has been our main emphasis, they give us practical methods for appraising policy proposals. Let us consider these contributions in turn.

The main questions raised by the approach at a general level are "What are the consequences of the proposed change for households and government revenue?" And "Are these consequences beneficial in the sense of providing an increase in social welfare?" These questions may seem at one level rather banal and obvious, but they do structure inquiry in a way that less formal approaches do not. Consideration of all households thus pushes us into a general equilibrium framework and tells us that changing taxes in one sector will affect revenue and welfare elsewhere. Specific formal models provide the means of pursuing these general equilibrium questions and not just simply noting that the effects may be present. Furthermore, the explicit statement of objectives raises the question of whether the tools currently being considered are the best way of promoting the objectives or whether there is some more direct method. If tariffs are suggested as ways of taxing luxury consumption or stimulating employment, for example, we can legitimately ask whether there is some other way of achieving similar results at lower cost. Similarly, if it is argued that indirect taxes should be used to improve income distribution, we can ask whether they should be combined with or replaced by other instruments that are targeted more closely toward the groups we would like to benefit.

A number of general principles and rules were derived and discussed in parts 1 and 4. Thus, as we saw in chapter 2, the standard theory of optimal taxation suggests that tax revenue is raised most efficiently by taxing goods or factors with inelastic demand or supply, although careful interpretation is required. In chapter 16 some simple checks were proposed to see whether taxes had been pushed beyond the point of maximum revenue so that reductions would improve both welfare and revenue. We emphasized the concept of the social marginal cost of revenue from different sources. If these are unequal, then welfare can be improved at constant revenue by a shift from a higher-cost source to one of lower cost. These costs can also be compared with the marginal benefits from different types of expenditure. A prominent theme was the uniformity of indirect taxes, and we examined (chapters 2, 3, 4) circumstances and tests that would tell us whether or not it was an attractive policy. Crucial determinants of the answer were the availability of redistributive tools outside indirect taxes, particularly whether optimal universal uniform lump-sum transfers were employed for redistribution purposes, and the structure of preferences.

The theoretical inquiry has therefore provided a variety of important lessons in terms of principles, methods of analysis, scrutiny of common proposals, and some warnings. The Ramsey-like rules thus provide useful intuition concerning which types of goods should be taxed. The social marginal cost of funds helps structure argument on reform. The discussion of uniformity showed us that simple-minded arguments must be used very carefully in this area, and we had many warnings that the answers to public finance questions depend crucially on the tools that are assumed to be available.

The approach we have adopted here places taxation firmly within the general theory of economic policy as described, for example, by Meade (1955a). This theory provides a valuable consistency over different areas of policy concerning, for example, taxation, industry, and trade. In this regard we emphasized the relationships between the theory of tax reform and shadow prices. The role of a shadow price is to capture the effects on welfare of an increase in the availability from the public sector of an extra unit of a given commodity after the readjustments required have worked through the general equilibrium. If changes in taxes cause a shift in demands from households, the consequences of those changed demands for welfare can be captured by the shadow prices. Thus shadow prices provide a very convenient way of summarizing general equilibrium consequences for welfare, allowing us in many cases to avoid the complications of an explicit general equilibrium model. We must remember, of course, that such a model would in principle be necessary to calculate the shadow prices, but once the calculation has been done, the shadow prices provide sufficient statistics for tax and industrial policy.

All these examples, and they are only examples, have given us valuable lessons. Our main concern, however, has been to demonstrate the empirical potential of the approach and ways in which it could be extended and modified to increase its usefulness in practice. We hope that the several empirical studies provided here, both of economywide reform and of individual sectors, show what can be done and indicate fruitful avenues for further work. We have placed special emphasis on the types of data that are required or should be collected and on ways of using the data that are likely to be available. The problem of data scarcity suggests a number of possible directions for research, some of which we will indicate below.

The structure of consumption and production and elasticities of demand and supply are central to the data requirements. For the analysis of marginal reform, we need only the existing distribution of consumption and production and local elasticities. For nonmarginal reform we need demand and supply functions over a range that may well lie beyond recent experience. Nonmarginal analysis thus places greater strains on our knowledge and requires stronger assumptions.

Although the less stringent demands for data constitute an advantage of the marginal approach, there is the obvious disadvantage that we can learn only about improving directions and not about how far we should go in these directions. The choice of policy is left open in the further sense that, if there is one welfare-improving direction, there are likely to be many. This ambiguity is not necessarily an overwhelming disadvantage, because our model will inevitably leave out much that is important to the policymaker. A menu from which the policymaker can choose may therefore be attractive. Thus the marginal and nonmarginal approaches, both of which are illustrated at a number of points in the book, should be seen as complementary, each with its compensating strengths and weaknesses. If we found an attractive nonmarginal reform under given assumptions, for example, it would be reassuring to check that the direction it embodies is also attractive from the point of view of the more robust marginal analysis.

In the empirical chapters the task has been, using the data and estimates described, to trace the consequences of possible tax changes for households and government explicitly. This work has generally involved models that allow us to derive changes in revenue and a money measure of the real income losses to different types of household. The first step, to calculate the incidence of policy changes, is in general the most difficult part and inevitably involves judgment as to the choice of an appropriate but tractable model, the ability to manipulate the chosen model, ingenuity and resourcefulness in using data that will often require stringent theoretical assumptions, and a substantial effort. We would not pretend that the implementation is always easy, but we trust we have shown that much is feasible. We hope and expect that the task will become easier with experience.

Although the analyses we have been advocating are sometimes difficult, we would suggest that they are the logical result of the simple and rational desire to evaluate government action in terms of its consequences. In this sense the attempt to predict those consequences is the natural way to proceed. This prediction is the central distinguishing feature of the approach. The next step, which is also crucial but in some ways easier, is the evaluation of the consequences. The value judgments required are subjective and embody the position of the commentator, although, as we argued in chapters 1 and 2, they are not arbitrary. Their use does not assume benevolent and coherent government but simply involves the question of how someone with particular values would judge the consequences of a reform. The answers should form a part of the political and economic process. We pursue the role of models of how governments do behave further in the next two sections.

Problems and Omissions

Many of the problems of implementation discussed in this book provide subjects for further research, and some specific suggestions are offered in the next section. Here we indicate some aspects that, although not ignored here, lie outside the approach we have been considering. These include the related issues of administration, rights and justice, and the role and behavior of government.

Although administration has been omitted from most of the formal analyses in the book, it has been significant for much of the discussion. Thus a prominent theme throughout the book was the analysis of tax policy in models where tax tools or handles were severely limited, and the extent of these limitations and reasons for them were examined carefully in part 2. We have not, however, provided a formal treatment of administration in our models or estimated its costs. The former, we judge, is unlikely to be illuminating, and although the latter is important, it requires detailed investigation of a kind that will be country specific and will involve rather different skills. Such inquiries would be valuable and would provide the economist with useful guides to model building. They would provide estimates of the costs of implementing the various policies that could be set against the benefits that have been the main focus of this book.

In a similar way some issues involving rights and justice have been embodied in the analysis, although they have rarely appeared explicitly. An example arises in the consideration of admissible tax tools. The full set of lump-sum taxes associated with the first best would, in principle, be based on detailed knowledge of individual preferences and abilities. We rule out such taxes partly because individuals have an incentive to conceal the relevant information (about their potential income earning ability, for example) but also because we have reservations about the rights of governments to collect and use this type of information. A second example is the choice of tax unit. This topic has not been discussed in detail in this book, and we have, on the whole, taken the household implicitly or explicitly as the unit of taxation. It is, however, commonly asserted that individuals have separate rights within the households for tax purposes, and in particular each spouse has the right to symmetrical and separate treatment. If this proposition is accepted, then quite strong constraints are imposed on the types of taxes that can be levied, for instance concerning levels and transferability of allowances for married couples. A third example concerns pensions. Some observers would argue that each individual has the right to a pension from the state in old age, whereas others would suggest that this is a matter of individual choice and that each person can allocate consumption over the life cycle as he or she wishes, with the corollary that the consequences of the choice must be accepted. It is possible that some of the arguments concerning rights can be fitted into the consequentialist framework we have been using, but others cannot (see, for example, Sen and Williams, 1982). We have seen that these arguments can and do play an important role in the analysis, but they leave open issues for which the consequentialist approach seems to be well suited. We would suggest, for example, that one such topic is the appropriate levels of taxation of different goods.

A prominent notion in public finance associated with ideas of justice has been "horizontal equity," and this has played little role in the analysis of the book. "Vertical equity" has been central throughout in the discussion of distribution involved in the ubiquitous equity-efficiency tradeoff. Horizontal equity concerns the like treatment of equals and requires us to describe what is meant when we say that two people or households are equal. We shall not pursue the question further except to note that *if* being equal in this sense is defined, then we can ask how any tax system that emerges fares relative to the principle of horizontal equity. It is of course necessary to decide not only the meaning of horizontal equity but also, where it conflicts with other principles, its ethical force.

Finally in this section we consider the role and behavior of government. In the models we have been analyzing, the government has coherent, unified, and largely benevolent objectives, captured in the social welfare function, and we search for ways in which the tools available to it can be used to improve this measure of welfare. Not that we believe governments can plausibly be described in this way; when we assert that a policy yields an improvement, we are simply saying that, if the model is a satisfactory description, and if your values are as described in the social welfare function, then you would describe the policy change as an improvement. The result then provides a valuable element in a discussion of economic policy. It does not settle the question. From this point of view we are led to ask whether the improvement would still be present if we changed the model and if we altered the values, because commentators will differ not only in their values but also in their views on how the world works. We would argue, therefore, that the approach should be of interest to people with values who wish to comment on policy proposals. Furthermore, there is no need from this point of view to regard the commentator as benevolent (although we would hope that he or she would be). One can, for example, use the social welfare function to represent the interests of just one household, or one can make it negatively related to the utility of other households, and so on.

The positive theory of government, that is, the attempt to model the behavior of government, is a separate topic and one that we have not considered in this book. The topic is important and of long standing and has recently been an active area of theoretical and applied research. It is possible, broadly speaking, to identify three main approaches that involve models of voting, of bureaucracy, and of interest groups. The purpose of these models is to derive the policies pursued by government within the model in contrast to the optimization of some exogenous criteria by the government in most of the models we have been discussing (although, as we have emphasized, we prefer to see these as modeling the commentator). Our purpose has been of a rather different type: we have been examining what the government should do if it had certain values.

We shall not attempt to summarize the positive theory here; we refer the reader to Atkinson and Stiglitz (1980, chap. 10) for a useful introduction to the literature. The question of the role of government does, however, raise interesting and important questions for tax design. If individuals wish to protect themselves from a government that may at some point be predatory or malevolent, for example, they may wish to place certain restrictions on what the government can do. An obvious example is the U.S. Constitution. The theory of how these restrictions might be selected for questions of taxation would provide an interesting topic for further research.

Further Work

Many of the theories we have been discussing are recent, and they have been applied to developing countries only in the last few years. It is therefore not surprising that we have encountered many problems for further research. Some of them must be investigated over a fairly long term, but others can be pursued immediately, and we would suggest that many of them are likely to be fruitful and interesting. Several of the authors have made their own suggestions for further work, and here we shall briefly draw out some subjects that seem to us to be interesting and promising. We consider them under three headings: extensions of the theory, the use of sparse data, and particular applied topics.

Extensions of the Theory

Some of the desired extensions of the theory that have been proposed provide topics that can be examined fairly readily, using techniques that are currently available, whereas others are more long term. In the former category, Diamond (in chapter 24) indicated the topics of grouping of commodities for tax purposes and models with noncompetitive behavior. The former problem is of particular importance to policymakers, and a number of considerations are noteworthy. Some separability theorems, for example (see chapters 2 and 4), suggest that certain groups of goods should be taxed at the same rate. We would not want to see the tax rates on close substitutes too far out of line. For administrative reasons it would be an advantage to have uniform rates for commodities sold through similar outlets. Thus this problem is researchable and could be pursued quite quickly.

The theory of tax and tariff policy in noncompetitive markets has closely followed developments of positive models (examples are Dixit, 1984b, Seade, 1985, and Stern, 1985). The first set of questions would concern incidence, that is, what happens to prices and real incomes in response to taxation in the models. These issues could lead fairly rapidly to applied studies (see below), particularly with regard to trade, to domestic large-scale industry, and to relations between government and foreign companies. The optimization of policy in such models is likely to come rather later.

The most tractable examples of non-market clearing models concern rationing, and in some models (see, for example, Guesnerie and Roberts, 1984), it is easy to show, for example, that a little rationing of a subsidized good is beneficial. To grasp this point intuitively, consider an equilibrium in which there is a subsidy on some good and no rationing. Now impose a ration that is a little smaller than current consumption of the good so that a consumer is shifted along the budget constraint in the direction of reduced consumption. The increase in government revenue is first order in the change, but the loss of utility is second order, because by assumption the individual's budget constraint was tangential to the indifference curve. More complex kinds of nonequilibrium models of the sort described in Diamond's chapter will prove more difficult to construct and to analyze, and the research time scale will be correspondingly longer. We will have to wait for positive theories to advance further.

A similar remark would fit some of the intertemporal problems described by Diamond. Here, we suspect, more applied and theoretical work on how individuals actually do allocate consumption over time and how intertemporal markets function will be necessary before we can have much confidence in models of intertemporal policy. In the meantime, however, we would not be overly pessimistic because, as we saw in chapter 5, some analysis of intertemporal policy is possible in simple aggregative models.

A major topic that has emerged at a number of points has been the size and frequency of policy change. Frequent small changes allow directions to be based more firmly on local knowledge and allow for error correction on the way. Larger steps are more likely to reveal new information (particularly about responses to the policy changes). On the other hand, change itself can be costly, and this consideration may make fewer, larger steps more sensible even if they are based on less secure empirical knowledge. The issues are not easy to capture formally, and we require some simple models to train intuition and provide insights. Careful empirical studies of large reforms would be valuable, especially if they confronted experience with prediction.

Tax incidence in models of production that are less simplistic than some of those in the book would be useful and should be feasible. We must carefully consider assumptions concerning the mobility of factors, but some simple yet instructive models are available (see, for example, chapter 11, and Dixit and Newbery, 1985, using the Ricardo-Viner model). Of particular importance is the effect of taxes on factor prices, a topic that has been featured at a number of points (see, for example, chapters 7, 13, 15, and 16) and for which the structure of factor markets and the model of production are crucial. The importance of capital in the production process would suggest a link with the dynamic models (see chapter 11).

Finally, on the theoretical extensions we would suggest closer examination of the links between the theory of reform and that of shadow prices. Shadow prices depend on how equilibrium is reestablished after an economy is perturbed by a project, and in many cases reform can be seen as a modification of the equilibrating mechanisms. Thus choice among types of reform should be reflected in the shadow prices we use, and it would be useful if we could establish simple rules connecting the two (for some initial thoughts, see Drèze and Stern, 1985).

The Use of Sparse Data

The problems of sparse data provide a set of questions for both theory and empirical work. Thus we can ask, following Deaton in chapter 4, how the theoretical assumptions that are made in order to get definite results on, for example, price responses in cross-section data will influence the public policy conclusions. If these influences are strong, as they appear to be, what should we conclude? As Deaton argued, the force of the assumptions concerning preferences will depend on the taxation and expenditure possibilities that are available. Should we deal with models in which uncertainty about parameters and structure is explicit? Can we transfer elasticities estimated in countries where richer data sets are available, and if so, under what circumstances? All of these questions require a judicious consideration of theory and empirical work, and research is likely to be both feasible and productive.

This discussion is based on the notion that the optimal levels for different policies may be very sensitive to assumptions regarding preferences and taxation possibilities. A related but different issue concerns the sensitivity of social welfare to these assumptions. Seen from this viewpoint, the sensitivity may be somewhat less marked (this possibility seemed to emerge, at least in the economy with identical consumers, in chapter 15, by Heady and Mitra). One line of research could involve experimenting with different assumptions and asking whether some class of policies does quite well across the broad range of these possibilities.

Further Applications

The methods described in this book could be helpful in research on many applied topics, and the book has already given and worked through a number of examples. The following topics seem to us to be important additional cases, although they obviously do not exhaust the possibilities.

Two points have repeatedly been emphasized. The collection of available tax tools exerts a strong influence on the rates at which those taxes should be set at the optimum. Second, the expenditure side of the budget could be analyzed using the same methods employed for the tax side. Those statements are actually strongly related, because many expenditure activities are very like taxation (with an opposite sign), so that the availability of different types of expenditure should itself influence tax policy. An important example concerns food policy. Thus a rationed food subsidy is like a lump-sum transfer, and its availability and coverage (see chapter 4) may well affect our view of tax rates, in particular the attractiveness of uniform tax rates. Food policies should therefore be a prime candidate in the analysis of the interaction of taxation and expenditure. The simple tools of reform analysis, for example the marginal value of public funds spent on the food subsidy, could be used directly here and its value compared with the marginal costs of funds from other sources, in particular indirect taxes. If the marginal cost of a dollar from any one indirect tax lies below the marginal value of the dollar from the food subsidy, then a case may be made for financing extra food subsidies from extra taxation on that good. It should be clear that similar analyses could be carried out for different types of public expenditure.

An important topic for applied work concerns the degree of aggregation of demand, and here we overlap with the problems mentioned under the heading of sparse data and extensions of the theory. With a given data set we could experiment with different degrees of aggregation to see how different the policy conclusions would appear. Thus if we had data on consumption distinguished by origin (imports or domestic production) and the corresponding demand functions, we could find separate taxes for the two types of good (supposing they are not perfect substitutes). These tax rates could then be compared with tax policies that might arise from the assumption that we could not distinguish by origin and tax policies in cases where we were forced to make ad hoc assumptions. The research could provide valuable lessons for cases where only the aggregate data were available. Similar examples could be generated for subclassifications of types of good.

Labor markets have been crucial to the analysis at a number of points, and over the years a sizable theoretical literature has emerged. We cannot be confident, however, of the effect of tax policy on factor prices and movements. Here we would suggest that more applied work deserves priority. Examples of questions that need to be answered are: what are the effects on the level and pattern of urban wages of a change in rural standards of living (for example, when the standard of living is altered by a change in the price of agricultural output)? What is the incidence of urban taxes and subsidies? Is it reasonable to suppose that migration equilibrates urban and rural after-tax real wage rates? If so, for which segments of the labor force? What repercussions, if any, does migration have on the wages of skilled workers? Over what time period does the migration adjustment work itself out? The availability of empirical data that might be used to address these questions is increasing and may already be adequate for the purpose. What has been lacking so far is the recognition that these questions were important for tax analysis.

When the operation of and interrelations between the various labor markets have been empirically clarified, it may be useful to construct simple computable general equilibrium models. Shifts in factor prices are a clear example of a general equilibrium matter. Tractable models for finding the response of factor prices to tax changes should be possible without extreme disaggregation, and we could therefore retain an intuitive grasp of how the models were working.

An omission from the applied work reported in the book has been the treatment of savings. The use of the tax system to encourage savings is often discussed, but data to show the effects are very rarely available. The positive studies that have been carried out provide no clear conclusion on the responsiveness of savings to interest rate changes. Hence a formal and applied analysis of the effects of tax incentives to saving is very problematic, and further work would be worthwhile only when data sets become available that do allow estimation of tax responsiveness.

Company taxation played a prominent role in the discussion of Mexican tax reform (chapter 12) but did not receive special attention in the theoretical part of the book except in chapter 23, on the taxation of foreign investment. In this area, however, fruitful applied studies have been carried out for developed countries (see, for example, Atkinson and Stiglitz, 1980; King, 1977), and it should be possible to extend some of the methods to developing countries. The application does, however, involve rather detailed knowledge of the particular legal system of a country and the way the corporation tax in that country functions. We cannot therefore expect to be able to transfer standard techniques in a mechanical fashion—something that may be less reprehensible with commodity taxation.

Finally we return to shadow prices. These have been calculated for many countries, and for marginal reform, they can be used to avoid the manifold difficulties of constructing a full general equilibrium model. Thus they provide a valuable tool for tax analysis that may be ready, awaiting use. It is important to check, however, whether the assumptions on the workings of the economy and of government policy that have been used are appropriate to the adjustments of the economy that might be anticipated from changing tax instruments. If the shadow prices are available, however, then we can summarize the general equilibrium reactions on welfare of a tax change by simply adding the partial effect on welfare of the tax change and the partial effect on shadow revenue (see chapter 4). Hence the shadow price calculations are a resource that could usefully be exploited in reform analysis.

Final Remarks

We hope this book has demonstrated the value of the formal and systematic analysis of tax policy. Although its contribution through pure theory in terms of ideas, questions, and principles is substantial, our main concern has been to show how that theory can be put to use in applied work. To do so, we have provided examples, developed the theory to make use of the data available, and indicated directions for further research.

The methods are in general terms very simply and natural—we ask about the consequences of a proposed change and then evaluate them. The application of the general idea can, however, involve a great deal of thought and hard work; the prospect of characterizing a complicated world using a simple model and poor data can be daunting. Nevertheless, such effort would appear unavoidable if the effects of policies are to be evaluated in a coherent way. Thus the task of developing simple methods is important as well as challenging. In our judgment the potential and appeal are great, and we recommend the future study, development, and application of the principles discussed in this book both to researchers and to practitioners.

Bibliography

Adams, C. 1982. *Fight, Flight, Fraud: The Story of Taxation.* Curaçao: Euro-Dutch.

Adler, M. 1979. "U. S. Taxation of U. S. Multinational Corporations: A Manual of Computation Techniques and Managerial Decision Rules." In M. Salant and G. Szego, eds., *International Finance and Trade,* vol. 2. Cambridge, Mass.: Ballinger.

Ahluwalia, M. S. 1974. "Income Inequality: Some Dimensions of the Problem." In H. Chenery, M. S. Ahluwalia, C. L. G. Bell, J. H. Duloy, and R. Jolly, *Redistribution with Growth.* New York: Oxford University Press.

Ahmad, E., and N. H. Stern. 1983a. "Effective Taxes and Tax Reform in India." Discussion Paper 25. University of Warwick, Development Economics Research Centre; processed.

————. 1983b. "Tax Reform, Pareto Improvements, and the Inverse Optimum." Discussion Paper 30. University of Warwick, Development Economics Research Centre; processed.

————. 1983c. "The Evaluation of Personal Income Taxes in India." Discussion Paper 36. University of Warwick, Development Economics Research Centre; processed.

————. 1984. "The Theory of Tax Reform and Indian Indirect Taxes." *Journal of Public Economics,* vol. 25, no. 3 (December), pp. 259–98.

————. 1986. "Tax Reform for Pakistan: Overview and Effective Taxes for 1975–76." *Pakistan Development Review,* vol. 25, no. 1 (Spring), pp. 43–72.

————. Forthcoming. *Tax Reform and Development: An Economic Analysis of the Indian Fiscal System.* Cambridge: Cambridge University Press.

Ahmad, E., D. Coady, and N. H. Stern. 1984. "Fiscal Reforms, Shadow Prices, and Effective Taxes in Pakistan: A Preliminary Analysis." Discussion Paper 48. University of Warwick, Development Economics Research Centre; processed.

————. 1986. "Shadow Prices and Commercial Policy for India." Discussion Paper 54. University of Warwick, Development Economics Research Centre; processed.

————. Forthcoming. "A Complete Set of Shadow Prices for Pakistan: Illustrations for 1975–76." *Pakistan Development Review.*

Ahn, C. Y., I. J. Singh, and L. Squire. 1981. "A Model of an Agricultural Household in a Multicrop Economy: The Case of Korea." *Review of Economics and Statistics,* vol. 68, no. 4 (November), pp. 520–25.

Alexander, L., and J. Simmons. 1975. *"The Determinants of School Achievement in Developing Countries: The Educational Production Function.* World Bank Staff Working Paper 201. Washington, D.C.

Anand, S., and V. Joshi. 1979. "Domestic Distortions, Income Distribution, and the Theory of Optimum Subsidy." *Economic Journal,* vol. 89, no. 354 (June), pp. 336–52.

Anderson, C. A., and M. J. Bowman. 1966. *Education and Economic Development.* Chicago: Aldine.

Anderson, K. 1981. "South Korean Agricultural Price and Trade Policies: Their Effects since 1955." Australian National University, Research School of Pacific Studies, Department of Economics; processed.

Anderson, L., and D. Windham, eds. 1982. *Education and Development*. Lexington, Mass.: Heath, Lexington.

Armitage, J., and R. Sabot. 1983. "Socioeconomic Background and the Returns to Schooling in Two Low Income Economies." World Bank, Development Research Department; processed.

Arnott, R. J., and M. Gersovitz. 1982. "Social Welfare Underpinning; or, Urban Bias and Unemployment." *Economic Journal*, vol. 96, no. 382 (June), pp. 413–24.

Arrow, K. J., and M. Kurz. 1969. "Optimal Public Investment Policy and Controllability with Fixed Savings Ratios." *Journal of Economic Theory*, vol. 1, no. 2 (August), pp. 141–77.

Arrow, K. J., and T. Scitovsky, eds. 1969. *Readings in Welfare Economics*. London: Allen and Unwin.

Ashenfelter, O., A. S. Deaton, and G. Solon. 1985. "Does It Make Sense to Collect Panel Data for Developing Countries?" Princeton University, Woodrow Wilson School, Research Program in Development Studies; processed.

Askari, H., and J. T. Cummings. 1976. *Agricultural Supply Response: A Survey of the Econometric Evidence*. New York: Praeger.

Atkinson, A. B. 1970. "On the Measurement of Inequality." *Journal of Economic Theory*, vol. 2, no. 3 (September), pp. 244–63.

———. 1973. "How Progressive Should Income Tax Be?" In M. Parkin and A. R. Nobay, eds., *Essays in Modern Economics*, pp. 90–109. London: Longman.

———. 1977. "Optimal Taxation and the Direct versus Indirect Tax Controversy." *Canadian Journal of Economics*, vol. 10, no. 4 (November), pp. 590–606.

Atkinson, A. B., and A. Sandmo. 1980. "Welfare Implications of the Taxation of Savings." *Economic Journal*, vol. 90, no. 359 (September), pp. 529–49.

Atkinson, A. B., and N. H. Stern. 1974. "Pigou, Taxation, and Public Goods." *Review of Economic Studies*, vol. 41, no. 125 (January), pp. 119–28.

Atkinson, A. B., and J. E. Stiglitz. 1972. "The Structure of Indirect Taxation and Economic Efficiency." *Journal of Public Economics*, vol. 1, no. 1 (April), pp. 97–119.

———. 1976. "The Design of Tax Structure: Direct versus Indirect Taxation." *Journal of Public Economics*, vol. 6, no. 1 (July–August), pp. 55–75.

———. 1980. *Lectures on Public Economics*. New York: McGraw-Hill.

Atkinson, A. B., N. H. Stern, and J. Gomulka. 1980. "On the Switch from Direct to Indirect Taxation." *Journal of Public Economics*, vol. 14, no. 2 (October), pp. 195–224.

Auerbach, A. J., L. J. Kotlikoff, and J. Skinner. 1983. "The Efficiency Gains from Dynamic Tax Reform." *International Economic Review*, vol. 24, no. 1 (February), pp. 81–100.

Baldwin, R. E. 1969. "The Case against Infant Industry Tariff Protection." *Journal of Political Economy*, vol. 77, no. 3 (May–June), pp. 295–305.

———. 1982. "The Political Economy of Protectionism." In J. N. Bhagwati, ed., *Import Competition and Response*, pp. 263–295. Chicago: University of Chicago Press.

Banerjee, B. 1983. "The Role of the Informal Sector in the Migration Process: A Test of Probabilistic Migration Models and Labor Market Segmentation for India." *Oxford Economic Papers*, vol. 35, no. 3 (November), pp. 399–422.

Barnum, H. N., and L. Squire. 1979. *A Model of an Agricultural Household: Theory and Evidence*. World Bank Staff Working Paper 27. Washington, D.C.

Batra, R. N. 1973. *Studies in the Pure Theory of International Trade*. London: Macmillan.

Batra, R. N., and R. Ramachandran. 1980. "Multinational Firms and the Theory of International Trade and Investment." *American Economic Review*, vol. 70, no. 3 (June), pp. 278–90.

Becker, G. S. 1964. *Human Capital*. New York: Columbia University Press.

———. 1965. "The Theory of the Allocation of Time." *Economic Journal*, vol. 75, no. 299 (September), pp. 493–517.

Berg, E. 1969. "Wage Structures in Less Developed Countries." In A. D. Smith, ed., *Wage Policy Issues in Economic Development*, pp. 294–337. London: Macmillan.

Berry, R. A., and R. H. Sabot. 1978. "Labor Market Performance in Developing Countries: A Survey." *World Development*, vol. 6, nos. 11–12 (November–December), pp. 1199–1249.

Bertrand, T. J., and R. Griffin. "Financing Education in Kenya." World Bank, Country Policy Department; processed.

Bertrand, T. J., and L. Squire. 1980. "The Relevance of the Dual Economy Model: A Case Study of Thailand." *Oxford Economic Papers*, vol. 32, no. 3 (November), pp. 480–511.

Bhagwati, J. N. 1971. "The Generalised Theory of Distortions and Welfare." In J. N. Bhagwati and others, eds., *Trade, Balance of Payments, and Growth: Essays in Honor of C. P. Kindleberger*. Amsterdam: North-Holland.

Bhagwati, J. N., and V. K. Ramaswami. 1963. "Domestic Distortions, Optimal Tariffs, and the Theory of Optimal Subsidy." *Journal of Political Economy*, vol. 71, no. 1 (February), pp. 44–50.

Bhagwati, J. N., and T. N. Srinivasan. 1973. "The General Equilibrium Theory of Effective Protection and Resource Allocation." *Journal of International Economics*, vol. 3, no. 3 (August), pp. 259–82.

———. 1974. "On Reanalyzing the Harris-Todaro Model: Policy Rankings in the Case of Sector-Specific Sticky Wages." *American Economic Review*, vol. 64, no. 3 (June), pp. 502–08.

———. 1980. "Revenue Seeking: A Generalization of the Theory of Tariffs." *Journal of Political Economy*, vol. 88, no. 6 (December), pp. 1069–87.

Binswanger, H., Y. Mundlak, Maw-cheng Yang, and A. Bowers. 1985. "Estimation of Aggregate Agricultural Supply Response from Time Series of Cross-Country Data." Working Paper 1985-3. World Bank, Commodity Studies and Project Division; processed.

Bird, R. M. 1974. *Taxing Agricultural Land in Developing Countries*. Cambridge, Mass.: Harvard University Press.

Birdsall, N. 1982. "Strategies for Analyzing Effects of User Charges in Social Sectors." World Bank, Country Policy Department; processed.

Blaug, M. 1973. *Education and the Employment Problem in Developing Countries*. Geneva: International Labour Organisation.

Blaug, M., R. Layard, and M. Woodhall. 1969. *The Causes of Graduate Unemployment in India*. London: Penguin.

Bliss, C. J. 1975. *Capital Theory and the Distribution of Income*. Amsterdam: North-Holland.

Bliss, C., and N. H. Stern. 1978. "Productivity, Wages, and Nutrition." *Journal of Development Economics*, vol. 5, no. 4 (December), pp. 363–98.

Boadway, R. 1978. "Public Investment Decision Rules in a Neo-Classical Growing Economy." *International Economic Review*, vol. 19, no. 2 (June), pp. 265–87.

―――. 1979. "Long-Run Tax Incidence: A Comparative Dynamic Approach." *Review of Economic Studies*, vol. 46, no. 144 (July), pp. 505–11.

Boissiere, M., J. Knight, and R. Sabot. 1985. "Earnings, Schooling, Ability, and Cognitive Skills." *American Economic Review*, vol. 75, no. 5 (December), pp. 1016–30.

Boiteux, M. 1956. "Sur la gestion des monopoles publics astreints l'équilibre budgetaire." *Econometrica*, vol. 24, no. 1 (January), pp. 22–40. (Translation in Boiteux, 1971.)

―――. 1971. "On the Management of Public Monopolies Subject to Budgetary Constraints." *Journal of Economic Theory*, vol. 3, no. 3 (September), pp. 219–40. (Translation of Boiteux, 1956.)

Bond, E. 1981. "Tax Holidays and Industry Behavior." *Review of Economics and Statistics*, vol. 63, no. 1 (February), pp. 88–95.

―――. 1982. "Optimal Transfer Pricing When Tax Rates Differ." *Southern Economic Journal*, vol. 47, no. 1 (July), pp. 191–200.

Bowen, A., and R. Sabot. 1983. "Education, Urbanization, and Family Size: Evidence from Nairobi." World Bank, Development Research Department.

Bowman, M. J., and R. Sabot. 1982. "Human Resources in Africa: A Continent in Rapid Change." Paper presented to the UNDP Conference on Technical Cooperation for the Development and Utilization of Human Resources in Africa. Libreville, Gabon. August.

Bradford, D. F. 1975. "Constraints on Government Investment Opportunities and the Choice of Discount Rate." *American Economic Review*, vol. 65, no. 5 (December), pp. 887–99.

Braverman, A., and J. S. Hammer. 1986. "Multi-Market Analysis of Agricultural Pricing in Senegal." In I. Singh, L. Squire, and J. Strauss, eds., *Agricultural Household Models: Extensions, Applications, and Policy*. Washington, D.C.: World Bank.

Braverman, A., C. Y. Ahn, and J. S. Hammer. 1983. *Alternative Agricultural Pricing Policies in the Republic of Korea: Their Implications for Government Deficits, Income Distribution, and Balance of Payments*. World Bank Staff Working Paper 621. Washington, D.C.

Braverman, A., J. S. Hammer, and A. S. Brandão. 1986. "Economic Analysis of Agricultural Pricing Policies in Brazil: The Wheat and Soybean Case." Revised. Discussion Paper. World Bank, Agriculture and Rural Development Department; processed.

Braverman, A., J. S. Hammer, and A. Gron. 1987. "Multimarket Analysis of Agricultural Price Policies in an Operational Context: The Case of Cyprus." *World Bank Economic Review*, vol. 1, no. 2, pp. 337–56.

Braverman, A., J. S. Hammer, and E. Jorgensen. 1983. "Agricultural Taxation and Trade Policies in Sierra Leone." World Bank, Country Policy Department; processed.

―――. 1985. *Reducing Input Subsidies to Livestock Producers in Cyprus: An Economic Analysis*. World Bank Staff Working Paper 782. Washington, D.C.

Braverman, A., J. S. Hammer, and J. Levinsohn. 1983. "Agricultural Pricing Policies in Senegal: Their Implications for Government Budget, Foreign Exchange, and Regional Income Distribution." World Bank, Country Policy Department; processed.

Braverman, A., J. S. Hammer, and J. Morduch. Forthcoming. "Wheat and Maize Price Policies in Hungary: Tradeoffs between Foreign Exchange and Government Revenue." *Agricultural Economics*.

Brecher, R. A. 1974. "Optimal Commercial Policy for a Minimum Wage Economy." *Journal of International Economics*, vol. 4, no. 2 (May), pp. 139–49.

Brecher, R. A., and C. F. Diaz Alejandro. 1977. "Tariffs, Foreign Capital, and Immiserizing Growth." *Journal of International Economics*, vol. 7, no. 4 (November), pp. 317–22.

Brecher, R. A., and R. Findlay. 1983. "Tariffs, Foreign Capital, and National Welfare with Sector-Specific Factors." *Journal of International Economics*, vol. 14, no. 3/4 (May), pp. 277–88.

Bridge, R. D., C. M. Judd, and P. R. Moock. 1979. *Determinants of Educational Outcomes*. Cambridge, Mass.: Ballinger.

Brown, G. T. 1978. "Agricultural Pricing Policies in Developing Countries." In T. W. Schultz, ed., *Distortions of Agricultural Incentives*. Bloomington: Indiana University Press.

Burdett, K., N. M. Kiefer, D. T. Mortensen, and G. R. Neumann. 1983. "Earnings, Unemployment, and the Allocation of Time over Time." Cornell University, Department of Economics; processed.

Cain, G. G., and H. W. Watts. 1973. *Income Maintenance and Labor Supply*. Chicago: Rand McNally.

Calvo, G. A., and R. B. Fernandez. 1983. "Competitive Banks and the Inflation Tax." *Economics Letters*, vol. 12, nos. 3–4, pp. 313–17.

Case, A., and L. Squire. 1984. "The Relative Merits of Alternative Approaches to Applied Welfare Economics." World Bank, Country Policy Department; processed.

Cavazos, M. 1976. "Nominal Implicit Protection in Mexico." Dirección de Estudios Económico-Hacendarios, Secretaría de Hacienda, México; processed.

Caves, R. E. 1982. *Multinational Enterprise and Economic Analysis*. Cambridge: Cambridge University Press.

Cervantes, J. 1982. "La inflación y la distribución del ingreso y la riqueza en México." In *Distribución del ingreso en México*. Mexico City: Banco de México.

Chalmley, C. 1983. "Taxation in Dynamic Economies: Some Problems and Methods." World Bank, Country Policy Department; processed.

Chelliah, R., H. J. Baas, and M. R. Kelly. 1975. "Tax Ratios and Tax Effort in Developing Countries, 1969–71." *International Monetary Fund Staff Papers*, vol. 22, no. 1 (March), pp. 187–205.

Christensen, L. R., D. W. Jorgenson, and L. J. Lau. 1975. "Transcendental Logarithmic Utility Functions." *American Economic Review*, vol. 65, no. 3 (June), pp. 367–83.

Cline, W. R. 1972. *Potential Effects of Income Redistribution in Economic Growth: Latin American Cases*. New York: Praeger.

———. 1975. "Distribution and Development: A Survey of Literature." *Journal of Development Economics*, vol. 1, no. 4 (February), pp. 359–400.

Cochrane, S. H. 1979. *Fertility and Education: What Do We Really Know?* Baltimore, Md.: Johns Hopkins University Press.

Corden, W. M. 1974. *Trade Policy and Economic Welfare*. Oxford: Clarendon Press.

———. 1984. "The Normative Theory of International Trade." In R. W. Jones and P. B. Kenen, eds., *Handbook of International Economics*. Amsterdam: North-Holland.

Corden, W. M., and R. Findlay. 1975. "Urban Unemployment, Intersectoral Capital Mobility, and Development Policy." *Economica*, vol. 42, no. 165 (February), pp. 59–78.

Corlett, W. J., and D. C. Hague. 1953. "Complementarity and the Excess Burden of Taxation." *Review of Economic Studies*, vol. 21, no. 1 (January), pp. 21–30.

Dalton, H. 1922/1967. *Principles of Public Finance*. Fairfield, N.J.: August M. Kelley, 1967.

Danube Weekly. 1984. September 4.

Dasgupta, P. S., and P. J. Hammond. 1980. "Fully Progressive Taxation." *Journal of Public Economics*, vol. 13, pp. 141–54.

Dasgupta, P. S., S. Marglin, and A. Sen. 1972. *Guidelines for Project Evaluation*. Sales No. E.78.II.B.3. New York: United Nations.

Deaton, A. S. 1974. "A Reconsideration of the Empirical Implications of Additive Preferences." *Economic Journal*, vol. 84, no. 334 (June), pp. 338–48.

———. 1979. "Optimally Uniform Commodity Taxes." *Economics Letters*, vol. 2, no. 4, pp. 357–61.

———. 1981. "Optimal Taxes and the Structure of Preferences." *Econometrica*, vol. 49, no. 5 (September), pp. 1245–60.

———. 1983. "An Explicit Solution to an Optimal Tax Problem." *Journal of Public Economics*, vol. 20, no. 3 (April), pp. 333–46.

———. 1984. "Issues in the Methodology of Multimarket Analysis of Agricultural Pricing Policies." Princeton University, Woodrow Wilson School; processed.

Deaton, A. S., and J. Muellbauer. 1980a. *Economics and Consumer Behavior*. New York: Cambridge University Press.

———. 1980b. "An Almost Ideal Demand System." *American Economic Review*, vol. 70, no. 3 (June), pp. 312–26.

Deaton, A. S., and N. H. Stern. 1985. "Optimally Uniform Commodity Taxes, Taste Differences, and Lump-Sum Grants." Discussion Paper 63. University of Warwick, Development Economics Research Centre; processed. Published in *Economics Letters*, vol. 20, no. 3, pp. 263–66.

Dervis, K., J. De Melo, and S. Robinson. 1982. *General Equilibrium Models for Development Policy*. New York: Cambridge University Press for the World Bank.

Diamond, P. A. 1969. "On the Economics of Tourism." *East African Economic Review*, vol. 2, pp. 53–62.

———. 1973. "Taxation and Public Production in a Growth Setting." In J. A. Mirrlees and N. H. Stern, eds., *Models of Economic Growth*. London: Macmillan.

———. 1975. "A Many-Person Ramsey Tax Rule." *Journal of Public Economics*, vol. 4, no. 4 (November), pp. 335–42.

———. 1984. *A Search-Equilibrium Approach to the Micro Foundations of Macroeconomics*. The Wicksell Lectures. Cambridge, Mass.: MIT Press.

Diamond, P. A., and J. A. Mirrlees. 1971. "Optimal Taxation and Public Production, Part I: Production Efficiency," and "Part II: Tax Rules." *American Economic Review*, vol. 61, no. 1 (March), pp. 8–27; no. 3 (June), pp. 261–78.

———. 1976. "Private Constant Returns and Public Shadow Prices." *Review of Economic Studies*, vol. 43, no. 133 (February), pp. 41–48.

Dixit, A. K. 1969. "Marketable Surplus and Dual Development." *Journal of Economic Theory*, vol. 1, no. 2 (May), pp. 203–19.

———. 1971. "Short-Run Equilibrium and Shadow Prices in a Dual Economy." *Oxford Economic Papers*, vol. 23, no. 3 (November), pp. 384–400.

———. 1973. "Models of Dual Economies." In J. A. Mirrlees and N. H. Stern, eds., *Models of Economic Growth*. London: Macmillan.

———. 1984a. "Taxation Theory in the Open Economy." Princeton University,

Woodrow Wilson School; processed. Published in A. J. Auerbach and M. S. Feldstein, eds., *Handbook of Public Economics*, vol. 1. Amsterdam: North-Holland, 1985.

———. 1984*b*. "International Trade Policy for Oligopolistic Industries." *Economic Journal*, supp., vol. 94, pp. 1–16.

Dixit, A. K., and D. M. G. Newbery. 1985. "Setting the Price of Oil in a Distorted Economy." *Economic Journal Conference Papers*, supp., vol. 95, pp. 71–82.

Dixit, A. K., and V. Norman. 1980. *Theory of International Trade*. Cambridge: Cambridge University Press.

Dixit, A. K., and N. H. Stern. 1974. "Determinants of Shadow Prices in Open Dual Economies." *Oxford Economic Papers*, vol. 26, no. 1 (March), pp. 42–53.

Drèze, J. H. 1964. "Some Post-War Contributions of French Economists to Theory and Public Policy." *American Economic Review*, vol. 54, supp., pp. 1–64.

Drèze, J. P. 1983. "On the Choice of Shadow Prices for Project Evaluation." Ph.D. diss., Indian Statistical Institute.

Drèze, J. P., and N. H. Stern. 1985. "The Theory of Cost-Benefit Analysis." Discussion Paper 85. Economic and Social Research Council, Programme on Taxation, Incentives, and the Distribution of Income, London School of Economics. In A. Auerbach and M. Feldstein, eds., *Handbook of Public Economics*. Amsterdam: North-Holland.

Drud, A. 1985. "CONOPT: A GRG Code for Large Sparse Dynamic Nonlinear Optimisation Problems." *Mathematical Programming*, vol. 31, pp. 153–91.

Duloy, J. H., and G. T. O'Mara. 1985. *Issues of Efficiency and Interdependence in Water Resources Investments: Lessons from the Indus Basin of Pakistan*. World Bank Staff Working Paper 665. Washington, D.C.

Dupuit, J. 1969. "On the Measurement of the Utility of Public Works." In K. J. Arrow and T. Scitovsky, eds., *Readings in Welfare Economics*. London: Allen and Unwin.

Dutton, J. 1982. "The Optimal Taxation of International Investment Income: A Comment." *Quarterly Journal of Economics*, vol. 97, no. 2 (May), pp. 373–80.

Eaton, J., and M. Gersovitz. 1981. "Debt with Potential Repudiation: Theoretical and Empirical Analysis." *Review of Economic Studies*, vol. 48, no. 152 (April), pp. 289–309.

———. 1983. "Country Risk: Economic Aspects." In R. J. Herring, ed., *Managing International Risk*. Cambridge: Cambridge University Press.

———. 1984. "A Theory of Expropriation and Deviations from Perfect Capital Mobility." *Economic Journal*, vol. 94, no. 373 (March), pp. 16–40.

Ebrill, L. P. 1984. "The Effects of Taxation on Labor Supply, Savings, and Investment in Developing Countries: A Survey of the Empirical Literature." International Monetary Fund; processed.

Eden, L. E. 1983. "Transfer Pricing Policies under Tariff Barriers." *Canadian Journal of Economics*, vol. 16, no. 4 (November), pp. 669–85.

Ehrenberg, R. G., and R. S. Smith. 1982. *Modern Labor Economics: Theory and Public Policy*. Glenview, Ill.: Scott, Foresman.

Ethier, W. 1977. "The Theory of Effective Protection in General Equilibrium: Effective-Rate Analogues of Nominal Rates." *Canadian Journal of Economics*, vol. 10, no. 2 (May), pp. 233–45.

Fair, R. C. 1971. "The Optimum Distribution of Income." *Quarterly Journal of Economics*, vol. 85, no. 4 (November), pp. 551–79.

Fei, J. C. H., and G. Ranis. 1961. "A Theory of Economic Development." *American Economic Review*, vol. 51, no. 4 (September), pp. 533–65.

——. 1964. *Development of the Labor Surplus Economy.* Homewood, Ill.: Irwin.

Feldstein, M. S. 1972. "Distributional Equity and the Optimal Structure of Public Prices." *American Economic Review,* vol. 62, no. 1 (March), pp. 32–36.

——. 1974. "Incidence of a Capital Income Tax in a Growing Economy with Variable Savings Rates." *Review of Economic Studies,* vol. 41, no. 128 (October), pp. 505–13.

Feldstein, M., and J. Green. 1983. "Why Do Companies Pay Dividends?" *American Economic Review,* vol. 73, no. 1 (March), pp. 17–30.

Feldstein, M., and D. Hartman. 1979. "The Optimal Taxation of Foreign Source Investment Income." *Quarterly Journal of Economics,* vol. 93, no. 4 (November), pp. 613–29.

Feldstein, M., and C. Horioka. 1980. "Domestic Saving and International Capital Flows." *Economic Journal,* vol. 90, no. 358 (June), pp. 314–29.

Fernandez, P. A. 1980. "Essays on Taxation in a Small Open Economy," Ph.D. diss. proposal, University of Chicago.

Fields, G. S. 1974. "The Private Demand for Education in Relation to Labor Market Conditions in Less Developed Countries." *Economic Journal,* vol. 84, no. 336 (December), pp. 906–25.

——. 1975a. "Higher Education and Income Distribution in a Less Developed Country." *Oxford Economic Papers,* vol. 27, no. 2 (July), pp. 245–59.

——. 1975b. "Rural-Urban Migration, Urban Unemployment and Underemployment, and Job Search Activity in LDCs." *Journal of Development Economics,* vol. 2, no. 2 (June), pp. 165–87.

——. 1979. "Lifetime Migration in Colombia: Tests of the Expected Income Hypothesis." *Population and Development Review,* vol. 5, no. 2 (June).

——. 1980. "Education and Income Distribution in Developing Countries: A Review of the Literature." In Timothy King, ed., *Education and Income.* World Bank Staff Working Paper 402. Washington, D.C.

——. 1982. "Place-to-Place Migration: Issues in Estimation and Some Evidence for Colombia." *Economic Development and Cultural Change,* vol. 30, no. 3 (April), pp. 539–58.

——. 1984. "Employment, Income Distribution, and Economic Growth in Seven Small Open Economies." *Economic Journal,* vol. 94, no. 373 (March), pp. 74–83.

Findlay, R., and S. Wellisz. 1982. "Endogenous Tariffs, the Political Economy of Trade Restrictions, and Welfare." In J. N. Bhagwati, ed., *Import Competition and Response.* Chicago: University of Chicago Press.

Fogelman, F., R. Guesnerie, and M. Quinzii. 1978. "Dynamic Processes for Tax Reform Theory." *Journal of Economic Theory,* vol. 17, no. 2 (April), pp. 200–26.

Food and Agriculture Organisation. Various years. *Trade Yearbook.* Rome: FAO.

Frank, C. R., Jr. 1968. "Urban Unemployment and Economic Growth in Africa." *Oxford Economic Papers,* vol. 20, no. 2 (July), pp. 250–74.

Frisch, R. 1959. "A Complete Scheme for Computing All Direct and Cross Demand Elasticities in a Model with Many Sectors." *Econometrica,* vol. 27, no. 2 (April), pp. 177–96.

Fullerton, D., J. B. Shoven, and J. Whalley. 1983. "Replacing the U.S. Income Tax with a Progressive Consumption Tax." *Journal of Public Economics,* vol. 20, no. 1 (February), pp. 3–23.

Gandhi, V. P. 1979. "Vertical Equity of General Sales Taxation in Developing Countries." Discussion Paper DM/79/52. International Monetary Fund; processed.

García Bullé, M. A. 1985. "Estimación de Ecuaciones con la variable dependiente rezagada como regresor: El caso de la demanda de dinero en México." Licenciado tesis, Instituto Tecnológico Autónomo de México.

Garnaut, R., and A. Clunies-Ross. 1974. "A New Tax for Natural Resource Projects." In M. Crommelin and A. R. Thompson, eds., Mineral Leasing as an Instrument of Public Policy. Vancouver: University of British Columbia.

———. 1983. Taxation of Mineral Rents. Oxford: Clarendon Press.

Gavan, J. D., and I. S. Chandrasekara. 1979. The Impact of Public Foodgrain Distribution on Food Consumption and Welfare in Sri Lanka. Research Report 13. Washington, D.C.: International Food Policy Research Institute.

Gehrels, F. 1971. "Optimal Restrictions on Foreign Trade and Investment." American Economic Review, vol. 61, no. 1 (March), pp. 147–59.

Gersovitz, M. 1983. "Trade, Capital Mobility, and Sovereign Immunity." Discussion Paper 108. Princeton University, Research Program in Development Studies.

Gil Díaz, F. 1982. "The Incidence of Taxes in Mexico: A Before and After Comparison." In P. Aspe and P. E. Sigmund, eds., The Political Economy of Income Distribution in Mexico. New York and London: Holmes and Meier.

Goldman, S. 1968. "Optimal Growth and Continual Planning Revision." Review of Economic Studies, vol. 35(2), no. 102 (April), pp. 143–54.

Goode, R. 1962. "Personal Income Tax in Latin America." In Joint Tax Program of the Organization of American States, International Bank for Reconstruction and Development, and the United Nations Economic Commission for Latin America, Fiscal Policy for Economic Growth in Latin America. Baltimore, Md.: Johns Hopkins University Press.

———. 1984. Government Finance in Developing Countries. Washington, D.C.: Brookings Institution.

Gordon, R. H., and J. D. Wilson. 1983. "An Examination of Multijurisdictional Corporate Income Taxes under Formula Apportionment." Working Paper. Bell Laboratories; processed.

Guesnerie, R., and K. W. S. Roberts. 1984. "Effective Policy Tools and Quantity Controls." Econometrica, vol. 52, no. 1 (January), pp. 59–86.

Guesnerie, R., and J. Seade. 1982. "Non-Linear Pricing in a Finite Economy." Journal of Public Economics, vol. 17, no. 2 (March), pp. 157–79.

Hall, R. E. 1972. "Turnover in the Labor Force." Brookings Papers on Economic Activity 3, vol. 3, no. 3, pp. 709–64.

Hamada, K. 1966. "Strategic Aspects of Taxation on Foreign Investment Income." Quarterly Journal of Economics, vol. 80, no. 3 (August), pp. 361–75.

Hansen, W. L., and B. A. Weisbrod. 1969. The Distribution of Costs and Benefits of Public Higher Education in California. Chicago: Markham.

———. 1970. Benefits, Costs, and Finance of Public Higher Education. Chicago: Markham.

Harberger, A. B. 1954. "Monopoly and Resource Allocation." American Economic Review: Papers and Proceedings, vol. 44, no. 2 (May), pp. 78–87.

———. 1962. "The Incidence of Corporate Income Tax." Journal of Political Economy, vol. 70, no. 3 (June), pp. 215–40.

———. 1971. "On Measuring the Social Opportunity Cost of Labor." International Labour Review, vol. 103, no. 6 (June), pp. 559–79.

———. 1978. "Perspectives on Capital and Technology, Etc." In M. J. Artis and A. R. Nobay, eds., Contemporary Economic Analysis, pp. 15–42. London: Croom Helm.

————. 1980. "Vignettes on the World Capital Market." *American Economic Review*, vol. 70, no. 2 (May), pp. 331–37.

Harris, R., with D. Case. 1984. *Trade, Industrial Policy, and Canadian Manufacturing*. Toronto, Ontario: Economic Council.

Harris, J. R., and M. P. Todaro. 1970. "Migration, Unemployment, and Development: A Two-Sector Analysis." *American Economic Review*, vol. 60, no. 1 (March), pp. 126–42.

Harsanyi, J. C. 1955. "Cardinal Welfare, Individualistic Ethics, and Inter-personal Comparisons of Utility." *Journal of Political Economy*, vol. 73, no. 4 (August), pp. 309–21.

Hart, O. D. 1979. "Monopolistic Competition in a Large Economy with Different Commodities." *Review of Economic Studies*, vol. 46, no. 1 (January), pp. 1–30.

————. 1983. "Optimal Labour Contracts under Asymmetric Information: An Introduction." *Review of Economic Studies*, vol. 50, no. 1 (January), pp. 3–36.

————. 1985. "Imperfect Competition in General Equilibrium: An Overview of Recent Work." In K. J. Arrow and S. Honkapohja, eds., *Frontiers of Economics*. Oxford: Blackwell.

Hartman, D. G. 1977. "Deferral of Taxes on Foreign Source Income." *National Tax Journal*, vol. 30, no. 4 (December), pp. 457–62.

Hasan, P., and D. C. Rao. 1979. *Korea: Policy Issues for Long-Term Development*. Baltimore, Md.: Johns Hopkins University Press.

Hausman, J. A. 1981a. "Exact Consumer's Surplus and Deadweight Loss." *American Economic Review*, vol. 41, no. 4 (September), pp. 662–76.

————. 1981b. "Labor Supply." In H. J. Aaron and J. A. Pechman, eds., *How Taxes Affect Economic Behavior*. Washington, D.C.: Brookings Institution.

————. 1983. "Taxes and Labor Supply," MIT, processed. Published in A. Auerbach and M. Feldstein, eds., *Handbook of Public Economics*, pp. 213–64. Amsterdam: North-Holland, 1985.

Heady, C. J., and P. K. Mitra. 1982. "Restricted Redistributive Taxation, Shadow Prices, and Trade Policy." *Journal of Public Economics*, vol. 17, no. 1 (March), pp. 1–22.

————. 1984. "Optimum Taxation and Shadow Pricing in a Developing Economy." Discussion Paper 83. World Bank, Development Research Department; processed.

Heckman, J. J., and T. MaCurdy. 1981. "New Methods for Estimating Labor Supply Functions: A Survey." In Ronald G. Ehrenberg, ed., *Research in Labor Economics*, vol. 4. Greenwich, Conn.: JAI Press.

Hinrichs, H. H. 1966. *A General Theory of Tax Structure Change during Economic Development*. Cambridge, Mass.: Harvard University Press.

Horst, T. 1971. "The Theory of the Multinational Firm: Optimal Behavior under Different Tariff and Tax Rates." *Journal of Political Economy*, vol. 79, no. 5 (September–October), pp. 1059–72.

————. 1977. "American Taxation of Multinational Firms." *American Economic Review*, vol. 67, no. 3 (June), pp. 376–89.

————. 1980. "A Note on the Optimal Taxation of International Investment Income." *Quarterly Journal of Economics*, vol. 94, no. 4 (June), pp. 793–98.

————. 1982. "The Optimal Taxation of International Investment Income: Reply." *Quarterly Journal of Economics*, vol. 97, no. 2 (May), p. 381.

Houthakker, H. S. 1960. "Additive Preferences." *Econometrica*, vol. 28, no. 2 (April), pp. 244–56.

Hughes, Gordon A. 1986. "A New Method for Estimating the Effects of Fuel Taxes: An Application to Thailand." *World Bank Economic Review*, vol. 1, no. 1 (September), pp. 65–101.

Hughes, G. A., and Islam, I. 1981. "Inequality in Indonesia: A Decomposition Analysis." *Bulletin of Indonesian Economic Studies*, vol. 17, no. 1 (March), pp. 42–71.

India, Karnataka Taxation Review Committee. 1982. *Report on State Taxes*. Bangalore: Taxation Review Committee.

India, Ministry of Finance. Various years. *All India Income Tax Statistics*. New Delhi: Ministry of Finance.

———. 1978. *Report of the Indirect Taxation Enquiry Committee*. New Delhi: Ministry of Finance.

———. 1981. *Indian Economic Statistics: Public Finance*. New Delhi: Ministry of Finance.

India, National Sample Survey Organisation. 1977. *Tables on Consumer Expenditure, Twenty-eighth Round, October 1973–June 1974*. New Delhi: NSSO.

India, Planning Commission. 1981. *A Technical Note on the Sixth Five Year Plan of India*. New Delhi: Planning Commission.

International Monetary Fund. 1984. *Government Finance Statistics Yearbook*, vol. 8. Washington, D.C.

Jallade, P. 1974. *Public Expenditures on Education and Income Distribution in Colombia*. Baltimore, Md.: Johns Hopkins University Press.

Jenkins, G. P. 1974. "Comment." In M. Crommelin and A. R. Thompson, eds., *Mineral Leasing as an Investment of Public Policy*. Vancouver: University of British Columbia.

Jenkins, G. P., and B. D. Wright. 1975. "Taxation of Income of Multi-National Corporations: The Case of the United States Petroleum Industry." *Review of Economics and Statistics*, vol. 57, no. 1 (February), pp. 1–11.

Johnson, H. G. 1965. "Optimal Tariff Intervention in the Presence of Domestic Distortions." In R. E. Baldwin and others, *Trade, Growth, and the Balance of Payments*. Skokie, Ill., and Amsterdam: Rand-McNally and North-Holland.

———. 1971. *Aspects of the Theory of Tariffs*. Cambridge, Mass.: Harvard University Press.

Jones, R. W. 1971. "A Three Factor Model in Theory, Trade, and History." In J. N. Bhagwati and others, eds., *Trade, Balance of Payments, and Growth: Essays in Honor of C. P. Kindleberger*. Amsterdam: North-Holland.

Jones, R. W., and P. B. Kenen, eds. 1984. *Handbook of International Economics*. Amsterdam: North-Holland.

Jorgenson, D. W. 1961. "The Development of a Dual Economy." *Economic Journal*, vol. 71(2), no. 62 (March), pp. 309–34.

———. 1967. "Surplus Agricultural Labour and the Development of a Dual Economy." *Oxford Economic Papers*, vol. 19, no. 3 (November), pp. 288–312.

Kaldor, N. 1956. *Indian Tax Reform: Report of a Survey*. New Delhi.

———. 1964. "A Memorandum on the Value-Added Tax." *Essays on Economic Policy, I*. London: Camelot Press.

———. 1966. *Causes of the Slow Rate of Economic Growth of the United Kingdom*. Cambridge: Cambridge University Press.

Kannappan, S. 1977. *Studies of Urban Labor Markets in Developing Areas*. Geneva: International Institute for Labour Studies.

―――. 1983. *Employment Problems and the Urban Labor Market in Developing Nations.* Ann Arbor: University of Michigan, Graduate School of Business Administration.

Kay, J. A., and M. A. King. 1983. *The British Tax System.* 3d ed. Oxford: Oxford University Press. (4th ed. 1986.)

Khan, M. A. 1980. "The Harris-Todaro Hypothesis and the Heckscher-Ohlin-Samuelson Trade Model: A Synthesis." *Journal of International Economics,* vol. 10, no. 4 (November), pp. 527–47.

Khandker, A. W. 1981. "Multinational Firms and the Theory of International Trade and Investment: A Correction and a Stronger Conclusion." *American Economic Review,* vol. 71, no. 3 (June), pp. 515–16.

Killingsworth, M. R. 1983. *Labor Supply.* Cambridge and New York: Cambridge University Press.

King, M. A. 1977. *Public Policy and the Corporation.* London: Chapman and Hall.

―――. 1980. "Savings and Taxation." In G. M. Heal and G. A. Hughes, eds., *Public Policy and the Tax System.* London: Allen and Unwin.

―――. 1983a. "Welfare Analysis of Tax Reforms Using Household Data." *Journal of Public Economics,* vol. 21, no. 2 (July), pp. 183–214.

―――. 1983b. "An Index of Inequality with Applications to Horizontal Equity and Social Mobility." *Econometrica,* vol. 51, no. 1 (January), pp. 99–116.

―――. 1984. "The Economics of Saving: A Survey of Recent Contributions." Working Paper 49. Economic and Social Research Council, Programme on Taxation, Incentives, and the Distribution of Income. January. London School of Economics.

King, M. A., and D. Fullerton. 1984. *The Taxation of Income from Capital: A Comparative Study of the U. S., U. K., Sweden, and West Germany.* Chicago: University of Chicago Press.

Knight, J., and R. Sabot. 1981. "The Returns to Education: Increasing with Experience or Decreasing with Expansion?" *Oxford Bulletin of Economics and Statistics,* vol. 43, no. 1 (February), pp. 51–72.

―――. 1983a. "Educational Expansion and the Kuznets Effect." *American Economic Review,* vol. 73, no. 5 (December), pp. 1132–36.

―――. 1983b. "Rates of Return to Educational Expansion: New Approaches." World Bank, Development Research Department; processed.

Kopits, G. F. 1972. "Dividend Behavior within the International Firm: A Cross-Country Analysis." *Review of Economics and Statistics,* vol. 54, no. 3 (August), pp. 339–42.

―――. 1976. "Taxation and Multinational Firm Behavior: A Critical Survey." *International Monetary Fund Staff Papers,* vol. 23, no. 3 (November), pp. 513–48.

Korea, Republic of. National Bureau of Statistics, Economic Planning Board. 1980. *Korea Statistical Yearbook.* Seoul: National Bureau of Statistics.

Kotlikoff, L. J. 1984. "Taxation and Savings — A Neoclassical Perspective." Working Paper 1302. National Bureau of Economic Research.

Krueger, A. O. 1974. "The Political Economy of a Rent-Seeking Society." *American Economic Review,* vol. 64, no. 3 (June), pp. 291–303.

―――. 1983. *Trade and Employment in Developing Countries.* Vol. 3. Chicago: University of Chicago Press for the National Bureau of Economic Research.

―――. 1984. "Trade Policies in Developing Countries." In R. W. Jones and P. B. Kenen, eds., *Handbook of International Economics.* Amsterdam: North-Holland.

Krueger, A. O., and B. Tuncer. 1982. "An Empirical Test of the Infant Industry Argument." *American Economic Review,* vol. 72, no. 5 (December), pp. 1142–52.

Kuznets, S. 1962. "Quantitative Aspects of the Economic Growth of Nations, VII: The Share and Structure of Consumption." *Economic Development and Cultural Change*, vol. 10, no. 2, pt. 2 (January), pp. 1–92.

Kydland, R. E., and E. C. Prescott. 1977. "Rules Rather than Discretion: The Inconsistency of Optimal Plans." *Journal of Political Economy*, vol. 85, no. 3 (June), pp. 513–48.

Kyrouz, M. E. 1975. "Foreign Tax Rates and Tax Bases." *National Tax Journal*, vol. 28, no. 1 (March), pp. 61–80.

Lau, L. J. 1976. "A Characterization of the Normalized Restricted Profit Function." *Journal of Economic Theory*, vol. 12, no. 1 (February), pp. 131–63.

————. 1978. "Some Applications of Profit Functions." In M. Fuss and D. McFadden, eds., *Production Economics: A Dual Approach to Theory and Applications* pp. 133–216. Amsterdam: North-Holland.

Lau, L. J., P. A. Yotopoulos, E. C. Chou, and W. L. Lim. 1981. "The Microeconomics of Distribution: A Simulation of the Farm Economy." *Journal of Policy Modelling*, vol. 3, no. 2 (May), pp. 175–206.

Lent, G. E. 1967. "Tax Incentives for Investment in Developing Countries." *International Monetary Fund Staff Papers*, vol. 14, no. 2 (July), pp. 249–323.

————. 1977. "Corporation Income Tax Structure in Developing Countries." *International Monetary Fund Staff Papers*, vol. 24, no. 3 (November), pp. 722–55.

Lewis, J. D., and S. Urata. 1983. *Turkey: Recent Economic Performance and Medium Term Prospects, 1979–1990.*" World Bank Staff Working Paper 602. Washington, D.C.

Lewis, W. A. 1954. "Economic Development with Unlimited Supplies of Labour." *Manchester School*, vol. 22, no. 2 (May), pp. 139–91.

Lipsey, R., and K. Lancaster. 1956–57. "The General Theory of Second Best." *Review of Economic Studies*, vol. 24, no. 63, pp. 11–32.

Lipton, M. 1977. *Why Poor People Stay Poor: Urban Bias in World Development.* Cambridge, Mass.: Harvard University Press.

Little, I. M. D., and J. A. Mirrlees. 1974. *Project Appraisal and Planning for Developing Countries*. London: Heinemann.

Little, I. M. D., D. Mazumdar, and J. Page. 1984. "Small Manufacturing Enterprises: A Comparative Study of India and Other Countries." World Bank, Development Research Department; processed.

Little, I. M. D., T. Scitovsky, and M. FG. Scott. 1970. *Industry and Trade in Some Developing Countries*. London: Oxford University Press.

Littlechild, S. C. 1981. "Misleading Calculations of the Social Costs of Monopoly Power." *Economic Journal*, vol. 91, no. 362 (June), pp. 348–63.

Lluch, C., A. A. Powell, and R. A. Williams. 1977. *Patterns in Household Demand and Saving*. New York: Oxford University Press.

McClure, C. E. 1974. "State Income Taxation of Multistate Corporations in the United States of America." In United Nations, *The Impact of Multinational Corporations on Development and on International Relations*. Technical Papers: Taxation, ST/ESA/11. New York: United Nations.

McCool, T. 1982. "Wage Subsidies and Distortionary Taxes in a Mobile Capital Harris-Todaro Model." *Economica*, vol. 49, no. 1 (February), pp. 69–79.

McCulloch, J. R. 1845/1975. *A Treatise on the Principles and Practical Influence of Taxation and the Funding System*. Scottish Economic Society Edition, D. P. O'Brien, ed. Edinburgh: Scottish Academic Press.

McKinnon, R. I. 1973. *Money and Capital in Economic Development.* Washington, D.C.: Brookings Institution.

Magee, S. 1976. *International Trade and Distortions in Factor Markets.* New York: Marcel Dekker.

Marglin, S. A. 1963. "The Social Rate of Discount and the Optimal Rate of Investment." *Quarterly Journal of Economics,* vol. 77, no. 1 (February), pp. 95–111.

————. 1976. *Value and Price in the Labour-Surplus Economy.* Oxford: Clarendon Press.

Marsden, K. 1983. "Taxes and Growth." *Finance and Development,* vol. 20, no. 3 (September), pp. 40–43.

Mazumdar, D. 1983. "Segmented Labor Markets in LDCs." *American Economic Review: Papers and Proceedings,* vol. 73, no. 2 (May), pp. 254–59.

Meade, J. E. 1955a. *Trade and Welfare.* London: Oxford University Press.

————. 1955b. "The Efficiency Effects of Direct and Indirect Taxation." In *Trade and Welfare Mathematical Supplement.* London: Oxford University Press.

————. 1978. *The Structure and Reform of Direct Taxation.* A Report of a Committee for the Institute of Fiscal Studies, Chaired by J. E. Meade. London: Allen and Unwin.

Mellor, J. W. 1978. *The New Economics of Growth.* Baltimore, Md.: Johns Hopkins University Press.

Mincer, J. 1974. *Schooling, Experience, and Earnings.* New York: National Bureau of Economic Research.

————. 1976. "Unemployment Effects of Minimum Wage Changes." *Journal of Political Economy,* vol. 84, no. 4, pt. 2 (August), pp. S 87–104.

Mirrlees, J. A. 1967. "Optimum Growth When Technology Is Changing." *Review of Economic Studies,* vol. 34 (1), no. 97 (January), pp. 95–124.

————. 1969. "The Dynamic Non-Substitution Theorem." *Review of Economic Studies,* vol. 36, no. 1 (January), pp. 67–76.

————. 1971. "An Exploration in the Theory of Optimum Income Taxation." *Review of Economic Studies,* vol. 38, no. 114 (April), pp. 175–208.

————. 1975. "A Pure Theory of Underdeveloped Economies." In L. G. Reynolds, ed., *Agriculture in Development Theory,* New Haven, Conn.: Yale University Press.

————. 1979. "The Theory of Optimal Taxation." In K. J. Arrow and M. D. Intrilligator, eds., *Handbook of Mathematical Economics.* Amsterdam: North-Holland.

Moon, P. Y. 1975. "The Evolution of Rice Policy in Korea." *Food Research Institute Studies,* vol. 14, no. 4, pp. 381–402.

Morawetz, D. 1981. *Why the Emperor's New Clothes Are Not Made in Colombia.* New York: Oxford University Press, World Bank.

Morey, E. R. 1984. "Consumer Surplus." *American Economic Review,* vol. 74, no. 1 (March), pp. 163–73.

Munk, K. J. 1980. "Optimal Taxation with Some Non-Taxable Commodities." *Review of Economic Studies,* vol. 47(4), no. 149 (July), pp. 755–66.

Musgrave, R. A. 1959. *The Theory of Public Finance.* New York: McGraw-Hill.

————. 1969. *Fiscal Systems.* New Haven, Conn.: Yale University Press.

Musgrave, R. A., and P. B. Musgrave. 1980. *Public Finance in Theory and Practice.* 3d ed. New York: McGraw-Hill.

Musgrave, R. A., and A. T. Peacock. 1967. *Classics in the Theory of Public Finance.* New York: Macmillan.

Mutén, L. 1982. "A Cascade Tax by Any Other Name." *Public Finance,* vol. 37, no. 2, pp. 263–68.

———. 1983. "Some Topical Issues concerning International Double Taxation." In S. Cnossen, ed., *Comparative Tax Studies*. Amsterdam: North-Holland.

Mutti, J. 1981. "Tax Incentives and the Repatriation Decisions of U.S. Multinational Corporations." *National Tax Journal*, vol. 34, no. 2 (June), pp. 241–48.

Nafziger, E. W. 1984. *The Economics of Developing Countries*. Belmont, Calif.: Wadsworth.

Neary, J. P. 1981. "On the Harris-Todaro Model with Intersectoral Capital Mobility." *Economica*, vol. 48, no. 191 (August), pp. 219–34.

Newbery, D. M. G. 1972. "Public Policy in the Dual Economy." *Economic Journal*, vol. 82, no. 326 (June), pp. 567–90.

Newbery, D. M. G., and J. E. Stiglitz. 1979. "Sharecropping, Risk Sharing and the Importance of Imperfect Information." In J. A. Roumasset, J.-M. Boussard, and I. J. Singh, eds., *Risk, Uncertainty and Agricultural Development*. New York: Agricultural Development Council.

———. 1981. *The Theory of Commodity Price Stabilization*. Oxford: Oxford University Press.

———. 1982. "Optimal Commodity Stockpiling Rules." *Oxford Economic Papers*, vol. 34, no. 3 (November), pp. 403–27.

Olson, M. 1965. *The Logic of Collective Action*. Cambridge, Mass.: Harvard University Press.

Organisation for Economic Co-operation and Development. 1963. *Labour Market Policy in Sweden*. Paris: OECD Review of Manpower and Social Policies.

Pearce, D. W., H. Sibert, and I. Walter, eds. 1984. *Risk and the Political Economy of Resource Management*. London: Macmillan.

Pencavel, J. H. 1982. "Unemployment and the Labor Supply Effects of the Seattle-Denver Income Maintenance Experiments." In R. G. Ehrenberg, ed., *Research in Labor Economics*, vol. 5. Greenwich, Conn.: JAI Press.

Phelps, E. S. 1973a. "Inflation in the Theory of Public Finance." *Swedish Journal of Economics*, vol. 75, no. 1, pp. 67–82.

———. 1973b. "The Taxation of Wage Income for Economic Justice." *Quarterly Journal of Economics*, vol. 87, no. 3 (August), pp. 331–54.

Pigou, A. C. 1947. *A Study in Public Finance*. London: Macmillan.

———. 1962. *The Economics of Welfare*. 4th ed. London: Macmillan.

Psacharopoulos, G. 1982. "Education as an Investment." *Finance and Development*, vol. 19, no. 3 (September), pp. 39–42.

Psacharopoulos, G., and K. Hinchliffe. 1973. *Returns to Education: An International Comparison*. New York: Elsevier.

Radhakrishna, R., and K. N. Murty. 1981. "Agricultural Prices, Income Distribution, and Demand Patterns in a Low Income Country." Paper presented to the Symposium on Economic Theory and Planning, Indian Statistical Institute, Bangalore.

Radian, A. 1980. *Resource Mobilization in Poor Countries: Implementing Tax Policies*. New Brunswick, N.J.: Transaction.

Ramaswami, V. K., and T. N. Srinivasan. 1971. "Tariff Structure and Resource Allocation in the Presence of Factor Substitution." In J. Bhagwati, ed., *Trade, Balance of Payments, and Growth*. Amsterdam: North-Holland.

Ramsey, F. P. 1927. "A Contribution to the Theory of Taxation." *Economic Journal*, vol. 37, no. 1 (March), pp. 47–61.

Rawls, J. 1971. *A Theory of Justice*. Cambridge, Mass.: Harvard University Press.

Reddaway, W. B. 1968. *Effects of U.K. Direct Investment Overseas (Final Report)*. Cambridge: Cambridge University Press.

Reyes Heroles, J. 1978. "Política fiscal y redistribución del ingreso." Licenciado tesis, Instituto Tecnológico Autónomo de México.

Reynolds, L. G. 1965. "Wages and Employment in a Labor Surplus Economy." *American Economic Review*, vol. 55, no. 1 (March), pp. 19–39.

———. 1973. "Labor in Less Developed Economies." In G. Somers, ed., *The Next Twenty-Five Years of Industrial Relations*. Madison, Wisc.: Industrial Relations Research Association.

Rosen, H. S. 1978. "The Measurement of Excess Burden with Explicit Utility Functions." *Journal of Political Economy*, supp., vol. 86, pp. S121–36.

———. 1980. "What Is Labor Supply and Do Taxes Affect It?" *American Economic Review: Papers and Proceedings*, vol. 70, no. 2 (May), pp. 171–76.

Sabot, R. H. 1977. "The Meaning and Measurement of Urban Surplus Labour." *Oxford Economic Papers*, vol. 29, no. 3 (November).

Sabot, R. H., ed. 1982. *Migration and the Labor Market in Developing Countries*. Boulder, Colo.: Westview.

Sah, R. K. 1978. "Egalitarian Commodity Taxes." University of Pennsylvania, Economic Research Unit; processed.

———. 1982a. "Comparison of Coupons, Queues, Rations, and Non-Intervention in Managing Scarcities." University of Pennsylvania, Center for Analysis of Developing Economies; processed.

———. 1982b. "A Welfare-Based Determination of Urban-Rural Prices." Paper presented at the World Bank seminar on public economics. Washington, D.C. June.

———. 1983a. "How Much Redistribution Is Possible through Indirect Taxes?" *Journal of Public Economics*, vol. 20, no. 1 (February), pp. 89–102.

———. 1983b. "Analysis of Intra-Household Consumption Allocations: A Methodology and Its Implementation." University of Pennsylvania, Center for Analysis of Developing Economies; processed.

Sah, R. K., and J. E. Stiglitz. 1984a. "The Economics of Price Scissors." *American Economic Review*, vol. 74, no. 1 (March), pp. 125–38.

———. 1984b. "Taxation and Pricing of Agricultural and Industrial Goods." Working Paper 1338. Cambridge, Mass.: National Bureau of Economic Research.

———. 1985a. "Price Scissors and the Structure of the Economy." Discussion Paper 478. Yale University, Economic Growth Center.

———. 1985b. "The Social Cost of Labor and Project Evaluation: A General Approach." *Journal of Public Economics*, vol. 28, no. 2 (November), pp. 135–64.

Samuelson, P. A. 1951. "Theory of Optimal Taxation." Memorandum to the U.S. Treasury. Published in *Journal of Public Economics*, vol. 30, no. 2 (July 1986), pp. 137–44.

Scandizzo, P., and C. Bruce. 1980. *Methodologies for Measuring Agricultural Price Intervention Effects*. World Bank Staff Working Paper 394. Washington, D.C.

Schultz, T. W., ed. 1978. *Distortions of Agricultural Incentives*. Bloomington: Indiana University Press.

Schumpeter, J. A. 1954. *Capitalism, Socialism, and Democracy*. 4th ed. London: Allen and Unwin.

Seade, J. 1977. "On the Shape of Optimal Tax Schedules." *Journal of Public Economics*, vol. 7, no. 2 (April), pp. 203–35.

————. 1985. "Profitable Cost Increases and the Shifting of Taxation: Equilibrium Responses of Markets in Oligopoly." Warwick Economic Research Paper 260. University of Warwick; processed. Forthcoming in *Journal of Public Economics.*

Sen, A. K. 1960. *Choice of Techniques.* Oxford: Blackwell.

————. 1966. "Peasants and Dualism with or without Surplus Labour." *Journal of Political Economy,* vol. 74, no. 5 (October), pp. 425–50.

————. 1967. "Isolation, Assurance, and the Social Rate of Discount." *Quarterly Journal of Economics,* vol. 81, no. 1 (February), pp. 112–24.

————. 1983. "Development: Which Way Now?" *Economic Journal,* vol. 93, no. 372 (December), pp. 745–62.

Sen, A. K., and B. Williams, eds. 1982. *Utilitarianism and Beyond.* Cambridge, England, and New York: Cambridge University Press.

Shah, S. M. S., and J. F. J. Toye. 1979. "Fiscal Incentives for Firms in Some Developing Countries: Survey and Critique." In J. F. J. Toye, ed., *Taxation and Economic Development.* London: Frank Cass.

Shaw, E. S. 1973. *Financial Deepening in Economic Development.* New York: Oxford University Press.

Shepherd, D., J. Turk, and Z. A. Silberston, eds. 1983. *Microeconomic Efficiency and Macroeconomic Performance.* Oxford: Philip Allan.

Shoup, C. S. 1974. "Taxation of Multinational Corporations." In United Nations, *The Impact of Multinational Corporations on Development and on International Relations,* Technical Papers: Taxation, ST/ESA/11. New York: United Nations.

Shoven, J. B. 1983. "Applied General Equilibrium Tax Modeling." *International Monetary Fund Staff Papers,* vol. 30, no. 2 (June), pp. 350–93.

Sidrauski, M. M. 1967. "Rational Choice and Patterns of Growth in a Monetary Economy." *American Economic Review: Papers and Proceedings,* vol. 57, pp. 534–44.

Singh, I. J., L. Squire, and J. Kirchner. 1984. "Agricultural Pricing Policies in Malawi." World Bank, Country Policy Department; processed.

Singh, I. J., L. Squire, and J. Strauss. 1986. "Agricultural Household Models: A Survey of Recent Findings and Their Policy Implications." *World Bank Economic Review,* vol. 1, no. 1 (September), pp. 149–80.

Smith, A. 1892. *The Wealth of Nations.* London: Routledge.

Solís, W. R. 1981. "The Firm's Cost of Capital in Mexico." Instituto Tecnológico Autónomo de México; processed.

Spence, A. M. 1975. "Monopoly, Quality, and Regulation." *Bell Journal of Economics,* vol. 6, no. 2 (Autumn), pp. 417–29.

————. 1977. "Nonlinear Prices and Welfare." *Journal of Public Economics,* vol. 8, no. 1 (August), pp. 1–18.

Squire, L. 1981. *Employment Policy in Developing Countries.* New York: Oxford University Press.

Srinivasan, T. N. 1984. "Development Strategy for the Last Two Decades of the Twentieth Century: Is the Success of Outward Orientation at an End?" Yale University, Economic Growth Center; processed.

Srinivasan, T. N., and J. N. Bhagwati. 1975. "Alternative Policy Rankings in a Large, Open Economy with Sector-Specific Minimum Wages." *Journal of Economic Theory,* vol. 11, no. 3 (December), pp. 356–71.

Starr, G. 1981. *Minimum Wage Fixing.* Geneva: International Labour Office.

Stern, N. H. 1972. "Optimum Development in a Dual Economy." *Review of Economic Studies,* vol. 39(2), no. 118 (April), pp. 171–84.

————. 1976. "On the Specification of Models of Optimum Income Taxation." *Journal of Public Economics*, vol. 6, nos. 1–2 (July–August), pp. 123–62.

————. 1977. "Welfare Weights and the Elasticity of the Marginal Valuation of Income." In M. Artis and R. Nobay, eds., *Modern Economic Analysis*. Oxford: Blackwell.

————. 1982. "Optimum Taxation with Errors in Administration." *Journal of Public Economics*, vol. 17, no. 2 (March), pp. 181–212.

————. 1983*a*. "Taxation for Efficiency." In D. Shepherd, J. Turk, and Z. A. Silberston, eds., *Microeconomic Efficiency and Macroeconomic Performance*. Oxford: Philip Allan.

————. 1983*b*. "Tax Reform: Income Distribution, Government Revenue, and Planning." *Indian Economic Review*, vol. 18, no. 1 (January–June), pp. 17–33.

————. 1984. "Optimal Taxation and Tax Policy." *International Monetary Fund Staff Papers*, vol. 31, no. 2 (June), pp. 339–78.

————. 1985. "The Effects of Taxation, Price Control, and Government Contracts in Oligopoly and Monopolistic Competition." Discussion Paper 60. University of Warwick; Development Economics Research Centre; processed. March. Forthcoming in *Journal of Public Economics*.

Sternberg, M. J. 1970. "The Economic Impact of the Latifundista." *Land Reform, Land Settlement, and Co-operatives*, no. 2, pp. 21–34.

Stiglitz, J. E. 1974*a*. "Alternative Theories of Wage Determination and Unemployment in LDCs: The Labour Turnover Model." *Quarterly Journal of Economics*, vol. 88, no. 2 (May), pp. 194–227.

————. 1974*b*. "Risk Sharing and Incentives in Sharecropping." *Review of Economic Studies*, vol. 41(2), no. 126 (April), pp. 219–56.

————. 1976. "The Efficiency Wage Hypothesis, Surplus Labour, and the Distribution of Income in LDCs." *Oxford Economic Papers*, vol. 28, no. 2 (June), pp. 185–207.

————. 1982*a*. "Alternative Theories of Wage Determination and Unemployment: The Efficiency Wage Model." In Mark Gersovitz and others, eds., *Theory and Experience of Economic Development*. New York: Allen and Unwin.

————. 1982*b*. "The Structure of Labor Markets and Shadow Prices in LDCs." In Richard H. Sabot, ed., *Migration and the Labor Market in Developing Countries*. Boulder, Colo.: Westview.

————. 1982*c*. "Taxation and Agricultural Pricing Policies, Cost-Benefit Analysis, and the Foreign Exchange Constraint." Princeton University; processed.

————. 1982*d*. "The Wage-Productivity Hypothesis: Its Economic Consequences and Policy Implications." Paper presented at the 1982 annual meeting of the American Economic Association, New York.

————. 1982*e*. "Self-Selection and Pareto Efficient Taxation." *Journal of Public Economics*, vol. 17, no. 2 (March), pp. 213–40.

Stiglitz, J. E., and P. S. Dasgupta. 1971. "Differential Taxation, Public Goods, and Economic Efficiency." *Review of Economic Studies*, vol. 38(2), no. 114 (April), pp. 151–74.

Stolper, W., and P. A. Samuelson. 1940. "Protection and Real Wages." *Review of Economic Studies*, vol. 9, no. 1 (November), pp. 58–73.

Stone, R. 1954. "Linear Expenditure Systems and Demand Analysis: An Application to the Pattern of British Demand." *Economic Journal*, vol. 64, no. 255 (September), pp. 511–27.

Summers, L. H., 1981. "Capital Taxation and Accumulation in a Life-Cycle Growth Model." *American Economic Review*, vol. 71, no. 4 (September), pp. 533–44.

Tait, A. A., W. L. M. Grätz, and B. J. Eichengreen. 1979. "International Comparison of Taxation for Selected Developing Countries, 1972–76." *International Monetary Fund Staff Papers*, vol. 26, no. 1 (March), pp. 123–56.

Tanzi, V. 1966. "Personal Income Taxation in Latin America: Obstacles and Possibilities." *National Tax Journal*, vol. 19, no. 2 (June), pp. 156–62.

————. 1973. "The Theory of Tax Structure Change during Economic Development: A Critical Survey." *Rivista di Diritto Finanziario e Scienza delle Finanze*, vol. 32, no. 2, pp. 199–208.

————. 1978. "Import Taxes and Economic Development." *Economia Internazionale*, vol. 31, nos. 3–4 (August–November), pp. 252–69.

————. 1981. "Taxation in Sub-Saharan Africa: A Statistical Evaluation." *International Monetary Fund Occasional Paper* 8 (October), pp. 43–73.

————. 1983. "Tax Systems and Policy Objectives in Developing Countries: General Principles and Diagnostic Tests." International Monetary Fund; processed.

Taylor, C. C., D. Ensminger, H. S. Johnson, and J. Joyce. 1965. *India's Roots of Democracy*. Calcutta: Orient Longmans.

Taylor, L. 1979. *Macro Models for Developing Countries*. New York: McGraw-Hill.

Theil, H. 1965. "The Information Approach to Demand Analysis." *Econometrica*, vol. 33, no. 1 (January), pp. 67–87.

Tidrick, G. M. 1975. "Wage Spillover and Unemployment in a Wage-Gap Economy: The Jamaica Case." *Economic Development and Cultural Change*, vol. 23, no. 2 (January), pp. 306–24.

Timmer, C. P., W. P. Falcon, and S. R. Pearson. 1983. *Food Policy Analysis*. Baltimore, Md.: Johns Hopkins University Press.

Tobin, J. 1975. "The General Equilibrium Approach to Monetary Theory." *Journal of Money, Credit and Banking*, vol. 1, no. 1 (February), pp. 15–29.

Todaro, M. P. 1969. "A Model of Labor Migration and Urban Unemployment in Less Developed Countries." *American Economic Review*, vol. 59, no. 1 (March), pp. 138–48.

————. 1971. "Income Expectations, Rural-Urban Migration, and Employment in Africa." *International Labour Review*, vol. 104 (November), pp. 387–413.

————. 1976. *Internal Migration in Developing Countries*. Geneva: International Labour Office.

Tolley, G. S., V. Thomas, and C. M. Wong. 1982. *Agricultural Price Policies and the Developing Countries*. Baltimore, Md.: Johns Hopkins University Press.

Toye, J. F. J. 1978. *Taxation and Economic Development: Twelve Critical Studies*. London: Frank Cass.

Turnham, D. 1971. *The Employment Problem in Less Developed Countries*. Paris: Organisation for Economic Co-operation and Development.

United Nations. 1968. *Manual of Land Tax Administration*. New York: United Nations, Department of Economic and Social Affairs.

Usher, D. 1977a. "The Welfare Economics of the Socialization of Commodities." *Journal of Public Economics*, vol. 8, no. 2 (October), pp. 151–68.

————. 1977b. "The Economics of Tax Incentives to Encourage Investment in Less Developed Countries." *Journal of Development Economics*, vol. 4, no. 2 (June), pp. 119–48.

van Wijnbergen, S. 1981. *Short-Run Macro-Economic Adjustment Policies in South Korea: A Quantitative Analysis*. World Bank Staff Working Paper 510. Washington, D.C.

————. 1982. "Stagflationary Effects of Monetary Stabilization Policies: A Quantitative Analysis of South Korea." *Journal of Development Economics*, vol. 10, no. 2 (April), pp. 133–69.

————. 1983. "Credit Policy, Inflation, and Growth in a Financially Repressed Economy." *Journal of Development Economics*. vol. 13, no. 2 (August–October), pp. 45–65.

Wade, R. 1979. "The Social Response to Irrigation: An Indian Case Study." *Journal of Development Studies*, vol. 16, no. 1 (October), pp. 3–26.

Wald, H. P. 1959. *Taxation of Agricultural Land in Underdeveloped Economies*. Cambridge, Mass.: Harvard University Press.

Weitzman, M. 1977. "Is the Price System or Rationing More Effective in Getting a Commodity to Those Who Need It Most?" *Bell Journal of Economics*, vol. 8, no. 2 (Autumn), pp. 517–24.

Welch, F. 1978. *Minimum Wages: Issues and Evidence*. Washington, D.C.: American Enterprise Institute.

Whalley, J. 1984. *"Trade, Industrial Policy, and Canadian Manufacturing*, by R. G. Harris (with the assistance of D. Case): A Review Article." *Canadian Journal of Economics*, vol. 17, no. 2 (May), pp. 387–98.

Wicksell, K. 1896/1967. "A New Principle of Just Taxation." In R. A. Musgrave and A. T. Peacock, *Classics in the Theory of Public Finance*, pp. 72–118. New York: Macmillan, 1967.

Williams, M. L. 1975. "The Extent and Significance of the Nationalization of Foreign-Owned Assets in Developing Countries, 1956–1972." *Oxford Economic Papers*, vol. 27, no. 2 (July), pp. 260–73.

Willig, R. D. 1978. "Incremental Consumer's Surplus and Hedonic Price Adjustment." *Journal of Economic Theory*, vol. 17, no. 2 (April), pp. 227–53.

Wilson, C. 1980. "The Nature of Equilibrium in Markets with Adverse Selection." *Bell Journal of Economics*, vol. 11, no. 1 (Spring), pp. 108–30.

Wilson, L. S., and M. L. Katz. 1983. "The Socialization of Commodities." *Journal of Public Economics*, vol. 20, no. 3 (April), pp. 347–56.

World Bank. 1980a. *Commodity Trade and Price Trends*. Baltimore, Md.: Johns Hopkins University Press.

————. 1980b. *Education*. Sector Policy Paper. Washington, D.C.

————. 1983. *World Development Report 1983*. New York: Oxford University Press.

————. 1984. *World Development Report 1984*. New York: Oxford University Press.

————. 1985. *World Development Report 1985*. New York: Oxford University Press.

Yabuuchi, S. 1982. "A Note on Tariff-Induced Capital Inflow and Immiserization in the Presence of Taxation of Foreign Profits." *Journal of International Economics*, vol. 12, no. 1/2 (February), pp. 183–89.

Yellen, J. L. 1984. "Efficiency Wage Models of Unemployment." *American Economic Review: Papers and Proceedings*, vol. 74, no. 2 (May), pp. 200–206.

Yotopoulos, P. A., and L. J. Lau. 1974. "On Modelling the Agricultural Sector in Developing Countries: An Integrated Approach of Micro and Macro-Economics." *Journal of Development Economics*, vol. 1, no. 2 (September), pp. 105–27.

Yotopoulos, P., and J. Nugent. 1976. *Economics of Development*. New York: Harper and Row.

Yusuf, S. and others. 1983. "Employment, Wages, and Manpower Policies in Korea." Report 4485-KO. World Bank, East Asia and Pacific Regional Office; processed.

Zymelman, M. 1982. "Education Expenditures in the 1970s." World Bank, Education Department; processed.

Affiliations of Contributors

The affiliations shown are those at the time of writing.

Ehtisham Ahmad	Deputy director, Development Economics Research Centre, Warwick University
Choong Yong Ahn	Professor of economics, Chung Ang University, Republic of Korea
Jane Armitage	Economist, Development Research Department, The World Bank
Anthony Atkinson	Professor of economics, London School of Economics
Christopher Bliss	Reader in international economics, Nuffield College, Oxford University
Avishay Braverman	Senior economist, Agriculture and Rural Development Department, The World Bank
Angus Deaton	Professor of economics and international affairs, Princeton University
Peter Diamond	Professor of economics, Massachusetts Institute of Technology
Gary Fields	Professor of economics, Cornell University
Mark Gersovitz	Senior research economist and public affairs analyst, Woodrow Wilson School of International and Public Affairs, Princeton University
Francisco Gil Díaz	Director of research, Banco de México
Jeffrey Hammer	Economist, Agriculture and Rural Development Department, The World Bank
Christopher Heady	Lecturer in economics, University College, London
Gordon Hughes	Professor of economics, Edinburgh University
Michael Katz	Assistant professor of economics, Princeton University
Pradeep Mitra	Senior economist, Country Policy Department, The World Bank

Richard Musgrave	H. H. Burbank professor of political economy, emeritus, Harvard University, and adjunct professor, University of California at Santa Cruz
David Newbery	Fellow of Churchill College and reader in economics, Cambridge University
Richard Sabot	Professor of economics, Williams College
Raaj Kumar Sah	Assistant professor of economics, Yale University
Nicholas Stern	Professor of economics, London School of Economics
Joseph Stiglitz	Professor of economics, Princeton University
Vito Tanzi	Director, Department of Fiscal Affairs, International Monetary Fund
Sweder van Wijnbergen	Senior economist, Country Policy Department, The World Bank

Index

The most recent World Bank publications are described in the catalog *New Publications*, which is issued in the spring and fall of each year. The complete backlist of publications is shown in the annual *Index of Publications*, which is of value principally to libraries and institutional purchasers. The latest edition of each is available free of charge from Publications Sales Unit, The World Bank, 1818 H Street, N.W., Washington, D.C. 20433, U.S.A., or from Publications, The World Bank, 66, avenue d'Iéna, 75116 Paris, France.